Architectural Diplomacy

ROME AND PARIS
IN THE LATE BAROQUE

Architectural Diplomacy

ROME AND PARIS
IN THE LATE BAROQUE

GIL R. SMITH

THE ARCHITECTURAL HISTORY FOUNDATION
New York, New York

The MIT Press   Cambridge, Massachusetts, and London, England

Library of Congress Cataloging in Publication Data
Smith, Gil R., 1952–
Architectural diplomacy: Rome and Paris in the late Baroque/Gil R. Smith.
p. cm.
Includes bibliographical references.
ISBN 0-262-19323-X
1. Architecture, Baroque—Competitions—Italy—Rome. 2. Architectural drawing—17th
century—Italy—Rome. 3. Accademia nazionale di San Luca—Influence. I. Title.
NA2706.I8S6 1992
720'.22'24563209032—dc20
92-6766 CIP

Gil Smith is Associate Professor of Architecture at Ball State University.
Designed and typeset by Bessas & Ackerman.

CONTENTS

List of Abbreviations

ASL   Archivio Storico dell'Accademia Nazionale di San Luca, Rome

Comptes   Guiffrey, *Comptes des Batiments du Roi sous le règne de Louis XIV.* Paris (1881–1901)

Conc. Acc.   Concorsi Accademici dell'Accademia di San Luca

Conc. Clem.   Concorsi Clementini dell'Accademia di San Luca

Corr.   Montaiglon and Guiffrey, *Correspondance des Directeurs de l'Académie de France à Rome avec les Surintendants des Batiments.* Paris (1887–88)

DEAU   *Dizionario Enciclopedico de Architettura ed Urbanistica*, ed. Paolo Portoghesi. Rome (1968)

JSAH   *Journal of the Society of Architectural Historians*

JWCI   *Journal of the Warbourg and Courtauld Institutes*

MEA   *Macmillan Encyclopedia of Architects*, ed. Adolf Placzek. New York (1982)

P-V   Lemonnier, *Procès-Verbaux de l'Académie Royale d'Architecture.* Paris (1911–29)

RJK   *Romisches Jahrbuch für Kunstgeschichte*

PREFACE

THIS WORK BEGAN MODESTLY as little more than a *catalogue raisonné* of a group of sixty-two architectural drawings linked at first only by proximity of date and the shared provenance of the Accademia di San Luca in Rome. They represent winning designs in architecture for the *Concorsi Accademici,* the earliest public student competitions at the Accademia, begun in 1677 on the occasion of its union with the French royal academies and continuing on and off until the end of the century. These were followed by the *Concorsi Clementini,* initiated in 1702 under the sponsorship of Clement XI, which represent their own separate and unified object of study (see the bibliography under Hellmut Hager [1981]). It seemed natural, therefore, to consider the earlier competition designs as a unit unto themselves, if only from the standpoint of typologies and methodologies at the hands of student architects in the waning years of the Roman Seicento.

However, my years as one of Hellmut Hager's students at The Pennsylvania State University, throughout the time he and we were occupied with the subject of the Accademia, taught me among other things not to take the drawings for granted as merely "student" or "academic" work. Deeper layers of meaning connecting them, beyond the range of skills and precedents they reflected, would reward a more comprehensive examination of both the drawings and the circumstances surrounding them, including the subsequent careers of the more successful students, the nature of instruction at the Accademia, the influences and tasks of its officers and patrons, and contemporary projects along thematic lines similar to those stipulated for the *concorsi.* As to the last, the general slump in building activity in Rome at the time gives these

designs an even more critical role as documents of existing trends in architectural thought.

At one level, the circumstances that unite the *Concorsi Accademici* are provided by the aggregation of the French and Roman academies in 1676–77, and the shifting fate of their association over the remainder of the century and beyond. The lesser or greater degree to which each design addressed this association, by fusing French to Roman elements, or largely ignored them in favor of native traditions, became the common ground by which the broader implications of the drawings could be defined. In their own way, the competition projects anticipated the next phase of the Baroque, in its international context, which would likewise derive inspiration from the legacies of Rome and Paris as a wider range of regional expressions emerged. It is this layer of meaning that I wish to explore, based on the premise that the *Concorsi Accademici* represent a unique and productive juncture between the French and Italian traditions.

But the implications of the competition designs were broader still. What was increasingly at issue was not just the synthesis of Roman and French motifs at a point in time when their temporal spheres of influence coincided. The concept of synthesis itself had attained significance, now that the Baroque had reached a crossroad between nearly playing itself out in Paris and Rome and flourishing in both cities again and throughout Europe during the subsequent half century. It was synthesis as design methodology that was being consciously pursued by the Accademia di San Luca, particularly by Carlo Fontana who would dominate it by the 1690s, as a means of revitalizing flagging traditions of Roman architecture. As a result, the *Concorsi Accademici* became an important source of inspiration for prominent architects of the next century, like Johann Bernhard Fischer von Erlach; Filippo Juvarra; the Swede, Nicodemus Tessin; and others across the continent, in their search for a progressive, though synthetic, Baroque language.

While the scope of what follows is largely confined to the exchanges between French and Roman architectural traditions in the last quarter of the seventeenth century, my work continues to make clear how much more there is to be said about the context of ideas at this crucial turning point of the Late Baroque. The exchanges between the academies of France and Rome, involving painting and sculpture as much as architecture, continued throughout the Settecento. And the position of the Accademia in exchanges between Rome and other national entities, like Austria, Poland, Spain, Great Britain, Sweden, Prussia, and Russia during the same period, has equal potential to reveal nuances in the complex pluralism of eighteenth-century style.

In realizing this book, I have several individuals to thank: the faculty in Art History at The Pennsylvania State University, and Hellmut Hager in particular, for their esteemed example; Henry Millon, of the Center for Advanced Study in the Visual Arts, for his gracious support; the staff of the Accademia di San Luca, and Giulia de Marchis and Angela Cipriani in particular, for their invaluable and courteous assistance in Rome; Susan Munshower and Christine Challingsworth, for their friendship and consultation on points of scholarship; and Carla, my wife, for her everlasting patience.

GIL R. SMITH
Ball State University
Muncie, Indiana

Architectural Diplomacy

ROME AND PARIS
IN THE LATE BAROQUE

I

AGGREGATION OF THE ROMAN AND FRENCH ACADEMIES:
UNION OF CONVENIENCE OR STRATEGIC ALLIANCE?

AS THE HIGH BAROQUE becomes the Late Baroque, there is a tangible sense either of a shift of the center, or perhaps of a multiplication of the centers, from which architectural cultures spring. The Baroque becomes, as all such coherent expressions seem inevitably to do in the cycles of Western art history, an "international style." It emerges from one source, Counter-Reformation Rome, and diversifies as it touches upon and reacts to the regional traditions or national interests it encounters, which absorb it in the effort to shake off their own dated provinciality. This has happened many times, with infinite variations from the Hellenistic period to the later Roman Empire, to Romanesque Europe after Charlemagne, to Gothic Europe after Suger, to the Renaissance Europe that ultimately sprang from Medicean Florence, to the "International Style" Modernism of our own time.

While the process presumably continues even now, the historian can try to reveal something of the current intricacies and dynamics of the phenomenon by studying its earlier stages. What interests the scholar first, however, are not the poles upon which the cycles of history turn so much as the minute details of the flux in between these poles, against which the validity of any general perspective will have to be tested. The present book asks one particular question of architectural affairs at the end of the seventeenth century, as the mechanisms of diversification come into play in the Late Baroque. Does the hub, upon which Baroque architecture turns, shift from its initial location in Rome to a new position, Paris, commanding more authority over events in the next phase of the Baroque? Or is this apparent shift only one part of a general process of dispersion

from one consistent center to the periphery of Baroque Europe?

The model that emerged during the rise of the comparatively young discipline of scholarship dedicated to the Baroque period is now less useful. Fated to deal with far more complex social situations and a greater wealth of material resources than was the case for earlier, well-established periods of study, scholars of the Baroque were inclined at first to restrict themselves to regional perspectives, tracing the waxing and waning of the fashion within certain geographic limits, or even relating to singular personalities. This reinforces the view that the Baroque is the sum of many largely independent and cyclic patterns of development, and that at any given moment one such pattern could be ascendant over the others in the influence it exerts over the whole. In such circumstances it is easy to mistake "forest" for "trees," and to impose overriding viewpoints that might neglect unexpected but no less important determinants.

From a remove of several centuries, it may appear in general that the star of Rome rises and falls between 1500 and 1700, to be overshadowed eventually by the rise of Paris from the time of Louis XIV on. It follows then that the other capitals of Europe avail themselves of first one and then the other light in finding their way through the complex of eighteenth-century tastes. Such a broad assessment persists largely due to the landmark work of those notable authorities who have laid claim to preeminence in their regional fields of scholarship.

For example, it is evident in reading *Art and Architecture in Italy: 1600–1750* that Rudolf Wittkower considered the election of Charles

LeBrun to the post of *principe,* or president, of the Roman Accademia di San Luca for 1676 to be the principal boundary marker between the temporal spheres of influence of Rome and Paris in the Late Baroque.[1] Certainly the event is critical (see below), and while Wittkower made his case intentionally with regard to Roman sculpture, his earlier text implies the same demarcation in architecture.[2] Anthony Blunt corroborated this premise in *Art and Architecture in France,* believing that the origin of French cultural supremacy over Rome in the eighteenth century could be traced directly to LeBrun's principate.[3]

This is a difficult presumption to test through the medium of Roman architecture, given the dearth of building activity in the city between 1675 and 1725.[4] But at the end of that period, when activity temporarily revives, Roman *gravitas,* its solemn and weighty classicism, still holds the upper hand over Parisian elegance in projects like the Trevi fountain, or the facades of S. Giovanni in Laterano, S. Maria Maggiore, or S. Croce in Gerusalemme. And any overt license in detailing or planning, in the work of Filippo Raguzzini, Alessandro Specchi, or Gabriele Valvassori, can more easily be interpreted in terms of Borromini's inspiration than that of the French court.[5] If the cues for the international character of architecture after 1675 came increasingly from Paris, or even exclusively after 1720, Rome remained resolute in maintaining its native traditions.

Questions still remain: how was this supposed shift in poles of influence understood in Rome after 1676; how did this city, with its artistic dominance spanning two centuries and traditions spanning millennia, view the trend toward the Gallic dictation of taste; could Rome's artistic community see, as clearly as hindsight allows, the implications for its supplantation by Paris? The mere circumstance of LeBrun's principate cannot in isolation answer such questions, but an examination of the particulars may.

Since the 1590s Rome had sustained a phenomenal burst of energy in all fields of creative endeavor; many of the projects then spawned were still in progress by 1675, while many others were still in need of attention. Though the harsh realities of economics and statecraft would severely deplete that energy for the next half century, it is difficult to imagine that any Roman, in the years just following LeBrun's election, could have conceived of his city as diminished somehow in the scheme of European culture. From his standpoint, Paris was still an upstart, the capital of a monarchy only recently reestablished as a world power but still provincial in its understanding of the achievements of the Renaissance, or its appreciation of Italian genius. The "failure" of Bernini's mission to the French court, and the rejection of all Italian proposals for the Louvre in 1665, must have been proof to Roman eyes against any claims of French superiority. The subordinate position of the French would have been all the more apparent from the Roman view since for nearly a century many of France's own great artists, Poussin among them, had come to Rome to perfect their art or even spend their lives.

Whatever attraction France held for Rome in general was as a new nation, which on the one hand provided a buffer or distraction for the old rivals for papal power in Italy—Spain and the Holy Roman Empire—and on the other imparted a youthful potential not only to the advantage of world affairs or Christian and aristocratic societies, but to the vigor of the arts as well. Parallels might have been drawn with the age of François I (1515–47), who had provided an outlet for many Italian artists set adrift by the Sack of Rome, but for the fact that the city had not seen better days since the Caesars. Rome was still the place to be for an artist, though the "Sun King" was on the rise, and any group or individual with keen need and foresight might align their fortunes with his.

This last, as will be seen, was the major inducement behind the election of LeBrun and the union of the French and St. Luke academies initiated during his term. From this union emerged the idea of public competitions between students of both academies in painting, sculpture, and architecture: the *Concorsi Accademici.* And the designs produced for the architectural competitions during the last quarter of the seventeenth century are in turn a convenient and productive resource, given the scarcity of actual commissions, for studying Roman attitudes toward the initial penetration of French building principles and practices that occurs at this juncture. The union of the academies and the architectural designs themselves form the principal focus of this study. A necessary preamble concerns the nature of instruction in architecture at the two academies prior to their aggregation.

ARCHITECTURE AT THE ACADEMIES TO 1675

The principal distinction that ultimately evolved during the 1660s between the French and Roman academies, and the one which affected every other difference whether administrative or instructional, had to do with the relationship between the academies and the local guilds. In both Rome and Paris the original intent in founding an academy had been the same: to create an institution under aristocratic protection which pooled the intellectual and material resources of the artistic community, and provided an environment of freedom and excellence not possible in the guild system. After Federico Zuccari opened the Accademia di San Luca in 1593, its role in relation to the Roman guilds, collectively called the *Compagnia,* was often wildly contested and redefined by papal decrees.[6] The balance of power was set in favor of the Accademia by Urban VIII, in an unsuccessful attempt to enforce his authority over the arts in the city, with the result that all artists and artisans were taxed to support the Accademia. But in effect, the guilds were not replaced by the academy; some, like the weavers, were even loosely allied with it. While there was regulation of artistic activity, it was not despotic, and in most instances the guilds could continue to function as they had in the past, even to the training of apprentices.[7]

Aside from its main regulatory or fiscal missions, the Accademia was essentially a clearinghouse of ideas, which provided fundamental theoretical instruction meant for apprentices from the studios of member artists. If the emphasis placed on its role as educator fluctuated from time to time, nevertheless only the direst circumstances

could entirely negate the Accademia's efforts in this area, held by Zuccari to be one of its primary responsibilities.[8] But here, too, the Accademia's function was viewed as supplemental to that of the artists' workshops, which were ultimately responsible for training the young students in the finer points of their respective disciplines.[9] At this stage, the academy provided weekly assignments and guidance by twelve academicians chosen for the purpose, in order to give its audience of apprentices, and the occasional dilettante aristocrat, proficiency in the more abstract principles of their art.[10] This minimal role would not be enhanced until much later in the seventeenth century, quite possibly due to the example of the French.[11]

In France, the Académie Royale de Peinture et Sculpture was formed in 1648 on the instigation of Charles LeBrun, based largely on the example of Rome, but intended to more radically suppress the confining rule of the *Maîtrise,* the company of Parisian guildmasters.[12] A unique argument behind this foundation was the benefit to be had for the monarchy, which could through the agency of its academy make its own decisions on commissions, and even on the character of the arts, and put them to royal service. Credit must be given to Jean-Baptiste Colbert for seeing the full potential of this during his first years as chief minister to Louis XIV, after 1661, and for putting LeBrun in control of the Académie with the aim of defining a suitable monarchical style.

Every aspect of the Académie, from instruction to disputation to practical application of ideas, was rededicated to Colbert's absolutist objectives, and given the same rigorous organization common to all of his efforts for the centralization of power.[13] This meant that the authority over artists once held by the individual guilds would be replaced by that of the monarchy. The separation between the *Maîtrise* and the Académie Royale was therefore complete, and decidedly more hostile when compared with the situation in Rome.[14] But while French artists had thus been given a much improved status and security, they had no more freedom; they had simply changed masters. In the process, the economic and educational controls and obligations once delegated to the guilds had to be codified for the academies, adding considerably to the role they played in France. In the absence of any similar direction and purpose, efforts at the Accademia were languishing by comparison.[15]

In his history of academies of art, Nikolaus Pevsner asserts that during the Seicento Italian academies began to shift their emphasis from the elevation of the status of artists to their education, but that, lacking the necessary authority or will to usurp that function of the workshops, the change could not be as dramatic in Italy as in Paris.[16] Yet the change for architecture at the Accademia in Rome is by no means a gradual one over the course of the century. It is limited, in fact, to barely two decades in the latter half of the 1600s, coincidental with the period of Colbert's efforts at reform in France.

Zuccari's high aspirations for instruction were met in the statutes of 1596, when the Accademia was given its monopoly over posing models for drawing from life, and later when the library was established and a list of courses was proposed: drawing, painting, sculpture, architecture, perspective, anatomy, and "d'ogn'altra cosa spettante alla professione."[17] But the *verbali,* that is, the minutes from the Accademia's meetings, give no indication that these ambitions were successfully achieved, any more than were the periodic debates scheduled for the edification of students. It was not until 1670 that posing of the nude was begun again in earnest,[18] and only in the following year were the lectures on theory officially reinstated by the capable orator Pietro Bellori.[19] Offering courses was at best a hit-or-miss proposition, depending on who was inclined to accept the onus, until in 1664 Carlo Maratti gave a rather stirring discourse on the value of study at the academy.[20] In that year, Alessandro Sbringa was made lecturer in perspective for the next academic season, which ran from May to October. But it was not until 1673, during the principate of Carlo Rainaldi, that regular instruction in perspective, anatomy, and architecture was instituted, and lectures were firmly established on every Sunday and holy day.[21]

The year 1673 marks a watershed for architects at the Accademia: formal instruction could now begin for students of their profession, and one of their number was, for only the third time in the history of the Accademia, raised to its head.[22] The fortunes of architecture at the Accademia had previously not been equal to those of painting and sculpture. Working from his experience at the Florentine academy, Zuccari had intended the academy in Rome to include architects, too, but the first two papal briefs establishing the Accademia had made no provision for them.[23] Still, Onorio Longhi and Giacomo della Porta were charter members, even though the latter was a reluctant lecturer. Zuccari was constrained to sit in for him, and, as he was inadequate to the task, the lectures in architecture lapsed shortly after the turn of the century. Until 1673, interest in the affairs of architecture at the Accademia was virtually dormant, with the exception of the period of Pietro da Cortona's principate and the work on the academy's church. But in 1673, Mattia de Rossi began the first organized lectures in architecture on Sunday afternoons;[24] two years later lectures in military architecture were begun under the direction of a captain of the papal guard.[25] Around the same time, the Accademia resumed its obligations in the valuation of architecture, which required them to mediate questions of cost in disputes between architects and their clients. In 1674, Rainaldi and de Rossi were appointed *stimatori,* or appraisers of architecture, they being among the most competent practitioners ever to hold that post.[26] They were also responsible for overseeing the efforts of that year's lecturer in architecture, Gregorio Tomassini, an untested assistant of Rainaldi's.[27] He was followed by Carlo Fontana in 1675.[28]

De Rossi and Fontana were two of Bernini's most capable students, along with Giambattista Contini, and by 1676 these four formed one half of the contingent of architects in the membership of the Accademia.[29] This "school" inevitably put its stamp on the last quarter of the Seicento at the Accademia, particularly since in that time the three heirs of Bernini each held the office of *principe* for a total of thirteen years. And these years turn out to be the most active as far as competition was concerned.

The idea of competitions and/or the awarding of prizes to students also dated back to the time of Zuccari,[30] who had earlier suggested the practice to the Florentine academy to stimulate both the students and the curriculum.[31] There is no certainty about how the idea was actualized in the absence of mention in the Accademia's minutes or any surviving designs. The intention at the earliest instance was to award modest prizes, like drawing equipment, to the best work in studying the model or following the assignments.[32] Being an internal function delegated to the professors themselves, no records were kept, and in any case it would appear that architects had no part in this process at all. It was not until 1663 that architects and sculptors were allowed to participate in the competitions (App. B, 1663, n. 1), and by that time competitions were to be held every three months. This can refer only to what were still in effect in-class competitions, as the brief time allotted for each *concorso* could have permitted nothing like the efforts required for the annual competitions held later in painting, sculpture, and architecture.

Throughout the history of the Accademia, however, the public display of student work had a particular importance, no doubt for the motivation of young artists whose work would not otherwise be seen by a wide audience. The occasion was ideally the feast day of St. Luke, the Accademia's patron (Festa di San Luca, 18 October), when the doors were opened to the public for the only time during the year.[33] At that time, the *doni,* or admission pieces, of new academicians would also be put on view, as a demonstration of the Accademia's achievements for the past year, which was of particular importance in explaining how the taxes supporting it were being spent.[34]

In 1664, Carlo Maratti put into effect his earnest reforms of the competitions, giving them a stature sufficient to use them in determining eligibility for membership in the Accademia (App. B, 1664, n. 4). The decrees registered in the *verbali* permitted professors in painting, sculpture, and architecture to recommend as *Accademico di Merito* anyone who had taken first honors in one

or more *concorsi,* and who met the other requirements such as age (30 years) and the submission of a *dono* in the form of their prizewinning work. These measures were taken not only to "animate everyone in their studies," but to glorify the beneficence of Pope Alexander VII, whose continued taxes made it all possible.

In view of their heightened significance, the *concorsi* were now reduced to two per year: one judged in May, when studies were set to begin, and the other on the Feast of St. Luke. And the intensification of interest in the *concorsi* brought more of their nature to light. The prizes to be awarded in May were a "Libro della Psiche" in parchment (first prize), a steel pen and penknife in a silver case (second), and a three-color print;[35] even their total value is known: five *scudi.*[36] Members were called upon to provide works to ornament the salon for the ceremonies on the third Sunday of May, when the prizewinning entries would be exhibited.[37] Poets were commissioned to read laudatory verses, Pietro Bellori was invited to give the keynote address, or discourse, and all living members as well as the governing prelates were invited to attend.

There is no earlier record of such pomp and circumstance applied to a competition, but apparently the one that followed on the Feast of St. Luke was meant to be the equal of its predecessor. In June, it was resolved again to open the competition in October to architects and sculptors, as well as to painters, and one Andrea Piscuglia was chosen to provide the *soggetto,* or topic, for the painters and to give the discourse.[38] Member sculptors and architects were to make their own choice for the *soggetti* in their fields (App. B, 1664, n. 6),[39] and the same entry indicates that their students were meant to compete at more than one level as well.[40] The *soggetti* were written up and placed on display on 13 June (App. B, 1664, n. 7), and the judging was scheduled for Sunday, 19 October, the day after the feast day.[41] Bernini is specifically mentioned among the prelates and gentry invited to attend, and his presence, given his previous indifference to the functions of the Accademia, by itself would have been an extraordinary event. Despite all of this preparation, something broke down, since by 16 November the *concorso* had yet to be held, and the delay was threatening the competition for May (App. B, 1664, n. 8).

The celebration of the *concorso* was finally scheduled for the second Sunday of February 1665 (App. B, 1665, n. 1), but the record conspicuously omits mention of the participation of architects. What this means is difficult to say, for despite intentions it was never certain that architectural students had as yet competed, and with no curriculum there may be no reason to expect them to have competed.

What is certain is that from this year on the idea of two annual *concorsi* was never again entertained. Indeed, for the next six years the question of whether *concorsi* were held at all is moot. In May of 1665, Girolamo Garofoli is asked to give the discourse and submit *soggetti* for the competition in October,[42] but come the time no mention of the celebration of the *concorso* appears in the *verbali*. For 1666, no reference is made to any *concorso,* and indeed it would appear from the minutes that very little business of any kind was carried on during Giovanni Grimaldi's principate. Orfeo Bosselli was the fourth artist to be offered the post of *principe* in 1667, but the first to accept, and only because in the last year of his long but undistinguished life he had energy for little else and could no doubt do with the honor. In June he was asked to give the discourse and provide the *soggetti* for October, and again in August (App. B, 1667, nn. 1, 2), but by September he had passed away, to be replaced by Pietro del Pò. No further mention is made of the *concorso*. It should be noted again that in the requests for *soggetti,* none were required for architecture.

For the next two years only the mundane affairs of the Accademia are recorded in the minutes: the acquisition and expenditure of funds, the regulation of the activities of artists, and the litigation of assessments. It may very well have been the absence of responsible attention to its obligations as an institution for education that led in 1670 to Pope Clement X's reduction of the taxes which supported it (see note 34), support which would be sorely missed. In response, Domenico Guidi, as mentioned above, reinstated the posing of models

for study in April 1670, but no other courses or any *concorsi* were as yet attempted.

In the ebb and flow of the tide of instruction at the Accademia, attention to the needs of the student of architecture was most often submerged. For the first seventy-five years of its existence, the Accademia was primarily a resource and haven for painters and sculptors, whose academic principles had been codified earlier, and who were more compatible with the idea of working from models, casts, or copies in the studio. Though Bernini and Pietro da Cortona were members, they were for this purpose sculptor or painter first, and made no use at all of the Accademia in their roles as architects. Where their architecture was not conceived in terms of their manual or pictorial arts, it was much more a product of inspiration than orientation, and had as little to do with "rules" as did Borromini's mason's aesthetic. The Accademia must have recognized that here, more than in any other instance, the job of instruction was best left to the master in the context of his own workshop, especially one of the stature of Bernini's.

But by the 1660s a generation of architects was appearing that *had* learned its art from the example of others, which implied that they in turn could communicate it to the next in terms that conformed to the needs of an academic structure. So it was that Carlo Fontana was raised to membership in 1667, and Carlo Rainaldi was called to the principate in 1673, the same year that Mattia de Rossi began the course in architecture, and G. B. Contini, the third of Bernini's best students, was made *Accademico di Merito.*[43] Also in 1673, the Accademia's house was put back in order with regard to instruction (App. B, 1673, n. 2), with entries "circa li studij" set aside specifically in the minutes, and a *concorso* arranged for the second year in a row, to include young architects this time (App. B, 1673, nn. 6–8).

So it appears that the fortunes of architecture and instruction at the Accademia had risen at the same time. But where the two fields merge, the fact remains that the concept of the application of "rules" to architecture for the purpose of teaching "correct" principles is not one that is native to Italy. Though the best treatises on architecture were by 1670 still the product of Italian minds—Palladio, Vignola, or Serlio—they had not been supplemented for nearly a century, during which time Italian architecture had continued to explore new paths. The use of these treatises as academic models is an idea more to be identified with the French after 1670. This suggests that the events of 1673 at the Accademia may have been anticipated in the previous year, during the principate of Charles Errard, when the *concorsi* had first been revived after the six-year lapse. At the time Errard was also director of the Académie de France in Rome, a satellite institution of the Académie Royale, and had been since its foundation in 1666. He was himself well versed in all the elements of French academicism, as a painter, decorator, and architect.[44] It is here that the threads of the histories of the French and Roman academies begin to weave themselves together, and Errard in many respects was responsible for the pattern that was woven.

Rome had been a second home to Errard since his youth. He had come there with his father from Nantes in the 1620s to enhance his already considerable drafting skills through the study of antiquity.[45] In this capacity he met the antiquarian Roland Fréart de Chambray, who was in Rome for the same purpose, and through him, on their return to Paris, was introduced to François Desnoyers, then *Surintendant des Bâtiments.* Desnoyers sent the two back to Rome under his patronage to conduct a thorough documentation of ancient and modern architectural ornament. During this longer stay Errard made his reputation in Roman artistic circles as a consummate draftsman, and in Roman society as a vigorous, upright, and commanding personality who was "fort adroit a l'épée."[46] Afterward, Desnoyers established de Chambray and Errard at his country estate at Dangu, where they collaborated on the *Parallèle de l'architecture antique et de la moderne.*[47] This was the first serious and scholarly attempt in the seventeenth century to assess the Renaissance authors on the orders against their ancient counterparts, and thereby to propose a rational theory of beauty derived from ancient usage, the didactic potential of which was well

suited to the needs of the fledgling Académie Royale. To this same end, and because of Palladio's comparative success in this light, they also published a translation of his treatise, *Les quatres livres d'architecture* (1650), which would become the cornerstone of the French academy's program in architecture.[48]

In the late 1640s, Errard began in earnest his career as a painter and decorator, designing and directing such work at the Palais Royal for Mazarin, at the royal chateaux at Versailles, Fontainebleau, and Saint-Germain-en-Laye, and at the Louvre where he was lodged with the rest of the artists to the crown. He was thus allied with them against the tyranny of the *Maîtrise,* and played a significant role in the foundation of the Académie Royale in 1648 and in its dealings thereafter with the *Maîtrise,* before all ties were severed in 1655.[49] Early on, Errard had attempted to keep the institution's finances in order. As one of four rectors in 1659 he had addressed the problem of lax instruction by calling the professors to task, and even offered his own services as teacher in some instances. Errard was in effect the elder statesman of the academy in its early years, with a greater role even than LeBrun, who is otherwise credited with the inspiration behind its formation.

But in the court of Louis XIV no one could be sure of his status for long. When the king took the reins of his government after 1661, Colbert became his chief minister. And Colbert, as *Surintendant des Bâtiments,* had recently been given an object lesson by his now disgraced predecessor Nicolas Fouquet in the effectiveness that a single monument, designed by a crack team of specialists, could have in enhancing personality. Vaux-le-Vicomte, with gardens by André LeNôtre, architecture by Louis LeVau, and decoration by Charles LeBrun, was an ill-timed demonstration of Fouquet's embezzled prestige, but one which Colbert recognized as appropriate to the aggrandizement of the monarchy. In consequence, the talents of LeNôtre, LeVau, and LeBrun were reapplied to that necessity, and the latter's star began its rise at the expense of Errard's. In 1663, LeBrun was made Chancellor of the Académie Royale for life, which gave him control on behalf of Colbert of all artistic endeavor in France for the next twenty years.[50]

One of LeBrun's first acts as chancellor was to revive the idea of sending some of the more accomplished students of the Académie Royale to Rome to continue their studies. This had been a provision in LeBrun's plans for the academy at the time of its founding, but for the next fifteen years the structuring and survival of the parent body itself were the primary concerns.[51] Now the solid foundation had finally been provided under Colbert's direction, and talk of a satellite in Rome could resume. At first, Poussin was considered for director of this school, which during a period of four years would provide support for a certain number of students chosen by the Académie. Letters requesting Poussin's acceptance of this responsibility were drawn up in 1664.[52] Competitions had already been held in April and July of 1663 to decide who would first be awarded the privilege (later called the *Prix-de-Rome*) of being sent to Rome to study, and three painters were singled out.[53] In September of the following year, a third competition was held which included a prize in sculpture.[54] But in neither the letters to Poussin nor the documents of the competitions is architecture mentioned as among the disciplines for which the new school would provide. This omission may reflect a realization, similar to that arrived at by the Accademia, that architecture could not yet be easily integrated into an academic curriculum, particularly under the direction of Poussin.

It is also of interest that both academies at the same time, 1663–64, placed emphasis on the role of competition: in Rome as a means of selecting members, and in Paris as a means of selecting students for advancement. In his speech to the Académie Royale in September of 1665, during his sojourn in Paris and work on the Louvre, Bernini also emphasized the value of competition and the stimulus to be found in prizes.[55] But this was no news to the French, as the letters to Poussin indicate that the royal endowment of prizes had been a common practice since the academy in Paris was founded. Therein lies an important distinction between the French and the

Romans, for the former had considerably greater resources for the stipulation of prizes and, as a result, more inducement for initiative in the competitions. Rather than drawing tools, books, or prints, the French could offer gold medals, or a display case in gold with a leather cover.[56] In its own, rather profane way, this is a measure of the stress placed on motivating students at the French academies, so that the next generation would know to whom it owed its allegiance in the matters of its art.

Despite continuing promises to the contrary, the students thus far chosen by competition had yet to be sent to Rome, since two more years would be required to find a suitable director for the school. Poussin had apparently balked at the idea, and in any event died on 19 November 1665, while in the meantime another competition was held.[57] The choice of a director was becoming a delicate one, and could not be based merely on convenience; he had to be as versed in academic organization as he was diplomatic in bearing. So it was that Errard could be recommended, and may indeed have recommended himself in order to be free of the shadow of LeBrun and the machinations of the French court.[58] "Errard se consolera de ne pas être le premier à Paris, puisqu'il va être le premier à Rome."[59] Errard seems also to have devised the first statutes for the new academy, which were read to the assembly in Paris in March of 1666.[60] Shortly afterward, the first group of *pensionnaires,* those students selected for boarding at the academy in Rome at royal expense, departed for Italy.

The statutes (App. B, 1666, n. 1) give the rector of the Académie de France in Rome complete authority in all things over the twelve *pensionnaires* established as the optimum number: six painters, four sculptors, and two architects. Not all of these places had been filled by the first rounds of competitions held in Paris. Some, particularly the architects, for whom there was as yet no academy through which to hold such competitions (see below), would arrive at the privilege by other means, presumably the influence of their patrons. This shadowy practice would have been business as usual for the French court, and makes it impossible to determine what merits recommended the architects that were chosen. Nevertheless, it appears that at the moment of its inception, the Académie de France in Rome would finally accommodate architects among its young artists.

In the statutes of the new academy, articles not dealing with the behavior of the students as Catholic gentlemen have to do with their activities as servants of the king, not as yet as artists in their own right. Hours not spent studying mathematics, geometry, anatomy, perspective, and architecture were to be spent at the command of the rector copying from originals. For architects, this amounted to the production of plans and elevations of Rome's monuments, most often palaces. In return, they would have the guidance of the rector, prizes for their best efforts, the facilities of the academy (which were necessarily limited at first), and one day off each week to pursue their own interests. But no one was allowed to produce any work other than for the king.

In nearly every instance, this work was in the form of copying from painting, sculpture, and architecture. When asked by Colbert for his advice about the academy in Rome in 1665, Bernini had offered the suggestion that students divide their time between copying and producing their own creative work, but only the first seems to have been taken to heart.[61] Perhaps there was an ulterior motive behind the foundation in Rome. Jean-Paul Alaux, historian of the Académie de France in Rome, does not find a coincidence but evidence of intent in the fact that the institution was started at the same time that the decision to move the court to Versailles was made.[62] Colbert and his successors considered their academy's branch in Rome to be an important source of ideas and artifacts for the decoration of Versailles. Copies were preferred only because originals were expensive, but literally or figuratively the principal objective was the spoliation of Italian art, as the majority of the correspondence between Colbert and the director in Rome reveals.[63] Copies of paintings could be turned into tapestries by the Gobelins factory under LeBrun's direction; original antique statuary or casts and models could be used to adorn the palace or the gardens. There was little part to play for architects,

since their contribution was not yet needed at Versailles, which was still in the capable hands of Louis LeVau. This would change during the 1670s, as will be seen in the next chapter.

What changed as well was the French academy's entire approach to architecture, which had, since 1648 and even during Colbert's initial reforms, been essentially excluded from the academy's domain. The result was that during the last decade of LeVau's life, after he had been given complete control over the king's building enterprises, his style was understood as Louis XIV's style. He was the French equivalent of Bernini, whose studio could dictate a particular practice or taste without arbitration on the part of the academy, with the only distinction being that LeVau, unlike Bernini, need not share the stage with any other architect. And so what control Colbert had exerted over the other arts after 1661 could not be so easily extended to architecture. Colbert had hoped to break this monopoly in 1664, when LeVau's designs for the east front of the Louvre were rejected and designs by Italian architects were solicited. Courting Bernini for the next two years to bring LeVau into line, Colbert was ultimately able to set up a committee of architects more receptive to his dominion, where LeVau shared credit with LeBrun and Claude Perrault for the genesis of the Louvre front in 1667.[64] On LeVau's death in 1670, Colbert merely expanded this committee to form the nucleus of the Académie Royale d'Architecture, which was opened in 1671.[65]

The vacancy left by the death of LeVau would be even more despotically filled by Jules Hardouin-Mansart after 1675, but in the meantime Colbert's committee of architects set about the task of codifying the "correct" principles of architecture to be uniformly applied in the France of Louis XIV. Most of the committee, as practicing architects in their own right, could call upon experience when giving advice on construction methods and the like, and in that capacity the "academy" functioned very well. In fact, the Académie d'Architecture was from the start and would remain until after the Revolution separate from the Académie de Peinture et Sculpture because on balance it dealt more with concrete matters than abstract ones. But Colbert's purposes, and an "academy" in the truest sense, required the establishment of authority in theoretical principles and in the education, or more to the point "molding," of the next generation of architects who must continue to follow the establishment line. For this the majority of the committee was less well equipped, and deferred instead to the architects of the past who had already written on their art, and to those special individuals, more than amateurs but less than architects, who were willing to interpret them.

These last were men like the physician Claude Perrault, who was certainly less of an architect than he imagined himself, but whose annotated translation of Vitruvius, *Les dix livres d'architecture* (1673), was the last and greatest of its kind.[66] With this and de Chambray's translation of Palladio, the preferred ancient and modern counterparts of a theoretical curriculum were in place, and attention could now turn to the other authors of treatises on the Orders. De Chambray had taken the first step with the *Parallèle* by simply graphically contrasting the proportions and measurements of the Orders as proposed by these authors, beginning with Palladio and going down the list in order of preference from Scamozzi, through Serlio, Vignola, Alberti, and others, and ending with the two Frenchmen, Bullant and de l'Orme. This hierarchy served to satisfy the academy as well, as it was based not on what the architects had built, but on how lucid and functional their writings were for use in teaching. Architects of equal stature in the Cinquecento, like Bramante, Sangallo, or Sansovino, or even the great names of the Seicento, were given no hearing because they had published nothing. And the more aberrant talents like Michelangelo and Borromini were altogether condemned not only because they flouted classical usage or their work was not put into print, but because it *could not* be translated into any readily communicable form.

The next step was to reshape this material into a comprehensive textbook, for use in the classroom, and to this end the first director of the Académie d'Architecture, François Blondel, devoted himself. He was a military engineer, a diplomat, and a professor of mathematics at the Académie de Science, who qualified as a gifted and well-traveled amateur in architecture with an inclination to theory and teaching rather than practice. The fact that Colbert put him at the head of his new academy in 1671 suggests that the minister saw the establishment of a curriculum to be a first order of business, and Blondel was set to the task immediately.[67] He established one meeting per week for the membership to debate the nature of "le bon goût," and two meetings per week for instruction in the "règlements" generated by these debates.[68] There were also to be lectures in the related fields of geometry, mechanics, hydraulics, fortifications, perspective, and even stonecutting. Blondel was the lecturer in architecture for the first years of the academy, and his lectures were compiled to form his *Cours d'Architecture,* which for the rest of the century was the principal organ of doctrinaire classicism.[69]

The first part of the *Cours,* published in 1675, presented a list of terms and a history of architecture, as preface to the by now standard comparisons between the orders of Vitruvius and those of Palladio, Vignola, and Scamozzi. In 1683, four parts were added which examined the individual elements of the Orders, and other details like arches, domes, doors and windows, stairs, chimneys, and even bridges and aqueducts, in relation to proportional principles which Blondel then more generally defined. His experience led him to the conclusion that beauty in architecture was a function of ideal proportions derived from simple ratios, constant throughout creation, which the ancients understood well and the moderns less so. In this claim he was immediately at odds with Perrault, who, in his studies of Vitruvius and his own work on the Orders which he published in 1683 as the *Ordonnance,* had decided that satisfactory proportions appear so only because men of genius had settled upon them intuitively, and their usage had conditioned what was beautiful.[70] Perrault's more daring assertion had less of a following in the seventeenth century, but in fact neither proposal was antithetical to academic thinking, since both required an architect to reason his own tastes from accepted precedents. Indeed, what appears in Perrault to be a more liberal attitude to the examples set by ancient and modern masters, was actually used by him to argue for much narrower guidelines, a "middle road," in the determination of proper proportions in French architecture.[71]

What the Académie d'Architecture now had was the makings of a debate on the precepts of beauty equivalent to that between the "Ancients" and "Moderns" which was then going on in their sister institution, the Académie de Peinture et Sculpture. The resolution of the argument (though of course it was irresolvable) thus became the theoretical apology for their existence, and they could consider themselves to have come of age. This was ideally suited to Colbert's purpose, as the debate was a smoke screen for his efforts to exert his will over practical building in France through the Académie d'Architecture.

The danger, of course, was that in this environment pedantic concerns would override all others, and this remains to date the principal criticism to be leveled at the Académie d'Architecture in the age of Louis XIV. To some extent this is true of the architecture of the age, which is of uniformly excellent quality and attentive to details, but cannot be recommended for inventiveness, or for thinking beyond the sum of the parts. Compromises could be accepted for the sake of richness and grandeur, if a general classical propriety was upheld in order to retain what was both beautiful and French. But the *Style Louis Quatorze* is just a measure of Colbert's success, as even Jules Hardouin-Mansart, whose towering ego was capable of passages of independent genius in the commissions that passed through his office, subordinated his one-man rule over building in the kingdom to the wishes of Colbert as long as the *Surintendant* lived.

Colbert's control of the Académie d'Architecture was perhaps even more insidious than it was for the painters and sculptors. The latter had at least gained some autonomy for their institution before voluntarily placing it in Colbert's trust after 1661, but the Académie d'Architecture existed solely on his sufferance. There were no patent letters filed until 1717, under the regency, which meant that the academy had no official existence during the reign of Louis XIV, and whatever privileges the academicians had were at the mercy of his *Surintendant des Bâtiments*.[72] Members could promote their own apprentices to the academy as students, but since their own tenures depended on the indulgence of the king, these choices were virtually in his hands as well. And most certainly the choice of which students would be sent to Rome belonged to him, or more correctly to his minister, Colbert. In the preface to his *Cours,* Blondel states that the promise had been made that a *grand prix* would be instituted to select students for that honor, as was already the case for students of the other academy. It was not until 1720, however, that the *Prix-de-Rome* was extended to include architects, so that, too, was handled arbitrarily in the meantime.[73] This system was quite vulnerable to whim, abuse, and nepotism, and the benefits of a curriculum steeped in dogmatism did little to counter their effects.

It should be said that Errard must be considered among the pedants rather than the practitioners of architecture, as up to the year of his departure for Rome his involvement other than in decoration had been totally literary. And even in 1666, when he was finally awarded a commission for the Church of the Assumption on the Rue St. Honoré, the design itself can be praised in the reasoning of its details but fails to please when taken as a whole (see Figs. 4–6).[74] The fact that the church was executed in his absence by a builder who was typically insensitive to the wishes of a professional architect is only a partial explanation.[75] Errard's church is actually one of the first casualties of French academicism applied at its most rational but least inspired level. Still, though he does not appear as such in the royal accounts, he refers to himself as "architecte du Roi" in the church registry at the time of his second marriage in 1675.[76] It is reasonable to assume, therefore, that in his role as rector of the Rome academy he would have upheld the interests of the young architects along with those of the painters and sculptors.

And so it was that in 1666 he brought with him to Rome a young architect by the name of

DuVivier, whose place among the first *pensionnaires* can only have been arranged by Errard as neither the Académie d'Architecture nor the means to select architects for Rome as yet existed.[77] DuVivier may have been intended to assist Errard on the designs for the Assumption church, which were sent from Rome to Paris, but he must have shown enough promise to deserve the privilege of his *pension*. His stay in Rome was extensive, as he still appears in the inventory of 1673 as one of two architects then in residence.[78] Although the monthly reports on the students required of Errard are not preserved intact, DuVivier probably would have spent the time making plans and elevations of Roman buildings when not working specifically for Errard. What becomes of him after 1673 is unknown, though he probably returned to Paris with Errard when the latter's first term as rector was over.

Those first six years for the Académie de France in Rome, between 1666 and 1673, were years of phenomenal progress. Starting with nothing more than letters of credit sufficient for the purchases that would have to be made, and housed at first in the home of the Abbé Saraca on the Janiculum,[79] the academy thrived under Errard's careful nurturing. By 1673, more commodious lodgings were arranged on the Tiber's left bank near S. Andrea della Valle,[80] and the academy was well provided with the necessary utensils and furnishings, even if the latter were a bit "monkish."[81] The stock of casts and engravings as models for the drawing classes was growing, a model had been hired, and the other business of the academy, sending copies back to Paris, was keeping pace. Funds from Paris were always generously forthcoming and well accounted for, and by 1673 the academy was able to support seventeen artists in residence, five more than the quota stipulated by the statutes.[82] Spirits were running high, to the point where the requirements for devoting time to copying and working only for the crown were being questioned by the students, but Errard's discipline was strict.[83]

Matters were so well in hand by 1670 that Errard was free to resume his membership in the Accademia di San Luca, and even to participate actively in its functions, after an absence of more than thirty years. He was invited to contribute to the decoration of the Accademia's salon (see note 44), and in November of the same year was one of the nominees for *principe*.[84] Though Giovanni Maria Morandi was elected to that post, Errard was appointed one of the two *pacieri* (peacemakers) for 1671,[85] and as such was responsible for quelling disputes between the professors and students, and assuring that they "all live quietly together in a Christian fashion."[86] From this vantage point it is certain that he would have been given a good idea of the state of education at the Accademia. In December of 1671 he was elected to the principate, so that his full expertise as an organizer and his imposing character could be brought to bear on conditions at the Roman academy.[87] Melchior Missirini (App. B, 1672, n. 1) credits him with putting in order many of the negotiations, assets, and disbursements of the Accademia, but more importantly he was responsible for reinstating the prize competitions.

In July 1672, the *concorso* on the Feast of St. Luke was established again (App. B, 1672, n. 3), and among the authors of the *soggetti* appears the name of an architect, from which it is possible to assume that students in that field were meant to compete.[88] In August and September, the *verbali* (App. B, 1672, nn. 4, 5) admonish all the professors to urge their students to expedite their entries, so that their work might be used to decorate the "piccola galleria" during the celebrations and become an example to others. Come October, however, the *concorso* had to be postponed as not enough dignitaries were able to attend, and the ugly question of expenses had to be confronted (App. B, 1672, n. 6).[89] The date for the *concorso* was ultimately set for the first Sunday in December, but still the money for prizes was lacking (App. B, 1672, n. 7). This problem with funds is difficult to understand, since so many of the *verbali* in this year are given over to the methods Errard successfully employed to compound the Accademia's income through the collection of dues and rents. Even the posing of models had been eliminated this year, so that if the money was going anywhere not much went to fulfill the Accademia's obligations in instruction. Nonetheless, it would appear that the *concorso* was carried out, as mention is made on 29 November of the submission of the competing designs.[90] With some fourteen prelates and princes in attendance, the event was not insignificant, and in this instance there is nothing to indicate that architects were not in fact involved.

There was still by this date no record kept at the Accademia of those who were awarded prizes in the *concorsi,* and the practice of retaining or even labeling winning designs was not yet routine. Therefore, the competitors themselves remain anonymous to us, but in this year of Errard's involvement something of them is known that is both enlightening and suggestive. A letter from Colbert dated 6 January 1673 (App. B, 1673, n. 1) congratulates Errard on the fact that in the Accademia's *concorso* of the previous year four French *pensionnaires* (both painters and sculptors) received prizes. Even if duplicate prizes were awarded at each level, this must represent a large proportion of the prizewinners, and French students would thus appear to have already been active in the functions of the Accademia. Errard had succeeded not only in bringing the Accademia's attention back to the *concorsi,* but in drawing their attention to his academy and its charges, and through them to French achievement in general. In other words, it was in Errard's principate that the process was begun whereby the French and Roman academies were reconciled to each other, while LeBrun's principate, and the union of the academies in 1677, represents what is in effect the climax of that process.

During his term of office in 1672, Errard was also able to achieve other goals that were not altogether selfless. In August he proposed several new candidates for *Accademico di Merito,* as his way of gaining favor for his own academy as well as with Bernini, who was still providing his services to the French in Rome.[91] Bernini's son, Paolo, was nominated in sculpture, and Mattia de Rossi, his prize pupil and assistant while in Paris, in architecture. De Rossi's conduct in Paris during Bernini's stay, and afterward, while working on the model for the Louvre, had gained him the respect of his French hosts, so his nomination was by no means a hollow gesture.[92] Errard also proposed one of his own students, the sculptor François Lespingolas, who had taken two prizes in the competitions for the trip to Rome, and who must have been one of Bernini's assistants in the work on Louis's equestrian portrait. The most important benefit of all was that de Rossi was now eligible to teach when architecture was added to the curriculum the following year.

In April 1672 Errard also introduced into the minutes of the Accademia his presentation, on behalf of the Académie Royale in Paris, of a book edited by Thomas Regnaudin, a sculptor in the king's service, containing the patents, privileges, statutes, and earliest meetings of the Académie de Peinture et Sculpture (App. B, 1672, n. 2). The Romans were thus given the most concise idea possible of what were the nature and potentials of French academic practice and patronage, and certainly Errard had been given the best possible opportunity to see what the Accademia had to offer. He should also, therefore, have been aware at this point that provision had been made in the statutes of 1607 for the aggregation of the Accademia di San Luca with similar institutions elsewhere, which made its facilities available to the members of such institutions.[93] In view of all this, and of the joint participation of French and Italian students in the *concorso,* it may be that already in 1672 Errard had conceived the idea of uniting the French and Roman academies, of making official what had been an experiment for him. After all, this would in the long run have most benefited the academy that was then in his care.

Indeed, this idea may have been one of the items discussed when Errard was shortly thereafter called back to the French court, at the conclusion of his first term as director.[94] When his good friend and one-time collaborator Noël Coypel appeared in Rome early in 1673 to relieve Errard in this post, Errard was reluctant to leave what had become his home to return to what was for him less welcome society.[95] He appeared before the Académie Royale to be heaped with their praises for his direction of the affairs of their satellite, and he must certainly have availed himself of the opportunity to supervise personally the work on his church, but neither of these was sufficient to bring him back to Paris in view of his wishes to the contrary. Colbert and LeBrun no doubt wished to confer with him directly about the affairs of their academy in Rome, but these were in order, for all intents and purposes, and likely held no real concerns for them that had not been answered in correspondence. More probably it was Errard's activities on behalf of the Accademia that they wanted to hear about. They would have needed to know whether he had compromised his own position as director of the French academy in Rome in accepting the duties of *principe,* but more importantly whether he had indeed seen any advantage for their interests in the temporary and unofficial union of the two academies. The reaction was apparently favorable, and it must have been during Errard's brief stay in Paris that the means for an officially sanctioned union of the academies was worked out, for he returned to Rome in the fall of 1675 to resume his position as rector, with the new title of *Directeur* of the Académie Royale, and fully empowered to initiate the process of unification.[96]

In the meantime, Carlo Rainaldi was *principe* at the Accademia in 1673, during which time he compounded the educational reforms begun by Errard. Instruction was firmly established on Sundays and feast days, with the posing of the nude and lectures in anatomy set aside for the mornings, and lectures in architecture and perspective for the afternoons (App. B, 1673, n. 2). The French had provided examples in their academies in both Paris and Rome of the effectiveness of a rigorous lecture schedule in maintaining the discipline of students. The Accademia had turned its attention to the curriculum as early as January (App. B, 1673, n. 3), at the same time that efforts toward a *concorso* in that year were initiated with a call for *soggetti.* In April, it was decreed that in the future the *soggetti* would be proposed by whoever was chosen to give the oration during the celebration of the *concorso* on the Feast of St. Luke (App. B, 1673, n. 4), and three weeks later one Michael Bruguères was elected to serve in this capacity.[97] In view of the fact that instruction in architecture

had begun for the first time under Mattia de Rossi's direction in May, competition was now open to his students as well, but by the end of that month there was as yet no *soggetto* in architecture (App. B, 1673, nn. 6, 7).

This must have been corrected a short time later as the posted announcement of the *concorso* written by Giuseppe Ghezzi as assistant to then secretary G. B. Passeri includes the topic for the architects: "il motivo del tempio da farsi Pianta, Facciata, e Spaccato" (App. B, 1673, n. 8).[98] While this contains what will become the standard injunction regarding the use of plan, elevation, and section drawings to present an architectural design, the topic itself is quite vague. There is no surprise in this since Bruguères had no competence in architecture, and the instructor in architecture had as yet no say in the matter. In the absence of submitted designs related to this *soggetto,* it is therefore impossible to attach any importance to the architectural portion of this competition, other than that it happened at all.

On 10 September (App. B, 1673, n. 9), "diligence" was encouraged in the production of designs for the forthcoming *concorso,* which was ultimately set for Sunday, 15 October (App. B, 1673, n. 10), with the judging to be done the week before.[99] Even Maratti and Errard had not succeeded in having the *concorso* celebrated on time, and the general success of this *concorso,* despite its lack of ceremony, is a tribute to Rainaldi. But what is known of this *concorso* is in large part due to the conscientious effort of Ghezzi, whose documentation of it repairs the lacunae in the *verbali,* which were very poorly kept by Passeri. There will be a number of occasions where Ghezzi must be thanked for his record of the details of the *Concorsi Accademici,* after he becomes secretary in his own right at the end of 1674.

But there is little record of the year 1674 itself and the principate of G. B. Gaulli, whose achievements were in any case more personal than institutional. According to the few entries in the *verbali* that appear during the first nine months of that year, Gregorio Tomassini was made lecturer in architecture, and later chosen to provide the *soggetto* for his students in the upcoming *concorso*

(App. B, 1674, n. 1). Tomassini had gained a new privilege for his office as lecturer, but he put it to use by merely repeating the theme of a "tempio" that had been proposed in 1673. It may be that he, too, was unprepared for such a responsibility, as he had no reputation as an architect, and even had to be supervised in his lectures by de Rossi and Rainaldi. In September, Ghezzi was made secretary, and he turned out to be ideally suited to the position as the minutes are consistently recorded for most of the rest of the century.[100] But with regard to the *concorso* of 1674, there was nothing to record, for in October it was decided to "transfer it to another, more opportune time" (App. B, 1674, n. 2). Why the opportunity was lost in this year is not reported, but it would seem that the Accademia had again put its fiscal concerns ahead of its mission to educate.

This action did not go unchallenged, however, and it was decided in September of the following year to reestablish the *concorso* in response to what must have been considerable objection to the competitions having lapsed at all (App. B, 1675, n. 1). The *concorso* was set for the second Sunday in November, to cap what had been an eventful year for the Accademia: new statutes were defined in 1675, some of which affected the *concorsi;*[101] the debates on theory continued on the subject of Raphael; the Holy Year was celebrated at the Accademia with considerable pomp; and a new symbol was adopted for use on the Accademia's diplomas.[102] This was to be an image of the Sun, with three rays, representing the three arts which were now equally represented at the Accademia, striking the Earth and bringing beauty symbolized by plants and flowers. In this year, as well, a union was struck between the Roman academy and its counterpart in Turin, and the first steps were taken toward forging the same links with the Académie Royale in Paris.

Carlo Fontana had been instructor in architecture for 1675, and so the first three instructors in architecture in the history of the Accademia, including Mattia de Rossi and Gregorio Tomassini, have now been accounted for. Some word about *how* they conducted their lectures would therefore be in order, were it not for an unfortunate lack of

specific information on the subject. All that remains from this period are the fifteen sheets of lessons on the orders by de Rossi's hand, two of which are illustrated in this volume (see Figs. 55, 56). These two are quite the most elaborate of the drawings, some of which represent only the barest outline of a pedestal. They are all too schematic to have demanded much of either de Rossi's or his students' time, which is disconcerting since these lessons were now pointed directly at young architects, and not merely at painters or sculptors who had earlier required only a passing familiarity with principles of classical architecture (Chapter III, note 8). With Mattia de Rossi in charge, surely there must have been more substance introduced into the curriculum.

If the methods of instructors in painting and sculpture can be used as a model, students in architecture would likewise have been assigned to render details of existing monuments by established masters, or to produce their own designs for minor architectural details based on earlier precedents. The architect/instructor would then be expected to comment on the student's work and provide advice for perfecting his skills with the tools and techniques of his art (how to work with pen and wash or how to draw a geometric figure, for example). Lectures in architectural theory very probably did not progress beyond a similarly elementary level, being limited to the "dos and don'ts" involved in the employment of the various orders in basic contexts, again as established by precedent. A more advanced experience for any particular student would depend upon his involvement in the work of his master's studio, as draftsman on the projects commissioned from it, at whatever level his master deemed him fit. But here, too, the ultimate source of his ideas was the sketches or assignments given him by his master, whether to define a particular detail or provide the final presentation drawing.

Within this system, the concept of "authority" would have been quite different from that which was being evolved for the Académie Royale d'Architecture during the years from 1671 to 1675. Granted, the treatises of Palladio, Vignola, and the rest of the Italians were also considered valuable visual resources in Rome, but only as examples and not as a hierarchy of what was "correct" and acceptable usage. They shared an equal place in the experience of any student of architecture in Rome with the city itself, and with its classical heritage that spanned millennia, and included many works by great architects whose fortes did not happen to be writing or critical analysis. In this rich and varied milieu, to establish one "authority" would exclude many others, and without a centralized power to assert that authority for its own ends, such a premise would not stand for long. A consistent theory of architectural beauty could not easily be found that would encompass both Michelangelo and Vignola, or Borromini and Bernini, or Vitruvius and nearly all of his ancient counterparts. And so where there was no single authority there were instead many, some of elevated stature and others of less, but none who was considered either superior to or separate from the whole.

What sounds like stylistic anarchy in comparison to the French was of course ameliorated by the context of Rome, where patronage predicated a general conformity to tastes that could be described only as Roman. But to precisely define such tastes to serve as the core of an academic theory would have been an impossible task, and perhaps by contemporary standards an undesirable one as it would have stifled the vitality of Roman architecture even more than did the decline in commissions. Even Fontana and de Rossi, students of the greatest master of the Roman Baroque, did not exist entirely in Bernini's shadow, either before or after his death in 1680. They were, in effect, their own authorities, and any young architect who did not wish to subordinate his talent to another's could hope to garner such authority for himself, answering only to the desires of the patron.

Of course for an academic curriculum to function effectively, the ability to make critical judgements, and to describe the better architectural decisions of the past and define the reasoning behind them, was a necessary start. But given the reluctance to establish an absolute authority in this regard, the alternative was to provide the students with several authorities in rapid succession from

which they could derive their own stylistic identity. So it was that in the first three years of architectural instruction at the Accademia three different architects had this responsibility, to be followed by a fourth, Felice della Greca, in 1676 (App. B, 1676, n. 3). This might also be the result of a reluctance on the part of the architects themselves to compromise their practices by becoming too involved in teaching, but this indirectly implies that the role of the architect as theoretician was viewed in Rome as a minor one compared to his role as innovator.

De Rossi and Fontana, with promising independent careers before them, would no doubt have seen it this way, and at no time after 1675 did either of them resubmit their services in teaching the architecture course at the Accademia. For them, and for the students in their workshops, the immediate and practical concerns of architecture held sway over the universal and timeless. But this is not true of Tomassini, who was at best a capable draftsman, and at worst a cabinet maker (see note 27). He may have conceived of a future for himself as a theoretician in architecture within the confines of the Accademia, just as Errard had found such a niche for himself in the French academy. Following the union of the academies in 1676, when Tomassini became instructor in architecture for extended periods of time, his methods alter the nature of such instruction after the example of the French and their obsession with the Orders, as the next chapter reveals. But before that occurred the architecture program at the Accademia remained without definition, and presumably without much value placed on it as a result. It may have still existed primarily for the benefit only of painters and sculptors, enabling them to know better the principles of the third visual art in relation to their own.

The advantage as early as 1673 belonged to the French, who in that year sent the first student trained at their Académie d'Architecture to Rome on a royal *pension* (though without a *Prix-de-Rome*). Simon Chupin arrived in the entourage of Noël Coypel when the latter came to take up his position as director for the period of Errard's visit to Paris.[103] Chupin was followed in 1674 by

Augustin D'Aviler (who was delayed until 1676; see Chapter II), and by Claude Desgots in 1675, by which time Errard had resumed the post of director, and was meant as well to be their tutor in drafting. Each of them was, however, already fully versed in the fundamental principles of architecture being set down by Blondel for the Parisian academy, needing only the experience of Rome to reach their maturity. They were, in effect, to have the blessings of both worlds: their technical skills and grasp of the literature of architecture had been formed by the strict regimens of Paris; their creative horizons would be expanded beyond the limitations of Parisian academicism by the variety of Rome.

It was only the rules of the French Academy in Rome that defined them as students, an expedient which allowed the academy in Paris to use them, as it did the painters and sculptors, to provide accurate measurements and renderings of Roman architecture. Their drawings could be used to test the theories of proportion then being weighed in Paris which depended so much on precision. But by now these young architects were above this, for indeed there were no other students of architecture anywhere in Europe who could boast their background, and their talents could be better applied elsewhere. This is confirmed by their performances in the *concorso* of 1677, which was occasioned by the aggregation of the French and Roman academies, and in which they achieved a signal victory.

THE UNION OF THE ACADEMIES

Late in 1675, Errard (then in his seventies) returned to Rome, delayed by his second marriage, and as the earliest sources would have it he did so already equipped with documents, and with new authority as *Directeur* of the Académie Royale, which enabled him to begin the process of joining the academies of Paris and Rome.[104] This would not be a loose association of the two schools in Rome as was the case in 1672 when he was head of both, but a formal unification of two sovereign institutions. A great deal of bureaucratic and diplomatic maneuvering was therefore in

order, much of which appears to have been worked out during Errard's stay in Paris as progress is made quickly and consistently thereafter.

LeBrun is presumed to have put forward the idea of the aggregation, but so much of the actual process was conducted *sub rosa* that it is difficult to say who made the first overtures.[105] The French would seem to have been the source only because matters were for the most part under their control, and they held the upper hand throughout the negotiations. But the Italians might just as well have initiated the idea, having seen what Errard could do in 1672, and what royal patronage had done for his academy, in the hope of reaping such benefits for themselves. Louis XIV's coffers had opened to finance his enterprises in Rome: commissions for sculpture and paintings, acquisitions of antiquities and copies, and an academy to oversee his interests. And that academy had begun to show the fruits of the well-ordered structure it had in common with its parent body. If either individually or as a group the Roman academicians could tap into any part of this, allying themselves with a foreign power was a small price to pay.

On the surface, it may be that Colbert, who after all has to be considered the prime motivator behind the actions of the French, conceived of the union in similar terms. Having access to the Accademia's resources would have been of some value to his academy in Rome, which would also be able to operate more effectively without the limitations that might otherwise apply to rival academies, but no dire effects had been felt before this. Moreover, the Accademia could presumably now work for him in dealing with Roman artists on royal commissions, like Bernini's equestrian portrait of Louis, but with the Louvre project Colbert had already demonstrated that France had little need for the contributions of Italians. Certainly none of the grand expectations for the union with regard to its effects on the arts in both France and Italy had any part in his scheme, since he was indifferent to such aesthetic arguments. The projected union might be seen to give more to the Italians, therefore, were it not for the fact that Colbert never pursued anything that did not in some way further his efforts to make France supreme in Europe. That French academicism should be the common language for the arts was crucial to this, to be sure, but Colbert's interests were more often directed to his mercantile policy, whereby he hoped to reset the balance of trade in France's favor. One particular regret of his in this regard was the expense required to compete in the market for Roman art or antiquities. If the union of the two academies should remove the hindrances which often plagued his agents (since they would no longer be representing an altogether foreign interest) and reduce the flow of capital needed to make their purchases, then it would in Colbert's mind achieve the greatest good.

The Italians seem to have had no inkling of these ulterior motives, and for the first few years of the union, while aspirations were still high, they remained oblivious to them. Instead, it was not long after Errard's return to Rome that the Accademia's officers enthusiastically set the process of aggregation in motion, though Errard himself remained conspicuously behind the scenes. Some idea of how unusual this particular process was in the history of the Accademia, and thus of its importance, can be had by comparing it to the aggregation with the Turin academy that had occurred earlier in 1675.

Provisions for such aggregations had existed since the statutes of 1607, the idea being that academicians from another Italian city would thereby be granted all the privileges of membership in the Accademia, and vice versa, so that artists from either city would be welcome to practice in the other without restraint. Advantage was not taken of this for nearly seventy years, however, perhaps because no need arose until the power of the urban academies began to manifest itself most remarkably in the late Seicento. Then, over the next several decades, many Italian academies were joined to the Accademia, beginning with the one in Turin and including those in Bologna, Parma, and Venice, as were the national academies of France, Austria, Spain, and Russia.[106] The Accademia need not have played a subservient role in any of these unions, since it had as much if not more to offer in the bargain as far as educational opportunity was concerned.

In fact, in the first instance it was the members of the ducal academy in Turin who petitioned the Accademia for their aggregation, in a letter dated 4 March 1675 and signed for them by the secretary of Duke Carlo Emmanuele II.[107] Their academy had had a late and uncertain start in 1652, providing protection and a modest status for the artists of the House of Savoy, which had only recently established its court in Turin, the principal city of its domains in Piedmont. In the latter part of the 1600s, the Dukes of Savoy were beginning to assert their autonomy from the French, under whose wing they had existed for centuries, and moving their capital south of the Alps was one way of doing so. In the next century they would achieve their end during the Wars for the Spanish Succession as allies of the Holy Roman Empire in their victory over the French, after which they had dominion over an independent Italian kingdom. In the meantime, the request for a union between the Roman academy and their own was no doubt part of the diplomatic game in which Piedmont's affiliations were redirected to the south.

These factors would have meant very little to the Accademia, of course, nor was the high purpose of the union diminished by them. If the culture of the Turin court was henceforth to be Italian, there was no better inspiration than Rome to which to turn; and the Roman academy had succeeded with little effort in having its authority, even to the full adoption of its rules, extended to another capital. And as a result the way was paved for later Roman artists like Filippo Juvarra (see Chapter II) to make their careers in a thriving Turin where opportunities were more abundant, and for Piedmontese students to hone their skills in Rome. All of this had been achieved by the exchange of two simple letters, the one mentioned above wherein the aggregation was proposed and the response of the Accademia which followed soon after. Both have little substance beyond the usual florid courtesies, but their tone leaves no doubt that in this matter deference was owed to the Romans, and that it was their importance that had been magnified.

In view of this, there is little validity in any assumption that the Accademia was forced to the union with the French academy by reason of a diminished faith in itself.[108] Both academies had begun to extend influence outside of their respective cities; both had learned something from the other during critical periods of their development; and both could derive advantages from their aggregation. While there were obvious differences in degree between Colbert's national academy and an urban foundation like the Accademia, they would have been paired as relative equals in this age of formality. And confronting each other as equals required that the affair be conducted with more ceremony and assurances than were necessary between the Accademia and its lesser Turinese counterpart. The question is whether in the final analysis the Accademia gave up more than it received in return.

The first overt move in the direction of the aggregation was made by the Italians. On 15 December 1675, Charles LeBrun was nominated *Accademico di Merito* by Carlo Maratti, in recognition of his "rare quality and eminence in the profession" (App. B, 1675, n. 2). Proposing an artist for this honor who was neither in residence in the city at the time, nor had any intention of returning in the future, was an extremely exceptional occurrence, which overlooked the spirit, if not the letter, of the Accademia's rules.[109] The wheels must have already been greased, however, for not only LeBrun's nomination, but his membership was accepted by the general congregation on the first ballot "with no objections, speaking as one," which is to say unanimously. A letter informing LeBrun of his new title and privileges was immediately posted by then secretary Giuseppe Ghezzi, filled, in the usual fashion, with a preponderance of laudatory and obsequious phraseology.

One week later, on 22 December, Domenico Guidi as acting *principe* accepted a motion from Maratti that LeBrun's name be added to the ballot for the election of the next year's *principe*, requiring an even more extraordinary subversion of the statutes.[110] Then the three whose names were already on the ballot, namely Mattia de Rossi, Lazzaro Baldi, and Giovanni Maria Morandi, conveniently renounced their own candidacies, thus handing LeBrun the post "per utilità grande e

decoro maggiore della nostra Accademia." This time the result was received with "minima discrepenza," an interesting semantic shift on Ghezzi's part which suggests that some members had been less intimidated by the speed with which they were faced with events, and were, at least minimally, able to cry foul. For it would seem that while "conspiracy" may be too strong a word for their conduct, certainly the hierarchy of the Accademia had orchestrated its actions to make LeBrun's elevation to office as quick and painless an operation as possible, over the heads of their constituency. While Errard does not appear in attendance at these meetings, his covert involvement in the plot is almost certain since his name was raised in nomination for *vice-principe*, giving him control in LeBrun's absence and on Colbert's behalf over the events which were to follow.

As for what may have prompted the "conspiracy" of the Italians, there is the possibility that devious or self-serving intent may have guided Domenico Guidi, according to Wittkower.[111] As acting head of the Accademia at the end of 1675, it was he who allowed the rules governing elections to be bent so that LeBrun could be made *principe*, and when the academies were joined in 1676 Guidi was repaid by being made a *recteur* of the Académie Royale, in accordance with the articles of the aggregation. Guidi was also awarded some of the commissions coming into Rome from Versailles, and though he had to accept designs from Paris (a stunning blow to Roman pride, as Wittkower points out) he may have appreciated most this addition to his international markets. Guidi was, after all, an artist little concerned with his art and more with his production, having devoted his studio's efforts to quantity rather than quality. This had set him at odds with the higher standards of the Accademia, as much as his mediocre handling of his master Algardi's idiom had cast him off from the Bernini camp. His ambitions were so great, however, that he was not averse to promoting himself by other means, and his support of the tactics of the French in achieving LeBrun's election was just one more way of doing so.

It is doubtful, though, that artists like Maratti

or Mattia de Rossi, or even lesser lights like Morandi and Baldi, would have been willing to compromise their reputations to such a degree. Their aim would have been to improve the system of which they were an accepted part, and not simply replace it with a system that might present them with more material advantages. By taking Maratti as the most important component of their group, the philosophical incentives behind embracing the French academy are more easily explained. Pietro Bellori's exposition before the Accademia of the classicist platform, in a speech he made in 1664 titled "L'idea," was the springboard not only for Maratti's Late Baroque classicism, but also for the doctrines of the Académie Royale as they were laid down under Colbert and LeBrun. Maratti and LeBrun were weighed as equals in epitomizing this style, characterized by empiricism and lucid principles that could be easily taught and disseminated.[112] For Colbert's purposes, this meant that a national style could be rapidly formulated and stringently maintained to suit his ends. But for Maratti and his party, the application of similar means to their academy might succeed in making it a bastion of academic classicism to stand against the unchecked exuberance of the High Baroque and its supporters, which explains why Errard was able to enlist their aid on behalf of LeBrun. Maratti perhaps hoped that an alliance with the French would elicit their aid in championing his cause, but indeed members of any of the other stylistic "schools" may have seen value in a French system that could give definition and direction to their particular art.

With regard to painting and sculpture, Maratti and the others may well have succeeded. While Guidi himself had no particular "style" to champion, his support of the French from 1675 on did give further legitimacy to the influence of their sculptors in Rome. As a result, the advocates of a purely Roman Baroque in sculpture, centered on Bernini, were compelled to define more precisely their alternative so as to make the choice clearer for their patrons; two readily distinguishable lines of development emerge. Maratti's classicism had to contend with the Berninesque idiom of G. B. Gaulli, who was also an important acade-

mician, or with followers of Pietro da Cortona like Lazzaro Baldi, and so each of these "schools" of painting needed to define its precepts more concisely as well. A strict academic context made the best laboratory in which to arrive at these definitions and prepare the next generation to meet its partisan challenges.

Another purpose of the present book is to explain what kind of laboratory for architecture the Accademia represented, as indicated by the competition designs, and what impact the French and their academics might have had on them, but painting and sculpture cannot be conveniently elaborated upon here. Suffice to say that while the classicists held the upper hand in painting into the eighteenth century, thanks principally to Maratti but in no small way to the Accademia as well, sculpture remained dominated by Bernini's influence. Though it may be possible to place a Roman artist of the period on either side of the argument between the "Ancients" and the "Moderns," as was the case in France at the time, there was certainly no equivalent orthodoxy established with regard to style, as the complex Roman artistic climate would tolerate none. Perhaps, in fairness, Maratti appreciated this fact, and wished to redesign the "laboratory" along French lines only for more efficient operation, and not to determine what experiments were to be allowed. However, there would still have been detractors who would have considered French methods to be a direct threat to the heterogeneous nature of Roman art. They, therefore, would have viewed this alliance as a surrender of Roman authority to the French in every important respect.

Whatever opposition there was seems to have expressed itself most dramatically in January of 1676. As was usual on the first day of the year, Errard appeared before the general congregation of the Accademia to accept his post and LeBrun's, and then proceeded to the election and appointment of his administrators. It is interesting to note that the principal parties thus far involved in LeBrun's election attained high offices for themselves as well: Guidi (*consigliere*, the closest advisor to the *principe*), de Rossi (*rettore*, the chief academic officer), Baldi (*censore*, supervising the conduct of the members), Maratti and Morandi (*sindici,* ruling on conformity to the statutes).[113] Another letter was drafted and sent to LeBrun telling him of his newest title, and recommending to him the qualities of his new deputy, Errard.[114] The French and their faction in the Accademia were now established in power, but the reaction of the opposition soon followed. In the meeting of 19 January it was announced, and recorded with a vehemence unusual for the *verbali,* that Raphael's painting of St. Luke, the Accademia's most treasured possession, had been turned to face the wall of the room in which it was stored, "to its detriment, due to the humidity and heat" (App. B, 1676, n. 1). This may very well have been the action of the group responsible for the "minima discrepenza" when LeBrun was elected, whereby their disaffection was symbolized by the painting, standing for Raphael or their patron saint, turning its back on the Accademia, which had delivered itself into the hands of foreigners. Their affront was answered by moving the painting to the main salon, where it could be watched over more easily, but no move was made to determine or reprimand those responsible. No retaliation was necessary because no further opposition was voiced, for within a short time the entire Accademia was given good reason not to regret its election of LeBrun. On 10 February, LeBrun wrote a response to the news of his elections, and was obsequious in his turn, expressing (with tongue in cheek) his surprise and his belief that the Accademia had done this only to honor him, and not actually to make use of him in a position for which he had "little merit."[115] And so he was pleased also by the choice of Errard to function in his stead. To avoid the delays that would occur should any attempt be made to govern from Paris, he effectively transferred his powers to Errard. Along with this letter, LeBrun forwarded his *dono,* in the form of a set of large engravings after his "Alexander" series, the work that had boosted him to preeminence in France, and other battle pictures. The size of this donation was already exceptional, but it was accompanied by a gift of sixty gold doubloons, with a value of 180 *scudi,* which represented no small part of the Accademia's

income for the year.[116] That the Romans did not in fact have to tolerate a rule from Paris, but at the same time could reap such profit from it, was enough, apparently, to silence the dissenters. Letters of patent were sent to LeBrun on 26 April (App. B, 1676, n. 2), bestowing on him all the rights, honors, and privileges of his position as *principe.* But in the meantime Errard had been about his business, and the opening of studies at the Accademia was set for the first Sunday in May, with six lecturers and six assistants to have charge over the posing of models. This represents a considerable augmentation of the efforts devoted to the students, although by 25 May it was realized that the appointment of lecturers in the other courses had been neglected (App. B, 1676, n. 3), and Felice della Greca was elected to serve in architecture.[117] On the same date, but with very little preamble, the proposal was made before the general congregation to proceed with the aggregation of the French and Roman academies.

Six days later Errard presented to a closed meeting of the officers of the Accademia a list of ten articles governing the union, compiled by the French but opened now to amendment by the Romans (App. B, 1676, n. 4). The texts of these articles, including the changes they made, became the official documents of the aggregation, and so were translated into Italian, French, and Latin, and stored at both academies.[118] Generally informative about the nature of the union as a diplomatic tool, the articles of conjunction also specifically made an impact on instruction at the two academies in ways relevant to the upcoming discussions.

Article 1 extended the guardianship of each academy's protector to the other, according them the honors and respect of both institutions, to the point where portraits of Colbert and Cardinal Barberini were to be venerated together in both Paris and Rome. This balanced exchange seems harmless on the face of it, but since the Romans had no interests to protect in Paris this article would be most functional for Colbert. The Romans did succeed, however, in deleting the stipulation of a vice-protector, whose presence would only have contributed to a semblance of *lèse majesté.*

Articles 2 and 3 bestowed the title of *Recteur* of the Académie Royale on any Roman who had previously held the position of *principe* of the Accademia. It then became possible for the Académie de France in Rome to employ the services of such an artist as teacher or adviser to its students, once he had sworn his fealty to their king and their statutes. He was also eligible for elected offices in the French academies, but while serving in any such capacity his authority would be shared equally with an assistant supplied by the French. Guidi took advantage of this opportunity after 1675, accepting the position of *recteur* to ingratiate himself further with the French by participating in their counsels, and indeed they gave him an inordinate amount of attention as a result, in the form of a commission for a group at Versailles.[119] But no other Roman was thus coerced into becoming a useful pawn for the French, while for the most part being denied a meaningful role in the affairs of the Paris academy.

Articles 4 and 5 gave members of either academy the right to be considered for membership in the other, so long as the justification for their first admission could be demonstrated and they were willing to accept the rules pertaining to the second. Given the much stricter regulation of membership in the Académie Royale, where difficult examinations were being required to establish proficiency in the style of Louis XIV, the Italians were put at a disadvantage here as well.

Article 6 granted access to the facilities of any one academy to students from the other academy who had been awarded prizes in its competitions (App. B, 1676, n. 10). This, too, was designed primarily to benefit the French at the time since only they had made provisions for sending students who had excelled in competition to Rome. The Accademia had neither the resources nor the inclination to send students to Paris on the same pretext, and the inconsistency of competition at the Accademia had not as yet singled out any student worthy of the trip. This article also specifically allowed for the participation of French *pensionnaires,* in Rome by virtue of their competitive edge, in the Accademia's *concorsi.* As a consequence the French were set for their important

victory in the *concorso* of 1677.

Disputation of the issues of theory and taste had by now become an important part of the life of both academies. Article 7 required their secretaries to record the contents of such debates within their own walls and to forward the texts to the other institution every three months. Since this was already standard procedure for the French, and since it may very well have been in this regard that artists like Maratti hoped to gain from the French (that is, in the codification of classical principles), then this article must have held the most attraction for the Italians. But as the French had earlier made these critical debates a cornerstone of their academic routine and function, and had been at it longer than the Romans and with more success, their exchanges would inevitably be one-sided for the time being. This article thus provided Colbert and his academies with another route whereby they could insinuate French ideas into Roman practice without having to suffer too much from the Italians.

Article 8 also gave the Romans pause, as it involved the method now prescribed for electing their *principe* (App. B, 1676, n. 8). Generously, the article opens the position of head of either academy to the membership of both, and nominations of those considered eligible to govern one of the institutions would be accepted from among the members of its opposite number. The problem with this was that two entirely different systems for choosing a presiding authority were in place at the academies. Only the *principe* of the Accademia was an annually elected post; the head of the Académie Royale was appointed by the king's minister, and LeBrun had been awarded that position for life. In effect, for the time being Article 8 could conceivably be invoked only by the French, so that each year one of their academicians must be included on the ballot for *principe.* They deferred to the authority of the Roman statutes for this purpose, but in doing so they gave up very little considering what they had effectively denied to the Italians. In response, the latter really had no choice but to accept what was on the surface an equal exchange, but they were able to amend the article so that two months' notice would have to be given by the nominating institution to be sure that there was time to act on their recommendations, and only the rectors of the Académie Royale, second in rank to LeBrun, would be eligible for election to *principe*.

Articles 9 and 10 were broadly designed to assure that the lines of communication remained open between the two academies. As a complement to Article 7, Article 9 called for them to keep each other appraised of their creative activities by exchanging drawings, engravings, or models after the work of their members. For the French this would add to the wealth of material already coming into Paris from their academy in Rome. The last article expressed a general hope for a continuing *entente* to guide the future transactions and correspondences of the academies. Despite the assurances of several authors that nothing fruitful ever came of this union,[120] or that it quite quickly reverted to complete independence for both,[121] or that the results for the Romans were only negative and betrayed their diminishing stature,[122] the beneficial effects of that *entente* can still be traced up to the end of the Seicento in the prizewinning designs from the architectural *concorsi*.

With the exception of the two alterations made by the Accademia officers in their closed meeting of 31 May, the articles of aggregation were accepted in their entirety and passed on to the general congregation of the Accademia on 7 June 1676, at which time they were approved and ratified unanimously (App. B, 1676, n. 5). In view of this it would seem that the Romans had eagerly and without remorse entered into a union with the Académie Royale under an agreement contrived in terms which favor the French at every point. This has brought many to the conclusion that in so doing the Accademia had proved itself at last incapable of withstanding the threat of an ambitious rival for the artistic attentions of Europe, and had thus relinquished its authority to Paris. But there is nothing in the language of the pact that intrinsically takes from the Italians while giving to the French; implicit in it is the incentive for the Accademia to bring itself up to the organizational standards of Paris, perhaps even to

establish its own satellite there, so that it might eventually make use of the aggregation to equal advantage. As has been said, it was just this kind of incentive that Maratti and the others might have hoped to derive in general from their association with the French. They were being shown what absolute authority could mean for institutions like their own, which since the Cinquecento had thrived on any support that the aristocratic order could give to their particular authority. Consider also that the Accademia's statutes, and therefore its preeminence in Rome, were still intact, that in fact the articles had given them a route into Paris that did not exist before, and that in the end nothing of Rome's stylistic independence had to be surrendered, and the perceived good of the aggregation may well have outweighed any long-term concerns. What the Romans failed to appreciate was that in their ecclesiastic context there could be no absolute authority, not even the pope, who could, like Louis XIV, remake the artistic life of Rome to suit himself and enlist the aid of the Accademia in the effort. But that they were shortsighted does not mean that they were submissive; from their standpoint, if not history's, the effects of the aggregation articles would be neutral at worst, and provocative at best, and the opportunity could not be missed.

On 24 July, LeBrun conveyed to the members of the Académie Royale the Accademia's tentative approval of the articles of conjunction, which response was well received (App. B, 1676, n. 7). The matter was then turned over to Colbert, and after deliberating for several months Louis XIV finally gave his consent for the union in November (App. B, 1676, n. 8). In the patent letters forwarded in the king's name to the Accademia, sentiments were phrased that the Romans must have been most anxious to hear.[123] They were to be involved along with their Parisian counterparts in the noble cause of bringing more glory to the crown, and at the same time "they could mutually contribute in elevating the arts to the highest point to which they had ever been taken." Louis's reasoning was stated quite succinctly: "We have been obliged to undertake that to which We have given life (the aggregation) by the malice of Our enemies, and the extreme jealousy that they have derived from the glory of Our Reign has not prevented Us from giving heed to the cultivation and stimulation within Our Realm of all that the sciences and the Fine Arts can contribute to the ornament and glory of Our Reign." By attaching itself to this ambition, the Accademia could be envisioned as one of the beneficiaries of the most powerful monarchical patronage and protection that had ever been devoted to academies of art, and which were now to be distributed between two great cities.

The Romans were again shown an immediate and tangible profit from their compliance. On 9 November they received a gift of 37 doubloons (111 *scudi*) from LeBrun to help defray the costs of their celebrations on the Feast of St. Luke.[124] Instances like this give substance to the aspirations held for the union, but appear also as no more than carrots dangled before a mule, or as tantalizing glimpses into the coffers that could now be opened for the Accademia. The bait was taken on the same day, when Mattia de Rossi, as *primo rettore*, moved that the usual procedures be waived so that LeBrun could be elected for a second term. There was still much to be done, and the French were apparently required to remain in charge.

On 21 December 1676, a letter from the membership of the Académie Royale was dispatched to Errard giving him their license to implement the aggregation. The next day the articles of conjunction were registered in the French parliament, and one week later the secretary of the Académie Royale, Henri Testelin, sent the Accademia the best wishes of Paris for the consummation of the union.[125] The tone in any such communication between the two academies was still neither superior nor deferential, but always equitable, and there can be no question that both were sincere in their shared respect and ideals. The Accademia's ultimate demonstration of this came on 31 January 1677, when the union was accepted and enthusiastically celebrated.[126] Letters from Louis XIV and the Cardinal Protector blessing the merger were read to the assembly, and Domenico Guidi was given his new title of *Recteur* of the Académie Royale.

The celebrations were conducted in the salon of the French academy buildings in Rome, where the Accademia had been holding its meetings since the first of the year under Errard's aegis as steward of both institutions. The attendance at these meetings had practically doubled by the time the aggregation became official, which is another indication of the new life that had been injected into the Accademia in the process. The ceremonies were allegorized in a painting commemorating the event which Charles Poerson, then a student of the French academy in Rome, would present to the academy in Paris as his reception piece in 1682.[127] In the painting, two feminine personifications of the academies are brought together in an alliance ordered by the god Apollo (read Louis) for their mutual benefit. The appropriate geographic references are made by river deities, the Seine to the right and the Tiber to the left, and scattered about are winged putti carrying the attributes of the arts and the arms of the academies, "temoignent leur joye de cette alliance et des avantages qui devoient en revenir aux arts du Dessein." Here, too, the two institutions were conceived of as equals. Errard also saw to it that the articles and patent letters which governed the union were carefully inscribed in Latin and sealed in a silver box wrapped in silk, then placed in a second box closed with gold clasps and covered with a cloth embroidered with *fleurs-de-lis*, to be preserved for posterity.[128]

It is obvious that at least in Rome the aggregation of the academies was meant to be a reverenced and momentous occasion, and Errard quite typically upheld the amenities. As LeBrun's deputy, it was of course he who had a direct impact on the affairs of the Accademia, and he applied himself as he had in 1672 to organizing those affairs with his usual rigor and energy, and for this he would always be gratefully remembered in Rome. In January 1677, he reappointed his officers from the previous year so that there would be no inconvenient interruption to their efforts either, and in April lectures were set to begin on time on the first of May at 10:00.[129] Melchior Missirini, the nineteenth-century historian of the Accademia, credits Errard with having begun during LeBrun's principate the complete renovation of the inventories and accounts of the academy and its church, and with the furnishing of the sacristy (App. B, 1678, n. 1). Errard was expected to continue this important work for the Accademia when he was elected to the principate in his own right again in 1678 (see Chapter III). But one achievement in 1677 that must have been close to his heart left an impression with the Italians as well: he "brought about the celebration of public competitions in art with a magnificence of which the Accademia had never before had an example."

This statement by Missirini is unique in that his history contains so few references to the Accademia's competitions prior to this date. It is now known that *concorsi* were in fact a common part of the classroom routine at the Accademia, and that even before Errard's arrival in Rome steps were being taken to amplify the importance of the *concorsi* in order to use them as a public demonstration of the abilities of the Accademia's students. Though the record of success was uneven, Errard was nevertheless building on a foundation that was already in place at the Accademia when he scheduled a *concorso* for the second year of LeBrun's principate. The difference is not one of kind, but of quality. As per Article 6 of the aggregation statutes, students from both academies could now compete together officially, which added considerably to the circumstance of this competition. The attention of all Rome, including its foreign quarters, would be drawn to this event,

which would test the mettle of the two academies whose union had been the talk of the city for the past year and a half. Involving as it did the pride of two great sovereignties, the public could expect a rare display of economic and visual wealth in conjunction with this particular *concorso*. And in the confrontation between two artistic and academic traditions, something more than the usual student production, rife with trivialities, could be expected. The Accademia itself was revitalized by the effort involved in preparing for the *concorso;* there was more space devoted to it in the *verbali,* and a better record kept of it than in any previous year. And of course the fact that the competition designs, including those in architecture, were preserved for the first time in this year as precious documents and resources distinguishes this *concorso* from those that came before.

Regardless of how hindsight might view them, the events surrounding the union of the French and Roman academies must have seemed at the time like the start of a new period of progress in the history of the Accademia. What progress was in fact made over the next quarter-century will be assessed against the examples provided by the subsequent *concorsi* and against the fortunes of the association between the French and the Romans. But for the moment, in 1677, the tone was undeniably optimistic, expectations ran high, and the results of the competition in architecture were by no means disappointing.

II

CONCORSO OF 1677

TO BE CONVINCED OF the distinction between the *concorso* of 1677 and its predecessors requires an examination of the unique circumstances surrounding it, and, most importantly, of the architectural entries that are the earliest competition drawings in the Accademia's collection. Missirini's brief statement, already mentioned, concerning the magnificence of the public competitions instituted by Errard helps, but is certainly not sufficient to demonstrate that the *concorso* of 1677 was exceptional unless the drawings themselves are considered. Let us reconstruct some of the other pertinent details and events that precede their submission on 11 November.[1]

Unfortunately, for this year, we do not know the name of the instructor in architecture at the Accademia, which is known to us in almost every other year of the Seicento since instruction began in that field in 1673. The *verbali* of 25 April 1677 establish the opening of classes in May, but no names of instructors are given. Based on the previous few years, candidates for that obligation could have been Felice della Greca (1676), Fontana (1675), Tomassini (1674), or Mattia de Rossi (1673). The last two were officers in both years of LeBrun's *principate*, but this gives no clue to their academic involvement during the same period.[2] Della Greca, who was instructor in 1676 and therefore the one most likely to have continued in the position, was already failing in his responsibilities, and may have been incapacitated by illness in 1677.[3] As for Fontana, the fact that he held no office in these years does not exclude the possibility of his being the lecturer, but he is perhaps the least likely of the four as his career seems to have been by far the most active.[4]

It is possible to arrive at an answer by indirect means, if we consider that the instructor in architecture was usually asked to provide the *soggetto* for the competition, and to participate in the judging. Only Gregorio Tomassini was called upon to fill both of these roles in 1677 (App. B, 1677, nn. 1, 5), and so it is reasonably certain that Tomassini was the Accademia's instructor in architecture for that year.

THE TASK

The *soggetti* for 1677 were not approved by the general congregation until the meeting of 15 August, at a time rather late in the year (App. B, 1677, n. 1). The reason may lie in the spirit of the aggregation articles, some months' delay being necessary to inform the Accademia's Parisian counterpart of the proposed tasks. But even more than a routine formality or an act of professional courtesy seems to have been at work here.

First mention of an author of the *soggetti* in painting and sculpture for 1677 is found in a French document of the following year.[5] Giovanni Pietro Bellori is therein credited with those tasks, and if other years are an indication, he would have been chosen for this sometime around the start of instruction in May, not, apparently, by the membership of the Accademia as no such nomination was voted on by them. And when the *soggetti* were finally approved in August, Bellori's name was still not mentioned (though Tomassini's was). This suggests that Bellori was the choice of the French, to whom it was most favorable.

Bellori was a professed Francophile, a friend and admirer of both Duquesnoy and Poussin, and in the latter half of the Seicento the most outspoken advocate of classicism, on the basis of which he was gaining continental recognition.[6] The same classicism that he routinely championed before the Accademia was finding fertile and uncontested ground in Colbert's academies and Louis XIV's France. And Bellori's *soggetti* seem to have sprung from a mind in sympathy with Colbert's own, as the topics both in painting and sculpture deal with events from the history of Alexander the Great, Louis's favorite allusive conceit.[7] Read as metaphor in seventeenth-century fashion, they equate the sovereignty, patronage, and ambitions of the two great monarchs for the benefit of those attuned to such thinking (certainly all academicians in Rome). Such bold, Grand Manner propaganda was to be expected of a LeBrun, but Bellori's motives may have been closer to those of Guidi or Maratti. He had no doubt been drawn into the same pro-French campaign that had climaxed in the union of the academies, and he wanted as well to capture the recognition and esteem of the French establishment while advocating an environment sympathetic to his ideals.[8]

Regardless of Bellori's motives, there seems to have been a connection between his *soggetti* and direct monetary benefit for the Accademia. In both French and Italian documents, mention of the competition tasks is often made together with the prize money donated by the crown. One instance of particular interest is in the *verbali* for 15 August, when Errard first announces that Colbert has sent the prize money and then presents the *soggetti* for the congregation's approval.[9] No doubt the membership could not have accepted one without accepting the other. But it is by no means sure that the Italians had any desire to question the *soggetti,* for their tenor must have been known within the Accademia some time before they were forwarded to Colbert and his academicians. The Romans must have made up their minds by then as it would have been too late afterward to make changes. In the final analysis, it should be remembered that it was Colbert's principal responsibility to ensure that events, including the *soggetti,* were flattering to Louis XIV. Bellori seems to have known this, Errard would certainly have encouraged it, and in the end the Accademia must have accepted it for reasons of

diplomacy and practicality.

By comparison, the nature of the architectural competition was much less political. As was usually the case for authors of the *soggetti* in painting and sculpture, Bellori had nothing to do with the task in architecture. He deferred instead to Gregorio Tomassini, whose task proposal was also accepted, without opposition, on 15 August.[10] Unlike earlier competitions at the Accademia, this first public *concorso* required that the tasks be displayed publicly, and it is fortunate that the posted description for architecture survives, written in a precise hand and complete with a site-plan sketch, stipulating at length the required details.[11]

The topic in architecture is essentially divided into two parts: a description of the building to be designed, and admonitions as to the methods the young architects were to use. As for the first, the church was to be octagonal, with seven altar spaces, a main and subsidiary entrances, and a sacristy or other apartments. A cupola and two bell towers were to be included, as well as a vestibule or portico at the facade; even a site plan was stipulated.[12] The rest was left "ad arbitrio dell'operante." The competitors were provided with what amounted to the preexisting conditions they would likely encounter in an actual commission, whether dictated by the terrain or the patron. Tomassini was apparently intent on testing the competitors not only on their proper use of theoretical principles, but also on their practical capabilities under the most realistic conditions. The only restraint lacking was that of funds, which was always too onerous for academic minds. Such an elaboration of the *soggetto* is exceptional before the eighteenth century and the *Concorsi Clementini.*

Tomassini's proscriptions on method, involving both quality and invention, are also unique. The first was to be ensured through the submission not of sketches but of carefully finished drawings outlined in pen and shaded in wash. The cautions against plagiarism take two forms: the design was not to be a copy of any other, antique or modern, or it would be barred from competition, nor was it to be the work of another presented as the competitor's original.[13] These seem to be perfectly ordinary requirements, which in some respects simply echo the policies of the Accademia. If Tomassini deemed it necessary to include his caveat in the text of the *soggetto*, and indeed with some firmness, it must have been to address problems not remedied in earlier competitions by statutes, decrees, or even accepted norms. The *soggetto* of 1677 was apparently designed to reverse a trend and to establish higher standards for the presentation methods of this first public competition.

Tomassini also proposed a topic for competition in a second class of architecture, which is as detailed in its descriptions of the task and prohibitions as that for the first class.[14] It called for the design of an altar in a niche with columns and entablature of the Corinthian Order, and may have been intended to relate to the octagonal church of the first *soggetto* (as was often the case in later *concorsi*). By choosing somewhat awkward dimensions for the space of the altar, Tomassini has again hypothesized a situation which challenges each competitor's practical as well as technical or theoretical skills. Perhaps he intended a third-class topic as well, setting the participants to rendering a part of an important monument, just as painters or sculptors in this class might be required to copy a detail of a work by one of the early masters.

It is reasonable to assume that there were no actual competitions in any but the first class of architecture before 1694, when second and third classes were added to conform with the practice in painting, for the simple reason that no drawings from these classes survive from before that date. Despite Tomassini's intentions in 1677, there was no competition in any but the first class for architects, at least none that was made public, and this was true also for the painters and sculptors in that particular year.[15] There appears to have been some restriction agreed upon which would allow only the most advanced students to compete. This *concorso*, the first to involve the unified academies, was meant to be as much a public spectacle as an academic function. By limiting competition to the best, the best results and the best impression were hoped for.

As to the part played in this spectacle by the architectural competition, there is a telling difference between Tomassini's first and second proposals, and between any two classes of competition, which diminishes the circumstance (and the pomp) of the lesser of the two. It has to do with invention. The altar *soggetto* was a test of technical skills, of drafting, measuring, proportioning, and detailing. Little was left to the student's imagination. He was not, in other words, confronted with much of a design problem and was required only to embellish. Tomassini's first *soggetto*, while quite specific about the nature of the building and its elements, provides considerable leeway for invention. Here the competitors were asked to address a particularly intriguing problem, to call upon their full design capabilities, and to embroil themselves in a topic of long-standing importance and current interest for both practical and theoretical architects.

In the twofold nature of the *soggetto*, the methodological stipulations are self-explanatory, but the typological elements invite an examination of the motives behind their selection. No allegorical tribute to Louis XIV could be construed from the architectural vocabulary Tomassini describes, or even a French connotation. In fact the bell towers and octagonal plan he required are entirely outside the French tradition, which had rejected towers along with the Gothic style and had settled upon the circle as best for planning centralized churches.[16] Certainly Tomassini's purpose was aimed toward a more practical end. His intention may have been to renew debate either on a particular design problem encountered in the real experience of Roman architects, or on one of long standing in the academic tradition, or on one concerned with the building history of a single monument. Such an opportunity would have been more than any young architect could have reasonably expected, even in anticipation of a relatively successful career. And for Tomassini to invite students to deal with a weighty theoretical problem was more generous than other academicians were usually willing to allow even their own charges. But if he did have such an end in mind, this alone would make the *concorso* of 1677 much more than a simple academic exercise.

To be sure of his purpose, one need only consider the clues Tomassini has given in his description of the building task. Centralized planning had been the cornerstone of architectural theory since the Quattrocento; beyond practical or liturgical requirements, it was the architect's "ideal" (and would remain so for some time, as the later *concorso* drawings attest). Of all the geometries proposed in this context, the octagon and Greek cross would, after the example of St. Peter's, constitute a vigorous tradition for church design in Italy, especially, it can be imagined, for academic conservatives faced with the unbridled variety of Baroque geometries. But much had happened to Michelangelo's church in the course of its construction. The nave and facade had cost the building its centrality, its portico, and the imposing aspect of its drum and dome (Fig. 1). And nearly half a century before 1677 there had been an abortive attempt to add bell towers to the facade (an idea which had not as yet been entirely abandoned). Each of these elements—octagon, portico, dome, and campanili—had been included in Tomassini's task description. One obvious conclusion is that he intended the competitors to reconsider the composition of St. Peter's.

Then there is the church of S. Agnese on the Piazza Navona, one of the Baroque progeny of St. Peter's, where decoration was still in progress in 1677, though the construction had been completed some ten years before (Figs. 2, 3). Principally the work of Carlo Rainaldi,[17] who had been *principe* of the Accademia in 1673 and the most recent Roman architect to hold that post, S. Agnese was almost certainly one of the projects on which Tomassini acted as Rainaldi's assistant. The church is composed of the same elements described in Tomassini's *soggetto,* with the exception of a portico or vestibule.[18] That particular feature had been omitted in Rainaldi's final design for S. Agnese and replaced by the concave front in order to improve the view of the drum and dome from the narrow piazza. In fact, S. Agnese succeeds, where St. Peter's ultimately failed, in integrating dome, facade, and towers. By stipulating a portico, Tomassini invited a further integration, and a final correction, if you will, of the vicissitudes of St. Peter's along more conservative lines than the

1 MICHELANGELO BUONARROTI: project facade for St. Peter's; Rome, after 1546 (from D. Fontana, *Della Trasportatione dell'Obelisco Vaticano*).

Baroque facade of S. Agnese. In such a way Tomassini could pay tribute to past masters of high academic standing while promoting further development of a type. From his warnings against plagiarism we can be sure he intended no mere imitation of Rainaldi's achievement, or indeed of any other's. What he must have hoped for instead was a progressive step in the evolution of centralized church design or in the resolution of problems related to it. It is not until the *concorsi* at the very end of the century, or more dramatically in the *Concorsi Clementini* of the early 1700s, that student architects are given comparable opportunities to deal with questions of practical reality and problem-solving. Perhaps the aggregation and joint competition of the academies occasioned Tomassini's ambitious means.

2 GIROLAMO & CARLO RAINALDI: Palazzo Pamphili and S. Agnese on the Piazza Navona; Rome, 1645–66 (photo: author).

On 15 August 1677, and for a time thereafter, the *concorso* was still meant to coincide with the Feast of St. Luke.[19] Approval for the *soggetti* had come some months later than usual, however, and while their content may have been understood enough for preliminary sketching to begin, a postponement became necessary. On 10 October, the *concorso* was moved to the octave after the commemoration of All Souls, and the firm date of Sunday, 14 November, was arrived at during the last meeting of October (App. B, 1677, nn. 4, 5). At the same time, certain members were chosen to fulfill special duties in preparation for the celebration of the *concorso*. Some were appointed to decorate the salon of the Accademia with works from

the *concorso* and the archives, others were delegated to invite the cardinals and nobility of Rome, and Bellori was elected to give the discourse and select the poets who would pay tribute to the event. The judges for the *concorso* were also chosen at this meeting, and in architecture they were Gregorio Tomassini, Mattia de Rossi, and Alessandro Sbringa (then *stimatore d'architettura,* or appraiser, along with Tomassini).

The submissions were received on the morning of Thursday, 11 November, following which there was a special meeting of the judges to administer the *prove,* and then select the prizewinners. The *prove* were extemporaneous examinations, this time using a topic suggested by Errard for the

31

3 CARLO RAINALDI: interior of S. Agnese (photo: Alinari).

when one considers the ease with which French draftsmanship could be distinguished from Italian. But for this year, with its diplomatic overtones, the pretense of objectivity was upheld.

The decisions of the judges in all three disciplines dramatically favored the French, but so did the odds. Of the seven entries in painting, four were submitted by French subjects, and the three prizes were finally awarded to *pensionnaires* of the French academy in Rome.[21] Eight entries were submitted in sculpture, of which four were from *pensionnaires* of the crown, and two of the prizes, first and third, descended on the French.[22] Though students of the Accademia were represented in the selection process, victory belonged almost entirely to the French. With the awarding of all three prizes in architecture to *pensionnaires* of the king, two thirds of the total student complement of the French academy had won distinction in the *concorso* of 1677. The winning architects were Simon Chupin (first),[23] Augustin D'Aviler (second), and Claude Desgots (third), but what is more remarkable still is that they seem to have been the *only* competitors in architecture.[24] Surely a competition of such magnitude would have attracted contenders from most of the studios in Rome with any connection to the academies. But perhaps after only a few years in existence the Accademia's architecture curriculum had yet to produce any qualified competitors. Or it may simply be that the French discouraged any and all Italian competition by the sheer weight of their reputations. After all, as mentioned before, they were only students in the eyes of their superiors; given their background, by Italian standards they were much more advanced.

Once the formalities of the *prove* had been satisfied, the nine architectural drawings were, along with all the other prizewinning pieces, turned over to the secretary, Giuseppe Ghezzi, at which time the names of the artists were inscribed as they now appear on the fronts of the drawings.[25] On the evening of 14 November, the *concorso* was celebrated in the salon of the Accademia, where the winning designs were displayed. The magnitude of the ceremony was exceptional, and the French, if not altogether impressed, were certainly pleased

painters and sculptors, and "a gli architetti un altra non meno della prima dificoltosa materia."[20] It is safe to presume that the architectural material was provided by Tomassini, and if nothing else is known it was certainly not intended to be a simple step. The topic could have ranged anywhere from a complex detail to a full elevation of a church or a palace, with the additional challenge of designing and rendering the item in a matter of a few hours, under close supervision, and with no other resources than paper, drafting tools, and a mind. In choosing the winners, the judges could then compare the effort of the *prove* to the unsupervised effort of several months represented by the competition entries. In this, and in the numbering rather than signing of the drawings, actions to ensure fairness seem to have been rigorous. Albeit, favoritism was still possible, especially by what they heard of it, and particularly by Bellori's speech and the selection of so many French prizewinners.[26] Errard, on behalf of LeBrun and Colbert, distributed the prizes—large gold medals whose cost had been donated by Louis XIV. Chupin received a medal worth eighteen *scudi,* D'Aviler one worth fifteen, and Desgots one worth nine.[27] In the other categories, there was equal reward for the French in all but the second prize for sculpture. Colbert had cast his bread upon the waters, but the waters had turned out to be almost exclusively French. Both the gold and the glory had returned to rest within the walls of his academy in Rome. While such an outcome no doubt pleased the *Surintendant,* there were added benefits to be derived from the *concorso* in architecture, relating to its place in the history of church design and the careers of the winning architects, which the French were not so quick to recognize.

THE COMPETITORS: CHUPIN, D'AVILER, DESGOTS

As each of the winning architects was a French *pensionnaire,* it would not be surprising to find them at pains to supplement the tradition called up by Tomassini with elements of French practice in the design of centralized churches. The degree to which this occurs, the proportions or balance struck between the two, may reveal some of the thinking of the architect, and his attitudes toward the architectural heritages of his homeland and his hosts. In turn, his place in the final outcome of the competition may tell us more of the motivations of his judges, and what their priorities were. Simon Chupin's first-place project is particularly illuminating in these respects.

Simon Chupin

Chupin is a rather forlorn figure among the first-prize winners of the *Concorsi Accademici.* The record of his existence is scant, and for every mention of his name a different spelling is used, as if to further diminish his consequence and confound his history.[28] He first appears as one of the

entourage listed in the passport of Noël Coypel, accompanying the new director to Rome in 1672.[29] If he was in his early twenties then, he was perhaps born around 1650. After his success in 1677, and his return to France, there are only occasional references to a "Chuppin" in the *Comptes.*[30] It is possible to conclude from these that he spent his later career as a draftsman, employed on crown commissions in the creation of working drawings. Other than this there is nothing known of him; he was a small cog in the vast machine controlled by the *Surintendant des Bâtiments.*

Understandably he has earned little attention since. Only the scope of the paperwork of Louis XIV's bureaucracy, and the thorough work of the first historians of the French academies, have saved him from near total oblivion.[31] And there are his drawings for the *concorso* of 1677, which for all we know are the only original work by Chupin, and represent the climax of an undistinguished, but certainly not atypical, architectural career. After all, for every great name in the history of architecture since the Renaissance there were several who rose no higher than the role of draftsman, but whose function was nonetheless indispensable. Most of the prizewinners at the Accademia began at this point, even if only a few had the talent to advance beyond it. If Chupin was not one of these, the niche he eventually found was still a contribution to his art, and to see his first-place design is to realize that it promised little more.

In a letter to Colbert of December 1676, in which Errard reports on the progress of the *pensionnaires,* Chupin is called a "submissive youth," which quality he applied to his studies.[32] Presumably this means he was a tractable rather than a speculative artist. Indeed, Errard goes on to say that Chupin "has no [sense of] design," without which he could not progress. And so he finds Chupin better suited for a military than a civil career, which is poor praise for an artist who had come as far as he had along the path prescribed for neophytes in Colbert's new order. Though there was as yet no *Prix-de-Rome* for architects, the choice of Chupin to fill the ranks of the Roman *pensionnaires* could not have been made lightly (unless it was politically calculated). Errard's judgement might reflect the usual attitude toward the individual held in the France of Louis XIV, where for each talent a role was to be found to which it was best suited, subordinate to the needs of the state. But as Chupin was to win the first prize in 1677, that judgement may have been premature. This remains to be seen.

Other than having his name appear at the head of the list of prizewinners in architecture, Chupin does not seem to have reaped any further benefit from his victory. The Accademia did not extend membership to him, as they would to three other prizewinning Frenchmen, none of them architects.[33] Unlike D'Aviler and Desgots, Chupin would no longer hold the attention of his superiors, for no report of his efforts or progress is made again until he appears in the royal accounts in 1682.

What little this tells us of the man Chupin can be supplemented by using his design to investigate his personality. It is almost as easily described as his life (Pls. 1–3 and App. A), conforming, in every respect except site dimensions, to the task and to his principal model, St. Peter's. To his credit, Chupin presented his judges with a comprehensive yet uncomplicated design. The elements described in the *soggetto* are joined together logically, functionally, and with an economy of means. But far exceeding this success is the stunning beauty of Chupin's draftsmanship, the skill with which he commands pen and brush in deriving a variety of linear and chiaroscuro effects for even the finest details, applying them with unfailing precision, without a slip of rule or compass. And even without those tools, in the freer passages required for the statuary, murals, or capitals, his touch is uncanny, almost inhuman. If when Chupin came to Rome in the company of painters (see note 31) he was training to be a painter himself, there would be no reason to reject such an idea on the basis of these drawings. But such skills are only one part of the Baroque concept of *disegno,* the balance having to do with the vagaries of invention. There are grounds for criticizing Chupin in this respect.

It should, in fairness, be remembered that the task description by its very nature limited invention somewhat with regard to the major features of the design, there being only so many ways to compose a cupola, towers, portico, seven altars, and a sacristy around an octagonal space. Chupin assembled the required elements efficiently and practicably. As to his adherence to the rules of classical architecture, Chupin's proportioning and detailing was essentially without fault. As to the suitability of the design, what his compatriots called its *convenance,* aside from the large arched windows in the design which betray his northern origins, Chupin's church could have been raised without offense anywhere in Baroque Rome.

Then, however, there are his models. It should not be remarkable that so much of Chupin's design recalls St. Peter's, if one accepts that Tomassini's motive in the *soggetto* may also have been to reexamine its design history. Chupin, like Michelangelo, began with the Greek-cross plan, inscribing it in an octagonal rather than a square ambulatory, no doubt getting his cue for this from the wording of the task. If this appears ingenuous now, it may have been ingenious by the standards of the time. The economy of the octagon gave Chupin room for his sacristies and for sound foundations for his towers without sacrificing the fluidity and logic of Michelangelo's original scheme.[34] Chupin left no doubt as to the object of his tribute, retaining from St. Peter's the giant Orders, the coffering of the vaults, the beveled piers, and most especially the cupola, which like most in Rome erected after St. Peter's quotes from its example. Even Chupin's Parisian sponsors would not have questioned his choice considering the context of the competition, as they too considered Michelangelo's the finest dome in Rome, if not in history.[35]

The result at least for the interior of Chupin's church was a well-integrated whole in close accord with a significant prototype. But in accomplishing this Chupin approached the interior more as a decorator than as an architect, painting and sculpture having drawn a considerable proportion of his attention. On the other hand, for the facade of his design, Chupin was not fortunate enough to have a suitable model available, one similarly revered and composed of a cupola, towers, and portico.[36] So it was here that his talents of architectural invention were to be most sorely tested, and where likewise he could depend less upon his interests and abilities in decoration to carry him through. Also, it must have been here that the judges' concerns as architects were most likely directed.

Chupin had to bring together previously dissociated elements, beginning with the cupola and the towers which he related to each other through their paired Corinthian columns. The belfries are oval in plan, but their concentric appearance and paired columns at the diagonals mark them as simplified versions of the uppermost stories of the towers of S. Agnese (see Fig. 2). This is no surprise if we accept that Tomassini's task description was also meant to address Rainaldi's design. But the power of Rainaldi's much taller towers, recommended by the urban space they were called upon to dominate, represented too immodest a means to Chupin, apparently. His towers are timid by comparison, as well as being otherwise poorly integrated with the whole. They are simply set on the corners of the building, with little or no proportional relation to the cupola (though their oval plan adjusts them to the differing widths in the perpendicular bays below). Lastly, the towers are situated in visual contact with the drum, which is not at all as satisfactory a solution as Rainaldi's.

Much the same can be said of the portico, which threatens to interfere with the view of the dome from in front of the facade. The only affinity between Chupin's temple front and the lost facade of Michelangelo's basilica, other than the existence of a colonnade and giant order in both, is his use of an Ionic order derived from the portico of Michelangelo's Palazzo dei Conservatori on the Capitoline hill. Chupin's interpretation thus establishes a proper classical sequence of superimposition: Ionic, to Corinthian, to Composite (the lantern). Such an academic refinement would have meant little to Michelangelo but everything to Chupin and his judges. The result is almost Palladian by comparison, which suggests where to look for Chupin's source in this instance.

To be sure, any number of ancient temples, including the Pantheon (see note 36), or architec-

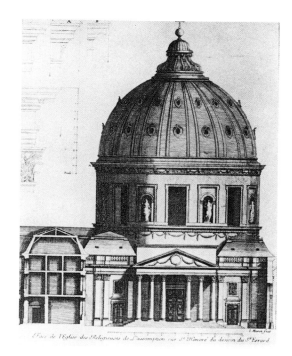

4 CHARLES ERRARD: facade elevation of the Church of the Assumption; Paris, 1670–76 (engraving: Marot).

tural treatises may have suggested themselves as models, but it is certain that Chupin was aware of a much more recent precedent, the facade of Errard's Church of the Assumption in Paris (Figs. 4–6). This was Errard's first and only complete design in the role of architect, and had just been finished in 1676.[37] As Errard was himself one of the finest draftsmen in Rome, he must be credited with imparting some of this skill to the virtuoso prodigy Chupin. There could be no better way for the young *pensionnaire* to pay homage to his director and master than to refer to Errard's achievement in his own design.

Still, the Assumption is part of a tradition of centralized design quite different from that evoked by Tomassini's *soggetto*. Intended for a convent of nuns, it is related typologically and compositionally to François Mansart's Church of the Visitation in Paris (1632–34, compare Figs. 6 and 7). Both employ the cylindrical nave space common to the century-long history of French centralized church planning, used for the purpose of accentuating the

5 ERRARD: section of the Church of the Assumption (engraving: Marot).

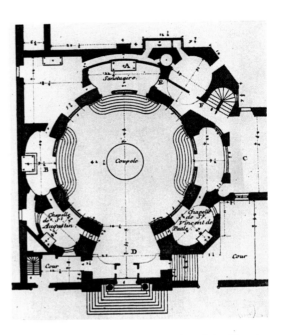

7 FRANÇOIS MANSART: project plan of the Church of the Visitation; Paris, 1632–34 (engraving: Marot).

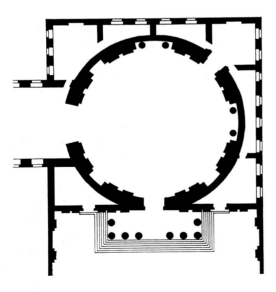

6 ERRARD: plan of the Church of the Assumption (graphic: Troy Thompson).

dome. Errard pursued this end even more intently by eliminating the extruded altar spaces of Mansart's plan, diminishing the substructure to a square no wider than the cylinder itself, and reducing the drum and dome to the purest of geometric profiles.[38] In the last is the influence of LeVau's dome for the Chapel of the Collège des Quatre Nations (begun 1662, Fig. 8), but the result for Errard's church was quite different. While LeVau's was considered the greatest example of French carpentry domes prior to that of the Invalides chapel (see note 35), Errard's earned the disfavor of the acerbic Blondel, and the popular sobriquet "sot dome."[39] The reason for this seems to have been the overpowering scale of the drum and dome, which dwarf the lower portions of the structure, but such would appear to have been Errard's intention.

Furthermore, his choice of the hexastyle Corinthian portico was calculated to advance further the dominance of the cupola. The lower parts of the drum of LeVau's chapel are obscured by the facade when viewed from the quay before it. In

8 LOUIS LEVAU: facade of the Chapel of the Collège des Quatre Nations; Paris, 1662–68 (engraving: Pérelle).

order to guarantee the visibility of his dome from the courtyard in front of his church, Errard had to find an alternative to any variations on the Vignolan front, with their high screening pediments. As an academician, and a scholar of Palladio, he would have been predisposed to a classical solution, and so found his alternative in the transept facade, also facing a courtyard, of LeMercier's Sorbonne chapel (1635–53, Fig. 9), where a temple front appeared for the first time in French classical architecture.[40] Suitably proportioned, such a temple front could be conveniently attached to the square base of Errard's church with no hindrance to the cupola. The resulting facade was praised for its detailing and "bon goût," as were the rest of the building's decorations, and its acoustics.[41] But the visual weight of the drum and dome is oppressive, and destructive to the ordinarily monumental aspect of such a portico, and so the criticism of Errard ensued.

In Rome in 1677, with this criticism still in the future and geographically remote in any case,

Chupin would have been free to emulate the course Errard had taken, since Errard's was after all one of the few significant central-plan churches in France. His tribute began in the interior decoration, where the Marian theme, and particularly the Assumption fresco, refers to the dedication of Errard's church.[42] In the arrangement of the facade, he also chose the best local model for his dome.[43] And as bell towers were out of fashion for the moment in France he turned inevitably to S. Agnese for his example, though his lack of familiarity with the motif resulted in its rather uninspired relationship to the whole. Most importantly, spurred by Tomassini's *soggetto,* the tradition of the Pantheon, and Errard's influence, he introduces a very classical temple front to the facade. In doing so he commendably did not repeat the proportional imbalance struck in Errard's church between portico and dome, but nevertheless some of the old problems remain.

The outer bays attached to either side of the portico as bases for the towers prevent the latter

DE L'EGLISE DE   LA SORBONNE.

9 JACQUES LEMERCIER: transept facade of the Chapel of the Sorbonne; Paris, 1635–53 (engraving: Blondel the younger).

from totally obstructing the view of the dome, but they also increase the horizontality of the facade. This resurrects one of the criticisms leveled at Maderno when substructures were added for the towers at St. Peter's after 1612. While the projection of the portico ameliorates this somewhat on Chupin's church facade, in the section it can be seen that the depth and height of the portico would cut off much of the cupola from any nearby viewpoint, despite the short nave. This situation, which had marred the effect of Michelangelo's basilica, was no doubt what Tomassini had hoped to see corrected.

Chupin's judges, including Tomassini, would not have missed this shortcoming of his design. To be able to overlook it, there must have been enough to recommend his effort: his flawless drafting, "correct" detailing, Italianate concept, or overall conservatism. They may even have appreciated Chupin's tribute to Errard, or his portico as something new and useful. Errard's judgement of Chupin in 1676 seems all the more valid, however. He was submissive, if for that we can read derivative, and he did lack a vital part of the design sense, if for that we can read invention. This assessment does not portend a future for Chupin beyond what has already been presumed: that he spent the 1680s in the royal employ, drafting, no doubt with admirable facility, the ideas of others. Whether he survives this brief span of activity in any greater capacity is not known, and even should works from his hand remain unattributed in some *cabinet des dessins,* they would probably add little to the sum of knowledge. Such a complete lack of consequence will prove extremely rare among first-prize winners at the Accademia, once the international reputation of the Accademia's *concorsi* is established. Before his right to the first prize is judged too harshly, the background of his compatriots, the level of their concern for the design problems inherent in Tomassini's challenge, and their subsequent successes and failures as architects, must be considered. In the meantime, it is sufficient to point out that from the standpoint of the French, who had devised their own system of advancement to meet their own ends in architecture, Chupin's victory meant nothing.

Augustin-Charles D'Aviler

In contrast to Chupin, the events in the life of Augustin-Charles D'Aviler leading up to his second-place effort in 1677 were certainly more dramatic.[44] He was born in Paris in 1653, of modest parentage that traced its origins to the city of Nancy in the as yet autonomous Duchy of Lorraine. Though D'Aviler's family had been established in Paris for some time, it had neither the resources nor the social stature to overcome its provinciality and secure a career for him in the usual fashion. It was by early demonstrating his talent and penchant for architecture that he earned his own way into the system, becoming one of the first students of the fledgling Académie Royale d'Architecture, apparently without powerful patronage or family backing. Subsequently, the Académie Royale chose D'Aviler as one of their first *pensionnaires* in Rome, for which position he departed Paris in September 1674.[45]

In the company of a fellow architect, Antoine Desgodetz, then also twenty-one years old and a favorite of the Académie Royale, and the antiquarian and numismatist Jean-Foy Vaillant, D'Aviler departed for Rome via Marseilles. At sea, their ship was pirated by an Algerian corsair, and they were taken as slaves to North Africa, where they were held for several months without talk of ransom. In his biography of D'Aviler, Mariette asserts that the young architect recognized the danger in practicing his art for his new masters, since to prove his usefulness might delay his release, "mais l'amour de son Art ne lui permit pas de dissimuler."[46] According to Mariette's account, D'Aviler did produce a design during his captivity, the plan and elevation of a mosque, which was eventually constructed in Tunis "dans la grande rue qui conduit au Fauxbourg de Babaluch. L'Architecture en est de fort bon goût." This is not apocryphal; Mariette got his information from D'Aviler's brother, and the reference is too specific to be spurious. In other words, D'Aviler had the Infidel to thank for the earliest execution of one of his designs. It would be fifteen years before he received equivalent encouragement from his own kind.

After more than a year in Moslem hands,

D'Aviler and the others were released on 22 February 1676, in a prisoner exchange arranged by Colbert. Once in Rome, D'Aviler came under the scrutiny of Errard, and through him Colbert, who had gone to some effort for his release and would be watching his progress carefully for the next four years. Errard's first report on D'Aviler, in his letter to Colbert of 2 December 1676 (App. B, 1676, n. 9), describes him as "sage," but deficient in the area of design, in which regard he would oversee his instruction. But whether he would address draftsmanship, which Errard was most capable to teach, or invention, in which there was less to recommend him, is difficult to say. D'Aviler's design (Pls. 4–6 and App. A) may provide an indication.

In his project, D'Aviler considered every practical contingency in the design of a suitable church, integrating them concisely as befit the requirements of the *soggetto* and the dictates of contemporary taste. He drew upon a number of sources to compose his solution to the problem put by Tomassini, but not without adding some part of himself. The drum and dome are drawn from those of St. Peter's, if perhaps by way of the more contemporary example provided by Maderno's cupola for S. Andrea della Valle (1620). However, the chain of semi-oval recesses around the drum, which D'Aviler created between the buttresses by using concave pilasters (see the quarter-plan, Plate 4), is a unique, organic conception in this context, and by no means out of place. The screening effect of the facade, provided by the projecting towers which create a low, broad front, conforms to the spirit of both Maderno's and Bernini's projects for St. Peter's, after the decision was made late to add the towers. But unlike Chupin, D'Aviler avoids the overstressed horizontality still existing at St. Peter's by means of compartmentalization, such that each bay is distinct from the others in accordance with its location. He effectively dissociated the towers from the porch by inserting between them deeply recessed bays, constricted between compound pilasters. The tension and chiaroscuro contrast thus provided removed the danger of planar monotony.

D'Aviler could call upon appropriate precedents for this approach as well. Maderno had himself hoped to "disconnect" the towers from the facade of St. Peter's, and avoid further conflict with the dome, by setting them on new bays at the extreme ends of the facade, and using the tension of compound pilasters to separate these bays from the others. The independence these tower bays would have had (Fig. 10) was destroyed when the campanili were left unfinished. During the pontificate of Innocent X, Bernini had proposed new alternatives after the failure of his first project to add towers over Maderno's substructures.[47] In one such proposal the towers are completely detached from the facade (Fig. 11) to relieve the stresses acting on the whole due to the shifting foundations of the towers. D'Aviler's inclusion of an open intervening bay between towers and portico recalls both of these attempts. He seems to have understood more of the history of the problem and the model than had Chupin, who depended more on a literal, simplistic interpretation.

The tetrastyle portico in D'Aviler's design is no doubt also derived from St. Peter's, where it had been a part of the facade, either freestanding or engaged, since Michelangelo's design (see Fig. 1). Bernini had hoped to reinstate the freestanding version "which would have broken up the uniform 'wall' of the facade," according to Wittkower,[48] but such was not to be. Tetrastyle porticoes were part of Rainaldi's final designs for the Twin Churches on the Piazza del Popolo (Fig. 12),[49] and of his facade of S. Agnese in an engaged version, either of which may be considered as D'Aviler's source, and there are French examples which may have supported this choice as well.[50] Whatever the case, the result is colored by a strict classicism in the proportions and planning of the portico which points to none of these precedents, and the same is true of his use of the Doric order.

In his later theoretical writing, D'Aviler was to align himself closely with the lessons of Roman antiquity, which his contemporaries, Rainaldi among them, had "forgotten," and he praised above all the Doric order as the precursor of the others. It was for what he saw as Vignola's fidelity to the clear values of antiquity that he would model his own treatise on that of the Cinquecento master. But in one instance he gave credit to an architect of his

10 CARLO MADERNO: project facade for St. Peter's; Rome, 1613 (engraving: M. Greuter).

own time and patrimony for the best modern use of the Doric: François Mansart and the domed facade of the Church of the Minims in Paris (1636, Fig. 13).[51] He compares Mansart's work favorably to Imperial monuments, and so a link between Mansart's facade and D'Aviler's would not be surprising. As a dome is the focal point of both, both use a screening front to displace the towers, and as if to make the association clear D'Aviler reuses the Doric. Without quoting directly, he has drawn upon the architectural heritage of his two homes in designing the facade. Such eclecticism, tempered by critical analysis and a capacity for innovation, marks him early as the serious student of his art later evinced by his writing.

Locating the towers was only one part of D'Aviler's approach to the problem implicit in Tomassini's task regarding the visibility of the dome. The short entrance arm of the Greek-cross plan, and the relatively low and shallow portico help in this respect, but even they would not be sufficient were it not for the socle which raises the cupola to where it can be seen from a vantage point quite close to the facade. This pedestal for the drum and dome is elegantly integrated into

11 GIANLORENZO BERNINI: project facade for St. Peter's; Rome, ca. 1650 (source: Biblioteca Apostolica Vaticana).

12 CARLO RAINALDI: facades of the Twin Churches on the Piazza del Popolo; Rome, 1662–79 (photo: author).

13 FRANÇOIS MANSART: facade of the Church of the Minims; Paris, ca. 1636 (destroyed, engraving: Pérelle).

the structural lines of both the exterior and interior of the church, and like the articulation of the drum is quite appropriately organic in its contours. It is unorthodox, to be sure, by the standards of the judges, but it is just the thing to reconcile the elements of the *soggetto*. It may also not have recommended itself to the Italians as its precedents are French.

The concept of a truncated dome opening into a second dome also has its origins in the architecture of François Mansart, who in academic eyes was still the brightest light in French architecture of the first half of the Seicento, if not the most popular personality. Among his buildings, variations on the opened vault exist in both secular and ecclesiastic contexts in numerous instances,[52] but for the purpose of this study no further mention need be made than of the Visitation church, which has already been introduced. A project drawing from the earlier stages of the design of this church (Figs. 14, 15) shows it in elevation and section in a state essentially as executed, except for changes in the roofing of the cupola. What the exterior drum and dome were eventually to dis-

guise was the existence of a smaller dome covering the oculus of the principal dome. In the absence of an interior drum, illumination is brought in through the lower dome by the four lights that coincide with the outer drum, creating what is called a sunken dome. There are reasons behind Mansart's method other than eccentricity.[53] Partly, there was the French antipathy for the drum of Italian usage, particularly in palace chapels which were the source for Mansart. But primarily he was concerned with two different designs: the interior

15 MANSART: facade of the Church of the Visitation (engraving: Mariette).

14 MANSART: project elevation/section for the Church of the Visitation (source: Archives Nationales, Paris).

and its pure geometry, and the exterior and its urban context. The second dome can be looked upon as a mannered adjustment between the two. The tendency has therefore always been to reduce the significance of the motif in view of Mansart's other successes and failures in the realization of the Visitation.

But it does not seem that later French architects were devoid of appreciation for the truncated dome's potential. LeVau's Chapel of the Quatre Nations, already mentioned above, is a case in point. Throughout the design history of this church, LeVau was faced with the awkward view of the cupola from the quay on which the church fronted.[54] Though he ultimately rejected his initial solution to the problem (perhaps unfortunately), in his early designs (Fig. 16) he introduced a truncated dome as a base, to raise drum and dome above the facade portico and its crowning attic. The direct correlations between LeVau's section drawing and D'Aviler's are undeniable, and easily explained. Errard very likely had a direct experience of the first projects for the Collège chapel, because of his own activities in Paris in the early 1660s, and he certainly would have passed his knowledge on to the students in Rome under the circumstances of the *concorso.* For his design, D'Aviler then moderated the verticality of LeVau's proportions, with some improvement in the result; and he took a cue from Mansart, adding four windows to the truncated dome and their light to that of the drum. Had D'Aviler's design been executed, it would have been one of the most well-lit churches of its kind.

A greater departure from LeVau and Mansart lies in the octagon of D'Aviler's plan, called for by the *soggetto,* but never espoused by French architects in centralized church-planning. In this instance, D'Aviler's models are necessarily Roman, for the most part S. Agnese and St. Peter's, but in deference to the tastes of his homeland he has eliminated pendentives, which would have been redundant in tandem with the truncated dome. The complex volumes involved in their use had never been satisfactory to the French, who preferred a continuity of circular plan from ground floor to dome.[55] What D'Aviler thus accomplished

was no less than the reconciliation of two traditions of building, using mechanisms which were alternately Roman and Parisian, to achieve what is in effect a very homogeneous and successful solution to Tomassini's task.

This happens with some inventive energy on D'Aviler's part, not only in the combination of disparate elements, but also in many details. There is the articulation of the drum to which reference was made previously. Any cupola, in its structure and surface, paraphrases the organic relation between skeleton and skin; there could be no more appropriate place to use a concave pilaster as a transitional device. In plan, the oblong chapels of the Sacrament and of the Madonna may be based on the chapels of Mansart's Visitation, but not directly. Even the tabernacles of these chapels are given distinctive treatments, and the high altar is embraced by two columns supporting entablatures on an oval plan, as though it were the Piazza of St. Peter's in miniature. There are many other details which D'Aviler created rather than borrowed.

D'Aviler's design thus satisfies in a number of ways: It answers the challenge of Tomassini's *soggetto* by means that are both progressive and traditionally grounded; it is also accurate and comprehensive in the details of both architectural ornament and construction. In the midst of all these accomplishments, D'Aviler did not sacrifice quality of drafting to any noticeable extent, even though close inspection reveals him to have been second to Chupin in this respect.[56] D'Aviler's relative deficiency in drawing is insignificant in comparison to his admirable success over Chupin in solving the design problem, however. In hindsight it may be difficult to find any reasonable justification for his receiving second prize, unless and until motives are included which may lie outside the limits of good architecture. The picture is not complete until D'Aviler's subsequent fortunes are traced and all of the designs have been examined.

D'Aviler need not have felt victimized by the Italian judges alone, for it was not long after the *concorso* of 1677 that his own countrymen began to frustrate his efforts. Recalling Errard's assessment of D'Aviler in 1676, it would seem from his drawings that he did in fact fall short of the per-

16 LOUIS LEVAU: second project section for the Chapel of the Collège des Quatre Nations (source: Archives Nationales, Paris).

fection in technique reached by Chupin, though both were obviously pupils of the same master, Errard. Still, the distinctions are too slight to be seen well in any but the original drawings. And if, as was proposed, Errard also meant invention when he spoke of *dessein,* there is no question of D'Aviler's advantage there. But the profit of his achievement was no better for D'Aviler than it had been for Chupin: his name appeared in documents and his drawings were viewed in public for a short time. With no offer of membership coming from the Accademia, he returned to his duties as a *pensionnaire* of the king. "He studied with an extreme ardor; he fixed his observation upon everything that he judged deserving of his attention, and measured with care those most beautiful antique and modern buildings that made [Rome] so recommendable."[57]

Despite this prose of Mariette's, wherever D'Aviler directed his attention, it was always under the watchful eye of Errard and subject to the approval and examination of Colbert. And even with his "extreme ardor," and his performance in 1677, it was another two years before he again drew the interest of Colbert, and the minister was anything but flattering. In a letter to Errard of 9 March 1679 (App. B, 1679, n. 2), Colbert refers to some drawings he had recently received from D'Aviler, including plans of the Palazzo Farnese, which he found satisfactory, but he did not find D'Aviler to be able to draw "well enough." Reginald Blomfield (IV, 16) took exception to this remark, pointing out that Colbert "knew as much about drawing as a washerwoman," and indeed the minister may only have been parroting Errard's judgement of three years before. In so doing he establishes his own authority, however, and declares that D'Aviler "could serve."

Colbert extends D'Aviler's stay in Rome, with an ulterior motive he reveals toward the end of his letter. Should Errard find the young man of sufficient "genius," he should put him to the task of investigating the elements of hydraulics, or "the different means of conducting and creating effects with water." D'Aviler would visit those sites in Italy where he could be shown the best examples of this, not to study fountain architecture, but to calculate the results of particular adjustments to the apertures and elevations of jets, or to the relative levels of fountain and source. Errard was to provide biweekly reports on the progress of this investigation.

Colbert's intention is quite transparent. The fountains of Versailles were perhaps the most pressing and complex project for the *Surintendant des Bâtiments*.[58] A student in Rome provided the best agent to report on Italian hydraulics, just as others had been used as copyists in providing decorations for Versailles. It is equally easy to imagine the effect of Colbert's uninformed judgements, and the unfulfilling chore he had assigned, on a promising young architect of D'Aviler's means and interests. It was not long before this fledgling personality revolted against the depersonalizing system. On 14 June, just three months later, Colbert writes that he is surprised to have received nothing new from D'Aviler, and asks Errard to prod him (App. B, 1679, n. 3). In the meantime, it seems that D'Aviler had been pressuring Errard to secure permission for his return to Paris, and his release from any further research into fountains. By 28 June, Colbert is prepared to acquiesce, provided D'Aviler could prove his claim that he had "gained some capacity in the conduction of waters" (App. B, 1679, nn. 5, 6). D'Aviler's later publications prove that he had, in fact, but it was nevertheless a headstrong individual who could in such a way court the displeasure of the *Surintendant*.[59]

In August of 1679, D'Aviler was on his way to France via Lombardy (App. B, 1679, n. 6), a favorite route for the architectural *pensionnaires* who could thereby add to their experience of ancient and modern building in Italy. Given D'Aviler's experiences on the trip to Rome, it would also be understandable if he had retained some aversion to taking the faster sea route. Still, after five years' absence, he was no doubt in a hurry to return home to a rewarding career, but he would not immediately be satisfied.

D'Aviler's progress and ambitions seem to have been routinely undermined by events and by those who held sway over his career. From the moment of his embarkation from Marseilles in

1674, his hopes were repeatedly dashed, only to be raised again before another obstacle was placed in his path. First came a year in Islamic captivity, climaxed by his design of a mosque, the construction of which he could not have seen before continuing on to Rome. After a year of training there D'Aviler placed second in competition to a compatriot with a superior hand but far inferior mind. His greatest pleasure no doubt came in studying and measuring Roman architecture and decoration, in which task he would have had the company of Antoine Desgodetz, his fellow prisoner in Algiers, who was in Rome for that same purpose.[60] This activity was abridged by Colbert's insistence that he turn his attention to the more practical side of his art, and study hydraulics. He was able to escape this onus, but if he had any sensitivity at all he must have realized that he was all too readily being identified as a technician rather than an artist.

As if to answer this, on his return to Paris late in 1679 he offered his services to the Académie d'Architecture in order to regain his academic footing. He first began a translation of Scamozzi's treatise, starting with the sixth book, on the orders, so that the members might have a copy to use in their discussions.[61] On 10 March 1681, however, they admonish D'Aviler to submit only the "pertinent" sections of the transcript, avoiding in future chapters on "exotic" subjects like Arab, Egyptian, or early Roman architecture.[62] It was apparently not D'Aviler's quite serious historical interests that concerned the Academy, but only the age-old debate on the orders. Later, on 19 July 1683, the assembly extended a rare privilege to a nonmember when D'Aviler was invited to read before them from the preface of his annotated translation of Vignola's treatise (which would form the basis of his *Cours*).[63] For several weeks he lectured to a very receptive audience of the great architects of his day, and his work was variously called "sound" and "ingenious." But on 23 August this brief flirtation with success was abruptly ended by the appearance before the membership of M. de Blainville, Colbert's son (who was being groomed as his successor), to demand that discussions on the theoretical and the antique cease and that the Académie redirect itself to the concrete

and immediate needs of the royal building works.[64]

In a way that must have been all too familiar by now, D'Aviler was forced to abandon temporarily his hope for a scholarly career, and to find a place in the practical realm. He had already attempted to impress upon the Académie d'Architecture his abilities in that area by submitting several renderings and original designs for their appraisal, beginning with a plan of the church and colonnade of St. Peter's which he donated on 30 December 1680.[65] It was considered "fort exact et fort grand," and so pleased the membership that it was displayed in their rooms at the Palais Royal. Their enthusiasm for D'Aviler, one of their first students, soon waned, however, when he began to submit original ideas. The first was a design for a triumphal arch, with straight lintels over the portals (possibly not unlike the central motif of the facade of his *concorso* design). Blondel, as the authority on triumphal arches (and little else), led the assembly in criticizing this choice since in his view lintels were better suited to temples. They also found fault with D'Aviler's design for a basilica "à l'Italienne," which carried high-pitched roofs "à la Française."[66] Later that same year (1681), D'Aviler made his first proposal for an actual building project, a dome for the order of the Annonciade at S. Denis.[67] In May 1684, he submitted a design for a communion chapel at St.-Jacques-la-Boucherie.[68] Neither case represented an actual commission, but in both instances the academicians had only criticisms to offer and changes to suggest. In a dozen years D'Aviler's status had yet to rise above that of a student.

To alter that status, the only route open to him in the Paris of the mid-1680s was to join the office of Jules Hardouin-Mansart, who had complete autocratic control over building activities in France. This D'Aviler did in the fall of 1684, serving as a draftsman for five years while continuing his work on the Scamozzi translation and the Vignola annotations. The latter was his most cherished undertaking, for with it he hoped to establish his own reputation and practice, and thus free himself from his unhappy association with Mansart.[69]

In the biography of D'Aviler attached to the later editions of his *Cours* (1756, pp. xxxvi–xxxvii), Mariette paints a rather innocuous picture of this association, seeing in it great advantage for D'Aviler at first: "M. Mansart … who knew of [D'Aviler's] merit, received him among the number of those who worked under him at the Bureau d'Architecture. There [D'Aviler] soon occupied one of the highest positions; and since nothing was done for the King that did not pass through his hands, the experience considerably augmented his knowledge." D'Aviler's eventual separation from Mansart's office was in Mariette's view no more than a normal part of the maturation process, like a fledgling leaving the nest: "… D'Aviler hoped to make himself a name, and to immediately present himself to Paris, by means of some building of good repute; but it began to appear that so long as he remained attached to M. Mansart, and worked under his orders, [D'Aviler] would be obliged to bury his pride, and grow to dislike his situation.…" However, from the letters D'Aviler wrote during the 1690s to his Parisian publisher, Langlois, Mariette derived a better idea of the relationship between D'Aviler and Mansart, and imparted it in his *Abecedario* (II, 66–67). One letter of September 1691 speaks of D'Aviler's treatment by Mansart "who, far from being favorable, worked against [D'Aviler] in the intent he had formed to have himself received into the Académie Royale d'Architecture. [D'Aviler] repented having lost five years of his time in the service of that architect."

The impression this leaves is not one of professional harmony, but of conflict between two indomitable personalities, the artist with ambition and the bureaucrat jealous of his station. Having once before risked defying Colbert, D'Aviler appears now to have been at odds with his successor, the new power in French architecture. It is true that as Mansart's draftsman D'Aviler would have been exposed to every important project then under way in France, but it is equally true that regardless of the community of talent at work on them Mansart's name alone would be attached to each. There must have been many occasions when D'Aviler felt the urge to comment on a project, with little disposition on Mansart's part to listen.

One such instance, when D'Aviler's own experience in the *concorso* of 1677 might have been of particular relevance, may have occurred during the design modifications and final construction of the Chapel of the Invalides (1679–91; see below, Fig. 50), which was also an Italianate, domed, and centralized church.

It was, therefore, an apparently bitter D'Aviler who left Mansart's immediate circle in 1689 to try on his own to find again a place in the academic domain. Consulting with several established architects, primarily François D'Orbay,[70] D'Aviler set about completing his commentary on Vignola, and transforming it into a comprehensive course in architecture. The *Cours d'Architecture qui comprend les ordres de Vignole* was published in 1691 as proof of the value of his combined scholarly and practical method and of the benefit he found in his Roman sojourn.[71] In his preface he restated the principle that Rome is the best place to learn architecture, if from ancient rather than modern examples. For him Italy's contemporary masters, particularly Pietro da Cortona, Rainaldi, and Borromini, "had divorced themselves from the rules of beautiful simplicity";[72] only the ancient Romans, who had adopted those rules directly from the Greeks, could successfully apply them in the grand manner.[73] But he did find Vignola to be an exception among the modern architects of Italy and France, because of his clear rules and close approximation of antique principles, and the elder Mansart has already been seen to have earned D'Aviler's praise and emulation.[74] In the quarrel between the "Ancients" and the "Moderns," between Blondel and Perrault, he seems, whenever he is concerned with theory at all, to be unable to commit himself to one or the other conviction. This would only have weakened his position with the French academy as it was then being defined.

More than a vehicle of theory, however, D'Aviler's treatise was intended as a practical guide to all matters related to architecture: masonry, carpentry, vaulting, ironwork, and paving; materials and construction; geometry and mechanics; even painting and sculpture.[75] Every detail of civil architecture is analyzed and illustrated with the utmost clarity, making the *Cours* an indispensable tool for any practicing architect concerned not only with design but execution. D'Aviler even included the elevations and plans of a typical house, "and a very good design it is" (Blomfield).[76]

Dealing as it does with secular architecture, the *Cours* contains nothing which can be directly related to D'Aviler's church design of 1677. But his work that year demonstrates that the core of his reasoning was already in place: a discriminating approach toward sources, a respect for traditional usage, and a concern for the practicalities and precisions of presentation. This philosophy did not achieve the highest honors for him in 1677, but perhaps it was for that reason that he pursued it so doggedly at the height of his career. He may very well have realized that for the benefit of future generations, the two natures of the architect, designer and builder, had to be reconciled within the academic context. No other published work before D'Aviler's had taken such a tack, and it earned him immediate and enduring acclaim, and the gratitude of a century of architectural students.

But D'Aviler did not remain in Paris to accept the acclaim. "Impatient to apply himself to more practical tasks,"[77] he was granted a commission to oversee the construction of a triumphal arch designed by D'Orbay for the city of Montpellier, in Languedoc.[78] Once he had arrived, in July of 1691, he was never to leave; he married there, and in 1693 he became architect to the province by appointment of the local *Intendant,* M. de Basville. His principal patron was the Roman Catholic Church, which was reestablishing itself in the region following the revocation of the Edict of Nantes (1685). But there was less of a need for churches than for palaces, and of these he designed one for the Archbishop Colbert in Toulouse, and another for the bishop of Beziers. The rest of his enviable activity in the South was spent in Carcassone, St.-Pons, Nîmes, and elsewhere, designing townhouses for the local gentry in the current Parisian mode.[79] It was in Nîmes, while planning the restoration of the Pont-du-Gard, that D'Aviler died in 1700, at age forty-seven, just one year after he was finally given membership in the Académie d'Architecture.

D'Aviler had come too late to his success, but in the brief span of his independent activity he had compiled an impressive oeuvre, and had introduced cosmopolitan tastes to the crude Languedocian palace tradition. In the same span of time, his reputation in Paris had grown as the value of his *Cours* was immediately recognized by members of the Académie, who had brought it into their discussion in 1691, and turned to it routinely thereafter.[80] The usefulness of D'Aviler's treatise was not blunted through a total of seven reprintings,[81] including the later Mariette editions, and it was not replaced as the most important academic sourcebook until the publication of the younger Blondel's *Cours d'Architecture* in the 1770s. As for his design for the *concorso* of 1677, it illustrates how early he had arrived at the principles and practices of his maturity, and underscores the tragedy both of his treatment at the hands of the French, and of a system which submerged so much promise beneath the cold waters of Hardouin-Mansart's dictatorial pretensions.

Claude Desgots

The last of the prizewinners, Claude Desgots, was the son of Pierre Desgots (d. 1688), a royal garden designer, and perhaps the grandson of another Desgots, who had designed the first gardens for the Palais Royal in 1635 for Cardinal Richelieu.[82] More importantly, he was the nephew of Louis XIV's great garden designer, André LeNôtre, with whom he began his career as assistant and disciple, sometime after 1663, at the park of Chantilly.[83] This would put his date of birth just before or after 1650, depending on when he had in fact first joined his uncle.

Desgots had what D'Aviler had not: a family history of royal patronage, an opportunity for experience which was his by birth, and a powerful relation as his advocate at court. According to Louis Hautecoeur (II, 114), it was Desgots's uncle who obtained him a place as a student of architecture at the Académie de France in Rome, which D'Aviler had had to win on merit. LeNôtre may have hoped that this training would raise Desgots from the second-class status granted most garden designers in the French architectural hierarchy, excepting only LeNôtre himself. To this end Desgots departed for Rome in July of 1675.[84]

It is evident from the drafting of his *concorso* design (Pls. 7–9 and App. A) that he, too, entered the tutelage of Errard. Nevertheless, there are many instances in his presentation where Desgots's drafting ability, satisfactory as it may be by some standards, falls far short of Chupin's or D'Aviler's. Yet in the same letter of 1676 in which Errard criticizes both Chupin and D'Aviler on this count, Desgots by comparison receives quite noncommittal handling (App. B, 1676, n. 9). He is called a "young man with a willingness to do well everything that is possible" (to paraphrase Errard's tortuous prose), which reflects favorably upon Desgots's attitude but says nothing of his ability. After a year in Rome, Desgots had given Errard far more opportunity to assess his skills than had D'Aviler, who arrived six months later. Errard's reluctance to express an opinion on Desgots's skills in 1676 creates the impression that he was withholding judgement on a student blessed with powerful backing. His courtier's instincts may have gotten the better of him.

Upon the evidence of Desgots's *concorso* entry in 1677, sufficient grounds certainly existed to criticize him much more than Chupin or D'Aviler on the basis of drafting. But this did not represent the limit of a contemporary definition of achievement in "design," as has already been seen. What is equally suspect is Desgots's originality in approaching his subject. There are abundant parallels between his project and D'Aviler's, too many to be explained as anything but the result of close collaboration, which was for both parties contrary to the spirit of the competition and the proscriptions phrased in Tomassini's *soggetto*. Where the parallels exist, however, Desgots's inferior abilities and design judgement make clear in which direction inspiration had passed. They used the same means to present their designs, for example green wash for the leading of the domes and a quarter-plan of the cupola, but Desgots's technique was much more careless and hurried, which suggests that the precedence in rendering was D'Aviler's. The same elements were used in both designs to articulate the drum, but Desgots's composition of the elements lacks the organic logic of D'Aviler's. The cupolas of similar pedigree are both carried on elevating bases which contain truncated domes, but the exterior of Desgots's socle is comparatively graceless, treated in a language of form and detail more appropriate to fortifications. Some or all of the beveled piers below the truncated domes in both interiors are penetrated by passages leading to diagonal chapels, but in Desgots's design these openings are spanned by a gutted pediment used in place of an arch. This device is mannered in the extreme and would set a classicist's teeth on edge. It betrays a naiveté in architectural matters only a garden designer could conscience.

It is obvious from these that D'Aviler and Desgots, though distinct in the levels of their talent, were working closely together in the formation of their ideas, but this is also understandable in view of their shared origins, professions, and circumstances, and in spite of their different social status. And no doubt Errard represents a juncture between them, and may ultimately have been the source for many of the ideas they held in common. The most important feature of Desgots's design, however, cannot be traced through his contacts at the French academy.

Desgots placed his bell towers to either side of the cupola, and on axis with it over the sacristies in his plan. This arrangement presents no danger of the campanili interfering with the view of the dome when the front of the church is approached from nearly any angle. Standing on its raised base, framed but not upstaged by the towers, and carried by the circular pedestal which is the lowest story of the church, the cupola is assured of its dominance in the scheme. Desgots, who showed only average skill and little independent thought up to this point, very likely did not come upon this ingenious solution to Tomassini's *soggetto* on his own either. Indeed it is not necessary to look far for the best and only possible source of inspiration, but some preamble is required, as well as some assumptions. And the time has come to consider more earnestly the role of Carlo Fontana in the *concorso* of 1677.

Though Fontana was probably not lecturing in architecture at the Accademia in that year, he was nevertheless master of the most important workshop in Rome, descended from Bernini, which included a number of student-apprentices. Their number would have been augmented by students from both academies, as allowed by Article 6 of the aggregation agreement and by Bernini's obligations to the French. As for Desgots, while nominally under the direction of Errard, he (and the other French architects) would have had access to Fontana's studio and advice, and to whatever of his projects were then in progress.

Had he taken this opportunity, Desgots would have found Fontana and his charges at work on the only church project of any importance to be considered by the recently anointed Pope Innocent XI. It was to be built within the Colosseum as part of the renovation of that monument, and dedicated to the *Ecclesia Triumphans*.[85] The funds for the project were preempted by the Turkish war, and the relief of Vienna, and so Innocent's dream died with him. But Fontana's project did not; he revived it nearly verbatim in his later treatise on the Colosseum: *L'Anfiteatro Flavio*.[86] A concentrically planned church was to have been placed at one end of the oval arena which would have been transformed into a vast arcaded piazza (Fig. 17), paraphrasing the Piazza of St. Peter's.[87] In elevation (Fig. 18), the church is composed of cupola, bell towers, and portico, which were the elements of Tomassini's *soggetto* in 1677. Since this was the most important project being conceived in Rome at the time, there is little reason to doubt that Desgots was aware, perhaps even intimately aware, of Fontana's designs in 1677. As they were thematically related to St. Peter's and Tomassini's task description, they would certainly have suggested themselves to Desgots as pertinent to the problem put to the competitors that year.

Opportunity and motive seem to have existed, and now for Desgots's method. In plan, there are numerous borrowings from the Colosseum church in his design: the concentricity (modified somewhat), the radiating chapels linked by a ring of

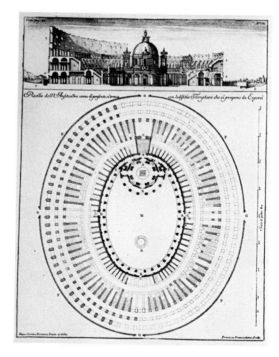

17 CARLO FONTANA: project plan for a church and piazza in the Colosseum; Rome, 1707 (from *Anfiteatro Flavio*).

corridors, and the sacristies on the lateral axis as substructures for the campanili.[88] The arrangement of the towers to either side of the cupola was chosen by Fontana to point up the proportional, geometric, and volumetric relationships between the church and the amphitheater. In addition, the campanili, as Hager points out, "frame the view [of the cupola] without blocking it."[89] In this regard Desgots must have seen the value of Fontana's idea for his own ends. In the absence of any other precedent, and accepting that there is little likelihood of Desgots having influenced Fontana in this, it seems reasonable, if not obvious, that Desgots derived his ingenuity in locating the towers of his church from a more fertile source. But this should not detract from his achievement, as his design, with its "circular" plan and temple front, is a distinctive contemporary version of the Pantheon. And, as will be seen, Filippo Juvarra, an architect of demonstrably greater talent, will not shrink from depending on Desgots's

18 FONTANA: project facade for a church in the Colosseum (from *Anfiteatro Flavio*).

design in his turn.

In the instances of poor design judgement on his part, in the close derivation of his design from those by Fontana and D'Aviler, and in his inferior drafting skill, Desgots raises doubts as to the legitimacy of his place at the Académie de France in Rome. He does not seem to have been as well prepared for the *concorso* of 1677 as either Chupin or D'Aviler, and justly deserved third prize only by virtue of the unique success of his design in solving the problem put by Tomassini. But the success is not altogether his. It is therefore fair to question why no indication of his deficiencies is given by Errard in his letter of 1676, when he was so quick to point out those he presumed to find in Chupin

and D'Aviler. If in Desgots's case he was limiting himself to mention of the young man's positive attitude, he all the more appears to have hedged the issue. And neither does Desgots's subsequent behavior support even this judgement.

In June of 1679, Colbert writes to Errard concerning Desgots: "LeNôtre will bring him home with him, and you may tell him what you have reported concerning his conduct" (App. B, 1679, n. 5). What the conduct was that deserved the attention of Desgots's illustrious uncle, then in Rome to study Italian gardens, and threatened to end Desgots's tenure in Rome, is not known.[90] During the previous February, Colbert had agreed with Errard's decision to reinstate Desgots into the Academy, which means that his offense had been serious enough to earn him a dismissal.[91] Unfortunately, Errard's part in this correspondence, which would give us the facts, does not survive. It suffices to remark that his opinion of Desgots was no longer noncommittal, and that Desgots's connections were no longer an assurance of protection.

Desgots did not return to Paris with his uncle, however. It was not until April of 1680, and at the request of his aged father, that he was allowed to depart for France, with his 200 *livres*, a passport from Colbert, and permission to visit Lombardy for two months.[92] While in this he may seem to have been treated like D'Aviler, he was also granted additional funds for his stay; having LeNôtre as his uncle still garnered him more consideration than his familially less fortunate comrades.[93] Most importantly, a position at his uncle's right hand was awaiting him on his return in 1680, and when his career resumed he was a garden designer again. But even more for this reason, Desgots, like his fellow prizewinners, would not have found his status significantly augmented either by his stay in Rome or by his performance in the *concorso* of 1677. He must have been relegated automatically to the subordinate station fixed for garden designers in French architecture, with at best the prospect of spending the next several years in the shadow of the greatest genius in that field that France would know. If he had any ambitions in architecture, which his sojourn in

Rome should have and was intended to have given him, they would soon have been extinguished by the same repressive climate in Paris that had inhibited the abler D'Aviler, and sent Chupin into oblivion.

Upon rejoining his uncle, Desgots reassumed his duties at the gardens of Chantilly, designing the celebrated labyrinth of the Parc de Sylvie (destroyed 1770).[94] Recognition was not forthcoming, however, until 1688 when, in the equivalent of a cultural exchange, his services as garden designer were donated to the new dynasty of England, and its new monarch, William of Orange. He worked there twelve years, replanning the gardens of Windsor Palace, then for a year in Holland at the gardens of Het Loo, returning home in 1700 heaped with the praise of his foreign patrons.[95] It seems Desgots, like D'Aviler, owed his first substantial opportunity and success to foreigners, rather than to those in Paris with nominal control over his destiny.[96] In 1699, upon the death of LeNôtre, his nephews, Desgots and Michel de Bouteux, succeeded him in the post of *Contrôleur des Bâtiments*. At this time, or slightly later, Desgots is first admitted to the Académie as an architect of the second rank, and the scope of his endeavors broadens.[97]

In the second decade of the new century, Desgots was granted two major commissions requiring the design of *châteaux* as well as attendant gardens: Sable, in Anjou, and Perrigny, in Burgundy.[98] There he could apply his uncle's ideals for the unification of architecture and garden, and in plan he is successful. But the architecture in both cases draws upon types and styles obsolete in Paris at the time, harking back to the previous two centuries.[99] This breach of taste is perhaps even more serious than D'Aviler's, who had at least brought something new to Languedoc.

Desgots's atavisms could be explained by the fact that he had had no experience in anything other than garden architecture for more than thirty years. Then, too, there was a general crisis in architectural direction during the last years of Louis XIV's reign and the first years of the Regency. After Hardouin-Mansart's death in 1708, French architects had gained some freedom but had lost the sense of purpose that French architecture had had in service to the monarchy, and it would not be easy to find again. Leaderless, French architects struggled to establish new directions and new names of international stature; Desgots was not one of these.

In 1720, Desgots was made architect of the first rank by the Académie d'Architecture upon his nomination and selection by the regent, the Duc d'Orleans.[100] Thereafter, he worked only as a garden designer, most importantly for the son of the regent at the Palais Royal, to which he returned in 1730, to the gardens first laid out by a Desgots nearly one hundred years before. Here, and at the parks of Bagnolet and St. Maur in Paris, he employed some of what he had learned of English garden design (he did not take LeNôtre's influence abroad without bringing something back for himself).[101] It was on this work that his fame in France rested,[102] but his death came soon afterward, in 1732.[103]

Because Desgots was principally a garden designer, because he came late to any major architectural activity (and that of questionable relevance), and because he had no academic or theoretical importance, the significance for him of the *concorso* of 1677 is moot. The trip to Italy certainly could have contributed to his repertoire of garden designs. But his shaky tenure at the Académie de France in Rome shows little discipline as an artist, and that is borne up by the relatively poor quality of his competition entry. There is much else to be deduced from his drawings: his dependence on examples set by his friend D'Aviler (who in turn may have learned about gardens from Desgots), his familiarity with works in the Fontana studio, and the effect on him of Errard as a drafting instructor (who may have been too lenient in Desgots's case). The church design itself is an altogether unique demonstration of his skills in that area, separated from any other architectural effort on his part by a gulf of thirty-five years, during which most of his professional development occurred. It is therefore nearly impossible to make any direct connections between Desgots the student and Desgots the successful garden designer.

There is an indirect insight to be derived, however. Desgots the student was much more up-to-date, even progressive, in his ideas than Desgots the designer of *châteaux* a generation later. Avoiding the conventions that associate conservativism with advanced age, other interpretations are possible. Either the academic environment in Rome during the 1670s was more conducive to progressive thinking than that in France just prior to the Rococo reform, or Desgots had been robbed of his forward-thinking potential by the intervening years and Mansart's intransigence. Through his own neglect and that of those responsible for his progress, including even LeNôtre, the spark of architectural talent struck tentatively in him by the *concorso* of 1677 failed to catch, and was ultimately doused by the unfavorable situation in Paris. If Desgots was less of a victim in this, it was due to the need for landscape architects that arose as LeNôtre retired in stages, leaving a considerable vacuum to fill for which Desgots was best qualified.

The Italians

When the catalog of the Accademia's competition drawings was compiled in 1974, it was assumed in the light of certain thematic similarities that Filippo di Leti's design for a church with a cupola and bell towers was an unclassified entry in the *concorso* of 1677.[104] When Tomassini's *soggetto* was discovered later, it became clear that di Leti's design did not conform to it,[105] and it can be dated instead to 1680 (see Chapter III). But knowing the *soggetto*, it is now possible to find other designs in the Accademia's collection which do conform to it, and to propose them as variations on its theme by Italian architects.

At present these drawings, comprising two separate designs attributed to anonymous architects, are listed as *doni accademici* in the Marconi catalog.[106] Perhaps, as this implies, they were ultimately gifts made to the Accademia as a condition of membership, but they may have originated as designs inspired by the *soggetto* of 1677, or even have been produced specifically for submission in competition that year, only to have been held back for whatever reason. There must have been some Italian architects who were eligible to compete in

1677, and any one of them, if eventually elected to the Accademia, would have found his competition-inspired project an acceptable *dono* in swift fulfillment of that obligation. Given the enormous prestige to be derived from participation in the historic event of the *concorso*, it is reasonable to assume that the closer a design conforms to Tomassini's *soggetto* the more probable it is that the design was intended for actual submission.

These arguments would be insupportable, or even unnecessary, were it not for the fact that the two designs in question are quite closely related to the topic in 1677. One of the two designs (Figs. 19, 20) corresponds exactly to Tomassini's task description, even to its planning on the stipulated site of 90 by 160 *palmi*, confining as those dimensions proved to be for the actual prizewinners. Consequently, there is little room to be daring. At the center is the octagon, from which radiate the shallow arms of a Greek cross and four diagonal chapels. A long axis is created by the vestibule to the west and the main altar space to the east, both of which are flanked by square rooms (for sacristies and other secondary functions) fitted into the corners of the rectangle. In the half-section, the absence of pendentives is revealing, and there is little other than the *coretti* in the bevels to connect this interior with St. Peter's or S. Agnese. Instead, the engaged columns in the angles of the octagon, and the statues above them in the drum, recall the articulation of Baldassare Longhena's S. Maria della Salute in Venice (Figs. 21, 22), as do the volutes buttressing the exterior of the cupola. The Salute is an obvious precedent in light of Tomassini's *soggetto*,[107] but still an unusual choice in the Roman context, suggesting an architect of northern Italian origin.

Another unique choice is made for the facade, seen in the half-elevation, where the architect rejects the antique portico used in the three French variations, in favor of a portico of more modern derivation. The central motif is a serliana, flanked by two bays, open below and closed above, which carry the campanili. The facade is generally of the block-portico type, in line with Bernini's S. Bibiana (1624–26, Fig. 23) or G. B. Soria's S. Gregorio Magno (1629–34), except for

19 ANONYMOUS (att. to G. B. Menicucci): plan for a domed and porticoed octagonal church with bell towers; ASL 2181 (Dono Accademico).

20 ANONYMOUS (Menicucci): section/elevation for the church in Figure 19; ASL 2182.

the towers. In other words, the traditions embodied in this design continue to be rooted in the period just preceding the High Baroque. Anthony Blunt, in one of his last works, specifically connected the facade type with a conservative, antibaroque style that both predates and runs concurrently with the High Baroque in Rome, its examples outnumbering the progressive masterpieces normally identified with the period.[108] The architect of this design would seem to have been an exponent of this vernacular trend, and given the strength of the trend this is no reason to condemn him. However, confined by the required site, the facade is no wider than the cupola, and

the towers almost completely eclipse the drum and dome. The cupola itself is therefore quite plain, and the architect's attention is given over more to his inventions for the facade and towers.

Regardless of whether there is any value in this decision, he does not fulfill the purpose that has been derived for the *soggetto* of 1677, which was to enhance the dominance of the dome in the context proposed by Tomassini. Indeed, had the architect provided the longitudinal section required by the task, it would have revealed that the dome is set too far back from the facade to be viewed advantageously from a proximate angle. In other words, this architect has followed the letter of the

21 BALDASSARE LONGHENA: interior of S. Maria della Salute; Venice, begun 1631 (photo: Alinari).

soggetto, but has not comprehended its intent; he provides no new insights into the problem of composing cupola, towers, and portico. And if his drafting technique, of a type common to Roman workshops, is of good quality, it nevertheless suffers in comparison to the facility of the French *pensionnaires.* Had he not had their work to contend with, he might rightfully have expected a prize under ordinary circumstances. But the fact remains that the design was not submitted, perhaps in complete awareness of how stiff the competition was, and was reserved instead as a suitable *dono.*

The second set of drawings related to the *concorso* of 1677 (Figs. 24–26) is more problematic, since it is planned on a site measuring nearly 225 by 340 *palmi,* and is derived from a circular rather than an octagonal geometry.[109] These deviations

from the *soggetto* may be attributable to license (since the French cared little about the site either), but the date of "1676" inscribed on each drawing is not so readily dismissed. As there was no competition in 1676, if the date is correct (and all too often the dates on the Seicento drawings are not; see Chapter III, note 92) then this was not a competition design. In that case, the close affinity between this design and the *soggetto* of the following year must be explained. And if it was a *dono,* the only candidate for its authorship is Felice della Greca, who became a member in January of 1676. But there are no stylistic grounds to support such an attribution, and it is by no means certain that della Greca was capable of even that much effort in the last year of his life.[110] It would be best, perhaps, to ignore the date for now and consider the stylistic evidence.

23 GIANLORENZO BERNINI: facade of S. Bibiana; Rome, 1624–26 (engraving: Falda).

22 LONGHENA: exterior of S. Maria della Salute (photo: Alinari).

The plan is truly concentric. The domed nave is surrounded by a circular ambulatory, and screened from it by eight pairs of columns. These are spaced more widely where the main axes open into the arms of a Greek cross, which continue the concentric geometry in the ribs of their vaults. Through the narrower bays below the cylindrical pendentives, the diagonal axes continue into four chapels with oblong plans which are also "bent" by the architect's compass. If this eight-part composition, reminiscent of Michelangelo's designs for S. Giovanni dei Fiorentini, can be accepted as a suitable interpretation of an octagonal plan, then the assumption that this *dono* was produced in conjunction with the *concorso* of 1677 becomes more reasonable.

The curvilinear interior spaces are effectively masked by the rectangular chambers that surround them, and reduce the external geometry to a simple rectilinear cross. The entrance arm is enclosed in a pseudodipteral peristyle with an octastyle front, mirrored at the east by a pseudo-

peripteral articulation in engaged columns. The effect is nearly that of an antique temple, run through by a transverse structure, were it not for the absence of pediments and the presence of the cupola.

The campanili are placed at the forward corners of the lateral wings, rather than at the front plane of the building, so as not to overlap the view of the dome but to frame it at a comfortable distance. Though the length of the nave and depth of the porch are already enough to hamper the visibility of the cupola, the latter is raised on a balustraded platform, or socle, provided by the interior vaults which reach a greater height than the outer shell of the building. And just to look at the facade elevation is to find a satisfactory composition of cupola, portico, and towers.

In his article on the Colosseum church, Hellmut Hager points out the affinity between this facade aspect and that of Fontana's shrine (though in the *dono* the towers are not strictly on axis with the dome), and the shared circularity of the church plans.[111] In the decade after 1675 Fontana was at work on many concentric designs, including churches, chapels, and the facade of S. Marcello al Corso (1682–84, see Fig. 87).[112] The pedigrees for these designs are to some extent Berninian, by way of projects like the Assunta in Ariccia (see Figs. 80–82), but in the early years of Fontana's stylistic independence the circular plan becomes his personal crusade. One very telling

24 ANONYMOUS: plan for a domed and porticoed circular church with bell towers; ASL 2178 (Dono Accademico).

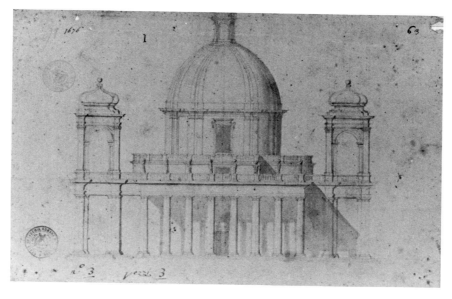

25 ANONYMOUS: facade elevation for the church in Figure 24; ASL 2179.

26 ANONYMOUS: longitudinal section for the church in Figure 24; ASL 2180.

example, in comparison with the *dono* now under discussion, is Fontana's first plan, discovered by Hager, for the Cappella Cybo in S. Maria del Popolo.[113] This plan (Fig. 27), generated by a compass from a single point, contrasts dramatically with the conventional cross-plan of the chapel as executed between 1682 and 1684 (see Fig. 132). But it is quite literally a miniaturized version of the *dono,* having an inner ring of four pairs of columns between which the alternately deep and shallow arms of an elongated cross project along concentric lines. Hager has also reconstructed the interior of Fontana's project (Fig. 28), and there, too, the similarities between it and the *dono* are apparent.[114] Only a reduction in scale from church to chapel has occurred, requiring as well the deletion of the drum, four pairs of columns, and the ambulatory.[115]

An early project (ca. 1635) by Pietro da Cortona for the Accademia's church of SS. Luca e Martina (Fig. 29) is justifiably considered by Hager to be the inspiration for Fontana's first Cybo chapel plan. Neither would it be inappropriate to suggest it as the source for the schematics of the *dono,* since they have in common an eight-part plan with diagonal chapels. After all, Cortona was a past *principe* of the Accademia (1634–37) and the architect of its church, and so his projects would have been known to and respected by both students and members.[116] But the *dono* does not so much start with Cortona's project as prefigure Fontana's—this is the only real clue to its authorship.

There is no reason to connect the grandiose design in Figures 24 to 26 directly with the more skilled hand of the pragmatic Fontana (the draw-

28 FONTANA: section reconstruction for the Cybo chapel (graphic: author).

27 CARLO FONTANA: project plan for the Cybo Chapel in S. Maria del Popolo; Rome, 1682 (source: Biblioteca dell'Istituto Nazionale d'Archeologia e Storia dell'Arte, Rome).

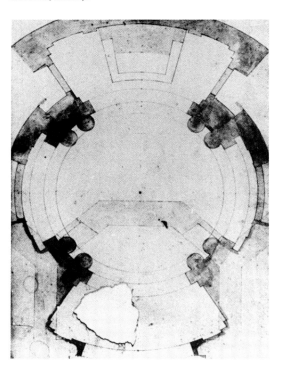

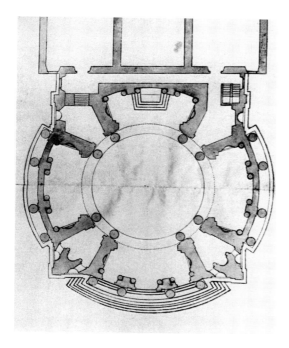

29 PIETRO DA CORTONA: copy of a project plan for SS. Luca e Martina; Rome, 1635 (source: Civico Gabinetto dei Disegni, Milan).

ings are not inked), and even less to suggest its influence on him. However, the possibility exists, given the number of close affinities in the *dono* with the work of Fontana after 1675, that it was executed by someone very close to him, perhaps even working under his direction or in his workshop. If the germ of the idea was the Colosseum church, then 1676 is probably too early a date; but if the date were 1677, or slightly later, then the genesis of Fontana's Cybo Chapel preceded the commission by several years. Perhaps the *concorso* of 1677 prompted Fontana to put the members of his studio to the task of designing a building along the lines of the *soggetto* of that year, using his own idioms. The project need not have been intended for the competition itself, but only as a donation to the Accademia. It could have been Fontana's contribution to the decorations of the salon of the Accademia during the celebration of the *concorso,* a gesture members were called upon to make by the statutes of 1675.[117]

The likelihood is greater that this second set

of drawings was intended only for purposes of display since there are two *dono* designs related to the *concorso* of 1677, but only one architect elected to membership in the years shortly after whose *dono* is not accounted for. The architect was Giovanni Battista Menicucci, who, along with several of the prizewinners in painting and sculpture in 1677, became *Accademico di Merito* on 10 July 1678.[118] He had in fact been nominated earlier, in 1673, only to receive a "votazione contraria,"[119] so his success the second time, with a vote of twenty-three out of twenty-six in favor, suggests he had done something in connection with the intervening *concorso* to earn the respect of the Accademia. As Menicucci had no involvement with Fontana's studio, the first *dono,* which responds only adequately to Tomassini's *soggetto,* is very probably attributable to him.

Granted, this rather awkward attribution is complicated further by how little we know about the undistinguished career of Menicucci. But it is perhaps this very lack of distinction which recommends him for the authorship of what is a quite ordinary design. His only important architectural activity dates from 1682 to 1684, when he and the Capuchin architect Mario Canepina completed the facade of S. Carlo al Corso from earlier designs.[120] We know nothing of his origins or experience before the 1670s, the most eventful decade of his life, during which he became a member of the *Congregazione dei Virtuosi* at the Pantheon (in 1675), and a member of the Accademia only a dozen years before his death.[121] In 1679 he was made instructor in architecture at the Accademia, a post usually delegated to new member-architects, but he was replaced by Tomassini the following year.[122] It seems he could not distinguish himself there, either.

THE OUTCOME

The Means of Evaluation

In assessing the findings of the judges in the *concorso* of 1677, the situation alone is evocative. Three Italians, one, Tomassini, the Accademia's instructor in architecture, and another, Mattia de Rossi, a favorite disciple of Bernini, were called upon to decide the fate in competition of three French *pensionnaires* who had no past or future in Roman architecture. This jury was certainly aware of the nature of its decision. The distinctive drafting style common to the three young architects, and the "French" passages in their designs, would easily have singled them out from any Italian competition long before their names were officially made known. Though almost every move made by the Accademia since the election of LeBrun to the principate appears to have been calculated to gain ground with the French, this would not have contributed to the motives of the judges in architecture as they had only French designs to judge. Of their number, only Mattia de Rossi had been directly involved in establishing the close ties between the Accademia and the French, which on his part had begun while in Paris working on the model of Bernini's Louvre design (see Fig. 71 and associated text). The rejection of that model and its effect on his master's reputation would not have made him an unqualified Francophile, however, and would certainly not have made him willing to conspire on their behalf. After all, he was also an artist with an advancing reputation in Rome and at the Accademia (he would be *principe* in 1681) which he would not have wanted to compromise with questionable judgements in 1677 in full view of the artistic community of the city. The same must to a lesser degree be true of Tomassini and Sbringa, who also had positions to protect.

The outcome may very well have been based more on academic than diplomatic criteria, and the Italians may have taken a more serious view of the purpose of the competition, as had Tomassini in the definition of the *soggetto*. In that case, Mattia de Rossi's first-hand experience of French methods, and his respect for them, would actually have been a boon to all three judges in reaching an objective criticism of the hybrid character of the designs. Such apologies aside, however, it was the nature of the times to find subjective and objective judgements equally valid, and this is very much true of the *concorsi accademici*.

Tomassini, a consummate draftsman in his own right, would certainly have found Chupin's first-place design (see Pls. 1–3) to be the most

skillfully drawn and detailed, and would no doubt have stressed this achievement in concert with the other judges. They would also have found Chupin's design to be the most "Roman," paraphrasing in so many respects Michelangelo's basilica in the Vatican. If no disdain can attach to the judges for awarding all prizes to the French, since only the French competed, their chauvinism in favoring what amounted to architectural treason on Chupin's part is more suspect. As to compliance with the task description, the judges would also have found Chupin's design to be appropriately aligned with the tradition Tomassini intended the competitors to address.

In the final analysis, however, Chupin's design did not answer to any appreciable extent the challenge implicit in Tomassini's *soggetto*. The judges would have noticed the homage Chupin paid to his sources for the facade—Errard, Michelangelo, and Rainaldi—but they would also have found the references weakened by the lack of cohesion; and the visibility of the dome is no better served in Chupin's design than in any of his prototypes. If the judges deemed the mere act of homage to be of greatest importance, then they compromised the intentions of the *soggetto* more in this instance than they had in the case of either D'Aviler or Desgots. But there is one other factor involved in this regard. Though Chupin is by no means daring in the search for a solution to the compositional problem, taking no liberties with traditional detailing or architectonic mechanisms, neither does he make any serious errors, and it may have been this sobriety with which the judges felt safest.

And finally, the judges may have been impressed with Chupin's concern for the program in painting and sculpture for his church. Mattia de Rossi in particular would have found such a unity of conception necessary to the definition of a great architect, along the lines of his own master, Bernini. Chupin did not demonstrate the potential for true greatness, but he attempts far more in the adornment of his design than D'Aviler or Desgots, who were not equipped for it. In contrast, de Rossi, Tomassini, and Sbringa may have determined that D'Aviler's conception was limited by his purely architectural interests. In the decor and mechanics of his church, and in the composition of the elements described in the *soggetto,* a much livelier but still exclusively architectural imagination was at work. That this could have counted against D'Aviler may seem contradictory at first in the context of what was, after all, a competition for architects. But in light of how close D'Aviler came to equaling Chupin's entry in draftsmanship and "Roman" references, and given the advantages D'Aviler's design held in displaying its cupola, there seem to be few directions left to turn in which to find the deciding factor in his second-place showing.

The truncated dome in D'Aviler's design may actually have been at the center of both his successes and failures before the judges. Despite its useful purpose in elevating the drum and dome, the truncated dome was still a remarkably "new" feature, completely unfamiliar to the Italian judges, with the possible exception of de Rossi. They would no doubt have viewed it as quite an unorthodox interpretation of the nature of a dome, and their first reactions were quite probably negative. Even had they had some introduction to this French idea, de Rossi, Tomassini, and Sbringa may ultimately have concluded, within the short period allotted for the judging, that such an unprecedented device had no appropriate place in an Italianate context, and Chupin's design gave them an alternative.

Just as D'Aviler's church was an architect's conception, the truncated dome was an architect's device. There was no theory behind it, no academic tradition, no suitable precedent, only practical necessity. To have been thus guided by artifice rather than art, to have stressed so strongly the mechanical aspects of his craft, D'Aviler came too close to lowering the station architecture was just then achieving within academic principles and the *Belle Arti.* Whether this affected the decisions of Mattia de Rossi is hard to say. Certainly he was no more open-minded than Bernini, but he knew from experience the difference between theory and practice. He had been exposed to French ideas during his sojourn in Paris, which may have prepared him for the truncated dome but need not

have predisposed him to accepting it. In the end, academic propriety may have been the overriding concern of all three judges, leading to an arbitrary decision that must have rankled the impetuous D'Aviler.

Desgots's "borrowing" of the truncated dome availed him even less in view of his inferior skills in drafting, proportions, and detailing, and he takes some liberties which, unlike D'Aviler's, do not always succeed, as in the treatments of the socle exterior or the bevels of the interior. There was still enough good in the design to overcome his questionable resources, however.

Most of the "good" is derived from projects of the 1670s by Fontana: the concentric plan, the location of the campanili, and even the plan of the diagonal chapels.[123] This would not have immediately condemned Desgots in academic eyes, especially since he gave Fontana's ideas, which were only on paper at the time, a unique interpretation. And in answer to Tomassini, Desgots's use of the socle and the towers on axis with the cupola makes for a successful compositional solution. But in the final analysis his precedents were not those that academicians could readily accept as established. It is unfortunate that his haste robbed him of a better showing, but posterity will nevertheless find some value in his design.

In essence three criteria carried weight in the selection of the prizewinners: drafting technique, respect for conventions or traditions, and a unity of conception encompassing all media. These happen to be the very qualities which could be reinforced by academic training, as in the French academic standards of "reason, rules, and the best masters." To achieve such conformity of thinking is what presumably brought the two academies together, and the judges in architecture, Mattia de Rossi in particular, must also have come to share these attitudes. And, since the French had more practice in applying these principles to architecture, their success without contention on the part of the Italians in 1677 is less surprising.

From the viewpoint of the present, even more enlightening are those qualities which did not carry enough weight to swing the balance in favor of the architecturally more adventurous. For example, mastery of architecture as a process or technology may have counted against D'Aviler, whose design is full of devices and clever solutions, as the most naive suggestions took first place. The relative modernity of his sources did not help Desgots, whose Fontana-inspired design was more up-to-date than those of D'Aviler and Chupin, which were derived from more "established" masters. Apparently being progressive or daring was not sanctioned, while being reactionary was, but this too was something only recently learned from the French by the Romans, who up to this time had put their faith in the intuitions of their modern masters.

The issue of conservatism as a criterion for success at the Accademia requires some further qualification with respect to the two Italian designs discussed earlier as corresponding to the *concorso* of 1677. The design herein attributed to G. B. Menicucci (see Figs. 19, 20), which was presumably withheld from competition in 1677, was certainly thematically conservative, adhering strictly to the letter of Tomassini's *soggetto* and avoiding the design problem implicit in it. But the competing architects were not penalized for lack of compliance with inconsequential aspects of the *soggetto;* Chupin exceeds the stipulated site dimensions by a factor of nearly six to one. Rather they were rewarded for their means, whether conventional or unconventional, of imparting visual weight to the cupola. Menicucci's design would also fit a purely temporal definition of "conservative" since it reflects tastes in place perhaps a decade before he was born, tastes to which Roman academicians might otherwise be expected to respond favorably.[124] Nevertheless, Menicucci's decision not to compete for a prize in 1677 suggests he had recognized that the field at that moment belonged to a new and progressive generation, skillfully represented by the French *pensionnaires*, and that his particular brand of conservatism would not then enjoy the academic standing it might have had when Vincenzo della Greca was lecturing on architecture at the Accademia in the late 1630s.[125]

Menicucci, in a sense the Italian champion, had not surrendered the field to the young Frenchmen; within the year he would be admitted to the Accademia while they were ignored. Instead, he and any other Italian contenders had temporarily given ground to the French, much as had the officers of the Accademia in turning it over to French administration. The short-term effect on prestige of succumbing to superior forces would be outweighed by the long-term benefits to be derived from giving the French the freedom of the arena of competition, bowing to their advantages and fresh perspectives, while carefully studying them.

The design submitted *hors de concours* from the Fontana studio (see Figs. 24–26) is revealing on the issue of conservatism, also. Despite Anthony Blunt's simplistic assignment of Fontana to the last stages of the anti-Baroque trend prior to the emergence of the Roman Rococo, there is too much in this design that is novel and dynamic to be construed as reactionary or even moderate.[126] In fact it matches in scale and approaches in technique the designs of the French, and is an equally daring and successful solution to the task. Along with the winning designs from 1677, it demonstrates that bold approaches were not dismissed either by the Accademia or the most influential studio in Rome. When these designs are later singled out by other architects as their inspiration, it becomes clear that, contrary to the usual preconceptions, the academic environment very often could be conducive to fruitful experimentation along lines which were of continuous concern to practical as well as theoretical architects, at least in Rome. The academic climate in France was not always so receptive.

The Process of Dissemination

Resting in the archives of the Accademia, the designs for the *concorso* of 1677 were virtually unknown outside of Rome and perhaps even quickly forgotten by the competitors themselves in the presence of more immediate concerns. But the problems they addressed and the methods used would continue to hold the attention of architects, particularly in Italy but elsewhere in Europe as well. Though what Chupin, D'Aviler, and Desgots had accomplished in 1677 was of little consequence to their superiors in Paris, their designs were to be a determinative resource for architects, both casually and intimately connected with the Accademia, who would at some time be occupied with similar problems requiring fresh approaches.

The first place to look for the legacy of these designs would be in the Accademia's collection of later prizewinning competition entries, which grew continuously from the seed planted in 1677 as a reference tool for teaching and study in the architecture curriculum. Those who aspired to do well in their own *concorsi* could learn from the most successful of their predecessors not only the finer qualities of drafting and classical usage, but also ideas. This could be all the more true of the drawings from the *concorso* of 1677, in cases where centralized churches were required, since those designs were generated by a rather serious purpose and for one of the most auspicious events in the history of the Roman academies—the aggregation with the French.[127]

The frequency with which later competitions turn to the centralized church type should not be taken as evidence of a retreat from practicality to idealism on the part of academic architecture in Italy. On the contrary, it mirrors quite closely the present perceptions, and surely the perceptions of the period, of definitive church design in the century from 1650 to 1750. After all, while longitudinal church design or rebuilding was still a staple commodity for architects, the conventions were in place and little room existed for experimentation on their part. The architects of the High Baroque had instead directed most of their imaginative energies to variations on the theme of the centralized church, and had tipped the scales in favor of that type with a momentum that carried well past the turn of the century, urged by the passion shared by architects since the Renaissance to indulge in the myriad possibilities of centrality. The changing nature of patronage since the mid-Seicento, from ecclesiastic to aristocratic or governmental, might also explain the unflagging vigor of the centralized church type. In the eyes of both Late Baroque architects and patrons, the opportunities for expression and invention in church

design were to be identified with projects like votive churches, or palatine, monastic, and family chapels where intimacy of scale, creative imagination, and centralized geometries were the rule, and funding was secular.

For its part, the *concorso* of 1677 in architecture was innocent of any pretense other than the analysis of a particular problem, and the hope that useful solutions might be produced under the guidance of Tomassini, Errard, and Fontana. But later architects more deeply concerned with the theme involved would not have missed the value of the designs in their researches. The *concorso* entries from the next century often verify this, but in many instances they also contrast sharply with the serious intent of the competition in 1677, and create the more usual impression of academic sterility as a result.

The earliest of the *Concorsi Clementini*, initiated by Clement XI in 1702, immediately points out the distinctions between it and its antecedents. The *soggetto*, calling for a church with a presbytery, college, and hospital, sounds like an amplification of the monastic college proposed in 1694 (see Chapter IV), and is interpreted by first-prize winner Alessandro Rossini as an enormous, Versailles-like complex of buildings, with two *cours d'honneur*, gardens, courtyards, and a Greek-cross basilica at the center (Fig. 30).[128] The church plays variously on the theme of St. Peter's, as had Chupin in 1677, but it is not approached as a contemporary design problem, only as a recapitulation of the Vatican basilica's Cinquecentesque design history. The annular corridors behind the apses, the Greek cross repeated in the quadrants of the square, and the towers at its four corners speak of the artist's awareness of the projects in Serlio's treatise, but there is nothing resourceful in this. It is only an ability to conceive on an imposing scale that has been rewarded; and only the antiquity of the sources, not their relevance to a particular problem (like the dominance of the cupola), was considered. Even the quality of Rossini's rendering has been obscured by scale.

Such grandiloquence comes just short of being a ruling principle in the Settecentesque *concorsi*, applied routinely to villas, palaces, academies,

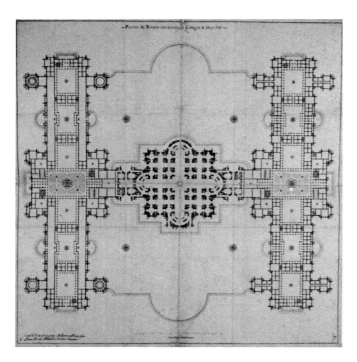

30 ALESSANDRO ROSSINI: plan for a basilica with college and hospital; ASL 63 (Conc. Clem. 1702).

piazzas, and even entire cities, as well as to ecclesiastic complexes. While centralized planning remains an almost universal constant, problem-solving for church design in this context becomes secondary to caprice and the selection of sources, with experimentation limited to endless variations on church facades or symmetrical geometries contrived for their own sake.[129]

Take, for example, the *concorso* in the first class for 1713, which required the design of a "tempio rotondo col suo magnifico portico," dedicated to four saints, each of whom would be allotted a separate domed chapel.[130] Though analogous to the *soggetto* of 1677, there was no implicit challenge in the task other than locating the proper prototype, found by the four prizewinners in the planimetric arrangement of Michelangelo's projects for S. Giovanni dei Fiorentini. Sebastian Demangeot took first place with two designs (one illustrated here as Figures 43 and 44) differentiated not by their plans but by their formal links, again, to Bramante's and Michelangelo's respective projects

for St. Peter's.[131] Pietro Passalaqua took second place with a design whose one (albeit significant) merit is the transverse oval vestibule at the facade, which he would later reuse in the remodeling of S. Croce (1743). Only Carlo Rè, a native of Piedmont who shared second prize with Passalaqua, turned for help to the *concorso* of 1677. His project (Figs. 31, 32), with its radiating plan, temple-front portico in advance of a hypostyle *in antis* at the facade, a solid geometric perimeter, and towers on the lateral axis flanking a Michelangelesque dome, relates directly to Desgots's design (cf. plates 7 and 8) in everything but scale. It only looks back, however, and cares even less for improving the cupola's aspect, since Rè rejects the other device Desgots had used to this end, the elevating socle, no doubt because of its still questionable academic propriety.

Themes similar to that in the first class of 1713 were chosen for the next two competitions: the design of a victory church in 1716, and in 1725 a papal sepulcher in tribute to the Accademia's recently deceased patron, Clement XI.[132] But again no clever solutions were sought, only the permutations possible in bringing together any number of architectural forms and planning mechanisms.

This is as yet not a complete explanation of the differences between the *Concorsi Clementini* and the *concorso* of 1677. When the subject of a freestanding church first appears in the former, in the second class of 1704, concern for composing the elements of dome, facade, and towers is absent both from the brief *soggetto* and the resulting designs.[133] At work here was a philosophy quite different from that in 1677, when the conditions of the *soggetto* challenged not just the skills but the resourcefulness of the architects involved. In relegating church design *per se* to the second class, the later *concorsi* could no longer reasonably invite or expect speculation in that regard.

If the eager but cautious student architects in the later competitions found no special value in the designs from 1677, this was not true for more discerning professionals who would obtain some reputation. For the latter the designs by Chupin, D'Aviler, and Desgots would have constituted an unparalleled opportunity to tap into a convenient

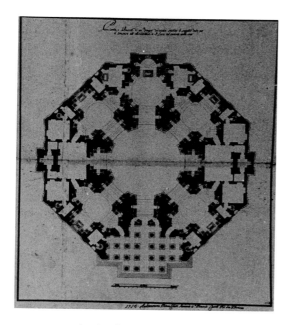

31 CARLO RÈ: plan for a centralized church with portico; ASL 271 (Conc. Clem. 1713).

32 RÈ: facade elevation for the church in Figure 31; ASL 272.

juncture between French and Italian traditions, a juncture formed at a moment when the French were free of their usual restraints. The next logical place to look for the influence of the designs from 1677 is therefore among the *doni accademici* of architects subsequently admitted to membership in the Accademia, since these drawings were often meant to relate to its activities or interests. In addition, the *doni* generally reflect a greater concern for the practical and the useful, while many times evincing a fascination with ideal, centralized planning. And so it is not surprising that the impression left by the designs from 1677 on certain important *doni* is immediately detectable.

Antonio Valerii, a Roman architect of some small consequence in the 1700s, was admitted to membership in the Accademia on 3 May 1696, after the submission of his design for an octangular church (Figs. 33, 34).[134] But he had first been nominated for *Accademico di Merito* in 1681, when he was in his early thirties and so just recently eligible for the post.[135] There is no way to account for this fifteen-year delay within the shadowy career of an architect who came to his fame so late in life, but it is possible that his *dono* design was conceived nearer to 1681, and given its final form only in 1696.[136] This is suggested by the close association between it and the *soggetto* of 1677, in the elements of facade towers, octagonal geometry, and cupola. The inspiration for the angled corridors running behind the piers of his church may, in fact, have been the octagonal ambulatory in Chupin's design (cf. Pl. 1).[137] There would be little cause to remark on this were it not for the fact that these corridors (here employed as sacristies) were reused by Valerii in a triangular pattern around the central vessel of his model for a new sacristy for St. Peter's (Fig. 35).[138] One of several models executed in competition in 1715, his project, though unexecuted, was virtually his only masterpiece, and is the culmination of an analytic process that may very well have included Chupin's design in 1677.

A stronger argument can be made, and has been made, for finding in the *concorso* of 1677 the roots of another and far more important *dono* design, that which Filippo Juvarra submitted to the

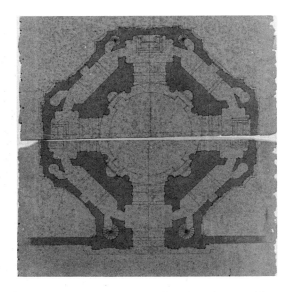

33 ANTONIO VALERII: plan for a domed octagonal church with bell towers; ASL 2106 (Dono Accademico, 1696).

34 VALERII: lateral section for the church in Figure 33; ASL 2107.

35 VALERII: plan of a project model for the new sacristy at St. Peter's; Rome, 1715 (graphic: Troy Thompson).

Accademia on 3 April 1707 (Fig. 36).[139] Juvarra had earned his eligibility for *Accademico di Merito* by winning first prize in the first class of the *concorso* of 1705 with a design for a villa that displayed a virtuoso talent (see Figs. 152, 153).[140] Whatever part of this skill he had not brought with him from Messina less than a year before was derived from his apprenticeship in the studio of Carlo Fontana, who put the final touches to Juvarra's provincial cast.[141] Much of the great architect he was to become at the court in Turin can already be seen in his *concorso* design and the later *dono*. But the latter is more instructive since in this admission piece his versatile mind was at work without the restrictions of a *soggetto* and his own particular interests could be revealed. In every essential, Juvarra had the same concerns in centralized church design as the *soggetto* in 1677.[142]

Juvarra's freestanding church is laid out on an octagonal plan, with four apsidal chapels at the diagonals of a Greek-cross interior, a temple-front portico at both of the symmetrical faces, and a pair of campanili, semidetached, on the lateral axis flanking the cupola. Like the *concorso* of 1677, his design is to be understood as a reappraisal of its major prototype, Rainaldi's S. Agnese, undertaken through the medium of Juvarra's typically eclectic but thorough and imaginative method. Nino

36 FILIPPO JUVARRA: plan and facade elevation for a domed and porticoed octagonal church with bell towers; ASL 2150 (Dono Accademico).

Carboneri considers Fontana's Colosseum church, the designs for which were being prepared for publication in 1707 (see Figs. 17, 18), to be the principal mechanism used in taking Juvarra from S. Agnese to his *dono,* since there are parallels not only in composition but also in the proportional unity between cupola and towers to be accounted for.[143] As an apprentice in Fontana's studio, Juvarra was of course intimately aware of the Colosseum project, but as a student at the Accademia he would also have known of the resources there, including the competition designs from 1677 to which his *dono* is allied by virtue of its grand cupola and porticoed facades.

The tetrastyle portico of Juvarra's design could as easily be compared to that used by D'Aviler in his church as to those of Rainaldi's Twin Churches, or Bernini's projects for St. Peter's. It does not compete with the cupola, but still it contributes to the dynamic counterpoint of void and solid, the mingling of interior and exterior spaces, and the scenographic vistas characteristic of the church and Juvarra's architecture in general. One of the section drawings Juvarra produced for this design (Fig. 37), now housed in the Berlin Kunstbibliothek, highlights another element held in common with designs from 1677: the intermediate socle zone above the first cornice that raises the cupola to its majestic height. He does not bring in the foreign device of the truncated dome, used by D'Aviler and Desgots for this purpose, nor does he return to the timeworn pendentive system, choosing instead to continue the octagonal geometry vertically along the structural lines of columns and ribs. The result is unquestionably Italianate, but has the quasi-Gothic character of what will become his personal Rococo idiom.[144]

The *dono* is emphatically Juvarra's in nature, but there is much in it in sympathy with the methods selected by the competitors in 1677 to confront the problems inherent in Tomassini's *soggetto.* Comparisons need only be drawn between the *dono* and Desgots's third-place design, since the Colosseum church is ancestor to both. In addition to the facade porticoes and the elevating socles they have in common, both architects chose, on Fontana's example, to locate the towers on the lat-

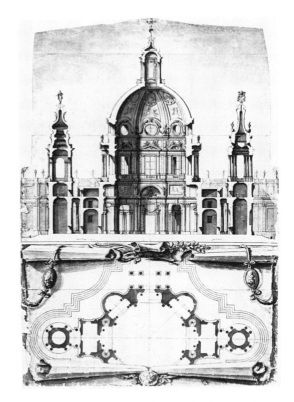

37 JUVARRA: plan and section for the church in Figure 36 (source: Kunstbibliothek, Staatliche Museen Preussischer Kulturbesitz, Berlin).

eral axis so as to frame rather than block the view of the cupola. Juvarra's version is again replete with more sophisticated adjustments to this scheme. The semidetached position of the cylindrical towers allows them to have their own considerably enhanced stature (like the towers of S. Agnese) without detracting from the cupola. But they are reunited with the church by the continuity of the cornices throughout (like the Colosseum church). The *dono*'s Michelangelesque (more correctly Cortonesque) cupola is akin to Desgots's, but is more thoroughly integrated with the whole because of the openness the drum colonnade shares with the upper stories of the towers and the portico below.[145]

Comparing interiors, Juvarra dismissed the value of the truncated dome, but took to heart the light-filled quality of Desgots's building, and provided large windows for the drum and a second ring of lights above them, rather than below in the socle. Both ground plans are also similarly open, though Juvarra is more orthodox in his usage and more scenographic in his conception. While Juvarra's architectural judgement, even as a student, was more consistently unerring than was Desgots's in 1677, he may nevertheless have identified with Desgots's thinking on open structure, since it would continue to occupy him in the course of his later work in Rome and Piedmont.[146] If it is difficult to accept this association between Juvarra's *dono* and Desgots's *concorso* design, there is still the Superga to consider, which represents the practical application of Juvarra's ideas on centralized church design.

It was for the construction of the Superga outside of Turin that Juvarra was called to Piedmont by King Vittorio Amadeo II in 1715.[147] Juvarra's initial sketches did not deviate far from the project of the previous architect, Antonio Bertola, but he may even then have been certain of the suitability of his *dono* design, with its impressive silhouette, to the mountaintop site.[148] His opportunity came in 1716, when it was decided to combine the building of the church and a nearby monastery into one project, requiring an entirely new design, to which the Superga was erected between 1717 and 1731 (Figs. 38–40). As executed, the church makes plain that Juvarra had succeeded in having at least some form of his *dono* design realized, though compromises had to be made in order to adjust the church to the site and the monastery. For example, the campanili had to be set back and fit into a wing of the residence, and much of the detailing was reduced, presumably for economic reasons.[149] What is intriguing to note is that the final result presents even more analogies to Desgots's project.

Firstly, Juvarra reduced the lower portion of the exterior of the church to the form of a broad cylinder, as a monumental base for the cupola, bringing the whole in line with the Pantheon, to which Desgots's project can also be compared. Then there is the elevating socle, and a cupola which is a great deal closer to the one designed by Desgots in 1677, particularly in articulation. For scenographic reasons, the towers and portico were

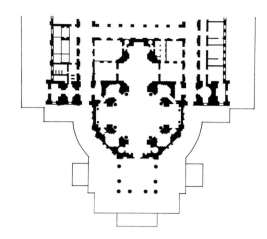

38 JUVARRA: plan of the Superga; Turin, 1717–31 (graphic: Troy Thompson).

extended well outside the perimeter of the church, since the complex is approached at an angle, but otherwise the similarities are enticing, and continue in plan and section. Both Juvarra and Desgots referred to S. Maria dei Miracoli (Fig. 41), the church by Rainaldi on the Piazza del Popolo completed by Carlo Fontana, for the distribution of the interior spaces. Juvarra's church also accommodates seven altars; and it is generated from an octagon, but in making the transition to the cylinder of the drum he contrives an entirely new device. Eight columns are inserted into the corners of the octagon to support the circular tension ring. This masterful solution, however unprecedented, is still very much in the spirit of Desgots's and D'Aviler's designs, which also avoided pendentives and introduced an innovative alternative.

In the final analysis, Juvarra is a far more sophisticated architect and decorator by the time of his own competition than any of the three prizewinners in 1677, and any proposed connections between their work and his cannot go unqualified. But neither can they be ignored, since the common ground provided by the Accademia and Fontana makes certain Juvarra's familiarity with the French designs. Just as Fontana may have advised Desgots and D'Aviler in 1677, he may also have encouraged Juvarra to include their work

39 JUVARRA: facade of the Superga (photo: Alinari).

40 JUVARRA: interior of the Superga (photo: author).

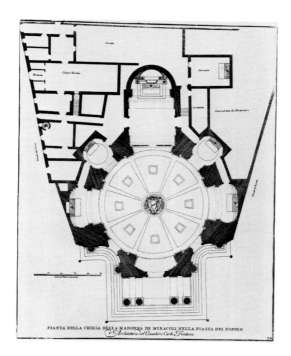

41 CARLO RAINALDI AND CARLO FONTANA:
plan of S. Maria dei Miracoli; Rome, 1662–75
(engraving: de Rossi).

in his researches, since their churches were more in line with his conception than Fontana's severely classical design for the Colosseum church. What Juvarra would have found was not necessarily inspiration, but a confirmation of the validity of his approach.

The Superga is not only the product of genius but also of an eclectic appetite that was not above feeding itself on any collateral effort, including that of a student like Desgots. This is only the first of several occasions where a connection can be drawn between a competition design and Juvarra's later work. The porticoed facade of Chupin's church from the *concorso* of 1677 (see Pl. 2) bears comparison with Juvarra's final design for the facade of S. Filippo Neri in Turin (1730; Fig. 42).[150] Juvarra's contemporaries—who doted on tradition, believed the end justified the means, and subordinated individual ideas to the common good of the "art" of architecture—would not have condemned his method. Even Desgots, who had used much the same method in deriving his *concorso* design, would probably have appreciated the Superga not as plagiarism but as the culmination of an evolutionary process in which he had played a significant role.

This process of evolution had, however, come close to expending itself in the Superga, as evidenced by the number of subsequent projects, both academic and practical, based on it or Juvarra's *dono*. In fact, Juvarra, or at least his thoughts on centralized design, would seem to have been the sole mechanism of transmission between the *concorso* of 1677 and later competitions. Juvarra was lecturer in architecture at the Accademia in 1707–8, immediately following his admission to membership, and in 1712 he taught perspective.[151] In the next year, the *Concorso Clementino* generated the first *soggetto* with ambitions similar to those in 1677, and it may have been Juvarra's experienced guidance which compelled Carlo Rè to refer, albeit all too literally, to Desgots's design for his second-prize project (see Fig. 32). One of Sébastien Demangeot's first-prize alternatives that year (Figs. 43, 44) merged Juvarra's *dono* with St. Peter's, in his own way answering the problems put by Tomassini's *soggetto* in 1677.

42 JUVARRA: facade of S. Filippo Neri; Turin, 1732–38 (photo: Alinari).

The call for a victory church in the *concorso* of 1716 was of course motivated by the project which had taken Juvarra from Rome to Turin. While in their ignorance no competitors could refer to the Superga itself, some still drew inspiration from the *dono* for locating the towers. And after 1716, any *concorso* design in which the juxtaposition of towers and cupola was of critical concern almost invariably aligned itself with the Superga.[152]

The impact of the Superga was felt continent-wide, as well. In Copenhagen, the royal Danish architect Nils Eigtwedt designed a great church for Frederick V as part of the Amalienborg complex (Fig. 45). This project, though never executed due to Eigtwedt's death in 1754, was based closely on the examples of the Superga and Juvarra's *dono,* which he had absorbed on his trip to Rome in the early 1730s.[153] The Superga was therefore not just a type, but an archetype for eighteenth-century Europe.

The coincidental definition of this new type,

43 SÉBASTIEN DEMANGEOT: facade elevation for a domed, centralized church with bell towers; ASL 266 (Conc. Clem. 1713).

44 DEMANGEOT: lateral section for the church in Figure 43; ASL 267.

just when a church of similar characteristics was being devised elsewhere, has troubled those architectural historians who are concerned with precedents and a verifiable process of dissemination. In 1715, Johann Bernhard Fischer von Erlach was chosen in competition with several other Austrian and European architects to execute the design for the Karlskirche in Vienna, dedicated to Emperor Charles VI's name-saint, Carlo Borromeo (Fig. 46). Because of Fischer's proven propensity for historical architecture, much more has been made of the allegorical content of this church than of its formal architectural qualities.[154] But in the latter, as in many other regards, the parallels with the Superga are striking and not easily explained in view of their proximate dates.

The Karlskirche was also a votive church, the construction of which had been promised by the emperor in return for divine relief for Vienna from a plague in 1713. Its siting was likewise similar to the Superga's; it was built on a hill outside the city

walls, facing the imperial palace, in an area that had been depopulated since the Turkish siege of 1683.[155] It was meant, therefore, to have a prominent aspect, to which end Fischer gave it an impressive silhouette composed of towers and a cupola.

Ignoring the Trajanic columns, which are part of the iconographic program, what is left are those elements which also characterize the exterior of the Superga: a nearly identical (though oval) cupola, a temple-front portico, and campanili at a comfortable remove from the drum and dome. This has been a cause of consternation for those who cannot decide if Juvarra influenced Fischer when he submitted his own design for the Karlskirche, or if Fischer's earlier conception had a telling effect on the Superga.[156] Then, too, the latter explanation does not account for Juvarra's *dono*.[157] In such a case it is always advisable to trace the roots of the designs in question to find their common nodes, and the *concorso* of 1677 provides

45 NILS EIGTWEDT: facade project for the Frederikskirke; Copenhagen, 1754 (source: Royal Danish Academy, Copenhagen).

46 J. B. FISCHER VON ERLACH: facade of the Karlskirche; Vienna, 1715–38 (photo: author).

that opportunity in this particular instance.

The cupola of the Karlskirche is one of an infinite number of variations on its theme, which include the Superga, Juvarra's *dono,* and the French designs from 1677. Its facade is more illuminating, beginning with the obvious feature of the portico. As this projects from the plane of the facade via the flanking concave walls, the connection is usually made to the facades of the Twin Churches on the Piazza del Popolo (see Fig. 12), which were also central to the designs from 1677. The hexastyle portico, until now loosely attributed to Fischer's historical interests, can also be seen to refer to the proposals of Chupin and Desgots, and through them to French classicism in general.

The Gallic characteristics of Fischer's architecture are often glossed over in view of the tastes of his time, but when he is so specific in the case of the Karlskirche, it is possible to propose quite an unexpected route for the acquisition of those characteristics. The bell towers, in particular, are not just in the nature of the pavilions common to French secular architecture, but are in their form and position directly comparable to the towers of François Mansart's facade of the Minims church (see Fig. 13). If indeed Fischer knew of this building from contemporary engravings, he may have been inspired to imitate it not only because conditions were the same, but because D'Aviler had used the same model in transposing from the screening facade of St. Peter's to the facade of his *concorso* design. It is possible to be convinced of the link between their designs merely by comparing the plan of the Karlskirche (Fig. 47), to that of D'Aviler's church (see Pl. 4). Fischer shares with the competitors in 1677 a capacity for formal analysis that surfaces in the Karlskirche not just as symbolism but as good architectural sense. If the question is how he gained his familiarity with the methods used in 1677, the answer is simple: he was there.

Fischer arrived in Rome in 1671, aged sixteen, to learn from experience, like many other young Austrians and the French *pensionnaires,* but to Hans Aurenhammer he was exceptional: "He, perhaps more than any of his contemporaries, entered into the spirit of the artistic creativity and scientific research that characterized the Rome of this period."[158] At the time, some of the last great urbanistic, architectural, and decorative projects of the High Baroque were in progress, and these were to have their effect on his later work. Fischer succeeded in insinuating himself into intellectual circles and the studio of Bernini, which was then in the hands of Carlo Fontana. He also made the acquaintance of Pietro Bellori, and when the French and Roman academies were united in 1676, he too was caught up in the popular acclaim for things French.[159] It was about this time that he abandoned his career as a sculptor and decorator, and took up architecture, immersing himself in its theory, history, and practice. The significance of the architectural competition in 1677, the ceremony of the *concorso,* the involvement of both Fontana and Bellori, and the participation of an international array of young talent, not unlike himself, would have combined for a spectacle he could not have missed. When the designs from the *concorso* were exhibited during the celebrations on 14 November, or were discussed in the halls of academe, the impressionable young Fischer must have come away with ideas that lingered in his memory, until he could apply them in 1715.[160]

It would seem, then, that in 1677 productive discourse and experimentation on centralized church design were pursued at the Accademia di San Luca, initiated by Tomassini and other member architects, the effects of which were felt not only in the *concorso* of that year, but forty years later in two principal monuments of the type. One looked back to derive its aura from the past, the other looked ahead and colored much of eighteenth-century usage, but both capitalized on a process of formal investigation nourished by an academic environment occupied not only with theory but with practice. Still to be considered, however, is the truncated dome, the device which of all the proposals made in 1677 was the most "French" and was so crucial to the success of D'Aviler's and Desgots's designs, but which played no direct part in either Juvarra's or Fischer's church.

Nor was the truncated dome to have a significant role in French architecture, which had spawned it. LeVau rejected his own first project

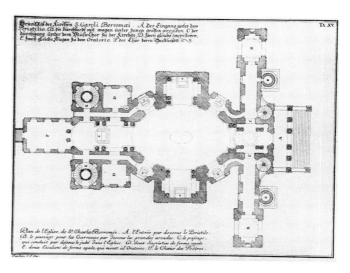

47 FISCHER: plan of the Karlskirche (from *Entwurff einer historischen Architectur*).

for the Chapel of the Collège des Quatre Nations, the direct antecedent for D'Aviler's and Desgots's designs, presumably because the truncated dome interrupted the continuity of the interior geometry, though it so adroitly enhanced the prospect of the cupola. When in the late 1670s the opportunity next came in France to use the device in the design of a domed centralized church, the Chapel of the Invalides in Paris, the truncated dome was included by the architect Jules Hardouin-Mansart, not as a base for the cupola but above the drum, opening into a second painted vault beyond (Fig. 48). In this and in many other particulars the younger Mansart is indebted to his uncle François and his designs for the Bourbon chapel at St.-Denis.[161]

Conceived like the latter on a radiating plan (Fig. 49), the Dome of the Invalides is the most accomplished example of this type in France, but D'Aviler's and Desgots's *concorso* designs are in line with it, too. In conformity with a taste for the Italian Baroque in French church architecture at the time, Hardouin-Mansart, like Chupin, blended much of the formal and decorative qualities of St. Peter's into his design, which determined the handling of the dome, the interior articulation, the high altar, and even the plan of the porticoed

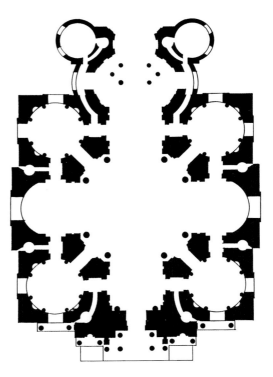

49 HARDOUIN-MANSART: plan of the Invalides chapel (graphic: Troy Thompson).

48 JULES HARDOUIN-MANSART: section of the Chapel of the Invalides; Paris, 1679–91 (engraving: Rondelet).

facade (Fig. 50). The two-story front advances in stages toward the center, like those of Roman churches, but the lower portion of the front is based on the Minims, as is that in D'Aviler's design. In fact, in his attempt to combine French and Italian traditions of centralized church design in the Invalides chapel, Hardouin-Mansart's ideas run parallel to the results of the *concorso* of 1677 (with the obvious exception of the bell towers). But the project for Hardouin-Mansart's chapel was initiated early in 1676, while the competitors were out of touch with events in Paris.[162] In that case, François Mansart's Bourbon chapel design may constitute a precedent for the designs from 1677, as well as for the Dome of the Invalides. But the only other valid conclusion that can be drawn is that novel approaches to centralized design were being tried in Paris and Rome at roughly the same time, and that more and more the *concorso* of 1677 appears to be an important point of exchange between the two lines of development.

Hardouin-Mansart's use of the truncated dome at the Invalides chapel has been compared to Guarini's at the church of Ste.-Anne-la-Royale in Paris (1662, destroyed), which had otherwise no good reputation in France. In both instances the truncated or open dome is a mechanism to control vertical vistas, framing layers of space, and it is in that sense that the motif becomes a part of Italian practice, rather than a supporting element for a cupola. Still, if not the function, then the form the device ultimately takes is very much like the form it had in both D'Aviler's and Desgots's designs.

Bernhard Kerber has discovered an early pro-

78

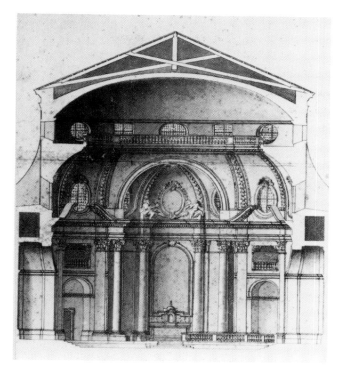

51 ANDREA POZZO: project section for the chapel of the Collegio Inglese; Rome, ca. 1680 (source: Collegio Inglese).

50 HARDOUIN-MANSART: view of the Invalides chapel (photo: Marburg/Art Resource, New York).

ject for the chapel of the Collegio Inglese in Rome, which he attributes to Andrea Pozzo and dates to about 1680 (Fig. 51).[163] Here the truncated dome has a purpose identical to that of the Invalides, constricting the view of the upper vault and hiding from sight the ring of windows that light it. The effect would be to enframe the vault fresco, and artificially separate it from its architectural context, a unique approach for Pozzo to the Baroque illusions at which he excelled. If the dating is correct, Pozzo could have had only an indirect knowledge of the Invalides dome, which had yet to reach the height of the drum by the early 1680s. He may have been aware of the general concept and been versed in the architecture of the elder Mansart or Guarini, but the form his truncated dome takes is more likely inspired by the French designs from 1677. Pozzo, too, was no doubt caught up in the excitement surrounding that *concorso* and the new ideas it presented. For him, as for all those who in the future would employ the truncated dome, it was not a practical expedient but a thoroughly Baroque mechanism well suited to a combined program of illusionistic architecture, painting, and sculpture.[164]

As such, it constitutes a primary part of the architectural vocabulary of one of the last truly Baroque artists of the Seicento, Antonio Gherardi. He was a member of the Accademia di San Luca in 1674. The first of his two major commissions was also realized in 1680, at which time he had completed the remodeling of the Avila family chapel in S. Maria in Trastevere, Rome.[165] To expand the cramped space of the chapel optically, he included illusionistically diminishing colonnades behind the altar and a truncated dome for the vault (Fig. 52). The latter supports what amounts to a second

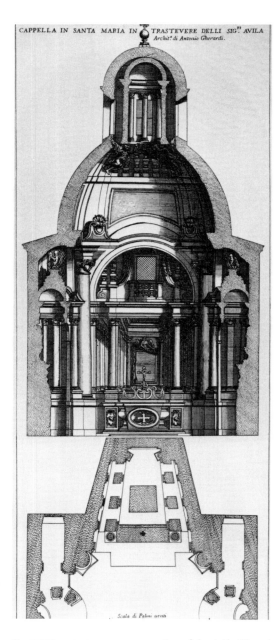

CAPPELLA IN SANTA MARIA IN TRASTEVERE DELLI SIG.ⁱⁱ AVILA
Archit.ᵗ di Antonio Gherardi.

Scala di Palmi uenti

52 ANTONIO GHERARDI: section of the Avila Chapel in S. Maria in Trastevere; Rome, 1678–80 (engraving: de Rossi).

dome on a drum (but is actually a much enlarged lantern) into which is inserted an Ionic *tempietto* carried as if miraculously by four putti. The idea fuses architecture, sculpture, and light to create a new, though fundamentally Berninesque, effect in which the truncated dome, "crowned" by a balustrade in relief, plays an essential part.

He achieved approximately the same result in the chapel dedicated to S. Cecilia, in S. Carlo ai Catinari in Rome, which he began in 1691 for the Congregazione dei Musici (Fig. 53). Above the truncated dome of this chapel is a light chamber, artificially treated like a second dome and drum, from which sculpted angels bearing musical instruments descend. In this instance, Gherardi has conceived of the truncated dome as a demarcation zone between earthly and spiritual realms. In both examples, he was undoubtedly inspired by D'Aviler and Desgots, whose efforts in 1677 would have had his eye as well, but his purpose is programmatic rather than practical, and quite Baroque.

Experimentation in Rome along these lines did not end here. Despite his conservative reputation, Carlo Fontana answered Gherardi's chapel of S. Cecilia with his own designs for the baptismal chapel at St. Peter's (see Fig. 107), into which light is directed from a chamber above through a tension ring supported by pendentives but carrying no cupola.[166] For this reason it may be possible to suggest Fontana as having introduced the truncated dome into the training of the Bavarian brothers Cosmas Damian and Egid Quirin Asam. The Asams came to Rome in 1711, Cosmas Damian to study painting at the Accademia, and Egid Quirin to study sculpture.[167] When they returned to Bavaria in 1714, they were completely Romanized decorators, and in collaboration they enjoyed a brief tenure as architects as well, before 1720, though it is as difficult to separate their architecture from their decoration as it is to distinguish their individual hands. Of two churches entirely the products of their joint invention, the earliest was the Benedictine abbey church at Weltenburg (1716–35, Fig. 54).[168]

This church is unique in their oeuvre and Bavarian architecture in general for the candor with which it refers to Roman Baroque motifs: in

53 GHERARDI: interior of the Cappella S. Cecilia in S. Carlo ai Catinari; Rome, 1691–1700 (photo: author).

54 COSMAS DAMIAN ASAM AND EGID QUIRIN ASAM: interior of the Benedictine abbey church; Weltenburg, 1716–35 (photo: Marburg/Art Resource, New York).

the oval plan, the articulation, the Berninesque tableau of St. George above the high altar lit from behind by the choir, and now the truncated dome. The purpose of the truncated dome is both programmatic and illusionistic: it bears a great crown iconographically linked to that offered to the Virgin in the Coronation fresco above, and separates real space from the miraculous space above lit by windows at the circumference of the vault. The drama in the fresco takes place within the feigned space of a *quadratura* drum and dome, illusionistically supported by the truncated dome below. The connection with Gherardi's S. Cecilia chapel is obvious, but since there the truncated dome is supported on pendentives, Kerber prefers to trace the lineage back to Pozzo's Collegio Inglese chapel (see note 175), where the association between vaults is identical to that at Weltenburg. It is now possible to follow the development back even further, to D'Aviler's and Desgots's designs, where the absence of pendentives was also of definitive importance. The only difference is that while for the French the truncated dome had a purely architectonic purpose, for the Italians it immediately developed as an illusionistic device which furthered the cause of the Baroque. And so the Asam church not only has a starting date in common with the Karlskirche and the Superga, but also formal links to the *concorso* of 1677.[169]

Tomassini, Carlo Fontana, and Charles Errard expressed certain interests in centralized church design which they seem to have encouraged their young charges to share. Through the fortuitous participation of the French in the *concorso* of 1677, and the inspiration of Carlo Fontana in particular, some novel thinking was injected into the flagging Italian tradition of church design. But by the same token, it was only the less rigidly dogmatic academic climate in Rome, which operated on the assumption that new ideas did not necessarily represent anarchy and were indeed essential to the vitality of any tradition, that gave the French a better opportunity for innovation than they would have had in Paris. Inadvertently, the pomp and ceremony of the *concorso,* combined with the vigorous approbation aimed at everything French,

gave the *concorso* projects a wider audience than they would otherwise have had. Their impression was made successively on Fischer, Juvarra, and the Asams, when each of them passed through Rome and into the circle of Fontana and the Accademia.

There was little of the kind of building in Rome or by the Church that might have exploited the proposals of 1677, and even academic experiments would lose touch with what had been achieved. It was not until Juvarra, Fischer, and the Asams were provided the opportunity by secular patronage to design churches of the same type at roughly the same time that the ambitions of 1677 were rekindled on a large scale. The irony is that while the theater in which the drama of Baroque architecture was being played had moved north to Turin, Vienna, Paris, and Bavaria, the script, at least for church design, was still being written in Rome. And while the competitors in the *concorso* of 1677 were French, just as the architects most often consulted in the next century would be French, the environment in which their ideas were nurtured was Roman. The importance of the *concorso* in architecture for 1677 thus reaches beyond the walls of the Accademia and of Rome, even beyond the boundaries of Italy and the temporal limit of the turn of the century, to give it a stature not usually associated with an academic competition. It is against this stature that the significance of the later *Concorsi Accademici* in the seventeenth century, and the achievements of their participating architects, must be measured.

But the significance of the *concorso* of 1677 should not be overstressed. Surely its relationship to the general phenomenon of the merging of French and Roman influence in the Late Baroque is a symptom and not a cause. The designs by Chupin, D'Aviler, and Desgots are simply a valuable part of the broader discourse on these issues current in Rome and Europe, discourse that may otherwise go largely unrecorded but to which Juvarra, Fischer, and the Asams would certainly also have had access. It is only the vicissitudes of time that have left the drawings from 1677 as such stark and singular testimony to that larger discourse which can be and has been deduced in any case from the architecture of the early 1700s.

The two sides, Italian and French, of Juvarra's architecture are characteristics already well documented in the literature on him.[170] He is as capable of Parisian elegance in his secular designs, as he is capable of Roman *bravura* in his church designs. Fischer was master of an even subtler fusion of the two traditions which he could apply universally, without regard for typology. Hans Sedlmayr made a life-long study of this aspect of Fischer, and of the Late Baroque in general, that has to the greatest extent shaped the existing view of the stylistic hegemony shared by France and Rome in Central Europe during this period.[171] In this view, the dichotomy of expression epitomized by Hardouin-Mansart's chapel at the Invalides in Paris is not an incident isolated to the court style of Louis XIV or to France alone.[172] Rather, it stands at the leading edge of a continent-wide trend toward synthesis of the two dominant Baroque traditions, a trend that can now include even the Asams, who were once perceived largely as unmitigated Bavarian Romanists.[173]

The evidence of the architecture is in effect too strong to question the combined influence of Paris and Rome on the Late Baroque. But on that same evidence it is still possible to question the means that gave rise to this end. Buildings from the period may reflect an unconscious adherence to norms accepted by all architects in response to the social and political milieu in which they practiced. In such cases the mechanisms for the transmission of ideas tend to be taken for granted, even trivialized: where did the architect go and what, in the form of buildings or engraved images, did he see? Or the objective of stylistic fusion may have been consciously pursued, in which case the experiences of the architects would have been deliberately shaped to include the thickest part of the debate and dialogue on architecture, and not just chance exposure to the built environment.

Such cases, which now include Fischer, Juvarra, the Asams, and the three young French architects who took the honors in 1677, are of increasing interest to scholars of the period because their experiences go deeper than the superficial cycle of innovation and influence, to the very core of architectural thought. Padre Pozzo made a career of synthesizing the ideas of Bernini, Borromini, Rainaldi, and other contemporaries in his definition of an architectural idiom in harmony with his extravagant methods in painting and sculpture.[174] His use of the truncated dome shortly after 1677 betrays an interest in adding French influence to the mix that is otherwise unexpected, as incompatible as the two tastes can be, but is more understandable in the context described above.[175] Another such product of the period was the Swede, Nicodemus Tessin, whose preparations to become architect to Charles XII took him throughout Europe, primarily France and Italy, in the 1670s and 1680s.[176] In Paris he was in contact with the architects of the court, and in Rome with Bernini and Carlo Fontana; his indirect contact with the academies of both cities can therefore be presumed. In Sweden, and abroad, his fame attached to his facility for design in both the French and Italian languages, and to a fluency not just in decor but in ideas that could have been learned only in the highest circles.

The *Concorsi Accademici* are here considered as insights into the circle of architectural intellects in Rome and not just as stopping points on the routes by which architectural motifs have been transmitted. The Accademia must be understood as a laboratory for ideas, most specifically for the crossbreeding of Roman and French ideas. Its effectiveness beyond the successes of 1677 will depend on maintaining an ability to respond to or even promote new ideas, anticipate or even contribute to future developments, and retain a prominent position in the minds of European architects regardless of its association with the French.

III

THE INTERIM YEARS: 1678 TO 1692

THE FATE OF RELATIONS BETWEEN PARIS AND ROME

1678

THE FORTUNES OF the *concorsi* after 1677 are intimately linked to those of the two academies and their union in the succeeding years. Just as public competition was first inspired by that union, it would seem that the ability to sustain the kind of effort needed for public competition depended on the willingness and resources of both parties to do so. And in an age that depended so heavily on adherence to the amenities, the factors of diplomacy and protocol must be considered as well in the uneven history of the *Concorsi Accademici*.

While Errard retained his office as director of the French in Rome, and while Colbert still lived to favor the role of Rome in the artistic affairs of the French monarchy, those factors combined to the advantage of the academies. But the phenomenon of the first competition could not easily be repeated. The *concorsi* of the next few years are inevitably anticlimactic by comparison. The intensity of the campaign in 1677 must have gone a long way toward depleting available energies, both of the academies for mounting such an enterprise and of the artistic community for supporting it.

This may, in part, explain the decision to hold no competition in 1678. Errard had been made *principe* in his own right at the end of 1677, in tribute to his achievements on behalf of LeBrun in making the previous two years a diplomatic and administrative success for the academies then under his jurisdiction.[1] But his principal goals during this, his second tenure as *principe,* involved the consolidation of gains made during the aggre-

gation period other than competition. His first official act, before the congregation in Rome and by letter to Paris, was to affirm the articles of aggregation.[2] His concern for the architectural appraisals of the Accademia for the coming year was underscored by his reappointment of Rainaldi and Mattia de Rossi as *stimatori d'architettura.* On 24 April, instruction was set to begin on the first Sunday of May, and to continue every Sunday and feast day thereafter at 10:00; Gregorio Tomassini was named again as lecturer in architecture.[3] Nine new members, an unprecedented number for one occasion, were nominated by Errard on 10 July, including three of the French *pensionnaires* who had won prizes the previous autumn, and the Italian architect Giovanni Battista Menicucci who had also contemplated competing (see Chapter II).[4] After a week had passed for the congregation to consider the candidates' suitabilities, all nine were accepted as dues-paying *Accademici di Merito,* in accordance with the statutes as modified by the articles of aggregation to include the French.[5] Missirini (App. B, 1678, n. 1) also credited Errard with updating the inventories of the Accademia and its church, and clarifying the accounts of its administrators, creditors, and debtors.

Emphasis was above all put on bringing the fiscal responsibilities of the Accademia into some semblance of order, more so than on pursuing academic advances. The priorities were no doubt mandated by the situation at the Accademia, and by its congregation, which had turned to Errard as much for his organizational skills as his academic inclinations. Solvency was viewed as a necessary antecedent to a healthy environment for learning and debate. Another benefit to the efficient functioning of the Accademia realized in this year was the re-election to the office of secretary of Giuseppe Ghezzi.[6] As a painter, Ghezzi epitomized the tenets of academicism to a degree that is admirable if one can accept the reasoning behind the taste. As that has not always been the case, there is little comment on him in later accounts of the period, but in his day he enjoyed a considerable reputation. This was particularly true with regard to his oratorical and critical skills, and in those respects he was an asset to the Accademia. He brought his thoroughness to bear as well on the minutes and reports of the Accademia from 1674 to 1711, and for this the historian is particularly grateful as his *verbali* are a lucid source of information. Such was presumably also the opinion of his fellow academicians, and for the rest of the century and into the next Ghezzi was given important roles to play in the *concorsi* in particular: writing *soggetti,* presenting discourses, and later publishing commemorative tracts on the events of the competitions.[7]

This year of reform and consolidation during Errard's principate would almost certainly have affected instruction in some way. Most significantly, the curriculum in architecture had, since its instigation in 1673, been operating under the aegis of instructors—Fontana, de Rossi, della Greca, and Tomassini—who had at best only a part-time interest in such affairs, and who represented, one can presume, their own separate and distinct attitudes and methods to the students under their charge in any year. Given Errard's intention to remove inconsistencies in the Accademia's operation, and given that one of the first objectives of the Académie d'Architecture was to codify the principles which would uniformly guide instruction there, it should be expected that the Accademia would also seek to achieve the same end, and by means modeled on those of the French. There is no direct evidence for such a process chronicled in the histories of the Accademia, but there are circumstances which support such a conclusion.

First among these is a group of fifteen drawings by Gregorio Tomassini, the Accademia's instructor in architecture in 1678, which represent his recommendations for the Classical Orders, carefully rendered in complete detail and with measurements. Preserved in the Accademia's archives as his lessons in architecture, they include the Doric and Corinthian Orders illustrated in Figures 57 and 58. His primary source was Vignola (*Regola delli cinque ordini* ... 1562), who for Tomassini as much as for D'Aviler and the rest of the academic community amounted to the highest modern published Roman authority on the subject. These exceptional drawings are not dated, but something more precise about when the drawings were made may be construed from why they were made. The fact that they are concerned with the Orders is not of itself remarkable, but the degree of attention devoted to them, not just as "visual aids" but as exquisite drawings, is quite revealing.

Previous mention has been made of the lessons on the Orders produced by Mattia de Rossi during his tenure as instructor in 1673.[8] His efforts amounted to little more than basic diagrams of the Orders (Figs. 55, 56), measured out in modules marked by prick holes, penciled in with rule and compass, hastily inked in outline only, with little or no fine detail and no accompanying text. They were no more than a temporary means of elucidation. Tomassini's drawings, magnificently rendered down to the most minute detail, on a fine grade of paper, and annotated with his thoughts on the Orders, send quite a different message. His was an almost obsessive preoccupation with the Orders, recorded in a manner that would assure that their impression endured not only for one year but for many, and it was an obsession his students were no doubt meant to share.

This attention to the Orders is enlightening, since it is so much in harmony with the predominant preoccupation of the French theorists as well (see Chapter I). French treatises, textbooks, and debates were almost entirely devoted to the Orders and the proportioning systems derived from them, whenever practical matters did not intrude, and this tendency had been reconfirmed at the outset for the Académie d'Architecture by its first director, Blondel. Ensuring consistency in this regard not only in the academic context but also in the establishment of a uniform French style

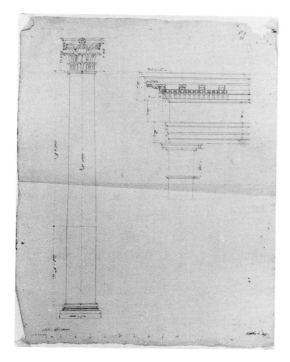

55 MATTIA DE ROSSI: lesson in the Corinthian order; ASL, uncataloged drawing.

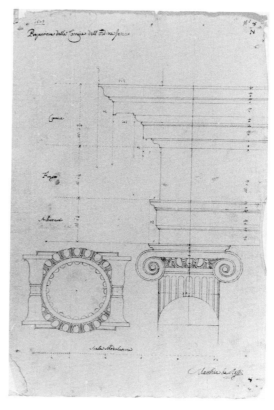

56 DE ROSSI: "proportione della cornice dell'ordine Ionico"; ASL, uncataloged drawing.

was the *raison d'être* of Blondel's academy. If the Roman academy was to continue to emulate the success of its French counterparts, it had to define a purpose for itself along the same lines—setting itself up as the principal arbiter of correct classical usage in Rome. If a concerted response to French stylistic discipline was to be upheld, then the dignity of contemporary Roman classicism demanded a consistent rigor in the adaptation of the Orders to architectural projects. The Accademia was logically the best qualified to train the architects of the next generation in these first principles. Tomassini's lessons may well have been the first attempt to establish such a role for its architectural curriculum, and the relatively quiet year of 1678 represented his best opportunity to work on the project. It may even be, given the finished state to which the drawings were taken, that Tomassini's Orders were also intended to form the nucleus of a textbook similar to Blondel's. While this did not come to pass, perhaps for lack of resources, it is true that until the turn of the century every

instructor in architecture after Tomassini was required to produce his own set of lessons on the Orders for submission to the Accademia's archives.

In 1678 the Feast of St. Luke was not celebrated by a *concorso*. Instead, the ceremony surrounding the feast day was augmented by a demonstration provided by the *Aggregati dei Recami*, a group of tapestry weavers who were affiliated with the Accademia.[9] This, too, was quite probably inspired by French example. Perhaps the most important mechanism for disseminating French taste to Europe existed in the Gobelins manufactory, which was in the business of turning designs by French artists and Italian masters into furnishings, including tapestries, that were in demand in palaces across the continent. To have recourse to their own means of producing such artifacts represented a further step in bringing the

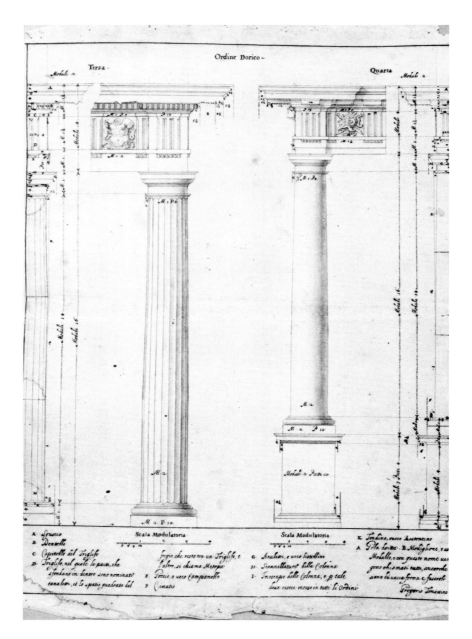

57 GREGORIO TOMASSINI: "Ordine Dorico"; ASL, uncataloged drawing.

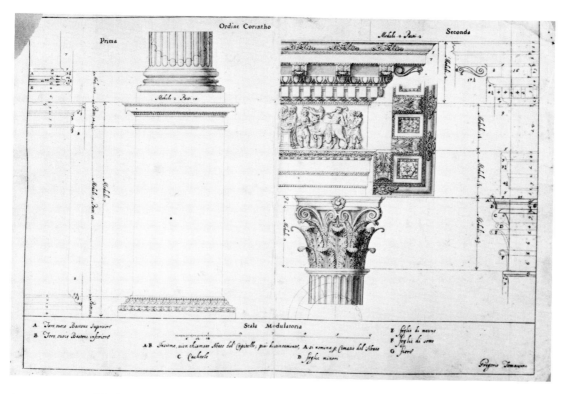

58 TOMASSINI: "Ordine Corintho"; ASL, uncataloged drawing.

Accademia's achievements in line with those of the French academies. The year closed with the election of Lazzaro Baldi to the office of *principe*, a painter in the Cortonesque style who is praised by Missirini for his piety and his charity to the poor, but who achieved very little on behalf of the Accademia in comparison to his immediate predecessors.[10] Errard returned to the comparative ease of his post as director of the French academy in Rome, but he would continue to make his presence at the Accademia known on behalf of the French.[11]

1679

Competition resumed in 1679, the congregation having resolved on 18 June to reestablish the *concorso* at the usual time, some five months later (App. B, 1679, n. 4). To Ghezzi went the task of defining the *soggetti* in painting and sculpture, and

the honor of presenting the oration on the day of the *concorso,* and to him is owed as well a debt of thanks for the excellent account of the *concorso* provided in his minutes. He recorded the first-class topics dealing with the Infancy of Moses, those of the second class on the Creation of Woman, and the third-class exercise which required a copy after one of the heads of old men from Raphael's frescoes in the Vatican *stanze.*[12] This documents the intent of the Accademia to hold competition in all three classes, in contrast to 1677, which was at least one way of recapturing some of the attention that would have been lost in the intervening two years.

Waning interest would also have followed from the fact that the French were incapable of holding their end up in competition due to a diminished enrollment at their academy in Rome.[13] There were five sculptors in attendance, but only one architect (Desgots), two painters, and one engraver. With three classes open to competition, the French had no hope of equaling the coup they had pulled off in 1677, and this may very well have been at the back of the minds of the Romans even then.

Since Desgots had already competed, and in any case was not in good standing with his superiors, the field in architecture was left open to the Italians. Ghezzi, like the authors of *soggetti* before him, deferred to another authority for the definition of the topic in architecture. This was Giovanni Battista Menicucci, one of the recent additions to the ranks of the congregation who had been made instructor in architecture as well as a chaplain of the Accademia during the previous few months.[14] There is no written record that survives of the *soggetto* in architecture, and so it must be reconstructed from the design which won the first and only prize in that category: Domenico Martinelli's design for a domed cruciform church with a towered and porticoed facade (Pls. 10–12).

Parallels between this theme and Tomassini's *soggetto* in 1677 suggest that what Menicucci had in mind, perhaps with Tomassini's encouragement, was the investigation of similar problems within the scheme of a longitudinal church, this time corresponding to Rainaldi's S. Maria in Campitelli (consecrated 1675), the plan of which is similar. Again the critical aspect of the design is the facade, but in contrast to the task in 1677 this could not have been meant to answer any pressing need or unresolved problem in Roman architecture. In conjunction with a longitudinal church, a towered facade had little relevance at all in Baroque Rome, but it does coincidentally relate to issues recently revived in Paris.[15]

These have to do with proposals for the facades of St.-Eustache and St.-Sulpice made by LeVau late in his career. For basilican churches in Paris, the medieval tradition of the towered facade had temporarily been displaced by the Vignolan type imported from Italy early in the seventeenth century, though the tradition still survived in the provinces. It reemerged in Paris during the eighteenth century, centering on the facades of St.-Sulpice (J. N. Servandoni, 1733–45)

and St.-Eustache (J. Hardouin-Mansart de Jouy, begun 1754), which for French classicists epitomized the reconciliation of the classical vocabulary with this type. The common origin of their development, however, should be traced to the period when LeVau was at work on both in the 1660s, since his facade designs would have required the same reconciliation.[16] St.-Eustache was particularly significant in that it had demonstrated in the early sixteenth century the continued strength of the Gothic church form despite the intrusion of classical detailing. It was Colbert, champion of all things French, whose parish church this was and who called on LeVau to provide a design for the facade to complete it, and thereby span the gap between France's earlier and contemporary primacy in the arts.[17] The issue of the classically defined towered facade was therefore quite topical for the French at this time, and the *concorso* of 1679 may very well have been planned to return the favor done by the French in 1677, when they responded to an issue equally topical for the Italians.

Most notable is the atmosphere of exchange between the two national interests that still existed in 1679. The French were at a loss as far as participating in the architectural *concorso* was concerned, but nonetheless some advantage was envisioned for them. And despite their reduced numbers they did compete in painting, and distinguished themselves again. Of the six prizes awarded in the first class for this medium, two were taken by French *pensionnaires,* and these two must have been the ones mentioned by Colbert in a memorandum to LeBrun (App. B, 1679, n. 7) as the *only* student painters then attending the French academy in Rome.[18] With a total of seven prizes awarded in the second and third classes of painting, the numbers favored the Italians, but the French painters have to be credited with 100 percent participation and 100 percent success.

In contrast, the fact that only one prize was awarded in both sculpture and architecture suggests that participation in these categories was not optimum on the part of either academy. The French sculptors were involved in other important work, making copies or assisting Bernini on the king's equestrian statue, and there were no qualified French architects. Where, then, were the Italians who might have made their gains in the absence of the French? It would seem that the Accademia had not yet recruited sufficient numbers from masters' studios in either medium to fill out their enrollment or to bring distinction on themselves in the competitions. At the root of the problem was the Accademia's insistence, modeled on French practice, that no student apprenticed to an independent workshop could compete.[19] This may have suited the French academies which had employed this method to wrest artistic sovereignty away from the *Maîtrise,* but in Rome where independent studios were still the rule, and included even Bernini's where much of the work of sculpture and architecture in the city was being done, the policy was not quite as workable.

Still, the *concorso* was held on schedule, on the Feast of St. Luke, and as Ghezzi's account would have it (emphasizing as it does his primary importance in the role of orator) it was handled with some ceremony. The prizes awarded were, however, considerably less impressive than the gold and silver medals of 1677. They consisted of silver pens in brass cases, and drafting compasses of brass "qualificati a proportione della qualità delle classi." In depending on its own resources rather than those of LeBrun for acquiring the prizes, some adjustments obviously had to be made. But this *concorso,* no matter how much it pales by comparison to that of 1677, was conducted with far more attention to detail, and more success, than any before the aggregation with the French.

In December, the passing of the Accademia's protector, Cardinal Francesco Barberini, was mourned, and his nephew Carlo, then papal legate to Urbino, was solicited to succeed him.[20] The process was all rather perfunctory, indicating that the Accademia had more interest in the noble friends it was making in Paris than in the aristocratic patronage it had once depended upon at home. In fairness, however, the Barberini had taken little more than a rubber-stamp approach to their function on behalf of the Accademia since

the papacy of Urban VIII—witness the cardinal's passive role in the aggregation proceedings.

1680

Giovanni Maria Morandi, a Tuscan painter with a Venetian style, assumed the office of *principe* in January of 1680, having held the post before, in 1671.[21] In both instances, he, like Baldi, was better remembered for his personal manner than for his achievements as artist and administrator. A lack of leadership was unfortunate since in this year many symptoms of a reversal of the Accademia's fortunes, which had been at a peak only two years before, were to manifest themselves. For example, to ensure that the posing of a model could continue when instruction began in May, Errard had to offer the services of the model hired by the French, which their statutes and the aggregation allowed, and which the Accademia gratefully accepted in view of their financial incapacity.[22] Attendance at the meetings for this year, recorded by the secretary on each occasion, was also dramatically declining, so that many meetings had to be cancelled in the absence of a quorum. If dues were also down in proportion, then an important part of the Accademia's revenues were in jeopardy.

Admirably, however, the Accademia still fulfilled its obligations in the area of architecture and with regard to competition. Rainaldi and Carlo Fontana were made *stimatori d'architettura,* and Tomassini was returned to the post of instructor. No doubt Menicucci had not met the standards of this position, and Tomassini may have been backing him up throughout the previous year, since he seems to have had a hand in the definition of the *soggetto* for that year and was ultimately involved in the judging as well. Both Menicucci and Tomassini were judges in 1680, and Tomassini had also been asked by Ghezzi to provide the *soggetto* in architecture (App. B, 1680, n. 3).

Following his own pattern, Tomassini proposed a church on a hexagonal plan this time, again with a towered facade (App. B, 1680, n. 4). The critical objective of this *soggetto* may have been an academic reappraisal of Borromini's "licentious"

59 FRANCESCO BORROMINI: perspective section of S. Ivo della Sapienza; Rome, 1642–50 (from *Opus Architectonicum*).

design for the church of S. Ivo (Fig. 59). But Borromini had never before drawn even this much attention from the academies, and the same could be said of the hexagon, which was considered to have more symbolic than formal value as a planning mechanism.[23] Though Tomassini may have derived the six-part plan as an expression of the unity of the three arts taught at the Accademia, the specific reference in the *soggetto* to five altars tends to negate that possibility.[24] The absence of sound purpose and precedent in Tomassini's task for 1680 makes it appear all the more fanciful in comparison with the two previous *concorsi,* and the requirement of towers, which held serious implications then, seems all the more idiosyncratic in this instance. As such the exercise would have been of dubious value for either the Italians or the French, but this element of the exchange was

already becoming less of a factor in the dealings of the academies.

Ghezzi's own *soggetti* for the three classes in painting and one class in sculpture were proposed on 30 May 1680. Four months later, when it was obvious that the competitors would not have time to complete their projects before the Feast of St. Luke, it was decided to postpone the *concorso* until December (App. B, 1680, n. 5). A date of 15 December was finally arrived at (App. B, 1680, n. 8), but in spite of the postponement, the number of competitors seems to have declined again.[25] No one competed at all in the second class of painting, and of four prizes in the first class only one was taken by an Italian, who shared second prize with a German student at the Accademia. French painters took first and third prize, the latter won by an artist who took first prize the previous year. One prize was again awarded in sculpture, to a Burgundian; in architecture, Domenico Martinelli was not only again the only prizewinner, his was also specifically recorded as the only entry (App. B, 1680, n. 9). The *prove* on the subject of Elias were administered, Ghezzi gave his oration on costume in art, and prizes of silver and brass pens were distributed. But without the added ceremony of the Feast of St. Luke, this *concorso* must have been a considerably poorer spectacle.[26]

A look now at Ghezzi's *soggetti* for 1680 will draw in the question of the diplomatic situation between Rome and Paris, and may explain the waning enthusiasm for academic affairs like the *concorsi.* The more obscure subject, that for the sculptors, is the more intriguing and, perhaps as a result, the most enlightening.[27] It refers to the assassination of Jehoash, King of Juda, by his own officers while asleep in his sickbed, in revenge for Jehoash's having ordered the stoning of the High Priest Zachariah in the temple court at Jerusalem. Zachariah had condemned Jehoash for allowing pagan priests to reestablish their cults in Jerusalem. Zachariah's father Jehoiada, high priest before him and once regent for Jehoash, had previously succeeded in casting out the foreign cult of Baal and rebuilding the temple of Yahweh. Assuming for the sake of argument that Jehoash represents Louis's monarchy, and the high priest the papacy, there is a telling analogy to be found here regarding attitudes in Rome toward the ecclesiastic policies of the French court.

The primary point of contention between the Vatican and Versailles by this time was Louis's assertion of France's right to self-determination without papal interference not only in temporal affairs, a notion of absolutism which by now most European monarchs could take for granted, but also in spiritual affairs, a notion of Gallicanism which Louis now chose to foment. When the French first established their satellite academy in Rome in 1666, a brittle atmosphere of stalemate already existed between Louis and then pope, Alexander VII. During the affair of the Corsican Guards in 1662, when Alexander's troops overzealously challenged the claim of Louis's ambassador to diplomatic immunity for the entire French quarter of Rome, Louis's extreme military response of occupying papal territory in France and Italy forced Alexander to make a humiliating apology. On the other hand, Louis, a devout Catholic, needed Alexander's aid in many matters of religious doctrine, especially in suppressing the Jansenist threat to orthodoxy. After Alexander's death, and throughout the 1670s, Louis's wars with the Dutch would present enough of a distraction to postpone his conflict with the papacy, calm the waters, and allow the Romans to at first accept and later extol a French authority in their midst, though limited to the realm of art and the academies.

A renewal of tensions was inevitable, however, so long as both the French clergy and the French crown insisted on an independent French church based on Erastian principles of divine right. Louis's new adversary was Pope Innocent XI (1676–89), who throughout his reign was immersed in a war of wills with the king over the issue of Gallicanism. The major weapon on Louis's side was the General Assembly of the French church which heartily endorsed his views on Gallican "liberties." Their day would come in 1682 when a meeting of their number, cast and staged by Louis, presented the famous Four Articles of Gallicanism: that the church had no jurisdiction in temporal matters, that the pope

was subject to a General Council of the Church in spiritual matters, that papal infallibility concerning doctrine was also open to question by the General Council, and that the pope could not usurp royal authority in affairs of the Gallican church. Louis no doubt also hoped to make a case for his being a good shepherd for his church through his policy of persecuting the Huguenots, which culminated inauspiciously with his revocation of the Edict of Nantes in 1685. Certainly this was the most dubious attainment of all, severely diminishing France's status as an enlightened nation in a Europe grown tired of the rhetoric and brutality of the Reformation.

Innocent's chief weapons in the conflict had already been put into play by the early 1680s. To answer Louis's claim of authority to name bishops and abbots, Innocent had only to withhold his necessary approval and let a post continue vacant, then sit back and watch the confusion in the French church mount as the number of empty cathedrae grew. Innocent also found a way to raise the international diplomatic prestige of the papacy again, while foiling French interests in that theater of "war." Louis had emerged victorious and increasingly ambitious from his wars of the 1670s, and with his eye on the imperial throne itself, he could tolerate no such alliance as that proposed by Innocent which would have joined the forces of the empire with Poland and others in turning back the Turks from Europe. Innocent was successful here, however, and the siege of Vienna was broken in 1683, along with Louis's hopes, for the time being.

By 1680 it was readily apparent to anyone, even a Roman intent on finding the good in French academicism in the arts, what Louis's real intentions were: the enhancement of his religious, economic, and diplomatic status in Europe at the expense of others. Also apparent was that Innocent XI was one of the French king's principal and inevitable antagonists in his attempts to realize these intentions. Innocent did not have the immediate or unqualified support of the artistic community of Rome in this; his concern was for the moral dignity of his office rather than its embellishment through any patronage of the fine arts, and his reign was a poor one as far as artistic activity in Rome was concerned. But if Ghezzi's *soggetti* in 1680 are any indication, then there had been a marked change in sentiment since the task descriptions in 1677 had so blatantly apotheosized the Sun King in his role as the Alexander of his day.

The topic in sculpture could be read in this fashion. The Bourbon dynasty had once, like Jehoash, been instrumental in restoring the True Faith in a land torn apart by apostasy, aided in this by their "high priests," the pope and the Church of Rome. Now that same dynasty had turned its back on the one true church, just as had Jehoash, urged on by priests who acknowledged a different authority from that ordained by God. Of course, in the analogous circumstance neither Louis nor Innocent is murdered, but the implications are there for serious moral injury both committed and suffered by the offending parties should the situation persist.[28] It is unlikely that any contemporary observer could have mistaken the meaning of this iconography. In light of this interpretation, it is also possible to suggest the motivation behind Ghezzi's subject for the first class in painting: the Judgement of Solomon. In that instance a wise king was faced with two who pleaded for his justice, one who would have the object of their pleas ripped in two to have that justice and another who would rather see it preserved whole. Solomon, of course, decided in favor of the latter, but the question in the air in Rome in 1680 was whether Louis would also be wise and see to it that the Catholic church remained whole.[29]

In truth, given the tone of Ghezzi's *soggetti* in 1680 it must have been difficult for any French student to conceive of participating in the *concorso* at all. Surely no sculptor who depended on the king's pension could have easily brought himself to model so controversial a subject as that proposed in his medium. It must be remembered, therefore, that it was in this medium that the French represented the greatest threat to Italian prestige.[30] Perhaps the Accademia was innocent of any politico-religious motive and wanted merely to frustrate the French, to turn the tables as they had been set in 1677, and give the Italians the

benefit of a propaganda that favored their interests. In other words, having learned the game from the French the Romans now hoped to beat them at it. Unfortunately, their students did not or could not respond in the numbers necessary to accomplish this conclusively.

It should also be emphasized that, then as much as now, issues were not likely so clearly defined that it was possible for every Roman to distinguish readily the right from the wrong with consistency. There almost certainly were academicians who could reconcile themselves to a continued alignment with the French. After all, Louis's claims, based as they were on some precedent, could not easily be refuted by the pope; Louis's methods could still be seen to carry with them a measure of success; and in any case, Innocent was not inclined to show himself to be the patron of the arts that Louis conspicuously was. All things considered, what was good about an alliance with the French academies in 1676 was still valid in 1680, and there would be those who both in spite of the diplomatic climate in Rome, and because of the artistic climate, would want to see that continue. One of these was Mattia de Rossi, who was in a position to do something about it in 1681.

1681

De Rossi was elected to the post of *principe* for 1681 on the preceding 1 December.[31] As an artist respected by both the Romans and the French, he was as competent as Errard to pursue the good intentions that had joined their academies half a decade before. One intention in particular that was fulfilled during de Rossi's first principate was that outlined in Article 7 of the aggregation statutes.[32] The secretaries of both academies were required to record accurately the debates on painting and sculpture that occurred in their respective meetings, so that this information might be exchanged and shared. These debates were rarely conducted at the Accademia, but they were perhaps the most important business in meetings of the Académie Royale. The stipulation that the content of current debates be reported to each other seems to have been neglected, however,[33] as in 1681 the Accademia was reduced to referring to Regnaudin's account of procedures at the Académie Royale that had been given to the Romans nearly ten years before.[34] Inspired by this document, which records monthly discussions on topics ranging from Raphael to the Venetians, and from the Laocoön to Poussin, the Accademia conducted its own debates on the primacy of painting.[35] Errard was routinely in attendance this year, so that presumably the content of these debates was transmitted, directly or indirectly, to Paris. Compliance with this aggregation article ends with this tentative first attempt, however, and the Accademia's future meetings are again concerned only with practical matters, seemingly oblivious of issues of theory.

Mattia de Rossi should perhaps be commended with seeing the error here and wishing to correct it as their union with the French had given them the wisdom and ability to do so. If the Accademia was to establish a role for itself in Rome equivalent to that of the French academies in Paris, it needed to augment its position as a clearinghouse of ideas and an arbiter of taste. As long as it neglected its opportunities in this respect, it would continue to be little more than the guarantor of the financial interests of its members that it had been from the start. Fundamental refinements like Tomassini's lessons in the Orders (he was continuing as instructor) could not be expected to effect such a dramatic change on their own. Given the repressive repercussions this change might have had in the otherwise pluralistic context of Rome, it is perhaps not regrettable that the Accademia was never inclined to take this step.

Enthusiasm for the *concorsi* continued to wane in 1681. On 17 May, Ghezzi presented his topics for the painters and sculptors, and recommended Tomassini to propose the topic in architecture (App. B, 1681, n. 2). Ghezzi's *soggetti* seem harmless on the surface: the Tower of Babel in the first class of painting, Samson destroying the temple of the Philistines in the first class of sculpture, and Noah's Ark in the second class of both media.[36] Any reading could be possible in these instances, and they may simply have been chosen for the drama or magnitude of the imagery. But in the

first of these topics, Ghezzi refers specifically to the tower as the work of Nimrod, a Babylonian hero-king not usually identified with the events in Genesis 11. The inference, then, is that divine wrath is not incurred by Noah's descendents in general, but by the "towering" ambition of one ruler in particular. The ambitions of the Sun King again provide the inevitable analogy, and invite a reconsideration of the motives behind the topic dealing with Samson, who was therein the instrument of divine wrath in the devastation of his persecutors. He might possibly be read as a symbol of the papacy, striking out against a hostile authority operating outside the bounds of the true faith.

Curiously enough, as it poses a threat to these assumptions, the *soggetto* in architecture in 1681, or at least the one prizewinning design, was more conciliatory. Tomassini's text does not survive, but Romano Carapecchia's entry provides the clues to its content (Pls. 16, 17). It must have called for designs of a palace facade of three stories with a rooftop belvedere. Carapecchia submitted two versions: one Italianate and one in a French style. Whether this was mandated by Tomassini's task description or not, it would indicate that the *concorso* in architecture was still conceived as a mechanism of exchange between the two traditions. No doubt the presence of Mattia de Rossi, consistently a friend of the French, in the office of *principe,* and his being an architect as well, were responsible for the perpetuation of this attitude.[37]

The fate of the *concorso* was again in doubt. A date of 12 October for the awards ceremony was first set in September, but at that time it was also decided that if there were not at least four competitors in each class there would be no prize in that category (App. B, 1681, n. 3). It would seem that in the Accademia's view a poor turnout would have had a more damaging effect on its credibility than the cancellation of a part of the competition. It may be, however, that this proscription threatened the entire *concorso*, as a general lassitude on the part of the students forced its postponement to 14 December (App. B, 1681, n. 4). The judging, by Tomassini and Menicucci, took place as scheduled on 13 December,[38] but the celebration of the *concorso* was postponed again until after the holidays (11 January 1682).[39]

The first class in painting was a particular success, with seven prizes being awarded: one first prize to a Pole, Giorgio (Jerzy) Szymonowicz; two second prizes divided between the German prizewinner of the previous year and a student from Piedmont; and two third and fourth prizes, only one of which was taken by a native Roman, the other three going to Italian provincials. Romans took all the prizes in the second and third classes of painting and the one prize in the third class of sculpture, but Francesco Maria Nocchieri of Ancona captured the first prize in the first class of the latter medium. The French were by now conspicuously absent from the ranks of the winners, and perhaps from competition altogether, but aside from Carapecchia the Romans had not particularly distinguished themselves either. Both they and the French were slowly losing their grip on the mastery of academic events in Rome, and with it went some of the foundations of their union as well.

Still, the *concorso* was accompanied by Ghezzi's grand oration on the three visual arts, and by the pomp and processional of the distribution of prizes by the Cardinal Protector and Mattia de Rossi: silver and brass pens and large gilt-leather portfolios. De Rossi's year as *principe* was thus ceremoniously brought to a close, and for his efforts during that year he received on this occasion the "applause and congratulations" not only of the noblemen in attendance, but of his fellow academicians. The process of replacing de Rossi had already begun the week before, when nominations were taken for the new ballot (*bussola*) required every three years for the principate.[40] Among the nominees for *principe* in 1682 were Charles Errard, G. B. Menicucci, and Carlo Fontana, but only G. B. Contini received the two-thirds majority of votes necessary to enter his name on the ballot.[41] The mood had changed dramatically from the time Errard could be shuffled into office without conforming to these usual processes, and Luigi Garzi, whose name was eventually drawn from the ballot for *principe,* was capable enough to set the course for the Accademia with no deference whatsoever to the French. The

pro-French party at the Accademia was now in eclipse.

1682

Garzi was a renowned painter of illusionistic ceilings in the traditions of Cortona and Garzi's master Andrea Sacchi.[42] He put much of this aside in his year as *principe* to devote himself to setting the curriculum in order, with particular regard to reestablishing the consistent posing of the nude, and putting his lecturers, including Tomassini in architecture, to the job of organizing the designs used as examples in class into bound sets. Ghezzi was to make a careful inventory of these works, with the exception of the lessons in architecture which were to be returned to Tomassini so that he could complete them and see to their binding.[43] The significance of these documents, in number and utility, for the conduct of lectures was now recognized officially, and their preservation became mandatory.

As for the competition in 1682, Ghezzi was again chosen to provide the *soggetti* in painting and sculpture (App. B, 1682, n. 2) and on 28 June he presented them to the congregation. If judged from the theme of Alexander the Great that ties them together, it may seem at first that Louis XIV was again, as in 1677, the object of the iconography.[44] But the secondary theme was Alexander's conquest of the East, in light of which a quite different interpretation seems likely in view of the trend over the past few years. In painting, the first-class topic dealt with Alexander's encounter with the Persian governor of Susa, leading a train of exotic animals and "precious gifts" from King Darius, intended to induce Alexander to turn aside from his path of conquest. For the second class, the image of the defeated Darius when found by the Macedonians, hidden in a cart of horse carcasses being carried from the battlefield, was required of the competitors. These subjects must be understood in terms of the most pressing issue for the papacy at the time: the new threat from the East, the Turks, and their rapid advance toward Vienna.

Innocent XI was in the process of gaining a diplomatic advantage over France by forming a Christian alliance centered on Emperor Leopold to turn back this threat, while patiently ignoring Louis's religious posturing, which was at its peak at the Gallican convention of 1682. Victory on the battlefields would not come for more than a year, but in Ghezzi's *soggetti* the Holy Roman Emperor becomes the Macedonian Emperor, accomplishing the disgrace of the Persian king as Rome might hope for the disgrace of the Sultan. A most subtle ignominy for Louis is thus also provided by usurping one of his favorite symbols, Alexander. The first-class topic in sculpture recalled the obscure moment in Alexander's history when, seeking a new king for the conquered city of Sidon, he was led to a man of the royal bloodline who was, however, no more than a poor gardener at the time. Abdolonyme was made king, though, and the message here may be that it is emperors who make kings, and not *vice versa,* despite Louis's ambitions to the contrary.

In architecture, Ghezzi again deferred to another authority for the definition of the *soggetto* (App. B, 1682, n. 3), but neither his name nor the task are recorded. The winning design (Pls. 18–20) would indicate that a circular-plan church with nine altars, a monumental facade, and towers to the rear was required, and the inspiration, for the task or the young architect, was presumably Bernini's Assunta in Ariccia—a belated tribute to the recently deceased master. The theme, then, was proudly Roman, but neither Rome nor France deserves credit for the victory in this category, as the winner was another Pole, Jan Reissner. Not only was the Accademia appearing to turn its back on the French by way of the iconography chosen for the competitions in painting and sculpture. In the selection of Reissner for a first prize, and Szymonowicz in painting the year before, the Accademia was now courting entirely different royal favor, that of Jan III Sobieski of Poland.

Sobieski was the most important link in the alliance that was destined to turn back the Turkish advance. His armies would prove instrumental in breaking the siege of Vienna the following year,

making him the hero of Christendom, and in the meantime it was his goodwill, and no longer Louis XIV's, that all of Rome was after. Add to this that Sobieski had, since being established on the throne in 1674, proven himself an avid patron of the arts, willing to extend his patronage and send two of his best young artists to Rome, and the attentions of the Accademia were assured.[45] Sobieski's reign as the last native king of Poland was largely one of peace and rebuilding following a long period of war and the rampages of armies of Swedes, Cossacks, and Tartars. He set the new example for his nobles by constructing a modern villa palace for his court at Wilanów, designed by a Roman architect and stage designer, Agostino Locci. He further gratified his appetite for the finer things by importing books, engravings, original art, and other artists, principally from the workshops of Roman masters like Maratti. And to foster a native capacity in the same arts, he had Szymonowicz and Reissner enrolled in the Accademia. The advantage in this for the Accademia was not only the market it opened in a new part of Europe, but also the growing perception that they were both a peninsular and a continental place of pilgrimage for young artists intent on an academic training. By comparison, the scope of the Académie de France in Rome was no more than national, and this perception would work to its disadvantage.

As *principe* in 1682, Garzi was devoted to insuring the success of the *concorso,* and on 6 September, its celebration was set to coincide with the Feast of St. Luke so that once again the ceremonies would be suitably dramatic (App. B, 1682, n. 4). No postponements occurred, and the designs were received on schedule on 4 October for the judging and the administering of the *prove.*[46] Once again Ghezzi's minutes provide some of the details of the events on the evening of 11 October, when the doors of the Accademia were opened to the people of Rome, who would have found the main salon "molto bene ornata de quadri o bassorilievi."[47] A Dr. Sinibaldi, physician and man of letters, gave the oration, and medals of silver and copper were distributed to the seventeen prizewinners in all categories.[48] The largest of the silver medals was worth only 2 *scudi,* but they were still much more meaningful than the prizes in the last few years, in that they bore a likeness of Innocent XI and were accompanied by a silk-trimmed diploma printed with the image of St. Luke. This *concorso* became a dramatic demonstration on the part of Garzi of the Accademia's intention and ability to conduct its affairs responsibly and grandly, now largely on its own initiative. The union with the French academies was for now almost completely forgotten.

1683

Giovanni Battista Contini, another architectural protégé of Bernini's, was elected *principe* for the year 1683, after having served the previous year as one of the *stimatori d'architettura.*[49] While it may be true that he was disinclined to carry out the duties of his office, occupied as he was with commissions outside of Rome, he was not altogether a neglectful overseer of the Accademia's affairs.[50] He appointed Carlo Rainaldi and Carlo Fontana as *stimatori* during his administration, made Tomassini his treasurer, and in a gesture of continuing good will toward the French gave Charles Errard the largely honorific title of *visitatore,* or visitor to the sick and bereaved. Notably, this was not a position from which any power derived. Most to Contini's credit, however, were the attention and financial support he directed toward the competition in the year of his principate, continuing the effort begun by Garzi the year before to assure the significance of this event in the Accademia's calendar. His most appreciated personal contribution was the money for the prizes to be awarded, which donation was gratefully acknowledged by the congregation on 30 May (App. B, 1683, n. 4). It was put to the purchase of medals in silver and copper, those for the winners in the first classes valued at up to 2 *scudi,* which were distributed when the *concorso* was celebrated on time again this year on 10 October.[51]

Relieved of the burden of providing the prizes, the Accademia approached its other obligations with respect to the *concorso* with more than the usual enthusiasm, and in this their secretary,

Ghezzi, was again instrumental. On 18 July he proposed the *soggetti* for painting and sculpture, on themes from ancient Roman history like Hannibal crossing the Alps, the death of Archimedes, or the construction of the Capitoline temples. The task in architecture was defined by Domenico Martinelli (App. B, 1683, n. 5), prizewinner in architecture in 1679 and 1680, who two months before had been made *Accademico di Merito* and lecturer in architecture in the absence of Tomassini.[52] Martinelli's *soggetto* called for the design of a garden villa, derived perhaps from the general Roman theme, or possibly alluding to Jan Sobieski's "Villa Nova" which was still in progress. This task had the potential to elicit designs for a building type as yet untried in the *Concorsi Accademici,* and one that offered the opportunity to elaborate on the setting to an unprecedented degree. Unfortunately, no design, not even that of the sole prizewinner, Vincenzo della Greca, survives in the archive, though his drawings must once have been among those mentioned by Ghezzi as adorning the main salon for the celebration of the *concorso* on 10 October (App. B, 1683, n. 7). A trio of judges had been selected in each medium on 19 September (App. B, 1683, n. 6), and those in architecture were the most illustrious the Accademia had to offer: de Rossi, Rainaldi, and Fontana (with Menicucci as alternate). At the same time Martinelli had been commissioned to see to the decoration of the academic chambers for the ceremonies, and according to Ghezzi these were attended by a throng of Rome's most distinguished inhabitants, and accompanied by poetry and music composed just for the occasion. Ghezzi himself gave the oration on the subject of architecture, in tribute no doubt to Contini as principal benefactor of the event. Prizes were limited to three in each class of painting and sculpture, so as not to overtax Contini's generosity, and there was sufficient participation in all but the second and third classes of sculpture to fill every category, and with an Italian in each.

The level of Ghezzi's excitement as indicated by his minutes seems always to have been determined by the level of his participation, as author of the *soggetti* or reader of the discourse. As such it is not advisable to weigh the significance of a *concorso* based entirely on his commentary, which might otherwise lead to the conclusion that the one in 1683 was the most magnificent to date. It would appear so all the more, however, in comparison to the futile efforts at continuing the competitions over the next eight years. And it is possibly no coincidence that both the Accademia and the French academy in Rome would experience a decline in their stature as institutions of learning during the same period. The evidence manifests itself immediately upon the attempt to elect a *principe* for 1684.

1684–1685

Giacinto Brandi, a Neapolitan painter, was originally chosen on 19 December to head the Accademia, having held the office once before in 1669.[53] But he declined the honor, claiming extenuating circumstances, an excuse usually rejected by the congregation as they could hardly let stand the notion that there was any business more serious than their own. It is possible, however, that despite what Contini had done for the Accademia the year before, they felt the need for an active *principe* rather than a figurehead. And so they passed over Brandi's slight and elected Ciro Ferri, a Cortonesque painter, in Rome to represent the Florentine Academy. Though this provided a potential link between the two institutions, Ferri totally neglected his duties and Contini was compelled to continue in his office. In the meantime, no meeting was held until 9 March, and it was not until 9 April that Brandi finally presented himself to be sworn in as *principe* for 1684.[54]

Fortunately, things were in hand in time for the arrangements to be made for the start of the academic season in May: Domenico Martinelli was to continue as lecturer in architecture, and the "usual" competition was to be held, with Brandi providing the *soggetti* (App. B, 1684, n. 1) and Agostino Scilla giving the discourse. Ghezzi was not involved at this level, nor was he apparently very active as secretary as the *verbali* for this year went mostly unrecorded.[55] Given Ghezzi's low profile, it is not surprising to find him betraying

so little interest in the affairs of the Accademia, but it is likely that the lack of interest was epidemic. Attendance was down considerably; during Innocent XI's reign, the bread-and-butter issue of commissions, of getting them and keeping them, was in all probability more important to the academicians than the luxury of pursuing their academic ideals or overseeing their joint interests. Commendably, however, this did not yet mean the demise of competition altogether.

The meeting of 3 September set the date of the *concorso* to again coincide with the Feast of St. Luke, with entries to be submitted on 8 October.[56] On that same date, new members were taken in, with their official induction to take place during the celebration of the *concorso*. It would seem from this that the competition did take place in 1684, but what it was like or who and what it involved cannot be determined. By this contrast the value of Ghezzi's participation in a *concorso* becomes even more obvious, but it is also possible that in the end there was very little to record about the *concorso* in 1684. This conclusion is based on the events of the following year, in which the first period of active public competition at the Accademia was brought to a close.

Brandi continued as *principe* in 1685, and Martinelli resumed his function as lecturer in architecture (Tomassini would not return from Naples until July).[57] The pattern of the previous year, of few meetings, low attendance, and sparse minutes, continued also, but some achievements with regard to competition and architecture were notable. Firstly, Martinelli was officially accepted into membership as *Accademico di Merito,* with his *dono* in the form of the fourteen sheets of lessons in architecture he had produced over the past three years (App. B, 1685, n. 1; cf. Figs. 61 and 62). These were to be displayed in the Accademia's salon during the celebration of the feast day, along with the lessons of the lecturer in perspective, Pier Francesco Garolli (App. B, 1685, n. 2). The implication is that there would be no competition entries to so adorn the salon, and in fact the reference made is specifically to the celebration of the feast day and not of a *concorso*. This, combined with the complete absence of any other mention of a *concorso* in this year, would seem to rule out the possibility of one having been held.

Whether one was contemplated is more difficult to ascertain, though again no direct evidence exists in the minutes. Even at this low ebb the enhancement of the competitions was still on the minds of the congregation. A sculptor, Giovanni Hamerani, upon being awarded his membership in the Accademia along with Martinelli on 7 October, was assigned the task for his *dono* of designing a medallion to be used for the prizes in future *concorsi*.[58] His dies became the property of the Accademia, but they could not have been used in any case in 1685, nor would there have been any use for them in the near future, until competition began in earnest again in the 1690s.

The French

While the process of reorganization at the Accademia set in motion by its union with the French would be a continuing one, pursued with varying degrees of intensity and success, what the French hoped for from the union were more tangible, short-term benefits. The aggregation opened doors that had previously been closed to them, as far as the acquisition of antiquities to be shipped back to Paris, and access to less portable artifacts for their student copyists were concerned. For example, the painter Louis de Boulogne was allowed into the Vatican to make copies from Raphael's frescoes, to be used as tapestry cartoons by the Gobelins weavers.[59] The sculptors Théodon and Nicolas Coustou had the great patrician collections of ancient vases and statuary made available to them for a similar purpose.[60] The manufactured goods modeled on these examples would adorn the palace and gardens of Versailles, and become an important source of revenue for Colbert's mercantile system when sold abroad. An engraver in the employ of the French, named Thomassin, could now work from the great masterpieces of Rome and send copies of altarpieces like Raphael's *Transfiguration* back to Paris.

It was pointed out earlier that architects participated in this as well, remitting plans, renderings, and details of all manner of Roman architecture. In researching local hydraulic techniques for possible incorporation at Versailles, both D'Aviler as *pensionnaire* on hand and LeNôtre during his visit to Rome in 1679 very likely depended on the license their affiliation with the Accademia gave them in examining Roman achievements in fountain design and science. Conceivably, much of the detailed information would have escaped them or been denied them had their reception by the owners of the gardens not been prepared by their ties to the Roman academy.

Paralleling this result, the French now also had access to the field of Roman artists connected with the Accademia, in filling certain commissions or providing lecturers for their students. They no longer had to compete at a disadvantage as foreigners, through agents or at higher prices, to have the benefit of that collective talent. A great deal of effort and patience had been expended by Paris previously to gain the good will and services of just one Roman artist, Bernini, but his incorrigible genius had often given them reason to question the wisdom of that expenditure. Now, by virtue of one diplomatic device, the services of a large body of artists, who conveniently shared their academic philosophies and stylistic ideals, was made available to the French without qualification. Commissions descended immediately upon Carlo Maratti and Domenico Guidi, who had been instrumental in forming the alliance with the French, for an altarpiece and sculpture group respectively.[61] Correspondence between Colbert and Errard almost exclusively dealt with these projects, with reports on the progress of students and artists at work for the crown, or urgings from Colbert to see to the timely execution of the work and that it be of the highest quality. Often addressed, too, were the arrangements for transporting antiquities, copies, casts like those of the column of Marcus Aurelius, and materials like pozzolana and marble, by sea from the port at Civita Vecchia to Paris. The first leg of this trip, normally complicated by customs formalities and expenses, was made easy by the now allied status of the French art establishment.

It is readily apparent, however, that nearly all of this was more subject to the local climate of opinion about the French than to the mere fact of the aggregation. The most important factor was that in the years just after the union, the early years of Innocent XI's pontificate, the French represented a source of income and an infusion of energy in an otherwise depressed art market in Rome. The active participation in both academies of Errard, with his sober disposition and single-minded attention to academic affairs, would certainly have had a beneficial influence during this period. That he was in large part responsible for keeping the two institutions on course toward their shared objective in education is made plain by how quickly they lost sight of these goals after his retirement. Even Colbert had taken a *laissez-faire* approach toward Errard's administration of the academy in Rome as a seat of learning, and that trust was not misplaced since during his tenure some of the finest artists of the next generation in France reached their maturity. It is reasonable to assume that the Accademia valued his presence as highly, but as tensions mounted and diplomatic relations disintegrated between Louis and the pope, one indomitable Frenchman was not enough to turn back the tide of public resentment. Nor, apparently, was the possibility of French commissions any longer sufficient inducement while alternative sources like the king of Poland could be found.

As the situation worsened, Errard inevitably found himself frustrated on all sides. The hostility of the Roman populace conspired against him in two ways. His youthful charges took to going about the streets of the city armed with swords, and answered their detractors, both in and outside the academy, with violence. Their tempers had been set on edge by the prevailing disquietude, and by 1681 Colbert and Errard were forced to respond by threatening expulsion for anyone who did not disarm himself.[62] The lodgings of the Académie de France in the Palazzo Caffarelli were at the mercy of their landlord, who by the early 1680s was making their position difficult by withholding their lease or requiring higher rents, another sign they were no longer welcome.[63] Errard made attempts to find new and better accommodations, but he was stymied here as well,

there being no one in the city willing to provide the property on a permanent basis.

Errard was also given reason to doubt the sincerity of his own superiors in their support of his academic endeavors. While leaving Errard to his own devices in that respect, it is still obvious from the bulk of his communications that Colbert's principal interest was in the artifacts being acquired or produced for export to France. In addition, Colbert had a tendency to neglect the fundamental role of his academy in Rome in providing a carefully supervised but encompassing experience of the art of that city. In his view, students were merely employees of the crown, who could be set one task, copying from some medium, and, providing they continued to do good work, be locked into that function for as long as he saw fit. It was not until 1677, compelled perhaps by Errard on behalf of his disgruntled students, that Colbert set the limit of their stay in Rome at three years.[64] This created its own problems, however, in that there was a tendency afterward to let enrollment slip below the optimum number of twelve. Measures taken to correct this in 1679 betray a marked change in attitude toward how the ranks of the academy in Rome should be filled. In identical letters to LeBrun and Charles Perrault in September of that year, Colbert solicited their recommendations for adding to the complement in Rome, chosen from the most capable students then at work in the academies of Paris (App. B, 1679, n. 7). Where these decisions had been made earlier through the mechanism of competition (with the exception of architecture), thus upholding a pretext of achievement for qualification, selection was now virtually in the hands of Colbert, through his immediate subordinates. The method of choice became arbitrary, based on convenience or patronage rather than demonstrated skill. Colbert could favor, for example, sculptors fluent in copying or casting to pursue his aims in that regard, and indeed in future years the roll of the academy in Rome was weighted rather heavily in favor of mediocre sculptors. He could also, of course, bestow pensions for Rome on the sons of courtiers or others to whom he was obligated or who had otherwise purchased the privilege.

Regardless of the benefits that might have been derived from these means for Colbert, it was Errard who suffered the consequences in the declining quality of his students, students best disposed in terms of ability and temperament to the menial tasks Colbert had in mind. In architecture specifically, the first replacement to arrive in 1679 was one Jean Champagne, but conveniently he was a sculptor as well and it was work of this kind that occupied him on Colbert's behalf.[65] In February of 1680, Pierre-Nicholas de L'Espine was admitted to the academy in Rome by Colbert's order at the request of de L'Espine's architect father.[66] He was already in Rome to study architecture, which saved the crown the expense of sending him, and there may have been other financial incentives provided as well. De L'Espine would know some success in the French system, becoming architect to the king and member of the Académie d'Architecture in the few years before his death in 1709, but there was nothing in his later career that suggests it was his talent that earned him this. Then in March of 1682, a young architect named Levasseur, a completely unknown quantity, was put in Errard's charge.[67] His name appears among the three *pensionnaires* in architecture mentioned in a lengthy accounting dispatched by Errard to Colbert in July of 1683.[68] The others were a Carbonet, perhaps the same who was later assistant to Robert de Cotte,[69] and Jacques Bruant the younger, son of an architect and nephew of Libéral Bruant, who would have a long and successful career in the Académie d'Architecture after receiving membership in 1699.[70] Of all of his fellows, he was no doubt the most deserving of the trip to Rome, but what he accomplished there, or whether it included competing with the Italians, is impossible to determine. It is again unfortunate that Errard's periodic reports on the progress of these students are lost, but it would not be inaccurate to say that their potential and opportunities had been much reduced in comparison to those of the architects present in 1677, when the aspirations of both academies in Rome were so high.

But the Accademia, which owed so much to Errard, had also begun to turn its back on him by the early 1680s. Some of the themes of the competitions were taking on a tone distinctly antagonistic

to his sovereign, and by 1683 he had been relegated to a bootless ceremonial position in the Accademia's administration. It speaks to his credit that in spite of this and the considerable burden of his duties as director of the French academy, he continued to attend the meetings of the Accademia to observe and contribute. Now in his late seventies, he was still a vigorous advocate for the academies and the goals he had set for them. It would take one final affront before he would step back from this.

Jean-Baptiste Colbert died on 6 September 1683, to be replaced in the office of *Surintendant des Bâtiments* by François-Michel LeTellier, Marquis de Louvois. This was a most unfortunate circumstance as much if not more for the Académie de France in Rome as for the academies in general. He was not a businessman like Colbert, but the minister for war, who had gained Louis's favor at the expense of Colbert during the French campaigns in the Low Countries. Louvois was no more versed in the arts than Colbert, but he had considerably less sympathy for them as a factor in establishing Louis's primacy in Europe. The machinery of the state was now to be almost entirely devoted to the military exploits of the crown, retaining only what there was of tangible and practical advantage in the rest of the system, and ignoring any aspect that might be remotely idealistic. This included the theoretical and educational pursuits of the French academies.

In Paris, while LeBrun remained head of the Académie Royale de Peinture et Sculpture, he was now passed over in the patronage of Louis and Louvois in favor of Pierre Mignard, his rival up to then for the eye of the king and therefore an enemy of the Académie, though his style was even more doctrinaire than LeBrun's.[71] At the same time, the academy was wallowing in the theoretical dispute between the Ancients and the Moderns, and its influence on the practical matters of production was severely shaken. The authority that Colbert had won for his academies not only in France but in Europe was largely lost, and most of the next two generations would be spent regaining it. With regard to architecture, much the same condition existed. The potential authority of the Académie d'Architecture had been usurped by the king's favorite, Hardouin-Mansart, and he exercised his dictatorial oversight of the practical domain while the Académie preoccupied itself with theory (see Chapter II).

In Rome, Colbert's man, Errard, was also passed over. Whether he deduced or it was made clear to him that his services, no matter how inestimable, would no longer be required under Louvois, Errard decided in 1684 to put aside the increasing aggravations of the directorship in Rome and retire to private life.[72] His last official act was to make an inventory of all the possessions of the academy before turning it over to his successor.[73] This document, an imposing list of plaster casts and terra-cotta reliefs, paintings and engravings, furniture and utensils, is a testament only to the material gains the academy had made during the fifteen years of Errard's tenure, after starting with nothing. His less quantifiable achievements in organizing both of the academies in Rome, and setting their standards as institutions of learning, can be understood only in terms of the history accounted thus far. His significance is undeniable, and his legacy, particularly for the Accademia which would eventually flourish beyond the gains made in the 1670s, is not so easily dismissed as was the man himself. After five years of peaceful retirement at his home near S. Maria della Pace, during which time diplomatic and academic relations between Paris and Rome completely collapsed, Errard finally succumbed to old age on 25 May 1689.[74]

Louvois's man was La Teulière, who was appointed to replace Errard as director in Rome in September of 1684, the choice having been based on convenience and Louvois's quite different expectations for the position, with disastrous consequences.[75] La Teulière was already in Rome by 1683, in the service of the king, supplied with more than 40,000 *livres* in notes of exchange for the acquisition of antiquities and works of art.[76] As an experienced collector and connoisseur he was qualified for this task, but he was no artist, so the wisdom in putting him in charge of the academy solely on the basis of his proximity is questionable. Louvois's intention may simply have been to use La Teulière as a collector rather than an administrator, and their correspondence would seem to bear this out. In his first letter to La Teulière, Louvois all but dismissed his lack of training as an artist, or of an academic background, with the implication that there were more important duties for him to perform. Essentially, he was to continue his efforts to acquire and expedite materials and works of art, as the king's agent, using his high academic status as a wedge in arranging the best bargains. To aid him in this, the budget of the academy of Rome, which had been maintained at somewhere between 10,000 and 15,000 *livres* before 1684, was raised to nearly 40,000 *livres* afterward.[77] This level was to drop consistently as the resources of the monarchy were devoted less to Versailles and the other royal palaces and more to the conduct of warfare. But the impression made immediately, nonetheless, from both the viewpoint of history and that of contemporary Rome, was that the office of director of the Académie de France would no longer be occupied by a minister of academic affairs for the crown, but by a procurer, though in the less profane sense of the word. Given this perception, and the prevailing diplomatic climate, relations between the Accademia and the Académie de France in Rome reached their lowest possible ebb in the 1680s.

To be fair, the blame should lie with Louvois in vulgarizing the director's role, and thereby compromising both the position and the institution it served in the eyes of Rome's artistic community. La Teulière, naive as he might have been upon taking the reigns of the academy, sincerely had its best interests at heart. What he could do was see to the adequate funding of the school, which netted only a small part of the total endowment provided for La Teulière and his purchases; and he quite often requested that the monies for academic activities be supplemented, though not always with complete success. During the 1690s, when Louis's military extravagances proved at last to be unsupportable without severe cutbacks elsewhere, and the academy in Rome was slated for closure, or at best the curtailment of most of its functions, it was La Teulière who struggled to keep the doors open, often at his own expense.[78]

La Teulière was a conscientious subject, as far as his frequent and lengthy reports to Louvois are concerned, but they have almost nothing whatever to do with the pedagogic aspects of his assignment, at first. In addition to his descriptions of items being sent on to Paris—various fine stones for carving, *objets-d'art,* and original works by Guidi, for example—and the means by which they were sent, he also provided occasional insights on the diplomatic situation. Any intelligence of this kind, while Louis's ambassadors were *personae non gratae,* was valuable, especially, in La Teulière's own words, "dans les conjonctures présentes, auprès d'un Pape du caractère de celuy qui règne présentement."[79] Innocent had not only made Louis uncomfortable by his stance on the Gallican question and in support of the emperor against the Turks, he was also proving to be a nuisance to the French academy in Rome. Other sources in the city had earlier indicated a growing resentment on the part of its citizens with regard to the recently invigorated French policy of despoliation now to be implemented by the academy under La Teulière.[80] The pope responded in early 1686 with a *bando* requiring his permission before any antiquities or works of art could be exported on foreign vessels, a move aimed directly at France.[81] The door that the French had been able to use with impunity before was closed, and the key was in Innocent's hands. Specific items, like Guidi's Versailles group, could still be shipped, but one more complication had been added to confound Louvois's ambition to adorn Louis's palaces by pillaging Rome.[82]

Provocation was answered with provocation. On 16 November 1687, Louis's new ambassador to Rome, replacing the recently deceased and far more tactful Cardinal d'Estrees, arrived in the city with an armed retinue determined to establish his right to police the French quarter. The Marquis de Lavardin no doubt had hoped to realize the same success in this ploy as had the Duc de Crequy in 1662 with the affair of the Corsican guards, but Innocent XI was not Alexander VII. His more coolly calculated response was to excommunicate the marquis and place the church of S. Luigi dei Francesi under interdict, which Louis countered by again occupying Avignon and threatening to advance on the Papal States. In this instance, answering the pope's spiritual power with military power created an inevitable deadlock, which persisted as long as Innocent was alive and Louis was distracted by the Bloodless Revolution against the Stuarts in England, and the shift in alliances it implied. The fragile peace that d'Estrees had been able to build between the two parties by his statesmanship was shattered, however, and from this point on Louvois withdrew his custom from Rome.[83]

This may have worked to La Teulière's advantage, since he was now both better prepared and more free to devote himself to the academy's educational functions. Beginning in February of 1688, and consistently thereafter, his letters to Paris comment on the work being done by the young *pensionnaires* on behalf of the crown.[84] His hand may even have been too heavy in putting them to these tasks, as the specter of student revolt that had plagued Errard at one time rose again. Louvois effectively put down this rebellion with the threat not only of expulsion, but of imprisonment.[85] What had moved the students to this action was, paradoxically, their talent, which did not let them accept lightly the roles of artisan or copyist forced on them by their dependence on the crown. The level of talent, as was true in Errard's time, had been boosted by the reinstitution in 1685 of the competitions for pensions in Rome.[86] As before, however, this privilege was extended only to painters and sculptors, and there would be no *pensionnaire* in architecture in Rome again until the next decade. Presumably, under the absolute rule of official taste by now established in that medium, and with the conviction of Hardouin-Mansart in particular that young architects need no longer look beyond France for their example, there was no one left to champion the value of a sojourn in Rome.

Aside from the reception his report on the student uprising was given, La Teulière's accounts of student activities or pleas for more funding were for the most part received with aloof disinterest by Louvois. But in 1690 he found an enthusiastic reader in Louvois's assistant, the Inspector General Édouard Colbert, Marquis de Villacerf, who was already being groomed as successor to the superintendency. Here was someone who saw eye to eye with La Teulière on the matter of the role of the branch in Rome within the French academic system: there were only certain students who could profit from the stay, and certain opportunities that the school should provide that would best profit them. Devoting time and resources to acquiring artifacts in a hostile market only detracted from this greater purpose. Villacerf shared La Teulière's sympathies on behalf of the *pensionnaires,* and having sensed this the director poured out his feelings in his letters not only about the students but about the academic and artistic environment in general in which they found themselves. After the death of Louvois in July of 1691, at which time Villacerf was made *Surintendant des Bâtiments* in his own right,[87] just the sheer volume of La Teulière's correspondence increased severalfold. His outlook, both academic and diplomatic, was still naive, and limited by his chauvinism in the areas of classical taste and national interest, but that he was disposed to be more loquacious is at least an indication of his heightened expectations as the last decade of the seventeenth century began.

Regrettably, it was not in Villacerf's power to satisfy La Teulière's hopes, as in that decade of Louis's most disastrous military exploits there would be virtually no funds made available to any of his academies, in Paris or Rome. This was all the more unfortunate since other circumstances had combined to raise the status of the French in Rome at just about the time that Villacerf came to power. An immediate plus in the French column was the death of Louvois, who had been intent on raiding the patrimony of Rome, and was guilty in world opinion as well of the atrocities committed by French troops against the Huguenots after 1685, and in the Palatinate in 1689. The death of Innocent XI two years before relieved most of the tensions that had existed between Paris and Rome since his assuming the Chair of St. Peter in 1676. Still, none of the issues that divided pope and monarch were conclusively decided; only the desire of the next two popes to be responsible spiritual shepherds, and to put aside the temptation to wield temporal power, reconciled them to Louis. For his part, the king no longer wished to complicate further his position in Europe by continuing his feud with the papacy. During Alexander VIII's pontificate (1689–91), both sides stepped back

from the brink of schism: Louis restored the occupied papal territories, his envoys would no longer enforce the "freedom of the quarter," and Alexander did not act on the issue of Gallican independence, until on his deathbed when he published a bull denouncing it.

From there the contest moved to the conclave of cardinals, where for six months pro- and anti-French candidates for the Holy See were debated, before the Neapolitan cardinal, Antonio Pignatelli, was elected to reign as Innocent XII (1691–1700). This choice was predicated on much more than compromise, however, as this Innocent personified a dramatic realignment of emphasis within the church. The new pope's primary objective was to restore order to his own house, and to quell the factional arguments, between orthodox and Jansenists, Jesuits and Quietists, that were threatening to dismember the church further, or diminish its doctrinal credibility. Louis became, in essence, the pope's ally in this, subduing the urge for independence amongst his clergy in return for Rome's acceptance of the royal rights that applied to French bishoprics. No ground had been gained or lost by either side, and Gallicanism still persisted; but considering what had been averted, and the damage that had been done to relations between the two over the past fifteen years, it was an important victory for the diplomatic prestige of both.

Innocent also tended to the problem of nepotism, one of the most enduring ills of the Vatican, and effectively put an end to it with his first bull. By such actions his people had the measure of their new pope, who would be guided by his piety, his high moral character, and his charity, rather than any worldly ambitions for his office. This was indeed the tone of La Teulière's letter to Villacerf on 17 July 1691, in which he reported optimistically on the nature of the new pope and did not neglect to mention Innocent's advanced age (seventy-seven).[88] It was a miscalculation to believe that this implied a more manageable temperament, but it was in any event a temperament that would not be so vehemently directed toward the French as Innocent XI's had been.

In fact, the French academy in Rome was soon given one very important reason to appreciate the new pope, for under his auspices its *pensionnaires* were provided much freer access to the art of the Vatican, and many of the other collections and palaces in the city that had been closed to them in more hostile times.[89] Innocent seems to have been moved to this by Carlo Maratti in particular, who had remained over the years an advocate for the French, and was one of the few artists in Rome that students of their academy could freely consult.[90] He was also, not coincidentally, one of the few artists in Rome still practicing a Late Baroque classicism in sympathy with the doctrines of their school. Since before the death of Innocent XI, Maratti was custodian of paintings in the Vatican and St. Peter's, and after the election of Alexander VIII he petitioned consistently for papal permission admitting French students to copy from them, and from the works of Raphael in particular.[91] Innocent XII's magnanimity was the greatest in this regard, and so by 1692 there was at least one visible sign that the breach between the French academy and its Roman hosts was beginning to close.

In that same year of 1692, competition resumed at the Accademia, and the results of the *concorso* in architecture might also be used to signify the opening of a new period of exchange between the two traditions. To be sure of this, however, requires a closer look at the *concorsi* of the first period of exchange to test that assumption against the events already accounted. The first of these was the competition held in 1679, two years after the one which marked both the initiation and the climax of that exchange.

Domenico Martinelli: Concorso of 1679

Entries for the competition in 1679 were submitted for judging on the morning of Sunday, 8 October, and the *prove,* the sketch examinations, were administered that afternoon.[92] The alacrity with which this process was carried out suggests that there were not very many entries to consider, and the exception made in architecture bears this out. The minutes indicate that Tomassini, judge in this year along with Alessandro Sbringa, had

only one design by one architect which required his evaluation, and finding it "di ottimo talento, e di crudità practica, e teorica" he pronounced it to be the winner of the first prize.[93] Though Domenico Martinelli had won essentially by default, this should not take away from his achievement, for as champion of the Italian cause in the face of the overwhelming French victory in 1677 his work stands up to theirs admirably. While there was no French *pensionnaire* to contend with, his design (see Pls. 10–12 and App. A)[94] excelled in those areas which had distinguished the work of the French in the previous *concorso.*

His command of pen and brush, using the traditional sepia ink of the Roman studios, was equal to that of even Simon Chupin in many passages. And like Chupin he included a comprehensive program of sculpture and painting alongside the architectural detail he lavished upon the design. In the range of his architectural decoration, and his attention to practical devices like the roofing of the church, he is much like D'Aviler. In other words, where the two French architects had intended to be comprehensive in their designs but reflected different attitudes, artist vs. architect, in their method, Martinelli intended to incorporate both senses in his design. In so doing, he arrived at a sum of the achievements of his two most competent predecessors, and by that measure he bested them. In presenting a design that was considerate of the rules of architecture, of the skills with which it was rendered, and of the building both as a unified display of the three arts and as a practical exercise, Martinelli fulfilled the principal expectations of his judges as they had been applied before to the *concorso* of 1677.

Martinelli's response to the design problem posed by Tomassini's *soggetto* is more essential to the purposes of this study, but no judgement can be made on how well he conformed to the task since it was from his design that its content has been reconstructed. The deduced intent of the task, to address an issue of particular moment to the French, is more enlightening, however, and transcends Martinelli's individual achievement. The motif of the towered facade with a colonnaded portico was apparently a given, a redefining of the task in 1677 in terms of the longitudinal church plan more appropriate to current French needs. The question of Italian prototypes seems less pertinent; Cortona's facade of S. Maria in Via Lata (Fig. 60) with its two-story open loggia and closed flanking bays may have been a resource for Martinelli, but it had no towers.

The influence of Cortona on Martinelli, as the first architecture student of any importance to come out of the academy that Cortona once served, is possible in other respects. This involves the quite mannered exuberance with which Martinelli approached the articulation of his design: the inverted scrolls used as nonfunctional brackets for the intermediate zone of the facade or the interior, or as volutes for the towers, or around the drum of the dome; the playful variety of door and window surrounds; the patterning of the nave vault; or the curious facade feature of small segmental pediments placed over paired columns below the belfries. But by comparison, even Cortona's work, like SS. Luca e Martina (see Fig. 111), appears severely classical. Martinelli's manner, and his method with regard to this design problem, was more likely conditioned by Tomassini, his tutor in architecture at the Accademia.[95] Only a later entry in the *verbali* (Chapter I, n. 27) gives the clue to Tomassini's orientation as a cabinet maker, but this is supported by the decorative elaboration he applied to his lessons in the Orders (see Figs. 57, 58). That Martinelli was affected by Tomassini's taste is evident in the close affinity between Tomassini's lessons and those Martinelli produced as his *dono* during his tenure as lecturer between 1683 and 1685 (Figs. 61, 62).[96] It is therefore quite probably a craftsman's aesthetic that explains the preponderance of contrived ornament applied to Martinelli's design. That Tomassini is to blame is underscored by how thoroughly Martinelli had discarded this taste in his mature work in Austria, such as for the Liechtenstein Palace in Vienna (1692–1705, Fig. 63). There he executed and modified the designs of Enrico Zuccalli in a reserved Berninesque taste, instilled by Carlo Fontana after Martinelli entered his studio in 1678.[97] It would not be productive to trace the development of his church architecture

60 PIETRO DA CORTONA: facade of S. Maria in Via Lata; Rome, 1658–62 (engraving: Vasi).

between the *concorso* design and the few and fragmentary examples of ecclesiastic architecture he executed later. Suffice to say it was Carlo Fontana, and not the Accademia, who gave him the discipline he needed to achieve a reputation.

The greater importance for Martinelli's design exists at the level of its typological relevance for French church architecture. In the late Baroque, the most daring experiments in towered facades were being conducted only by the French, who hoped to reintroduce the type to their tradition of basilican churches. LeVau's designs for the rebuilding of St.-Sulpice in Paris (1655) were a first attempt, but his plans were not accepted and he was replaced by Daniel Gittard.[98] What Gittard's intentions were is not known, since the project was put on hold between 1675 and 1718, but they may have paralleled LeVau's. Gittard's own variation on the theme, the facade of St.-Jacques-du-Haut-Pas (Fig. 64), which he designed in 1675, may reflect LeVau's influence, though only in a crude way.[99] The insertion of a tetrastyle temple front between the towers was totally inadequate to the spirit of France's monumental facade tradition. What LeVau was capable of in a similar circumstance is better illustrated by his design for the facade of St.-Eustache (Fig. 65), which carried the Orders across two stories with a pediment above the recessed central bay and between the two towers. This solution was much

61 DOMENICO MARTINELLI: "Dorico"; ASL, uncataloged drawing.

62 MARTINELLI: "Corintio"; ASL, uncataloged drawing.

more consistent with the scheme of a Gothic facade, since the church is Late Gothic, while at the same time it was in line with French classicism in the Grand Manner (cf. Hardouin-Mansart's Invalides chapel, see Fig. 50).[100]

Somehow this design, or another like it, must have been communicated to Martinelli, whose facade composition in 1679, in general layout and in many details, corresponds to LeVau's. Aside from the two distinct tastes in ornament, the only notable differences are the absence of a pediment in Martinelli's design, his use of the double loggia in response to the supposed task, and the transposition of the zone of relief sculpture from above the second story to above the first. The latter tactic is in fact an improvement, bringing this zone closer to eye level, and avoiding the discontinuity that exists in this zone as it moves through the pediment in LeVau's design. The absence of a pedi-

ment in Martinelli's project enhances the unity of his facade as well; this was still a daring move as no Roman facade, including Cortona's S. Maria in Via Lata, was complete without its pediment.

In his very Italianate way, then, Martinelli not only responded to a French design problem but also to a French design. He had duplicated in reverse the circumstances of the *concorso* of 1677 in which French architects had successfully brought French ideas to bear on an Italian design problem and an Italian design, Rainaldi's S. Agnese. Regardless of how much less of an event the *concorso* of 1679 was compared to that of 1677, the desire to promote exchange between the French and Roman traditions was still very much in force. What should be emphasized is that the human factors that had pursued this end in 1677 were still in place: Tomassini as instructor in architecture, Fontana as the master of Martinelli's stu-

63 ENRICO ZUCCALLI AND D. MARTINELLI:
facade of the Liechtenstein Palace; Vienna, 1692–1705
(photo: Marburg/Art Resource, New York).

64 DANIEL GITTARD: project facade for St.-Jacques-
du-Haut-Pas; Paris, 1675 (engraving: Marot).

dio, and Errard as director of the French academy and the most likely source of ideas from his tradition. And, as was the case for the designs generated in 1677, it is not so much the direct influence of Martinelli's design that can be documented by examples, but rather the influence of the general debate on the issues addressed in his design, which would have surfaced in the Accademia and in Rome at the time of the *concorso*.

For instance, Mattia de Rossi, a not disinterested party when it came to matters of moment to the French, investigated the theme of the towered and porticoed facade in his design for the collegiate church of the Assunta in Valmontone (begun 1686, Fig. 66). Here a single-story portico on a recessed (concave) plan joins two campanili. The longitudinal nave of this church is a domed oval, whose cupola is framed by the bell towers and which therefore incorporates principles that had been fuel for the *concorso* in 1677. This is not

meant to say that de Rossi's design is derived in any way from either the competition designs or any collateral examples, but only that he too was caught up in the possibilities raised when academic attention was directed to the specific issues contained in the *concorsi* of 1677 and 1679. There is undeniably nothing French about de Rossi's facade design, either, but still it is an entity unique in Italian architecture, a hybrid of ideas brought into focus during the academic union in which he had been involved. The *concorso* of 1679 otherwise had no legacy for later Italian church design, but appropriately so since the problem defined for it was more peculiar to French ecclesiastic architecture.

As in 1677, the good intentions shared by the Accademia and the Académie de France in Rome did not extend to the royal academies in Paris. The chauvinistic attitudes of the art establishment under Louis XIV would not have been receptive

65 LOUIS LEVAU: project facade for St.-Eustache; Paris, 1660s (engraving: Patté).

66 MATTIA DE ROSSI: facade of S. Maria dell'Assunta; Valmontone, 1686–98 (photo: Brogi/Alinari).

to any ideas originating from foreign sources. So the *concorso* of 1679 had no repercussions there whatsoever, until 1752, when Servandoni proposed the final facade project for St.-Sulpice (Fig. 67) along lines not far removed from Martinelli's design.[101] Prior to this writing, no author has ever identified a precedent for this facade, other than S. Maria in Via Lata (Hautecoeur), believing it instead to be unique, though flawed rather than inspired. The gap in time and geography that separates Martinelli's design from Servandoni's could have been spanned by the Accademia. Servandoni, a theater designer whose facade of St.-Sulpice was the only permanent highlight of his career, studied drafting and architectural perspective in Rome at

an early age. He would have been there while Charles Poerson was director of the Académie de France and occasionally *principe* of the Accademia (see Chapter V). Therefore, Servandoni would likely have had access to the Accademia's archive, and Martinelli's finely executed drawings would certainly have had his attention.

There is another possibility, provided by the fact that Giles-Marie Oppenord, Servandoni's predecessor at St.-Sulpice, was the *premier* student of architecture at the Académie de France in Rome during the 1690s (see Chapter IV). He, too, would have referred to the Accademia's collection as a necessary part of his experience in rendering, and may have been aware enough of Martinelli's

67 JEAN-GEROME SERVANDONI: facade of
St.-Sulpice; Paris, begun 1735 (engraving: Blondel
the younger).

work to communicate it to Servandoni, directly or
through his own designs. What makes it all the
more likely for both young men to have sought
out Martinelli's project was the fact that it was
meant to relate to a French design problem, that is
to their own tradition. Aside from a greater reserve
in ornament and classical usage, Martinelli's design
was modified very little by Servandoni's invention
by the time the facade of St.-Sulpice was realized.

It is no surprise, then, to find that Martinelli
would be the greater architect. Given his status as
the most outstanding student of the Accademia's
fledgling program in architecture, his experience
in Fontana's studio after 1678, and his tenure as

instructor in architecture at the Accademia
between 1683 and 1685, Martinelli represented
the finest product of Roman academic training
available in 1690. It was this that recommended
him to the patronage of Viennese nobility at the
court of Leopold I, attentions Carlo Fontana was
also cultivating.[102] For the fifteen years between
1690 and 1705, except for a year in Rome
(1699–1700), Martinelli was able to hold his own
against up-and-coming native talents like Fischer
and Johann Lukas von Hildebrandt in satisfying
the Austrian taste for Italian fashion in palace
architecture. He returned to Rome in 1705 to
resume his station as lecturer in architecture, by
then boasting a laudable international reputation.[103] He retired to his birthplace in Lucca two
years before his death in 1718.

FILIPPO DI LETI:
CONCORSO OF 1680

In 1680 Martinelli was again the only competitor
and the only prizewinner in architecture (App. B,
1680, n. 9), but his 1680 design does not survive
as such in the Accademia's archive. However,
contained in the nine bound volumes of drawings collected by Martinelli over his lifetime, and
now deposited in the Bertarelli collection in
Milan, is a design which offers the possibility of
its being a copy of Martinelli's 1680 entry, if not
the original itself.[104] The drawing (Fig. 68), signed
by Martinelli, represents a domed, centralized
church with bell towers, consistent with the task
description in 1680 (App. B, 1680, n. 4), though
in the absence of a plan it is difficult to determine if it is hexagonal as the *soggetto* stipulates.
Certainly, it is both in style and technique identical to Martinelli's presentation in 1679, and that
makes the date of 1680 and the provenance of academic competition much more likely. Upon this
assumption, it is interesting to note how little
development he had undergone after another year
in Fontana's studio; he seems to have matured
slowly.

But in fairness to Martinelli the *concorso* in
1680 had not provided him with any special challenge. By this year, the union of the academies had

ceased to motivate the use of the *concorsi* to investigate issues, whether topical or high-minded, that were pertinent to the interest of either the French or the Romans. There was little left of the atmosphere of open intellectual exchange that had made the first two *concorsi* important marketplaces for ideas. This, together with the fact that hexagonal churches had as little a future as a past, should leave no hope of finding a legacy for the *concorso* in architecture of 1680, and there is none.[105] It is moot, therefore, whether anything more momentous can be derived from the rediscovery of Martinelli's project. But there is a project related to this *concorso* that does survive in the Accademia's archive, and may have some value by way of contrast with Martinelli's approach.

This design is known from three drawings (Pls. 13–15 and App. A), bearing in several places and various hands the name of the architect Filippo di Leti. Their attribution to him is therefore reasonable, but their assignment to the *concorso* in 1677, by whoever is responsible for the inscriptions on the reverse of the plan (App. A, n. 13), is not. Di Leti's drawings, along with many others from the seventeenth-century competitions, were incorrectly dated during an inventory of the archive conducted in 1756.[106] Di Leti does not appear in the *verbali* as a competitor in 1677, nor in any other year, and his project is thematically quite distinct from the task in 1677. It corresponds exactly, however, to Tomassini's *soggetto* for 1680, even to the measurement of the site that was stipulated on the posted announcement. Therefore, di Leti's project would most likely have been conceived in conjunction with the *concorso* of 1680, but it was not submitted along with Martinelli's, which was the only official entry. The alternative means by which the Accademia acquired drawings was as admission pieces, or *doni,* and the *verbali* indicate that this was the route for di Leti's design.

On 15 September 1680, Filippo di Leti and another young Roman architect were proposed as *Accademici di Merito* by then *principe* Giovanni Morandi (App. B, 1680, n. 6). Two members were assigned to verify their suitability in time for the next meeting, on 6 October, at which time they were accepted into membership by unanimous

68 DOMENICO MARTINELLI: project elevation for a domed hexagonal (?) church with bell towers; 1680 (?) (source: Civico Gabinetto dei Disegni, Milan).

acclamation, on the condition that they submit their *doni* within the six months required by the statutes.[107] Should di Leti have been at work on a project for the *concorso,* the tasks for which had been publicized in June, he could not, as a probationary member, have entered it in competition in December. He could, however, have presented it as "qualche opera di studio per i giovani" in conformity with the stipulations put on his *dono,* but there is still some question as to whether it was accepted.[108] Di Leti was not in fact officially inducted into the ranks of the Accademia until

1692 (App. B, 1692, n. 2), upon the satisfactory submission of a *dono*.[109]

Di Leti's only remarkable architectural achievement came at the end of his life: the restoration of S. Giovanni Evangelista in Montecelio for the Borghese family (1705–10).[110] The nave is quite ordinary, with apse and side chapels, corresponding to the preexisting edifice. The facade (Fig. 69), however, consists of a two-story rectangular front with cylindrical bell towers of one story above the outside bays, which is a singular variation on the theme. But it is no more than that—a legacy, in other words, of the obsession that Tomassini, di Leti's instructor in architecture, has betrayed in his *soggetti*. As part of a whole the towered facade of S. Giovanni means very little, and this is even more true of his *dono* design based on the *soggetto* for 1680.

The facade of the *dono* (see Pl. 14) was quite literally a two-dimensional conception; with its relief elements only minimally indicated by thin bands of cast shadow it contrasts starkly with the shaded contours of the cupola to which it has been applied like a paper cutout. The lack of integration between the church and its facade is no more evident than at the towers themselves. Not only have these been inserted independent of the erstwhile horizontal unity of the second story, but di Leti also did not explain how they are affected by the vaults of the side chapels which must necessarily abut them. Plan and section do not resolve this question either, though a resolution should be critical for a design that was, after all, fundamentally concerned with bringing hexagonal church and towered facade together.

There are other weaknesses in both di Leti's design and his methods of presentation. He was wasteful of space, which is displaced by a great deal more masonry fabric than a church of this size should require (see Pl. 13), rather than letting the site suggest a more efficient arrangement. The six piers that support the dome are a structural truth that is denied visually by the sharp fold in the wall that occurs at each pier (see Pl. 15), and by the arches above them that seem to disappear into each other. Di Leti was apparently ignorant of the reasoning behind the attempts made since

69 FILIPPO DE LETI: facade of S. Giovanni Evangelista; Montecelio, 1705–10 (photo: Getty Center for the History of Art and the Humanities, Santa Monica).

the fifteenth century to "strengthen" such corners with more considerate articulation. He was also ignorant of the proper conventions for plans; he represented the situation at both the first and second levels of the church without distinguishing them, adding to the confusion about how the zone of the vaults is to be treated on the exterior. There is little hope of reconciling the windows into the vaults of the side chapels with the articulation of the lower story. Other aspects of the design have not been given enough thought, like the side entrances that branch off into the side chapels rather than lead directly into the main space. It is his frequently demonstrated inability to think his design choices through that detracts from di Leti's earnest response to the *soggetto*.

The quality of his draftsmanship varies considerably, from hand drawn to finely rendered passages, but in general his technique is commendable, especially in his section drawing. The ornamental details of his church, though sparse and ordinary even when of Mannerist derivation, still contribute positively to the whole. Despite the flaws in some of the design elements of his church, the project was nonetheless up to competition standards. Doubtless it would not have withstood comparison with Martinelli's prizewinning entry, but as it turned out it did not have to do so. With di Leti's nomination to membership just prior to the celebration of the *concorso*, his design could have legitimately become his *dono*. Though his ultimate acceptance into the Accademia was postponed until 1692, it would not appear to have been the result of a missing or even unacceptable *dono*. Rather, di Leti may have run up against one of the Accademia's oldest rules for membership: that the candidate be thirty years of age.[111]

It is surely no coincidence that, within two months of the nomination of di Leti and two others as *Accademici di Merito*, a motion was passed unanimously by the congregation to enforce that statutory requirement (App. B, 1680, n. 7), both for nominations as well as admissions into membership.[112] If 1692 was the earliest year that di Leti was eligible to meet the age requirement, he would then have been eighteen in 1680 (and, incidentally, forty-nine at the time of his death in 1711). His comparative youth at the time the hexagonal church design was produced could explain his naiveté about the consequences of his design choices, or about presentation methods. Di Leti's is not an inspired design, but his youthful effort is not entirely devoid of worth.

At the turn of the century, di Leti was sharing responsibility for the lectures in architecture at the Accademia with more readily identified talents like Antonio Valerii, Carlo Bizzaccheri, Carlo Buratti, Sebastiano Cipriani, and Francesco Fontana.[113] It seems that the Accademia was prepared to equate di Leti with these others; at least he belongs more appropriately to their emerging generation. Di Leti's church in Montecelio, therefore, might better be considered the first tangible achievement of a career cut short before its potential was reached, rather than the last gasp of an

unpromising career begun much earlier.[114] Despite its relative mediocrity, di Leti's *dono* is an important resource for providing a better understanding of his position in the scheme of things. And, too, it provides an insight into the state of affairs at the academies in Rome, which must be blamed for the uninspiring context that produced it.

ROMANO CARAPECCHIA: CONCORSO OF 1681

Tomassini's *soggetto* for 1681 of a palace facade, reconstructed from Romano Carapecchia's prizewinning project (Pls. 16, 17, and App. A), represented a considerable break with Tomassini's own pattern of churches with towered facades, an issue that had demonstrably grown tired with overuse. This turnabout alone would certainly have fanned the interest of competitors, since the possibility of addressing an entirely new typology in competition would have inevitably stood them out not only against their immediate rivals, but against the winners of the previous *concorsi*.[115] Carapecchia's two variations on the theme, one reserved and the other elaborate, were perhaps his way of further highlighting his efforts, if not called for by the *soggetto* itself which would have been unusual. Either way, Carapecchia's is an intriguing proposal: two superficially identical facades subtly differentiated to conform to two distinct tastes. The central seven bays of the first facade (see Pl. 16) project forward, like those of its prototype, Bernini's Palazzo Chigi (1664, Fig. 70), framed by compound colossal Tuscan pilasters. Instead, what project on the second facade (see Pl. 17) are the two pairs of outermost bays, like the pavilion corners of the French tradition. Ornamental details distinguish the two further. The ground story of the second variant is treated with banded rustication accenting the horizontal joints—again a French convention. And the alternation of pediments that occurs horizontally above the windows of the *piano nobile* in the first variant (still in conformity with the Chigi Palace), happens vertically in each bay of the second. The latter is generally more ornate (note the foliate Corinthian capitals, and paired columns at the entrance), as though

70 GIANLORENZO BERNINI: facade of the Chigi Palace; Rome, 1664 (engraving: Falda).

71 BERNINI: third project facade for the Louvre; Paris, 1665 (engraving: Marot).

speaking to a taste for embellishment rather than a proper Roman *gravitas*. At first it may seem altogether that Carapecchia, or the *soggetto,* did not intend to resolve two traditions, as had the *concorsi* in 1677 and 1679, but merely to propose two alternatives for the consideration of his audience. But here, too, the insinuations are more subtle.

To begin with, there is a Berninian prototype for Carapecchia's second design as well: none other than the final project for the Louvre extension (Fig. 71) which the French had accepted from Bernini in 1665. The connections continue from there. Mattia de Rossi, *principe* in 1681, had been in charge of the execution of the model for Bernini's project while in Paris; Pascoli's biography of Carlo Fontana, who acquired Bernini's studio, mentions Carapecchia as one of Fontana's more promising students.[116] Carapecchia was therefore firmly within the Bernini camp, and his project, guided by de Rossi or Fontana or both, was in an important sense a tribute to the master of them all, who had passed away at the end of the previous year, leaving a last generation of his students in the care of his immediate successors. But there is more to Carapecchia's projects than a hollow gesture, or a simple choice of provenance. Not only does his second design perhaps reveal indirectly more about Bernini's last Louvre project than Marot's rudimentary engravings, which allow only a limited appreciation of the bare essentials of the building now that the model is lost, but Carapecchia apparently intended to advance the project further. The clue to this is the crowning belvedere that is common to both of his variations, and was almost certainly a requirement of the *soggetto.*

Accepting that Bernini's own intention in his designs for the Louvre was to bring the traditions of French palace design in contact with his own, this would seem to be a reasonable point of departure for Carapecchia as well. After all, the objectives of the *soggetti* in 1677 and 1679 were different only in that they involved church design. Also, the same *dramatis personae* were in place this year: Mattia de Rossi, Carlo Fontana, Gregorio Tomassini, and Charles Errard behind the scenes. For them, on behalf of their medium, the first two

concorsi were opportunities for constructive dialogue, and de Rossi and Tomassini provided the same opportunity again in 1681.

It would be better to consider Carapecchia's two designs not as alternatives, but rather as points on a line of development. The first, the more "Roman" facade, represents the simple Berninian ideal, with the added feature of the rooftop belvedere common to Italian villas and palaces.[117] This becomes the template for the "French" facade, which despite the change in taste with respect to detailing retains the most telling characteristics of the original: the Italianate fenestration, block form, balustrade, and Colossal Order. There would, in other words, be no mistaking this in, say, a Parisian context for anything but a Roman-inspired building—exactly the kind of statement in which Bernini would have reveled. Presumably Carapecchia's judges, Tomassini and Menicucci, could see the advantage in so frank a declaration of Roman determination as well.

The belvedere participates in this on a different level. In the translation from "Roman" to "French" facade, Carapecchia gave this device an elliptical rather than a rectangular plan, and in that he was at his most objective and circumspect. The gesture is equivalent to that made by Bernini in his first design for the Louvre (Fig. 72), in which he included what Robert Berger has defined as a "drum-without-dome."[118] Berger traced the motif from the incomplete dome of St. Peter's into the French vocabulary of forms via an imaginary *château* project by Antoine LePautre (Fig. 73), and designs by him, LeVau, and Mansart for the new wing of the Louvre. The latter were among the projects sent to Rome for Bernini's comments, and very likely inspired him to propose the "drum-without-dome" motif as part of his own scheme, in deference to the French. But the device in truth had no real "tradition" of use in France, and no doubt looked as unwarranted to Colbert as it would originally have to Bernini, and so the Louvre project moved on. The myth persisted in Rome in 1681, however, and Carapecchia repeated Bernini's homage to the French, though it amounted to Bernini's error.

Mattia de Rossi was himself an agent in the

72 BERNINI: first project facade for the Louvre; 1664 (source: Cabinet des Dessins, The Louvre Museum).

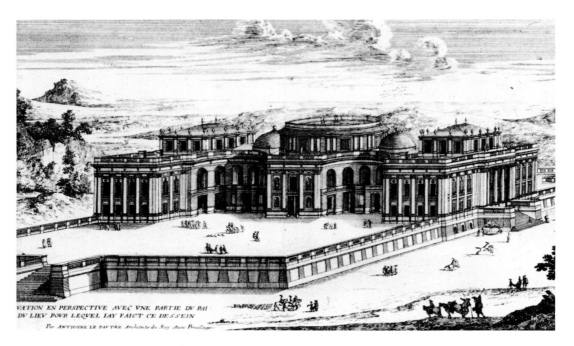

73 ANTOINE LEPAUTRE: project for an ideal *château* (from *Desseins de plusieurs palais*).

perpetuation of the myth. His *dono* (Fig. 74), submitted in July of 1673, nearly one year after his nomination to membership, was a design for a small *casino*, a miniature conflation of both LePautre's ideal *château* and Bernini's first Louvre project. Here a circular drum lit by oculi acts as a belvedere, and rests on a cylindrical salon surrounded by two stories of rooms that square off the plan like a Palladian rotunda. De Rossi's design has none of the homogeneous qualities of his precedents, however; the drum seems as foreign to his building as it does to both the French and Roman traditions. Since he was *principe* in 1681, though, his project no doubt is what suggested to Tomassini the topic for consideration in the *concorso* of that year. Carapecchia's aim was to bring the drum more in line with the Italian tradition by interpreting it in a more recognizable belvedere form which is better integrated with the whole. In this, and in many other respects of his design, he surpassed de Rossi's *dono*.

A new tradition would eventually be forged for the "drum-without-dome" based on a reading of it as a coronal symbol. This may have been apropos of some of the Louvre projects, but Bernini's point seems more to have been the link with LePautre.[119] Certainly Carapecchia's belvedere is nothing more than functional, rather than symbolic, given its obvious derivation from the square-planned version. After all, a monarchical emblem manifested in this way would not have readily suggested itself as such to a Roman architect unused to thinking in those terms. But in Vienna, where so many princely families coexisted and contested with each other to build architectural symbols of their rank and power, such an emblem could be appreciated immediately and therefore easily marketed.

Rome may still have been the route whereby this idea made its way from Paris to Vienna, however, since the Austrian architects who made use of the "drum-without-dome" motif were themselves trained in the papal capital. Johann Lukas von Hildebrandt was one of these, a student of Carlo Fontana in the early 1690s, who took advantage of several opportunities to propose the "drum-without-dome" as part of his palace designs. One

74 MATTIA DE ROSSI: facade elevation for a casino; ASL 2100 (Dono Accademico).

was for the garden palace of Prince Mansfeld-Fondi, now the Schwarzenberg Garden Palace (Fig. 75).[120] This was Hildebrandt's first major, nonmilitary commission upon making his way to Vienna in 1697. According to Robert Berger, of the two versions Hildebrandt proposed, the prince chose the one with the "drum-without-dome" crowning the salon, rather than the one with the ogival dome that came too close to usurping the form of the Imperial crown, though the prince actually possessed crowns of both "open" and "closed" type. This project was taken over by Fischer von Erlach when Prince Schwarzenberg purchased the property after the death of Mansfeld-Fondi in 1715. Work resumed on the left half of the palace in 1720, but Fischer retained much of the sense of Hildebrandt's design, with

75 J. B. FISCHER VON ERLACH: Schwarzenberg Garden Palace; Vienna, 1697 (from *Entwurff einer historischen Architectur*).

only some practical changes being made to the crowning portion of the salon. Though the two were rivals, such sensitivity on Fischer's part was possible because indeed many of Hildebrandt's ideas had been inspired by Fischer in the first place. The "drum-without-dome" solution at the Schwarzenberg palace was anticipated by Fischer's Schloss Engelhartstetten (1693), also in the Vienna suburbs, but his ideal for the type had been defined as well no later than 1697, in a project for a *Lustgartengebäude* (Fig. 76).[121]

Fischer's variations on the *maison de plaisance* theme are said to be his most original architecture, but the parallels between this design, which had so great an influence on Fischer's imitators in the provinces, and Carapecchia's "French" palace, cannot be ignored. Their shared descent from Bernini's first Louvre project (see Fig. 72) only begins to explain these correspondences, and does not exclude Carapecchia's *concorso* projects from a list of Fischer's possible precedents. Fischer was still in Rome in 1681, and he may have again been

encouraged by his mentor, Carlo Fontana, to familiarize himself not only with the results of the *concorso* for that year but also with any of the debates it might have provoked.[122] Carapecchia's competition entry was a by-product of those debates, which were presumably involved with the fusion of Roman and French palace design along the lines established by Bernini. Fischer's use of arches between pilasters to open his belvedere, rather than the oculi used in every other instance of a "drum-without-dome" to light the vault of a salon, points directly to Carapecchia's drawings. In effect, Fischer combined the straight-lined and curvilinear versions of Carapecchia's belvedere into one very powerful architectural element in harmony with a facade composition that goes only a little beyond what had already been achieved between Bernini and Carapecchia.

Another "by-product" of the debate in 1681 was a design (Fig. 77), anonymous but by an apparently Italian hand, for a casino that stands somewhere between Carapecchia's and Fischer's

76 FISCHER: project for an ideal garden pavilion (from *Entwurff einer historischen Architectur*).

concepts. Now in the Kunstbibliothek in Berlin, the drawing's origins can be traced to Rome in the latter part of the Seicento, if for no other reason than its correspondence to the *concorso* of 1681, though other evidence of connoisseurship readily supports this. The drawing's connection with Fischer is much less certain, but the formal links between it and his *Lustgartengebäude* are inarguable, as was put forward by Hellmut Lorenz in his 1979 article on the type in Fischer's *oeuvre* (see note 121). It is at least safe to say that this anonymous design provides another mirror for the discourse on the issue of the rooftop belvedere that was current in Rome in the 1680s.

Carapecchia was not an unimportant participant in these developments. His project advanced beyond what preceded it (notably de Rossi's *dono*), and was a possible factor in what came after (particularly Fischer's ideal garden palace). In his own time, however, French and Roman traditions of palace design would continue to diverge, heedless of the intentions of a small group of architects in

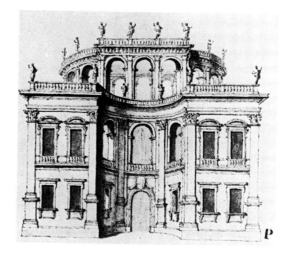

77 ANONYMOUS (Italian): design for a casino; late 1600s (source: Kunstbibliothek, Berlin).

121

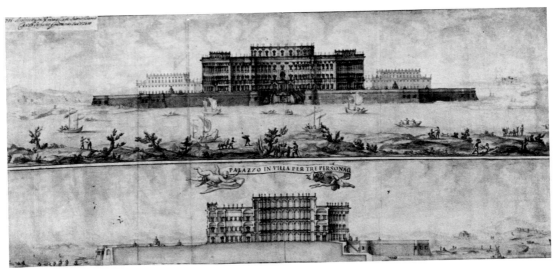

78 CARLO STEFANO FONTANA: elevation and section for a villa for three dignitaries; ASL 144 (Conc. Clem. 1705).

Rome in 1681, and the domeless drum itself would have a very spotty history in the eighteenth century.[123] The legacy of Carapecchia's effort does extend into later projects at the Accademia, the first-class *concorsi* of 1692 and 1696 for example, and the "drum-without-dome" bore especially interesting fruit.[124] In a project for a palatial villa for three dignitaries, with which he took second prize in the *Concorso Clementino* of 1705 in the first class (Fig. 78), Carlo Stefano Fontana, nephew of Carlo, included the drum as the fourth story of a central circular courtyard that projects above the roofline in a manner different from Carapecchia's in little more than scale. The link between the two young architects was, of course, the elder Fontana, who was involved in the genesis of both of their projects.[125] By recommending the drum to ring a courtyard rather than light a salon, while retaining it as a functional belvedere, Fontana (the elder most likely) gave the motif what amounts to its ultimate legitimacy and worth. Unfortunately, there would be no development beyond this point.[126]

Despite his accomplishments, Carapecchia was never offered membership in the Accademia.

He was content to remain within his master's shadow, as one of Carlo Fontana's best draftsmen, until Fontana's death in 1714. Sometime between then and 1726 he left Rome altogether, at the invitation of Prince Vaini for whom he had once worked, to establish himself on Malta as architect to its order of knights, and eventually as a knight himself. A few documented buildings, including the facade of S. Giovanni in Calibità on the Tiber island, and a volume of drawings at the Courtauld Institute, constitute the record of the independent workings of this architect's mind, to which his *concorso* design makes a significant contribution.[127]

JAN REISSNER OF POLAND: CONCORSO OF 1682

Jan Reissner's prizewinning design for this year (Pls. 18–20) is rendered with a quality equal to many but second to no other competitor in the seventeenth century.[128] Despite its obvious derivation from a specific model, it is intriguing in certain of its design elements. In two important respects it represents an exceptional resource for the present study: First, its theme does not respond to either the French or Roman traditions but only to the work of one architect, Bernini; second, it had little relevance for Reissner's development as an artist, since the career he pursued was that of a painter of illusionistic perspectives. He may already have been leaning in this direction while a student at the Accademia. Though the decree conferring membership on him on 1 November 1682 (App. B, 1682, n. 5) refers specifically to his enrollment in the architecture curriculum, his *dono* appears to have been in the form of a figural painting.[129] His principal employment after returning to Poland was as a painter/decorator, first at the palace of Jan III Sobieski in Wilanów (1682–96), and later at the parochial church of Wegrowie during its rebuilding by Carlo Carlone (1703–6).[130] His interests in perspective and architecture while at the Accademia may have put him in contact with the Jesuit painter Andrea Pozzo, who had recently arrived in Rome and would soon be at work on the ceiling of S. Ignazio. Pozzo, too, saw no legitimate distinction between his roles as designer of feigned and designer of real architecture, and if anything gave preeminence to painting (see Chapter II, note 174).

Reissner's drawings prepare the way for accepting this particular arrangement of his priorities. Not only are they well crafted using the tools of drafting, which would have stood him well in any medium, but the elaboration and skillful execution of the decoration in sculpture and painting betray the artist's intent to establish his fluency in those arts too.[131] Like Simon Chupin in 1677, Reissner may have understood that success in a *concorso* depended on such a demonstration. But it may also have been the situation in his native land that mandated his comprehensive approach. His sovereign, Jan Sobieski, in a manner consistent with the times, had initiated a cultural exchange between his country and Italy. The Italians had had the advantage at the start, just as they had in Austria, and many mediocre talents made their way north from Italy to find a place already prepared for them in the patronage of the Polish nobility. Reissner was virtually one of the first from his nation to be sent to the wellspring of Rome, in the hope of establishing a native pool of

talent upon which that patronage could draw. In doing so, he, like Fischer who was first a sculptor, applied himself to the study of more than one medium to make the most of his stay in Rome, and to make his services more competitive at home.[132]

Appearances to the contrary, it is not at all certain that Reissner entirely put aside his interest in architecture, even though in Poland he was in demand only as a decorator. When he was occupied at the palace at Wilanów a new feature was added to it: a three-bay belvedere above the central block overlooking the *cour d'honneur* (1686–92, Fig. 79).[133] It is very nearly identical to the belvedere in Romano Carapecchia's Italian palace design of 1681 (see Pl. 16). Reissner, who may even have contemplated competing in 1681, seems the best candidate for having suggested this device as the "latest thing" in Rome to the builder-in-charge at Wilanów, Agostino Locci, whose father had been Roman but who was unversed in contemporary Italian taste. With Reissner at hand as a native-born artist who had that necessary experience, it would have been natural for Locci to turn to him for advice in updating the palace.

It may be, then, that the architectural promise that Reissner showed in his *concorso* design did not go altogether unfulfilled. Nevertheless, whether because of the still vital craft traditions of Poland, or its vassal status, both politically and culturally, with respect to the major European powers at the time, Reissner's training and achievement abroad did not appreciably affect his status at home. Domenico Martinelli, on the other hand, whose abilities and experiences as a student in Rome ran parallel to Reissner's in many respects, found his own training to be an enormous boon to his acceptance by an Austrian clientele.[134] Both Martinelli and Reissner employed the same presentation methods (sepia line and wash and a *scala modulatoria* for measurement), included similar motifs (the scalelike tile work for the surfacing of domes), and displayed the same technique (the drafting of column capitals) in their *concorso* designs (compare Pls. 12 and 19). All of this points up their common participation in the architecture curriculum at the Accademia under

79 AGOSTINO LOCCI: garden facade of the Palace of Jan III Sobieski; Wilanów, 1677–92 (photo: E. Kupiecki; from *Polish Architecture*).

the direction of Tomassini. The latter must be commended for having instilled in both artists a nearly equivalent skill in rendering, one which could be compared without reproach to the abilities of the French under Errard's direction. Martinelli's enthusiasm for architectural ornament is quite distinct from Reissner's restraint, however, and herein may lie the evidence of an important divergence in the circumstances of their training leading up to their respective *concorsi*. In 1679 and 1680, Martinelli had been in the studio of Carlo Fontana for only a year or two, and the influence of that master's Late Baroque classicism, which Martinelli's later work would reveal, had yet to have its fullest effect. In 1682, Reissner's design was the result of what was certainly a much more extensive association with that school of taste and of what was possibly a longer affiliation with Fontana's studio.

The theme of Reissner's project in 1682 made this connection inevitable. The initial model was

another project by Bernini, the church of S. Maria dell'Assunzione in Ariccia (1662–64, Figs. 80–82); the premise was a more conventional interpretation, based on Carlo Fontana's projects for S. Maria di Montesanto (ca. 1665; Hager, "Zwillingskirchen," p. 211). The latter explains the typically Roman drum and dome of Reissner's design, and the two-story facade that replaces the Assunta's arcaded temple-front portico. Reissner's immersion in the Berninesque mode went much deeper than this, however.

In plan Reissner suppressed the lateral axis of his church by the same means Bernini had applied at S. Andrea al Quirinale (1658–76, Figs. 83, 84), that is, by closing it off with piers rather than chapels. He also emphasized the longitudinal axis on S. Andrea's example, setting off the main altar and entrance bays from the minor chapels by interposing narrower bays. The latter give onto the facade and access the sacristies, and into their upper halves *coretti* are inserted. To further high-

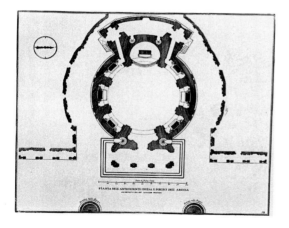

80 GIANLORENZO BERNINI: plan of S. Maria dell'Assunzione; Ariccia, 1662–64 (engraving: de Rossi).

81 BERNINI: exterior of the Assunta (photo: author).

light them, the main altar and entrance bays are trabeated rather than arcuated, like the aedicula framing the apse of S. Andrea. In each of Bernini's churches, the Assunta and S. Andrea included, a chain of garlands carried by angels marks the springing of the dome, at the boundary between the lower and upper zones of the church, as though separating the earthly and spiritual realms that are symbolized by the rational architecture below the cornice and the irrational juxtaposition of coffering and ribs in the vault. Reissner used the same device, albeit less enigmatically, to border the vision of Heaven he projected for the intrados of the dome of his church. Throughout Bernini's church and chapel designs (especially S. Andrea) altar spaces are distinguished by different qualities of architecture, space, ornament, or light. The last he considered to be the most effective, and Reissner, too, has given the main altar space of his church an independent zone of light provided by a window behind the altar and by illumination from the vault.[135]

It is obvious from the Barberini stemma which Reissner indicated above the main portal of his church that he wanted it to mean something to the Accademia's protector, the Cardinal Barberini; another Berninesque prototype would have presented itself for this purpose. In fact, the first church architecture Bernini ever designed was

82 BERNINI: lateral section of the Assunta (engraving: de Rossi).

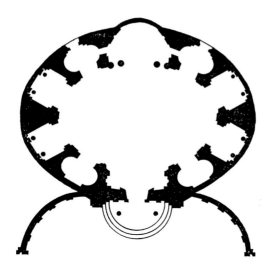

83 BERNINI: plan of S. Andrea al Quirinale; Rome, 1658–76 (graphic: Troy Thompson).

84 BERNINI: lateral section of S. Andrea (engraving: Nuvolone).

commissioned by Urban VIII, the Barberini pope, in 1624: the porticoed facade of S. Bibiana (see Fig. 23). Conceived when a much younger Bernini was beginning to establish himself as an architect, and before the middle decades of the century when he and the High Baroque matured together, the block facade with its palatine scheme is innocently conservative. Yet there is an implied dynamic in it, produced by the layering of the facade's articulation, and by its silhouette that optically extends the central aedicula forward along with the benediction loggia it contains. In both its form and function the facade of Reissner's church is nearly a replica of S. Bibiana's except that Reissner again more literally interpreted Bernini and actually extended the central aedicula forward to a depth of one bay. This gave him room above the narthex for a chamber leading to the benediction loggia and overlooking the nave through an aedicula that repeats the one at the facade. With this balcony for the use of dignitaries, Reissner gave full expression to an imperial or royal church in the language of Bernini, perhaps with his future service to Jan Sobieski in mind (if not merely the *soggetto*).

One of the few shortcomings of Reissner's drawings is that the modeling of the facade elevation in wash does not sufficiently represent its extreme variations in depth. Only the plan does this, and there, too, an additional plastic manipulation of the facade can be seen, where its outside bays curl inward on a slightly concave plan and present the two tiers of paired columns on their lateral faces at an oblique angle to the plane of the paired columns of the portico. The closest Bernini came to this kind of enframement for a church facade were the low, concave walls that extend to either side of the aedicular front of S. Andrea (see Fig. 83). Carlo Fontana's church facades have much more of this element of Baroque movement about them, and depending upon how the facade of Reissner's church is to be read, since it can be read essentially two ways (Fig. 85), different Fontanesque arrangements are suggested. If its flanks are to be seen as obliquely receding, that is when the column articulation is considered, the upper story of Fontana's S. Rita da Cascia (now S. Biagio in Campitelli, Fig. 86) comes to mind.[136] There are other correspondences between the two as well, like the boldly projecting central aediculae, or the slightly concave flanking bays. If Reissner's facade design is to be seen as curving forward to either side of the central portico, that is, when the wall architecture is considered, the facade of S. Marcello al Corso (Fig. 87) is evoked, and the more so since its entrance portal is also framed by paired columns.

The fact that the facade of Reissner's church can be interpreted in many ways, with only qualified references to possible models, speaks to his independent creative strength. The dialogue he expressed between column and wall, while in the language of the Baroque in general, is given a unique interpretation; his design does not invite further theoretical refinement as much as it begs for its execution, so that it might become a singular part of the family of Roman Baroque facades. Still, there is enough in it to suggest that Reissner went beyond the original Berninesque derivation to include in his researches the efforts of the most active heir to the recently deceased master. Fontana may have been more to Reissner than just a source. Like Tomassini's other promising student, Domenico Martinelli, Reissner may already have been taken into Fontana's studio.[137]

Reissner did avail himself of important opportunities to assert his independence, however. One was the dome fresco, while the facade, compiled from several examples but distinct from all of them, was another. But the balance of the exterior treatment of his church represents an even more daring departure. It begins with cylindrical swellings of the outside wall, between the side chapels, which effectively become pedestals for the statues that ring the church above the first cornice. These projections impart a rhythm to the first story, accenting the long curve of the building's perimeter with their more convex contours in counterpoint to the hemispherical domes above the chapels. With the main drum and dome establishing the theme, Reissner orchestrated a symphony of curvilinear volumes that is unprecedented for a Roman church. The closest one can come to it in the Italian Renaissance tradition are the studies for domed churches which appear in Leonardo's sketchbooks (Fig. 88), and which were formative for Bramante's designs for St. Peter's, but they

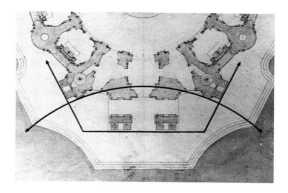

85 JAN REISSNER: detail of Plate 18 (graphic: Troy Thompson).

86 CARLO FONTANA: facade of S. Biagio in Campitelli; Rome, 1665 (photo: author).

87 FONTANA: facade of S. Marcello al Corso; Rome, 1682–84 (photo: author).

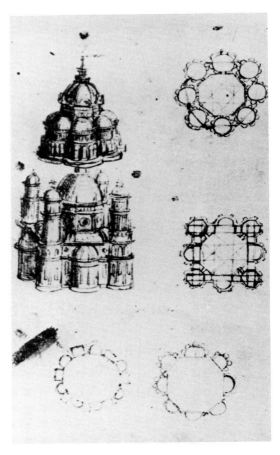

88 LEONARDO DA VINCI: projects for domed centralized churches; MS. B, ca. 1490 (source: Institut de France, Paris).

would not have been known to Reissner. The Byzantine flavor of these sketches recommends a more exotic stimulus to Reissner's invention, perhaps the medieval churches of Russia and the Ukraine, which might have been within his ken.[138] Even so, his design is completely in harmony with the Roman Baroque language in which he expresses it, and it is truly original as a result.

Reissner could not be blamed, then, for wanting to preserve what was most unique in his church, and this may explain why the bell towers included in his section drawing appear so out of place. These would have been required by the *soggetto*'s presumed reference to Bernini's Assunta, where the campanili were placed to the rear of the church to orient them to the town on the hillside behind it. But Reissner was evidently reluctant to make them a part of his design, and he took strong measures to put them out of context. First, he used the Doric Order, which occurs nowhere

else in the church; then he put them in unworkable positions so that they must inevitably abut the drum; finally, their square plan cannot reasonably be adjusted to the geometries of the walls beneath them, or to those of the church in general, any more than their elevations can be reconciled with the rest of the second story. Reissner was no doubt motivated by the simple fact that the towers must detract from the exterior composition; it was to be understood from the contradictions contained in the towers that they do not belong to his conception. He may have been urged to retain them at the last, by Tomassini or Fontana, so that the reference to Bernini's master-

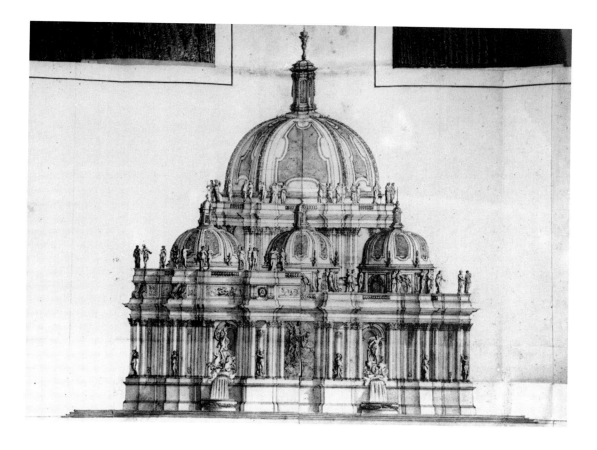

89 DOMENICO MARTINELLI: project elevation of a mausoleum for Jan III Sobieski; ca. 1689 (source: Civico Gabinetto dei Disegni, Milan).

piece would remain intact for the sake of judging his adherence to the *soggetto*.

The unusual arrangement of lobed walls and smaller domes around the main cupola, which the towers adversely affect, cannot be fully appreciated in any of the three drawings, including the facade elevation, that survive in the archive to document Reissner's design. There are references, however, in an inventory (App. B, 1683, n. 1) and on the reverse of the plan (App. A, no. 18), to a fourth drawing which was once a part of Reissner's entry. Since he had already provided the plan, facade elevation, and section normally required of the competitors, the extra rendering would probably have been informative of some aspect of the church that these three views could not have anticipated.

It therefore may likely have been a side elevation, but in that form it does not survive in the Accademia's archive. Its fate may not be impossible to establish, however.

Late in the reign of Jan III Sobieski, Domenico Martinelli made contact with the Polish court to recommend himself as architect for various projects, including a monastic college, and a royal sepulchral chapel (Fig. 89).[139] This latter design, which survives in the Martinelli sketchbooks in Milan, consists of a central-plan building with a main cupola surrounded by a ring of smaller domes. The coincidences between this design and Reissner's competition project, as well as the coincidences within the careers of the two architects, are sufficient to suggest that Martinelli may have largely depended upon his recollection of Reissner's design in deriving his own concept. In fact, his memory may have been aided by the missing drawing, which could have entered his possession while he was instructor in architecture after 1683, since his drawing is also a lateral view. In recommending a project to a Polish king, what better means to use than reference to a project by a Polish architect which no one in Poland but that architect could have known; brazen, perhaps, but not outside the realm of contemporary behavior.

Still, even by this measure, Reissner's efforts in this *concorso* were exceptional, and the more so since they were completed in the little more than three months between the posting of the *soggetti* on 28 June, and the judging of the *concorso* entries on 4 October.[140] Within a month he was on his way home to Poland, armed with his new membership in the Accademia but fated to a comparative obscurity in the affairs of Baroque art.[141] His *concorso* design, which recommends him for higher attainments, had little influence on events beyond Martinelli's project. One important factor must have been that the *concorso* in architecture of 1682 had itself much less of an interested audience because of the shift in motive it entailed. Rather than calling for the resolution of a design problem or of two design traditions, the *soggetto* to which Reissner responded required him only to acknowledge the achievements of an already legendary genius, and his own creative personality, which he himself did not submerge, would have been dwarfed in the eyes of most observers. While competitors still might not have shrunk from having their work compared to Bernini's in this way, the public would have found such a confrontation less engaging than the ones between France and Rome on earlier occasions, because they were more evenly matched. The tributary intent of the Accademia may have been commendable, but it marked the end of the brief period of experimentation that had been initiated by the aggregation with the French, and removed the stimulus to exchange ideas that had been so fruitful in the *concorsi* of 1677, 1679, and 1681. It will be ten years before those higher ideals can again be detected in the results of a *concorso*.

THE HIATUS OF 1683 TO 1691

One reason why the loss of the prizewinning design for the *concorso* of 1683 is so lamentable is that it begins the decade-long gap in evidence of serious purpose for the competitions earlier than need be. While the younger Vincenzo della Greca, who took the prize in this year is virtually an unknown quantity, the circumstances under which he competed would have made his entry quite useful for analysis.[142] The garden-villa theme of the *soggetto* avoided the domed-church-with-bell-towers formula that had dominated the previous competitions, and struck out in a direction ripe with potential for the near future of European architecture, when the villa-palace type would know its heyday. The associations with Sobieski's palace at Wilanów, in the year of his victory over the Turks at Vienna, added new diplomatic overtones to the expected discourse between the rich villa traditions of both France and Italy. In the absence of della Greca's drawings it is impossible to know to what degree any of the above had its effect on his project. It is also impossible to know whether his first-prize effort in 1683, and the training that prepared him for it, promised anything more for him than the obscurity into which he subsequently descended. Of the prizewinners in this early period of competition at the Accademia, della Greca was the last, and as such the one whose years of study more completely coincided with the most critical years of the union between the French and Roman academies. Whether or not this left a mark on his conception for the villa palace, his *concorso* design would have provided the final opportunity to judge the prevailing attitudes toward that union just prior to its practical dissolution.

With a change in leadership and objectives, the French academies and their satellite in Rome magnified the breach that had already begun to form between them and the Accademia as a result of failing diplomacy. For their part, the Romans, too, grew increasingly lax in their oversight of academic affairs, perhaps discouraged by the ease with which the vaunted French system could be corrupted, though more likely preoccupied with their individual livelihoods as the artistically impoverished reign of Innocent XI dragged on beyond its first decade. Domenico Martinelli's lessons on the Orders (see above and Figs. 61, 62), which were submitted to earn his membership in 1685 (App. B, 1685, n. 2), included many unfinished renderings, and the content as a whole was incomplete by the standards set in Tomassini's earlier "textbook." Over the two years it took him to produce this *dono,* presumably other, more lucrative interests had the greater part of his attention. The fact that a new set of lessons was commissioned at all would seem to indicate that the Accademia was again asserting its preference for models rather than rules. Though Martinelli's Orders are even more in line with Vignola's than Tomassini's had been, they are much more extensively annotated, and in effect personalized. The objective of a fundamental authority that had motivated the French may never have been altogether shared by the Romans, for after all Tomassini was not a Blondel nor was Martinelli a Perrault. But whatever consistency there might have been in the curriculum was seriously imperiled by returning to the practice of changing the authority with the instructor. It was abandoned completely when Francesco Fontana took over in that role in the 1690s (see Chapter IV). Of course, avoiding the implantation of doctrine in pluralistic Rome is not to be lamented; this is just another measure of how difficult it was to graft French practices onto the Roman vine.

Disenchantment with the idea of continuing to advance the functions of the Accademia descended even from its highest office. In 1683, Contini was generous in his support of the *concorso* for that year, with spectacular results that unfortunately cannot be corroborated by della Greca's winning architectural design. But as *principe* Contini had none of the interest in the other affairs of the Accademia that, for example, Mattia de Rossi had had in 1681. And after Contini it was difficult to find anyone even willing to serve in the office in the limited capacity that he had. Giacinto Brandi practically had to be coerced into accepting the principate in 1684 some four months after his election; even so he

was reelected for the following year. In the meantime, active attendance at the Accademia's general congregations was sharply declining, so that even the most routine business was not being conducted, and by 1685 neither were competitions, though instruction was somehow maintained.

Into this rather distressing state of affairs came Carlo Fontana in his first year as *principe* in 1686, and the means by which he came to the honor might seem all too symptomatic by now. Filippo Lauri was actually the first to have his name drawn by lot from the five on the ballot, but when members were sent to inform his of his election they failed because of his "continue indispositioni."[143] More likely he had simply avoided what was becoming a dubious honor. So it was that Carlo Fontana's name was next drawn by lot from the ballot, or *bussola.* Since at the time he was directing one of the most active studios in Rome it might be expected that he, too, would decline to serve, but he did not. He admitted to his constituents that his work might keep him away, and so he saw to the election of a *vice-principe,* Morandi (App. B, 1686, n. 1), to act in his stead, but in fact Fontana was in attendance at every meeting save the last of the year, when it came time to elect a new *principe.* Not only he, but nearly all of the Accademia's member architects were conspicuously active: Menicucci and Tomassini as *visitatori,* Contini and de Rossi as *stimatori,* and Martinelli as lecturer; they routinely comprised more than one third of the membership in attendance at the meetings.

This enthusiasm on the part of their number is not hard to understand. They had seen the status of their medium rise within the Accademia at the same time that the Accademia's fortunes were burgeoning due to the impetus provided by its association with the French. It was in their interest not to let the momentum subside, or at least not to lose any more ground than had already been lost in such a short time. Fontana had a personal interest in this also. While he could easily match Mattia de Rossi with his reputation as a practitioner, he did not have the academic credentials that his fellow graduate of the Bernini studio had.[144] This was his first opportunity to show how effectively he could bear the standard of academe, in a direct and public way. Having been neglected, like every other artist in Rome, by Innocent XI, he now had been given the chance to crown his *de facto* prominence with accomplishments in a distinguished and titled position.

Aside from enforcing the decrees concerning the admission of new members, Fontana's actions were taken principally on behalf of the economic welfare of the Accademia.[145] He reduced the honorary stipends awarded to artists, "shrewdly" restricted the expenses of the Accademia, and fought doggedly on its behalf with the deputies of S. Euphemia for a share in the legacy of Pietro da Cortona. In an effort to rouse the interest of both members and Rome in general, a *concorso* was to be held again, with Fontana providing the *soggetti* (App. B, 1686, n. 2). When the Feast of St. Luke arrived, however, it was celebrated "moderately" (App. B, 1686, n. 3), and did not include a competition. It would seem that the dwindling financial resources of the Accademia in the 1680s have deprived posterity both of Fontana's thematic intentions for this *concorso,* and of the results his energetic advocacy would certainly have otherwise generated.

Ciro Ferri was elected *principe* for 1687, but he did not appear in person to be sworn in as the statutes required. Fontana sought him out personally, but was told that Ferri considered himself too occupied to serve, and so Fontana was asked to resume the principate.[146] When Charles LeBrun had in his own time served two consecutive terms as *principe* it was indeed a tribute to the benefits the Accademia was seeing under his rule. For Fontana, a considerable amount of the glory had worn away, and with it much of the enthusiasm he had displayed in the previous year. He attended fewer of the meetings this year, and the meetings were themselves taking place less often than the statutes required. St. Luke's feast day was again celebrated without pomp, and without a *concorso* (App. B, 1687, n. 1); in 1688 the feast was celebrated "with every possible parsimony" (App. B, 1688, n. 1). In this first year of Ludovico Gemignani's principate, the painters' governance was again aided by several of the member architects, but now there was only one

uncompromisable objective: to overcome the Accademia's debilitating burden of debt.[147] Since dues were an important resource in these hard times, the election of even one new member was treated as a very significant event, and the loss of a member could be ill afforded.[148]

In 1689, the last year of his life, G. B. Menicucci was no longer able to fulfill his duties as one of the Accademia's chaplains, and so he was replaced by the second in the Accademia's line of priest/architects, Domenico Martinelli, who was still conducting the classes in architecture (App. B, 1689, n. 1). The following year, 1690, saw both the death of Menicucci, and the departure of Martinelli for Austria (App. B, 1690, n. 1) to escape the moribund contexts of the Accademia and Rome, thus in short order reducing the roster of the architects at the academy by two.

But the corner was about to be turned; Innocent XI had gone to his reward in 1689, and Rome could anticipate some kind of renewal in artistic activity. As a sign of their own emergence from stasis, the Accademia, at the end of Gemignani's second year as *principe,* elected Mattia de Rossi to his second term in that office "à unica voce senza alcuna discrepenza."[149] The congregation was severely depleted, so that they even had to dispense with the usual procedures for choosing the *principe,* naming de Rossi by acclamation. The honor fell to him no doubt because the *accademici* remembered the important role he had played in the affairs of the Accademia when its stature had last crested some ten years before. He had a considerably greater deficit to overcome this time, however, so that what little he did achieve over the next few years was still remarkable.

A year of consolidation in 1690 was closed with another modest celebration of the Feast of St. Luke (App. B, 1690, n. 2); in the absence of Martinelli it cannot even be said with certainty that instruction in architecture was offered that year, though it had yet to be neglected even in those hard times.[150] In 1691, de Rossi was almost nonchalantly reconfirmed as *principe,* again forgoing statutory procedures, and in August, together with Tomassini as instructor in architecture, he made his most concerted effort to reverse the tide of apathy. Having reminded the presiding congregation of their obligations as an academy, he proposed to reinstitute the *concorsi*, "in order to animate the young students" (App. B, 1691, n. 1), and set the secretary, Ghezzi, to the task of defining and publicizing the *soggetti*. The late start would not have allowed the *concorso* to be conducted in October, as was preferred, and so the events were scheduled for January of the following year (App. B, 1692, n. 1), with submissions on the twentieth, judging on the twenty-fifth, and the awarding of prizes on the twenty-seventh.[151] There were twenty-five submissions altogether, and seventeen prizes were awarded in three classes of painting, three of sculpture, and one of architecture. The low ratio of entries to prizes made for quite favorable odds, and the one prizewinner in architecture, Filippo Barigioni (App. B, 1692, n. 3), would have been one of the few if not the only competitor in his field. However, this should not detract from either his accomplishment or the significance of the *concorso* in general.

After all, there had been no event like it attempted since 1683, and nearly all of the principals who had been so active in fostering the *concorsi* a decade earlier were again in place: Tomassini, de Rossi, and Carlo Fontana, who were each at some time Barigioni's teacher (see below). Even the French academy in Rome, just recently reconciled with their Roman hosts due to the changing diplomatic environment, had rejoined the audience of interested observers who can be presumed to have been lured by the Accademia's renewed ambitions. The French were in fact the audience most likely being played to by the choice of subject in architecture for this *concorso*. Ghezzi's (or Tomassini's) task descriptions do not survive, but working from Barigioni's drawings (Pls. 21–24 and App. A), a palace design fusing French and Italian modes seems again to have been required, as it had been in 1681, though the scale had increased. All of this was undoubtedly calculated to demonstrate a rejuvenation on the part of the Accademia, to impart a sense of picking up where it had left off eight years before as though there had been no hiatus. Barigioni's design participates grandly in the effort.

FILIPPO BARIGIONI: CONCORSO OF 1692

Like so many Roman architects active in the Settecento, the details of Barigioni's career have not until recently been given very serious scrutiny.[152] This neglect left some erroneous assumptions about his origins, which eventually conflicted with the emerging documentation; his *concorso* design turns out to be central to the issues. His birth was at one time dated to 1690,[153] or slightly earlier, and this was perpetuated in all the lexicons despite the fact that the same sources, on the authority of Pascoli's *Lives*, call him a student of de Rossi, who died in 1695. Then there was the problem of his *concorso* drawings, which were incorrectly dated "1681" by a zealous but misinformed archivist in 1756 (see note 92). Obviously, if the same Filippo Barigioni was meant in all instances, some reconciliation of the dates was necessary.

Such a reconciliation first confronted Hellmut Hager in his monograph on Juvarra's design of 1715 for a new sacristy at St. Peter's, for which he considered Barigioni's palace project an important prototype (see below).[154] It was he who discovered the registration of Filippo's baptism in 1672 at the parish church of S. Marco in Rome, signed by his father, Giovanni Battista, an artisan in leather.[155] The Barigionis were apparently a large clan of artisans, many of whom were in fact affiliated with the Accademia through the *Aggregati degli Indoratori*, a union of gilders, and attended academic meetings (without voting rights, of course) throughout the 1680s and 1690s.[156] The Accademia would therefore have been available to them as a mechanism for elevating the status of one of their number, in this case Filippo, to that of a professional artist. He had first, however, to be accepted into a studio, and, having moved the date of his birth back eighteen years, his apprenticeship to Mattia de Rossi becomes a much more reasonable assertion. If, as was usual, Barigioni was in his midteens at the time, the date would have been sometime in the years 1686 to 1688, which would mean that he was simultaneously hearing lectures at the Accademia by Martinelli, and later by Tomassini.

Together, these three architects would have had some five years to instill in Barigioni the drafting skills and dedication necessary to excel in the *concorso* of 1692, and the documents now establish (App. B, 1692, n. 3) that it was in this competition, and not that of 1681, that he took first-prize honors.

He did so with a commendable effort with regard to his presentation: four sheets—two plans, a facade elevation, and a section—in larger than usual dimensions, and renderings in the finest possible hand. He also enhanced his drawings with color: blue for the surrounding moat, and green for the esplanade that borders it on the ground plan. It was his drafting skill that recommended him to Carlo Fontana's studio after de Rossi's untimely death in 1695, and it was his use of color which distinguished him from Fontana's other assistants, who were otherwise equally skilled, and indeed from the master himself.[157] The scope of his conception far exceeds Carapecchia's in 1681 (this explains why at one time Carapecchia's design was mistaken for a second-class entry), but this may have been a function of their different *soggetti*. Otherwise, the two projects are not all that dissimilar (cf. plates 16 and 17), which suggests that the fundamental premise for both was the same, and that an amplification in scale and beyond the facade was now the objective.

In fact, Barigioni's palace could be royal, as evidenced by the crown above the escutcheon surmounting the centermost window of the *piano nobile* (see Pl. 23), which made Bernini's Louvre project thematically appropriate as a model, where for Carapecchia it had been stylistically appropriate. This distinction will be important since so many of the circumstances are otherwise the same. De Rossi, who had worked on Bernini's model in Paris, was *principe* both in 1681 and 1692, and the *soggetti* and the judging in both of those years were no doubt the result as much of deference to him as to his master. Both projects were in elevation intended to integrate Italianate elements, like the belvedere, the crowning balustrade, the fenestration, and the Colossal Order, into a French scheme with corner pavilions and rusticated ground story. In that sense, Barigioni is building

upon the same traditions that were previously mentioned with respect to Carapecchia's project. However, Barigioni advances the idea in a direction which not only magnifies the grandeur of the palace, but also makes it more "French." Although he rejected the elliptical plan for the belvedere (which was after all more a link to Bernini than to the French), the facade of twenty-five bays now allowed him to introduce a projecting frontispiece of three bays, boldly marking the entrance and the ceremonial axis leading to the majestic staircases in the rear wing (see Pl. 21). The pavilions are accented by their beveled corners and the extensions of the banded rustication into the upper stories. The interior rooms are enfiladed in accordance with French practice, with their doors lined up along sight lines conspicuously marked by Barigioni. Even the moat, at the level of the battered basement, bridged at front and rear, refers directly to French *château* design, and the Louvre specifically (Fig. 90).

Salons were already a part of the repertoire of forms shared by both the Italian and French traditions, but by incorporating one into the ceremonial procession circulating through the spine of his building (see Pls. 22, 24) Barigioni behaved more like a French designer than an Italian one. Symmetry along the central spine required the doubling of the main courtyard, which seems a harmless enough solution but was nonetheless unprecedented and daring for a student unless, as in this case, it was founded on a programmatic purpose. The fenestration and the Colossal Order still betray the hand of an Italian architect, but even here the repetition of the bay around the entire exterior and the courtyards to include the garden front, while varying it only at the pavilions, is more like the overstatement that is typical of Versailles (Fig. 91) than of any Italian palace (as yet). What Barigioni in effect did was to offer again, now long after the fact, a royal palace block that mimicked the French mode—its scale, massing, planning, and articulation—as it might be appropriate to the Louvre, only thinly disguised by Italianate detailing. He had, in fact, paid even more lip service to the French manner than had Bernini more than a quarter-century before, and,

90 LOUIS LEVAU, CLAUDE PERRAULT, AND CHARLES LEBRUN: East facade of the Louvre; Paris, 1667–70 (photo: Giraudon/Art Resource, New York).

91 LOUIS LEVAU AND JULES HARDOUIN-MANSART: garden facade of the Chateau at Versailles; 1669–85 (photo: Alinari).

92 FILIPPO JUVARRA: project model for the new sacristy of St. Peter's; Rome, 1715 (photo: Museo Civico, Turin).

after all, Bernini had then had to operate under the close supervision of his patrons.

The question becomes one of why Barigioni, who was under no such pressure, chose to be so blatant in his emulation of the French. The motivation must almost certainly have come from his master, de Rossi, who may still have been harboring some affection for the French, and some regrets about the disappointing end to which the affair of Bernini's Louvre project had been brought. If so, Barigioni's project is more a lament for the past than an augury for the future. This, too, may reflect the demoralized atmosphere at the Accademia, whose members had approved the topic, and whose judges had chosen Barigioni's work as a means of commiserating with their French counterparts in Rome, whom they had tentatively begun to reembrace.

But this does not diminish Barigioni's achievement. He had come through some of the worst years for both the Accademia and Roman artistic activity in general, having acquired a bravura drafting style and a laudable architectural sense. Like those who had been the most successful in earlier *concorsi,* he thought through every aspect of his building, even the masonry vaults and carpentry roofs (see the section), and rendered them considerably. Though distinctions are minute, his may be the finest hand of any of the Italian prizewinners up to his time, coming closest to the virtuoso skill of the French in 1677 and certainly surpassing them in the coloristic variety of his drawings which makes them so pictorially attractive. And while his palace project amounted to a visionary extreme in the Rome of 1693, this did not mean it would not eventually have some relevance and some influence.

Two authors have already remarked on this. As mentioned above, Hager finds that Juvarra made reference to Barigioni's design in the model he made for the competition for the new sacristy of St. Peter's in 1716 (Fig. 92).[158] Similar are the articulations of the two buildings, their pavilion corners (angled in Juvarra's version), and the dominant central ceremonial axis running between two courtyards, into which Juvarra inserted his domed sacristy roughly where Barigioni's salon had been. The links between Juvarra and Barigioni were the Accademia itself, at which they were both students, and Carlo Fontana, in whose studio they both had worked. As noted before, Juvarra made frequent use of the Accademia's archive, no doubt

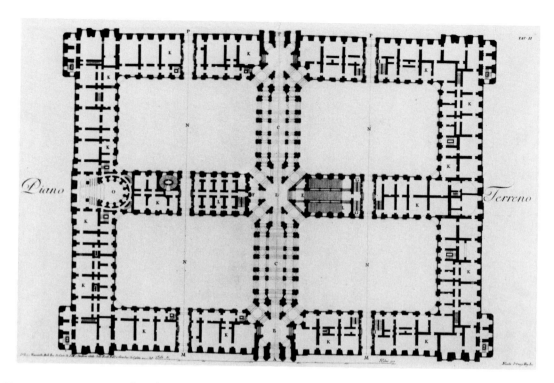

93 LUIGI VANVITELLI: plan of the Royal Palace at Caserta; begun 1752 (from *Dichiarazione dei disegni di Caserta*).

on the advice of Fontana, and capitalized on this experience in later designs.

Bernardo Vittone, who came to Rome and the Accademia from the Piedmont, employed the same tactics several times himself. Werner Oechslin draws comparisons between his project for the Royal Palace in Turin of 1736 and Barigioni's project.[159] Vittone's borrowing is less subtle than Juvarra's but more appropriate since he was designing a royal palace for an important Italian monarch whose kingdom had cultural links with the French.

There was another important Italian monarch emerging in the eighteenth century who did not need such a feeble pretense, but simply needed his own Versailles. Charles III, one of the most enlightened of despots and himself of the Bourbon line, became king by conquest of Naples and Sicily in 1735. As ruler of this large territory, and next in line to the Spanish succession, he was compelled to provide for himself a residence befitting his rank, at Caserta, and to this end he recalled to

Naples the sculptor/architect Luigi Vanvitelli around 1750. Vanvitelli had studied in Rome, and had entered the Accademia after receiving distinction in the 1732 competition for the facade of S. Giovanni in Laterano. In designing Charles's palace, he had nearly twenty years of additional experience as an itinerant architect on which to draw, but he, too, reached back into his experience at the Accademia to inform his solution for Caserta (Figs. 93, 94).

Rudolf Wittkower called Caserta "the overwhelmingly impressive swan song of the Italian Baroque," into which had gone "the experience of Italian and French architects accumulated over a period of more than a hundred years."[160] But most of that experience as evoked at Caserta was already harvested by Barigioni in his design of 1692. Most remarkably, the two exterior articulations are virtually identical: the rusticated ground stories supporting continuous colossal Composite Orders, the pavilion corners and frontispieces, and the

94 VANVITELLI: garden facade of the Royal Palace at Caserta (from *Dichiarazione dei desegni di Caserta*).

window pediments whose segmental and triangular forms alternate both vertically and horizontally. Caserta was even projected to have belvederi over the corner pavilions, in lieu of that over the frontispiece in Barigioni's design, which Vanvitelli replaced with a pediment. The only substantial difference is in the scale of the two projects, and this is true also in plan where the courtyard of Vanvitelli's palace is subdivided by building wings which accommodate the principal ceremonial processions. The scenographic vistas provided by these wings are for Wittkower the most striking aspect of Vanvitelli's design, but they, too, are anticipated on a smaller scale by Barigioni's design.[161]

So despite the reminiscent qualities of Barigioni's *concorso* entry, occasioned by the almost maudlin spirit of the Accademia, his palace could still have a far-reaching and significant impact on the future of Italian palace design. And despite the flagging fortunes of the Accademia in 1692, it still had the energy to perpetuate its role as a focus of ideas and a vital resource for the dissemination of those ideas to posterity. From this standpoint it was still the venerable institution it had been ten to fifteen years before. Also carried over from this period was the interest in fusing French and Roman

architectural traditions, but this is perhaps the most surprising since the union of their academies should have ended for all intents and purposes by 1684. De Rossi, and to some extent Tomassini, must be given credit for upholding this custom, as well as for preparing Barigioni to address it on his own part.

De Rossi, Tomassini, and the Accademia had done well by Barigioni. While the Accademia of 1692 was a shadow of its former self, the promise that Barigioni had shown was fulfilled in the same way that Martinelli's had been in 1680. His victory in the *concorso* was followed by his service in the studio of de Rossi, and later that of Carlo Fontana, in which he achieved a high station. Barigioni's independent career began in 1702, at the age of thirty, after which he became one of the most active Roman architects of the first half of the Settecento, though oddly enough he would never be offered membership in the Accademia in recognition of this achievement or of his earlier attainments as a student. His alma mater may have spurned him because he would have few large architectural commissions to his credit, but this would have been unjust given the depressed economy in Rome during the early 1700s. Vanvitelli and Ferdinando Fuga attained membership in the Accademia on the strength of their performances in the competition for the facade of S. Giovanni in 1732, and with little else to their credit. Barigioni, on the other hand, could already boast a list of accomplishments when he provided his own design for the facade in 1725, but no overtures were ever forthcoming from the Accademia.[162]

Most of Barigioni's activity was involved with engineering projects (bridges and aqueducts), the completion or restoration of existing structures (chapels, palaces, and basilicas), ephemeral architecture (catafalques and conclaves), or minor architectural endeavors of his own (altars, chapels, fountains)—enough so that he may not have wanted the distraction of being *Accademico di Merito*.[163] In this work, and wherever his own artistic personality emerges, he can be seen to have put aside the nostalgia for the Grand Manner Baroque that his *concorso* design emanated in favor of an elegant delicacy and restraint more consistent with the Roman Rococo. His most important commission, for the expansion and restoration of the Palazzo Testa Piccolomini in Rome (1718–19, Fig. 95), was articulated in dramatic contrast to the design from 1692, which may tend to indicate that his motives in that year were imposed upon him from outside. Barigioni died in 1753, having compiled an oeuvre of which no architect of his day could be ashamed, but which history, until now, has tended to ignore in the absence of major monuments that bear his name.

95 FILIPPO BARIGIONI: facade on the Via della Dataria of the Testa Piccolomini Palace; Rome, 1718–19 (photo: author).

Though the *concorso* of 1692 was carried off effectively, it was not enough to urge the Accademia out of the doldrums in which it had languished for nine years. There being no other candidate with an interest in the position, de Rossi was reconfirmed as *principe* for a third year in April of 1692.[164] Faced with what were referred to as "many inconveniences" and "continuing expenses," his first official act was to close down instruction for that academic year (App. B, 1692, n. 4). The Accademia had rarely been forced to this juncture, and not at all during the hardest times of the past decade, but there was now neither the faculty

available to supervise the lessons, nor money to pay them or to hire models, and the doors simply had to be closed. Even the Feast of St. Luke was to be celebrated as it had in the previous year (App. B, 1692, n. 5), which is to say moderately. There was only one other meeting held at all between October of 1692 and April of the following year, when instruction was resumed but with drastic cutbacks in expenditures.[165] On 15 February 1693, de Rossi had again been acclaimed as *principe*, but his only important official act came when the congregation met, after a lapse in meetings of nearly five months, on 20 September to accept his recommendation of Francesco Fontana, son of his rival Carlo, for membership.[166] Francesco and others, including Antonio Valerii, who must then still have been a novice at the Accademia, were put to the task of decorating the salon with paintings and drawings for the upcoming Feast of St. Luke.

Though no *concorso* was projected, this still marks a slight upward turn in the aspirations of the Accademia.

On 10 January 1694, de Rossi requested that he be excused from serving another year as *principe* (App. B, 1694, n. 1); perhaps he was already beginning to feel his death closing in on him. In the election of the new *principe,* only three nominations were entered on the ballot; the requirement that five names be selected was passed over by the congregation with the usual lack of enthusiasm. Carlo Fontana's name was drawn, and he was there to be sworn in, as well as to officiate in the induction of his son Francesco into membership. The advent of this father-and-son team would mark the true turnaround for the Accademia as it girded itself to meet the challenge to its pride represented by the approach of its hundredth anniversary. The elder Fontana, both as *principe* and acting through his son who would become instructor in architecture, was to spur the Accademia on to achievements it had not realized since the aggregation with the French, and would in fact take it beyond what it had been capable of at that time. The *concorsi* in architecture of 1694 and 1696 would visually dramatize the effects.

IV

CONCORSI OF 1694 AND 1696

CARLO FONTANA AND THE CENTENARY OF THE ACCADEMIA

THE PRESENCE IN 1694 of the two Fontanas, Carlo as *principe* and Francesco in charge of the architecture curriculum, seems to have had an immediately salubrious effect on the Accademia. Courses of instruction were resumed in a timely fashion in May, and concurrently a *concorso* was scheduled, with Ghezzi again in charge of defining and publicizing the *soggetti* (App. B, 1694, n. 2). The general congregations of the membership soon regained their earlier regularity, and the numbers attending gradually increased as well. Both the elder and younger Fontana were always in attendance, operating like a team and determined to set an appropriate example for the others who, with the exception of the member architects, had been guilty over the past decade of a severe neglect of their duties as academicians.

Several factors besides Carlo Fontana's hands at the helm may help to explain this rejuvenation of interest. The momentum was first imparted during de Rossi's last term of office and his successful attempt to bring off a competition in 1691. It would continue to gain energy from Innocent XII's pontificate, during which the decline in artistic activity that had plagued Innocent XI's reign was reversed, though it would never again reach the levels of Alexander VII's day. With their incomes more secure, some Roman artists could better afford to devote a part of their attentions to loftier issues. More to the point, now that competition among themselves for their basic bread and butter was becoming a thing of the past, they had again to consider their status relative to each other in less mercenary and more high-principled terms.

Now that their financial crisis was receding, they could return to the haven of academic ideals and theory that they had established to distinguish themselves from the guild members, whose venal motives they had once forsworn along with their craft traditions.

Carlo Fontana was no less influenced by these motives than any of his fellow *accademici*. In terms of commissions and students in his charge, his may have been by far the most lucrative practice in Rome even at the nadir of activity in the 1680s. Still, he had been given ample reason to suppose that this kind of success was not the only measure being applied to his standing in the profession. He had not been able to use his principate in 1686–87 as effectively as had de Rossi in 1681 and 1690–93, either for his own benefit or that of the Accademia.[1] Specifically, de Rossi had not only added to the academy's prestige, by consummating *concorsi* during both of his terms of office, but also to his own, by presiding over architectural competitions on themes directly related to his own work. To Fontana, an egotist of the first water, it may have been just this kind of maneuvering that accounted for de Rossi's greater popularity despite what Fontana perceived as a lesser talent.[2] Likewise had Mattia parlayed his closer relationship with their master Bernini into the position of Architect to St. Peter's after Bernini's death; though it availed de Rossi little in the way of work during Innocent XI's reign, there was still enormous distinction attached to the title. Fontana probably considered himself more deserving of it.[3] Even earlier, Fontana had witnessed the rise of de Rossi's star at the Accademia, buoyed up by his reputation with the French at the time of the aggregation of the academies. Certainly Fontana would have seen little coincidence in the fact that just as de Rossi had again attained the ultimate in academic office in the early 1690s, the French academy in Rome was beginning to set its own house back in order following its dismal record in the preceding decade (see Chapter III). To more generous minds, no small part of de Rossi's success would have been credited to his diplomatic mien and personable nature; but to Fontana, who lacked both, he would have seemed mostly to have been blessed by circumstances. The circumstance of Fontana's second principate became one that he was determined to work to his benefit, and not just to the Accademia's, as he had tried to do (without much support) in 1686–87.

Other circumstances were shifting to Fontana's advantage as well, regarding his status relative to both de Rossi and the French party in Rome. Principally involved was the project for the baptismal chapel at St. Peter's, but his rivalry with Mattia over the building went back slightly earlier, to the mid-1680s and a dispute over the condition of the dome of Michelangelo's basilica, at which time Fontana found de Rossi's historical knowledge to be suspect.[4] In a typically pragmatic fashion, Fontana set about demonstrating his superiority along those lines by compiling a definitive history of the construction of the church, published in 1694 as *Il Tempio Vaticano*. In this account, he also took the opportunity to propose to Innocent XII his ideas for the completion of Bernini's *piazza* (by adding enclosing wings extending into the *Borgo*), and to amplify his achievement in having been awarded the final commission for the remodeling of the baptistry. As this was the first important project to come out of Innocent XII's reign, and the first overt display of papal patronage in nearly fifteen years, competition for the commission was intense from the outset.[5]

Fontana emerged as Innocent's artist-of-choice from a field of some twelve participants, who had produced over thirty designs.[6] Among the contenders: de Rossi, Architect to St. Peter's at the time, who did at least succeed in having a model executed alongside Fontana's in the early stages of the winnowing-out process; and Carlo Maratti, Custodian of Paintings for the Vatican (the equiv-

alent in his medium of de Rossi's position), whose heretofore unhinted architectural ambitions generated two designs without success. In effect, Fontana had bested the Vatican's champions, both of whom were held in high esteem as well by the French and Roman academies. Next to fall (or be nudged) from grace was Domenico Guidi, sculptor and one-time friend of the French, whose models for the figures that would adorn the chapel were not received favorably by the pope when he inspected progress on the designs in June of 1693. Again it was Fontana's work that was preferred, and Guidi's subsequent contributions would be second to Fontana's control of the project, just as were Maratti's paintings when Fontana's final design for the chapel was being completed in 1697.[7] Also under Fontana's direction would have come Guidi's assistants: a Frenchman and member of the Accademia since 1678, Jean-Baptiste Théodon; his close friend and collaborator, Lorenzo Ottoni; and a Burgundian émigré, Michel Maille (Maglia).[8] The first two of these were components of the French "school" that had begun to manifest itself in Roman sculpture since the death of Bernini (Wittkower, p. 433f), but their inclinations would now also be subordinated to Fontana's overall command.

By thus winning the commission for the baptistry of St. Peter's, Fontana had achieved a signal victory in the eyes of the French partisans in Rome at several levels: over de Rossi and Maratti, their supporters in the Accademia as well as before the pope or in the artistic community in general; over Guidi, who in his greed had once stooped to accepting direction from LeBrun for a commission from Louis XIV (see Chapter I); and over an emerging generation of French-aligned sculptors.[9] Despite the self-satisfied air with which Fontana reports of his accomplishment in his own published account of the history of the chapel, he does not gloat over it with any rancor toward the French, who had overlooked him before that time.[10] In fact, the other primary source of information about the initial design stages for the baptistry are letters to Paris from La Teulière, then director of the French academy in Rome, and one of the principal observers of events there on behalf of French interests (see notes 6 and 8). La Teulière's intimate knowledge of the details of the baptistry's history suggests that more than its status as an important public commission was at work, and that Fontana, rather than spurning his attention, had actually sought it out. There is other evidence to support this assumption.

In the last decade of the seventeenth century, Fontana enjoyed his greatest public prominence, not only because of his position at the Accademia or his direction of the most important project in Rome, but also because he was his own best publicist. *Il Tempio Vaticano* was the first of several books both imagined and realized by Fontana that took a decidedly different cue from Palladio than that which still guided so much academic training. Instead of being concerned with theory and the Orders, which were the starting point for virtually every serious treatise in architecture since the sixteenth century, and especially for French authors, Fontana's books were unabashed advertisements: of his abilities as a designer, an antiquarian, and a historian.[11] His more down-to-earth, if self-serving, appreciation of Palladio's motives does more than just set him apart from the French in that respect, though he may have consciously intended this effect. It also further underscores the distinction between attitudes held in the French academies (and at certain times at the Accademia), and those prevailing in Roman studios, toward the means by which young tastes were to be shaped. For Fontana, as for the architects before him who had determined the definitive trends of the Italian Baroque, authority rested not with antiquity or even the more recent past, but with the individual genius of an artist when properly informed by the past.

Despite his doctrinal differences with the French, Fontana seems to have maintained a liaison with them through the Académie de France in Rome. When its director, La Teulière, first mentions the competition for the baptistry in his correspondence of 25 March 1692 with Colbert de Villacerf, the *Surintendant des Bâtiments,* he was getting his information from Lorenzo Ottoni, who was then an assistant on the project.[12] When La Teulière next writes of the project, on 8 December

1693, his knowledge was then gained from the text of Fontana's *Il Tempio Vaticano,* which he could have seen only in manuscript form or in early proofs since the book was in press at the time.[13] It is reasonable to assume that he was most likely made privy to that kind of material by the author himself.

Fontana's direct contact with La Teulière is confirmed in a subsequent report by the latter to Villacerf on the status of the printing of *Il Tempio Vaticano,* copies of which had been promised as gifts to Louis XIV, as well as to the emperor and the king of Spain (and other heads of state) by the building committee for St. Peter's, the *Fabbrica.*[14] La Teulière apparently had Fontana's personal assurance that he would be kept informed of the progress on the printing. It is significant that by this time (9 February 1694), Fontana was himself at the head of an academy, and that at least in this small way the lines of communication were again open between the Accademia and its French counterpart. But Fontana did not handle La Teulière as an equal. *Il Tempio Vaticano* was not just his introduction to the court of Louis XIV. It was also his demonstration of the skills in design and scholarship held by the artist now in charge of the Accademia—skills which Louis's representative for affairs of art in Rome, a mere collector, patently lacked. Fontana, with his usual tactlessness, even went so far as to bypass La Teulière and place the copy of his book destined for Louis directly into the hands of the French ambassador to the Vatican, Cardinal Forbin-Janson.[15]

Nonetheless, Fontana continued to funnel information about his activities in Rome through La Teulière to Paris. On 18 January 1695, La Teulière sent on to Villacerf a plan of another of the pope's pet projects, the conversion of the Palazzo Ludovisi in Montecitorio (left incomplete decades before by Bernini) into the *Curia Innocenziana.*[16] He followed this a week later with five line engravings, four showing Carlo Fontana's intentions for the site (see below), and one a plan of the preexisting ancient Roman context.[17] These must have been taken from Fontana's report on the project, published on Innocent's order on 16 October 1694.[18] Again, typically, Fontana used this opportunity to make grand proposals for the elaboration of the project, as a means of recommending his services in place of Mattia de Rossi under whom it had begun, and indeed this time to actually exaggerate his role in the conception of the project as though de Rossi had none at all. As before, an important part of his strategy was to demonstrate his qualifications as a historian by reconstructing the uses made of the site in antiquity which related to the function of the *curia*.[19]

Though dismayed by the potential costs, the pope was impressed enough by the magnitude of Fontana's thinking to approve the publication of his treatise, and public enthusiasm followed. La Teulière was made aware of the project through the same means, and in passing this awareness on to Paris, he was moved to say of Fontana's designs that, "S'il pouvoit estre achevé, il seroit d'une grande commodité pour les gens qui ont des affaires en cette Cour, dont le nombre est plus grand que dans pas une autre."[20] As the element of commodiousness was crucial to good design in France, this amounts to quite high praise, and Fontana seems now to have made his name there.

In February of 1695, it was decided to relocate the customs house, the *Dogana di Terra,* which Innocent had originally intended to include in the ground story of his *curia* as a source of revenue for the poor.[21] The new edifice would incorporate the ruins of the Temple of Hadrian on the nearby Piazza di Pietra, and Francesco Fontana would be in charge. In September, La Teulière communicated to Villacerf that both buildings, Carlo's *curia* and Francesco's *dogana,* were "fort avancés."[22] A third papal project, the *Dogana di Ripa Grande,* which Carlo also took over from Mattia de Rossi, is mentioned as finished. In February of 1696, the subject of La Teulière's report was "un Théâtre magnifique pour l'Opéra public, sous la conduitte de M. d'Alibert, François, Introducteur des Ambassadeurs auprès la Reyne de Suede...."[23] This refers to the expansion of the *Teatro Tor di Nona,* Carlo Fontana's ill-fated project for Queen Christina, and La Teulière again had Fontana's personal assurance that when engravings of his designs were made he would supply La Teulière with the first proofs. La Teulière in turn promised

them to Villacerf (with more than his usual obsequiousness, as though he were anxious to pass them on), but no proofs were forthcoming.[24]

Even if there had been no specific references to the direct contact between Fontana and La Teulière, as there were with regard to *Il Tempio Vaticano* and the work on the *Teatro Tor di Nona,* there would be reason to suspect its existence. For instance, La Teulière, no doubt because of his complete lack of background in the medium, betrayed absolutely no interest in current events in architecture in his correspondences, except for those projects of Fontana's mentioned above. Indeed, the activities of no other Roman artist are featured as prominently in his missives, or in fact at all, unless they related to the work of his students or other French artists active in Rome. His critical approach to architecture was limited entirely to what he could glean secondhand from books, which makes it unlikely that he could have or would have informed himself first hand of what was new on the scene in Rome; he would have had to have been led to it.[25] The lacunae in the communiqués from Paris to the academy in Rome prevent certainty, but it seems from the tone of La Teulière's letters that Villacerf was as interested in hearing about Fontana's projects as Fontana was in promoting them, and either or both could have steered La Teulière to his objectives. As a result, Fontana had succeeded in insinuating his name into the cognizance of official circles in Paris in time to assume the position left vacant therein by the death of Mattia de Rossi in August of 1695.

It was at about this time that Fontana may have been sounded out by Cardinal Forbin-Janson, then the French *chargé d'affaires,* as the architect for a project of his: the expansion of a monastic complex located in his domains as Bishop of Beauvais.[26] All that came of this commission, if such it was, was a set of finished plan and section drawings. However, no matter how tentatively, Fontana had his foot in the door to an extent that no Italian architect had since the Louvre competition, and this in its small way is a credit to his publicity campaign.

The French were by no means the only or even the principal target of that campaign. With *Il*

Tempio Vaticano Fontana courted the attention of all Catholic heads of state throughout Europe. Frederick Augustus, Elector of Saxony and later King of Poland, got his copy directly from Fontana during a tour incognito of Rome and the Vatican in 1694.[27] Augustus repaid his guide by making Fontana a Polish count in 1699. The custom Fontana wished most to cultivate was that of the empire, and the copy of his book sent to Vienna may very well have had the desired effect. In 1696, the new imperial ambassador, Count Georg Adam Martinitz, arrived at the papal court and immediately passed on the request of the prince of the House of Liechtenstein that Fontana submit designs for his garden palace in Landskron, Bohemia.[28] Shortly thereafter, Fontana was consulted by Martinitz's in-laws, the Sternbergs, concerning the design of a palace in Prague.[29] No commission was forthcoming in either of these instances,[30] but Martinitz himself engaged Fontana's services before departing from Rome in 1700, for designs for the remodeling of his palace in Prague.[31] During the 1690s, most of whatever energies not expended by Fontana's studio on papal or ecclesiastic projects in Rome or its environs were devoted to Austrian palace projects, and the proportion of the latter was not small.

Fontana had thus made substantial inroads in forging an international reputation for himself; no doubt he hoped that in the end his name would come as easily to the lips of every courtier in Europe as did Bernini's a generation before. But the Europe of his day was already quite different. Modern nations were forming with well-integrated and mature cultural identities which looked less to the example of Rome or Italy, and more to their own devices. The seed which Fontana had tried to sow could not take root where the ground was not prepared for it, or where the native flora was hostile to it, as in France; it might flourish to a degree in the shallow soil of Poland or Austria, but it would not thrive. Fontana was a Roman by disposition and training, and in Rome above all could he expect his harvest to be abundant.[32] By the end of the century Fontana was unquestionably the leading architect in Rome, thanks in part to his status with the pope, in part to his publica-

tions, and in part to the fact that those nearest competitors who had not actually left Rome for greener pastures were probably working for him.

Fontana earned another laurel with the work he did to improve the fortunes of the Accademia during his second principate. Having first reestablished some consistency in the Accademia's meetings, in the participation of its membership, in the offering of instruction, and in the collection of revenues, the advent of the *concorso* for 1694 spelled an opportunity for Fontana to make public the profit his leadership held for the Roman academy. For example, it seems that the Accademia's main salon was in a poor state of repair and therefore unsuitable for the celebration of the *concorso* (App. B, 1694, n. 3). It was Fontana who petitioned a Roman senator, Marchese Ottavio Riario, for the use of the great hall of the Palazzo Nuovo, which was conveniently located on the Capitoline hill adjacent to the academy buildings. The Marchese, who repeated the favor in subsequent years and in turn was made *Accademico d'Honore* in 1695 (App. B, 1695, n. 2), bestowed the necessary permission.[33] For the first time the ceremonies of the *concorso* could be conducted in a setting that was not only more appropriate to their intended spectacle but also both literally and figuratively at the heart of the city.[34] Compounding this achievement, Fontana contributed the funds for the prizes to be awarded, "medals in silver and silver plate in sizes proportional to the classes" (App. B, 1694, n. 5), for which it seems the dies made by Giovanni Hamerani exactly ten years before may have been resurrected.

On 17 October 1694, the Sunday before the Feast of St. Luke, Fontana presided over the distribution of prizes in the new venue, and handing out the medals for architecture must have been particularly gratifying for him. For the first time since the public *concorsi* had been initiated there were competitions in three classes of architecture; architecture had finally been put on a par with painting. In the three classes a total of seven prizes were distributed. The magnitude of the task for each class had also been adjusted accordingly: For the first class, a large, multifunction building complex tested the competitors' abilities as facilities planners as well as designers; for the second, a building of basic type challenged them as once had the sole *soggetto* in architecture in each previous *concorso;* and for the third, a copy after the work of a recognized master was the exercise usual at this level for all media.

The distinction here is double-edged, for not only had Fontana apparently mandated the change that made architecture the equal of the other media in competition, but he may also have been largely responsible for the increased enrollment of students in architecture that made their showing possible. Not since the victory of the French in 1677 had there been more than one prizewinner in architecture, or at times even more than one eligible competitor, and now there had been seven. While Ludovico Rusconi-Sassi (winner of one of two first prizes in the third class) is the only one of their number as yet to be documented as a student of Fontana's (see below), it is possible on the basis of style and technique to link most of the rest to his tutelage: Pompeo Ferrari (first class/first prize), Alessandro Sperone (second class/first prize), Alessandro Rossini (the other first prize in the third class), and Filippo Ottoni (third class/second prize).[35] With Fontana's son Francesco directing the course in architecture at the Accademia, just as he quite probably was overseeing the efforts of his father's apprentices, and with a number of those apprentices making up most if not all of the enrollment in that course, the Accademia in essence became an extension of Fontana's studio.

Parallels have already been drawn between Fontana and Jules Hardouin-Mansart on the basis of their respective monopolies on building activity and patronage in Rome and France, but now another factor can be added. Both in their time had succeeded in circumventing the boundaries between the institutions designated to inform the taste of student architects and the studios destined to employ them. To Fontana's credit, he had achieved this end without recourse to the bureaucratic intricacies that had made the same result a forgone conclusion in Paris, but the French had nevertheless provided him the example. How much of an example is verified by the use to which the *concorsi* in architecture were put now that

Fontana's studio had begun to mingle with the Accademia.

The texts of the *soggetti* for the *concorso* of 1694 have not been preserved, but Giuseppe Ghezzi was again in charge of collecting and publicizing them (App. B, 1694, n. 2). If he remained true to his usual form, he would have solicited the tasks in architecture from the instructor, who was Francesco Fontana, and with Carlo overshadowing things this gesture would appear all the more unavoidable. All doubt should be removed once the topic for the first class has been reconstructed from the labeling on Ferrari's plan (see Pl. 25), where the left side is ranked around a cloister, the right consists of classrooms, and a church and service wing separate them along the central axis. The generic type is that of a monastic college, but the specific reference must be to Carlo Fontana's own project for the Jesuit college at Loyola, Spain (Figs. 96, 97). This had been Fontana's most important commission of the 1680s, awarded him by the General of the Society shortly after 1681 (though construction did not begin until 1689 and continued well into the eighteenth century).[36] On the practical side, this theme made for quite a comprehensive test of all of the design skills expected of a first-class competitor, barring considerations of building context or topography. But it is also reasonable to expect a promotional side to the purpose behind the choice of subject. The Fontanas were in effect publicizing what had been the elder Fontana's only important project abroad, indeed his largest independent commission, up to that time. Dating as it does from a time when he was less of a public figure, and fated by its nature to have little local exposure, this design might otherwise have been forgotten amidst the attention being accorded his activities in the 1690s. The first-class competition in 1694 thus became an opportunity for Carlo Fontana to remind Rome of his earlier, equally impressive, accomplishments.[37]

There is another permutation to the choice of tasks in 1694, having to do with the connection between the Accademia's architecture curriculum and Fontana's studio. There is no hard evidence from around 1694 for the process by which apprentices in a studio progressed through the

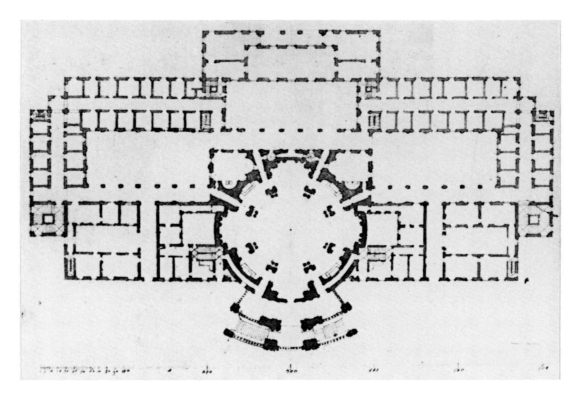

96 CARLO FONTANA: copy of a project plan for the Jesuit College; Loyola, 1680s (source: private collection, Rome).

ranks, to the point where they would be allowed to execute presentation or working drawings after their master's designs, and then to their release into the real world and the pursuit of their independent ideas. In the case of Fontana's studio, some valuable insight is given by two biographies of Juvarra, which cover a later period, that of his attachment to Fontana's workshop after 1704.[38] The two accounts are quite at odds as to Juvarra's first experiences with his Roman master, but each may contain a part of the truth. The longer version gives his first task as drawing a Corinthian capital, which he executed with such skill that he was then sent to copy from Michelangelo's Campidoglio, presumably the next stage in his education. In the shorter version his first test was to design a palace, in which he betrayed so much of his provincial origins (Messina) that Fontana admonished him to forget all he had learned up to that moment,

and in effect open his mind to what Fontana had to teach him. From there Juvarra proceeded to copy from a range of existing monuments, but above all the example to follow would be Fontana's. This accords with what has already been deduced above about the latter's methods and attitudes regarding the formation of an architect, as opposed to those which were more purely academic. Fontana was not recommending his "style" or any other as the absolute authority, but rather his empirical approach as the best model. Interestingly, this history also contains elements which are consistent with the experiences of the architecture students at the Accademia in 1694.

First of all, Francesco Fontana, like his immediate predecessors in the position of instructor, was compelled to produce a set of lessons on the Orders, but his are distinct from the earlier ones, though not by reason of inferior ability (Fig. 98;

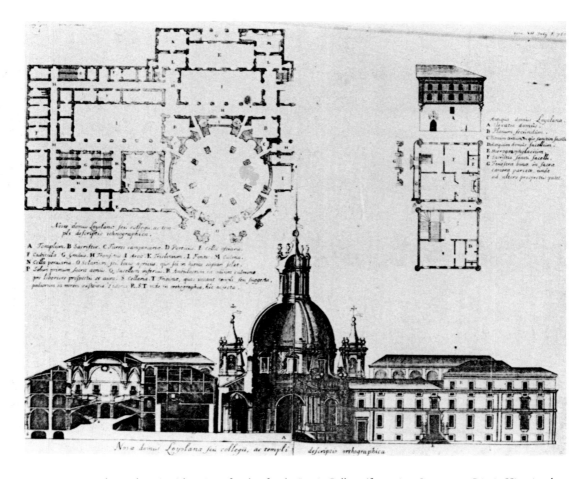

97 FONTANA: plan and section/elevation of a plan for the Jesuit College (from *Acta Sanctorum: Diario Historico de Loyola*).

compare Figs. 58 and 62). Fontana's are not the carefully modeled and finely detailed examples that Tomassini and Martinelli had presented after labors of two or more years, but rather are simple outline drawings which measure out the basic elements of the Orders; in that they are more like de Rossi's lessons of 1673 (compare Fig. 55).[39] The difference is crucial. Again, as when the curriculum was first introduced, the Orders were not to be an all-consuming preoccupation, but merely a starting point. Fontana's lessons even provide a sense of how rapid the pace of this stage was, for most of them are dated to the exact day, beginning when studies were opened on the first of May, and extending into June of 1694, by which time the more complex Orders were reached. He paused

momentarily in the midst of this to render fully two examples in order to edify his pupils and reveal his own skills (Figs. 99, 100), but otherwise, rendering, detailing, or sculptural embellishment were not to distract them. Neither, apparently, was the issue of "correctness," for in choosing subjects for his renderings Fontana went to extremes: from the ancient ideal for the Ionic capital (preferred, incidentally, by Tomassini and Martinelli), to the personalized variation from Michelangelo's Palazzo dei Conservatori. The "quarrel" between the Ancients and the Moderns, into which the French academies had descended and become mired, was of no concern, it seems. In effect, Fontana's students were treated only as young architects, not as painters, sculptors, or theoreticians, more so than

148

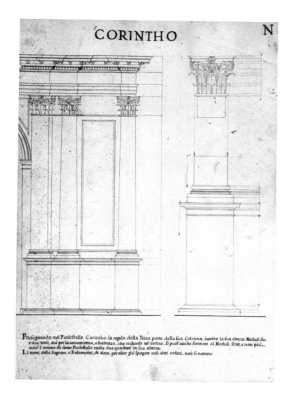

98 FRANCESCO FONTANA: "Corintho"; ASL, uncataloged drawing.

99 F. FONTANA: "Ionico Moderno"; ASL, uncataloged drawing.

100 F. FONTANA: "Ionico Antico"; ASL, uncataloged drawing.

in any earlier curriculum, perhaps because there were now so many more architects in it. A fundamental understanding of the Orders was something to be obtained early, and quickly, and then put aside for more important business.

The important business was the study of architecture *in situ,* not in classrooms or from books. By sketching, measuring, and rendering existing buildings, students of the Fontanas could not only improve their techniques in those areas as well as they could by any other means, they could also learn from the best examples in Rome how to plan a building, how to proportion and articulate it, or how to make the best use of site and context. Put bluntly, architecture is a manipulation of space, and requires a three-dimensional awareness impossible to gain by just two-dimensional means. Students of architecture had to be recognized as unique in this way, and the development of their architectural judgement therefore depended on extramural experiences, of the kind that would be encouraged for Juvarra. Francesco Fontana encouraged the same for his charges at the Accademia by giving a tangible goal for their efforts: the chance to win prizes in a third-class competition by executing renderings after a particular monument. Again the drawings themselves (cf. Pl. 37) are the clue to the specific topic in this case: an end bay of the Palazzo dei Conservatori on the Campidoglio. It was to this very site, so near the Accademia, that Carlo Fontana would supposedly refer Juvarra for study ten years later.

As a student progressed in Fontana's studio, he would conceivably be given gradually more complex projects of his master's on which to work as a draftsman. This now became the logic of the successive classes of competition in architecture at the Accademia, though there the students would be challenged to produce original designs. In the second class in 1694, reading from Alessandro Sperone's winning entry (see Pls. 34–36), the task was a chapel, dedicated to St. Luke, for attachment to another building, perhaps the Accademia. This exercise was for those with the requisite intermediate skills, equivalent to what they might expect to be allowed to work on in the studio. The first-class *soggetto,* the monastic college, could be attempted by only the most advanced students. The idea of graduating the first-prize winner in this highest class into the ranks of the Accademia, and thereby conferring professional status on him, now made a good deal more sense than it ever had since Maratti first decreed the practice in 1664 (see Chapter I and App. B, 1664, n. 4).

The architecture curriculum had finally been brought up to the standards of curricula in the other media. No longer was it a subsidiary discipline, serving *per se* very few architects; now it was recognized as an equal and independent entity, with its own means. Its students, now greater in number, were encouraged to draw directly from models appropriate to *their* art, and were motivated by the *concorsi* at year's end, which recognized the value of each stage of their development. Their objectives were not to be obscured by issues more suited to the other arts, unless or until they displayed the maturity to deal with them. This achievement resulted, it would seem, from the

identity that now existed between the academy's curriculum and Fontana's workshop; the benefits do not appear to have been Fontana's alone.

For young architects, the qualities that before this had distinguished an academic from a workshop training (theoretical vs. practical) made both desirable. But the efforts involved in attaining them had made it difficult for an apprentice to reap the best of both experiences before age thirty, the age of majority for their profession, which was for the time already middle age. Martinelli, for example, having pursued his career at the Accademia while also an assistant in Fontana's studio, did not receive his membership in the former until age thirty-five and he did not begin his independent work in earnest until age forty. With conformity now established between instruction at the Accademia and in Fontana's studio, the two experiences could coalesce into one more efficient process, which was conceivably greater than the sum of its parts and a legitimate precursor of the nineteenth-century Beaux-Arts tradition.

Fontana's accomplishments on behalf of the Accademia were aired publicly upon the celebration of the *concorso* of 1694, in mid-October, on the Campidoglio. The entries had been submitted for judging, and the *prove* administered, on the preceding Sunday (App. B, 1694, n. 3); the jury in architecture was composed of Fontana's closest peers in the spheres of practice and academics: de Rossi and Tomassini.[40] They were thus confronted directly with the results of Fontana's reformation of the architecture curriculum. On the day of the *concorso,* Ghezzi paid his tribute to the *principe* with a discourse on architecture written especially for the occasion (though perhaps reviving some of what he said when Contini was *principe* in 1683); it was presented by his son, for whom he had ambitions as an orator (App. B, 1694, n. 5).

The Accademia's Centenary

The centennial year of 1695 was cause for academy-wide celebration and self-congratulation. For that year Fontana, who continued as *principe* by acclamation rather than election,[41] set aside the *concorsi* (along with any further purpose he had for the architecture competitions) in favor of other ceremonies.[42] Ghezzi was put in charge of events, to assure that they be "conspicuous" but "decorous," and include "all possible demonstrations and pomp" (App. B, 1695, n. 1). To bankroll these intentions, "spontaneous contributions" were collected from every active member, even from those who had had the foresight not to attend the meeting on 20 February when the decisions were made. Special deputies (Lorenzo Ottoni and G. B. Théodon, Fontana's assistants at the baptistry) were sent to accost them for their share. The membership was also considerably augmented this year by the election of eight *Accademici d'Honore,* including Senator Riario, and the admission of several new *Accademici di Merito,* including the first woman, Teresa Raimondi Velli, a Roman miniaturist.[43] With attendance already higher than it had been for nearly all of the past two decades, the influx of revenues must have seemed like a flood.

The usual climax would have come with the ceremonies on the Feast of St. Luke in 1695, conducted again on the Campidoglio (App. B, 1695, n. 2) and capped by Ghezzi's oration on the quality of the arts in Rome, and the city's long history as the wellspring of European culture.[44] But those festivities only marked the opening of a Secular Year of celebrations, a revival of an ancient imperial tradition marking every hundredth anniversary of the city of Rome with games, and with rites performed on the Capitol itself.[45] The new Secular Year proclaimed by the city government and the pope established a year-long celebration in honor of the Accademia's centennial, climaxing on the Feast of St. Luke for 1696, and inviting the sustained attention of every Roman. Fontana and his academicians were determined to make the best use of center stage.

Fontana's first act on being reconfirmed as *principe* in January of 1696 was to appoint several members to the task of painting "portraits" of the Accademia's founders and benefactors—popes, prelates, and princes.[46] These comprised only a part of the decorations prepared for all of the Accademia's public spaces, its church, salon, and grounds, as well as for the Palazzo Nuovo and the Piazza del Campidoglio which had become extensions of them. Old works by past and present members were put out on display alongside new works, in all media, in order to illustrate the history of the Accademia. Fontana himself contributed ephemeral decorations for the Campidoglio, and tapestries were loaned by the Colonna family for the same purpose (App. B, 1696, n. 8). The *verbali* for this year keep an impressive account of the gifts coming in to the Accademia, primarily in the form of money, and of the dues and rents collected, all of which were necessary to fund the elaborate and continuing spectacle. Stone tablets were inscribed and affixed to the academy's walls in commemoration of the artists and pontiffs who had given it its start, of the Barberini (their noble protectors), and even of Innocent XII (who was more of a patron to Fontana than to the Accademia as a whole).

Ghezzi kept a record of the events surrounding the Secular Year, publishing them in the first of the Accademia's *relazioni,* or annual reports (though they would not appear annually until the eighteenth century).[47] Each *relazione* focused primarily on the *concorso* for its respective year, and the first was no different, for the centenary competition that was withheld in 1695 was now to be carried out as part of the Secular Year celebrations. As such, it was counted on to be the most spectacular event of its kind, eclipsing even, and perhaps with intent, the aggregation competition of 1677 that had been conducted under French auspices. It is no surprise that the architectural *concorsi* orchestrated by the Fontanas were meant to carry a large share of the burden to impress. They could hope in that way to overcome the crushing blow to the pride of Roman architects suffered when Chupin, D'Aviler, and Desgots had won their victory virtually unchallenged by any equivalent local talent. Carlo Fontana had observed this defeat firsthand, and may even in a small way have contributed indirectly to it (see Chapter II); in the intervening years he had yet to see Italian competitors assembled who could better the accomplishments of those three Frenchmen. Now his chance had come.

Francesco Fontana put together an unprecedented set of *soggetti* (App. B, 1696, nn. 1–3) for 1696. In the first class, the participants were to design, for a royal patron, a villa palace for the

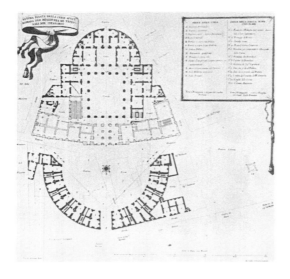

101 CARLO FONTANA: project plan for the *Curia Innocenziana;* Rome, 1694 (engraving: Specchi).

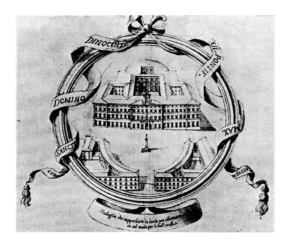

102 FONTANA: perspective study for a medallion commemorating the *Curia Innocenziana* (source: private collection, Rome).

separate residence of four dignitaries, fronted by a piazza for public tournaments; around the piazza were to be located the stables and carriage houses. There are echoes in the last two stipulations of Carlo Fontana's earliest and grandest projects for the *Curia Innocenziana* (see above), which included at one point plans for a semicircular piazza having the same purpose and disposition (Figs. 101, 102). Otherwise the idea of such a palace seems only a bold fantasy, particularly in the context of Rome, where there was no royal patronage and where a palace made up of four independent residences could be considered extravagant, to say the least.[48]

Reading between the lines of the *soggetto,* the title of "monarch" could be applied to only a few heads of state. If one supposes the reference to be to Louis XIV, who after all had been most numerously referred to in the previous *concorsi,* then the question remains as to who the four dignitaries were to be. Keeping in mind the academic setting, one possibility suggests itself. The four dignitaries—and it is important to realize that they are not specified as noblemen—may be the four rectors of the Académie Royale de Peinture et Sculpture, its principal governing body after the director (now Mignard) and the *surintendant* (now Colbert de Villacerf).[49] Granted, there is no way to verify this guess, and the project would still be a fantasy. But the *soggetto* in the first class for 1696, at least in the magnitude of its conception, was meant to speak to sensibilities more Grand Manner French than anything else.

Another clue to the reasoning of the theme comes from the specific mention in the *soggetto* of the "place [for] public tournaments" before the palace, and the stables facing it. Such a situation existed at Versailles, once Hardouin-Mansart had completed the *Grande* and *Petite Écuries* in 1683 (Fig. 103), to the sustained awe of the rest of Europe. What would have been palaces in their own right anywhere else, surpassing the needs and aspirations of most of the rulers on the continent, were home to several hundred horses and their attendants at the *château* of the Sun King. While the requirements of the first-class *soggetto* in 1696 were modest by comparison to Versailles, there was still something tongue-in-cheek about the ref-

103 JULES HARDOUIN-MANSART: the *Grande* and *Petite Écuries;* Versailles, 1679–83 (engraving: Pérelle).

erences, a subtle goad to the arrogance and pretensions of contemporary French architecture, which had, since the Louvre project, dared to put itself above the example of Rome. The implicit challenge for the French was to repeat their performance in 1677 and demonstrate that the expertise for defining the architecture of absolute monarchy was truly exclusive to them, or stand by while Roman hands were put to the task.

The Fontanas must have known, and may have counted on the fact, that they had the French in Rome at a disadvantage in 1696. The next volley in their assault came with the second-class topic, which called for the design of a church for the above villa, on a site measuring 100 by 80 *palmi.* The building itself would be rather small, but just the type required a level of thought and ability equivalent to what was needed for the com-

petition in 1677 (see Chapter II). In other words, what had once been first-class material for competition was now deemed fit for students who had reached only an intermediate stage of development. What might look on the one hand as a concession to the maturity of the Accademia's architectural curriculum was also a veiled insult to the French victors in 1677, whose level of competence was thus diminished by inference.

Finally, there was the *soggetto* for the third class, which asked not for a rendering of an existing building, but for an original design of a Doric portal for the same villa. The Fontanas now had such confidence in their methods and their students that even the most callow competitor could be expected to produce novel work.[50] In every class, therefore, the *soggetti* in architecture were calculated to make a point: about the value of the

153

improvements made to the architecture curriculum, or about how much it had outgrown whatever the French had had to offer.

There are more subtle associations, between the competition topics and Fontana, that come from the fact that Fontana was also occupied throughout 1696 on his own project for a villa palace, a miniature Versailles. This was the Liechtenstein palace at Landskron, mentioned earlier and in note 28, for which Fontana was invited to present designs early in the year, though his final proposals were not submitted to the patron until December. The proposal which conformed most closely with Prince Liechtenstein's requirements (Figs. 104, 105) included two stable wings separated from the main palace block by a vast esplanade. The palace proper was subdivided at the *piano nobile* into two sets of apartments (rather than four) sharing, along the central axis, a grand staircase and circular salon, the latter housed in an octagonal tower crowned by a belvedere/cupola.

Differences aside, there can be little doubt that main points of the commission from the prince had actually been incorporated into the *soggetti* in 1696. The chapel and ornate portal that Liechtenstein had stipulated for his villa were neglected by Fontana in his projects, but became the subject matter for the second- and third-class *concorsi*. The same ploy Fontana had used in 1694 to enhance public awareness of one of his more distant and less noticed projects was used again. The difference this time was that the project to which the competitors were to refer was itself only in the design stages. This is an important distinction, for it meant that Fontana and his students were simultaneously at work on kindred projects, and applying the same methods to their generation, ostensibly independently. Fontana projects the image of a master confident enough of his charges' abilities to allow them the illusion of being practicing architects in competition with him.

For the Secular Year 1696, the *concorso* was to be celebrated separately, before the Feast of St. Luke, on 30 September, presumably so that the *concorso's* now more elaborate festivities would not mar the solemnity, or poignancy, of the patron's

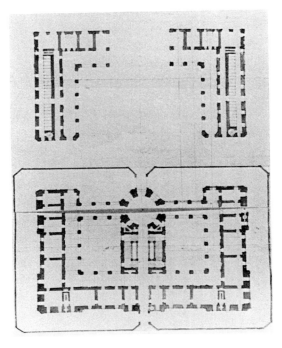

104 CARLO FONTANA: project plan (proposed) for the Liechtenstein Garden Palace; Landskron, 1696 (source: Windsor Castle, Royal Library, Her Majesty Queen Elizabeth II).

feast day. Submissions were scheduled for Friday, 15 September, and the administration of the *prove* for the following Sunday, with the winners to be chosen in the meantime (App. B, 1696, n. 4). The judges in architecture were Tomassini and Contini, and the documents indicate that there seems to have been a much greater show made of ensuring impartiality in this year than in any other.[51] Each entry was assigned a letter of the alphabet, up to the letter "Z" (which hints at a field of two dozen competitors throughout all three classes in all three arts, but does not prove it). Once the three winners were selected in each class, their letters were turned over to the secretary, who would have kept the record of their names (App. B., 1696, n. 5). Then the *prove* examinations were used to determine if what each winning architect could produce on the spur of the moment corresponded, in hand and ability, to what he had submitted as his effort of several months. The *prove* topics are also preserved for the first time in this year (App.

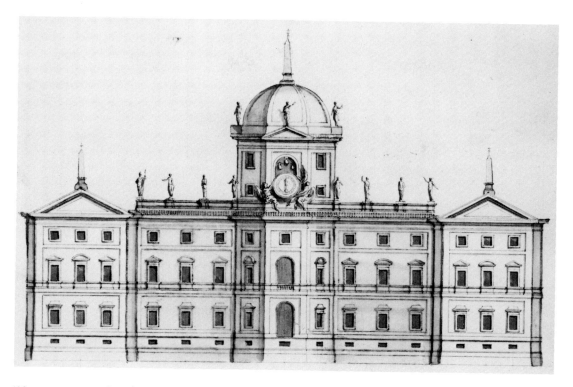

105 FONTANA: project elevation for Liechtenstein Garden Palace plan (source: Windsor Castle, Royal Library, Her Majesty Queen Elizabeth II).

B, 1696, n. 6). They, too, press home the point that these young architects had more mettle than their predecessors, for the assignments now to be followed in the course of two hours might once have been suitable for an entire *concorso:* a church facade (first class), a decorated niche (second), and a Corinthian capital (third).

Somehow at this point Ghezzi became confused, so that the list he made of the names of the prizewinners and their identifying letters (App. B, 1696, n. 7) does not correspond in its order to that made by the judges.[52] All was set right in time for the celebrations (App. B, 1696, n. 9). Nevertheless, the system intended to guarantee impartiality was not foolproof, and may therefore not have been tamperproof, but at least it appeared to be so, and that, to contemporary observers, was all that mattered. For the purpose of the present study, however, total objectivity would not be a reasonable expectation. No architect who might have been

involved in the handling of the entries would have missed the evidence of techniques or ideas enough to avoid some preconception of their origin, general or specific, except perhaps for Contini, but even he was not a complete outsider. A detached jury would have been a certainty only if it had been made up of artists who had no affiliation with either the Accademia's architecture curriculum or Fontana's studio, for it would seem from the drawings that nearly all of the participants were products of both. The one glaring exception (and a puzzling one as will be seen) that no one could have missed was the entry by the Paris-trained architect Charles Derbais, whose second-prize design in the first class (see Pls. 44–46) stood out for several reasons, some intentional and some not. With his successful participation, the French had returned to haunt the *concorsi* at the moment of the Accademia's greatest triumph; why his work was recognized when it could as easily have been passed over is intriguing.

With the judging complete, the winning entries in all media were put on public display in the Accademia's salon for an entire week so that Rome might assess the veracity of the jury's decisions. On the morning of 30 September, the day of the *concorso,* a "sumptuous" mass was offered, by no less than a bishop, in SS. Luca e Martina, accompanied by music composed especially for the occasion.[53] Later, in the evening, the distribution of prizes took place in the great hall of the Palazzo Nuovo, which Carlo Fontana's temporary architecture had turned into a "splendid" theater, according to the *verbali.* Much of Rome's nobility was in attendance to hear the recitation of original works of poetry and oratory, including Ghezzi's discourse (given voice again by his son), and to witness the awards ceremony, which was presided over by the Cardinal Protector, Carlo Barberini, and other members of the College present with him. The prizes were medals struck to new designs made by Giovanni Hamerani: on the obverse, the image of St. Luke painting the Virgin, the emblem of the Accademia; on the reverse, a symbol of the century past (in the form of a serpent devouring its tail), and appropriate inscriptions.[54] The latter read as follows:

> L'Accademia de' Pittori, Scultori, ed
> Architetti di Roma per la celebrazione
> dell'anno secolare 1696 sotto il Principato
> del Cavaliere Carlo Fontana

The medals were of gold, the like of which the Accademia had not seen since 1677, but the funds came now from their own overflowing coffers, not from Paris. And this time the prizes were distributed across three classes in all media, a luxury that could not have been subsidized in 1677 (see Chapter I). The Accademia was rightfully celebrating its new-found vitality, and its new-found identity, asserted in the motto on the medals, as the equal representative of each of the three major arts for the city of Rome. The name of Carlo Fontana appears conspicuously everywhere, not only on the medals but also in the *relazione* and the *verbali,* in token of his guiding hand.

With the Accademia in effect drained by these exertions, the balance of Fontana's principate appears more a period of recuperation (a veritable bed rest), in comparison to its first three years. On 4 November 1696, almost the entire meeting of the congregation was spent trying to decide how to dispose of or make a place for all of the decorations from the Secular Year celebrations.[55] After that, nearly half a year goes by before the members meet again to arrange for the opening of the academic season (presumably with Francesco Fontana again instructor in architecture), and to approve nonchalantly the continuation of Carlo in the office of *principe*. His only action worth noting in this year was the nomination as *Accademici di Merito* of three of his students, who may also have participated in the centenary competition: Sebastiano Cipriani, Carlo Francesco Bizzacheri, and Carlo Buratti.[56] They and another of their number, Antonio Valerii, admitted the previous year, together with Francesco Fontana would comprise a generation of offshoots of the Fontana studio that would be active at the Accademia in plotting the course of its architecture curriculum into the next century.

After another lapse of several months, the congregation met again in April of 1698 to see to its obligations regarding instruction, with Buratti appointed as lecturer in architecture. Also noted was the passing of Tomassini, their treasurer and once the doyen of the architecture faculty, part of whose legacy was to go toward the prizes for future *concorsi.*[57] Francesco Fontana, who had displaced him as instructor, assumed the post of *vice-principe,* under his father who was reconfirmed in his office. Objections were finally raised, however, to this practice of acting on decisions by acclamation, among others by Lazzaro Baldi, who moved the proposal that the congregation return to the idea of the secret ballot, the *bussola,* for the election of the *principe*.[58] Fontana's principate thus came to an end on 31 December 1698, when G. B. Buoncore's name was drawn from the ballot.[59] His death the following May brought his *vice-principe,* Carlo Maratti, back into the office he had not held since 1664–65 (and then with considerable distinction; see Chapter I), which effectively opened a new era in the Accademia's history.[60]

Consideration of this period is reserved for Chapter V.

The French Academies

The robust vigor of the Accademia during Carlo Fontana's second principate contrasts sharply with conditions at both the Académie Royale in Paris and its satellite in Rome for the same period.[61] Authority in Paris had been transferred to individuals considerably less devoted to the academic system built by their predecessors: the Marquis de Louvois, *Surintendant des Bâtiments* after Colbert from 1683; and Pierre Mignard, Director of the Académie Royale after LeBrun from 1690. With the slackening of their interest, the academy slipped deeper into the morass of the dispute between the *Poussinistes* and *Rubenistes,* which quickly eroded its doctrinal foundation. The ascendance of the Moderns replaced rules with license in contemporary taste, emasculating the arguments for either an established stylistic authority or a pedagogical means of disseminating it. The lectures in theory at the academy, which had established its power base, were increasingly replaced by lectures on the lives of past members by the academy's secretary and historian, Guillet de St. Georges. Whatever interest Louis XIV had in his academies was formed by Colbert. What absorbed Louis after the death of that minister was more his personal interest in waging war. His campaigns against the League of Augsburg, which dragged on for nearly a decade before ending with the Treaty of Ryswick in 1697, were particularly devastating to the state treasury. The grant set aside for the support of the Académie Royale was diverted to the wars, and the Académie was ordered to close its doors in 1694. The academicians requested that they be allowed instead to continue their activities without pay, and, impressed by their earnestness, Louis partially restored their grant.[62] Much the same curtailments were suffered by the Académie de France in Rome.

Circumstances for the Académie d'Architecture in Paris were only somewhat different, partly because from its beginning in 1671 Colbert intended it to be detached from the Académie de Peinture et Sculpture and more subject to central authority. And however else Louis XIV felt about the other arts or the academies, he loved building, as Versailles singularly attests. The principal function of the Académie d'Architecture was to consult on the practical matters of the royal works, in order to assure conformity to the consensus regarding "correct" style, as well as to the ones regarding proper methods of construction.[63] The theoretical disputes of the academy, like the major one between François Blondel and Claude Perrault, were only a means toward that end. So too were the students the academy produced; they were destined to perpetuate the consensus. At Colbert's insistence, theory was to be formulated early, and then set aside so that the academy could devote itself to practicalities. Thus it was that the objectives of the academy became synonymous with those of the office of the king's architect, Jules Hardouin-Mansart. The two effectively operated as one, both to train young architects and to assure compliance with authority, which more and more became focused on Hardouin-Mansart himself.[64] As a result of his despotic control, the Académie d'Architecture could not be threatened by the same conflict of taste that toppled its sister institution from grace, at least not during Hardouin-Mansart's lifetime. By the same token, however, French architecture would not be loosed from the bonds of doctrine until well into the next century and never to the revolutionary degree that can be detected in painting and sculpture from the *Régence* on. And its status did not make the Académie d'Architecture safe from the shortfalls of the 1690s, either, for it, too, was asked to suspend its activities in 1694.[65] This was avoided only when its membership likewise offered to continue without compensation.

La Teulière, director of the academy in Rome, weathered the storm in much the same way, though the threat to him was greater as it could have meant a permanent end to his operations, and possibly more disheartening as he was just starting to acquire a knack for his job (see Chapter III). Colbert de Villacerf, *surintendant* since 1691, was sympathetic to the need for an agency in Rome that could see to the welfare of the young

French artists who still went there to broaden their experiences, and he gave La Teulière what support he could. But the majority of opinion in Paris no longer admitted to the necessity of a stay in Rome. Antiquity and *disegno,* for which Rome still offered the best models, no longer commanded much respect from the *Rubenistes,* and French architecture was quite content with its native exemplar, Hardouin-Mansart. Villacerf informed La Teulière of the king's decisions regarding the royal academies in May of 1694.[66] Sessions were to be suspended in Paris. Since it was even more expensive to maintain the branch in Rome, it could expect the same fate. Professors at home might donate their services to keep their institutions open, but there was no way that La Teulière could have for free the local instructors and models, or the supplies and space for his students, that his academy would need to function. A subsistence level of funding would be considered only if immediate and drastic economizing measures, like cutbacks in personnel and pensions, were enacted.

Even before 1694 La Teulière is often found defending his position as director in Rome, or the actions of the man responsible for it, Louvois, whom he much admired. At other times he had been forced to plead for monies from Paris to cover even the most routine expenditures of the academy, though he himself was never delinquent in his own accounting. In the days of Louvois it had been possible to run the academy adequately on the surplus remaining after purchases of works of art were made, but those days were long past. Villacerf did not employ the academy as a go-between or factory, and shipments from Rome to Paris were most often limited to what could be sent by post: drawings and engravings, books, medals, or small *objets d'art*. Even these were rarely financed by Paris, but seem to have been sent for the most part on La Teulière's own initiative, in a desperate attempt to remind his superiors that his academy was in fact strategically located in a vital center for the arts. The collapse of the industry in reproductions at the Académie de France in Rome was a blow not only to its prestige at home, and its economic well-being as a result, but also to its enrollment, since there was

no longer the need for a large labor force disguised as students.

By October of 1691 there were, in fact, only four students receiving a pension from the academy in Rome: two painters and two sculptors.[67] Several other young French artists were in the city, and La Teulière kept an eye on them as well, but they were there "a ses frais"; the academy had no use for them and could not support them.[68] As for the four *pensionnaires,* La Teulière spoke highly of them in his appraisals of their efforts, and judged them worthy of privileges not accorded to earlier students. The sculptors were allowed to do independent work, and the painters were proposed to continue the project of recording Raphael's frescoes in the Vatican *Stanze* in cartoons for the Gobelins tapestry works.[69] Mignard, however, in consultation with Villacerf, did not believe that students could devote the time or skill necessary to that task, and he recommended the job be given over to established professionals.[70] At the same time, he also suggested that Raphael was no longer a suitable model for impressionable young Frenchmen, which shows how far the pendulum of taste had swung, and how wide the gulf between Paris and Rome had grown, even as early as 1691.

With no work for his students, dwindling finances, and few apologists for his cause in Paris, La Teulière's position was already dangerously untenable by 1692. This explains the edge of panic that can be sensed in much of his correspondence around that time,[71] particularly in several quite long letters to Villacerf which plead for recognition from Paris of La Teulière's own efforts, of the accomplishments and foresight of both his and Villacerf's predecessors in founding and nurturing the academy in Rome, and of the plight of his students who had been set adrift in a city largely hostile to them.[72] Goaded by the latter, he often vented his frustrations with the Italians. He included even Maratti, who, though he had been instrumental in getting the French their renewed access to the Vatican, had simultaneously been complaining to the pope about not being paid for earlier work for the king.[73] But Maratti and other Roman artists, like Domenico Guidi, Giovanni

Maria Morandi, or G. B. Gaulli, all eminent members of the Accademia, would also be of assistance to La Teulière in his hour of need, providing constructive commentary on the work of his students.[74] This suggests that a vestige of the aggregation accords remained in effect, regarding the availability of one faculty to the other institution. And given that de Rossi was at this time *principe* of the Accademia, it is very likely that other components of those accords were observed as well, as they had been just before and during his first principate in 1681. The resources of the Accademia may have been available to La Teulière's charges, making up some of the differences between what he could provide and what they needed.

Bereft of support from Paris, and devoid as he once was of an academic or artistic background, La Teulière would have had difficulty pulling the French academy in Rome through this trying time on his own devices, without some kind of informed assistance. Nineteenth-century historians, who were as yet unaware that La Teulière existed, even went so far as to suggest that the aggregation accords may have been invoked to put the Accademia's *principe* in charge at the French academy during a supposed lapse in its directorship from 1684 to 1699.[75] Though this was not the case, it is possible that La Teulière may have accepted some informal direction from the Romans, in deference to the earlier association between their academies, and de Rossi would have been quite willing and able to give it. The motive he, or any academician who followed his lead, may have had need be no different from what it was at the time of the aggregation: to ensure his being remembered at the French court. As has been seen, Carlo Fontana brought the same motive with him to the post of *principe* in 1694, and his already documented contact with La Teulière may have included the extension of institutional courtesies.

With the situation improving for Roman artists, La Teulière needed "friends" in the papal court far more than the Italians needed any in Paris, for at the very same time that his academy was faced with closure it was also faced with eviction. The pope, in casting around for a location for a general hospital for the city, had settled upon

the Palazzo Caffarelli, which housed the French academy.[76] On a visit to inspect the building, however, Innocent was so surprised by the academy's impressive inventory of statuary and equipment, and so swayed by the inconvenience to relocate it, that he retracted his decision.[77] Innocent made this visit in the company of an unidentified architect; either de Rossi or Carlo Fontana, each of whom was involved at this time on the *Curia Innocenziana,* could have been the pope's adviser in this case, and might even have prompted the pontiff to make his fortuitous discovery. Circumstantial though it may be, there is evidence for an informal and unstated bond between the Accademia di San Luca and the Académie de France in Rome to their mutual benefit in the 1690s, forged from the remnants of the aggregation of 1676.[78]

For La Teulière, faced in 1694 with the necessity of cutbacks, even a limited revival of the aggregation accords, which after all had never been abrogated, provided a means to alleviate some of his problems. To save the academy in Rome, Villacerf had called upon him to make reductions across the board: in student pensions (he even suggested sending two of what were then five *pensionnaires* home), in the faculty (the professors of mathematics and anatomy were dismissed), in the time for which the live model was hired, in the expenditures on supplies, and in the space leased for the academy's use.[79] If the Accademia could be opened to the French, however, making available to them its lecturers, models, and other resources, La Teulière could recoup most of what he would have to sacrifice. The only exception would be the funds for pensions and supplies, which La Teulière eventually had to contribute himself, in the vain hope of someday being reimbursed. But perhaps he had foreseen an additional objective in rebuilding ties between the two academies.

This can best be sensed in his lengthy letter of response to Villacerf's demands for a retrenchment at the school in Rome, in which La Teulière fought doggedly to be allowed to continue at the *status quo.*[80] His reasons were couched in references that are peculiarly nonacademic. To paraphrase him: Rome was an international focus of diplomacy, rife with intrigues, and the French academy there was an important rallying point for partisans of the king, who must uphold the French cause within a "théâtre exposé." His previous and subsequent dispatches often contain accounts of the impressions made on foreign visitors to the academy, and on the local climate of opinion regarding Louis's war against the League.[81] La Teulière's academy could no longer exist in the isolation to which it had been relegated in the 1680s if it was to be prominent in the "théâtre exposé" on which he intended to report. A resumption of relations with the Accademia was a readily accessible route to this end, as well as to gaining the favor, whether papal, civil, or professional, that the French academy now needed to secure its very existence.

This albeit conjectural conclusion, made for want of primary documentation, is nonetheless necessary if it is to be possible to establish the sort of academic experience a young French architect could expect to be provided when in Rome. After all, La Teulière was at best an amateur in the fields of painting and sculpture, who had absolutely no initiation in the art of architecture. And yet, in the 1690s, after a lapse of several years, Paris was again sending student architects to Rome to receive their final instruction under La Teulière's direction. Among them was Giles-Marie Oppenord, whose name is the most prominent gracing the roll of architects pensioned at the academy in Rome in the seventeenth century. There is no disagreement in the scholarship that Oppenord's nearly seven years of study at Rome (1692–99) were critical to the development of his mature style, which was central to the Rococo.[82] But the sources are also too willing to take for granted the part La Teulière played in organizing his studies. For the first two years of his stay, Oppenord was neither housed at nor pensioned by the impoverished academy, so even if La Teulière were adequate to the task he had little control over the youth's activities.[83] From the start, therefore, Oppenord was free to pursue his own interests in all manner of Roman Baroque ornament.[84] For Oppenord's entire tenure in Rome, La Teulière was never able to put together more of an impression of him than that

he was personable, imaginative, energetic, and an extremely competent draftsman.[85]

As for the work Oppenord was charged to do in Rome, Villacerf, who had sent him there and was intent on his progress, tried many times to dictate to him in the same way that Colbert had to D'Aviler in the 1670s (see Chapter II), but La Teulière was no Errard when it came to implementing such wishes. When Oppenord was finally granted a pension in 1694,[86] he was to employ himself with the study of the figure, from the antique and from Raphael, like any other student academician; Villacerf apparently had plans to put him in charge of the statuary at Versailles.[87] To La Teulière's eye, Oppenord acquitted himself well in this regard, even to the point of working on his own figure group in marble,[88] but at the same time he devoted himself in earnest to a recording of modern Roman architecture and decoration.

La Teulière makes mention in his letters of Oppenord's detailed studies after Vignola's Villa Caprarola, and the great basilicas of Rome built or remodeled since St. Peter's: S. Giovanni in Laterano, S. Ignazio, and S. Andrea della Valle (including Michelangelo's Strozzi Chapel).[89] There are also numerous references to the several volumes of sketches that Oppenord was producing, and the six that survive (distributed between the Louvre, the Kunstbibliothek in Berlin, and the Cooper Hewitt Museum in New York) attest to his fascination with the works of Bernini, Borromini, Pietro da Cortona, and their contemporaries.[90] In other words, with the exception of Vignola, Oppenord was discovering a Rome that no other French academician had ever been allowed to see. Like a child let loose in a candy shop, he gorged himself in particular on the plastic qualities of Roman planning, articulation, and ornament, which would once have been denied him, but which would now inform his personal Rococo idiom. Not even Villacerf's injunctions to verify the measurements of ancient architecture made in the 1680s by Desgodetz, or to study Italian garden design,[91] could distract Oppenord from his investigations.

At this point, in 1696, La Teulière came to Oppenord's defense with some observations on architecture in Rome that are surprisingly well developed for someone who had as yet shown no independent capacity for such. As for verifying Desgodetz's measurements, it was La Teulière's opinion that Rome's ancient monuments had been so eroded or buried by time that it would be impossible to be precise about the original proportions, and so other sites outside the city, or even in Greece or Syria, might be better for this purpose.[92] To his thinking, the study of motifs rather than proportions would be more productive; to this end, an experience of architecture outside the treatises of the past was essential, and the architecture of the last one hundred years in Rome provided the richest resource for instruction.[93] La Teulière's advice was meant to read as though it were his own, but this cannot be reconciled with either his background or his silence on architectural philosophy up to this time. He may have been transmitting Oppenord's own arguments, but it must be remembered that what they were arguing for was directly contrary to the ideologies of the French architectural establishment, and could therefore have posed a serious threat to both of their careers. They could be sure of themselves only with a recognized authority backing up their opinions, and on the face of it the authority they could have been counting on was Carlo Fontana's.

It was Fontana who impressed upon his students the need to learn by sketching and rendering from the more recent examples of Rome's great architectural tradition, rather than by refining the details or measurements of a deeper past. It was his eclectic method, distilled over the preceding few generations of that tradition, that encouraged an encompassing experience of all of its elements, and not just what had been labored about in the literature. To see Oppenord's sketchbooks is to come upon something totally unexpected from a French academic, but something familiar to anyone who had witnessed the same intensity of effort and scope of attention, the same hunger, in the volumes of sketches produced by Juvarra a decade later as a pupil of Fontana. The differences in the two oeuvres are mostly a function of the two architects' orientations to their medium: Oppenord the decorator, and Juvarra the

scenographic composer. Otherwise the spirits that they reveal, if not the drawing techniques, are quite similar.

Part of the explanation, perhaps a large part, is that Oppenord was less fettered than architecture students at the Académie de France in Rome when Errard was their master, and therefore more subject to the influence of general Roman attitudes. But with the assurance of a unity between Fontana's studio and the architecture curriculum at the Accademia, and the possibility of covert relations between the Accademia and its French counterpart, it may be that a direct route was open to Fontana's counsel for Oppenord. He would have been forced to take that route because he could have had no counsel of any kind on architectural matters from his own academy. And he would have been attracted by the reputation Fontana's workshop then had with regard to the work it was doing and the young drafting talent it represented. The situation is comparable to that in 1677, when Fontana's links with the Accademia were weaker but those of the French academy were stronger, and when Claude Desgots in particular took the same route to inform his design for the *concorso* of that year (see Chapter II). And as in that earlier instance, it is not necessary to suppose that Oppenord actually worked in any capacity in Fontana's studio, but only that he had access to it, and could learn from its example.[94]

For better or worse, depending on whether one mourns the fate of the Baroque as it gives way to the Rococo, it would seem that the learning environment in which Oppenord found himself in Rome, and the freedom and empiricism he encountered there, helped to determine the role he would play in that change of taste. It may not be wise to exaggerate Carlo Fontana's part in this, any more than it would be to exaggerate Oppenord's contributions to the Rococo. Still, taking even the broadest Roman view, it would have appeared that the city now had something to offer by way of example to the French in return for the rigorous organizational model that had been provided to them in the 1670s. The French system was perceivably breaking up on the rocks of its own conservatism (in the case of the Académie Royale), or pinioning itself into immobility (in the case of the Académie d'Architecture), and could very well learn something of advantage from the more liberal approach of Fontana or the Accademia. Oppenord was certainly not immune to the consequences, and just how infected he was is underscored by his treatment upon his return to Paris in 1699.

Villacerf may have had plans for Oppenord, but in that same year Villacerf retired, for reasons of health and the intimidations of high office in Louis's court.[95] Jules Hardouin-Mansart was now superintendent and in supreme command of all architectural thought and action. Oppenord, having for so long been outside the reach of Hardouin-Mansart's authority, had developed inclinations antithetical to it, and therefore received little official recognition. He did not emerge fully into the history of French architecture until the *Régence,* as the favorite of the Duc d'Orleans, for whom he remodeled the Palais Royal.[96] His most intriguing design there was for the Salon d'Angle (1719–20, Fig. 106), which once joined the apartments to the gallery at the corner of the *piano nobile,* but has since been destroyed. In it, the lower coved vault opened up, through a balustraded oculus of mixed-line contour, into a second vaulted chamber; the four windows around the circumference of the latter thus became an indirect source of illumination for the space below. The motif is similar in conception to the elder Mansart's staircase at Blois, but even more, because the light chamber has only that function and is treated like a drum and dome, to Carlo Fontana's final design for the baptistry of St. Peter's (Fig. 107),[97] and to Gherardi's chapel of S. Cecilia (see Fig. 53), both of which were near completion before Oppenord left Rome.

Given these precedents, Oppenord's salon becomes an offshoot of the line of thought that has already been traced with regard to the designs for the *concorso* of 1677, when the idea of the truncated dome was first introduced to Rome by French students of architecture (see Chapter II; compare Pl. 6). Oppenord in effect closed the collateral branch of the motif's development then opened by his fellow countrymen, by rejoining it to the parent tradition. Whether he appreciated

his achievement in this same way depends on how deeply he delved into the Accademia's archive, which would have attracted him with its examples of fine draftsmanship.[98] Of the possible goads to the generation of Oppenord's salon design—the baptistry, the designs from 1677, or the academic inquiries that linked them—any one or all three would have been reinforced by whatever connection can now be assumed between Oppenord and Fontana's studio, or between the two academies in Rome.

Hardouin-Mansart proceeded to work his mischief at the Académie de France in Rome, just as he did everywhere else, when it came under his jurisdiction in 1699. After narrowly escaping disenfranchisement five years earlier, La Teulière would have at first noticed a distinct improvement in the official attitude toward his stewardship. When the crisis in 1694 was past, Villacerf wrote to La Teulière to assure him that there was no one in Paris bearing witness against him, and that he should have no fear for his position.[99] La Teulière had no doubt struck the right chord with his willingness to put up a good front (even though scraping by and often at his own cost) and his promise to pass on the gossip of Rome. For the moment this was all that was required of him. Then, near the end of hostilities in 1697, came impressions of a return to normalcy, with the resumption of shipments of works of art, copies, and materials from Civita Vecchia to Paris, and the reinstitution of the competitions for pensions in Rome.[100] La Teulière already had five very talented artists under his care, with a community of unpensioned artists loosely tied to him; now more could be expected to arrive and with the best credentials. But when Hardouin-Mansart took over the superintendency, La Teulière seems to have known what to expect. His first two letters to his new superior are perhaps the most groveling of all, as he begged to be allowed to continue in the king's service as director of his academy in Rome. At first Mansart consented, but then he arranged for the appointment of the painter René-Antoine Houasse to replace La Teulière.[101] This action has been put down as one of the usual base intrigues of Louis's court, and indeed Mansart not only

106 GILES-MARIE OPPENORD: section of the Salon d'Angle in the Palais Royal; Paris, 1719–20 (source: Cooper-Hewitt Museum of the Smithsonian Institution/Art Resource, New York; gift of the Council).

107 CARLO FONTANA: interior of the baptistry of St. Peter's; Rome, 1696 (engraving: de Rossi).

played false with La Teulière but denied him just compensation for the expenses he had incurred.[102] But if there was reasonable intent at all, it may just be that it was time to put aside the role of the academy in Rome as factory, or purchasing agent, or tool of diplomacy, and to make it again an academy of artists with an artist in charge. With the close of the seventeenth century, an era was ending at the Académie de France in Rome, just as one was at the Accademia.

COMPETITIONS IN THE FIRST CLASS: POMPEO FERRARI

Besides the principate of Carlo Fontana and the centennial year at the Accademia, another factor which binds together the *concorsi* of 1694 and 1696 is the participation of Pompeo Ferrari, who

took first prize for the first class in both years. One of the last of a line of Italian architects who played out their careers in Poland, he has had little attention in the general literature, though the sources on Polish architecture credit him with no small contribution there.[103] The date of birth usually given for him (1660) is not at all certain, since it seems to have been arrived at from the dates inscribed on his competition entries (1678 and 1681; App. A, nos. 25–27, 41–43), which like so many others were erroneously applied in 1756.[104] His origins are no doubt Roman, and on the basis of his mature work he is even called a "follower of Borromini,"[105] but this must be given some qualification. His technique in his winning drawings betrays a precision and coloration identical to what was practiced in Carlo Fontana's studio, and as the latter was at one with the architecture pro-

gram at the Accademia at this time, it is more reasonable to call Ferrari a student of Fontana. This
can be justified on the grounds of style, as well,
but would still be consistent with a Borrominian
tendency in Ferrari's work, given how open to all
Roman strains Fontana's curriculum proves to be
in general.

1694

The inspiration behind the topic in the first class
for 1694, as derived already from Ferrari's own
entry (Pls. 25–27 and App. A), was Fontana's
Jesuit college at Loyola (see Figs. 96, 97). But a
much grander urban scale of more than one thou-
sand Roman feet along the front was apparently
stipulated, and in the absence of a publicized
soggetto it cannot be certain what further latitude
was allowed the competitors in generating their
own variations on the theme. At this point, it is
helpful for reasons of visual clarity to refer to the
copies made from Ferrari's entry, in half-plan and
half-elevation, by Bernardo Vittone (Figs. 108,
109), when he was a student at the Accademia in
the years before 1732.[106] Vittone's action has its
own significance (see below), but his copies simply
make it easier to read the details of Ferrari's elaborate and extensive project. Though Ferrari's drawings are larger in size than any from earlier
competitions, the scale was not conducive to
detailing. Still, he devoted considerable invention
to it, particularly with regard to the flanking residential and instructional wings. Both at their
facades and around their courtyards there are window and door surrounds of a sophisticated elegance that could easily be labeled Roman Rococo
were the college built twenty-five years later. As it
stands, it would seem at least that Ferrari anticipated the Borrominian revival that would color
the architecture of that period. It is difficult to
detect this revival occurring in anything being
built in Rome at the end of the seventeenth century, and most of all in Fontana's work, so one
must attribute Ferrari's venture to the academic
freedom of the Accademia.[107] But that freedom
had been imparted by Fontana himself, through
the medium of his studio and its methods, and a

feel for its dramatic impact can be had by comparing Ferrari's design to Barigioni's palace of 1692
(see Pl. 23), with its *retardataire* references.

There are other Borrominian devices in
Ferrari's design, like the portal jambs along the
front that are splayed outward at a daring angle, or
the reentrant corners at four points around the
exterior that are filled in to ease their harshness.
The interior plan is run through by uninterrupted
corridors from the front portals to the back wall,
or from side to side, which pick up the courtyard
porticoes on their way, like an expanded version of
Borromini's Filippine Monastery in Rome (Fig.
110). These form the grid for the layout of the
rooms, which are so lucidly, logically, and efficiently arranged that Ferrari's labels are almost
superfluous. The architect had taken into account
both the adornment of his building and the
requirements of communal living, and neither had
suffered.

Ferrari took advantage of the symmetry suggested for his project by Fontana's college, and
tried to magnify the effect of the juxtaposition
between the church of S. Agnese and the Palazzo
Pamphili on the Piazza Navona (see Fig. 2).[108]
Indeed, he has created a creditable urban presence
for the building, with a succession of wall panels,
framed by Composite pilasters, that crescendo in
size and layer forward in space to climax beneath
the seven-bay *belvederi,* before receding again to
adjoin the church facade. In this, each flank of the
facade is comparable to the main front of the
Palazzo Montecitorio, on which Fontana was at
work (Fig. 111), though in detail they are of two
different persuasions.

Ferrari's church is proportionally larger than
the chapel Fontana provided for his college, but in
devising his church Ferrari was otherwise quite
conservative by comparison to the rest of his project. This is particularly true of the cupola and the
interior aspect, which are nothing more than ordinary. Even the facade, which aimed at something
new, can be explained in terms of its models. The
campanili, brought forward from positions behind
Fontana's church (where they were oriented to an
isolated monastery, not a city), are meager reflec-
tions of those at S. Agnese, and less successful in

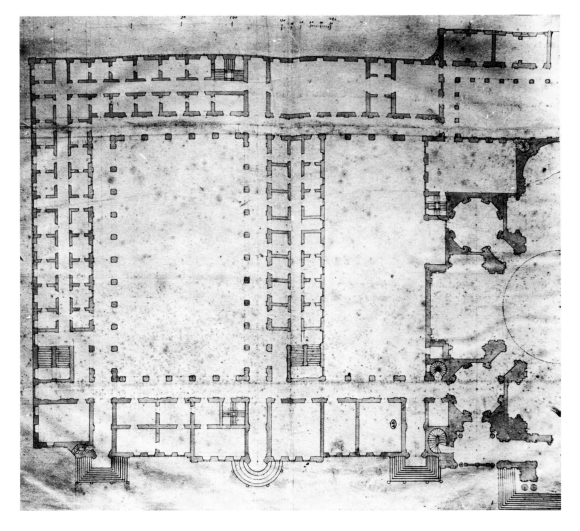

108 BERNARDO VITTONE: half-plan copy of Plate 25 (source: Musée des Arts Décoratifs/Sully-Jaulnes, Paris).

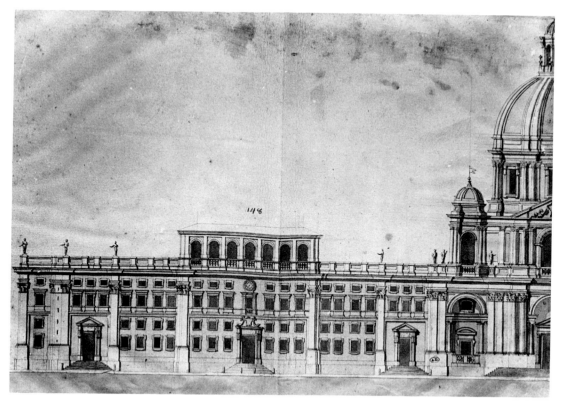

109 VITTONE: half-elevation copy of Plate 26 (source: Musée des Arts Décoratifs/Sully-Jaulnes, Paris).

that they interfere with a view of the cupola, as does the second story. The elements of the facade are well integrated by continuous cornices, in a method Fontana himself preferred, but this is only a two-dimensional way of seeing the problem. In addition, the convex arcaded portico of Fontana's chapel (see Fig. 97), which adds three-dimensional force to its facade, has been so flattened out and broadened by Ferrari as to be timid by comparison. There is serendipity in the chiaroscuro effect of the widely separated arches opening into the deep porch, which almost prefigures the cavernous eighteenth-century facades of S. Giovanni in Laterano or S. Maria Maggiore, but the choice of situating the visual weight of the bell towers over the two outside voids was not a good one. Ferrari seems to have been unable to learn from the ideas put forth by the French in 1677 about how to compose a cupola, facade towers, and portico.

Nevertheless, Ferrari did learn something from the French, though not directly from their contributions in that earlier competition. The plan of his church (Pl. 25, see Fig. 108), with circular spaces at the diagonals, passageways connecting them to the main vessel through the piers, and a layered facade, is derived from Hardouin-Mansart's plan for the Invalides chapel in Paris (see Fig. 49). Ferrari's intriguing choice for the starting point of his design for the church did not particularly inspire him thereafter, however; set upon the plan is a routinely Roman building. Mansart's corner chapels, which were part of an inscribing ambulatory, and were intended to house the tombs of the Bourbon dynasty, have been trivialized by Ferrari into vestibules that give entry to the church from the rest of the complex.[109] In fairness, it may be that Ferrari's knowledge of the Invalides chapel was limited to some notion of the plan, since the

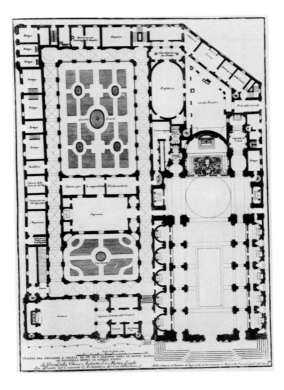

110 FRANCESCO BORROMINI: plan of the
Monastery of S. Filippo Neri; Rome, begun 1637
(engraving: de Rossi).

fabric of Mansart's church had been completed
only two years earlier.[110] But with regard to his
church, Ferrari still seems to have been incapable
of integrating two-dimensional sets of information
into a satisfying whole.[111]

Since the reference to the French church can
only be read in the plan of Ferrari's design, one
wonders why it appears there at all, so prominently and with so little modification. It should be
remembered that the competitions again had an
audience much like the one they had had in 1677,
including not just the Accademia's membership
but the entire international artistic community of
Rome, of which the French were once more a recognized part. Ferrari may have wished to demonstrate the broad scope of his eclecticism in terms
which his public could readily appreciate, but
which could not be misinterpreted as unseemly
plagiarism; the template of Mansart's plan was

used to shape an obviously Roman church. But
there is an edge of magnanimity to his gesture that
should be traced to a higher source than an academy student. Borrowing a motif from a foreign
tradition well known for its intransigence was a
blow aimed at Mansart's own pretensions, which
could be the reason his church was singled out.
There was not even an element of tribute left in
the gesture, for what was to have been his
Bourbon sepulcher had been exploited for quite a
different purpose, and had lost a great deal in
translation. What had been championed instead
was Carlo Fontana's method, which could pick up
or discard ideas at will, based solely on their usefulness and not on either the place or time of their
origin or an arbitrary hierarchy of "propriété." The
message had been phrased so that the French
could readily understand it.

For his models in 1694 Ferrari chose architects
as yet unvenerated: Borromini, Rainaldi, Fontana,
and Hardouin-Mansart. Just to see these four associated together in one design is a curiosity. In one
sense, Ferrari connected Fontana and Hardouin-
Mansart, between whom comparisons have already
been drawn on the basis of their equivalent status
in Rome and Paris respectively. As for Hardouin-
Mansart's and Fontana's association in the design
with Borromini and Rainaldi, the French, in their
disdain for the license of the latter, would have
been far more uncomfortable with this than the
Romans. Ferrari's barb may have been intentional,
to dramatize the difference between the pluralism
of Rome and Fontana's studio, and the narcissism
of Paris, Mansart's domain. The final point is dri-
ven home by literally burying the one French
attribute of the design beneath an exultantly
Roman edifice, as if to redress the wrong done to
Roman self-determination and superiority seventeen years before.

Such nuances of architectural design diplomacy would certainly have been beyond a mere
student, and would have been impressed on Ferrari
only from above. Left to his own devices, he may
have preferred to continue his Borrominian experiments into the church; or church design may not
have been one of his strong points, in which case
he would surely have needed coaching. His coach

111 G. BERNINI AND CARLO FONTANA: the *Curia Innocenziana* (Palazzo Montecitorio); Rome, begun 1650 (engraving: Piranesi).

may have been Francesco Fontana, but the source of the meaning contained in his design was probably Carlo. After all, the elder Fontana was then in the midst of trying to reach the French by other means: through his designs, his publications, or the Accademia's cooperation with the French academy in Rome. The *concorso* of 1694 provided a public vehicle for his efforts, and La Teulière and the rest of the French community of artists in Rome would have been on hand to receive the message being communicated on several levels: the Accademia was again master of its own house.[112]

The designs by the other two prizewinners in the first class in 1694 (Pls. 28–33 and App. A) had little part in this "diplomacy," except to show by contrast the best that could be expected of students who had drawn less benefit from Fontana's example. Andrea della Valle and Carlo Ravassi

were provincial Italians, from Tuscany and Lombardy respectively, who had probably spent only the one year of Francesco Fontana's instructorship thus far in any intimate contact with the Fontana studio. As a result, their draftsmanship, design sense, and presentation techniques are considerably inferior to the standards set by that workshop. And yet they are enough like each other in those respects to indicate that they had shared some common influence since coming to Rome.

Assigning credit for their tutelage would not be kind, since della Valle and Ravassi were abominable draftsmen when compared to any other prizewinning competitor in the early history of the Accademia's *concorsi*. They rise above their own standards only in their section drawings; perhaps the monotony of the detailing in both cases gave them the required edge. Their plans can only be

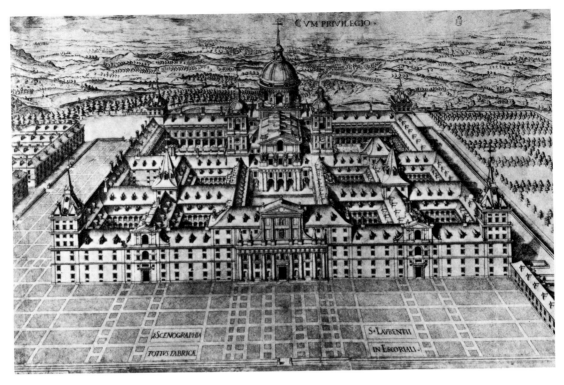

112 J. B. DE TOLEDO AND J. DE HERRERA: the Escorial; Madrid, begun 1563 (engraving: P. Perrer).

described as labyrinthine; for the sake of compre-hension, their designs should have had the labels that Ferrari had included unnecessarily. But there are other indications of questionable competence, beyond their technical failings, which include errors that no novice architect in any reputable Roman studio could be expected to make. They did not know how many steps made up a flight of stairs, or how to accomplish a consistent ridge line by varying the pitch of the roofs. Whoever had initiated della Valle's and Ravassi's training in Rome was either not equipped for the challenge represented by their provincial talents, or was not impressed enough by them to devote the necessary effort to remaking those talents. Their brief expo-sure to the Fontana studio in advance of the com-petition in 1694 would have made for little more progress, especially since their approach to the topic in that year distances them further from Fontana's circle.

They went to their work with an entirely dif-ferent model in mind from Fontana's Loyola com-plex, which had presumably inspired the task for the *concorso* and had guided Ferrari's concept. For their inspiration, della Valle and Ravassi chose (or had chosen for them) another Spanish monastic college, the Escorial in Madrid, Philip II's royal retreat by the architects Juan Bautista de Toledo and Juan de Herrera (Fig. 112).[113] This reference lies behind the more pretentious scale of their pro-jects and certain details like the roof dormers. They even made specific use of the perspective view of the monastery produced in 1587 by the Flemish artist Peter Perrer, to inform their efforts at presenting their designs. They understood this model only superficially, however, and the results are unsatisfactory.

Their numerous mistakes in judgement show them to have been incapable of conceiving their designs as the logical integration of masses and volumes; their lack of this sixth sense essential to an architectural talent is amplified by their perspective views, which constituted a choice of presentation method that could sorely test the skills of even the best draftsman. Their decision to proceed with this technique, when their designs could easily have withstood presentation in plan, elevation, and section as prescribed in general for the competitions, is an indication of how dependent upon Perrer's view they ultimately were. Like that view, della Valle's and Ravassi's bird's-eye renderings are not true perspectives, but oblique isometric projections with convergence forced upon them to mimic the perspective effect. Their shorthand method saved them many of the complex geometric operations that would otherwise have been needed, but by the same token it is questionable whether any additional information beyond what is in the plans and sections is given. In the Fontana circle, such methods were reserved for circumstances where only one rudimentary view of a building was possible, such as in medals, and Figure 102 provides an example of this specific to the *Curia Innocenziana* that may also have informed della Valle and Ravassi. But in their designs, and at their hands, given the level of detail required for competition, their approach creates more problems than it solves.

Where their perspective views could have done the most good, that is in making clear the spatial compositions of the elements of their churches, the two stopped completely short of Perrer's success. They indicated the church fronts only in flat projection, and then devised flimsy architectural fictions in perspective behind them to try to cover up their actions. The fictions are transparent, and the designs are in fact diminished by them even more than if straightforward facade elevations had been presented instead. The church was, after all, meant to be the climax of the facade, but treating it as a stage flat applied to the visually distracting isometric projection effectively drains it of that potential. In neither design was much thought given to the churches; each was simply inserted into its surroundings without concern for coherent integration. Della Valle's is a woefully prosaic recapitulation of the Accademia's own church, Pietro da Cortona's SS. Luca e Martina (Figs. 113, 114), combined at the facade with ele-

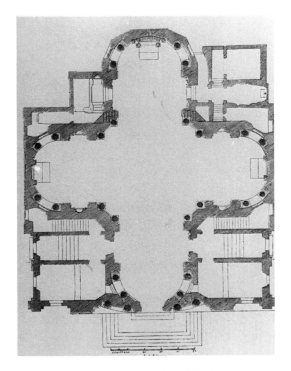

113 PIETRO DA CORTONA: plan of SS. Luca e Martina; Rome, 1635–64 (engraving: Venturini).

ments derived from Cortona's S. Maria della Pace (Fig. 115). The offspring of this union was a mongrel, devoid of the spirited ornamental or scenographic qualities of its progenitors, and crowned rather indifferently with the mandatory but innocuous bell towers. Ravassi's church is a somewhat more original and more richly ornamented variation on the Roman longitudinal-oval type, but his plan shows him to have been totally unprepared to deal with that particular centralized geometry.[114] His facade design is based on the facade of S. Caterina a Magnanapoli (Fig. 116), but it can be seen in section to be not at all the logical consequence of the interior situation, and can therefore be condemned on that count.

It is only a slight difference in the degree of criticism that can be leveled at both of them on all counts that separates della Valle's second-prize from Ravassi's third-prize effort. Otherwise, their entries were by far outclassed by Ferrari's and in previous years might well have been withheld

114 PIETRO DA CORTONA: facade of SS. Luca e Martina (photo: author).

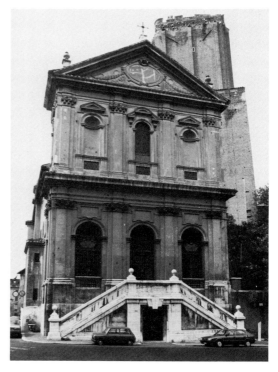

116 G. B. SORIA: facade of S. Caterina a Magnanapoli; Rome, 1638–40 (photo: author).

115 PIETRO DA CORTONA: facade of S. Maria della Pace; Rome, 1656–58 (engraving: Vasi).

from competition or passed over for any award. But in 1694, Fontana wanted to put the *concorso* in architecture on a par with those in the other media, and so three prizes had to be dispensed, fortunately for della Valle and Ravassi. In actuality, however, everyone gained. The Accademia had more in the way of architectural designs to display to the public when the *concorso* was celebrated, and the second- and third-place designs were at least good enough to be impressive under those circumstances. Fontana gained, too, in that it would have been obvious, to everyone with the least amount of professional awareness, whose tutelage had been responsible for Ferrari's competitive advantage.

1696

Even so, it was wise of Fontana to postpone the next *concorso* until the end of the Secular Year, so that those of his students who were back in the

117 CARLO MADERNO AND G. BERNINI: facade of the Barberini Palace; Rome, 1628–33 (engraving: Piranesi).

ranks could have time to advance themselves sufficiently to allow for full participation in the upper
classes. For the *concorso* of 1696, with time in
abundance, each class was also given an incremen-
tally greater task, in order to guarantee an
unequaled spectacle. In this year of stiffer competition and more demanding topics, an even more
mature Ferrari was no less equal to the challenge,
taking first prize in the first class again.[115] He handled the topic of a villa palace for four dignitaries
with the same poise with which he had addressed
his monastic college (with the exception of his
facade drawing where haste obscured his drafting
ability; Pls. 41–43). But this time he was prepared
to be a bit more resourceful, and to demonstrate
his fluency in an alternative stylistic language and
his grasp of a different typology. The language is
much more that of his master, Fontana, and
Baroque classicism in general, and Ferrari's palace
facade can therefore more aptly be compared with
the Palazzo Montecitorio (see Fig. 111) in its window enframements.

In accordance with the villa setting, Ferrari
lessened the severity of his model by articulating
his palace with pilaster strips rather than a
Colossal Order, and by pairing together the windows on the corner pavilions to create a more
informal rhythm. It also seems that Ferrari wished
to refer to another monument in the Berninian
line, the Palazzo Barberini (Fig. 117), which had
been Bernini's first experience in palace design, in
collaboration with his own master, Carlo
Maderno. Not only was this the family palace of
the Accademia's Cardinal Protector, but it had also
been conceived by Maderno in terms of a subur-
ban villa.[116] It is therefore the more likely source of
Ferrari's pilaster strip articulation, and unquestionably the source of the motif of the frontispiece
set between *avant-corps*. Ferrari even applied a
similar architectural scheme to his frontispiece,
though reducing it to five bays: an engaged Tuscan
order for the first-story arcade, Ionic for the second, and pilasters (Tuscan again rather than
Corinthian) for the third. He modified his model

in order to ease the transitions: from fenestration to arcading, by merging the two in the outside bays of the frontispiece and along its third story; and from pilaster strips to engaged columns, by using pilasters at the extremes of the frontispiece. He could have learned these lessons from Michelangelo's alterations to the courtyard and river facade of the Palazzo Farnese.

The most unusual characteristic of the Palazzo Barberini is that its frontispiece, in function and articulation, is a substitute for the courtyard elevation that the palace lacks. Because of the traditional layout of Ferrari's block palace, its ground-story vestibules open in successive stages toward the central courtyard rather than the facade, but in this more usual context Ferrari was in fact more original in his thinking. In the plan (see Pl. 41), there is the same organizational logic that was detected in his design for 1694. The private apartments of the four residents are grouped at the corners, and separated from one another by the spaces at the center of each wing that are devoted to public use: *sala terrena, salone,* and *belvedere* (see the section, Pl. 43). Each set of apartments is provided with a private courtyard as well, of circular plan, and here for the first and only time Ferrari turned to his textbooks for inspiration. The smaller courts are based on the representation in Serlio's treatise of Bramante's unexecuted project for the piazza of the *Tempietto* at S. Pietro in Montorio (Fig. 118).[117]

The centralized geometries of these *cortili* facilitate the reading of Ferrari's project as four autonomous *palazzetti* that have come together at the major axes of a new palace block, the main courtyard of which they share in common. The connection is made through the porticoes of all five courts, which are joined through two stories at the corners of the main courtyard, and by the extension at these same points of the cylindrical volume of the minor courts into the cubic volume of the major one. Such a transformation of an otherwise drab corner into an occasion for architectural drama again betrays Ferrari's sympathy for Borromini's accomplishments, the most pertinent of which in this case would be the cloister of the Trinitarian monastery of S. Carlino (Fig. 119).

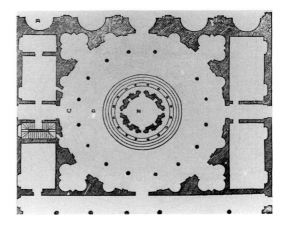

118 DONATO BRAMANTE: project plan for the courtyard and *Tempietto* at S. Pietro in Montorio; Rome, 1503 (engraving: Serlio).

With the third story of each circular court in Ferrari's project receding deeply in a taut arc away from the adjacent straight wings, the corners of the main courtyard become the focal point of an interplay of rectilinear and curvilinear planes and volumes, and of a variety of intriguing scenographic vistas. One's attention is drawn appropriately to the corners since it is in the diagonal directions that the individual residences lie.

The effect would have been analogous to that envisioned by Carlo Fontana in his unaccepted projects for the courtyard of the *Curia Innocenziana* (Fig. 120). The possibilities were no doubt impressed upon Ferrari directly while a student of the Fontanas in 1694, but he arrived at a unique, and perhaps even independent, expression of them. This is less true of his solution for the piazza in front of his palace, as defined by the semicircular plan of the stables opposite it. Here there is no mistaking the reference to one of Fontana's early projects for the curia, which included offices for the notaries in the place where Ferrari has indicated quarters for the grooms and stablehands (see Figs. 101, 102). Still, Ferrari was more himself in his considerate articulation of these utilitarian structures, which after all form an important part of the view from the main front of the palace, and in his efficient arrangement of their parts within awkward boundaries.

119 FRANCESCO BORROMINI: cloister of the Monastery of S. Carlo alle Quattro
Fontane; Rome, 1638–41 (photo: author).

120 CARLO FONTANA: project perspective for the courtyard of the *Curia Innocenziana;* Rome, 1694 (source: Windsor Castle, Royal Library, Her Majesty Queen Elizabeth II).

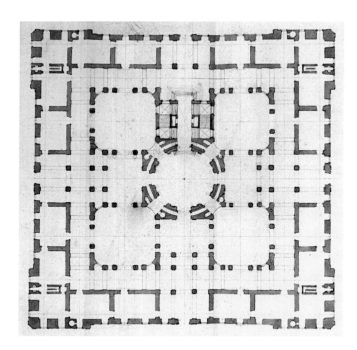

121 FONTANA: project plan (preferred) for the Liechtenstein Garden Palace (source: Windsor Castle, Royal Library, Her Majesty Queen Elizabeth II).

The connection between the first-class *soggetto* in 1696 and Fontana's project for the Liechtenstein villa sheds a singular light on the relationship between the master and his apprentice Ferrari. In addition to the practical solution to the prince's demands that Fontana submitted (see Figs. 104, 105), he had also devoted considerable time and paper to his first idealized projects for the palace. One such project (Fig. 121) was brought to quite a finished state of rendering, and apparently proposed to the prince in the hope of converting him to Fontana's ideals.[118] The actual pursuit of those ideals seems to have been of greatest importance to Fontana, and not surprisingly those same ideals appear in Ferrari's plan for his palace block in 1696 (see Pl. 41).

Fontana apparently preferred a centralized scheme, with the tower at the focus and the rest of the building disposed within the limits of a square and divided into four equal quadrants by the corridors radiating from the tower. As in Ferrari's scheme, each quadrant would thus be provided with its own courtyard, linked to the others by the common portico ringing the interior of the perimeter wings of the building. Each quadrant also contains a separate set of apartments (twice the number required by Liechtenstein but equal to the number required by the *soggetto*), and is pavilioned at the corner. There are several significant exceptions to exact parallel between Fontana's and Ferrari's designs. The common ground in Fontana's palace was the rotunda, and not a central courtyard, which gives his design the sense of a Romanized Palladian villa, and stands for his own allusion to a sixteenth-century treatise. The four diagonal courts in Fontana's plan are square, since for him a circular geometry was appropriate only at the center; but the corners of his *cortili* are blunted in Borrominian fashion, just as those of Ferrari's major courtyard were.

Even their two facade elevations (see Fig. 105 and Pl. 42) represent departures within basic commonalities. What derives from this is an appreciation of how alike the thinking of the two architects had become, yet how different the products of their thinking could be. The first was a function of their intimacy up to this time, while the second was a result both of the advantages adhering to their empiric method, and of their contrasting personalities. Though Ferrari had yet to define an idiom for himself, he could not, by the same token, be described as idiosyncratic. Fontana was perhaps one of the last of the Baroque architects who could be saddled with such a label, some would say to the detriment of his position in the history of style. On the other hand, in Ferrari he had formed one of the architects of the Settecento, a generation which could move at random through the legacy left them by the Baroque century to select whatever stylistic means suited a particular end. How close the turning point was in 1696 can be felt upon the observation of how difficult it would be to choose one design, Fontana's or Ferrari's, as superior to the other.

There are, after all, passages of brilliance in Ferrari's project which are illuminated all the more by a comparison with Carlo Pacenti's third-place entry for the first class in 1696 (Pls. 47–49 and App. A). According to the inscriptions on his drawings, Pacenti was also a Roman, and the techniques and skill evident in his rendering suggest that he was tutored in it by the Fontana workshop. Add to this the general similarities between

his presentation and Ferrari's and it seems certain that the two had worked in close proximity, most likely in Fontana's studio.

The crux of Pacenti's design was the transverse-oval esplanade between his villa palace and stables, taking a cue from Piazza S. Pietro, a project that had involved Fontana and figured prominently in his *Tempio Vaticano*. Pacenti's imagination was nearly expended with his employment of the oval, however, and in fact he became so much a slave to it that his design suffered. He simplistically planned the stables and carriage houses to follow the outline and radii of the oval, oblivious to the awkwardnesses this caused, and showing none of the ingenuity Ferrari had shown under similar circumstances. The opposite side of the oval was used to determine the plan of one palace facade, and from there the three other facades as well, with deep reentrant angles at the corners to join them. Unfortunately he chose an ordinary square plan for the interior court which does not interact at all with the dynamic of the exterior, and between the two he was left with a confused jumble of rooms "calculated" to adjust to the two opposed geometries. There is none of the lucidity that is to be found in Ferrari's arrangement, and that a villa usually called for. Indeed, it is not immediately clear how the four sets of apartments would divide themselves among the available spaces. Pentimenti on his ground plan (App. A, no. 47) indicate that Pacenti had at one time intended to dissociate the apartments as Ferrari had, at the center of each wing through the intervention of commodious vestibules, salons, and staircases. He retained this solution at the main palace front, but altered it at the other three into something much more humble, each time with a different but smaller stairway, so that the subdivisions are no longer clear.[119]

The chapel in Pacenti's design (H on the plan) is another interesting element, despite its incidental relationship to the whole. From its Greek-cross plan, four roughly square forms extend outward in the diagonal directions, the two at the front representing the towers which are thus skewed at a forty-five-degree angle to the entrance bay. The resulting diffraction of light and surface across the facade was the closest Pacenti came to working in a Borrominian mode, since the broad concave facades of the palace cannot be understood in the same terms. Pacenti positioned the church front at one open end of the oval piazza, mirroring it at the other end with, of all things, an aviary that mimics it in appearance and is visible in the elevation drawing (see Pl. 48). Church and aviary are necessarily off axis because of the extent of the stable wings, but nevertheless an attractive view of them, asymmetrically framed by the palace and stables, could be had upon entering the forecourt. Indeed, for all of the approaches to the complex, Pacenti seems to have kept in mind the variety and quality of the views, and arrival from between or around the stable wings would be particularly dramatic visually.

If Pacenti learned this lesson well, he was an average student otherwise. His drafting was certainly more developed than his judgement (in this he was like most novice architects of his day), but he took few opportunities to show his skill through architectural decoration. The elevation of Pacenti's palace for the most part refers to Carlo Fontana's most significant palace project, the Palazzo Montecitorio (see Fig. 111). Though different in plan, the two fronts are nearly identical in composition and articulation. Pacenti made only some minor changes: He rusticated the ground story (replacing quoins with herms); he extended the engaged portico at the entry to seven bays; he replaced the campanile with a belvedere (which is, by the way, reminiscent of Fontana's cupola for the Liechtenstein project, without the dome; cf. Fig. 105); and he surmounted the windows of his second *piano nobile* with a series of broken pediments.

Upon comparative analysis, it is understandable that Ferrari's design was awarded a higher place in the *concorso* of 1696 than Pacenti's. But Pacenti had nevertheless presented a considerably greater challenge to Ferrari than the latter's competition two years before, and had narrowed the gap between first and third place while the level of accomplishment in both was being raised. And behind their efforts the hand of Fontana is readily detected: defining their task, determining their

method, molding their skills, and providing their examples. Their success was his success, and the *concorso* of 1696, which celebrated the rejuvenation of the Accademia and of Roman pride, became his tribute as well. The tribute was not only to Fontana the architect and teacher, but to the *principe* who had elevated the status of the architectural *concorsi,* and had seen to it that advanced design judgement was rewarded as much as advanced skill, and familiarity with recent ideas as much as respect for the timeless. In consequence, it is difficult to understand why the judges in architecture, Tomassini and Contini, in the presence of their colleague Fontana, saw fit to award the second prize in the first class in 1696 to the design by the French architectural student Charles Derbais (Pls. 44–46 and App. A).

Derbais's participation in the *concorso* is not the problem. That door was presumably opened by the resumption of tentative relations between the two academies in Rome over the preceding few years. Though Derbais was not an official *pensionnaire* of his academy, a loose interpretation of the two-decades-old aggregation articles could have gained him access to the competition, especially if he had some tie with a Roman studio (Fontana's?). It is even possible, though by no means certain, that the French academy's prized pupil, Giles Oppenord, contemplated submitting an entry of his own to this *concorso*.[120] As mentioned in an earlier context, the attention of the French would have been inevitably drawn to the *concorso* by the *soggetto,* which seems to have been phrased intentionally to be a gauntlet thrown at their feet. The underlying French theme could even explain the vague references to Bernini's Louvre projects (cf. Figs. 71 and 72) in Pacenti's design, or to the plan of his model project (Fig. 122) in Ferrari's. Rather than being upstaged, the French turn out to have had at least one champion who could meet the challenge, and come away with second prize. But the problem lies in that showing, for by most of the standards of good design, including some espoused by Derbais's own tradition, his *château* is execrable.

Knowing what he was up against, Derbais did try to enhance his entry: His section and perspective renderings (see Pls. 45, 46) were of gigantic length (eight and eleven feet respectively). They are overwhelming advertisements of the drafting precision that could be expected of any French student, even when working in their characteristic but taxing monochromatic technique. The gradations of shading Derbais used to distinguish various qualities of light and space in these two drawings are particularly fine. Also, the perspective is a true one, for the first time in the history of the *concorsi*. On the basis of presentation, Derbais gave his judges ample reason to consider his effort. But then Derbais tried to compound the impression his project might have by amplifying the scale of the building itself, and from this point on his actions turned against him.

As Derbais provided no measurement on the drawings, it is necessary to derive the scale indirectly. The only convenient unit to work from is one of the horse stalls in the stable wings, which if taken to be about five feet in span makes the dimension of the site approximately 900 by 1,400 feet. The smallest room in the habitable wings of the *château* would be roughly 60 by 100 feet in size; each courtyard would be 600 feet square. The magnitude of this conception is worthy of Louis XIV, perhaps, but as a villa for four court dignitaries it goes beyond the Grand Manner to the ridiculous. Derbais continued to belabor his point by combining elements from the articulative schemes of the Louvre and Versailles (cf. Figs. 90 and 91) and applying the mix uniformly to the exterior of his palace, almost entirely without pause, accent, or any indication of sculpture to provide relief. This is not an intimate villa retreat as the Italians would have it; its rhetoric is ponderous in the extreme and could never be integrated with a plantation, but could only dominate it.

Though Derbais had captured the essence of Versailles, it is doubtful that his design would have been any more tolerable to contemporary French tastes. The stylistic language in which it was expressed was already falling out of fashion, and the scheme of the plan—three residential wings overlooking a *cours d'honneur,* closed off at the front (the stable court is to the rear in Derbais's project) by a low screening wall with a portal at its

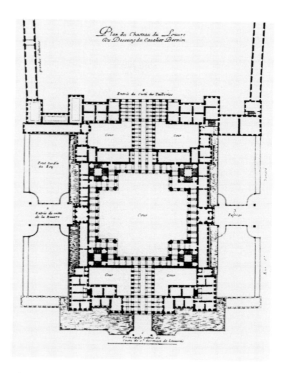

122 GIANLORENZO BERNINI: third project plan for the Louvre; Paris, 1665 (engraving: Marot).

center—refers to a tradition of *château* design even more out-of-date. A more timely aspect of Derbais's design was his provision of four grand staircases (two are combined at the center of the transverse wing), presumably one for each of the four sets of apartments though the demarcations are not altogether clear. Judging from the one stair hall that appears in section in Derbais's drawings (see Pl. 45), he seems to have been uncertain how to make them work as expanding zones of space and light, as the occasions for architectural drama that they usually were in the hands of great European architects. This is all the more unfortunate since the staircases were the only opportunities he had given himself to highlight his design. Otherwise, the interior spaces are undifferentiated, either by form or function; missing are the galleries, salons, antechambers, and cabinets that would have normally enriched that experience. As a whole, Derbais's design has all the *convénance* and *comodité* of an incredibly large barracks.

The only qualities which could conceivably have recommended Derbais's entry to his judges were the impressive size and craftsmanship of the drawings, the grandeur of his conception, and the exterior detailing. The jurors, with their limited perception of the French system, may have lulled themselves into believing that Derbais was among the best talents that that system had produced, but in fact Derbais was merely the epitome of both its successes and its failures. His receipt of the second prize in 1696, as overly generous as it may appear in hindsight, was therefore both a tribute to the former and a revelation of the latter made plain for all in Rome to witness. Derbais's project became the perfect foil for those submitted by Fontana's students. From the standpoint of design in the formal or practical senses, the Roman architects must have seemed better prepared for their task. Derbais's level of technical excellence, akin to that displayed by Chupin in 1677, no longer had priority over a well-developed or progressive design judgement. To this extent, Carlo Fontana had successfully reestablished the priorities to favor the design skills he had set about to inculcate in his students, and which Ferrari exemplified. In view of this, however, it remains a mystery why Derbais was awarded a higher prize than Pacenti, whose design skills were much closer to Ferrari's.

It is interesting to note that prior to the *concorso* in 1696 the French hierarchy had not been able to cope with Derbais with the same assurance that Colbert and Errard had approached the students in Rome twenty years before. Colbert de Villacerf was not even aware that Derbais was in Rome, until apprised of the fact by the young man's father (a minor artisan in the royal employ; App. B, 1697, n. 1) after he had already been there three years. Up to that time Derbais was apparently self-taught; he had not been a student in Paris, nor was he a *pensionnaire* in Rome. His participation in the *concorso* of 1696 would, therefore, from the French point of view, have been completely unwarranted and unsanctioned. Also, his accomplishment in winning over the judges becomes more remarkable, if less representative of what could otherwise be legitimately expected of a fully initiated French competitor, viz. Oppenord.

But if the Romans were misled, so too was La Teulière, who forwarded his impressions of Derbais to Villacerf to satisfy the *surintendant's* belated curiosity (App. B, 1697, n. 2).

Those impressions appear to have been gleaned at second hand, for by the time La Teulière looked in on Derbais he had been gone a month on a trip through northern Italy to broaden his experience of "the great Italian villas." This was a commendable intention since his *concorso* design had shown him to be totally ignorant of that tradition. According to La Teulière, who admitted only to having talked to some of Derbais's friends and seen some of his drawings, Derbais had applied himself well during his three years in Rome. La Teulière even accepted the word of Derbais's *confrères* that he in fact knew more than his drawings revealed, but that he was too modest and reserved to let it show. However, his *concorso* drawings were by no means modest, either in their dimensions or in their frank expression of his origins, origins he could not see beyond even after three years of study in Rome. La Teulière unwittingly took credit for Derbais's lack of sophistication by claiming to have advised him in his work, but that he in truth had little or no direct contact with Derbais is suggested by the lack of mention in his letter of Derbais's success in the *concorso* of 1696.

La Teulière was unprepared either to accept the significance of that news, or to pass it on to his superiors and thereby cast his own role in Rome in a lesser light. Whichever was the case, if Carlo Fontana had hoped by the *concorso* of 1696 to send a message to Paris, La Teulière in this one instance proved to be a hindrance to him. The small mind and the smaller character of the director of the French academy in Rome, whose instincts for self-preservation guided his every action, created a bottleneck in communications between the Accademia and Paris. Fontana's attempts to establish his dominance over La Teulière, and in that way reverse the flow of the information channel, from Rome to Paris, seem in the end to have been altogether fruitless.

The breakdown in communications was also costly to the careers of French architectural students in Rome, whether *pensionnaires* or not. From his vantage in 1677, Errard had actually been able to determine to a large extent the paths that prizewinners would take through their professions. La Teulière, on the other hand, had cut Oppenord off from adequate supervision, and by the time he returned home he was out of step with his contemporaries, so that his gifts lay dormant for twenty years. Derbais slipped so far out of La Teulière's grasp that he was never heard from again, and may never even have returned from Venice (App. B, 1697, nn. 3, 4). Pacenti, who had shown a somewhat greater measure of promise, but had had to accept a lower place, was less deserving of his fate. The chance to redeem himself in competition would not arrive for six more years, so in the meantime he may simply have resigned himself to the prospect of continuing his architectural career in a subordinate role, possibly as one of Fontana's draftsmen. His subsequent anonymity is the only certainty.

Just or not, the decisions of the judges in 1696 at least reflect the judgement of history much more than they had in 1677, when the lowest prize was awarded to the architect destined for the most recognition in his own time. Like Desgots, it was Ferrari who was received into aristocratic patronage immediately upon his final success in the *concorsi*. Desgots seems also to have been the one most affected by Fontana's example during his stay in Rome, much as was Ferrari in 1696. Fontana had, in these two respects, reversed the sense of the first-class competition in architecture, in all probability with conscious intent.

Ferrari in Poland

Ferrari was invited to Poland so soon after his victory in 1696 that there appears not to have been time to bestow on him membership in the Accademia, which should otherwise have been due him as a matter of course following his performances in the previous two *concorsi*. Still, it could very well have been his efforts in 1696 which directly earned him an invitation from one of Europe's great luminaries, Stanislaus Leszczynski, who intended Ferrari to continue the work on his ancestral castle at Rydzyna, in Greater Poland. The situation there was somewhat analogous to the topic in 1696, in that it involved a block-plan palace (Figs. 123, 124). Leszczynski no doubt also wished to extend his rivalry with Augustus of Saxony, German claimant to the Polish throne, into the arena of architectural patronage, and knowing of Carlo Fontana's overtures to Augustus he could have followed that same route back to find his own Italian designer. Ferrari may therefore have been dispatched to Poland upon the specific recommendations of Fontana.

Unfortunately, Ferrari's work for Leszczynski was obscured by various circumstances. Most of the Rydzyna palace was the product of local traditions of planning, massing, and detailing; only the stairhall added to the north facade (see Fig. 124), with its Colossal Order, balustrade, and Italianate portal and balcony, betrays the hand of Ferrari. Then in 1704 work was halted when Charles XII of Sweden overran Poland in the early stages of the Northern War (1700–21), and put Stanislaus I

123 POMPEO FERRARI: plan of the Leszczynski (Sulkowski) Palace; Rydzyna, begun 1696 (graphic: Troy Thompson).

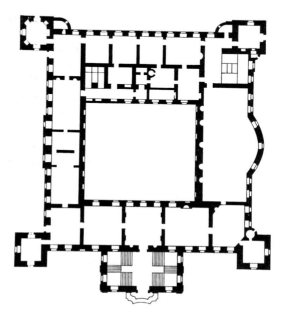

124 FERRARI: facade of the Leszczynski Palace (photo: from *Polish Architecture*).

on the throne. During the internal strife that followed, the palace at Rydzyna was damaged, and
the Leszczynski Palace in Warsaw that Ferrari had
also designed was destroyed (1707).[121] In 1709,
Russian victories over Sweden allowed Augustus to
return to Poland, driving Stanislaus I into exile in
France, and putting an end to Ferrari's source of
noble patronage. The Rydzyna estates were purchased in a dilapidated condition in 1736, the year
of Ferrari's death, by the Sulkowski family, and
the subsequent remodeling by the German architect Charles Martin Frantz obliterated much of
the earlier work.[122]

After 1709, Ferrari had to seek out ecclesiastic
commissions to sustain himself in Poland. Over
the next quarter-century, even if only by dint of a
lack of competition, his activities along those lines
will turn out to be definitive for Baroque church
typology in Greater Poland, a region with thriving
local traditions but lying virtually at the fringe of
European culture. There, his cosmopolitan sophistication had no equal.

Ferrari's career as a church designer in Poland
began as the assistant to a fellow émigré, Giovanni

Catenacci, on several of the projects the latter had
initiated after the late 1670s.[123] At Sw. Mikolaj in
Leszno, near Rydzyna, Ferrari added the domed
chancel to a vessel whose form Catenacci had otherwise derived from local variations on the hall-
church type. The two also collaborated on the
church of the Philippine abbey at Gostyń, the
designs for which were forwarded from Venice by
Baldassare Longhena on the model of the Salute.[124]

Projects like these have marked Ferrari as a
specialist in domed, centralized spaces, and his
association with Catenacci tainted him as a conservative as well. Indeed, his church design for the
concorso of 1694 (see Pls. 25–27) seems to indicate
that he had set off in that direction from the
beginning, and the fact that Carlo Fontana can
also be described as a conservative architect interested in centralized planning must have much to
do with this. One of Ferrari's independently
designed churches in Poland, that of Sw.Sw. Piotr i
Pawel in Obrzycko (1714, Fig. 125), with its symmetry on two axes and its elemental geometry,
proclaims his debt to the chapel architecture of his
Roman master more plainly than any other (see

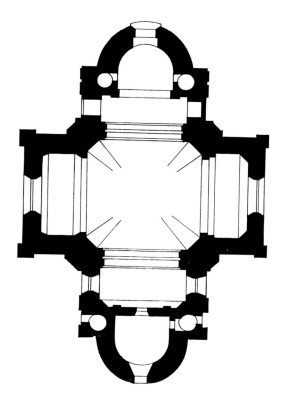

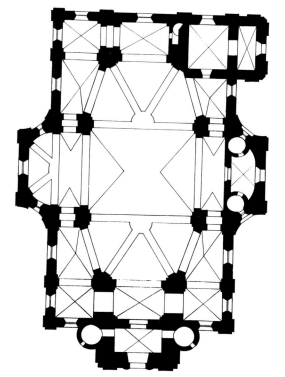

125 FERRARI: plan of Sw.Sw. Piotr i Pawel; Obrzycko, begun 1714 (graphic: Troy Thompson).

126 FERRARI: plan of Sw. Krzyz; Leszno, begun 1707 (graphic: Troy Thompson).

below and Fig. 27). But by this time he had finally come into his own in church design, and his most important work in that field was slave neither to prototypes nor to Fontana's ideals. Rather, he married local custom to the concept of centrality by means of an architectural language that has been called Borrominesque, and the results are his most original architecture.

The German Lutheran community of Leszno commissioned the design of their Church of the Holy Cross from Ferrari in 1707 (Figs. 126, 127). Beginning with a traditional hall church, he turned the central nave into an elongated octagon formed by eight piers and extended the space in the cardinal directions into apses, like the arms of a Greek-cross church. Surrounding the main vessel in the manner of a hall church is a nearly continuous ambulatory, containing additional tiers of seating, which fits the whole into the traditionally

rectangular contours of the exterior. The ends of the transept that emerge from the north and south are returned to the exterior envelope by means of concave bays, which were a part of the repertoire Ferrari brought with him from Rome (cf. the Twin Churches on Piazza del Popolo, Fig. 12). More telling, however, is the interior aspect, which combines the planimetric device of Borromini's S. Carlino (the elongated Greek cross) with the architectonic Gothicisms of his Philippine oratory or his chapel for the Collegio di Propaganda Fide (Fig. 128). Ferrari's methods allowed him to reconcile his Roman background with locally lingering medieval building practices, and the functional centrality required for a protestant preaching church.

Ferrari's design was not unparalleled; similar departures can be found throughout Central Europe during the early eighteenth century, and

127 FERRARI: nave interior of Sw. Krzyz (photo: from *Polish Architecture*).

128 FRANCESCO BORROMINI: section of the Cappella Re Magi at the Collegio di Propaganda Fide; Rome, 1654–67 (engraving: de Rossi).

for similar reasons. Borromini's style was simply very compatible with the traditions of northern masons. But what Ferrari had achieved in Leszno was certainly unique for the time and place, and would eventually give him his reputation. He was commissioned to duplicate the Leszno church in 1720 for the Cistercian nunnery in Owinska, and again in 1725 for the parish church in Wschowa.[125] For these two Roman Catholic foundations, he merely altered the design to exclude balcony seating, and to include a shallow oval dome over the octagon. This type, once defined by Ferrari on the plain of the Warta, also had an influence elsewhere in Poland, particularly on a line of churches built a generation later around Lublin.[126] When noble patronage returned to him in 1727, that of the Potocki family, he built their chapel in the cathedral of Gniezno as a version in miniature of his personal Rococo idiom, with bold Borrominian convolutions (Fig. 129).[127]

For the monument which crowned his career Ferrari deviated from his own most successful model, a fact that bears witness to his continuing evolvement as an artist, even into his sixties. The

project was to complete another church begun by Catenacci, the abbey church of the Cistercians at Ląd, where at some time in the building history the decision had been made to reverse the orientation, making the original nave the choir and constructing a new nave on the other side of the transept (Figs. 130, 131). Ferrari initiated his reworking of the nave in 1728, and finished it in 1735, the year before his death. There is in his conception some remnant of the concentric vision of Fontana, but the interior is for the most part a *tour de force* of Borrominesque or even Guarinesque architecture.[128]

In plan the usual nave and side chapels were abandoned in favor again of an elongated octagon, but this shape has been further manipulated so that the walls between the piers either disappear into the voids at the corners, or recede concavely to accept the side altars, in contrast with the convexly projecting entrance vestibule. The organic tension between structural skeleton and mural

129 POMPEO FERRARI: vault of the Potocki Chapel, Cathedral of Our Lady; Gniezno, 1727–30 (photo: Z. Swiechowski; from *Polish Architecture*).

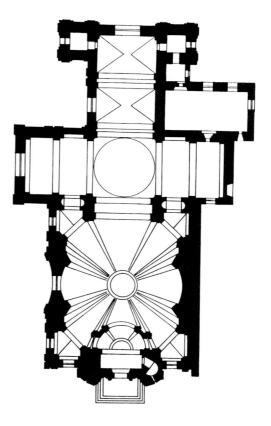

130 FERRARI: plan of the Cistercian Abbey Church; Ląd, nave begun 1728 (graphic: Troy Thompson).

skin that Ferrari thus established, and continued into the ribbed domical vault, is every bit appropriate to the language in which he has chosen to express himself. He added to the tension by doubling the articulation to either side of the lateral chapels, making their inward pressure more powerful as they compel the participant deeper into the church and toward the main altar. His nave is therefore not detached and self-serving, but is intimately a part of the whole program. What he has done here is to avoid the clichés of Counter-Reformation church architecture, or a too-literal Gothic formula. Instead, he created a building, in terms quite proudly Roman, which could easily withstand comparison to the Rococo churches of his progressive contemporaries further south.

Though he had been forced by circumstances to change his emphasis from palace to church architecture, and in the process had grown considerably beyond his earlier design abilities, it is still possible to make valid connections between

Ferrari's *concorso* projects and the accomplishments of his subsequent career. To the degree that this is true, he is unlike every other prizewinner in the first class of architecture throughout the *Concorsi Accademici*: Simon Chupin (1677) and Romano Carapecchia (1681) were to have no substantial futures to which to compare their earliest designs; Claude Desgots (1677) and Jan Reissner (1682) went on to excel in professions for which their *concorso* designs had little if any relevance; Augustin D'Aviler (1677) came closest in his entry to prefiguring his later interests, but those interests, formed by standards at the French and Roman academies that were different for his day, turned out to be more theoretical than practical, and so can provide only indirect correspondences to his *concorso* design. In the obvious drafting skills

131 FERRARI: interior of the Cistercian Abbey Church (photo: E. Kupiecki; from *Polish Architecture*).

that Domenico Martinelli (1679) and Filippo Barigioni (1692) displayed in their competition projects, was the promise of their future success. But they were to have their design intellects reshaped by Carlo Fontana soon after their victories in the *concorsi,* and it was undoubtedly more to his influence that they owed their mature talents. Ferrari was the first student of architecture, with successes in both competition and career, to have had the influence of Fontana directly by way of the Accademia.

COMPETITIONS IN THE SECOND AND THIRD CLASSES: ALESSANDRO ROSSINI AND LUDOVICO RUSCONI-SASSI

Consideration of the twenty drawings that make up the prizewinning entries for the second- and third-class *concorsi* in 1694 and 1696 will be relatively brief, for two reasons. First, it would ill serve the coherence of the present book to deflect its attentions too far from the first-class competitions, which are central to its arguments and consistent with its chronology. Otherwise, the weight of visual documentation would tip the balance against the earlier *concorsi,* when there were no competitions in the other classes. Second, the efforts of Ludovico Rusconi-Sassi, and his rivals in 1694 and 1696 for second- and third-class honors, have previously been analyzed in detail by Cathie Cook Kelly in her monographic dissertation on the former.[129] Third, with the exception of the second-class *soggetto* in 1696, the themes for these lesser *concorsi* tend to be trivial in comparison to those encountered in the first-class competitions.

For example, Alessandro Sperone's chapel design, which captured the sole prize in the second class for 1694 (App. B, 1694, n. 5; Pls. 34–36 and App. A), was an earnest but otherwise unremarkable effort. The lateral section, showing the image of St. Luke painting the Virgin in the altarpiece, makes plain the dedication of the chapel to the Accademia's patron saint. Whether this was stipulated by the task, now lost, or intuited by Sperone, it provided him with a handy model, the Accademia's church of SS. Luca e Martina, which every student knew well from daily experience.

From the plan of Cortona's church (see Fig. 113), Sperone derived a Greek-cross form that abridged the salient features of the original in accommodating them to the more modest situation. Of the four pairs of recessed aediculae which flank the altars and entrance portal of Cortona's church, Sperone found room for two, one at each end of the main axis. At the piers, where Cortona had inset columns between the bevels and pilasters bordering the arms of the cross, Sperone removed the bevels and four of the eight columns, so that the pendentives each spring from one point above one column. This is certainly a unique solution in Roman architecture, but not so daring if one follows the simple process of reduction that led to it.[130]

In the longitudinal section (see Pl. 36) Sperone included ornamentation (window and niche surrounds; a broken pediment) which might also be described as Cortonesque. But in this instance there is a more apt comparison available, with a project that is not only functionally related and corresponds on several points of articulation, but would also have been well within Sperone's ken. This was Carlo Fontana's Cybo family chapel in S. Maria del Popolo, which had been completed ten years before (Fig. 132). What Sperone gave that project, aside from an interpretation in terms of the Accademia's church, was the symmetry on two axes that Fontana had not been able to realize from his early projects for his chapel (cf. Figs. 26 and 27).

Sperone's direct association with Fontana is easily established because of the connection between the Fontana studio and the Accademia in 1694; because of Sperone's mastery of the Fontana studio drafting techniques; and because of the other directions in which he took his design. For the oval altarpiece carried by angels (see Pl. 35), his example was Bernini, who used the identical device on two separate occasions, one of which is illustrated here (Fig. 133). Another Berninesque device was the indirect light provided for Sperone's altarpiece by windows to either side of the apse, which is similar in layout and effect to Bernini's Cappella Raymondi in S. Pietro in Montorio (Fig. 134), though there a hidden light source is located above the altarpiece as well. From that source Sperone also took the motif of the

132 CARLO FONTANA: Half-plan and longitudinal section of the Cappella Cybo in S. Maria del Popolo; Rome, 1682–84 (engraving: de Rossi).

roundel carried by putti in the apse vault. One final borrowing, this time from the Bernini school in general, was the ring of oval windows in the drum, adapted from Contini's Cappella d'Elci in S. Sabina (Fig. 135).[131]

Sperone was a good student who had taken to heart Fontana's advice to go out and learn from a range of Roman monuments that might be useful to his design intentions. To his credit, he has assembled the parts well and there is no disharmony between them; his draftsmanship, and his skill in sculptural imagery, must have been gratifying to see in a second-class competitor. But in fact Sperone did not go very far to find his sources, and bringing them together did not inspire him to anything particularly new—the whole is not

133 GIANLORENZO BERNINI: lateral section of Cappella de Silva in S. Isidoro; Rome, 1660–63 (engraving: de Rossi).

135 G. B. CONTINI: Cappella d'Elci in S. Sabina; Rome, begun 1671 (photo: author).

134 BERNINI: interior of the Cappella Raymondi in S. Pietro in Montorio; Rome, 1638–48 (photo: author).

greater than the sum of its parts. He seems never to have risen above the level of this first and only accomplishment.[132]

More impressive results were expected of the second-class competitors in the Secular Year of 1696, and those competitors had in fact already groomed themselves for the challenge by participating in the third class in 1694, an advantage no previous entrant will have had. Alessandro Rossini and Ludovico Rusconi-Sassi, after sharing first prize in the third class in 1694, went on essentially to repeat that showing in the second and then the first classes of the next two *concorsi*. It is difficult to be more exact about the importance of their victory in 1694, however, since all they were given to do, after all, was to render a detail from an existing building, a bay from the Palazzo dei Conservatori on the Capitoline. Even the judges seem to have been unsure of how to handle this class of competition, since they were forced to award two first prizes (App. B, 1694, n. 5), but this had happened before in other media. What is required to distinguish

one entry from another is the quantification of quite minor differences in the handling of tools, or in fidelity to detail and nuances of chiaroscuro (App. A, nos. 37–40). It is nearly impossible to say why Rusconi-Sassi's entry (Pls. 38, 39) was considered by the judges to be second to Rossini's (Pl. 37), when in some respects the former's skills were greater. Their giving a lower place to Filippo Ottoni's entry (Pl. 40) is slightly easier to understand, since his rendering skills were less developed, but his use of wash was actually more successful in recreating the relief of Michelangelo's architecture. And as far as the accuracy of their measurements is concerned, all three entries could have been traced from one image, were their scales not somewhat different.

In retrospect, and perhaps even from the vantage point of the Roman public, the third-class *concorso* for 1694 was not so much a competition as an exercise for the architects involved, and it lacked drama. The fact that Ferrari and Sperone had little or no serious competition in their classes would not have sparked much more excitement in the spectators when the *concorso* was celebrated. The measures Fontana and the Accademia took to enhance the magnitude of the architectural competitions in honor of the Accademia's centennial must in part have been devised as a remedy for ennui. The *concorso* in the second class in 1696 would be enlivened by Rossini's and Rusconi-Sassi's participation, now that they had together won first prize in the third class of 1694.[133] But in the third class of 1696, something more than just a larger field of worthy competitors was needed, and so it was decided to make the test one of design abilities and not just of technical skills.

Unfortunately, the entries by the first two prizewinners in the third class for 1696, Bartolomeo Santini (Pls. 59, 60) and Giovanni Antonio Sevalle (Pl. 61), are architecturally rather undistinguished. They adhere stringently to the line of the *soggetto,* a monumental gateway for a villa (App. B, 1696, n. 3), and to the lessons in the Tuscan Doric Order provided for them by Francesco Fontana. The stipulation of three bays urged both architects to conceive of their gateways as triumphal arches, and to reinforce that idea through sculptural decoration. Sevalle's second-prize solution was quite simplistic on all counts: the architecture is severe, but for the projection of the central bay, and the statuary consists merely of six crude parodies of antique heroic figures crowning the balustrade. The scheme of Santini's first-prize design is not fundamentally different from Sevalle's, but it is much more elaborate, and executed with far more patience and skill. He included Tuscan pilasters at the extremes of the gateway, and volutes where it abuts the walls, and he retained a Doric frieze in the entablature, where the metopes bear reliefs of trophies. He continued the martial iconography into the sculpture around the royal escutcheon, and into the oval supraportal reliefs in the outside bays, but he mitigated it with the female figures above the balustrade which personify other aristocratic virtues besides belligerence.

In this case, there can be little dispute over Santini's deserving the higher award, despite the fact that both he and Sevalle seem to have started

from an all-too-common ground. A true air of competition could now be readily detected in even the lowest class of architecture within the *concorsi*. Santini's flair for expressing himself as architect and artist at so early a stage of development, and for relating his design to the general theme of the *concorso,* would have reflected all the greater upon the Fontana studio, which was responsible for his talent and his inspiration. His achievement, as well as Sevalle's, could easily have recalled to the people of Rome the three-bay Doric portal that Carlo Fontana had realized for the entrance to the *Curia Innocenziana* (cf. Fig. 107), thus compouding Fontana's personal gain through the mechanism of the competitions.[134]

There is an irony in this for the winner of the third prize in the third class for 1696, Giuseppe Parà. His entry (Pl. 62) was the only one of the three to interpret the *portone* required by the *soggetto* as the main portal of the villa palace rather than as the gateway to the villa proper. By incorporating the three openings called for by the *soggetto,* Parà equated his portal functionally with that of Fontana's *curia,* though stylistically it is anything but Fontanesque. The point of departure suggested to him by the three doors was not a triumphal arch, but a church facade, an association made apparent in the means by which he presented his design. The broad lower story, encompassing the three entrances, embraces the center like a Baroque church front, through the proliferation and advancement of its articulation. Above, the balcony reads like the upper bay of such a facade, with its Ionic Order an extension of Doric elements below, and cutaway renderings of flanking bays in place of volutes. In essence, he reversed the logic of the facade of the Phillipine oratory (Fig. 136), which Borromini conceived in terms of palatine architecture, but subtlety of that kind was perhaps beyond the thinking of a student like Parà. Still, much of the ornamentation of his portal could genuinely be called Borrominesque, in the sense that it is fancifully derived from craft work. Judging from many of the details, like open-work, scrollwork, or beaded moldings, pendant garlands, and scallop shells, the craft in question seems to have been cabinetry, which raises the

136 FRANCESCO BORROMINI: facade of the
Oratory of S. Filippo Neri; Rome, 1640–50 (photo:
author).

possibility that some of the responsibility for Parà's
training may have been Tomassini's, whose craft
orientation to architecture has been remarked
upon previously.

In view of this, Tomassini was probably the most
vocal advocate of Parà's design among the judges for
the *concorso* of 1696. Fontana and Contini, in their
conservatism, would not have accepted the language
in which it was submitted, but Fontana's much
more broadly based eclecticism might have toler-
ated it. After all, in Parà's project the jury had
been presented with an entry that was far more
thoughtful, imaginative, and painstaking then
either of the others. The fact that his did not conform to the gateway type may have given them an
excuse to disregard those qualities and to place
him below Santini and Sevalle, but as the *soggetto*
was not specific they could not ignore him. A clear
statement of the Accademia's stylistic preferences

had been made, but at the same time Fontana's
philosophy of the value of Roman pluralism,
which now the curriculum in architecture had
come to share, had made it necessary to confront
divergent tendencies in their students. Awarding
the third prize to Parà in effect gave license to
every young architect whose interests did not lie
entirely along the establishment line. Again, it
appears that in the last of the *Concorsi Accademici,*
some of the first inroads of the Borrominian
revival of the Roman Settecento are made into the
dominant classicism of the Late Baroque.

A similar conclusion pertains to the competition in the second class for 1696. Rossini, in repeating his first-prize showing of two years before in the
third class, seems to have known exactly what steps
to take to get the jury to respond favorably to his
entry, and to have learned his lessons from the
concorso of 1694. He related the plan of his villa
chapel (Pls. 50–52 and App. A) to that of the
Accademia's church (see Fig. 113), through its
Greek-cross plan and dominant longitudinal axis.
His treatment of the piers beneath the pendentives is much closer to Cortona's, however. In that
detail, and in the squared-off altar recesses, his
plan also has an affinity with Fontana's Cybo
Chapel (see Fig. 132), while Rossini's section
drawing (see Pl. 52) points to that comparison
even more dramatically.

Inspired by Ferrari's reference to a Parisian
church in the plan of his chapel for 1694 (see Pl.
25), Rossini also inserted centrally planned
vestibules in the angles between the arms of his
church, which link the side portals of the facade to
the entrance arm, and the main altar space to the
service rooms at the rear. He actually had his own
French precedent to guide him here, though, and
one more appropriate to his topic. As early as 1688,
Louis XIV had been contemplating the construction of a new chapel for his own "villa" at
Versailles.[135] The chapel that now stands was begun
by Hardouin-Mansart in 1699, but other projects
had been proposed by him prior to that, and one
of them, a variation on his Invalides church, had
been engraved (Fig. 137). There are striking correspondences between Hardouin-Mansart's plan and
Rossini's: the octagonal vestibules in the corners

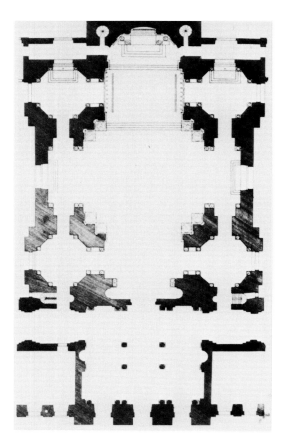

137 JULES HARDOUIN-MANSART: project plan for the chapel at Versailles; ca. 1684 (source: Bibliothèque Nationale, Paris).

and the articulation of the piers.

Hardouin-Mansart's project was not published, and so for Rossini to have known of it presupposes that a copy had been passed on to him somehow. Perhaps one was available to him in the Fontana studio, one that Fontana himself had acquired through his connections with Paris. The implication is that not only was Fontana passing information about his activities on to La Teulière, but was receiving information about Mansart's activities from him as well. By insinuating French motifs into the competition designs of his students, Fontana could remind the French partisans among the observers of the *concorsi* that the Accademia had not forgotten the aspirations

expressed at the time of its aggregation with the Académie Royale. The Romans were still willing to mingle the French tradition with their own in the name of progress for the arts in general. The hidden barb, however, was that while France might occasionally produce a planning device or articulative motif deserving of inclusion in the repertoire, Rome knew itself to be the more vital source of nearly everything else pertaining to architecture, aside from hubris.

Take, for example, the facade of Rossini's chapel (see Pl. 51). Only in the Mediterranean climate of Italy was the tradition of a freestanding villa chapel upheld; the chapels of French *châteaux* were attached, and therefore incurred no facade development. French churches had in many other instances deferred to Roman prototypes for their facades, so here was nearly uncontested Roman design territory. As if sensing this, or perhaps merely having apprised himself of the methods of earlier prizewinners, Rossini devoted most of his originality to the facade of his chapel, while making it a comprehensive and comprehensible variation on Roman types. In plan, the facade steps forward toward the center, with columns only to either side of the main portal. The articulation is continued into the narrower upper story, as per the typical Roman Baroque facades, but Rossini replaced the volutes with sculptured figures. To adjust the chapel to its villa context, he crowned the outside bays with balustrades, which along with the projecting central aediculae relate his facade to Bernini's for S. Bibiana (see Fig. 23). In deference to the alternative Roman line, that of Borromini, he framed the doorways with eared moldings, and made use of the specific device of the "unfinished" capital for the outermost pilasters, which borrows from the facade of the Oratory (see Fig. 136). There is more logic to his usage, however, in that his facade would diminish in detail while receding in space.

That logic should have satisfied Rossini's judges, who might otherwise have found the motif to be alien to the conventionality of his design. So, in the end, the simple directness of his project, and his conformity to establishment ideals, along with his excellent draftsmanship, earned him a first prize. Before one rushes to label Rossini, the Accademia, and Fontana's studio as arch-conservative or repressive on this evidence, however, one should consider that in actuality Rossini had in most respects found the middle road: between Bernini and Borromini, between Paris and Rome, between Fontana and Cortona, and even in some respects between convention and his own imagination. This makes him a moderate, not a conservative, much as Ferrari had shown himself to be in both of his *concorso* designs. Rossini may have been a model of restraint, of self-imposed discipline, and certainly this was what the Accademia and Fontana wanted to encourage. But in doing so there was no willingness to restrain selectivity from without, and thereby build walls between the students and the architectural legacy of the city. Indeed, to isolate them was impossible; Rome was around them and a part of them. It is to the credit of Fontana and his ideological fellows that they not only acknowledged this state of affairs, and allowed students free rein to explore in directions they themselves did not frequent, but that they also rewarded such efforts in competition. The entries of the next two prizewinners in the second class for the *concorso* of 1696 are proof enough of this.

The design by Rusconi-Sassi (Pls. 53–55 and App. A), the only competitor in 1694 and 1696 whom Pascoli specifically names as a student of Fontana (see above), departs the farthest from his master's idiom. The chapel is rife with Borrominesque qualities. The interior plan undulates along the lines of a Greek cross, approximating but not duplicating the effect of Borromini's plan for S. Carlino (Fig. 138) due to the seemingly obligatory reference to SS. Luca e Martina (see Fig. 113). The convex bulge of the piers, between the inset columns, continues into the pendentives but must be reversed for the concavity of the tension ring. The contradictions and tensions inherent in this are wholly Borrominian. Above the pendentives, and visible in section and elevation, is a cupola whose form is recognizably derived from Sperone's of two years before (though the oval windows are horizontal rather than vertical; cf. Pl. 35), but whose pedigree is generally traceable to the Bernini school (see above). On the

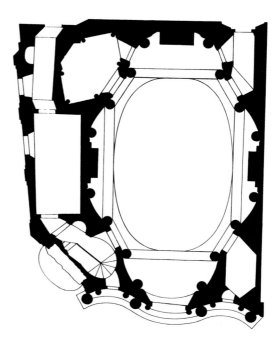

138 FRANCESCO BORROMINI: plan of the Church of S. Carlo alle Quattro Fontane; Rome, begun 1638 (graphic: Troy Thompson).

exterior, however, Rusconi-Sassi has tried, within the limits of his wash technique, to indicate that the panels of the dome swell outward between the ribs, and are answered by concave bays in the crowning lantern. Here Borromini's S. Ivo (Fig. 139), comes to mind, but not so much that the traditional sense of Rusconi-Sassi's cupola disappears. He, too, walked a line between heretofore separate Roman traditions, while leaning much more than Rossini toward the thrill of Borromini's aberrance. This is apparent as well in some of Rusconi-Sassi's decorative details, around the main altar (see Pl. 55), and on the facade, which by itself could stand for the whole of his design concept.

In two dimensions, the scheme of the facade is traditional, with narrow outside bays flanking a projecting entrance bay, and volutes clasping the narrower upper story (see Pl. 54). However, the convex center responds dramatically to the outward pressure of the entrance arm of the interior Greek cross, in paraphrase of both Cortona's SS. Luca e Martina (see Fig. 114) and Borromini's S.

139 BORROMINI: S. Ivo alla Sapienza; Rome, 1641–60 (photo: Alinari).

Carlino (Fig. 140). The layering of Rusconi-Sassi's facade, from convex projection, to the plane of the side bays, to the plane of the church behind, also paraphrases Cortona's facade for S. Maria della Pace (see Fig. 115), while the dome, which has already shown traces of Borromini's influence, is another variation on a Cortona design, that for the dome of S. Carlo al Corso (1668, Fig. 141). The whole of the chapel is in essence a conflation of Cortona's and Borromini's architecture, tempered by its traditional scheme, and confident in its Borrominian ornament (compare the frames of the niches and upper windows of the facade to similar details on the facade of the Oratory, Fig. 136). The charm of Rusconi-Sassi's facade design, which lies in its Baroque spatial effects, cannot readily be appreciated in flat projection.

What can be appreciated is how little lip service Rusconi-Sassi paid to the ideals of Late Baroque classicism, or to the architecture of his master, Carlo Fontana. Aside from fragmentary references to the facade of S. Marcello al Corso (see Fig. 87), in the relief medallion and broken pediment above the entrance portal of his chapel, Rusconi-Sassi nearly altogether ignored Fontana's legacy. This, and his less disciplined drafting hand, explain his finishing second to Rossini in the second-class *concorso* of 1696. Though he had undeniably devoted more creative thought to his design, he had come down too much on the side of the more licentious masters of the High Baroque, whose disposition the Accademia could never entirely condone so long as there were students like Rossini willing to work within proscribed limits of taste. But by phrasing his challenge to coincide with customary chapel forms, Rusconi-Sassi made sure that it could not be disregarded, either, and his judges could still reassure themselves that his models were thoroughly Roman. In the heady atmosphere of Roman *amour-propre* which the Accademia's Secular Year had generated, there was perhaps no more important criterion. Some students, intoxicated by the greater liberality of the curriculum under Fontana, had to be expected to cast yearning eyes in heretofore less countenanced directions, and the *concorsi* had now to allow for them.

Another such student was Basilio Spinelli, winner of the third prize in the second class for 1696 (Pls. 56–58 and App. A), and also a Roman. In plan (Pl. 56), his Greek-cross chapel again takes a cue from the Accademia's church, but this time from Cortona's earlier, concentric, project design (see Fig. 29). This project seems to have been well known to the students of the Accademia (see Chapter II, note 82), but Spinelli could also have been affected by Carlo Fontana's experiments in concentric church planning (compare Figs. 24–28). The one church design presented to the Accademia by the Fontana school in 1677 (see Chapter II) in particular bears comparison to Spinelli's in plan (compare Fig. 24 and Pl. 56) and in section (compare Fig. 26 and Pl. 58), and would also have been accessible to Spinelli. His bold columnar articulation of the interior further underscores this comparison. Aside from a difference of opinion as to how to delineate pendentives over a circular plan, Spinelli's methods, motifs, and detailing are within the range of Fontanesque possibilities; the cupola is especially doctrinaire. But the fact that he chose to follow the most daring line of development ever pursued by Fontana, that of the concentric plan, is significant, just as is his use of cylindrical vestibules at the front angles of the chapel to link the side entrances of the facade to the nave through the piers. He probably appropriated these from Pompeo Ferrari's monastery chapel design for 1694 (see Pl. 25), rather than from the original French source, but the intention was no doubt the same. The circular vestibules and nave were tokens of Spinelli's identification with two of Fontana's academic fascinations: with ideal geometries, and with the adaptation of French themes to Roman practice. All that remained was to savor a wider range of Roman influences, to which he, like his fellow competitors, gave fullest expression in the design of the facade of his chapel (see Pl. 57).

The scheme of Spinelli's facade as a whole is rather unusual, but the derivation of the important parts can be easily understood. The outside bays, for example, which contain the secondary entrances to the chapel, are both concave and angled sharply backward, like those on the facades

140 BORROMINI: facade of S. Carlo alle Quattro Fontane; Rome, 1665–67 (photo: Alinari).

141 PIETRO DA CORTONA: dome of S. Carlo al Corso; Rome, 1668–69 (photo: author).

of Rainaldi's Twin Churches on the Piazza del Popolo (see Fig. 12). At the center, an oval *tempietto* formed of six columns is set halfway into the principal plane of the facade, providing a platform for the balcony in its concave recess above. Here, again, it is as though Spinelli had conflated Borromini's facade of the Oratory and Cortona's S. Maria della Pace, much as Rusconi-Sassi had done, but with quite a different result.

The difference is that in Rusconi-Sassi's design, no matter what taste it betrayed, recognizably Roman formulas were left intact. Spinelli's plan, facade, and pendentives in the section deviate too far from the conventions. Also, many of the elements of his design are not well integrated into the whole. In plan, the flat or apsidal end walls of the arms do not seem appropriate to the concentric theme. At the facade, the balcony has little prominence, and the intermediate bays are too neutral in comparison to the others. Most

unfortunately, the cupola is entirely out of touch with what is beneath it, either in section or elevation, whether with regard to proportioning, articulation, or the simple fact that it is so ordinary while the rest of Spinelli's conception was not. His design is therefore proof of the difficulty of serving two "masters," of responding to both normative urges and the lure of the unorthodox.

In retrospect, it is worthwhile to point out the parallels between the decisions of the judges in the second class for 1696, and those in 1677 when the topic was the same, though only Tomassini was on both juries. First prize was awarded to the young architect who least compromised his staid Roman and French models, and presented the most sober result. Second prize went to the more daring and original designer, who called upon a wider, and in that an inevitably less acceptable range of influences, and integrated them into an entirely new but coherent entity. Third went to the architect who tried to do both, and ended up doing neither as well. It may seem from this that little had changed in twenty years of the Accademia's history, but in fact some important priorities had been adjusted. Skill in drafting, or in rendering the Orders, or in incorporating sculpture and painting into the building program, were now less likely to rescue a bad design, for indeed Spinelli has bested his competition in all of these. At the same time, there seems to have been less of an emphasis on fidelity to eminent models, and more of one on adopting motifs solely on the basis of utility, and adapting them to an otherwise original conception. While the judges continued in their efforts to advance a particular stylistic orientation, the three designs were still assessed largely on their architectural merits. This had not been the case in 1677, and indeed has never been so discernible as it is in this particular *concorso*. Carlo Fontana's leadership of the Accademia, and its affiliation with his workshop, are the single most important factors in the change.

Another thing that did not change, however, is that the instincts of the judges were again inconsistent with the findings of history. When Rusconi-Sassi and Rossini shared first prize a second time in 1702, in the first-class competition for

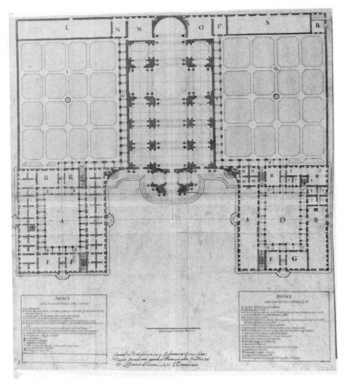

142 LUDOVICO RUSCONI-SASSI: plan for a basilica with college and hospital; ASL 68 (Conc. Clem. 1702).

the first of the *Concorsi Clementini* (see Chapter V), it seems to have been because the former had learned to play by the rules of the game. To his credit, he did not try to match Rossini's grandiose (even ridiculous) planning and historicism (cf. Fig. 30), but he did cool his Borrominian ardor considerably (Figs. 142, 143). All that he retained as part of his personal idiom was the central projection of the church facade, though here it is rectilinear in plan; all that is Borrominesque in his design seems to have been guided by Pompeo Ferrari's prizewinning project from 1694 (see Pls. 25, 26). Their subjects were similar—monastic college with chapel, and basilica with college and hospital—and Rusconi-Sassi could well have studied Ferrari's project to learn just how far he could safely take his deviating interests. His answer must have been "not far," for all that is left of Borromini's vocabulary are the concave wings masking the corners of the piazza to either side of the church facade. That

facade is as conservative as, indeed is nearly identical to, Ferrari's chapel front (compare Fig. 143 and Pl. 26). Lest one read into this a more repressive atmosphere building at the Accademia, it should be noted that the altar designs in the second class for 1702 include some Borrominian qualities, and the task in the third class was to render one of Borromini's niches in S. Giovanni.[136] A similar pattern will persist through several subsequent *concorsi,* but the implications of that are reserved for discussion in the next chapter. For now it remains legitimate to say that while inquiry into all Roman design options was encouraged, those who settled into the establishment line received higher reward.

Despite being consistently favored by the judges over Rusconi-Sassi, however, Rossini did not altogether fulfill his early promise. After some twelve more years in Rome without accomplishment, he went to the German states to offer his services as draftsman, surveyor, and *Baumeister.*[137] He was for a time an assistant to Johann Dientzenhofer, and his name is attached to several building programs, but to very little original architecture. His activity ceased after 1736, when he would have been in his sixties, and the record of his life ceases rather ingloriously at that point as well.

The year 1736 was also the year of Rusconi-Sassi's death,[138] but the mark he left on the history of architecture over an equivalent life span was much more substantial than Rossini's, and furthermore was accomplished in Rome itself, which was still no small feat. Immediately upon leaving the Accademia in 1702 he came under the patronage of the Ottoboni family, and remained there for the rest of his life. Like his master, Fontana, he made his name principally in the area of chapel design, but unlike Fontana he could vary his style rather unselfconsciously between a conservative idiom (Cappella Paolucci, San Marcello al Corso, 1723–24),[139] and a Borrominian one (Cappella Odescalchi, Fig. 144). In the completion of San Salvatore in Lauro (1727–33), he designed a Cortonesque cupola.[140] Indeed, the only mode in which Rusconi-Sassi declined to work was Bernini's, which put him outside the bounds of Late Baroque classicism, and made him, as Kelly rightly points out in her monograph on him, one

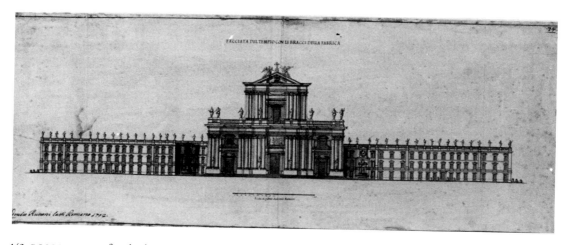

143 ROSCONI-SASSI: facade elevation for the project in Figure 142; ASL 69.

of the early pioneers of the Borrominian revival and the Roman Rococo.[141] What made that movement distinct from general European fashion was its fidelity to the full Roman vocabulary and grammar of architecture—the same language that Rusconi-Sassi and others had had reinforced for them by their studies at the Accademia and in Fontana's workshop, and in which Rusconi-Sassi had become particularly fluent.

In 1724 Rusconi-Sassi was made *Accademico di Merito* upon the submission of his *dono* drawing (Fig. 145).[142] That design, for a church facade, virtually encapsulates his entire career. It harks back to his formative years, through references to features of his *concorso* entries: the convex center of his chapel facade for 1696 (cf. Pl. 54); the scheme of his church facade for 1702, and that of its source, Ferrari's project for 1694 (cf. Fig. 143 and Pl. 26). The pediment of his *dono* design recalls his most successful project, the Odescalchi family chapel (see Fig. 144). The *dono* also looks ahead, to his model entry in the competition for the facade of S. Giovanni in Laterano (Fig. 146), which, though one of the dozens of submissions, was certainly for him his most important endeavor.[143]

The new front for S. Giovanni, Christianity's first official church and the cathedral of Rome, had a preeminent place in the individual and collective imaginations of Rome's artistic and religious communities. The Accademia became an

144 RUSCONI-SASSI: Odescalchi Chapel in SS. Apostoli; Rome, 1719–22 (photo: Alinari).

145 RUSCONI-SASSI: plan and elevation for a church facade; ASL 2183 (Dono Accademico).

important forum for ideas related to the project when in 1705 a facade design for S. Giovanni was selected for the *soggetto* in the second-class *concorso*.[144] By that time, Innocent XII had already held his own competition for the project, in anticipation of the Holy Year in 1700, and Carlo Fontana, perhaps along with many of his students, seems to have participated in it.[145] The genesis of Rusconi-Sassi's design may very well begin at this point, since it shows the attitudes he had formed as a student to be substantially intact thirty years later. The lower register, with its Colossal Order spanning two stories, picks up the theme of the facade of St. Peter's, while the upper register, a false front with enframing volutes, refers to the general tradition of Roman Baroque facades. The centermost bay, however, is characterized below by its convex plan and at the apex by a mixed-line pediment which are the hallmarks of Rusconi-Sassi's Borrominian repertory. The oval vestibule which causes the convexity is responded to in the upper register by a concave aedicula; inserted between them is a dome and lantern which fulfills the same compositional function as the "sentry-box" on the facade of Borromini's S. Carlino (see Fig. 139).[146]

Regardless of what critical judgements were then or could now be applied to Rusconi-Sassi's model, his "style" deserves special consideration. What distinguished the Roman Rococo from contemporary continental trends was its devotion to its own Seicentesque heritage, and the often opposing philosophies that comprised it.[147] In fact, so open was the Rome of the Settecento to the coexistence of different "schools" that success at times depended on an architect's ability to shift from one mode to another, but attempts to actually fuse divergent lines were rare and difficult. On that basis, however, it is reasonable to argue that such attempts, set against a predominant background of nostalgia, represent a legitimately progressive trend, seeking to advance Roman architecture by mixing breeds. Rusconi-Sassi must be recognized as a component of this trend in much the same way that Juvarra was; and, modern prejudices notwithstanding, the Accademia and Carlo Fontana have to be recognized as having provided the liberal learning environment that produced

146 RUSCONI-SASSI: model for the facade of S. Giovanni in Laterano; Rome, 1732 (photo: Rev. Fabbrica di S. Pietro in Vaticano).

them. The nature of the Roman architectural market, which was severely depressed in the first quarter of the eighteenth century, and of Roman taste, which became increasingly revivalist, may have cost Rusconi-Sassi his reputation with later historians, who ignored him until recently, but upon his death he had the respect of Rome.[148]

THE LEGACY OF THE COMPETITIONS

The *concorsi* during Carlo Fontana's principate have implications for how such events would be conducted in the eighteenth century, but that is a subject for the final chapter of this book. As has been the case before, however, particularly with regard to the *concorso* of 1677, specific topics and designs from 1694 and 1696 have implications for projects both within and outside the Accademia. For example, the motif of diagonal chapels reached through the piers of a centralized church, which Ferrari and Spinelli legitimized in their 1694 and 1696 projects respectively, was picked up by Ferdinando Reif in his plan for a church (Fig. 147) that won third prize in the second class of the

147 FERDINANDO REIF: plan for a church; ASL 129 (Conc. Clem. 1704).

148 FILIPPO OTTONI: plan for a public curia; ASL 119 (Conc. Clem. 1704).

Concorso Clementino of 1704. In the same year, in the first-class project for a public curia, Filippo Ottoni incorporated semicircular wings in his third-place plan (Fig. 148), which were apparently inspired by Carlo Fontana's *Curia Innocenziana* (see Fig. 101), just as was Ferrari's use of the device in 1696.[149] For the same project in 1704, Gabriele Valvassori's second-prize plan, with its transverse oval piazza (Fig. 149), and even to some extent the building elevation fronting on it (Fig. 150), can be explained through reference to Carlo Pacenti's project for 1696. There are as well echoes of both Ferrari's and Pacenti's palace projects in Kaspar Barzanka's first-prize plan for the first class in 1704 (Fig. 151). These connections are not hard to understand, since the situation at the Accademia had not changed much between 1696 and 1704. Carlo Fontana still loomed large as its emeritus in architectural affairs; his students and his son Francesco still dominated the faculty in architecture. And while Clement XI's name was attached to the competitions of the early eighteenth century it was Fontana who had set the pattern for them, and his own projects still provided topics for the *soggetti*. The entrants in 1704 therefore had a strong incentive to look to the accomplishments of those who had met with success under similar circumstances.

Nevertheless, it would not be as productive to trace the transmission of specific motifs into later competition designs, or into architectural practice, as it has proved to be with respect to the earlier *Concorsi Accademici*. For the emphasis had now been effectively shifted from the introduction of innovative motifs to the synthesis of motifs from an established repertoire, and for this Fontana bears the responsibility. The scale of the projects in the first few public competitions, and the contact during that time with the French on equal terms, seems to have invited the application of new or even hybrid motifs to rather ordinary themes: in 1677, the truncated dome and lateral towers for centralized churches; in 1679, the towered facade with double loggia for longitudinal churches; in 1681, the elliptical belvedere for palaces.[150] After Fontana's principate the stress would be on the themes of the *soggetti* themselves,

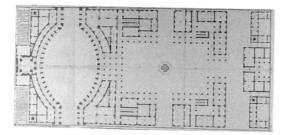

149 GABRIELE VALVASSORI: plan for a public curia; ASL 115 (Conc. Clem. 1704).

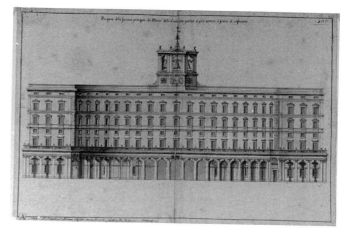

150 VALVASSORI: facade elevation for plan in Figure 149; ASL 116.

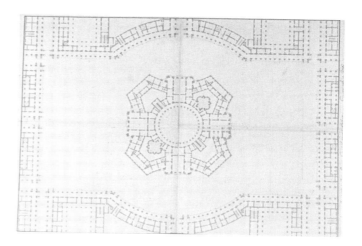

151 KASPAR BARZANKA: plan for a public curia; ASL 106 (Conc. Clem. 1704).

on their scope, their unusual (sometimes multiple, often contrived) functions, and the elaboration they required. Innovations on the level of smaller-scale motifs of planning or formal elements of design tend to be engulfed by such a context. Competitors expended their creative energies instead on a more appropriate response to the tone of the tasks, by demonstrating the scope of their knowledge of existing motifs, by bringing them together in unusual and often all-too-contrived juxtapositions, and by elaboration. Perhaps this was the best way to prepare the majority of the students for the secondary roles in the profession with which most architects had to be content, but the fact remains that very few eighteenth-century competitors emerged from the Accademia with their integrity intact. The most important of these, and the one who figures most prominently in the significance of the centenary competitions, was Filippo Juvarra.

On the issue of themes, Juvarra was given reason to reflect on that of the *concorso* of 1696 when he competed in the first class for 1705, with the subject of a villa palace for three dignitaries rather than four.[151] The gimmick of changing the number to change the geometry shows how topic-oriented the *concorsi* had become over the preceding decade, but Juvarra rose above such shallowness by overwhelming his audience with a virtuoso display of the scope of his thinking, and the quality of his skills (Figs. 152, 153). For all that, there is nothing innately new among the elements which make up his design; what is new is the synthesis itself. In it, it is possible to find only generic similarities between his approach and Ferrari's in 1696, since they both harken back to Versailles, and both of

152 FILIPPO JUVARRA: plan for a villa for three dignitaries; ASL 140 (Conc. Clem. 1705).

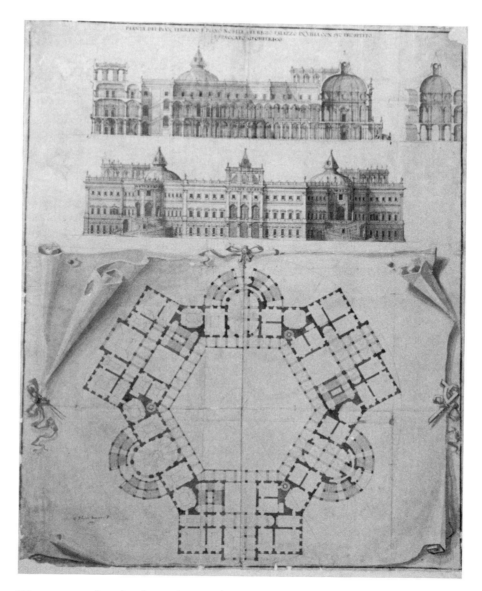

153 JUVARRA: plan, elevation, and section for the villa palace in Figure 152; ASL 141.

their palace blocks are planned on the same principle. Each set of apartments has a private courtyard in addition to the common central court, and each is joined to the others at the salons. Without more specific links between their efforts, all that can be said is that the thematic discussions within the Accademia likely informed both architects. But, since the ultimate result of Juvarra's experiments along such lines was the Palazzo Stupinigi for the King of Piedmont (Fig. 154), one of the finest Rococo villa palaces, those discussions have more importance than one might be willing to admit at first.[152]

The same can be said of the academic discussions which were probably engendered by Fontana's monastic college at Loyola, and which culminated in the task for the *concorso* of 1694 in the first class. Those discussions could have had implications for Fischer von Erlach, who had been in Rome up to the early 1680s, when he designed his monastic college and church of the Holy Trinity in Salzburg in 1694 for Archbishop Thun (Fig. 155). This represents an exasperating coincidence, for were Fischer in Rome at the time he could easily have submitted his design to the *concorso,* as it is identical in its basic composition to the three prizewinning designs. Otherwise, speculation about any direct connections between his college and events in Rome in 1694 is difficult, even though both he and Carlo Ravassi, winner of the third prize that year, designed their churches on a longitudinal oval plan. The only detectable commonality is the genesis of all the projects from Fontana's Jesuit college, which seems to have fostered a heightened level of inquiry into the theme within the Accademia that affected Fischer as well. This last is no surprise since Fischer has already been shown to have learned other useful lessons through his associations with Fontana and the Accademia while in Rome.

Much the same can be said of Juvarra, and with even more assurance because of the length and the more intimate nature of his associations. So much more involved was he that he came away touched not only by ideas but by specific motifs, like lateral towers for freestanding centralized churches (see Chapter II), or corner pavilions for

palaces (see Chapter III). It is again no surprise, therefore, to find him to have singled out the one motif in the centenary competitions that can truly be said to be new to Roman architecture. This was the church plan based on Hardouin-Mansart's Invalides chapel that appears so emphatically in Pompeo Ferrari's design for his monastic college chapel of 1694 (see Pl. 25). Juvarra's initial ideas for his first project in Turin, the Superga (see Chapter II; Fig. 156), which was once intended to house the tombs of the House of Savoy, were modeled after Hardouin-Mansart's chapel, which he in turn had derived from his uncle's projects for the Bourbon sepulcher.[153] When the design intentions for the Superga were dramatically altered, Juvarra transferred his experiments with the motif to the design of the chapel of the royal hunting lodge at Venaria Reale.[154]

Juvarra's first project for this chapel (Figs. 157, 158) takes its cue from Hardouin-Mansart's own variations on the type, which he devised as his first project for the royal chapel at Louis XIV's "hunting lodge," Versailles (see above, and Fig. 137). Such associations were symptomatic of Vittorio Amadeo's intent to match his court against Louis's; Juvarra's design was even divided into an "upper" and "lower" church like its French counterpart. Until now it has been necessary to construe that Juvarra had actually turned his attention to Paris to inform himself about these developments. But as has been shown, Hardouin-Mansart's ideas had previously been filtered through the Accademia in Rome, and had even been "Romanized" by Rossini in his first-prize chapel design for 1696 (see Pls. 50–52). Having seen before how much use Juvarra made in his studies of the Accademia's archive, and how much influence the ideas contained in the drawings could have on him, no doubt with Fontana's encouragement, this means for transmitting motifs should no longer be unexpected, or unacceptable.

As the design for the chapel evolved, Juvarra turned to other competition projects to aid his thinking. His preliminary sketch of the plan of the second project (Fig. 159) is a conflation of Rusconi-Sassi's and Spinelli's chapel projects for 1696 (Pls. 53, 56), which was to include both the

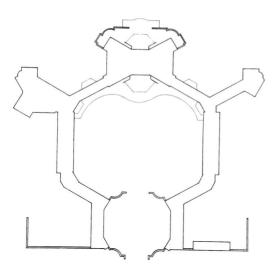

154 JUVARRA: plan of the Stupinigi Palace; Turin, 1729–33 (graphic: Troy Thompson).

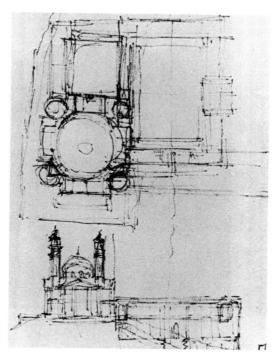

156 FILIPPO JUVARRA: first project sketch for the Superga; Turin, 1715 (source: Museo Civico, Turin).

155 J. B. FISCHER VON ERLACH: Holy Trinity Church and college; Salzburg, 1694 (photo: author).

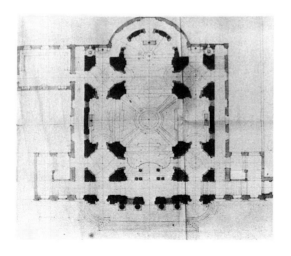

157 JUVARRA: first project plan for the chapel of the royal hunting lodge; Venaria Reale, 1716 (source: Archivio di Stato, Turin).

former's convex facade expression and the latter's diagonal vestibules opening through the forward piers of the crossing. This step took him to the final version for the chapel's plan (Fig. 160), where four circular chambers (vestibules and chapels) are inserted into the angles between the arms of the Greek cross. Again, it has been assumed until now that Juvarra's was a direct reference to Hardouin-Mansart's Invalides chapel, but the route by which its form came to him could more likely have been an indirect one, via the Accademia and Pompeo Ferrari's chapel project of 1694. Juvarra of course had somewhat different intentions for the facade of his chapel, but likewise they need not be explained in terms of LeVau's Collège des Quatre Nations (see Fig. 8), but can instead be linked to Rusconi-Sassi's facade project for the first-class competition in 1702 (see Figs. 142, 143). There one can handily find the concave wings flanking

158 JUVARRA: first project section for the chapel at Venaria Reale (source: Biblioteca Nazionale Universitaria, Turin).

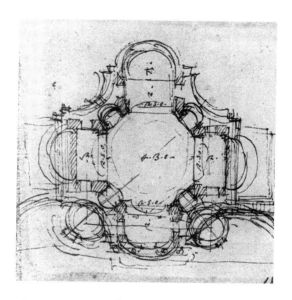

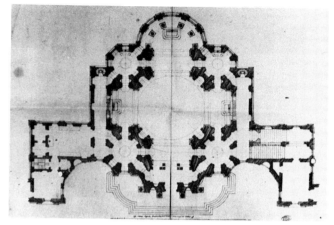

160 JUVARRA: final project plan for chapel at Venaria Reale; 1719 (source: Archivio di Stato, Turin).

159 JUVARRA: second project sketch for chapel at Venaria Reale (source: Museo Civico, Turin).

the two-story church front (which was itself apparently an offshoot of Ferrari's design; cf. Pl. 26), and these elements have considerable affinity with Juvarra's uncompleted facade for the chapel in Venaria Reale (Fig. 161). The unfinished drum above Juvarra's facade closes the circle of influence by pointing to the cupola of Ferrari's design.

Juvarra's interest in the work of Ferrari and Rusconi-Sassi is understandable since they all shared a fascination with the architecture of Borromini. Where his predecessors had been taken in by Borromini's language of decoration and space manipulation, however, Juvarra was more captivated by what Richard Pommer called the "open structures" of architects like Borromini and Guarini.[155] This was what also attracted him to Hardouin-Mansart's chapel planning schemes, though the most dramatic openings in those structures, the ones through the piers, were closed up by sculptural niches in Juvarra's final project, presumably for programmatic reasons (Fig. 162). This was an unfortunate compromise, destroying the diagonal vistas which were an important part of the spatial sequences Juvarra had staged by opening the

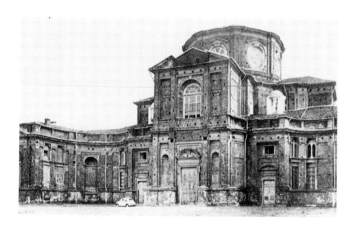

161 JUVARRA: facade of chapel at Venaria Reale (photo: Museo Civico, Turin).

162 JUVARRA: interior of chapel at Venaria Reale (photo: Museo Civico, Turin).

structure, and diminishing the lighting effects he must have hoped for as well. Still the building is a striking example of the quite sophisticated personal idiom Juvarra was developing. If its place in the history of architecture is therefore assured, then the significance of the drawings from the centenary competitions, which must have been quite instructive for Juvarra, is also guaranteed. As had been the case in 1677, and occasionally since, the drawings produced for the *concorsi* prove to have been a vital resource for later Roman architects, and for Juvarra in particular, in the formulation of their own ideas. Most consistently, it was French motifs that took root in the *concorso* designs and scattered seed into the Italian tradition. This seems to have been true regardless of the state of the relations between the French and Roman academies, as though the thirst for novelty transcended diplomatic conditions.

Individuals may therefore have been even more powerful motivators than community opinion. Fontana opened Juvarra's mind, and Juvarra in his turn urged a follower of his own to be receptive in the same way. When Bernardo Vittone came to Rome from Piedmont to join the Accademia's curriculum in architecture, he may already have prepared himself to make a study of Ferrari's college project of 1694 (cf. Figs. 105 and 106). It is one of only three *concorso* projects, the others being Barzanka's *curia* project of 1704 and a second-class church project from the same year, that he copied in exact detail and incorporated in his sketchbooks, now stored in the Musée des Arts Décoratifs, Paris. He included them among his studies of and variations on projects by Juvarra (like the 1707 *dono*) and Carlo Fontana (like the Liechtenstein palace projects), which shows the respect he had for the student work. He devoted considerable attention to Ferrari's project, so that his use of a similar church-planning scheme should

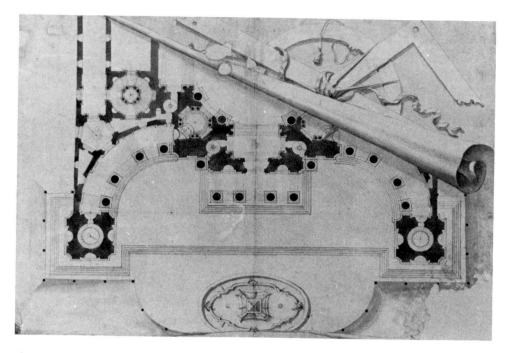

163 BERNARDO VITTONE: plan for a centralized church with bell towers; ASL 2176 (Dono Accademico).

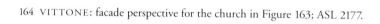

164 VITTONE: facade perspective for the church in Figure 163; ASL 2177.

not be unanticipated. It appears in his own *dono* project, a college chapel not coincidentally, which he submitted to the Accademia in 1733 in token of his being made a member, just before his return to the North (Figs. 163, 164).[156] There one finds the circular vestibules, giving access to the central vessel through the piers between the cross arms and reached from the porticoes of the concave wings flanking the facade. The latter elements, which culminate in bell towers and are no doubt modeled on Juvarra's partially unrealized intentions for the chapel of Venaria Reale, illustrate that what is really under examination here is an entire family of centralized church motifs, that include issues raised in 1677 as well (see Chapter II). They

were the progeny of French and Roman parentage, with the Accademia acting as go-between. In effect, the process of exchange that had begun so auspiciously in 1677 had yet to run its course by the end of the century, and continued to have repercussions well into the next. Albeit Vittone's mature style had little to do with what transpired for him in Rome; his activities there at least show how close his thinking was to Juvarra's in the early stages of his career. Again, the common ground is the Accademia, and by now a fairly complete idea can be had of the fertile environment it provided for the germination of architectural ideas during the last quarter of the Seicento, and the first quarter-century of its association with the French.

V

SYNTHESIS AS DESIGN IMPERATIVE AT THE CROSSROADS OF THE LATE BAROQUE

THE MENDELIAN ANALOGIES hinted at in the preceding chapter could form the starting point for these concluding remarks. To do so may strain the limits of this form of reasoning, as it requires that historical lines of architectural development be conceived of in terms of genetic principles. But once this method is used as a way of illuminating a point, the logical argument that seems to derive inevitably from it can stand on its own virtues.

Rome at the close of the High Baroque, just before Bernini's death, was a pool of architectural "genetic" resources, motifs if one prefers, which taken together determined the character of the city's built environment for the Seicento. Inbreeding, or the limitation of the future offshoots of that tradition to only a select number of resources, would have threatened the vigor of the Roman line. After all, at its origins the High Baroque had depended for its vitality on ideas brought in from outside: from the south by Bernini, from the north by Borromini, and from Tuscany by Pietro da Cortona. Rome was the essential incubator, providing the conditions favorable to the cultivation of those ideas, and to the nurture of their issue. The viability of the bloodline depended upon the continuous injection of new "genetic" material from more distant lines, which Rome could always have from the foreign artists who visited or settled there. Earlier in the Baroque, this was less true for architecture than for painting or sculpture, but by the last quarter of the seventeenth century foreigners were consistently making their way to Rome to study and contribute in that medium as well. Still, as most critics would have it, the art of Carlo Maratti and Domenico Guidi, of Mattia de Rossi and Carlo Fontana, of the membership of the Accademia in general, showed the effects of stylistic self-fertilization.

It seems from the evidence addressed in this book that those same academicians had struck upon a course of action intended to counter those effects. The union of the French and Roman academies could be construed as the merging of two separate bloodlines for the purpose of improving the health of both. The biological analogy would probably have escaped the parties involved, and for most the motives were indeed political, economic, or methodological rather than artistic. But the architectural competitions, which were a dramatic fruit of that union, do incorporate elements whose history disconcertingly invites an assessment in genetic terms. In 1677, the "gene" for the truncated dome was introduced into the Roman tradition, and the attribute reappears numerous times in the descendants of that line, even when it is transplanted to Austria or Germany. In later competitions, the "genes" for a towered and porticoed facade, or for an elliptical belvedere, are in a sense revitalized by the mixture of resources. Even motifs of Roman origin, like Fontana's lateral towers for centralized churches, which might otherwise have languished along with Roman architecture in general at the end of the Seicento, were invigorated in the process of cross-fertilization. Roman types that had become particularly sterile, like the urban palace, were given new life through contact with the French line.

Then, in the 1690s, the competitions accepted not only motifs popularized in France by Hardouin-Mansart, but also inspiration from one of Rome's own collateral lines of development, one that had split off from the mainstream earlier in the century. Borromini's idiom was one which the Accademia would once have preferred to neglect and allow to die out. The usual view is that academies in general practiced a form of architectural eugenics, working to ensure the integrity of the classical inheritance through the careful selection of a design's antecedence or pedigree, and the exclusion of aberrant characteristics. There can be little argument that such intentions were what had brought the French and Roman academies together in 1676. But in the mingling of their classical "genetic" resources there came a perhaps unanticipated result. Not only were the old lines strengthened, but new characteristics began to appear as well. With regard to the architectural competition designs at least, it was their new elements that gave them the sense of being progressive, of advancing the possibilities in Roman architecture when there was so little being built to achieve that end. A particular motif, like LeVau's truncated dome, could by itself still be considered aberrant, or foreign to the pure, classical bloodline, but what it contributed could also be exciting and suggestive, as it was for the succeeding generation of architects. The new attributes were merely a symptom of the vitality imparted to the Roman and French lineages beyond the point of their conjunction. With no clear perception of cause and effect, Carlo Fontana had enough of a grasp of the benefits of this marriage to be able to encourage that two approaches be taken by his students when they were competing in such large numbers during his second principate. On the one hand, they actively sought out the new, like the plan of the Invalides chapel, while on the other they sought to breed his Berninian line with Cortona's, or with Borromini's more divergent branch.

It may just be that one must credit Fontana with recognizing that while he himself was well beyond deriving any benefit from such an exercise, devoted as he was by then to his Late Baroque classicism, Rome's architectural tradition could still gain from it. After all, his own design for the baptistry of St. Peter's owed something to the long-term effects of the *concorso* of 1677, when the French and Roman lines had first been crossbred. Perhaps from his vantage it would not have been proper for any mature architect with a reputation for preserving conservative ideals to compromise them through experiments in hybridization. But the Accademia provided a safe laboratory, where students under his or his son's supervision, whose youth implied no stylistic preconceptions or interests to protect, could pursue such experimentation, and yet pose no danger to the mainstream. Useful resources could be gleaned from the results without threatening the architectural environment at large. In their role as "technicians" in this laboratory, Fontana's students were well prepared by his training, which exposed them to all the best of Rome's architectural resources, in effect to "engineer" new strains by recombining Roman lines that had previously diverged. At the same time, the necessity of attaching the local bloodline to a foreign one was obviated, presumably to the gratification of staunch defenders of Rome's preeminence, like Fontana. The union with the French may have provided the example, but by comprehending the numerous opportunities available for cross-fertilization between correlative lines within Rome itself, Fontana's studio, the Accademia, and their students could regain command of their inheritance, and maintain its viability for at least another generation.

To be sure, parallels drawn between modern methods of genetic research and manipulation, and Roman Baroque architecture, are potentially uncomfortable. Were it not for the elegance with which they illustrate matters central to this study, there would be no temptation to use them. Reason dictates that the mechanisms involved in either context cannot be the same, but the analogies persist nevertheless even beyond the twenty-five-year scope of the present topic. For indeed, in the second quarter of the eighteenth century there is a brief flowering of Roman architectural activity, the equivalent of the Rococo elsewhere in Europe, which can be defined only in terms of the blending of indigenous trends, rather than in terms of international influences. The germination of this phenomenon could be traced to events at the Accademia from the 1690s on. And Carlo Fontana's part in this must be reevaluated as well. He has always been accepted as one of the most important teachers of the Baroque based simply on the numbers of his students, but now something more about the progressive nature and quality of the learning experience he provided, and its ramifications for the future, can be inferred.[1] At the same time, the enlightened actions of the Accademia in giving Fontana free rein have to be admitted, in contradiction to those who would insist on academies having had only a repressive effect.

Of course there is nothing in all of this that can be transposed outside of the architecture program at the Accademia. Even its painting and sculpture curricula do not seem to have been so favorably blessed by circumstances. The architects who held the office of *principe* for long periods of time between 1675 and 1700—Charles Errard, Mattia de Rossi, and Carlo Fontana—were quite active on behalf of the Accademia and their medium. *Principi* from the ranks of painters and sculptors were almost criminally ineffectual by comparison, and so it is no wonder that architecture made such remarkable gains in its academic stature during those years, even to the point where it was virtually supreme by the turn of the century. By that time also, the *Concorsi Accademici* had brought no important young painters or sculptors to light, even though there had been more prizes, and more classes, for them. Prizewinners in architecture, however, had been set on paths not only toward local fame, as was the case with Barigioni and Rusconi-Sassi, but also into the international scene, viz. Martinelli, Carapecchia, Reissner, Ferrari, Rossini, and later Juvarra. The archive of drawings discussed here, which was the product of their efforts, becomes a very compact and inviting reference source, full of intriguing ideas, which later students at the Accademia, and architects in general, will often find very useful. This is true only to a limited extent of the much larger body of architectural designs produced in the competitions of the eighteenth century in either France or Rome (see below).

So it would seem that only in the realm of architecture at the Accademia was the charter with which it was presented by its aggregation with the French academy pursued with any great diligence. In fact this was the case to such a degree that stu-

dents were eventually able to look beyond the link to Paris, which would prove to have little return for them, to reexamine the too often neglected variegations in their own legacy, and to broaden the scope of their aspirations so that they could again perceive a route toward progress in, and an international purpose for, Roman architecture.

In light of this, previous generalizations about the status of Rome relative to France in the determination of the future course of architectural history, based on the evidence of the aggregation of 1676, are not entirely satisfactory. According to Jean-Paul Alaux, the union of the two academies bore no appreciable fruit for either party; both followed independent courses afterward, until ultimately Rome was eclipsed by the rise to eminence of the French sphere of influence later in the eighteenth century.[2] The long-term view of history and hindsight might support this, but it is doubtful that the Romans would have agreed to such an assessment in the decade just before and after 1700. Less convincing still is Nikolaus Pevsner's assertion that upon the aggregation the Accademia di San Luca had surrendered its authority to Paris "without opposition."[3] Surely a debt was owed to the French by the Accademia, which saw so many improvements in the way it conducted itself after the union, but this point, which Alaux missed, was one that Pevsner tended to exaggerate.

Organizationally, the Accademia had undergone some enhancement thanks to French example and administration; the "business" of being an academy of artists was something they better understood after 1676, even though for a while they were still not successful at it. Within two decades Carlo Fontana had mastered the craft. As for instruction, it did not take long at all for the Accademia to be able to match the drafting skills of its students against the accomplished hands of French *pensionnaires*—Domenico Martinelli was proof of that in 1679. The Romans had even toyed with the idea of introducing theory into their program by methods consistent with French academic practice. But pedantic rigor could never sit well with the Romans; that distinction formed the single most impenetrable barrier between the two academies, and in that regard their independent development was inevitable. It is by no means clear at this time, however, that the French development was destined to gain the upper hand, or that it in fact represented progress. At the Accademia, instruction had matured so rapidly that in 1696 rules of technique or theory were no longer ends in themselves, but simply means toward the end of good design, of which any student of well-rounded experience and good judgement was capable. The alliance with the French had boosted the Accademia through a potentially difficult time, but by the end of the century, the Accademia had regained its sense of self-worth, at least in matters of architecture, and was again setting its own course. In contrast, the situation at the academies in Paris was by no means as favorable.

Subsequent to the judgement he passed on the Accademia, Pevsner himself admitted that the crisis engendered in Paris by the dispute between the Ancients and Moderns had severely undermined the mandate of the academies, as much if not more than had the reduction of royal revenues. The Accademia had not been victimized by any such crisis; in fact it is evident that Fontana had opened its doors readily to ideas that could once have been considered antithetical to the establishment line. When the French academy tried to close those doors, it found itself torn apart by factional disputes. Other doors had closed around Jules Hardouin-Mansart, who had successfully imposed himself as the dictator of architectural tastes in the kingdom, effectively extinguishing all contrary notions and for a brief time the lamp of French influence abroad as well. There can be no clearer distinction between the uses made of the respective responsible positions of Hardouin-Mansart and Fontana. Rome could not afford to build as Louis XIV still could, but the atmosphere there was much healthier for constructive debate on the progress of architecture.

To continue the earlier analogy, the experiment in cross-fertilization that the French had initiated in 1676, for "the greater glory of the Arts," as Louis himself once put it, had not been entered into by them with the same enthusiasm with which the Romans greeted it. The exchange never passed in any but one direction, for there was no

way that Paris would ever allow the royal architectural bloodline to be contaminated by outside influences. Their academies had been devised for that very purpose, after all, unlike the Accademia which had to comport itself within a much more heterogeneous environment of taste. The mixing of stylistic strains was therefore something that the Romans by their nature were more inclined to accept. At first, the classicizing party at the Accademia had hoped to strengthen its line through contact with their French counterparts, and for nearly two decades they remained receptive to an influx of foreign ideas which then became a part of the local "genetic" make-up, or the repertoire of motifs available to them. But their gestures went consistently unrequited. Even Fontana, through his liaisons with La Teulière, was unable to make inroads for Roman ideas into French territory. Rebuffed, the Romans looked to their own devices, and sought to make the exchange between domestic lines of development, understanding that any line cut off from new ideas is destined to weaken and expire. The French clearly had no appreciation of this, and their policy of insulation made it a foregone conclusion that upon the death of Hardouin-Mansart, which came in 1708, the *Style Louis Quatorze* would no longer be a viable line. After its demise, several years passed before a new line, the Rococo, replaced it with sufficient vigor to stand the test of time (though it too would be short-lived).

The door between Paris and Rome, which by 1696 the latter was less inclined to notice, was threatened with closure altogether by the French early in the 1700s. In 1704, Charles Poerson became the director of the Académie de France in Rome. He had been a student of that same institution when the aggregation took effect (see Chapter I), and had been the beneficiary of all that it and the sojourn in Rome were believed then to offer. Yet in 1707 he was moved to propose the abolition of the satellite branch in a letter to Hardouin-Mansart, with the observation that there "was not much good architecture in Rome" (this from a painter), and better examples could be provided for students in France by Hardouin-Mansart himself.[4] Tensions in Rome were still making it uncomfortable for the French, and what Poerson suggested was effectively a retreat. In the same letter, he encouraged that French students be allowed to travel through northern Italy instead, to learn from Lombard and Venetian example, all of which was proof for Pevsner that the French no longer considered Rome to be the fountainhead. The pressures to vacate were more likely diplomatic than artistic, however, for in time, after Hardouin-Mansart and Louis XIV had passed away, and tensions had eased, Poerson could even see his way clear to accepting the office of *principe* of the Accademia, following in the footsteps of Errard, from 1714 to 1718, and again in 1721–22. This amounts to an admission on the part of the French that they still prized their association with the Romans, especially as it pertained to the union of the academies, which still survived after nearly half a century. Poerson's earlier comments regarding the value of study in Lombardy and the Veneto thus sound more as if he was affected by Roman attitudes toward the broadening of a student's base of experience, as practiced by the Fontanas at the Accademia. The picture that emerges is unquestionably one in which Rome has the upper hand.

This is no more apparent than when one considers the flurry of activity at the Accademia during the first decade of the Settecento, and the earliest history of the *Concorsi Clementini*. These competitions were sponsored by Clement XI, who became pope in 1700 and involved himself in the doings of the Accademia as no pope had since Urban VIII. He made his presence felt most appreciably in the diversion of papal funds to subsidize the prizes in the public competitions, which would thereafter bear his name.[5] With this certain source of revenue, it was actually possible to hold the competitions annually between 1702 and 1711, and Clement's interest may even have extended as far as having some say in the definition of the *soggetti*. His authority reached into the running of the academy as well. When he came to the throne, he found Carlo Maratti holding the office of *principe* (see Chapter IV), and named him to that position for life;[6] through Maratti, Clement would make his wishes known to the Accademia for the next decade or more.

It sounds very much as though Clement had been made well aware of the kind of benefit that might be derived by exercising his patronage in favor of the Accademia. Through it his influence on artistic activity could be more widespread and enduring, with a greater return on his investment than actual commissions for work would have brought. By his actions most of the artists of Rome would have been devoted to the greater glory of his reign, and of his domain, the Church, through the activities of the Accademia. For its part, the Accademia could now have what it had sought after in vain in 1676: aristocratic patronage of the highest order. While substantial commissions were still to be few and far between, a generation of students could nevertheless be reminded where their loyalties as artists lay—with the traditions of Papal Rome. The French academies under Louis XIV had been both positive and negative examples in this regard. If Clement was to make use of the Accademia effectively, he could not stifle it through too despotic a hold, but must let it follow a course set for it by those best qualified to understand its needs and objectives. And if there was anyone in a position to set the course for the Accademia in the area of architecture, it was Carlo Fontana, who may also have interpreted for Clement the lessons to be learned from the French miscalculation of the ideal association between an enlightened sovereign and his academy of artists.

To his great disappointment, it must be presumed, Fontana had not been in the position to be named *principe* for life. He had missed that opportunity by virtue of having stepped down from the office two years before Clement XI bestowed the honor on the *principe* presiding in 1700, who was Maratti. In view of the animosity that existed between Fontana and Maratti even before this, one can be sure that this circumstance did not sit altogether well with Fontana, but it is not the case that Fontana was in any way slighted or passed over by the pope.[7] Instead, he was made "first counselor" to the Accademia in matters of architecture, his own position for life that gave him control over what concerned him most, the Accademia's curriculum in architecture.[8] From that vantage he could continue the progress in that area that he initiated in the 1690s, with his son Francesco and other graduates of his studio providing instruction, setting competition tasks, and judging entries. As a result, the architectural components of the *Concorsi Clementini* rather routinely adhered to the pattern established by the competitions in 1694 and 1696.

That pattern was resumed with the first *Concorso Clementino* in 1702, for which the *soggetti* were revived from two years before (App. B, 1700, n. 1), when academic activities, including competition, had been curtailed following the death of Innocent XII and the election of Clement XI. The tasks in architecture for 1702 began in the first class with a cathedral church, overlooking a large *piazza,* which was to be flanked by a chapter house and a hospital. As was true in the *concorsi* for 1694 and 1696, this project is reminiscent of one of Fontana's own: the extension of the *piazza* of St. Peter's which he proposed in *Il Tempio Vaticano* (see Chapter IV). In other words, the topic was calculated again to aggrandize his own accomplishments, while advancing the talents of his students. For the second class in 1702, the task was to design a high altar for the cathedral, the principal point of departure being the *baldacchino* of St. Peter's, which had been Fontana's point of departure for the altar of S. Maria in Traspontina (1674). Here was a subject matter ideally suited to the abilities of students at the intermediate level. Then in the third class, competitors were to render a niche from the nave of S. Giovanni in Laterano, which had been remodeled by Borromini just prior to 1650. Where Borromini had been an implicit option for student investigations in 1694 and 1696, his work had now been specifically recommended for close examination. There is perhaps no clearer testimony to the liberality of Fontana's curriculum.

The adoption without revision of the architectural *soggetti* from 1700 as the ones for 1702 and the first *Concorso Clementino* also clearly testifies to the fact that the Accademia under Maratti and Clement XI wanted the Fontana reforms to continue unchecked.[9] To this end, Fontana's son Francesco was retained as *vice-principe* after 1700, and as instructor in architecture along with other students of his father and G. B. Contini, his father's *confrère* from the Bernini "school." The number of lecturers, one for each month of the academic season as had long been the case for painting, again assured against the rise of a single dominant authority that might at too early a stage limit a student's experience to a single line of thought. Breadth of exposure was the key to the success of the Fontana method, and the competitions were the test.

In 1703, the test took the form it had had in 1696, when all three *soggetti* were related to one imaginary building complex. This time it was a pontifical palace, the kind of project that, had it ever really been contemplated, would have naturally fallen to Fontana as premier papal architect and Rome's greatest living practitioner of his art.[10] In the absence of a legitimate commission of such grand scope, his students could still have the chance to cut their creative teeth on a visionary one. In the first-class competition for the palace proper, prizes were awarded to entries from Fontana's nephew Carlo Stefano, Francesco Ferrari (perhaps related to Pompeo; see Chapter IV), and two young architects of some consequence in Rome later on: Antonio Canevari and Gabriele Valvassori. The competition in the second class for the salon of the palace attracted the participation of another French *pensionnaire,* Jean Cotelle, who took second prize. In the third class, the task of a garden gateway was as potentially mundane as it had proved to be in 1696, but the first-prize winner, Francesco Bianchi, made the most of the opportunity with a very fine and comprehensive design. In all, ten prizes were awarded in the three classes of architecture, and a uniformly well executed and conceived body of drawings was produced.

And so it continued rather consistently for the next ten years.[11] In the first-class *concorsi,* the visionary themes ranged from great private villas (1705, 1707, and 1710) to public complexes (1704 and 1706), from magnificent city churches (1713) to proud academies of art (1708 and 1709). During this period, but at no other time in the history of the *Concorsi Clementini,* one task was assigned in the first class that related to a project that was actually envisioned: in 1711 designs were required for a new sacristy for St. Peter's, an idea that was very close to Clement XI's heart. It had become the rule for first-class *soggetti* to deal with buildings for which a vast scale or multiple uses were imagined, to test the student's adaptability to various functional or theoretical planimetric requirements. Since this was usually meant as a measure of practical competence in a hypothetical situation, one could often look in vain for anything of interest at levels of invention beyond planning, that is until signs of real genius emerge, as in Filippo Juvarra's villa design of 1705 (see Chapter IV). General competency was certainly not an unreasonable objective, until it is made the only objective, as the French had done. What made the system at the Accademia more effective was that when genius emerged, though it did so rarely, it could be recognized and nurtured rather than suppressed.

The methods employed in defining the competitions in architecture at the Accademia seem to have been intended to serve this end. It was the second-class topics that urged the participants to be daring and experimental, to give full expression to their creative identity, as a part of the intermediate process of growth between simple technical competency and a general professional ability (as had been the case in 1696 with Ludovico Rusconi-Sassi; see Chapter IV). In the second-class competitions of the early eighteenth century, a wide range of types—chapels, altars, tombs, salons, staircases, portals—were proposed as subjects, where the scale and succinctness of the problem virtually invited the student to be new and different in order to stand out. Here, too, were the kinds of projects they could actually expect to be working on some day, as opposed to the dream world of the first class. In fact, it more often fell to this category to deal with topical problems of design, like the facade of S. Giovanni (1705) or the Trevi fountain (1706).

Success at each stage was predicated on accomplishment at the previous level. One could not be a competent professional in the first class without the judgement learned in the second, and one could not proceed to the second until one had learned to read the book of Roman architecture

upon which that judgement would be based. The preferred means of testing achievement in the third class was, therefore, to send students out to measure and render architectural details, but in preferred source to which they were sent. In the first dozen years of the *Concorsi Clementini,* the youngest competitors were directed to copy the work of Borromini three times (1702, 1710, and 1711), Bernini three times (1704, 1706, and 1707), and Pietro da Cortona twice (1709 and 1713). In 1705, so as not to mislead them with only the great names of the High Baroque, they were even sent to render the portal of Flaminio Ponzio's Sciarra-Colonna palace. Their treatment could not have been more evenhanded in this.

Still, an unfortunate dissent emerged. Students, whether in Paris or Rome, were never entirely convinced of the necessity of copying as a pedagogical tool, so neither were they content to tolerate it for very long. Regrettably, some of the painters and sculptors had begun to give vent to their frustrations in the churches and palaces to which they had been admitted for their studies. Because of their scandalous behavior, in 1706 it was decided to exclude the third class from competition in the following year as punishment.[12] Francesco Fontana, then acting *principe,* had been absent when that decision was made, and when he returned he overturned it, because it was prejudicial to the architects. Competition in the third class was now an important factor in their advancement through the architecture curriculum. Also, they had not precipitated the problem because extramural study was critical to their art, and they would never have compromised their welcome throughout Rome by such behavior. After all, painters and sculptors could study from drawings, prints, or models in the classroom, but an architect had to study his art in the streets. Sets of engravings, like Domenico de Rossi's *Studio d'Architettura Civile* (1703), were increasingly available, but they were no substitute for the buildings themselves.

The general congregation of the Accademia, including even some of the member architects, opposed Francesco; the rebellious attitude of the students was too galling. The matter was referred to Pope Clement, and he, advised perhaps by Carlo Fontana, angrily sided with Francesco and reinstated the third-class competitions for 1707. In that year the topic for the architects in the third class was the facade of the Barberini palace, which was at least a challenging rendering. The following year, an original topic was again proposed for the third class (a church portal), perhaps by way of appeasement, but the idea was poorly received, and was never revived again. This may seem like a sorry incident in the history of the Accademia, but it actually speaks highly of the level of involvement on the part of the students, and of those teachers, like Francesco Fontana, who were advocates on their behalf. Something like that atmosphere had existed at the French academies a few decades earlier, but it had long since evaporated.

The French were also far from being able to sustain the intensity of activity and inquiry that is evident during the earliest *Concorsi Clementini* at the Accademia. With royal favor withdrawn, their infrequent competitions were minor internal affairs, not the great public spectacles that the Roman versions were. The *concorsi* were still celebrated on the Campidoglio, with elaborate ceremony, poetry, music, and art, and were climaxed by the awarding of silver and gold medallions of fine workmanship. The spectacle was not only for Rome, but also for those who came to Rome just to see it, or who read about it in the descriptive tracts published each year by Giuseppe Ghezzi. The competitors themselves came from throughout Italy—Messina, Parma, Milan, Turin, Como—and from Poland and France. Rome was the object of European attention, as it had always been, even in spite of the lack of substantial artistic production. Affairs were continuing at the Accademia as they had been initiated by Carlo Fontana in the 1690s, the only difference being that because of the attentions and generosity of their great and noble patron, Clement XI, the pace was much more invigorating.

That pace did not persist beyond the death of Carlo Fontana in 1714, and several years would pass between competitions in the future. Because of this, he appears all the more to have been the principal motivator behind the success of the Accademia in the fulfillment of its educational

mission as the seventeenth century became the eighteenth. However, his passing was not overtly mourned by the Accademia, undoubtedly because his habit of extolling his personal accomplishments had made him few friends.[13] The effect has been to obscure both then and now what were his accomplishments on behalf of others, the implications of which are much subtler. His worth is just beginning to be measured through the abilities of the numerous students who passed through his studio and in several instances became great architects. It is hoped that this book also makes clear what a useful teaching institution the Accademia had become since he joined the faculty in 1675, thanks in large part to his direct influence. After all, it must be realized that if ego were to be a negative factor in the determination of an artist's historical stature, then the reputations of Leonardo and Michelangelo, of Bernini and Borromini, would have to be reassessed as well.

But the principal objective here has been to illuminate the progress in architectural pedagogy at the Accademia against the background of its relationship with the French academies after 1675. Simple pronouncements, rooted in a generally valid historical picture which gives the French institutions the larger role in determining the future course of "modern" taste, are not satisfactory when exposed to the detailed evidence from more focused spans of time and place. For instance, it can no longer be upheld that Paris and Rome returned to being oblivious of each other soon after their union. The *Concorsi Accademici* prove that at least the Accademia was keeping tabs on its French counterparts, and understood what standards it was to weigh itself against, but if so it seems unlikely that the French could not sense the competitive atmosphere for themselves.

Neither can it be at all possible any longer to view the aggregation of 1676 as a "surrender" on the part of the Romans, regardless of the admittedly broad-scoped judgements of historians like Wittkower, Blunt, or Pevsner. More accurately, the union was a strategic alliance, entered into to bring the Romans the benefits of French pedantic and organizational rigor, but not so they could make themselves over in the image of the French.

That would have been impossible under any circumstances, given the pluralism of stylistic and theoretical attitudes extant in Rome. The aim of the Accademia seems to have been to bring order to its own house, to clear the air of nagging logistical problems, so that it could better see and realize its own goals as an academic institution. The attempts to fuse the French and Roman architectural traditions in the first of the *Concorsi Accademici* became something of a pretext, an attempt to find through design a middle ground between the two traditions in every academic respect, and to present a united front that would advance the cause of the visual arts. The Accademia's purposes may have been lofty, unobtainable, even naive, but the architectural drawings indicate that the Romans were pursuing their ends doggedly as late as the 1690s. To have conceived their means to such ends in any terms, even merely architectural, presupposes that at worst the Romans were willing to grant equal stature to French ideas, but by no means to cave in entirely to them.

Once it had become obvious to the Romans that the French had long since abandoned unilaterally the pretext of shared objectives for the arts, they were well prepared to look to themselves for the definition of new objectives. And by then the efficient mechanisms were in place to pursue them, thanks to the contributions to method made by the French. The festive centenary of the Accademia, and the inspiration of Carlo Fontana, had also restored Rome's confidence in and fascination with its own architectural heritage. The middle ground could then be established between Roman traditions, and progress resumed from there. Once this plateau of self-realization and self-assertion had been reached, during Fontana's second principate, it was sustained well into the next century by the generation of designers responsible for the surge of building activity that came during the second quarter of the Settecento. During this period, the so-called Roman Rococo, Roman architecture, though diverse, remained expressively Roman.

If Rome was indeed on the decline as an artistic capital at this time, the Romans had apparently not been informed. With scholarly hindsight, it

may be tempting to retrace the path taken in the evolution of taste backward and find an arbitrary point where the torch was passed from Rome to Paris. But from their vantage the Romans could not have seen that they had turned off onto a route doomed to extinguish itself, while Paris was attaining pride of place as the new artistic capital of Europe. To be fair, there would be many other threads of stylistic development cut short upon the fall of the *Ancien Régime,* and buried behind the wall of the social and cultural revolution engendered by the rise of industry and nationalism. And, in the final analysis, it is not reasonable at all to assume that the transfer of power occurred at a specific moment, rather than over an extended period during which neither side was aware of what was happening. The evidence of the *Concorsi Accademici* in architecture cannot be reconciled with the image of an Accademia that had submitted passively to its fate, any more than the sad situation at the royal academies in Paris in the early 1700s presaged great things to come.

When Charles Poerson became *principe* of the Accademia in 1714, the year of Fontana's death, the Roman school was at its peak, while the academies of France were at their nadir. When Charles Errard had been in a similar situation, as director of the satellite in Rome and *principe* at the Accademia some forty years before, things had been different, for then the royal academies were passing the quiescent Accademia on the way up. Poerson could not have missed the discrepancy, for he had been present as a student in Rome at the earlier instance. In the interim, the Accademia had attached itself to the French long enough to gain the momentum necessary to carry it to new heights of achievement, while the Paris academies were faltering as a consequence of their inflexibility. But by 1715, the year of Louis XIV's death and the advent of the Regency, those academies were just a few years away from their own recovery and the forging of a new and significant purpose for themselves in French Rococo society. With their roles reversed, with the Accademia now in a position to preach to the French and show them a way out of their doldrums, it would be of interest to find whether their union under

Poerson was a fleeting gesture, or whether there is evidence for an exchange of ideas, this time from south to north, over an extended period of time.

Such evidence has already been presented in a prefatory way by Hellmut Hager in an article which uses the eighteenth-century competition topics and designs from both the French and Roman academies to make a case for communication between the two.[14] Regular competition for the *Prix-de-Rome* did not resume in Paris until 1720, at which time students of architecture were officially allowed to participate, as they had not been since their academy was opened in 1671. Now the documents of student activity at the Académie d'Architecture were beginning to appear in numbers sufficient to analyze trends, and what Hager found was that Roman motifs, Roman design ideas, and even the subject matter of Roman competitions, were intruding into French academic practices, most remarkably by the middle of the century. The most telling observation to be made is that since the Parisian competitions were meant to single out promising talents to send to Rome, for those students the experience of Roman issues and events was still before them. What knowledge they had prior to this had to have been filtered through the Académie d'Architecture itself, perhaps by way of professors who had previously been to Rome. Whatever the mechanism of transmission, France was showing itself to be receptive to influence from abroad, from Rome specifically, to a degree that had not been possible during the reign of Louis XIV. Indeed, it is somewhat a surprise to find so much openness affecting the actions of the Académie d'Architecture, even in the eighteenth century when absolutism had only been replaced by nationalism. However, there is no escaping the evidence, or the opportunity that Poerson's principate provided to renew the ties between the academies. By 1720 the doors were again open to exchange between Paris and Rome, and the good intentions that had brought them together in 1676, but which diplomatic and philosophical differences had kept them from pursuing, could be restored as the common ground shared by institutions which viewed each other on equal terms.

In a sense, Hager's article is an appropriate epilog. It substantiates the conclusion that throughout the fluctuating history of the association between the Accademia and the French academies, and regardless of the preconceptions of previous scholarship, it was the Romans who were leading at several turns in pursuit of the goal of improving the academy system. They achieved their ends through the formalization of the *concorsi,* building first on French example, but then adapting competition to their own particular needs at the end of the seventeenth century, and laying the groundwork for a resurgence of Roman architecture in the 1720s and 1730s. So potent was their example that the French, who once felt there was nothing useful to be learned from outside their sphere, accepted Roman influence in reforming their own efforts. It was not until the middle of the eighteenth century that the two institutions can finally be said to be following roughly parallel lines of development, with some contact running between them, and only later will the French academies rise to preeminence. The instability of their association from 1675 to 1725, however, cannot be blamed on the Romans, who in that time patiently pursued their objectives as a school of art to take the Accademia systematically from its lowest ebb to its highest level of achievement. Ulterior motives on the part of the French, most of which had little connection with the progress of architectural education within their purview, were responsible for swinging the pendulum of the development of their own academies to either side of the steady direction followed by the Romans.

It is the contention of this concluding chapter that it was the integrity and energy of the Romans in the fulfillment of their goals that guaranteed the effectiveness of their academy as a resource for architects and architectural design into the eighteenth century. The designs from the *Concorsi Accademici* in architecture, found in the preceding chapters to have been the direct result of those circumstances, were essential to much of importance that was built later, and justifiably support the conclusion. Amid the complex pattern of lines of stylistic development being woven in the eighteenth century, it is increasingly unwise to neglect the period's Europe-wide academic activity for the lure of France alone. Refining our understanding of this crucial juncture, when modern concepts of "taste" were in embryo, depends upon a more encompassing per-

spective of the institutional factors at work. Consideration of the Accademia's role restores more of the rich and intricate tapestry of architectural history between the seventeenth and eighteenth centuries.

Appendix A
Catalog of the Drawings

In view of the information brought to light since the first publication of the drawings, the present catalog has been reorganized to comply with the new chronology proposed in this volume. The original numbering used in the catalog of the Accademia di San Luca's collection of architectural drawings (Marconi et al., [1974]), and still used to retrieve drawings, is indicated in parentheses for each entry. It should also be noted that since many of the drawings underwent extensive conservation in the early 1980s, mention of their physical condition will be limited to instances where the readability of the design has been compromised. Measurements are given first in centimeters and then in inches, height preceding width.

1 (ASL 1)
SIMON CHUPIN

first prize, 1677
plan for a domed and porticoed octagonal church
   with bell towers
70 x 51 (27.5 x 20)
gray pen and gray wash

reverse: "no. 6 pezzi 3" & "H" in pen; "1" in
   pencil
obverse: "Simone Sciupagn po. p'mio 1677" in
   pen, upper border; "no. 1—N" in pen, upper
   right corner; "Canne Sei" in pen, adjacent to
   scale bar

2 (ASL 2)
SIMON CHUPIN

first prize, 1677
facade elevation for above
71 x 58 (28 x 22.75)
gray pen and gray wash

reverse: "/ne Sciupagn po. premio" in pen
   (trimmed left); "391" in pencil
obverse: "<u>N 6</u>" in pen, upper right corner;
   "Canne Sei" in pen, adjacent to scale bar; "Pa.
   Classe Simone Sciupagn po. p'mio 16/" in
   pen, lower right (trimmed right)

3 (ASL 3)
SIMON CHUPIN

first prize, 1677
longitudinal section for above
64 x 52 (25.25 x 20.5)
gray pen and gray wash

reverse: "Architettura di/" in red chalk (trimmed
   right); "398" in pencil
obverse: "/anta del Campanile" in pen, upper left
   (trimmed left); "Pianta della Cuppola" in
   pen, upper right; "Canne Sei" in pen, adjacent to scale bar

In the course of time, the sheets on which Chupin executed his design have been badly stained or torn, and apparently trimmed to their present size, which would indicate much handling for whatever purpose. But the images remain intact, and reveal a superlative degree of precision in his use of the tools of drafting and shading. Chupin demonstrates a technical skill unsurpassed by any of the other competitors from the *Concorsi Accademici*. There is a uniformly excellent quality of pen and wash that applies not only to the rendering of architectural detail, but also to the sculpture and fresco decoration he includes in the elevation and section drawings.

    Chupin's church occupies a site considerably larger (approximately 240 x 330 *palmi*) than the one stipulated by the task, but that is not exceptional when compared to his fellow competitors (see below). A hexastyle portico extends for five of the seven bays of the facade, with access to the church provided by one major and two minor portals. The interior is a Greek cross, having a domed octagon at the center. Angled corridors behind the beveled piers supporting the pendentives link the ends of the cross arms to form a continuous ambulatory of octagonal plan. In these corridors, opposite the piers, are four semi-oval altar niches, which with the main and transept altars bring the total to the required seven. And compactly inserted within the corners of the rectangle are the sacristies and ancillary spaces also mentioned in the task.

Of the exterior elevations, with their unpretentious pilaster articulations, only the facade holds any interest, incorporating as it does the principal features of cupola, campanili, and portico. The latter, with Ionic columns derived from Michelangelo's on the Campidoglio, is spaced more widely at the center, and is flanked by two bays below the towers, framed by compound pilasters. The giant order spans two stories at the facade, the first carrying sculpture niches alternating with the portals and the second balustraded windows with arched lintels. The sculptural elaboration of the facade is limited to the four niche statues and a relief panel above the central portal. The freestanding figures are nondescript, more like studies after antique models of the draped male figure than any saints in the litany. But the relief panel may have some connection with the royal theme of the *concorso,* as it appears to be an interpretation of the task in sculpture (Chapter II, note 7).

Chupin's designs for the interior paintings are more readily identifiable as appropriately Christian in subject matter, though they are still quite conventional, if not banal. From ground to lantern along the centerline: the altarpiece depicts St. Luke painting an icon of the Virgin; in the lunette above is the Assumption, flanked by Evangelists in the pendentives; in the dome, Mary resides in heaven, as Queen or Intercessor. A unified Marian theme is achieved, but certainly this pedestrian iconography holds no interest in comparison to the fanatic care with which it and every other

aspect of the design is realized. There are no errors or *pentimenti* whatsoever. This would have made Chupin's drawings an invaluable reference, which can explain their rather worn condition.

Returning to the exterior, the campanili above the outside bays of the facade are of one story, and oval plan, oriented with their long axes parallel to the front. The choice of one story, which all the competitors made, prevented the campanili from competing with the dome visually in the two-dimensional environment of the drawing. Above the crossing, the cupola stands on a plain base, its drum articulated by eight pairs of freestanding Corinthian columns which alternate with large, splayed-arch windows.

Every competitor in the *Concorsi Accademici* had his "showpiece," the drawing on which he expended the most effort, or which revealed the most of his design or talent. For many, Chupin included, that showpiece was the section, where different conditions of light, and the opportunity for decorative detailing, invited the most earnest display of technique, and of the viability of a design. In Chupin's section, each architectural motif is sculpturally embellished or texturally enhanced. The pilasters of the giant order, now with more florid Corinthian capitals, are fluted, as are those of the drum, and moldings of all kinds are given a variety of carved patterns. Each segment of the bands of coffering in the barrel vaults is supplied with a rosette, carefully and delicately drawn. Architecturally there is little of interest, however, aside from the *coretti* high in the bevels of the piers or overlooking the main altar, or the simple aedicular frames for the altarpieces. The decor, beyond the paintings mentioned above, is completed by the statuary niches in the bevels of the crossing, relief panels over doors, angels supporting the painted altarpieces in the ambulatory, pairs of reclining figures above the round-headed vault windows, and winged cherubic heads in the spandrels above the windows of the drum.

4 (ASL 4)

AUGUSTIN-CHARLES D'AVILER

second prize, 1677
plan for a domed and porticoed octagonal church
    with bell towers
71 x 60 (28 x 23.5)
gray pen and gray wash

reverse: "no. 5 pezzi 3" & "H" in pen;
    "<u>1677</u>/P'ma Classe/Agostino Daviler" &
    "394" in pencil

obverse: "Pianta della Cuppola" in pen, upper
    left; "Pianta del Campanile" in pen, upper
    right; "Sagrestia" in pen, behind main altar;
    "Capella del Santissimo" in pen, left of main
    altar; "Capella della Madonna" in pen, right
    of main altar; "Il Sacro Fonte" in pen, in
    right facade tower; "Palmi 10" & "Canne V"
    in pen, adjacent to scale bar; "Agostino
    d'Aviler 2o. premio 1677" in pen, lower left

5 (ASL 5)

AUGUSTIN-CHARLES D'AVILER

second prize, 1677
facade elevation for above
66 x 47 (26 x 18.5)
gray pen and gray and green washes

reverse: "393" in pencil
obverse: "Palmi 10" & "Canne V" in pen, adja-
    cent to scale bar; "Agostino Daviler 2o. P.
    1677" in pen, lower left

6 (ASL 6)

AUGUSTIN-CHARLES D'AVILER

second prize, 1677
longitudinal section for above
68 x 51 (26.75 x 20)
gray pen and gray wash

reverse: "Agostino Daviler 2o. Premio 1677" in
    pen; "392" in pencil
obverse: "Palmi 10" & "Canne V" in pen, adja-
    cent to scale bar

D'Aviler's church was planned on an irregular site,
the maximum dimensions of which are about 230
by 300 *palmi*, meaning that he, too, ignored that
particular condition of Tomassini's *soggetto*. The
complex polygonal outline of the plan is generated
by the variety of chapel spaces that surround the

domed octagon at the center. In the cardinal
directions are the arms of the Greek cross leading
to the entrance, the secondary altars on the transverse axis, and the main altar at the east with a
rectangular sacristy behind it. To either side of the
main altar are the chapel of the Holy Sacrament
(left) and the Lady Chapel (right), which are
oblong spaces situated perpendicular to the diagonal axes of the plan. They are entered through
arched openings in the bevels below the pendentives, echoing the altar niches which face them
across the octagon and bring the total number of
altars to seven as required by the task description.
The altars are marked on the plan with Roman
numerals beginning to the left of the entrance and
proceeding clockwise, so that the main altar is
number IV.

    The bases of the campanili enclose the church
front, but project beyond the diameter of the
church proper for half their width. They are
square in plan but house two circular chapels, each
with an additional altar to the rear, the one on the
right reserved for baptisms. A tetrastyle portico
precedes the main entrance to the church, with
secondary entrances between it and the towers
leading into the west arm, the tower chapels, and
staircases giving onto the second story.

    The articulation of the facade begins with the
giant Doric order of the portico, and continues in
classical sequence to the Ionic order of the belfries,
and the Composite order of the drum. The central
bay of the portico is set apart by its greater span,
and the height of the main portal. The latter inter-
rupts the continuity of the string courses of the
flanking bays, which have been divided between
an ornately framed oval panel above, and a statuary niche below. The outside bays, below the belfries, are also wider in span, and crossed not by the
string course, but by arched moldings framing the
tall windows that light the tower chapels, below
the small windows that light their vaults. Between
the towers and the portico are recessed bays for
the minor portals, opening deeply into the chambers behind them as do the balustraded balconies
above.

    The cupola, raised on a flared base, has large
arched windows in the drum alternating with

paired engaged columns. The angles between buttresses and window bays are masked by concave pilasters (see the quarter-plan in Plate 4). The cupola's socle reaches a height nearly equal to the uppermost cornices of the towers, and is pierced by four large lights. In section this socle can be seen to house a truncated dome, which serves as the mechanism of transition from the octagon of the lower story to the circle of the drum, having its own source of light in the manner of a sunken dome.

The section (see Pl. 6) is also D'Aviler's "showpiece," and so there is much else that he elaborates upon in it. He does not, however, either in elevation or section, devote any effort to rendering painted or sculpted decoration. There are, in fact, only the four statues at the facade. His is rather an architect's elaboration, taking the form of nonfigural carving or stucco decoration, or the details of the architecture itself. For the interior in particular, D'Aviler orchestrated stucco work to highlight specific features within the main architectural theme, like the *coretti* in the upper part of the bevels or in the cross arms, the soffits of the arches, the surfaces of niches and vaults, the ribs and moldings in the socle, or the spandrels in the drum. D'Aviler provides plinths for sculpture and surfaces for paint, but goes no further. In his role as architect he leaves such work to others, and proceeds to the practical needs of the building, like the carpentry of the roofs and false dome, or the iron cinches of the domes, or even the mechanism of the bells shown in the tower section.

While at first glance his hand may appear to be as fine as Chupin's, there is evidence in the quality of line or the presence of *pentimenti* (altar number I) that D'Aviler was not altogether as capable a draftsman as Chupin. The heavier line that defines the balusters in D'Aviler's design, a result of their being rendered freehand, further distances his work from Chupin's more consistent quality of line. In his elevation and section drawings D'Aviler came closest to emulating the quality of Chupin's draftsmanship, lacking only the last increment of sureness or sheer physical skill necessary for perfection. This is not to say that D'Aviler was any less meticulous in the agonizing application of fine detail, from the Orders to the tabernacles of the altars. In fact, it may safely be said that though second to Chupin with regard to the care taken in rendering, D'Aviler was nevertheless several orders of magnitude ahead of the vast majority of competitors, French or otherwise, in the *Concorsi Accademici*. And while D'Aviler was not as concerned as Chupin with the inclusion of details of painting or sculpture, he was far more thorough in the elaboration of architectural details, both practical and decorative. For the Orders he includes even the smallest details, like guttae, and the stucco decoration is rendered so intricately that its finer passages are often obscured by the marbled texture of the paper. Though his skill with tools falls just short of Chupin's, the comprehensive nature of his design ultimately distinguishes D'Aviler from his compatriot, and from most of those who follow.

It should also be noted that D'Aviler has used green wash to indicate those parts of the elevation which would be sheathed in lead, such as roofs and domes, as protection from the elements. Since this does not have the strength of a convention for French draftsmen, it is interesting to note that Desgots, whose drawings so often correspond with D'Aviler's in other regards, also uses the same technique in his third-prize elevation (see corresponding text).

7 (ASL 7)
CLAUDE DESGOTS

third prize, 1677
plan for a domed and porticoed octagonal church
    with bell towers
66 x 51 (26 x 20)
gray pen and gray wash

reverse: "no. 4 pezzi 3" & "H" in pen;
    "1677/P'ma Classe/Claudio di Go" & "399"
    in pencil
obverse: "no. 12 N" in pen, upper right corner;
    "Canne" in pen, adjacent to scale bar;
    "Claudio di Go 3o. premio 1677" in pen,
    lower left

8 (ASL 8)
CLAUDE DESGOTS

third prize, 1677
facade elevation for above
70 x 50 (27.5 x 19.75)
gray pen and gray and green washes

reverse: "409" in pencil
obverse: "no. 13 N" in pen, upper right corner;
"Canne" in pen, adjacent to scale bar;
"Claudio di Go 3o. premio 1677" in pen,
lower left

9 (ASL 9)
CLAUDE DESGOTS

third prize, 1677
longitudinal section for above
70 x 60 (27.5 x 23.75)
gray pen and gray wash

reverse: "cartella III B" in pen; "410" in pencil;
"Se. Claudio di Go 3o. po." in pen; "no. po.
del Se. Claudio di Go" in pen (inverted)
obverse: "no. 14 N" in pen, upper right corner;
"Pianta della Cuppolla" in pen, upper left;
"Pianta del Campagnille" in pen, upper right;
"Canne" & "Palmi 10" in pen, adjacent to
scale bar; "Claudio di Go 3o. premio 1677"
in pen, lower left

Though it first appears to be concentric, the organizing geometry of the plan of Desgots's church is that of the octagon used to define the centralized nave from which the shallow arms of a Greek cross project. The eastern arm connects with a smaller cross-space, of oblong dimensions, housing the main altar, and side altars are situated in the transverse arms. At the diagonals are four circular chapels linked to the nave through the bevels of the octagon, bringing the number of altars to seven. A ring of corridors joins these chapels to the sanctuary, the recessed portico of the facade, and two quasi-oval sacristies behind the side altars. Around the perimeter of the building, Desgots had rounded the vertices of the octagon, and placed shallow aedicular projections between them on line with the altars, effectively suggesting a more circular arrangement for the exterior. This he does on a site measuring roughly 260 *palmi* in diameter.

At the west, this "circle" is flattened to accommodate the hexastyle facade portico, with a second pair of columns *in antis* behind it. This appears prominently in the elevation (Pl. 8), with the flanks of the building receding to either side, and the cupola and towers above. Aside from the giant Corinthian Order of the main body of the church, the only other details at this level are angels bearing a stemma atop the main portal, and two tiers of windows around its circumference. The latter were an afterthought, since some overlap a string course at the base of the capitals, but they are unfortunate as well in that they are awkwardly positioned and proportioned, and have nothing to do with the situation indicated in the plan. There are no windows behind the diagonal altars, nor are such large windows necessary to light the staircases in the corners of the octagon.

Desgots's drafting skill is in general considerably removed from both Chupin's and D'Aviler's. In plan, the hastily penned bounding lines have been blurred by the washes, which if properly applied first were not allowed to dry, or which were perhaps inappropriately applied afterward. His compass-drawn and ruled lines have a tendency either to overrun or not reach their measured limits, and there are *pentimenti,* most notably the column second from the left on the portico, which was initially drawn off-center. His statuary, at which he is less skilled than his compatriots, is applied in a heavy hand often directly over architectural lines. There is in Desgots's manner repeated evidence for a haste and carelessness not found in the other prizewinners. He rightfully expends the most effort on the various Orders: Corinthian for the Colossal Orders, the campanili, and the interior of the drum; Composite for the lantern and the exterior of the drum; and Ionic for the minor Order of the first interior story. But even in these instances, which were most vulnerable to academic scrutiny, his apparent rush to complete the work has abbreviated much of the precision and detail necessary for the best result.

Desgots's method is in some respects comparable to D'Aviler's, for example in the use of green wash for leaded surfaces or the freehand coarseness of the balusters in the elevation. Desgots's design in certain elements often echoed D'Aviler's as well. Concave pilasters are used by both in conjunction with the engaged order to articulate the exterior of the drum. But the sequence is changed by Desgots so that the columns flank the windows, and the pilasters embrace the projecting buttresses (see the quarter-plan in Plate 9). The semi-oval effect so pronounced in D'Aviler's version is suppressed as a result. Another detail they hold in common is the socle used to raise the cupola, and to house a truncated dome, but in Desgots's church it does so without grace, with severe lines and an imposing mass. The belfries in Desgots's design are also akin to D'Aviler's, composed of four simple aediculae, but again devoid of delicacy or lightness. The positioning of these towers is distinct from that in the other designs, however, as they are not on line with the facade of the portico, but are on axis with the cupola, placed to either side of it above the sacristies.

Desgots's section drawing (Pl. 9) again underscores the links between his design and D'Aviler's, particularly in the use of the truncated dome. This feature is also lit in Desgots's design by four large windows, and serves the same purpose, replacing the pendentives over the octagonal plan. However, Desgots's shortcomings in drafting continue into his section to the point where it is difficult to say which drawing is his best effort, his "showpiece." He admits to his own lack of skill by avoiding the degree of decorative detail found in the other competitors' sections, excluding even the fluting of the columns and pilasters. In the articulation of the bevels of the octagon he proves himself more inadequate still. These open into the diagonal chapels through rectangular windows above aedicular portals, the columns of which support open-bed pediments which have been stripped of their gables, an unprecedented and therefore potentially unacceptable solution in this context.

10 (ASL 26)
DOMENICO MARTINELLI

first prize, 1679
plan for a domed Latin-cross church with bell
  towers

55 x 42 (21.75 x 16.5)
brown pen and brown wash

reverse: "no. 15 pezzi 3" & "H" in pen
obverse: "Scala dj Pj. 40" in pen, adjacent to scale
  bar; "Pj. 6 1/2" in pen, adjacent to lateral
  entrance at NW corner of plan; "131" in pencil, lower left corner; "Primo Premio
  Domenico Martinelli 1679" in pen, lower left

11 (ASL 27)
DOMENICO MARTINELLI

first prize, 1679
facade elevation for above
56 x 42 (22 x 16.5)
brown pen and brown wash

reverse: "1679/P'ma Classe/D. Domenico
  Martinelli" in pencil; "357" in pencil;
  "Cartella A/Scaffole A" in pen
obverse: "no. 29 N" in pen, upper right corner;
  "Scale Modulatorie" in pen, adjacent to scale
  bars; "Primo Premio—D. Domenico
  Martinelli 1679" in pen, lower left

12 (ASL 28)
DOMENICO MARTINELLI

first prize, 1679
longitudinal section for above
42 x 55 (16.5 x 21.75)
brown pen and brown and gray washes

reverse: "411" in pencil
obverse: "131" in pencil, upper left corner; "no.
  30 N" in pen, upper right corner; "Scala dj
  Palmj 20" in pen, adjacent to scale bar;
  "Primo Premio—D. Domenico Martinelli
  1679" in pen, lower left

Though severely water damaged, Martinelli's drawings nonetheless retain the original beauty of their execution both in line and wash. In fact, with respect to his handling of tools there can be little distinction between his skill and that of the French in 1677, other than in his choice of a reddish-brown ink instead of a uniform gray. The only *pentimento* is a small spiral staircase added over the wash to the right of the main portal in the plan, providing access to a small balcony, which is above that portal facing the nave; it appears in the section drawing. What might be considered an inconsequential detail must have been required by Martinelli to satisfy his own sense of completeness, a sense that extended to the inclusion of privies just behind the towers.

The plan is of a Latin-cross, Gesu-type church set roughly within the confines of a rectangle of 180 by 120 *palmi*. At the facade the entry portico of three bays is slightly recessed between the bell towers, which are square-planned but heavily articulated. To either side of the nave are single chapels, oblong on the transverse axis; these are flanked by doorways leading to staircases and corridors that are also accessible from separate recessed portals at the sides of the church. The domed crossing is surrounded by a square circulation path, the corners of which include the corridors at the adjacent end of the nave, and two vestibules at the opposite side that admit to smaller circular stairs and the sacristies in the corners of the site. The main altar is in a semicircular apse, while the altars at the ends of the transept are set behind screening colonnades.

The facade elevation (Pl. 11) is again a finely detailed and skillfully rendered drawing, even though at times the linear elements proliferate to the point where distinctions between pen and brush are difficult to make (a major drawback to the use of one ink). The details are more freely rendered than in Chupin's and D'Aviler's drawings two years earlier, but this does not detract from their quality. Their abundance comes closer to doing that. The elements of the Corinthian Order in the first story, and the Composite Orders above, are obscured by the variety of architectural and sculptural motifs that pattern the facade. It is only Martinelli's uncanny precision that overcomes these effects, and makes the details fascinating rather than overbearing.

The form of the facade, which is analyzed in the text, is much simpler than the details. The plan scheme of portico between tower bays is repeated in the second story with its loggia; between the two is a mezzanine with sculpted panels between single or double volute scrolls. The uppermost story of each tower is narrower than the ones below, with slender volute scrolls to either side,

and a diminutive cupola above. The sculpture includes the numerously rendered statues of female saints in the first-story niches, and male saints above the second cornice. The relief panels in the mezzanine with scenes of the Annunciation (left), the Nativity (right), and the Adoration of the Magi, or the panels in the second-story loggia depicting the Assumption and a miraculous vision of the Virgin all suggest a unified Marian theme. But even this profusion of sculpture is equaled by the plastic variety of the architectural ornament.

Just as it was for the French, the section (Pl. 12) was Martinelli's "showpiece," a virtuoso display of his skills and the efficacy of his design. Every opportunity is taken by him to elaborate on the architectural, sculptural, and now painted decoration of the interior section. There is only the main Corinthian Order to contend with as far as classical detailing is concerned, but every other element—the frames of windows, doors, and *coretti,* or the surfaces of ribs, cross vaults, and barrel vaults—receives its own unique and lavish embellishment. And as for figural decoration, there are the reliefs of Old and New Testament scenes in the mezzanine, and the murals depicting the Community of Heaven in the dome and apse vaults, though only the Assumption altarpiece in the transept chapel can be specifically linked to the facade iconography.

The readability of this drawing is fortunately not affected by the tears which disrupt the border at several points, and again indicate extensive handling. Nor does the water stain across the lower half of the drawing present any problem in this regard, though it has caused the gray wash that Martinelli reserved for the fluting of the interior Order to run. His use of this uncharacteristically coloristic device seems to have been for purely pictorial reasons rather than for clarity, though the latter is not ill-served in this. But there are instances where Martinelli has undermined the clarity of his design through a peculiar idiosyncracy which has window and door surrounds receding obliquely to the left behind their frames, presumably as a rudimentary attempt at a perspective effect. This causes no serious problems except for the facade vestibule and loggia, which appear to curve inward in section but do not do so in plan. This is a minor shortcoming, to be sure, in a design which is for the most part extremely informative of its nature, particularly with respect to the tower and roof sections, and the dome half-section/elevation.

The latter is most intriguing, since it is unanticipated by any reference in plan or elevation to the specifics of its form. The quite small piers at the corners of the crossing in plan would have made a grand cupola of Roman type an impossibility from the standpoint of statics, and Martinelli's is wisely much more demure. On the interior, the hemispherical dome rests directly on a tension ring of corbel brackets rather than a drum, which is replaced by a series of circular windows set into the dome just above its spring line. On the exterior these windows do occupy a drum, crowned by a balustrade and articulated by volutes, into which the tiled surface of the dome appears therefore to sink.

13 (ASL 10)
FILIPPO DI LETI

unclassified, 1680
plan for a domed hexagonal church with bell
    towers
61 x 48 (24 x 18.75)
brown pen and gray wash

reverse: "no. 7 pezzi 3" & "H" in pen;
    "Progetti/d'Architettura/<u>1677</u>/Anno" in pen-
    cil; "<u>1677</u>/P'ma Classe/Filippo di Leti" in
    pencil (inverted); "395" in pencil (inverted)
obverse: "Di Leti" in pencil, lower left; "Filippo
    Letti" in pencil, lower left; "Schala di palmi
    Romani, con che s'e fatto il presente
    Disegno" in pen, adjacent to scale bar

14 (ASL 11)
FILIPPO DI LETI

unclassified, 1680
facade elevation for above
72 x 47 (28.25 x 18.75)
brown pen and gray wash

reverse: "Filipo Letti" in red pencil; "404" in pen-
    cil
obverse: "no. 4" (crossed out) & "N 5" in pen,
    upper right corner; "Filippo di Leti 2°. 1677"
    in pen, lower left

15 (ASL 12)
FILIPPO DI LETI

unclassified, 1680
longitudinal section for above
61 x 48 (24 x 18.75)
brown pen and gray wash

reverse: "396" in blue pencil
obverse: (image only)

Here in di Leti's drawings is the first use in competition of the brown pen and gray wash technique which would become the hallmark of Italian draftsmen in the subsequent *concorsi*. Based on the convention in use after the example set by the studios of Bernini and Fontana (see the text), it was a workshop expedient designed, particularly in elevation and section, to ease the optical separation between line and shade which the earlier competitors had attained only through agonizing precision. That is not to say that the presentation quality of their drawings could not still be matched using this technique, but for di Leti this was hardly the case. Both his line and his wash are coarsely applied, and his measurements are not always exact. In other words, his is rather closer in quality to an early draft than a final presentation. The plan is disappointing for the clumsily drawn arcs of the balusters and engaged colonettes, the ingenuous use of wash to outline steps, or for di Leti's ignorance of the best conventions for drawing a readable ground plan. There is no single plane taken through the building for this purpose, and so the first-story pilasters overlap the windows into the vaults of the side chapels. Di Leti's use of the two-color scheme almost seems to permit or even invite an abandonment of precise technique, which he perhaps lacks in any case.

The plan is fit precisely into the site specified in Tomassini's *soggetto* (App. B, 1680, n. 4): a transverse rectangle of 60 by 70 *palmi* extended to the rear by one of 20 by 30 *palmi*. From the hexagonal nave six trapezoidal arms extend, constricting the spaces prior to each of the four semicircular side chapels, the rectangular main altar, and the facade portal. This sets two of the side chapels into the far corners of the main block, but leaves gaps between the other two chapels and the near corners that are filled by the bell towers and the passages leading to them. Lateral entries access Y-plan corridors that lead to the side arms of the hexagon.

In his other drawings, di Leti redeemed himself somewhat in the care with which he executed the linear detail, as in the rendering of the Corinthian Order of the first story and campanili, or the Ionic of the lantern, in the facade elevation (Pl. 14). Also, in his use of wash he seems to have recognized his own limitations, and chosen a nearly perpendicular light source that required the least amount of shading. Only the oblique sides of the dome are cast in shadow, with variations in tone conforming to the orientation of the light but unmodulated in the absence of curved surfaces. But even if di Leti has come to grips with the limits of his ability, the elevation still looks incomplete in comparison to designs which were actually submitted in competition (see the text). The form of the facade is quite simple, being a typically Roman, two-story volute front, with campanili attached to its sides, and the dome and lantern to the rear are equally plain.

In his section, di Leti does not answer the questions raised in the elevation as to the manner in which the facade towers engage the vaults or the windows of the side chapels adjacent to them. And he raises further questions about the treatment of the exterior above the first cornice, where the vaults of the main and side altars must somehow be integrated into a second story. How, for example, are the rectangular windows of this story to be reconciled with the apsidal vaults of the side chapels in which they appear? How is the higher vault of the main altar to be accommodated? Still, there can be no hesitation in distinguishing this drawing from his others with respect to technique, as he has here employed a full range of values in line and wash, picking out the details of the main Corinthian Order and the turn of every wall surface with a skill he had thus far not revealed. Even the stippling used to indicate the section through masonry, an unusual and laborious technique, is, if unnecessary, not totally unsatisfactory. But if this was his best effort, it only serves to further point out the inadequacies of his other drawings, and to contrast his work with the prizewinning designs from the *Concorsi Accademici* in general. Despite the better impression left by his drafting, the architecture of the interior is still quite plain.

16 (ASL 54)
ROMANO CARAPECCHIA

first prize, 1681
facade elevation for a palace, first variant
28 x 42 (11 x 16.5)
brown pen and gray wash

reverse: "354" in pencil
obverse: "-44-" in pen, upper right corner; "1681 2a. Classe Romano Fortunato Carapecchia" in pen, lower left

17 (ASL 55)
ROMANO CARAPECCHIA

first prize, 1681
facade elevation for a palace, second variant
27 x 42 (10.75 x 16.5)
brown pen and gray wash

reverse: "I" (crossed out) & "F" in pencil; "329" in pencil
obverse: "no. 19 pezzi 2" & "H" in pen, upper left corner; "-43-" in pen, upper right corner; "1681 Romano Fortunato Carapecchia" in pen, lower left

In this, the only instance in the seventeenth century when two variations on the theme were presented by the same architect, Carapecchia demonstrated to better advantage than had di Leti the potential of the brown pen and gray wash technique. For example, though the statues above the cornice are indicated only by a few quick strokes of pen and brush, they are consistent in their nature with even the most detailed portions of the designs. And when in some respects Carapecchia's hand is relatively coarse, as in passages where more labor is required like a main portal or belvedere, his deft management of a variety of values still gives the impression of refinement where often it may not exist. This is the mark of an experienced and facile draftsman. Even if the two designs, conservative (variant 1) and elaborate (variant 2), are compared, his technique produces a uniformity that requires a second look to see the differences that otherwise distinguish them. These differences, which are thoroughly described in the text, involve both taste and economy, as though he were making alternate proposals to an actual patron. His accomplished draftsmanship adds to the illusion of a practicing rather than a student architect.

18 (ASL 56)
JAN REISSNER

first prize, 1682
plan for a domed circular church with bell towers
75 x 48 (29.5 x 19)
brown pen and brown wash

reverse: "no. 24 pezzi 4" & "H" in pen; "1682/P'ma Classe/Gio. Reisner" in pencil; "no. 24 dissegni d'arc't'ra de giovani concorrenti" in pencil; "356 bis" in pencil
obverse: "58 N" in pen, upper right corner; "Giovanni Reizner Polacco" in pen, lower border; "Scala Modulatoria" in pen, adjacent to scale bar

19 (ASL 57)
JAN REISSNER

first prize, 1682
facade elevation for above
74 x 48 (29.25 x 19)
brown pen and brown wash

reverse: "1682/cartello A" in pen; "Reizner 1682" & "355" in pencil
obverse: "no. 59" in pen, upper right corner; "Giovanni Reizner Pollacco Po. premio 1682" in pen, lower border

20 (ASL 58)
JAN REISSNER

first prize, 1682
longitudinal section for above
53 x 69 (20.75 x 27.25)
brown pen and brown wash

reverse: "1682/cartella A" in pen; "356" in pencil
obverse: "No." (crossed out) & "60/N" in pen, upper right corner; "Giovanni Reizner Pollacco Po. premio 1682" in pen, lower border

Reissner's plan bears a scale of modules rather than *palmi,* and so it is possible only to approximate the size of the church at about 150 to 200 *palmi* in length. The plan is otherwise that of a circular church, ringed by two sets of four identical, roughly square-planned chapels at the sides, and the facade and main-altar complexes at front and rear. In plan the most intriguing elements are the semicylindrical projections of the outer wall that are placed between the chapels, and are slightly visible at the sides of the elevation (Pl. 19). These provide a visual counterpoint in alternation with the domes of the chapels.

The facade consists of a two-story portico/loggia, one bay wide and one deep, flanked by concave bays also of two stories, the upper story being coincident and contiguous with the drum of the cupola. The articulation throughout interior and exterior is by single pilasters, except at the facade where there are double columns through both stories framing the front of the porch, and on the receding angles at the extremes of the facade. The three portals of the facade, repeated in the second story as two lateral windows and the door to the balcony, lead to the nave through three passages linked at their midpoints to each other and to the stairways leading to the upper narthex. This last constitutes an access to the facade balcony as well as being open to the nave, presumably to provide a noble vantage point both for services and for overlooking the public space in front of the church.

The main entry bay of the nave is set off from the chapels by narrower intermediate bays, an arrangement which is mirrored at the opposite side at the presbytery. There the minor bays give onto passages leading to the two sacristies that are situated in the corners of the rectangular projection at the rear of the church. The passages are again joined at their midpoints to the main altar space in the center and to stairways at the sides. The sacristies are linked by a passage which runs behind the presbytery, and through which light is passed to the main altar by way of windows in both walls of the passage. The main altar is also lit by windows in its coved vault, and by a curious campaniform lantern. (The issue of what *is* the main altar is moot, since the central altar and ciborium indicated in plan do not appear in section and may have been an afterthought. This may explain the appearance of a reliquary tomb under the main altar in the section, added later in a heavier hand to compensate for the disparity.)

There is much to remind us in these drawings of Martinelli's slightly earlier efforts: the brown pen and wash technique, the use of a "scala modulatoria," and the excellent draftsmanship. Reissner would, after all, have learned his mastery of his tools from the same source, Gregorio Tomassini (see the text), and was aided in the figural decoration by his additional background as a painter. He populated the exterior of his design with statues of male saints above the first cornice, and female above the second. Over the portal two putti flank the Barberini stemma, in tribute to the Cardinal Protector. These details, and those of the Corinthian and Composite Orders of the first and second stories respectively, are executed with consummate skill.

Inadequacies exist, however, in two regards. First, he has tried to draw the ribs of the dome using arcs of only one center, which resulted in a bulbous rather than a stilted effect. The statuary above the second cornice may have been intended to disguise this problem, since they, like the consoles at the top of each rib, were added later over the original penned lines of the cupola. More unfortunate is the fact that his shading is not varied enough to make tangible the dynamic spatial movement of the exterior, and in this regard the missing fourth drawing (referred to on the back of Reissner's plan), which may have shown the rear or flank of the church, could have been most informative.

In the section, Reissner brings all of his talents to bear, as draftsman and designer, and as architect and decorator. He has provided a detailed look at his iconographic scheme: scenes of miracles and martyrdom in the side-chapel altarpieces and mezzanine reliefs; angels with garlands at the springing of the dome; and the lively sketch of the fresco in the dome depicting the Fall of the Rebel Angels (an odd but intriguing choice for this location). All of the finely rendered Orders are repeated from the exterior, including the minor Ionic Order used for the windows of the drum and the lantern. However, it is in this context that the treatment of the bell towers seems out of place, as the Doric Order was used for them in stark contrast with the balance of the design. Also, the question of the placement of the towers arises, as they come dangerously close to abutting the drum. As the plan does not resolve this problem, it is possible that the missing drawing did, or that it might explain why the Doric was used. Were it not for Reissner's model (see the text) one might almost consider the towers to be another afterthought. Final mention should go to Reissner's idiosyncratic inclusion of a field or ground of hastily applied brown wash to suggest *terra firma,* an unnecessary convention when it is so undeveloped.

21 (ASL 41)
FILIPPO BARIGIONI

first prize, 1692
ground plan for a palace
57 x 83 (22.5 x 32.75)
brown pen and gray, blue, and green washes

reverse: "no. 20 pezzi 4" & "H" in pen;
"1681/P'ma Classe/Filippo Barigioni" &
"385" in pencil
obverse: "Pianta del Piano Terreno" in pen, upper
border; "Scala de palmi Cento Romani" in
pen, adjacent to scale bar; "Ponte" in pen, at
ends of short axis; "Fossa" in pen, at ends of
long axis; "Cortile" in pen, left and right of
center; "Cortile Pensile" in pen, upper left
and right

22 (ASL 42)
FILIPPO BARIGIONI

first prize, 1692
main-floor plan for above
57 x 83 (22.5 x 32.75)
brown pen and gray wash

reverse: "Barigioni/1681" & "1681" in pencil;
    "386" in pencil
obverse: "Pianta del Piano Nobile" in pen, upper
    border; "Scala de palmi Cento Romani" in
    pen, lower border (no scale bar); "Prima
    Classe Po. Premio" in pen, lower left;
    "Filippo Bariglioni 1681" in pen, lower right;
    "Sala" in pen, center; "Cortile" in pen, left
    and right of center; "Vestibolo" in pen, above
    center; "Cortile pensile" in pen, upper left
    and right

23 (ASL 43)
FILIPPO BARIGIONI

first prize, 1692
facade elevation for above
35 x 90 (13.75 x 35.5)
brown pen and blue and gray washes

reverse: "383" in pencil
obverse: "No. 47" in pen, upper right corner;
    "Filippo Barigioni Po. Premio 1681" in pen,
    lower left; "fossa che recinge il Palazzo" in
    pen, lower left and right

24 (ASL 44)
FILIPPO BARIGIONI

first prize, 1692
lateral section for above
34 x 84 (13.5 x 33)
brown pen and gray wash

reverse: "384" in pencil; "Barigioni" in white
    chalk
obverse: "No. 48" in pen, upper right corner;
    "Filippo Barigioni Po. Premio" in pen, lower
    left; "fossa che recinge il Palazzo" in pen,
    lower left and right

Barigioni's ground plan is possibly the most beautifully executed of those from the early *concorsi,* not only due to his fine touch with pen and brush but also for the use of color: blue wash for the water of the moat (*fossa,* indicated also in elevation and section at the level of the battered basement),

and a green boundary to signify the surrounding terrain. The plan of the *piano nobile* (Pl. 22) is slightly less even in the quality of the wash, and lacks the element of color, but is still informative on several important points regarding the exterior articulation (see the text). The interior articulation is stark, indeed nonexistent, as though Barigioni had left a clean slate for the decorator. The issue for him was the architecture, which consists of four wings of apartments *enfilade* (indicated by dashed lines of sight) around a rectangular plan with a front of 700 *palmi.* At the corners of these wings are pavilions of square plan with beveled angles, in each of which chapels are placed at every floor. Interior to these wings are two courtyards separated by another wing running along the short axis of the plan.

This last wing contains the principal public and ceremonial spaces. In the ground plan there is a *sala terrena* running the length of the building axis, connecting the triple portals of the entry and garden fronts through three continuous passageways defined by piers supporting a low vault. Along its middle length this wing is open at the ground floor to the two courtyards, and actually forms the fourth arms of the porticoes surrounding them. At the garden end of the central wing, and at right angles to it, are two grand dog-leg staircases, lit by lightwells at their turnings, which lead on the *piano nobile* to a vestibule covered with another low vault on doubled columns. From here the circulation route turns back onto the central wing to enter the main salon through three doorways. This salon is therefore satisfactorily lit by two tiers of windows overlooking the courtyards. It is followed in turn by a smaller salon at the front of the palace, above which is the rooftop belvedere, again of three bays.

The general articulation of the exterior and courtyards of the palace is the same: a colossal Order of Corinthian pilasters on a ground story of banded rustication, with a crowning entablature and balustrade. Window enframements vary from the plain treatment of the pavilion fenestration (where banded rustication is used throughout) to the aedicular surrounds and alternating pediments of the windows between the colossal pilasters. The frontispiece of the facade (Pl. 23) is accented by its projecting plan, larger and more elaborate fenestration, paired Doric columns at the triple portal, and the crowning belvedere. Statuary is limited to that above the balustrades of the main cornice and crowning belvedere, except for the stemma above the center window of the main floor. Though this bears no device, it is surmounted by a diadem, which is what suggests that Barigioni's design, and presumably the original task description, was meant to provide for a royal purpose.

As indicated in the text, Barigioni's elevation bears a lengthy comparison to Carapecchia's, on the basis not only of style but of technique. Using the brown pen and gray wash of his predecessor, Barigioni also achieved a uniform quality with a hand that varied from the quick sketches of the statues to the detailed work on the Orders. There are no grounds for criticizing Barigioni on any aspect of the drafting. The only major distinction between Carapecchia's and Barigioni's designs is of course their relative scales, where the scope of the latter project may have engendered a greater advantage in the brown and gray scheme. The ability of the artist who employs it to realize form with an economy of means and suggest refinement rather than meticulously render it increases with the reduction of the scale, though it is best served by an artist with Barigioni's rare skill.

One comment alone need be made here regarding the treatment of the first-story arcades along the courtyards and through the entrance hall in the section (Pl. 24). The apertures are left blank, a convention he used elsewhere in the elevation when a window was thrown into shadow by some part of the building, which does enhance the sense of volume. But to use such a method for the entire length of the arcades gives a false impression of openness, and would seem to have called instead for further architectural detailing, even if it must be immersed in shadow.

25 (ASL 17)
POMPEO FERRARI

first class, first prize, 1694
plan for a monastic college and chapel
53 x 111 (20.75 x 43.75)

brown pen and gray wash

reverse: "1681" (crossed out) & "1678/P'ma Classe/Pompeo Ferrari" in pencil; "362" in pencil
obverse: "279" in pencil, upper left corner; "19" in pen, upper right corner; "Pianta Terrena … Del'Edificio" in pen, upper border; "Scala di Palmi 200 Romani" in pen, adjacent to scale bar; "Prima Classe dell'Architettura Pompeo Ferrari Romano Primo Premio" in pen, lower left

The following parts of the plan are labeled in pen reading from left to right and top to bottom:

"Dispenza, Granaro, Farinaro, Forno, Stufa"; "Ambulatorij, Refettorio, Lavamani (2), Cucina, Cortile di Servitio, Passo, Portaria"; "Spetiaria, Sagrestia"; "Cortile Maestro del Claustro, Cortile, Tempio, Cortile, Cortile del Colleggio"; "Scola" (variously, around the right courtyard)

26 (ASL 18)
POMPEO FERRARI

first class, first prize, 1694
facade elevation for above
53 x 110 (20.75 x 43.25)
brown pen and gray wash

reverse: (no markings)
obverse: "279" in pencil, upper left corner; "20" in pen, upper right corner; "Prospetto" in pen, upper border; "Scala di Palmi 200 Romani" in pen, adjacent to scale bar; "Prima Classe dell'Architettura Pompeo Ferrari Romano Primo Premio 1681" in pen, lower left

27 (ASL 19)
POMPEO FERRARI

first class, first prize, 1694
lateral section for above
53 x 111 (20.75 x 43.75)
brown pen and gray and brown washes

reverse: "381" in pencil
obverse: "21" in pen, upper right corner; "Profilo" in pen, upper border; "Scala di Palmi 200 Romani" in pen, adjacent to scale bar; "Prima Classe dell'Architettura Pompeo Ferrari Romano Primo Premio 1681" in pen, lower left (date corrected in pencil to read "1678")

Ferrari's design, described rather fully in the text and labeled as it is so extensively, needs little more commentary here with regard to its architecture. Some minor, though still thoughtful, nuances of plan are worth pointing to in support of conclusions drawn in the text regarding Ferrari's maturity as a designer. The circulation grid, formed by passageways running tangentially to the four large courtyards, has main staircases located conveniently near those of its intersections that are along the front of the complex, where the public spaces and abbot's apartments are located. Minor circulation paths added in the monastery (to the left in the plan, Pl. 25) assure that each monk's cell can be reached or exited by a number of routes useful in the course of daily activities or in times of emergency, yet still remain private. Each cell and classroom also has access to abundant light and air via exterior windows and courtyards. The service wing is set off to the rear, so that its noise or cooking fires would not disturb the rest of the complex; and even here, around a fifth courtyard, the conveniences of light and air, and an efficient arrangement of space and circulation, have been seen to.

Into this system, the plan of the Greek-cross chapel seems not as well integrated, except for the fact that the two of its circular vestibules that are nearest the facade are intersected on axis by the two main corridors running parallel to the fronts of the monastery and college complexes. These two spaces therefore become important circulation nodes linking the church, the institution, and the public space outside. Otherwise, the chapel acts as a barrier between college and monastery, but in the interests of a cloistered environment this is perhaps desirable. In any case, Ferrari's motivations in the church plan, as discussed in the text, are distinct from those for the remainder of the complex, and the lack of integration may merely reflect this.

These design issues are left largely to the text, but his draftsmanship deserves further remark here. It was extremely competent in most respects, except for the dome and portions of the balustrade to the left of the church in the elevation drawing. There brown wash appears to have mixed with the gray used otherwise throughout, either because he began working those areas in brown only to change his mind, or because the brown ink of the penned lines in those areas had been allowed to run into the gray wash.

Otherwise, Ferrari's command of the two-color technique and its potentialities was superior, and indeed he expanded upon the latter. The detailing is somewhat complex: the Composite is used for the Colossal Order of the outside wings, Corinthian for that of the chapel, Ionic for the minor Order of the chapel facade, and Composite again for the upper facade and drum. To this may be added the decoration of portals, lanterns, and the like, but in rendering at such a small scale Ferrari wisely avoided overworking the details, allowing the contrasts between line and wash to suggest the refinements. He also created a broad spectrum of wash values which convincingly layer the many planes of the facade. His greatest success with this lies in the treatment of the areas between the towers and the drum, where the architecture is clearly defined using gray wash only and no line, thus achieving an atmospheric perspective.

In section, Ferrari combines brown and gray washes with purposeful intent, and not by accident. It gives him a third color, essentially, and therefore a greater range for indicating light effects. He put it to use in the outer courtyards to differentiate the shadows cast by a building wing, a loggia vault, or a doorway, thus giving a clear picture of the volumes involved. One problem with shading does exist, in the columns of the minor Order in the bevels below the pendentives, where the wash is too heavily applied.

Ferrari carries the variety of exterior articulation into the interior: an Ionic Order over a Tuscan for the arcades of the outer courtyards; pilaster strips for the inner courts, of which only the left is arcaded; and Corinthian major and Composite minor Orders for the chapel. Each door and window surround is also minutely rendered.

28 (ASL 20)

ANDREA DELLA VALLE

first class, second prize, 1694
plan for a monastic college and chapel
55 x 77 (21.5 x 30.25)
brown pen and gray wash

reverse: "no. 9 pezzi 3" & "H" in pen;
"1678/P'ma Classe/ Andrea di Nicol'Angelo"
in pencil
obverse: "22" in pen, upper right corner; "Prima
Classe dell'Architettura Andrea di
Nicolangelo della Valle da Città di Penna
Secondo Premio" in pen, lower border

29 (ASL 21)

ANDREA DELLA VALLE

first class, second prize, 1694
lateral and longitudinal sections for above
55 x 77 (21.5 x 30.25)
brown pen and gray wash

reverse: "Della Valle" in pencil
obverse: "23" in pen, upper right corner; "Prima
Classe dell'Architettura Andrea di
Nicolangelo della Valle da Città di Penna
Secondo Premio" in pen, lower border

30 (ASL 22)

ANDREA DELLA VALLE

first class, second prize, 1694
perspective for above
55 x 77 (21.5 x 30.25)
brown pen and gray wash

reverse: "363" in pencil
obverse: "43" in pencil, upper left corner; "24" in
pen, upper right corner; "1678 Prima Classe
dell'Architettura Andrea di Nicolangelo della
Valle da Città di Penna Secondo Premio" in
pen, lower border

With della Valle's design comes the first occasion
since 1677 to appraise the efforts of a second-prize
winner, and the comparison is not a gratifying
one. In the plan, he presents himself as a careless
draftsman, as it is rife with *pentimenti*. To the left
and rear-left there are traces of an entire two
wings later replaced by those which now mirror
the right side at a slightly farther remove from the

center lines. Since the differences between the two
arrangements are negligible, there is no telling
what prompted the change at the time of this final
draft—whether della Valle wanted greater symmetry or increased scale, or whether he simply measured incorrectly. In all three of his drawings, della
Valle included in the lower portion of the sheet a
scale bar marked from "10" through "300," presumably in Roman *palmi* (though this is not indicated) which would make his complex slightly
smaller in its front dimension than Ferrari's.

With regard to *pentimenti,* some alterations to
the facade of the chapel can be detected as well.
The ramp of stairs that leads to the portals was
once semicircular, where now it is polygonal. This
change was no doubt made to correspond to the
predominantly polygonal plans of the arms of the
Greek-cross church, a tactic which was its own
means to the end of simplifying the demands of
the design as far as draftsmanship was concerned.
And to the right of the recess that contains the
facade there is an indication of a convex bay
turned toward the center which was replaced with
the straight-line oblique bay now at both ends of
this recess.

Della Valle's lack of conviction in design is
matched by his technical failings. Many of his
chalked guidelines have not been removed, and
many of his inked lines, particularly those which
are curved or dashed, are applied in haste without
compass or rule. As for the application of wash,
the values vary noticeably in the columns of the
church, and several of the shorter lengths of wall
in the right side of the plan have not been shaded
at all.

Still, for all the uneven qualities of his drafting, della Valle's plan is functional and readable,
with the exception of the semiannular space
behind the chapel, the purpose of which is not
readily ascertainable. But neither here nor in his
other drawings does he adequately resolve questions regarding the integrations between the
chapel and the building wings that enclose it.
Despite its apparent complexity, della Valle's
design, like Ferrari's, otherwise requires little more
description than that already afforded it in the text
or provided by the drawings.

In view of the plan, and the perspective rendering to come, the two sections (Pl. 29) are refreshingly well drawn, with a great deal more composure on della Valle's part in defining details and shading. As a result, this becomes his showpiece. The lateral section is taken through the three courtyards to the rear of the plan, each of which is articulated with correctly superimposed Orders across three stories of arcaded *loggie* and an attic. The longitudinal section is taken through the chapel, with its Corinthian major Order, and doubled Composite columns in the drum. Amidst the refinements here and in other decorative details, it is disappointing to notice that he used circles for each of the windows in the dome when two of them should have been distorted by their angles into ovals. On the positive side, della Valle has correctly indicated the location of each doorway, window, staircase, and vault with unusually sober consistency. And while there may be some confusion in the roof lines, which could easily have been avoided, this is not, as it would be for Ravassi (see below), a major problem. However, if the junction between chapel and college is somewhat clearer here, there are still questions which might have been better answered by a third section, but are only compounded by the perspective drawing.

Regardless of why della Valle chose a perspective view to present his exterior elevation (Pl. 30, see the text), he was patently unprepared to undertake such a task. First of all, it is not a true perspective rendering, but rather a variation on an oblique projection, with a vanishing point used to improve the stereoscopic effect. The facade is placed parallel to the picture plane as though in a normal elevation, while the rest of the building extends behind it with all dimensions and proportions intact, except those that are horizontal which diminish to create the effect of convergence. Such a tactic eliminates the complex calculations necessary for true perspective, but involves its own inherent distortions and difficulties, and therefore had no real advantage either for della Valle or the clarity of the drawing. His most glaring failure lay in not even attempting within this system to fully develop the chapel, which is replaced in the third dimension by a curiously improvised square structure having the appearance of a large arcaded belvedere. When della Valle continued to improvise behind the chapel, with roofs and terraces pulled from thin air, he further muddled the issue of how the church is integrated with the college. His own uncertainty about how this system works is evidenced by several *pentimenti:* around his whimsical belvedere, along the wing just to the left of the chapel, and at the rearmost wing. Though at this point he understood the necessity for consistent ridgelines, he did not always guess correctly about the pitch of the roofs, and often misdrew the lines of intersection between them. And two ridgelines, to the right and left of the chapel, represent what are simply physical impossibilities in any three-dimensional space.

Other problems are again the product of haste. Many of the dormers had to be redrawn to face down the slope of the roofs (some of those facing upslope can still be seen to the rear and center of the complex). Part of the far left courtyard at the front of the complex had to be removed to make way for an overlapping wing, and the court to the right of the chapel is missing the vertical line at its corner. Della Valle's shading technique is rudimentary as well, reserved to indicate the volumes of the roofs, and the cast shadows of the courtyards and the building. Aside from the dome, there is no attempt to represent the spatial variety of the chapel facade in wash. The Corinthian Order of the chapel, and the towers and lantern, are rather crudely rendered, as are the poorly proportioned superimposed Orders of the adjacent wings. The towers are also off-center with the bays below them, and the rhythm of the bays and windows of the building front is quite unsophisticated.

Two further observations should be made. To the left side of the perspective, the outlines of the lower limits of the courtyards, and the left wing, are indicated with dashed lines. And finally, enough of the open rear courts of the complex can be seen to know that they are articulated like the others.

31 (ASL 23)

CARLO AMBROSIO RAVASSI

first class, third prize, 1694
plan for a monastic college and chapel
55 x 79 (21.5 x 31)
brown pen and gray wash

reverse: "no. 8 pezzi 3" & "H" in pen;
  "1678/P'ma Classe/Carlo Antonio Ravassi" in
  pencil; "no. 69" in pen; "368" in pencil
obverse: "25" in pen, upper right corner; "Prima
  Classe dell'Architettura Carlo Ambrosio
  Ravassi Milanese Terzo Premio" in pen, lower
  left; "48" in pencil, lower right corner
  (inverted)

32 (ASL 24)

CARLO AMBROSIO RAVASSI

first class, third prize, 1694
lateral and longitudinal sections for above
55 x 79 (21.5 x 31)
brown pen and gray wash

reverse: "1678" in pen; "376" & "24" in pencil
obverse: "27" in pen, upper right corner; "Prima
  Classe dell'Architettura Carlo Ambrosio
  Ravassi Milanese Terzo Premio" in pen, lower
  border

33 (ASL 25)

CARLO AMBROSIO RAVASSI

first class, third prize, 1694
perspective for above
55 x 79 (21.5 x 31)
brown pen and gray wash

reverse: "366" in pencil
obverse: "26" in pen, upper right corner; "Prima
  Classe dell'Architettura Carlo Ambrosio
  Ravassi Milanese Terzo Premio 1678" in pen,
  lower border

Ravassi also included a scale bar in the lower portion of each drawing, unlabeled but marked from
"10" through "300," putting the front dimension
of his building somewhere between Ferrari's and
della Valle's. Most other characteristics of his
design and presentation bear comparison to della
Valle's methods, as inadequate as they might be
for a model. Their projects are similar in plan dis-

position, though Ravassi makes provision for far
more rooms than any single institution of this
kind could possibly need. And they both betray a
similar lack of drawing skill.

Penned lines drawn freehand are numerous in
Ravassi's plan (Pl. 31), resulting in an uneven
quality in that respect, matched by the uneven
application of wash. Most striking is the darker
shading Ravassi used for the plan of the chapel,
which only emphasizes the fact that it has been
clumsily inserted into the college complex. The
geometry of this chapel gave him particular trouble, no more so than when he used the radii of the
oval drawn from a single focus, together with its
perimeter, to define the outline of the diagonal
chapels, distorting them unnecessarily. As a result,
the altars in these chapels cannot face the center of
the church. To avoid calling attention to this, he
has drawn only one of the altars in addition to the
main double altar (back to back) and a side altar.

Like della Valle, Ravassi put his best effort
into the section drawings (Pl. 32). The one parallel to the long axis runs through the court enclosing the apse of the chapel, and since the planning
is asymmetric a varied sequence of courtyards is
intersected. The two to the far left and near right,
of four bays each, are articulated through three
stories of *loggie* in a Doric-Tuscan-Ionic sequence;
those to the near left and far right, of seven and
ten bays respectively, are in a Tuscan-Ionic-
Corinthian sequence; that in the center, of ten
bays, is unarticulated. Ravassi also expended some
thought on the articulation of the salons and
chapels opened along this section, providing them
with a Corinthian Order.

The short section is dominated by the chapel,
wherein the Corinthian Order is carefully detailed
and most of the curved surfaces properly shaded
(note the piers). Ravassi wisely avoided applying
wash to the main and side altars, which are
minutely detailed in line through their four tiers.
The few *pentimenti* resulted when the lines of the
apse vault were reconsidered, but otherwise the
church and its facade and towers are well rendered. Major problems occur outside the chapel
proper. First, the section does not continue along
the short axis, but shifts to the left after the rear-

most wing to cut through half a series of chambers, a portico, and one of the rear courtyards. This is not as informative as it is confusing. Second, there is above the apse and the courtyard wing behind the chapel a depiction of the arcaded terrace which Ravassi used in his perspective drawing, as had della Valle, as a substitute for the dome he could not draw illusionistically. The inclusion of this nonexistent motif in section is merely a ruse calculated to draw attention away from his deficiency. And too, like della Valle, a consistent ridgeline seems to have escaped Ravassi, with the worst effects to be found in his own perspective rendering.

Virtually everywhere more than two ridgelines meet in his own oblique projection (Pl. 33), Ravassi incorrectly represented how such a junction must logically have appeared. In trying to generate the impossible solids that result he fails, and often it is impossible to overlook. This is only his worst handling of the several problems that go along with his adoption of della Valle's method. Then there is the obvious discrepancy between the chapel rendered in a flat projection, and the arcaded terrace which replaces it in the third dimension. Including this sham feature in the section, and then brushing in the shadow of the "flat" dome in the perspective, can be construed as insensitive to the sophistication of his audience.

Other of Ravassi's methods are of a kind with della Valle's: Both included dormers in the perspective, though neither show them in section; both used dashed lines to indicate the full volumes of the courtyards, though Ravassi was more thorough in this. While their articulation schemes are similar, Ravassi was more considerate here, as well. This is particularly true of the front of his college, where he limits himself to pilaster strips, and organizes the bays and windows more satisfactorily.

34 (ASL 29)
ALESSANDRO SPERONE

second class, first prize, 1694
plan for a chapel
54 x 39 (21.25 x 15.25)
brown pen and gray wash

reverse: "374" in pencil
obverse: "34" in pen, upper right corner; "Scala di P'mi 50 Romani" in pen, adjacent to scale bar; "Seconda Classe dell'Architettura Alessandro Speroni Romano Primo Premio 1679" in pen, lower border

35 (ASL 30)
ALESSANDRO SPERONE

second class, first prize, 1694
lateral section for above
54 x 39 (21.25 x 15.25)
brown pen and gray wash

reverse: "373" in pencil
obverse: "35" in pen, upper right corner; "30" in pencil, upper left; "Scala di P'mi 20 Romani" in pen, adjacent to scale bar; "Seconda Classe dell'Architettura Alessandro Speroni Romano Primo Premio" in pen, lower border

36 (ASL 31)
ALESSANDRO SPERONE

second class, first prize, 1694
longitudinal section for above
54 x 78 (21.25 x 30.75)
brown pen and gray wash

reverse: "1679 ?/Speroni" in pencil; "no. 13 pezzi 3" & "H" in pen; "372" in pencil
obverse: "36" in pen, upper right corner; "Scala di P'mi 40 Romani" in pen, adjacent to scale bar; "Seconda Classe dell'Architettura Alessandro Speroni Romano Po. Premio" in pen, lower left

Here are the first examples of prizewinning drawings in the second class of architecture from the *Concorsi Accademici*. All three of Sperone's drawings are badly damaged by water stains in the lower half, but the images are still clean and intact, except for the ground plan. Moisture was not at fault there, however, as there seems to have been a brown wash applied to the plan to accent the interior moldings, which has caused the adjoining penned lines to migrate. Speroni did not understand his medium very well in this regard, for even the more successfully rendered section drawings have in many instances lost their crispness of line due to the actions of a gray wash that had not been given sufficient time to dry. The effects are most prevalent where the wash was thinnest and therefore more watery. This is unfortunate since Sperone's drafting skills, the quality of line and the modulation of shading, are otherwise quite good for a simple design in the second class. His facility is most apparent in the details of the Corinthian Order and in the sculptural decoration. There is an oval relief carried by angels over the main altar in the short section, which bears the image of St. Luke, patron of artists, and provides the clue to the chapel's dedication (see the text). Two cherubs support a medallion in the apse vault, and three male saints appear in the long section, two in niches above the portals, and one kneeling on a cushion on the transverse axis. Above this saint, in the tympanum of the cross arm, is a thermal window glazed in a grid pattern of lines of gray wash, and fronted by a broken segmental pediment. Higher still is the simple cupola, with elliptical windows in the drum standing on the ends of their long axes. Beyond this and the discussion in the text, there is little else to describe here.

37 (ASL 15)
ALESSANDRO ROSSINI

third class, first prize, 1694
rendering of a bay of the facade of the
    Conservators' Palace, Rome
54 x 72 (21.25 x 28.25)
brown pen and gray wash

reverse: "Rotini 1677" in pencil; "H" & "No.
    148" in pen; "Copie/Campidoglio" in pencil;
    "no. 1 pezzo 1" in pen; "360" in pencil
obverse: "15" in pen, upper right corner; "1677"
    in pen, lower left corner; "Terza Classe
    dell'Architettura Alessandro Rosini Romano
    Primo Premio" in pen, lower left

Descriptions in the third class, where renderings of an existing building were the task, are not required at all. For the first to win a prize in a third-class competition, Rossini demonstrated considerable skill with the tools of his profession, but his handling is somewhat broad, particularly

in the abbreviated detailing of the Corinthian pilaster capitals. And though he uses a wide spectrum of wash values, it often tends to suggest more depth than there actually is in parts of Michelangelo's scheme. While the lower part of the bay seems appropriately cavernous, the upper part does not appear shallow enough. Nonetheless, he was thorough and precise, even using the plan to show the continuity of Michelangelo's design, and his broad handling imparts a lively quality to the sculptural details.

38 (ASL 13)
LUDOVICO RUSCONI-SASSI

third class, second first prize, 1694
plan of a bay of the facade of the Conservators'
    Palace, Rome
54 x 36 (21.25 x 14.25)
brown pen and gray wash

reverse: "No. 146" in pen; "359" in pencil
obverse: "82" in pencil, upper left corner; "16" in
    pen, upper right corner; "1677" in pen, lower
    left corner; "Terza Classe dell'Architettura
    Ludovico Rusconi Sassi Romano Po. Premio
    So." in pen, lower border

39 (ASL 14)
LUDOVICO RUSCONI-SASSI

third class, second first prize, 1694
rendering of the same
54 x 36 (21.25 x 14.25)
brown pen and gray wash

reverse: "no. 2 pezzi 2" in pen; "No. 148" in pen
    (crossed out); "358" in pencil
obverse: "17" in pen, upper right corner; "1687"
    (crossed out) & "<u>1677</u>" in pen, lower left corner; "Terza Classe dell'Architettura Ludovico
    Rusconi Sassi Romano Po. Premio So." in
    pen, lower border

For Rusconi-Sassi the guiding principal was control, from the meticulously stippled center lines of the plan to the carefully detailed Corinthian capitals of the Colossal Order. His penwork is much finer than Rossini's, though some lines have been blurred by moisture, and his wash is confined to precisely demarcated fields, though a narrow range of values creates too shallow an overall effect. Still, the amount and precision of detail is remarkable for such a youthful talent.

40 (ASL 16)
FILIPPO OTTONI

third class, second prize, 1694
rendering of a bay of the facade of the
   Conservators' Palace, Rome
54 x 72 (21.25 x 28.25)
brown pen and gray wash

reverse: "No. 147" in pen (crossed out); "Ottone
   1677" in pencil; "no. 3 pezzo 1" & "H" in
   pen; "1677" in pen
obverse: "18" in pen, upper right corner; "1677"
   in pen, lower left; "Terza Classe
   dell'Architettura Filippo Ottone Romano
   Secondo Premio" in pen, lower left

Ottoni was not the equal of the others in the quality of his wash or line, as his touch was too uneven, and the decorative details are rather awkwardly rendered. But the correct details are there, and he, like the others, has provided a faultlessly measured and proportioned copy of the original. In addition, he succeeds beyond the efforts of his fellows in the use of wash to accurately represent the contrast between the closed and open stories of the bay by properly varying the shading.

41 (ASL 45)
POMPEO FERRARI

first class, first prize, 1696
plan for a villa for four dignitaries
110 x 53 (43.25 x 20.75)
brown pen and gray wash

reverse: "no. 10 pezzi 3" & "H" in pen; "1678?"
   (crossed out) & "1681/pma classe/Pompeo
   Ferrari" in pencil; "382 - cartelli B" in pen
obverse: "Pianta" in pen, upper border; "49" in
   pen, upper right corner; "148" in pencil,
   lower left corner; "Scala di palmi trecento
   Romani" in pen, adjacent to scale bar; "Di
   Pompeo Ferrari Romano Nella Prima Classe
   dell'Architettura Primo Premio" in pen, lower
   left

42 (ASL 46)
POMPEO FERRARI

first class, first prize, 1696
facade elevation for above
36 x 53 (14.25 x 20.34)
brown pen and gray wash

reverse: "408" in pencil; "cartelli B" in pen
obverse: "50" in pen, & "148" in pencil, upper
   right corner; "Prospetto" in pen, upper border; "Scala di palmi trecento Romani" in pen,
   adjacent to scale bar; "Di Pompeo Ferrari
   Romano Nella Prima Classe dell'Architettura
   Primo Premio" in pen, lower left

43 (ASL 47)
POMPEO FERRARI

first class, first prize, 1696
longitudinal section for above
47 x 104 (18.5 x 41)
brown pen and gray wash

reverse: "400" in pencil; "c. B" in pen
obverse: "148" in pencil, upper left corner;
   "Spaccato" in pen, upper border; "51" in pen,
   upper right corner; "Scala di palmi trecento
   Romani" in pen, adjacent to scale bar; "1678"
   (crossed out) & "Prima Ce. P. Premio
   Pompeo Ferrari Romano 1681" in pen, lower
   left

The edges of these drawings are damaged where the acids of the heavily applied brown ink of the borders have eaten through the paper, but neither this nor some slight water staining at their peripheries has jeopardized the readability of either the images or the inscriptions. In the plan (Pl. 41), where Ferrari's draftsmanship is otherwise quite fine, there is also the faint impression of the word *Spaccato* to the left of center between villa and stable, caused when that inscription was likewise too liberally applied to the section and bled through to the plan. Shortcomings in technique or judgement continue in the other drawings as well.

This is particularly true of the facade elevation (Pl. 42) where the image has been marred by the migration of the ink of the penned lines, primarily in the center of the drawing. The problem is most prevalent where the wash is used most (the recessed central bays and the ground story with its banded rustication indicated in gray), and where the detail is greatest (the frontispiece with its superimposed Orders). Apparently, too little time was taken between the applications of wash and line, a rare slip on Ferrari's part in either this or his earlier first-prize effort, but one which does seem to plague his elevations. In addition, the ruled gray-wash lines of the rustication pass carelessly over other details and do not terminate precisely. And the quality of line in the cornice, balustrade, and belvedere is inferior. Finally, to indicate the capitals of the Ionic Order of the frontispiece at the *piano nobile,* he uses two arcs tacked onto the sides of a rectangular band, a hurried and inaccurate method. All of this is disappointing to find coming from the hand of Ferrari, and detracts from an otherwise excellent design and presentation.

The section (Pl. 43), Ferrari's showpiece, is more of the quality to be expected from him, although there are a few small areas where again the penned ink has migrated. Above all, it is his use of wash that is most gratifying, more specifically his ability to represent the various layers of the villa section, the different characteristics of cast shadows, or the curve and angles of the stable wing. And as he had in the elevation drawing for his 1694 design (Pl. 26), he uses wash without line for a subtle but effective illusion. Where before competitors had settled for a simple field of wash to indicate *terra firma,* or had made no indication at all, Ferrari creates an entire garden landscape as environment for his villa, depicted in gray wash between and to either side of the palace block and stables. The absence of linear detail prevents the landscape from presenting a distraction, while imparting a sense of atmosphere and depth that completes the overall pictorial effect. As a result, this is one of the most beautiful drawings from the seventeenth-century competitions.

It takes some care to read from the plan to the section, especially at the ultimate story with its terrace bounding the courtyard and the four circular courts at its corners. As complicated as that situation is, it speaks well of Ferrari's architectural sense that no discrepancies are to be found in the rendering. Indeed, where other competitors (includ-

ing Pacenti, see below) seem faced with insurmountable contradictions when mixing their planning geometries, Ferrari finds opportunities for architectural advantage. The corners of the courtyard mentioned above and in the text are a case in point, but the stable complexes include others. The segmental wings facing the tournament ground in front of the palace contain regular square-plan grooms' apartments. The wedges of wall that result between each chamber in this splayed arrangement are not wasted, but are used to enclose privies. The juxtapositions between these curvilinear wings and the other rectilinear wings of the stables enclose exercise courts of potentially awkward plan, each having one particularly sharp angle. Into these otherwise useless spaces Ferrari inserted staircases of unique triangular plan, lit from the interior courts.

44 (ASL 48)
CHARLES DERBAIS

first class, second prize, 1696
plan for a villa for four dignitaries
76 x 52 (30 x 20.5)
gray pen and gray wash

reverse: "Berbais" & "389" in pencil; "1681" in pen
obverse: "Y" in pen, upper left corner (inverted); "57" in pen, upper right corner; "1681 Di Carlo Derbais Parigino Nella Prima Classe dell'Architettura Secondo Premio" in pen, lower border

45 (ASL 49)
CHARLES DERBAIS

first class, second prize, 1696
longitudinal section for above
54 x 246 (21.25 x 96.75)
gray pen and gray and blue washes

reverse: "387" & "90" in pencil; "Berbais" in pencil
obverse: "55" in pen, upper right corner; "Di Carlo Derbais Parigino Nella Prima Classe dell'Architettura Secondo Premio" in pen, lower border

46 (ASL 50)
CHARLES DERBAIS

first class, second prize, 1696
perspective for above
56 x 335 (22 x 132)
gray pen and gray wash

reverse: "338" in pencil; "no. 16 pezzi 3?_" &
    "H" in pen; "<u>1681</u>/Pma Classe/(D)erbais" &
    "Berbais <u>1681</u>" in pencil
obverse: "Di Carlo Derbais Parigino Nella Prima
    Classe dell' Architettura Secondo Premio
    1681" in pen, lower border

There is no scale indicated on any of Derbais's three drawings, but if he was serious about the number and size of the horse stalls in the lower half of the plan (Pl. 44), the scale of the rooms is colossal, even ridiculous, as is the number of horses (more than 400) and the space devoted to them. Using one stall as a module, the length of the complex works out to exceed the 1,000 feet that was presumably required by the task. The planning of the rooms is naively simplistic, achieved through an arrhythmic sequence of walls placed across the uniform width of the wings, to the point where functional aspects are included only in afterthought: secondary staircases inserted into the corners of rooms, or fireplace masonry attached to the walls. Only the three stair halls are elaborated in accordance with their ceremonial function, providing access to the four partitioned sections of the palace. Still, though it may be monotonous, Derbais's plan is well drawn, in the uniform gray ink preferred by the French.

The section drawing (Pl. 45) is actually more of an elevation. It makes its impression initially by virtue of its size (two and one-half meters); to be stored it had to be folded seven times. The scale was an advantage to Derbais, since it gave him a greater margin for precision in the rendering of detail and the application of washes. In technique, therefore, this drawing is generally quite fine. Derbais has used a blue wash for the roofs of his complex, as D'Aviler and Desgots had used green in 1677. The simple, classical lines of his architecture required no involved modulations of shading or complex geometries of arrangement. The long files of doubled Doric pilasters on the stable wing, or the Corinthian Order of doubled columns superimposed over the Doric for the porticoes of the *cour d'honneur,* create a lavish effect without requiring a variety of detail, albeit the door and window frames of the *corps de logis* are elaborated somewhat. Also, the size of the drawing tends to diminish the monotony, as only a small portion can be viewed closely at one time, and diminishes the effects of the few *pentimenti,* like that of a ninth chimney centered over the stable wing.

The section through the main stair hall, at the center of the drawing, is the most difficult part of the rendering, but was very well handled nonetheless. The situation in depth is accurately depicted by the various stages of the wash, and within these shadows the articulation of the far walls with niches and pilasters is shown. The two ramps of stairs converging at the second story can be seen, though without their balustrades, and without a clear idea of how the awkwardly arranged columns, and the vaults they support, relate to the staircase. But this last is a minor drawback.

Derbais's panoramic view of his palace (Pl. 46) is the largest drawing (over 3 meters) of those from the *Concorsi Accademici,* and is also the only one rendered in true perspective, unlike the two oblique projections from the previous competition. Add to this the precision of his proportioning and detail, and the elegant sculpting of the masses in light, and Derbais has given his idea a majestic tangibility that no earlier competition design could have gained through alternate means. By its size, the drawing becomes in effect a two-dimensional model. Or it could be conceived of as a scroll to be read from right to left, as Derbais has rendered the details more completely on the right, or fully lit side of the building, while abbreviating details to the left, or shadowed side. In the background, the far wing is also fully detailed, if compactly so due to the convergence. He has imparted an atmospheric perspective not by obscuring these details, but by varying the shading from the deep black of the foreground fenestration to the lighter tones at the rear. Apart from any stylistic criteria, this is an excellent drawing. For this reason, one must applaud as well his decision not to include sculpture, though he has included the pedestals, for if he were not equally skilled at its rendering it would have lessened his success.

47 (ASL 51)
CARLO PACENTI

first class, third prize, 1696
plan for a villa for four dignitaries
74 x 100 (29.25 x 39.25)
brown pen and gray wash

reverse: "<u>1681</u>/Pma Classe/Carlo Pacenti" in pencil; "167" & "<u>406</u>" in pencil; "no. 17 pezzi 3" & "H" in pen; "no. 73" & "c. B" in pen
obverse: "52" in pen, upper right corner; "Indice/Delle cose notabili nel presente disegnio
  A Cortile del palazzo maggiore
  B Piaza o vero teatro
  C Porticale
  D Remesse per il comedo no36/caroze in tutte
  E Stalle per il comed. di no120/cavalli in tutti
  F Cortilij per il comedo delle fialle
  G Portone maggiore di detta villa
  H Chiesa
  I Uceliera per tortore o olivo
  L Fontane
  M Viali" in pen, upper left; "Di Carlo Pacenti Romano Nella Prima Classe dell'Architettura Terzo Premio" in pen, lower left

48 (ASL 52)
CARLO PACENTI:

first class, third prize, 1696
longitudinal elevation for above
53 x 95 (20.75 x 37.5)
brown pen and gray and blue washes

reverse: "<u>167</u>" & "405" in pencil; "Pacenti" in white chalk; "Cartella B" in pen
obverse: "53" in pen, upper right corner; "Di Carlo Pacenti Romano Nella Prima Classe dell'Architettura Terzo Premio 1681" in pen, lower left; "E" in pen, lower right corner

49 (ASL 53)
CARLO PACENTI

first class, third prize, 1696
longitudinal section for above
43 x 95 (17 x 37.5)
brown pen and gray and blue washes

reverse: "407" & "3" in pencil; "<u>1681</u>/Pacenti" & "167" in pencil; "Pacenti" in white chalk
obverse: "54" in pen, upper right corner; "Di Carlo Pacenti Romano Nella Prima Classe dell'Architettura Terzo Premio" in pen, lower left; "E" in pen, lower right corner

When first examined firsthand by the author in July of 1983, Pacenti's drawings, particularly the plan (Pl. 47), were in the worst condition of any of the seventeenth-century competition entries: rotting from mold, brittle and splitting at the creases, crumbling at the edges, and almost completely discolored. The reason for this is perhaps the opposite of those drawings which have been handled too often. Pacenti's drawings may have been stored too long in dampness without being brought out into the air and light. It is fortunate that his fine work is for the most part unaffected by the state of the paper; only the lower right corner of the villa block in plan has been obscured in its details by the intrusion of moisture. Pacenti's efforts were particularly vulnerable to this as his touch was extremely delicate. His technique was the opposite of Derbais's, working on a small scale in minute detail—detail so fine that the brush applying the wash often could not be kept within the chalked boundaries of the preliminary drawing. In fairness, this was not the fault of Pacenti's handling of his tools, which was otherwise superb, but of overextending himself beyond reasonable physical limits.

The most serious criticism to be leveled at him involves a major design change made in this final presentation drawing. Three *pentimenti* reveal that his original intent was to have four matching entrance halls, with staircases to one side identical to that in the wing facing the oval piazza. While the disposition of the latter was retained, the other halls were reduced in size, along with their attendant staircases which were each given different plans, including the one oval, and this required alterations to the planning of the rooms as well.

With regard to planning, Pacenti highlights Ferrari's success in reconciling otherwise opposed geometries (see above). The stable wings on half-oval plan, in juxtaposition with the rectilinear walls of the exercise terraces behind them, create the awkward angles and useless spaces that Ferrari's wisdom overcame. And Pacenti unwisely allowed the radii of the oval piazza to dictate the placement of the partition walls between the carriage stalls in the stable wings, giving rise to a sequence of varied, but equally bizarre spaces. In the palace block, the curved fronts made enfilading difficult, but Pacenti still lined the doorways up along a slight angle to secure an equivalent vista. The lack of concordance between the exterior and courtyard plans of this block defied Pacenti, who was left with a mazelike jumble of apartments, in four equal sets repeated in each quadrant of the plan. Into the protrudent angles of the palace, he inserted minor stairways and cabinets, as if finding useful purpose for these awkward spaces in Ferrari's best fashion. But by this time the wisest choice would have been to abandon his scheme altogether.

Pacenti used the blue wash for the waters of the four fountains visible in elevation and section (Pls. 48, 49), included potted shrubs along the garden wall, and placed statuary above the Doric colonnade of the facade and the arcaded porticoes of the stable wing. This provides more of a setting than had Derbais for his villa, if less than had Ferrari for his. Still, Pacenti was the equal of both in technique, displaying a deft handling of pen and brush, and in other respects he was more daring than they. Though not skilled at sketching sculpture, he nonetheless included it, even to the point of using herms for the compound bases of the Colossal Order at the corners of the palace. He designed more curving surfaces into the complex than had the others, and, more importantly, successfully rendered them. If he was timid about expanding on architectural details, what adornment there is was well executed: the Corinthian Colossal Order of the palace and the false church front, the Tuscan arcades of the stables, and the

ground story of the palace with its freestanding Doric colonnade at the frontispiece and rustication in two tones (brown for the horizontal joints and gray for the vertical).

These drawings must still be criticized, however, for the cruder quality of line used for the *belvederi* centered above each palace wing, and for certain *pentimenti*. In the elevation, the near belvedere has had the round frames of its smallest windows made square, and a segmental pediment above the clock tower of the stable wing has been replaced by a bell. Also, like Barigioni in 1692, Pacenti left the arches of the stable portico blank, so that an otherwise comprehensive drawing appears less complete. In the section, Pacenti has simply taken a cut through each of the buildings in the elevation, without concern for the centerline which does not, in fact, pass through the stable wing or the false church front. As such, it adds little to what can be understood from the plan and elevation drawings, except for the *loggie* of the interior courtyard and their correctly superimposed Orders and Palladian central bays. But it is the most carefully rendered of the three, with only one *pentimento,* in the campanili of the church front where a middle set of openings has been deleted with white chalk.

50 (ASL 32)
ALESSANDRO ROSSINI

second class, first prize, 1696
plan for a chapel for the same villa
51 x 36 (20 x 14.25)
brown pen and gray wash

reverse: "28" & "379" in pencil; "no. 14 pezzi 3"
   & "H" in pen
obverse: "Di Alessandro Rosini Romano Nella
   Seconda Classe dell'Architettura Primo
   Premio" in pen, upper border (inverted);
   "1679" (inverted) & "31" in pen, upper right
   corner; "Di Alessandro Rosini Romano Nella
   Seconda Classe dell'Architettura Primo
   Premio" in pen, lower border; "O" in pen,
   lower right corner

51 (ASL 33)
ALESSANDRO ROSSINI

second class, first prize, 1696
facade elevation for above
51 x 36 (20 x 14.25)
brown pen and gray wash

reverse: "377" in pencil
obverse: "8" in pencil, upper left corner; "32" in
pen, upper right corner; "1679" in pen, lower
left corner; "Di Alessandro Rosini Romano
Nella Seconda Classe dell'Architettura primo
Premio" in pen, lower border; "O" in pen,
lower right corner

52 (ASL 34)
ALESSANDRO ROSSINI

second class, first prize, 1696
lateral section for above
51 x 36 (20 x 14.25)
brown pen and gray wash

reverse: "378" in pencil
obverse: "33" in pen, upper right corner; "1679"
in pen, lower left corner; "Di Alessandro
Rosini Romano Nella Seconda Classe
dell'Architettura Primo Premio" in pen, lower
border; "O" in pen, lower right corner

Rossini's mastery of his tools in these drawings
was once more satisfactory, even though in elevation and section some of the penned lines have
migrated into areas of wash. This is particularly
true of the interior entablature and capitals. The
architectural scheme is simple but elegant, and the
sculptural decorations few but fluently rendered.
The palatine nature of the chapel is indicated by
the crown above the stemma in the upper portion
of the facade, and that over the altarpiece in the
section. The Corinthian Order is used for the
main interior and exterior stories, with curious,
partially blank capitals used for the compound
pilasters that frame the facade, so that detail
diminishes as the outer bays recede. The upper
story of the facade is articulated in the Composite
Order, with freestanding columns inside compound piers. The latter features appear freestanding as well, due to the cast shadow Rossini
represents to the right of the left-hand pier, but are

probably not so since he uses the same convention
below where the pilasters are certainly not freestanding.

53 (ASL 35)
LUDOVICO RUSCONI-SASSI

second class, second prize, 1696
plan for a chapel for the same villa
61 x 46 (24 x 18)
brown pen and gray wash

reverse: "371" in pencil; "no. 11 pezzi 3" & "H"
in pen; "1679/Seconda Classe/Ludovico
Rusconi" in pencil; "no. 103" in pen
obverse: "40" in pen, upper right corner; "Pianta
del Tempio Secondo il Sito Dato" in pen,
upper border; "Palmi Cento" in pen, center
(along longitudinal axis); "Palmi Ottanta" in
pen, center (along lateral axis); "Scala di
palmi Cinquanta Romani" in pen, adjacent
to scale bar; "Di Ludovico Rusconi Sassi
Nella Seconda Classe dell'Architettura
Secondo Premio" in pen, lower border; "H"
in pen, lower right corner

On the left side of the plan are delineated the
bases and lower moldings of the interior articulation, while on the right are the outlines of the capitals and cornices.

54 (ASL 36)
LUDOVICO RUSCONI-SASSI

second class, second prize, 1696
facade elevation for above
61 x 46 (24 x 18)
brown pen and gray wash

reverse: "369" in pencil
obverse: "41" in pen, upper right corner;
"Prospetto e Facciata Esteriore del Tempio"
in pen, upper border; "Scala di Palmi
Cinquanta Romani" in pen, adjacent to scale
bar; "Di Ludovico Rusconi Sassi Nella
Seconda Classe dell'Architettura Secondo
Premio 1679" in pen, lower left; "H" in pen,
lower right corner

55 (ASL 37)

LUDOVICO RUSCONI-SASSI

second class, second prize, 1696
lateral section for above
61 x 46 (24 x 18)
brown pen and gray wash

reverse: "370" in pencil; "1679" in pen
obverse: "42" in pen, upper right corner;
"Prospetto Interiore del Tempio" in pen,
upper border; "Scala di Palmi Cinquanta
Romani" in pen, adjacent to scale bar; "/o
Rusconi Sassi Romano Nella Seconda Classe
dell'Architettura Secondo Premio" in pen,
lower left (torn at left); "H" in pen, lower
right corner

All three of Rusconi-Sassi's drawings were once
coated on the back with a thick size for mounting
on canvas (the weave was still visible before
restoration in 1983), which was a common practice for displaying drawings. But for some reason
the size was never removed from these drawings,
with the result that the plan and section have been
severely stained, damaged by vermin attracted to
the organic glue, and made more brittle than usual
so that their edges have crumbled and the sheets
are badly torn in several places. One tear some
thirty centimeters long extends into the image area
of the section, near the ground line, but again, and
fortunately, the readability of the design has not
been seriously affected.

Rusconi-Sassi used a brown ink so dark as to
be almost black, and in this concentration it has
proved to be quite vulnerable to the moisture of
the wash, so that his quality of line suffers where it
comes in contact with wash that has not been
allowed to dry thoroughly. This is to be the more
regretted as he was otherwise capable of a very
fine, even superior command of pen and brush.
The facade elevation (Pl. 54) is particularly subject
to this problem, though an early binding of its
edges with glued strips of paper has preserved it
from tearing. Aside from the blurred lines, the
exterior view is quite fine from the standpoint of
Rusconi-Sassi's handling of light and shade modu-
lated across a variety of surfaces: the convex, two-
story central entry bay; the outer bays stepped

back (for lateral entries) from the volute bays
immediately adjacent to the central projection; and
the convex/concave contours of the cupola. And
his is a virtuoso touch with sculptural and architectural decoration.

The Composite is the only Order used for
both the exterior and interior articulations (that
on the exterior has been simplified by reducing the
acanthus leaves to vertical notches), and only for
the ground story. The rest of the architectural
ornament of the interior (Pl. 55) is quite severe in
comparison to the exterior, which is more imagi-
natively detailed and was likely his showpiece for
this design. While in the elevation Rusconi-Sassi
renders well the three-dimensional form of the
convex segments of the facade and dome, he is not
as convincing, through line or wash, about the
curvature of the bevels and pendentives in the section, which are the result of the sinuous Greek-
cross plan. He also avoided using anything but a
compass to draw the dome windows, by conceiving of them as oblongs rather than ovals, that
become circles when viewed at a forty-five-degree
angle. This is not an entirely precise method. In
section, the problem of lines blurring is most pronounced around the altarpiece where the wash is
heaviest.

56 (ASL 38)

BASILIO SPINELLI

second class, third prize, 1696
plan for a chapel for the same villa
51 x 37 (20 x 14.5)
brown pen and gray wash

reverse: "380" in pencil; "no. 36" & "no. 12 pezzi
3" in pen
obverse: "37" in pen, upper right corner; "Di
Basilio Spinelli Romano Nella Seconda Classe
dell'Architettura Terzo Premio" in pen, lower
border; "N" in pen, lower right corner

57 (ASL 39)
BASILIO SPINELLI

second class, third prize, 1696
facade elevation for above
51 x 37 (20 x 14.5)
brown pen and gray wash

reverse: "375" in pencil
obverse: "Di Basilio Spinelli Romano/Nella
Seconda Classe dell'Arch'ra/Terzo Premio
1679" in pen, upper left corner; "38" in pen,
upper right corner

58 (ASL 40)
BASILIO SPINELLI

second class, third prize, 1696
lateral section for above
51 x 37 (20 x 14.5)
brown pen and gray wash

reverse: "376" in pencil
obverse: "Di Basilio Spinelli Romano/Nella
Seconda Classe dell'Arch'ra/Terzo Premio" in
pen, upper left corner; "39" in pen, upper
right corner; "N" in pen, lower right corner

Each of Spinelli's drawings is coated with size on
the back, but they are less adversely affected than
Rusconi-Sassi's, since only the plan (Pl. 56) is
slightly stained. The artist's technique was also less
than optimum here in several respects. The wash
is too pale and uneven in tone, and the line quality varies considerably, from the relatively pallid
compass-drawn lines to the dark and heavy stippled lines. This stippling was employed to delineate the features both below the level through
which the plan is taken (the steps and altars) and
above (statuary niches, cornices, and the ribs of
domes), which is an unorthodox and potentially
confusing convention.

On the facade elevation (Pl. 57), there is a bad
tear at the right of the lower margin, which
includes a small portion of the image where it
closely crowds the border, but no important detail
is affected. The design itself required considerable
patience on Spinelli's part in the application of the
wash, because of the variously curving surfaces of
the facade: concave in the central bay with a convexly projecting oval *tempietto* porch; parallel to

the picture plane in the next bays outward; concave and obliquely receding in the outermost bays.
In contrast with the plan, however, his skills now
appear to have been adequate to the task, more like
those of a painter as his rendering of light effects is
almost photographic in its precision. In fact there
are passages, like the lantern dome, where he has
let the wash alone define the form, since no tool
could have easily aided him in penning its lines.

The exterior Orders are superimposed as follows: Tuscan for the ground story, Ionic for the
drum, and Composite for the lantern. In addition,
he has devised an original iconographic program
for the sculpture. In the mezzanine, the two outside relief panels are not readily decipherable, but
the two inside represent the Donation of the Keys
(left) and Moses with the Brazen Serpent. Above
the central balcony are the stemma and crown for
a royal chapel, and six statues are arranged along
the top of the facade. The three to the left are
Saints Longinus, Mary Magdalene, and Helena
with their attributes, while those to the right are
pagan personifications of Time, Abundance, and
Justice with theirs. These last are the only ones
that have any obvious relevance to the theme.

The section (Pl. 58) is as thoroughly detailed
and well rendered in line and wash as Spinelli's
elevation drawing, from the Corinthian major
Order to the Composite drum and lantern. In the
vaults above the statuary niches in the side chapels
to left and right, frescoes depicting St. Luke painting, as well as his sitters, the Virgin and Child, are
indicated. The salient feature of the cylindrical
nave of this Greek-cross church is discussed in
detail in the text, along with the cylindrical
vestibules in the front angles of the cross. But
there is cause here for a note concerning a convention of architectural representation. When pendentives are used above a cylindrical ground plan,
as here, the arches of the cross arms curve in the
third dimension as well as in the second, so that in
section it should actually be rendered as a double,
or ogival, curve. It was the usual practice for
Baroque draftsmen, like Spinelli, to treat this as an
arc of one curve only, though usually not inverted
as it is here.

59 (ASL 59)

BARTOLOMEO SANTINI

third class, first prize, 1696
plan for a gate for the same villa
36 x 78 (14.25 x 30.75)
brown pen and gray wash

reverse: "no. 23 pezzi 2" & "H" in pen; "Santini"
& "402" in pencil
obverse: "54" in pencil, upper left corner; "67" in
pen, upper right corner; "Palmi cinquanta
Romani" & "Scala di Mo'li Trenta" in pen,
adjacent to scale bars; "1682" in pen, lower
left corner; "Di Bartolomeo Santini Romano
Nella Terza Classe dell'Architettura Primo
Premio" in pen, lower left; "M" in pen, lower
right corner

60 (ASL 60)

BARTOLOMEO SANTINI

third class, first prize, 1696
elevation for above
50 x 76 (19.75 x 30)
brown pen and gray wash

reverse: "no. 134" & "c. B" in pen; "1682" &
"401" in pencil; "Santini" in pen
obverse: "66" in pen, upper right corner; "Palmi
cinquanta Romani" & "Scala di Mo'li Trenta"
in pen, adjacent to scale bars; "1682" in pen,
lower left corner; "Di Bartolomeo Santini
Romano Nella Terza Classe dell'Architettura
Primo Premio" in pen, lower left; "M" in
pen, lower right corner

To the left of the plan, the outlines of capitals and
cornices are marked out, while to the right are the
outlines of bases and moldings. Both the plan and
the elevation are rendered quite competently,
except for the outer iron gates where the heavily
applied brown ink has migrated.

Santini seems to have preferred to direct his
attentions to the gate's sculptural embellishment,
for which the Doric architecture required by the
task is but a simple framework. The program follows a martial theme, interpreting the gate as an
arch of triumph in conjunction with the royal
context. The oval reliefs in the outside bays bear
scenes of a mounted knight galloping through
flames on the left, and of a king and soldiers sacri-

ficing at an altar on the right. The metope reliefs
are of arms and armor, and the stemma and crown
above, on a pedestal with the image of a river god,
are surrounded by trophies and angels heralding
triumph. The eight statues along the balustrade
consist of various female personifications related to
Peace and Plenty. While these details are often
uninspired and naive in their handling, the total
effect is successful, and augmented by the landscape setting to either side, indicated in gray wash
as in Ferrari's first-class design.

61 (ASL 61)

GIOVANNI ANTONIO SEVALLE

third class, second prize, 1696
plan and elevation for a gate for the same villa
71 x 53 (28 x 20.75)
brown pen and gray wash

reverse: "Sevalle 1682" in pencil; "no. 22 unico"
& "H" in pen; "1682 no. 135" in pen; "403"
in pencil & "c. B" in pen (inverted)
obverse: "58" in pencil, upper left corner; "69" in
pen, upper right corner; "1682" in pen, lower
left corner; "Di Gio. Antonio Sevalle Torinese
Nella Terza Classe dell'Architettura Secondo
Premio" in pen, lower left; "Eschelle de Dix
Modules" in pen, adjacent to scale bar; "Z" in
pen, lower right corner

Sevalle's design is even simpler, and his work more
poorly done, than Santini's. The pen and brush-
work are of uneven quality, and there is even a fin-
gerprint in ink below the far left column. The six
statues along the balustrade are quite badly rendered, and are seemingly copied from antique
examples without regard for iconography. The
crown and stemma and the attached garlands
above the central arch are applied over the
markedly projecting entablature in ignorance of
how this might practically be achieved. And in the
flanking walls the inked lines have migrated into
the areas of wash. Above these he, too, includes a
suggestion of landscape in gray wash.

62 (ASL 62)

GIUSEPPE PARÀ

third class, third prize, 1696
plan and elevation of a portal for the same villa
79 x 80 (31 x 31.5)
brown pen and gray wash

reverse: "no. 21 unico" in pen; "no. 49" & "1682"
  in pen; "390" in pencil
obverse: "68" in pen, upper right corner; "1682"
  in pen, lower left corner; "Di Giuseppe Parà
  Romano Nella Terza Classe dell'Architettura
  Terzo Premio" in pen, lower left; "X" in pen,
  lower right corner

With a technique far superior to Sevalle's, Parà proposed an entrance portal for the villa, rather than a gate, and went beyond the Doric Order of the ground story to include the Ionic of the central balcony above. There are trophies in the metopes, and the crown and stemma above the balcony, but otherwise the decoration is of an architectural rather than a sculptural nature. The panels, moldings, balustrades, pediments, and door and window surrounds are fancifully and precisely detailed. The only shortcoming was Parà's tendency to overextend penned lines, or leave chalked lines in, particularly in the plan and the cutaway sections above.

APPENDIX B
SOURCES AND DOCUMENTS

1663

1. (30 September) "Fu fatto decreto che debbano concorrere anco li scultori, e li architetti alla concorrenza del disegno per ogni tre mesi, et il primo pross'o si facci per la fine di Novembre." ASL, vol. 43, fol. 149.

2. (11 November) "Fu discorso e risoluto che per l'ultima festa di Natale pross'a di facci la mostra dei disegni delli giovani concorrenti, e fu data la cura al sig. Carlo Cesi." ASL, vol. 43, fol. 151.

1664

1. (20 April) "Fu fatto decreto che alli giovani che fanno li disegni d'Inventione gli si diano dei premij, e dai à quelli che copiano, et al quarto in toccalapis." ASL, vol. 43, fol. 159; vol. 44, fol. 5.

2. (4 May) "Che non havendo il Sig. Domenico Guidi ordinati li premij destinati per li giovani concorrenti, li facci fare il Sig. Carlo Cesi Seg'rio, ma che non excedino la valuta di scudi cinque in tutto." ASL, vol. 43, fol. 159; vol. 44, fol. 6.

3. (18 May) "Fu fatto decreto che li disegni de li giovani concorrenti si mostrino per domenica pross'a e che il sudetto discorso si reciti l'altra domenica seguente." ASL, vol. 43, fol. 160; vol. 44, fol. 7.

4. (18 May) "Fu proposto e decretato il Modo di creare gli Accademici nella sottoscritta forma.

"Acciò ogni professore, si di pittura, come di scultura et architettura, habbia campo con il proprio merito di restare honorato con il titolo d'Acad'co cioe di maestro si decreta in conformità de Premi, e statuti del Ppe., e Cong'ne Acad'ca nel sottoscritto modo:

"Che ogni uno di quelli, che hà ottenuto il premio per primo due volte, o vero una volta al meno possa dipingere in tela però d'Imperatore, e non meno l'istesso soggetto, che si da per l'inventione, et esponerlo à concorrenza, concedendo à questi effetto licenza à chi non è stato mai il primo possa di non concorrere lui che una volta tale sia giudicato ma che lui siano i premij guadagnati e che di questi sarà giudicato il migliore si dichiari Academico con la Bussola in conformità delli statuti.

"Se alcuno che prima non hà concorso con i disegni varrà concorrere con il quadro non possa senza espressa licenza della Cong'ne Acad'ca quale essendo il soggetto cognito, e meritevole gli la concede.

"Che non possa in nesun modo concorrere chi dipinge per le Botteghe vietatolo l'istessi statuti decretando di non di procedere con quelli rigorosamente per l'avenire in rigore.

"Che non possa concorrere ne con disegni ne con altro chi prima non si è scritto nel libro dove sono notati gl'altri professori studenti.

"Che nisuno possa concorrere con il quadro se non passa l'età di venticinqu'anni, et havendo concorso con i disegni si compiacerà d'aspettare fino à detto tempo in conformità de statuti.

"Che chi resta Academico lasci il suo quadro al Acad'a in conformità del obligo, e statuti, testituendo pero gl'altri ai concorrenti.

"Che à chi resta academico si dia il privilegio specificando il modo con il quale ha ricento l'honore.

"Che detto concorso si faccia due volte l'anno, l'uno per il mese di Maggio, e l'altro per la festa di S. Luca nostro protettore d'Ottobre.

"Finalmente, che ciò si fà non solo per animare ogn'uno à li studij, e che il forestiero professore possa portare in patria la conferm(azion)e del proprio valore, ma che chi fatiga partecipi de gl'honori che godono gl'Academici concessi da sommi pontefici, e degl'altri, che si spera concedera la santità d'Alessandro Settimo.

"L'istesso per i sig'ri scultori, e architetti a quali si darà anco per l'avenire il soggetto." ASL, vol. 43, fol. 160; vol. 44, fol. 7.

5. (8 June) "Che la Cong'ne risolva se che dovrà dare il soggetto e fare il discorso per ottobre si per i pittori come per i scultori e architetti." ASL, vol. 43, fol. 161; vol. 44, fols. 7–8.

6. (22 June) "Fu pregato il S're Andrea Piscuglia per dare il soggetto d'inventione, e per fare il discorso, quale prontamente favorita l'Acad'a, e gia ha dato il soggetto se però sarà approvata.

   "Che i Sig'ri scultori e architetti diano il soggetto per i giovani, si per l'inventione come per copiare." ASL, vol. 44, fol. 10.

7. (13 July) "Che si e publicato et affisso il pensiero dell'istoria d'inventione." ASL, vol. 43, fol. 163; vol. 44, fol. 12.

8. (16 November) "Che deve sbrigarsi presto il concorso altrim(en)te l'altro soggetto per maggio non vi sara tempi." ASL, vol. 44, fol. 21.

1665

1. (11 January) "Che per la 2a. Domenica di Febrario si faccia il concorso, ma che però i giovani tanto pittori come scultori per la Domenica anteced(en)te debbiano mostrare il loro disegno, e basso rilievo." ASL, vol. 44, fol. 24.

1666

1. (11 February) "Statuts et Règlement que le Roy veut et ordonne estre observés dans l'Académie de peinture, sculpture et architecture, que Sa Majesté a résolu d'establir dans la ville de Rome pour l'instruction des jeunes Peintres, Sculpteurs, et Architectes Francois, qui y seront envoyés pour estudier, attestés par Nous, Jean-Baptiste Colbert, conseiller ordinaire du Roy en tous ses Conseils, etc., suivant le pouvoir à nous donné par Sa Majesté.

   "I. L'Académie … sera composée de douze jeunes hommes, Francois, … scavoir: six Peintres, quatre Sculpteurs et deux Architectes, sous la conduite et direction d'un Peintre du Roy, qui sera

estably Recteur de la dite Académie, auquel ils seront obligez d'obéir avec toute sorte de soumissions et de respects….

   "V. Le nombre des douze estudians ne pourra estre augmenté, pour quelque occasion que ce soit; mais, lorsqu'il viendra à vacquer quelque place, le Surintendant des Bastimens …, à qui il appartient d'y pourvoir, en sera averty par le (Recteur), et sera très humblement supplié de préférer ceux qui auront remporté les Prix de l'Académie, en conformité de ses statuts….

   "VIII. Ils estudieront tous les jours deux heures l'arithmétique, géométrie, perspective et architecture, aux heures qui seront prescrites et qui auront esté données aux Maisters qu'ils auront pour cet effet, et le reste du temps sera par eux employé suivant la destination qui en aura esté faicte par leur Recteur….

   "X.… ils ne peuvent jamais copier, ou exécuter aucune chose, sans son (the Rector's) conseil ou son consentement, à peine d'estre exclus de ladite Académie.

   "XI. Et, comme l'expérience fait connoistre que la plupart de ceux qui vont à Rome n'en reviennent pas plus scavans qu'ils y sont alles, ce qui provient de leurs desbauches ou de ce qu'au lieu d'estudier d'apres les bonnes choses qui devroient former leur génie, ils s'amusent a travailler pour les uns et pour les autres et perdent absolument leur temps et leur fortune pour un gain de rien qui ne leur fait aucun profit, Sa Majesté deffend absolument à tous ceux qui auront l'honneur d'estre entretenus dans ladite Académie de travailler pour qui que ce soit que pour Sa Majesté, voulant que … les Architectes (fassent des copies) les plans et les élévations de tous les beaux palais et edifices, tant de Rome que des environs, le tout suivant les ordres du Recteur de ladite Académie …

   "XV. Il sera, tous les ans, proposé un Prix aux dits estudians, qui sera donné, le jour de Saint-Louis, à celui qui en aura esté jugé le plus digne." *Corr.*, vol. I, pp. 8–11, n. 14.

2. (24 October) "Fu detto dal sudo. Sige. Principe che per rappresentare a N. Sig're la spesa e il bisogno che ha la nostra Accademia per mantenere gli studij del disegno sarebbe bene (se però cosi pace a nostri sig'ri Congregati) di donargli uno dei disegni dei giovani concorrenti acciòche più facilmente s'induca a farsi la gratia del sudo. Breve (i.e. that of Urban VIII, 1633)." ASL, vol. 43, fol. 180; vol. 44, fol. 36.

1667

1. (16 June) "Fu discorso, e concluso che per l'ottava della festa prossima di San Luca si facci il concorso del disegno de giovani virtuosi concorrenti, e che il sudetto Sige. Orfeo (Bosselli) Prencipe dia il soggetto che serva un per li Pittori, quanto per i scultori." ASL, vol. 43, fol. 186.

2. (14 August) "Fu concluso, che il Sige. Prencipe istesso dia il soggetto qual serva per pittori, e scultori." ASL, vol. 44, fol. 42.

1672

1. (n.d.) "L'onore del primo posto Accademico dopo il Morando, fu conferito a Carlo Errard Architetto. Ei si occupò dice il Milizia a misurare, e disegnare in Roma le migliori opere de Architettura moderna per farne una giunta al paralello d'Architettura di Chambray. Architettò per Parigi la Chiesa della Sunta presso Sant'Onorato. Fu l'Errard uomo industre, ed attivo, grave anche nel suo porgere, ed autorevole, per cui l'Accademia l'osservava con distinzione. Egli fissò alcuni ordini sulla dispensa de premj agli Allievi dell'Accademia: vendicò le ragioni accademiche sulle disposizioni testamentarie del Muziano: fece accrescere il numero de'Ritratti de'Pittori Accademici, e varj importanti articoli di contestazione su i negozj dell'Accademia felicemente compose." Missirini, Titolo LXXX, pp. 130–31.

2. (19 April) "Fu da me segretario presentata dal Sige. Principe, et Accademici una lettera mandata di Parigi con un libro dal D. Tomaso Regnaudin (sculptor to Louis XIV, member of the Royal Academy and the Parisian Academy of St. Luke; book titled *L'Établissement de l'Académie Royale de Peinture et Sculpture*) ... per lettere, e patenti del Ré, verificati in parlamento. In esso sono bellusimi privilegi doni e rendite (by Louis) per istabilimato e nobilità di quest'atte, con gli statuti, et più in do. libro li sono le conferenze fatti nella meda. accademia Reale, il tutto stampato in quarto in lingua Francese." ASL, vol. 44, fol. 67.

3. (17 July) "Fu ancora decretato che per il concorso da farsi per la festa di san Luca il Sige. Carlo Cesi faccia l'orazione. Per li Soggetti dell'Inventione

de'disegni fu data cura al Se. Pietro del Pò et al Se. Fabritio Chiari, che diano parte al Sudo. Bernetti....

"È solita per la festa di S. Luca dar campo à giovani che esserviano la sittua e fare il concorso, e mettere li soggetti sopra il quale li fa detto concorso." ASL, vol. 43, fol. 212; vol. 44, fol. 69.

4. (7 August) "Che ogni Accademico deve esortare i loro giovani a fare i disegni accio il giorno della conferenza sia copioso di disegni, e modelli.

"Che saria anco bene mettere bassirilievi e disegni di quelli, che sono stati premiati nella piccola galleria con i loro nomi, si per ornam(en)te, come per dar animo a gli altri." ASL, vol. 44, fol. 72.

5. (4 September) "Che è necessario ogni accademico esorti li suoi giovani si pittori, come scultori a fare il soggetto dato, acciòche il concorso non resti povero." ASL, vol. 44, fol. 75.

6. (30 October) "Il concorso, se che deve farsi, poiche è bene di riguardone alle spese, et al mancam(en)to del denaro, e che in vole per il compim(en)to delle cornici di i ritratti." ASL, vol. 44, fol. 80.

7. (20 November) "Circa il concorso, di già in conformità e s'intimo per la pa. domenica di Xbre.

"Vi vole il denaro per i premij." ASL, vol. 44, fol. 82.

1673

1. (6 January) Colbert to Errard: "J'ay esté bien ayse d'apprendre, par la relation que vous avez envóyee à M. du Metz de ce qui s'est passé en l'Académie de Saint-Luc, que les Prix ayent esté emportez par quatre Peintre ou Sculpteurs francois. C'est une marque que vous vous estes bien appliqué à leur élévation et qu'ils ont aussy bien correspondu aux instructions que vous leur avez données." *Corr.*, vol. I, p. 42, n. 73.

2. (n.d.) "Appresso l'Errard diresse gli affari del Romano Collegio degli Artisti in qualità di Principe Carlo Rainaldi, del cui merito si è di sopra ragionato. Il Rainaldi frattanto stabili: 1.

Che li studj delle buone Arti nell'Accademia si facciano tanto le Feste di Precetto che le Feste di devozione. 2. Che alla mattina di dia il disegno del nudo colla lezione dell'Anatomia; e il giorno s'insegni l'Architettura, e la Prospettiva, venendo eletti per Professori in Notomia: Carlo Cesi; Architettura: Mattia de Rossi; Prospettiva: Pietro del Pò. 3. Che in fin d'Anno vi sia un discorso sull'Arte, e per quell'Anno fosse l'Oratore Giovan Battista Passari." Missirini, Titolo LXXXI, p. 131.

3. (29 January) "È necessario d'incominciare à rimettere i studij, come era il solito, e dare i soggetti per i disegni di bassirilievo, et altro." ASL, vol. 44, fol. 86.

4. (9 April) "Si deve dar ordine … à chi deve far il discorso, dia il soggetto per il disegno d'Inventione." ASL, vol. 44, fol. 90.

5. (30 April) "Circa li Studij … primieramente bisogna stabilire se che deve dar lettione tanto di architettura (Mattia de Rossi), prospettiva e notomia." ASL, vol. 43, fol. 222; vol. 44, fol. 92.

6. (n.d.) "Vogliono in oltre secondo il consueto si faccino le concorrenze, si per i giovani Pittori, come anche per Scultori, et Architetti in conformità de' Soggetti. Arch. Mattia de Rossi; … (signed) G. Ghezzi." ASL, misc. docs., Secolo XVII.

7. (28 May) "Circa li Studij … il Sige. Passeri hà dato il soggetto per li pittori e scultori, resta quella della 2a. classe de pittori, e le che devono disegnare i giovani dall'opere.

"In oltre resta ciò che devono fare gl'architetti, e le grandezza.

"Che possa concorrere con il quadro della meda. istoria, chi una volta hà havuto il premio per il po. da esser fatto Accad'co." ASL, vol. 44, fol. 93.

8. (n.d.) "Desiderando il Sig. Ppe. et Accademici del Disegno che ogni giorno s'ammiri maggior profitto nei Giovani Professori di Pittura, Scultura et Architettura, espongono però i soliti soggetti per la prossima concorrenza nella festa di S. Luca …

"Per i Giovani Architetti il motivo del tempio da farsi Pianta, Facciata, e Spaccato.…

"Di più, se alcuno vuol concorrere per esser dichiarato Accad'co di Merito, potrà dipingere la med'a Historia di Annibale (the first class subject in painting) in tela d'Imperatore, che riconosciuto abile sarà ammesso; quando, che nò, se gli venderà il suo quadro.…

"Farà il Discorso per quel giorno il med'mo Sig. Michele Burgheres (or Bruguerres: Accademico di Gratia, 1670 [ASL, vol. 43, fol. 199]; chosen for the discourse 30 April, 1673 [ASL, vol. 44, fol. 92]) che hà dato li soggetti. (signed) Giuseppe Ghezzi." ASL, misc. docs., Secolo XVII.

9. (10 September) "Si avvicina il concorso è bene far diligenza, in siano disegni." ASL, vol. 44, fol. 96.

10. (1 October) "Che li Premij se si devono dare denari ò robba.

"Per la domenica li 15 8bre si deve far il concorso." ASL, vol. 44, fol. 97.

1674

1. (1 July) "Per li architetti fu dato dal Tomassini il disegno d'un tempio da farsi pianta, facciata e spaccato." ASL, vol. 43, fol. 232.

2. (4 October) "Che il concorso de premij si trasferitoli ad altro tempo più opp(ortu)ne." ASL, vol. 44, fol. 110.

1675

1. (21 September) "Sarebbe bene di stabilire il giorno del concorso per quelli hanno fatigato lui da due anni rintrosamente, i quali ne hanno mostrato con molti le loro doglianze, onde pare si dovrebbe evitare magior longhezza.

"Fu stabilito il giorno del concorso per la 2a. doma. di 9bre futuro, e fu eletto il Se. Giov. Ba. Passeri benchè assente, per haver la risposta dal Se. Coppa circa il discorso, che doveva fare." ASL, vol. 45, fol. 24.

2. (15 December) "Il Se. Carlo Maratti propose per accademico di merito il Se. Carlo LeBrun pittore,

appresto il Rè Christianissimo benchè assente, con rappresentare le sta lui rare qualità et eminenza nella professione, e la stima che si ne fà universalm(en)te, accio per tante qualità riguardevoli fusse accetato per accademico senza correre altra bussola.

"Fu da tutta la Cong'ne lo data la suda. proposit(io)ne e senza alcuna discrepenza à unica voce senza correre altra bussola fu accetato per Accademico di Merito il sudo. Se. Carlo LeBrun." ASL, vol. 45, fol. 28; vol. 46, fol. 8.

1676

1. (19 January) "Il quadro di S. Luca dipinto da Rafaele che sia riposto nel no'ro Arch'io <u>voltato al muro</u> ('!!!' in margin) par suo gran detrimento si per l'humido e caldo." ASL, vol. 45, fol. 33; vol. 46, fol. 10.

2. (26 April) "Fu spedita la patente in persona del Se. Carlo LeBrun no'ro Pren'pe in conformità del decreto fatto nella precedente Congregaz'ne." ASL, vol. 45, fol. 36.

3. (25 May) "Perche nella precedente cong'ne non furono deputati li maestri che nella pre(se)nte stagione d'essere lettione … sarebbe bene venire all'elettione.

"Fu deputati et eletto … per la prospettiva il Sige. Pietro del Pò, per l'architettura il Se. Felice della Greca (Acc. di Merito 19 January 1676 [ASL, vol. 45, fol. 33])." ASL, vol. 45, fol. 40.

4. (31 May) "Nella qual Congregaz'ne (secret, officers only) in esequiz(io)ne del desiderio altrevolte havutosi di far l'unione della Reale Acad'a del Disegno di Francia à questa nostra di Roma, il Sige. Carlo Errard al presente V. Prencipe della nostra Accademia presento a detta Congregaz'ne e per essere a me Segretario per parte di detta Accademia Reale una scrittura di diece capitoli, concernenti la medesima unione quale da me ricevuta e letto il suo tenore à voce alta e intelligibile, fu allora da Sigi. Academici Congregati riposto e risoluto … (text of articles in Missirini, pp. 140–41).

"Che quanto al primo capitolo circa l'espositione de Ritratti dei Sig'ri Protettori d'Ambedue l'Academici da farsi in ciascheduna d'esse ricende-

volme'te, pareva bene fatto; mà che per il contrario, non era bene fare l'elettione d'un Vice-Protettore che per ciò di cassatte questa conditione da do. capitolo.

"Circa el Capo. 8° fu risoluto in l'aggiungette che nel ne farsi la bussola per l'elettione de Prencipe della no'ra Acada., ogni volta fra li cinque soggetti soliti da rinbussolarsi vi ne dovette essere uno francese mà che però sia stato Rettore nell'Academia di Parigi, e che per ciò due mesi prima della rinnovaz'ne della bussola si debba avvitare in francia acciò possa mandarsi … in tempo la nomina dei tali soggetti capaci di questa cauza.

"Nel resto furono tutti gli altri accettati, e risolva che quando così piaccia alla nostra congregaz'ne generale da intimarsi in conformità de'statuti, et in oltre a Sigi. Superiori si facci l'unione suda., et intanto si mandi da me segretario la copia de medesimi capitoli con le informationi, e dichiarationi sudete a Sigi. dell'Accademia di Francia." ASL, vol. 45, fols. 40–41.

5. (7 June) "Nella qual congregaz'ne furono letti li dieci capitoli della Reale Accademia del Disegno di Francia per haver l'unione a questa nostra di Roma, e furono à unica voce da tutta da. congregaz'ne approvati, ratificando et approvando in oltre la congregazione segreta sopra sià fatta." ASL, vol. 45, fol. 41.

6. (7 June) "Per non essersi mai indica il Se. Felice della Greca a dar lettione d'architettura conforme all'elett'ne fatta in sua persona, fu pregato il Se. Francesco Rosa a ricordarglilo." ASL, vol. 45, fol. 41.

7. (24 July) "En ce jour, Monsieur Le Brun a dit à la Compagnie que Messieurs de l'Académie de Rome ont resceu très agréablement le projet de jonction de deux Académies que Monsieur Errard leurs a présanté, et les ont approuvé généralement, en y adjoutant, pour gratifier l'Académie Royale, que, dans le nombre des sujets que l'on met ordinairement en la boussole pour eslire leur Prince, il y sera toujours mis a l'avenir le nom de quelqu'un de l'Académie Royale, pourveu qu'il ait passé en la charge de Recteur.… L'Académie, apprenant avec beaucoup de joie l'estat de ces choses et en attendant l'entier accomplissement, pour tesmoigner les ressentimentz qu'elle a de l'afection que Messieurs

de l'Académie de Rome ont faict paroistre pour la jonction, la Compagnie a procede à la nomination de l'un d'iceux en la qualité de Recteur.… " *P-V,* vol. II, pp. 90–91.

8. (28 November) "Ce jour, l'Académie assemblée, a esté rapporte que Monseigneur Colbert, ayant faict la grace a l'Académie d'obtenir du Roy l'approbation des articles de jonction de lad. Académie avec celle de Rome.… " *P-V,* vol. II, p. 95.

9. (2 December) Errard to Colbert: "Les Pensionères sont treize en nombre, savoir, quatre Peintre, scinq Seculpteurs, quatre Architectes.…

"Sur quoy j'oserois dire, Monseigneur, à Vostre Excellance que les Srs. Leconte, Seculptuer, et Mesier, Architecte, mérite un chatiment examplère et d'estre excleus de l'Académie, car, s'ilz y demeuroits, ilz mèteront toujours le trouble, la disansion et la désobéisance parmy leurs camarades.…

"Le Sr. Davilers, Architecte, qui est l'un de seux que Vostre Exselance a délivré de l'exclavage des Teurs, est un garson sage, lequel s'aplique à l'éteude. Il luy manque du dessein, lequel il a besoin d'eteudier, comme je luy faitz présentement apliquer.

"Le Sr. Des Gotz, Architecte, et neveu de M. Le Nostre, et un jeune garson qui a volonté de faire quelque choze de bon et y faict son possible.

"Le Sr. Cheupein est un garson soumis, qui s'aplique à l'éteude de l'Architecteure. Je croy qu'il réheusira mieux à la militère qu'à la civile, n'éant pas de dessein, lequel est la baze et le fondement de se bel art, et sans lequel il est impossible d'y venir bien abil homme.

"Le Sr. Mesier, architecte, est un garson sans esprict et sans espérance qu'il fasse jamais rien de bien; extravagant, sans respect, sans aplication à l'éteude, dans laquelle il receulle et n'y faict auqun profict, qui mérite d'estre excleus de l'Académie ausy bien que Leconte, et mesme sans leur donner à l'un et à l'autre les deux cens livres que Vostre Excellance a la bonté d'acorder à seux qui ont faict leur devoir pour leur retour en France, pour servir d'exemple et tenir les autres dans leur devoir." *Corr.,* vol. I, pp. 62–64, n. 110.

10. (22 December) "Articoli per la congiunzione dell'Accademia Reale di Pittura, e Scultura di Francia coll'Accademia Romana di S. Luca …

"Articolo 6. Che gli studenti, che avranno

riportato qualche premio nell'Accademia di Roma, essendo in Parigi, potranno godere de'medesimi vantaggi di quelli dell'Accademia Reale, come di essere ammessi a disegnare il modello, ed altre cose simili, che godono li studenti dell'Accademia Reale di Francia; e potranno reciprocamente li permiati di Francia entrare nella concorrenza del premio, e generalmente in tutti gli esercizj dell'Accademia di Roma, purchè abbiano un attestato sottoscritto dagli officiali della loro Accademia, e si sottomettano agli ordini, ed alle discipline stabilite.…

"Articolo 8. Che sarà libero a tutte due le Accademie quando lo giudicheranno a proposito fare l'elezione del loro Principe, e Capo, ed ammettere nel numero de'soggetti quelli, che troveranno degni di questo onore, ancorchè assenti, purchè abbiano qualche Persona per farne esercitar le funzioni in loro luogo. A questo effetto ciascuna delle due Accademie si farà reciprocamente una lista di quelli che potranno meritare questa dignità, la qual lista si rinoverà due mesi avanti a fine di potersi informare de'nomi che avranno eletto.… " Missirini, Titolo LXXXVI, pp. 140–41.

1677

1. (15 August) "In oltre do. Sige. Errard chiede parte che Monsieur Colbert, Protett'e dell'Acada. Reale di Parigi, havea trasmessi li premij per il concorso da farsi dei giovani studenti delle nostri professioni per il giorno della festa di S. Luca.…

"Per li Architetti, fu confermato il pensiero e materia data gl'anni à dietro dal Sige. Gregorio Tomassini no'ro Academico Architetto, la quale fu risoluto s'eseguitte senza altro pensiero." ASL, vol. 45, fol. 48.

2. (n.d.) "Per l'Anno 1677 nel giorno di S. Luca; Soggetto per li Giovani Concorrenti per il Disegno d'Architettura. Si doverà fare un tempio ottangolo, di sett'altari, con il Maggiore, Porta Grande in facciata, et altre porte, secondo parrà, ad arbitro dell'operante, con Sagristie et appartamenti habitabili attuali per detto tempio, con cuppola, due campanili, vestibolo ò Porticho avanti per trattenimento del popolo, del quale se ne doverà fare Pianta, spaccato per il Lungo, e facciata in elevatione per di fuori, che sia ornato di tutti gl'ornamenti appartenenti ad un tempio, il tutto sia finito con diligenza, e ben perfezionato, e non sia altrimenti schizzo accennato, ma ben tirato di penna con suoi chiari, e scuri d'acquarella, o altro, che

non sia copiato da nessun disegno, o Tempio Anticho, per che altrimenti, non si metterà in concorso con gl'altri disegni, e sia fatto da se medesimo, e non d'altri, per che li si farà fare il rincontro alla presenza delli Mastri nell'Accademia, e trovando il rincontro differente dal disegno, s'annullarà e si leverà dal concorso, il tutto doverà farsi nel presente sito di lunghezza palmi 160 e di larghezza palmi 90 (site plan appended). (signed) G. Tomassini." ASL, misc. docs., Secolo XVII.

3. (n.d.) "Secondo Soggetto per li giovani concorrenti per il disegno d'Architettura (site plan appended).

"Si doverà fare un altare centinato di ordine corintho che vi siino 4 colonne con suo architrave, frogio e cornice, sopra frontispitii mezzanino requadramenti, et altri ornati, secondo parà all'operanti, che sia bon-disegno e toccato di penna et acquerello, ò altro, è non sia fatto d'altri ma da se stesso perche altrimenti si farà, e conterrà nell'modo detto nell'antredenti disegni per il tempio ottangolo, il sito del qualo sarà larghezza palmi 49 1/4 e centinato 53 di alttezza fino tutto il cornicione palmi 66 3/4 e di sopradetti fino tutto il mezzanino ad arbitro del'operanti. (signed) Gregorio Tomassini." ASL, misc. docs., Secolo XVII.

4. (10 October) "Circa il concorso de studij sopra li pensieri dati fu trasferito e stabilito … per la ottava dopo la commemoratione de Defunti, e che per ciò le ne publichi la resolutione…." ASL, vol 45, fol. 50.

5. (31 October) "Fu detto in oltre che dovendosi fare il concorso bene stabilire la giornata precisa e cosi fu risoluto di farette nella seconda domenica di Novembre futuro che sarà li 14 del med'o.

"Et anche fu risoluto che la stanza dell'Acada. dove si farà do. concorso si debba apparare de quadri et à quest'effetto furono deputati per do. apparato li Sigi. Fran'co Rosa et Ippolito Lioni con l'assistanza anche del Sige. Pietro del Pò.

"Per fare il discorso fu eletto il Sige. Gio. Pietro Bellori, il quale se prese s'assunto di fare l'invito de'poeti.

"Per ricevere li disegni de concorrenti e giudicarli furono eletti cioè … per l'architettura li Sigi. Greg. Tomassini, Alessandro Sbringa, e Mattia de Rossi.…

"Il giorno per ricevere li disegni … fu stabilito il Giovedi à matina precedente al do. concorso anche in oltre si debba far fare a concorrenti la prova del loro sapere con altri pensieri à parte da cavarsi à sorte et uno basterà per tutti, ed acciò le cose sude. siano note à ciascheduno fu ordinato se ne formatte e si affigette ne luoghi publici." ASL, vol. 45, fol. 51.

6. (11 November) "Premij consistenti in medaglie d'oro di valuta per li primi di scudi dieceotto, per li secondi di scudi quindici, per li terzi di scudi nove." ASL, vol. 45, fol. 52.

1678

1. (n.d.) "Compiuto il Principato del le Brun l'Accademia credette usare sua liberalità, e riconoscenza verso Carlo Errard, che del le Brun avea con molta lode sostenuto le veci: perchè nell'anno 1678 suo principe assoluto lo dichiarò. Mentre l'Errard tenea il posto di Carlo fece celebrare pubblici concorsi d'arte con una magnificenza di cui l'Accademia non aveva ancora avuto esempio: fornì di arredi, e di supellettili la sagrestia della Chiesa: fece registrare memorie di grato animo verso la generosità di Pietro di Cortona, ed impose gravi responsabilità ai custodi degli effetti dell'Accademia. Nel tempo poi del suo personale governo fece rinovare gl'inventarj de tutte la proprietà accademiche, e della Chiesa, colla descrizione d'ogni minimo particolare, e mise in chiaro tutti li conti degli amministratori, creditori, e debitori dell'Accademia; se non che in quell'anno Errard infermò, e sostennero il suo posto nella condizione de Vice Principe quando il Maratta, e quando il Morandi." Missirini, Titolo LXXXVII, pp. 142–43.

2. (16 January) "Essendosi fatta istanza dal Se. Carlo Errard d'havere una fede delle trè congregationi fatte sopra lo stabilimento dell'unione da farsi con l'Academia Reale di Francia à questa nostra di Roma, una cioè fatta sotto (31 May 1676; 7 June 1676; 31 January 1677) ad affeto di poterla mandare in Parigi a li Sigi. di detta Academia. Li Sudi. Sigi. Academici come da. nominati e congregati unica, e unica voce si contentarono si datte, e speditte da. fede." ASL, vols. 45, fols. 53–54.

3. (April) "Comme les prix envoyes tous les ans par le Roy a l'Académie de Rome, dit de Saint-Luc, devoient estre donnes à ceux qui reussiroient le mieux dans le travail qu'on proposeroit a la jeunesse, M. Bellori fut nommé pour choisir les histoires qui seroient traitées. Alexandre le Grand coupant le noeud gordien servit de sujet aux peintres, et les sculpteurs eurent celuy du fameux Dinocrate se présentant le mesme Alexandre, habille en Hercule et luy portant le plan du mont Athos…. L'affluence du monde fut telle qu'à peine MM. les cardinaux Nini, Rospigliosi, Carpegna et Spada y purent entrer. M. Bellori fit d'abord un discours très eloquent et très recherche sur les avantages des arts qui faisoient l'employ de l'Académie et sur l'estime que les roys et les républiques en avoient toujours marquée…. Il s'entendit sur les graces dont le Roy fait continuellement sentir les effets aux Académies et rapportá les termes des lettres patentes que Sa Majesté a données pour la jonction qui s'en est faite…. Le mérite de M. Lebrun, prince de cette Academie, fut fort elevé, et l'heure s'avançant insensiblement fit penser a donner les prix. Ils consistoient en de riches medailles d'or; et ceux qui en avoient esté Jugez dignes les receurent de la main du vice-prince (Errard). Arnaud Bucci de Saint-Omer (Arnould de Vuez), jeune etudiant de l'Académie royale de France, Alexandre, Parisien, et Louis Boulogne, étudiants de la mesme Académie, emporterent ceux de la peinture. Ceux qui estoient destinez pour les sculpteurs furent donnez a Simon Hurterelle, de la mesme Académie françoise, a Francois Nouhieri, de la ville d'Ancone, eleve du sieur Guide (Domenico Guidi), et a Jean Thirdon (Theodon), jeune Francois de la mesme Académie; et ceux des architectes a Simon Sciupagne (Chupin), a Augustin d'Arelier (D'Aviler), et a Claude de Go (Desgots), tous trois jeunes étudians de la mesme Académie royale." *Corr.*, vol. VI, p. 434–35, n. 2706.

4. (5 April) Henri Testelin, Secretary of the French Academy, to Errard: "La Relation de ce qui s'est passé en la sérémonie de la distribution des prix qui ontz esté envoyez de France a l'Académie de Saint-Luc, à Rome, a esté si agréablement resceue de toute nostre Compagnie lorsque Monsieur Lebrun luy en a fait lecture en une assemblée générale, l'ayant fait traduire en Francois, que toute cette assemblée résolut unanimement de vous en remersier et de vous suplier de tesmoigner à Messieurs de ceste célèbre Académie le ressentiment qu'elle a des soins qu'ilz prennent pour l'illustration de nos arts. C'est aussy pour en donner des marques publiques que Monsieur Lebrun a jugé à propos de la faire imprimer, avec l'excélent Discours de Monsieur Bellory, auquel on ne peur donner assez de louange. Recevez donc, Monsieur, les tesmoignage de ressentiments, d'afection et des voeux continuelz pour vostre conservation, que l'Académie vous présente par ma plume, en suportant sa foiblesse selon vostre indulgence accoutumée…. " *Corr.*, vol. I, p. 73, n. 124.

1679

1. (17 February) Colbert to Errard: "Vous avez bien fait de remettre à l'Académie le nommé Desgots…." *Corr.*, vol. I, p. 76, n. 132.

2. (9 March) Colbert to Errard: "Continuez toujours à faire travailler les Élèves à achever les ouvrages qu'ils ont commences.

"J'ay vu les plans du Palais Farnèse et des églises que Davillers a envoyés; j'en suis assez satisfait, mais je n'ay pas trouvé qu'il dissinast assez bien, et ainsy il fault qu'il se fortifie dans le dessin. Comme vous me faites scavoir que c'est un garcon qui peut servir, dites-luy que je veux qu'il demeure encore à Rome, et qu'il continue à lever le plan des plus beaux Palais et des plus belles Églises.

"Et, si vous luy trouvez assez de génie, je serois bien ayse qu'il s'appliquast à tout ce qui peut concerner les eaux, c'est-à-dire les sources, les niveaux, les conduites, les aqueducs, les différens effets des eaux; qu'il visitast avec soin tout ce qu'il y a de beau de cette nature dans toute l'Italie; qu'il s'appliquast meme à faire les calculs de ce que chaque ajustage de fontaines distribue d'eau par jour suivant son ouverture et elevation, et mesme si les eaux s'élèvent à la mesme hauteur que leurs sources, ou quelle diminution il s'y trouvé.

"En cas que vous croyiez qu'il ayt du génie pour cette sorte de travail, vous pouvez luy former une instruction sur ma lettre, et dites-luy de me rendre compte de ce qu'il fera tous les quinze jours." *Corr.*, vol. I, p. 79, n. 134.

3. (14 June) Colbert to Errard: "Je m'étonne de n'avoir recu aucunes nouvelles de Davillers. Faites-moy scavoir s'il travaille à ce que je luy ay ordonne, et tenez la main à ce qu'il ayt visité généralement

toutes les conduites des eaux et des fontaines d'Italie et qu'il m'en envoye les mémoires auparavant que de revenir." *Corr.*, vol. I, p. 83, n. 142.

4. (18 June) "Fu risoluto che in quest'anno per il tempo solito si facci il concorso di giovani studioli dello no'ri professioni … et essendo stato data l'ingumbenza a me seg'rio (Ghezzi) di dare li soggetti da esprimersi.…

"Per gl'architetti, fu ordinato al Sige. Gio. Ba. Menicucci (instructor in architecture 16 April, 1679 [ASL, vol. 45, p. 65; vol. 46, p. 25]) ne dia il pensiero et operatione.… " ASL, vol. 45, p. 67.

5. (28 June) Colbert to Errard: "A l'égard de Desgots, le Sieur Le Nostre le ramènera avec luy, et vous luy direz ce que vous avez reconnu de sa conduite.

"Je doute fort que Davillers soit aussy habile sur le fait des eaux qu'il en est persuadé; mais, puisqu'il a une grande envie de revenir icy, il seroit peut-estre inutile de le retenir davantage. Dites-luy seulement que, dans son retour, il examine soigneusement tout ce qui regarde les eaux." *Corr.*, vol. I, p. 84, n. 145.

6. (23 August) Colbert to Errard: "Je suis bien aise d'apprendre, par votre lettre du 2 de ce mois que Davillers soit allé visiter la Lombardie. Je verray à son retour s'il a quelque capacité pour la conduite des eaux." *Corr.*, vol. I, p. 87, n. 150.

7. (15 September) Colbert to LeBrun: "Il n'y a plus dans l'Académie de Rome que cinq Sculpteurs, un Architecte (Desgots), deux Paintres, et un Graveur, et, comme il est nécessaire d'en tenir toujours un nombre plus considérable, je vous prie de conférer avec M. Perrault de tous les Élèves qui vont a l'Académie, pour faire choix des plus habiles pour envoyer à Rome." *Corr.*, vol. I, p. 89, n. 153.

1680

1. (6 April) Colbert to Errard: "Le père de Desgots, qui est à l'Académie, m'a demandé le congé de son fils pour retourner en France. Je vous l'envoye, et vous pouvez luy donner de quoy s'entretenir pendant deux mois qu'il visitera la Lombardie, outre les 200 livres qui sont accordées a tous les Pensionnaires de l'Académie qui retournent en

France par mon ordre.… (Passport appended) "Estant informe que le nommé Desgots, Architecte, étant présentement dans l'Académie de peinture, sculpture et architecture établie par ordre du Roy à Rome, a finy les trois années aux-quelles nous avons fixé le temps du séjour des Élèves dans l'Académie, par le Règlement par nous fair le 28 octobre de l'Année 1677, en vertu du pouvoir à nous donné par Sa Majesté, mandons et ordonnons au Sr. Errard, Directeur de ladite Académie, d'accorder le congé audit Desgots pour retourner en France." *Corr.*, vol I, p. 96, n. 170.

2. (8 April) "Volendosi dunque provedere del modello per l'ignudo, il Sige. Carlo Errard per beneficar l'Accademia offersi e fu accettato il suo modello, con molti ringratiamenti." ASL, vol. 45, fol. 80; vol. 46, fol. 33.

3. (30 May) "Furono proposti da me Seg'rio (Ghezzi) li pensieri da eseguirsi per il futuro concorso stabilito a farsi nel solito tempo e … per l'architettura si prese l'ingumbenza il Se. Gregorio Tomassini Architetto di darme il pensiero." ASL, vol. 45, fol. 81.

4. (n.d.) "So(ggetto per) i Giovani (Archi)tetti (site plan appended). Sito per un tempio che dovrà essere un esagono nel quale vi vanno cinque altari con il maggiore, due porte laterali e da piedi la porta principale e due campanili in facciata. Pianta e spaccati. (signed) G. Tomassini." ASL, misc. docs., Secolo XVII.

5. (15 September) "Perche si è veduto che quelli che vogliano in quest'anno concorrere nella no'ra Acada. per l'honore de premij non hanno sufficiente tempo per compire le loro fatighe fu à medo. prorogano il tempo per il mese de Xbre futuro per il giorno da stabilirsi quindici giorni avanti e ciò si debba affigere nella no'ra Acad'a." ASL, vol. 45, fol. 84; vol. 46, fol. 36.

6. (15 September) "Furono proposti dal nostro principe per accademici di Merito … li Sigi. Marco Antonio Piaselli e Filippo Leti architetti Romani … per l'informatione dell'habilità di quali furono deputati à prendere informatione li Si. Fabritio Chiari e Gio. Batta. Buoncore per la sussequente Cong'ne darando li sudi. quando siano vinti in conformita del nostro statuti prima d'essere il possesso, cioè il pittore di portare il

quadro e gl'architetti di portare qualche opera di studio per li giovani, e non altrimente.... " ASL, vol. 45, fol. 84; vol. 46, fol. 36.

7. (10 November) "Fu risoluto à unica voce che in avvenire non si possi eleggere e ricevere nesuno Academico di Merito se non farà costare, oltre li necessarij requisiti contenuti ne nostri statuti, d'haver compita l'eta d'anni trenta, e non altrimente, e facendosi altrimenti l'intendi per nullo, et illegitimo e come mà fatto stato ne proposto, ne accettato.... " ASL, vol. 45, fol. 86.

8. (10 November) "Il concorso prorogato sino al mese di Xbre futuro, fu risoluto di fatti, e dia li premij alli giovani concorrenti per li 15 Xbre futo. con che per li 13 do. habbiano portati li loro disegni … conforme al solito, e nel modo e forma si vedera espresso nell'editto speciale da affigersi à publica vista nella sala della no'ra Academia." ASL, vol. 45, fol. 86.

9. (15 December) "Essendosi concorso solamente Domo. Martinelli fu anche a lui destinato il premio senz'altra giudicatura." ASL, vol. 45, fol. 87.

1681

1. (n.d.) "Sotto il governo del (Mattia) de Rossi l'Accademia Francese fece dono all'Accademia di Roma de'suoi statuti, inviati da Tommaso Regnaudin (see 1672, n. 1) scultore del Re con tutte le lettere patenti, e privilegj accordati a quella da Sua Maestà Cristianissima. E ciò che fu più grato era, che quell'illustre corpo communicava pure sette conferenze tenute da suoi professori intorno le cose dell'arte, in via comparativa sulle opere de'migliori Maestri. Queste dispute furono introdotte ad insinuazione del Colbert, e conosciute utilissime, come quelle, che univano l'insegnamento all'essempio. Le riunioni a quest'oggetto si fecero nella sala Accademica, o nel gabinetto de'quadri del Re ogni primo sabbato del mese, e furono precedute sempre da una allocuzione. Il Signor LeBrun, come cancelliere, ne fece l'apertura." Missirini, Titolo XC, pp. 144–45.

2. (17 May) "Per essersi gia stabilito il concorso per il solito tempo da farsi da giovani studiosi delle no'ri professioni, furono da me segretario (Ghezzi) proposti li pensieri da eseguirsi.... Per l'architettura, fu data l'ingumbenza al Se. Gregorio Tomassini che ne debba publicare il pensiero." ASL, vol. 45, fol. 91.

3. (7 September) " … che per la meno li concorrenti siano quattro per classe, altrimente non si facci." ASL, vol. 45, fol. 93.

4. (5 October) "Essendosi veduto che li giovani concorrenti non hanno all'ordine li loro studij e disegni fu risoluto prorogare il tempo … conforme fu prorogato per li 14 di Decembre futuro." ASL, vol. 45, fol. 93; vol. 46, fol. 42.

5. (13 December) "Fu intimata cong'ne particolare per giudicare li disegni . . . portati da giovani del concorso, conforme fu fatto, e si dirà precisam'te nel registro di do. concorso, fatto sotto il di 11 Gen. 1682." ASL, vol. 45, fol. 95.

1682

1. (4 January) "In fine fu stabilito che per doma. prossima undici del corrente si sollennizi il concorso per dar li premij." ASL, vol. 45, fol. 95.

2. (24 May) "Avvicinandosi il tempo del concorso, fu data l'ingumbenza a me Seg'rio (Ghezzi) di dar fuori li soggetti da eseguirsi col farli affigere nella nostra sala Academica." ASL, vol. 45, fol. 102.

3. (28 June) Soggetti: "Per l'architettura si dara a parte." ASL, vol. 45, fol. 102.

4. (6 September) "Fu stabilito che per li undeci d'Ottobre futuro si facci la sollennità del concorso in modo che li giovani debbano haver portato infallantemente i loro disegnj per li 4 del sudo., altrim'te non saranno più ricevuti e sopra di ciò si ne debba affigere l'edita nella sala acad'a." ASL, vol. 45, fol. 103.

5. (1 November) "Fu rappresentato del Se. Luigi Garzi no'ro Pnpe. essergli stato fatto istanza dall'Em(inentisi)me Sige. Card. Carlo Barberini no'ro Protettore voler honorare Giovanni Raisner Polacco che attende alli Studij dell'architettura; et debbe nel concorso del p(rese)nte Anno il Primo Premio nella Prima Classe dell'Architettura d'ammetterlo nel numero degl'Academici Studenti e dargline la patente necessaria. Il che benissimo e ponderatamente considerato da tutti li Si. Congregati fu accetto e ricevuto do. Giovanni Raisner Polacco per nostro academico studente, et ordinato a me Seg'rio gli ne spediteli le patente necessarie, ogni volta però habbi prima adempito l'obligo ingiunteli dal nostro statuto di portare il quadro dipinto di sua mano per farlo rimanere in utile della nostra Accademia e non altrimente." ASL, vol. 45, fol. 107.

1683

1. (n.d.) "Hosso d'Inventario delle Robbe dell'Accad'a esistenti nelle sue stanze … Concorsi, 1682 … 4 disegni d'Arch're de Giov. Reisner Polacco." ASL, misc. docs., Secolo XVII.

2. (14 February) "Essendo andato a Napoli chiamato dal quel Vice Re il Se. Gregorio Tomassini no'ro Camerlengo fu stimato bene eleggere un altro in suo luogo." ASL, vol. 45, fol. 110.

3. (25 April) Lecturers: "Per l'architettura, essendosi considerate le qualità sufficientissime del Sige. D. Domenico Martinelli Lucchese Architetto per esser dichiarato no'ro Academico di Merito; tutti li Sudi. Sigi. Congregati à unica voce, e senza alcuna discrepenza lo dichiaravono tale, e per il debito, che in conformità de no'ri statuti e decreti fatti è tenuto pagare con dar qualche cosi di sua mano e professione alla no'ra Acada. Li Sudi. Sigi. Congi. risolvenno che il sudo. D. Martinelli nella p'nte stagione, et apertura de studij dia lettione d'Architettura, con che le lettioni originali, che egli darà restiro a beneficio della no'ra Acada., e in tal forma haverà adempito il debito, e non altrimente." ASL, vol. 45, fol. 110; vol. 46, fol. 49.

4. (30 May) "Fu poi risoluto dal do. Sige. Prencipe (Contini) che si facci il concorso de giovani studiosi delle no're professioni esitendosi egli far la spesa delli premij senza gravari punto la no'ra

Acada. si che per la pa. festa prossima si ne debba affigger l'editto nella sala academica con li pensieri ò soggetti da eseguirsi dandone à me Seg'rio (Ghezzi) l'ingumbenza, il che udito da Sudi. Congi. ringratiarono il do. Se. Pnpe. con particolari espress'ni." ASL, vol. 45, fol. 111.

5. (18 July) "Per lo stabilimento fattosi del concorso de giovani fu già affiso l'editto nella sala accademica nel quale furono publicati gl'infri. pensieri da eseguirsi, concepiti da me Seg'rio in esecut'ne dell'ordine e decreto fatto nella precede. cong'ne e sono gl'infri …

"Per l'architettura essendo stata data l'ingumbenza al Se. D. Domo. Martinelli, in quest'anno deputato Maestro per le lettioni d'Architettura, chiede quegli per soggetto da eseguirsi: Pianta e spaccato d'un palazzo nobile in villa a beneplacito.

"Tutti li sudi. soggetti furono da me dati, come correlativi e mischiati con l'Architettura à caggione d'essere il nostro Prencipe Architetto." ASL, vol. 45, fol. 112.

6. (19 September) "Approssinandosi il tempo di sollennizare il concorso de premij fu stimato esser necessario venire all'elettione de giudici.… Architettura: Mattia de Rossi, Carlo Rainaldi, Carlo Fontana (alternate: G. B. Menicucci)." ASL, vol. 45, fol. 113.

7. (8 October) Prizes: "Arch'a 1a. cl. Vincenzo della Greca 1o.

"Giunto poi il giorno di doma. diece d'Ottobre giorno stabilito per la sollennità del concorso, fu veduta la gran sala Accademica ornata non solo con tutti li disegni … de concorrenti, disposti per ordinanza, assieme con le prove fatte, come sa. all'improviso, ma con diversi quadri scelti e rari di diversi Professori Antichi e Moderni (e venuta l'hora vigesima intimata, non mancò la quantità del gran popolo di far calca per la gara).… " ASL, vol. 45, fol. 114.

1684

1. (9 April) "Fu risoluto si facci il solito concorso de giovani studiosi delle no're Professioni nel modo se è fatto negl'anni precedenti e à dare li soggetti si prete l'ingumbenza il Se. Giacinto Brandi nostro Principe." ASL, vol. 45, fol. 118.

1685

1. (7 October) "Fu ammesso all no'ra Acada. e sui congi. il Sige. D. Domo. Martinelli Architetto, havendo adempito al suo obligo con haver dato e consegnato al no'ro custode dell'Academia le lettioni Academiche dato sopra li cinque ordini d'Arch'ra alli giovani studenti, essendo preceduto prima al do. possesso il giuram'te di fidelm'te osservare il nostro statuto … " ASL, vol. 45, fol. 122; vol. 46, fol. 54.

2. (7 October) "Fu risoluto di facci la festa seconda al solito …
   "Che li Sigi. Festaroli apparino la sala Academica, non potendosi de quadri, si facci con le lettioni di prospettiva et architettura date dalli Sigi. Pier Frano. Garolli e Domo. Martinelli." ASL, vol. 45, fol. 122; vol. 46, fol. 54.

1686

1. (31 March) "Il Sige. Pnpe. (Carlo Fontana) conoscendo che per le sue grandi occupat'ni può avvenire che alcune volte non possa intervenire alle congregat'ni per tanto ha pensato di elegire per suo V. Prencipe come eletto il Se. Giov. Ma. Morandi con le facoltà necese. et opp'ne." ASL, vol. 45, fol. 126.

2. (25 April) "Fu anche risoluto si facci il concorso e per dar li sogetti si preso l'ingumbenza il medo. Cav. Fontana no'ro prencipe." ASL, vol. 45, fol. 127; vol. 46, fol. 57.

3. (13 October) "Avvicinandosi la festa di S. Luca fu risoluto si celebri moderatamente conforme al solito." ASL, vol. 45, fol. 130.

1687

1. (21 September) "Essendo vicina la festa di S. Luca fu ordinato si sollennizzi al solito." ASL, vol. 45, fol. 136.

1688

1. (3 October) "Avvicinandosi la festa di S. Luca fu

risoluto di celebri con ogni parsimonia possibile." ASL, vol. 45, fol. 142; vol. 46, fol. 64.

1689

1. (27 March) "Volendo il Se. D. Gio. Batta. Menicucci Architetto al quale fu data una delle cappellanie lasciate nella no'ra chiesa … renunciarla à dispositione della no'ra Cong'ne quindi è che havendo io Seg'rio per sua parte ciò rappresentato in questa adunanza, li sudi. Sigi. Congregati elletero in suo luogo il Se. D. Domo. Martinelli nostro Academico." ASL, vol. 45, fol. 143; vol. 46, fol. 65.

1690

1. (30 April) "Havendo dimandato licentia il Sige. D. Domo. Martinelli di partarsi fuori di Roma, per affair d'Architettura, autiche molto lontano da Roma, dove pensa tratenersi per breve spatio di tempo, hà supplicato ancora la gratia di ritenere e far esevertare la cappellania della no'ra Cong'ne.… " ASL, vol. 45, fol. 145.

2. (8 October) "Avvicinandosi la festa di S. Luca, fu risoluto si facci nella conformità dell'anno passato." ASL, vol. 45, fol. 148.

1691

1. (10 August) " … ad ogni modo volendosi che servire anche come Academia fu discorso dal no'ro Se. Pnpe. (Mattia de Rossi) che havendo egli risoluto in quest'anno di fare il concorso per animare li giovani studenti al profitto, ordinò che si concepissere li soggetti da darsi alle solite classi e s'affiggesero con darne la totale ingumbenza à me Seg'rio (Ghezzi), tanto circa li pensieri quanto in sua la regenza per l'effettuaz'ne." ASL, vol. 45, fol. 149.

1692

1. (6 January) "Per sollennizare il concorso de premij già altre volte stabilito fu risoluto che si publichi nel modo solito, cioè che per il giorno di S. Sebastiano 20 corrente li giovani portino li loro disegni … che poi per li 25 si farà la giudicatura e per li 27 la sollennità del concorso." ASL, vol. 45, fol. 151.

2. (13 January) "Nella qual Cong'ne comparrero li Sigi. Filippo Leti Architetti, e David Coninghi Pittore, quali havendo adempito al loro debito per esser nel numero de nostri Academici; in conformità del no'ro statuto, e decreti, furono ammessi al solito giuramento e dato all'uno e l'altro il solito possesso." ASL, vol. 45, fol. 152; vol. 46, fol. 70.

3. (20 January) "Concorso dell'Anno 1692 e nomi de premiati ... Prima classe dell'architettura, Sig. Filippo Barigioni Romano, 4 pezzi, Primo Premio. . . . (signed) Mattia de Rossi." ASL, misc. docs. Secolo XVII.

4. (25 April) "A cagione di molti incommodi, e spese continue, che hà la nostra Accada., fu risoluto che per quest'anno non si aprino gli studij." ASL, vol. 45, fol. 153.

5. (5 October) "Essendo vicina la festa di S. Luca, fu risoluto si sollennizi in conformità dell'anno passato, tanto circa l'apparato quanto ad ogni altra cosa." ASL, vol. 45, fol. 153.

1694

1. (10 January) "Non volendo il Se. Matthia de Rossi, no'ro Pnpe., piu continuare nel suo principato, contutto die gli fusse à unica voce offerta la conferma, ad ogni modo egli con modestissima e legitima scusa d'impotenza ottenne la licenza....

"Havendo il Se. Frano. Fontana Archo. sin dalla festa di S. Luca dato il suo disegno per ricevere il posto d'Accademico essendo di già stato ammesso per tale hoggi gli fu dato il possesso." ASL, vol. 45, fol. 155; vol. 46, fol. 74.

2. (25 April) "Fu risoluto si aprino gli studij per sabbato pross(im)o primo di Maggio, nel modo risoluto nella precedente congreg'ne e che in oltre si affighino nella sala Accademica li pensieri per fare il concorso di premij e fu dato l'ingumbenza à me Seg'rio (Ghezzi) di sceglierli e publicarli conforme al solito." ASL, vol. 45, fol. 157.

3. (3 October) "Fu risoluto che si stabilitoli la sollennità del concorso, e per ciò fu detto, che essendo difettola, et invalida la sala della no'ra Accademia per non esser sicuro in solaio, fu risoluto che stante il cortesitt'ne beneplacito ottenuto dal no'ro Sige.

Pnpe. dall'Ecc'mo Senatore si debba fare nella gran sala del nuovo Palazzo di Campidoglio....

"Che per Doma. pross(im)a 10 del corrente li giovani debbano haver portati li loro disegni per la matina nella qle. doveranno fare anche le prove....

"Il giorno poi doppo il pranzo si farà il giuditio." ASL, vol. 45, fol. 158; vol. 46, fol. 79.

4. (n.d.) "Venuto poi il giorno sudo. delli 17 fu sollennizito il concorso nella sala di campidoglio e li premiati furono quelli che vedono scritti in un foglio che si conserva in filza intitolata 'scritture diverso.'" ASL, vol. 45, fol. 158 (marginal).

5. (17 October) "Concorso solennizzato in Campidoglio alli 17 ottobre 1694. Architettura Prima Classe Primo Premio Pompeo Ferrari Romano Secondo Premio Andrea di Nicolò Angelo della Valle Terzo Premio Carlo Ambrosio Ravassi. Architettura Seconda Classe Primo Premio Alessandro Sperone Romano. Architettura Terza Classe Primo Premio Alessandro Rossini Romano e Ludovico Rusconi Sassi Secondo Premio Filippo Ottoni Romano. Li soprascritti giovani furono li premiati e li premij furono di Medaglie d'Argento et altre di argento dorato a proportione delle classi nelle questi si vedeva impresso da una parte S. Luca e d'altra un motto alludente esso premio, il tutto a spese del Cav. Carlo Fontana Arch'o e Principe....

"Il discorso accademico fu fatto da me Giuseppe Ghezzi Segretario, sopra l'architettura, ma fu dato da Placidio Eusebio Ghezzi, mio figlio, nell'una e nell'altra legge dottore, nell'eta di anni 22." ASL, misc. docs., Secolo XVII.

1695

1. (20 February) "Corre l'anno Centesimo che fu eretta la no'ra Accademia e per esser cosa cospicua e degna di memoria fu proposto esser bene sollennizarlo con ogni dimostrat'ne e pompa possibile; il che con ponderata maturità considerato fu risoluto si facci con ogni dovuto decoro, e che intanto io Segretario disponessi il modo, e la materia più propria per effettuarlo, e datti una lista de riventi Accademici per esigerne una spontanea contributione conforme feci, e li presenti sottoscrittore, e per gl'altri furono deputati li Sigi. Lorenzo Ottone e Gio. Theodone." ASL, vol. 45, fol. 159.

2. (31 July) "Essendosi risoluto di celebrare il centesimo, fu determinato si sollennizzi nella gran sala
del campidoglio, essendo pronto il Ecc'me
Senatore (Marchese Ottavio Riario: *Acc. d'Honore*
as of 2 October [ASL, fol. 45, fol. 163]) à farne il
favore che per ciò fu ordinato si adorni con ogni
maggior pompa." ASL, fol. 45, fol. 162.

1696

1. (n.d.) Soggetto for the first class: "Desiderando
un monarca nel stabilito posto d'un ampla e
deliziosa villa costruire da'fondamenti una mag-
nifica e ben spartita abitation per il ricetto di
quattro personaggi che nei dovuti tempi dovranno
in essa separatamente habitarvi. Si dovrà con tal
effetto con nobile e vaga simetria delineare pianta,
spaccato e prospetto di una sontuosa e reale habitatione distribuita secondo il fine suddetto col situ-
arvi inoltre avanti al principal prospetto
dell'edificio una spaziosa piazza destinata alle pub-
bliche giostre nel contorno della quale si dovranno
collocare le officine necessarie de stalle rimesse et
altro attinente al Real edificio." Ghezzi, *Il
Centesimo ... dell'Accademia* (1696).

2. (n.d.) Soggetto for the second class: "Inherendo
all'intentione suddetta si disegnarà pianta, profilo e
prospetto di una vaga e raccolta chiesola da erigersi
contigua al suddetto regio edificio per il dovuto
servitio de personaggi suddetti qual tempietto
dovrà occupare il sito obbligato di palmi 100 di
longhezza e palmi 80 di larghezza." Ghezzi (1696).

3. (n.d.) Soggetto for the third class: "Per terminare
parimenti nel suddetto regio edificio le parti, si
formerà nella proportione dorica pianta et alzata
del portone principale de detta villa distinta in tre
vani et ornato con colonne e pilastri attinenti a
detto ordine." Ghezzi (1696).

4. (10 September) "Avvicinandosi dunque il tempo
da sollennizato do. centesimo fu risoluto et ordinato che per tutto venerdi prosso. li Giovani hab-
bino portato li loro disegni, bassirilievi, et
architetture, e che per la Doma. susseguente si faccino le prove." ASL, vol. 45, fol. 166.

5. (n.d.) Judging:
"p'ma classe d'Architettura
il disegno del R, p'mo
il disegno del Y, secondo
il disegno del E, terzo
"2a. classe d'Architettura
il disegno dell'O, p'mo
il disegno dell'H, secondo
il disegno del N, terzo
"3a. classe d'Architettura
il disegno del M, p'mo
il disegno del Z, secondo
il disegno del X, terzo."
ASL, misc. docs., Secolo XVII.

6. (n.d.) Prove estempore: first class, "Prospetto
principale di una facciata di un tempietto in
larghezza determinata di palma ottanta;" second
class, "Nicchia ornata in un tempio magnifico;"
third class, "Cornice con capitello d'ordine
corintho." ASL, misc. docs., Secolo XVII.

7. (n.d.) Assignment of prizes:
"P'ma Classe 1° Pompeo Ferrari (R)
2° Giov. Anto. Savelle, Piemontese (Z)
3° Carlo Derbais, Parigi (Y)
4° Carlo Pacenti, Rom'o (E)
"2'da Classe 1° Alessandro Rossini, Rom'o (O)
2° Basilio Spinelli, Rom'o (N)
3o Giuseppe Rossi, Pied. (L)*
*line crossed out
4° Lud. Rusconi Sassi, Rom'o (H)
"3'za Classe 1° Giuseppe Para, Rom'o (M)
2° Bartolomeo Santini, Rom'o (X)."
ASL, misc. docs., Secolo XVII.

8. (30 September) "In questo giorno fu sollennizato
il Centesimo della nostra Accademia ... nella gran
sala del Campidoglio fatta splendidam'te e con sin-
golarità non più veduta apparare per opera del
Sige. Cav. Carlo Fontana no'ro Pnpe. con gl'arazzi
singolari, e rinomati dell'Ecc'ma Casa Colonna...."
ASL, vol. 45, fol. 166.

9. (30 September) Awarding of prizes:
   "1ª Classe 1º Pompeo Ferrari
             2º Carlo Derbais
             3º Carlo Pacenti
   "2ª Classe 1º Alessandro Rossini
             2º Ludovico Rusconi Sassi
             3º Basilio Spinelli
   "3ª Classe 1º Bartolomeo Santini
             2º Giovanni Antonio Savalle
             3º Giuseppe Para."
   ASL, misc. docs., Secolo XVII.

1697

1. (3 February) Villacerf to La Teulière: "Il y a à
   Rome le fils de Derbois, marbrier, qui est depuis
   trois ans et s'instruit dans l'Architecture; vous me
   ferez plaisir de l'aider de vos conseils et de lui faire
   tout le plaisir que vous pourrés." *Corr.*, vol. II, p.
   290, n. 777.

2. (26 February) La Teulière to Villacerf: "J'auray
   soing, comme je dois, du Sr. Derbais, suivant vos
   ordres, Monsieur, en cas qu'il revienne icy, d'ou il
   est party, il y a environ un mois, dans le dessein de
   s'en retourner en France, qu'il changea néantmoins
   à Florence, jugeant, à ce qu'on m'a dit, qu'il luy
   seroit plus utile de voir toutes les grandes villes
   d'Italie où il y a quelque chose de remarquable. Il
   a écrit de Venise à un de ses amis, que j'ay prié de
   s'informer avecque luy de ce qu'il prétend faire,
   affin de vous en rendre conte. Je puis vous assurer
   cependant, Monsieur, que c'est un très bon garcon,
   qui s'est appliqué pendant qu'il a esté à Rome; il
   m'a fait voir divers desseins qu'il avoit fait qui
   estoient bien, et, sur les avis que je lui donnois, il
   me paroissoit avoir e l'entente; mais j'ay sceu d'un
   jeune Peintre Francois, qu'il fréquentoit et qui se
   distingue fort en toute manière, que le Sr. Derbais
   en sait plus qu'il n'en fait paroitre, estant fort mo-
   deste et réservé à se produire. S'il revient icy, vous
   pouvés estre, Monsieur, bien persuadé que je
   l'ayderay de tout ce qui dépendra de moy, regar-
   dant comme une bonne fortune toutes les occasions qui s'offrent de m'employer à quelque chose
   qui puisse vous plaire." *Corr.*, vol. II, p. 294, n.
   783.

3. (17 March) Villacerf to La Teulière: "Je suis sur-
   pris que le Sr. Derbais ne soit plus à Rome; s'il y
   revient, je vous prie de me le faire savoir." *Corr.*,
   vol. II, p. 297, n. 786.

4. (9 April) La Teuliere to Villacerf: "Si le Sr.
   Derbais revient de Venise à Rome, je ne man-
   queray, suivant vos ordres, de vous donner avis."
   Corr., vol. II, p. 302, n. 792.

1699

1. (5 April) Lecturers: "Per l'architettura, non
   potendo sempre un solo maestro supplire a tutto il
   tempo, fu fatta l'infra. elettione:
   Maggio, Filippo Leti
   Giugno, Antonio Valerij
   Luglio, Carlo Bizzaccheri
   Augusto, Carlo Buratti
   Settembre, Sebastiano Cipriani."
   ASL, vol. 45, fol. 177; vol. 46, fol. 97.

1700

1. (n.d.) Soggetti: "Archit'ra P'ma Classe: Si delinearà Pianta, Spaccato, e Prospetto di un magnifico,
   e sonsuoso tempio da fabricarsi in una celebra
   città, con situare avanti la principal piazza, di qo.
   due bracci laterali di fabrica, qual formando
   ornato, e teatro anteriore servino susseguente-
   mente da un lato per uso, et habitatione di un
   insigne capitolo e clero destinato al aiuto di do.
   tempio e dal altro per un ospedal grande di da.
   città, con due officine annesse e necessarie per il
   servitio di esso, e suoi ministeri.

   "2ª Classe: Si delinearà Pianta, e Prospetto du
   un capo altare magnifico da farsi nella fronte della
   nave maestra de do. tempio.

   "3ª Classe: Si copiarà proportionalmente una
   delle nichie ornata di colonne esistenti nella nave
   principale della Basilica di S. Giovanni in
   Laterano." ASL, misc. docs., Secolo XVII.

CHRONOLOGY OF THE COMPETITIONS

YEAR Day of Ceremony	CLASS Subject	PRIZEWINNERS/PLATES (in rank order)		PRINCIPE Instructor in Architecture
1677 (14 Nov)	First: octagonal church with bell towers	Chupin D'Aviler Desgots	1–3 4–6 7–9	LeBrun Tomassini
1679 (18 Oct)	First: longitudinal church with bell towers	Martinelli	10–12	Baldi Tomassini
1680 (15 Dec)	First: hexagonal church with bell towers	Martinelli	(Fig. 68)	Morandi Tomassini
1681 (11 Jan 1682)	First: palace	Carapecchia	16–17	de Rossi Tomassini
1682 (11 Oct)	First: circular church with bell towers	Reissner	18–20	Garzi Tomassini
1683 (10 Oct)	First: villa palace	della Greca	(lost)	Contini Martinelli
1692 (27 Jan)	First: palace	Barigioni	21–24	de Rossi Tomassini
1694 (17 Oct)	First: monastic college	Ferrari della Valle Ravassi	25–27 28–30 31–33	Fontana, C. Fontana, F.
	Second: chapel	Sperone	34–36	
	Third: one bay of Conservators' Palace	Rossini Rusconi-Sassi Ottoni	37 38–39 40	
1696 (20 Sept)	First: villa palace for four dignitaries	Ferrari Derbais Pacenti	41–43 44–46 47–49	Fontana, C. Fontana, F.
	Second: villa chapel	Rossini Rusconi-Sassi Spinelli	50–52 53–55 56–58	
	Third: villa gate	Santini Sevalle Parà	59–60 61 62	

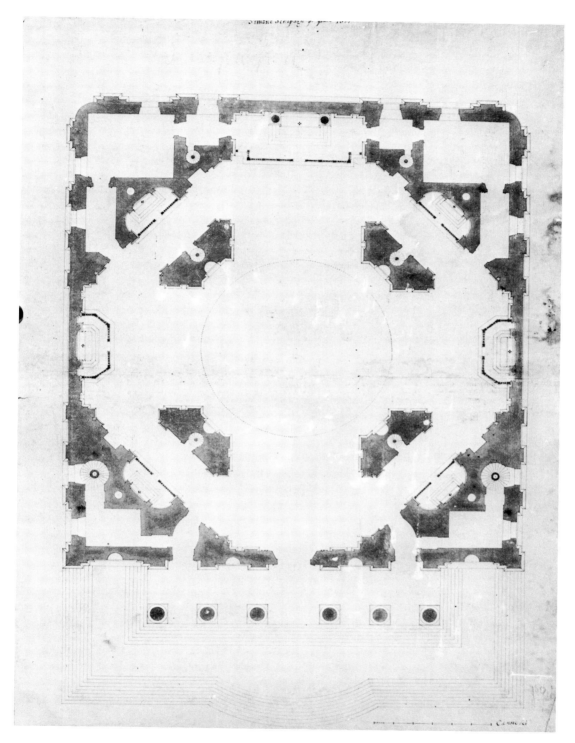

1 SIMON CHUPIN: plan for a domed and porticoed octagonal church with bell towers; ASL 1 (Conc. Acc. 1677).

2 CHUPIN: facade elevation for the church in Plate 1; ASL 2.

Pianta del Campanile

Pianta della Cuppola

3 CHUPIN: longitudinal section for the church in Plate 1; ASL 3.

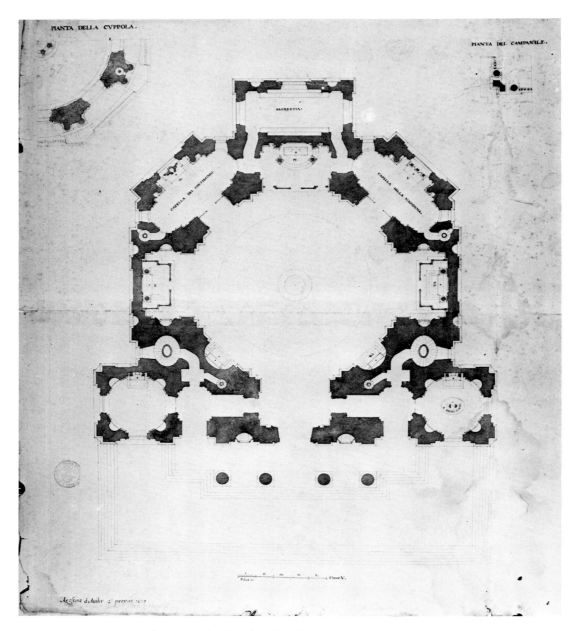

4 AUGUSTIN-CHARLES D'AVILER: plan for a domed and porticoed octagonal church with bell towers; ASL 4 (Conc. Acc. 1677).

5 D'AVILER: facade elevation for the church in Plate 4; ASL 5.

6 D'AVILER: longitudinal section for the church in Plate 4; ASL 6.

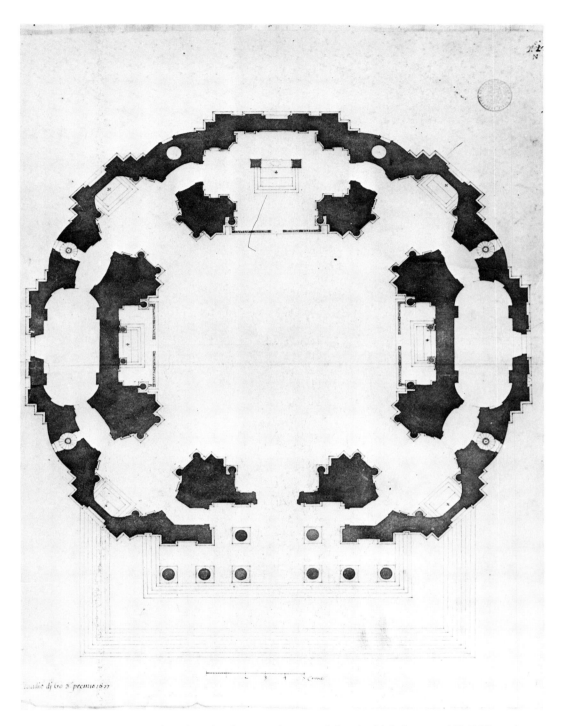

7 CLAUDE DESGOTS: plan for a domed and porticoed octagonal church with bell towers; ASL 7 (Conc. Acc. 1677).

8 DESGOTS: facade elevation for the church in Plate 7; ASL 8.

9 DESGOTS: longitudinal section for the church in Plate 7; ASL 9.

10 DOMENICO MARTINELLI: plan for a domed Latin-cross church with bell towers; ASL 26 (Conc. Acc. 1679).

11 MARTINELLI: facade elevation for the church in Plate 10; ASL 27.

12 MARTINELLI: longitudinal section for the church in Plate 10; ASL 28.

13 FILIPPO DI LETI: plan for a domed hexagonal
church with bell towers; ASL 10 (Dono Accademico).

14 DI LETI: facade elevation for the church in Plate
13; ASL 11.

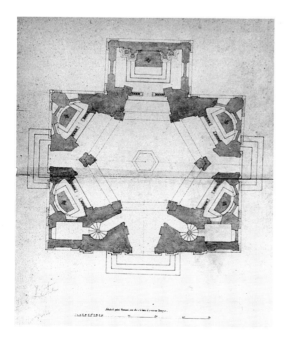

15 DI LETI: longitudinal section for the church in Plate 13; ASL 12.

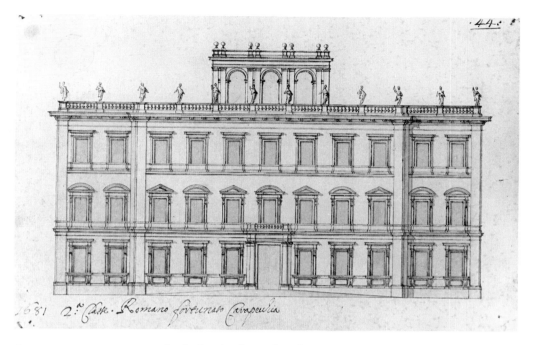

16 ROMANO CARAPECCHIA: facade elevation for a palace, first variant; ASL 54 (Conc. Acc. 1681).

17 CARAPECCHIA: facade elevation for a palace, second variant; ASL 55.

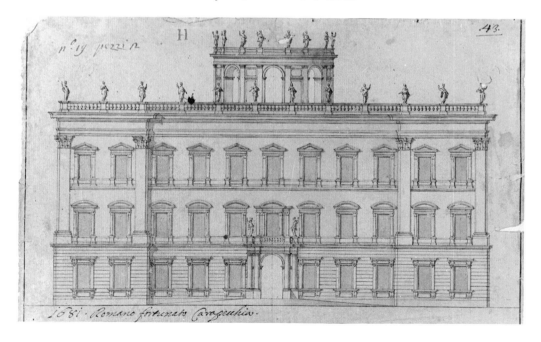

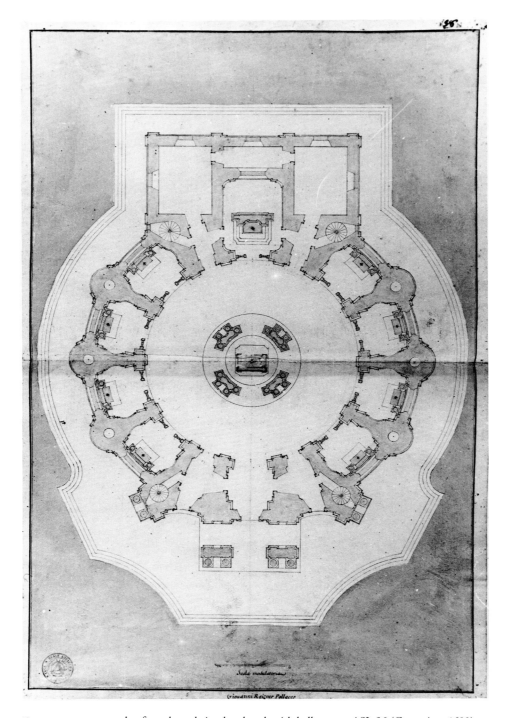

18 JAN REISSNER: plan for a domed circular church with bell towers; ASL 56 (Conc. Acc. 1682).

19 REISSNER: facade elevation for the church in Plate 18; ASL 57.

20 REISSNER: longitudinal section for the church in Plate 18; ASL 58.

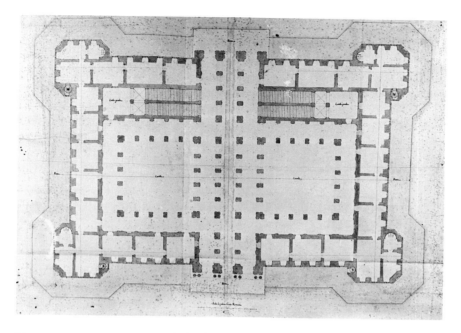

21 FILIPPO BARIGIONI: ground plan for a palace; ASL 41 (Conc. Acc. 1692).

22 BARIGIONI: main-floor plan for the palace in Plate 21; ASL 42.

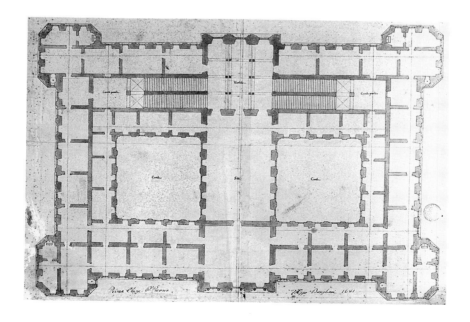

23 BARIGIONI: facade elevation for the palace in Plate 21; ASL 43.

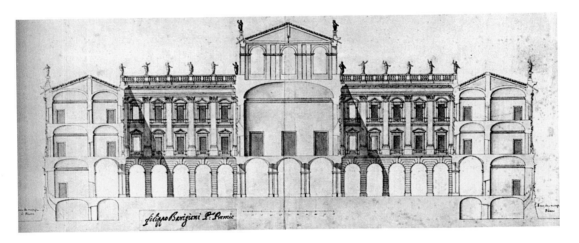

24 BARIGIONI: lateral section for the palace in Plate 21; ASL 44.

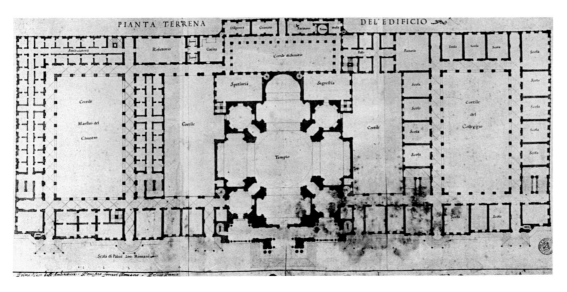

25 POMPEO FERRARI: plan for a monastic college and chapel; ASL 17 (Conc. Acc. 1694).

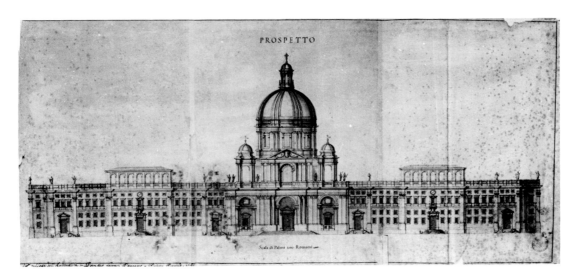

26 FERRARI: facade elevation for the college in Plate 25; ASL 18.

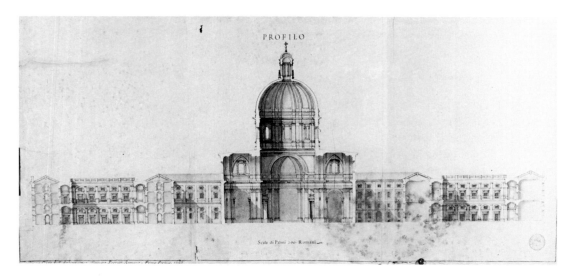

27 FERRARI: lateral section for the college in Plate 25; ASL 19.

28 ANDREA DELLA VALLE: plan for a monastic college and chapel; ASL 20 (Conc. Acc. 1694).

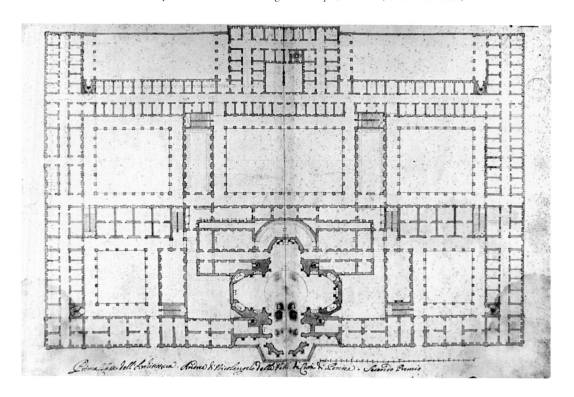

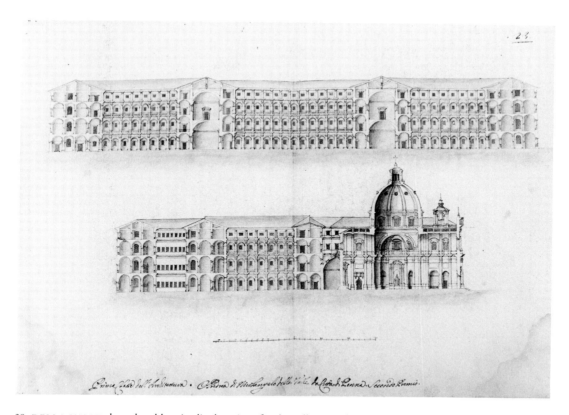

29 DELLA VALLE: lateral and longitudinal sections for the college in Plate 28; ASL 21.

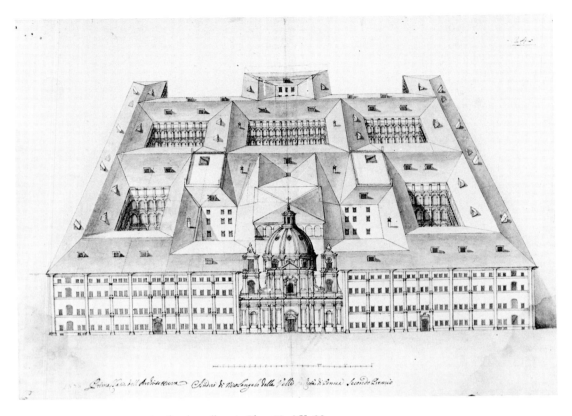

30 DELLA VALLE: perspective for the college in Plate 28; ASL 22

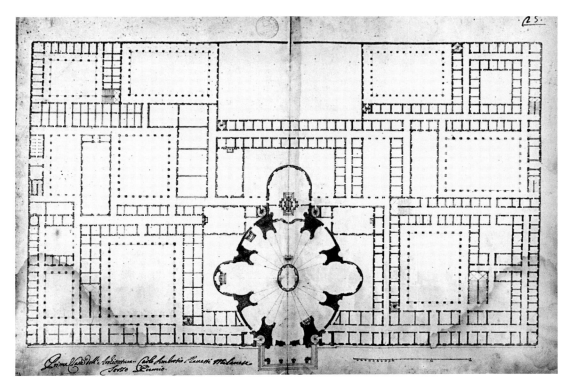

31 CARLO AMBROSIO RAVASSI: plan for a monastic college and chapel; ASL 23 (Conc. Acc. 1694).

32 RAVASSI: lateral and longitudinal sections for the college in Plate 31; ASL 24.

33 RAVASSI: perspective for the college in Plate 31; ASL 25.

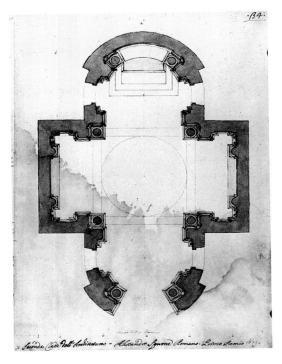

34 ALESSANDRO SPERONE: plan for a chapel; ASL 29 (Conc. Acc. 1694, second class).

35 SPERONE: lateral section for the chapel in Plate 34; ASL 30.

36 SPERONE: longitudinal section for the chapel in Plate 34; ASL 31.

37 ALESSANDRO ROSSINI: rendering of a bay of the facade of the Conservators' Palace, Rome; ASL 15 (Conc. Acc. 1694, third class).

38 LUDOVICO RUSCONI-SASSI: plan of a bay of the
Conservators' Palace; ASL 13 (Conc. Acc. 1694).

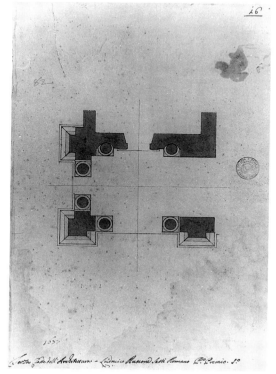

39 RUSCONI-SASSI: rendering of a bay of the
Conservators' Palace; ASL 14.

40 FILIPPO OTTONI: rendering of a bay of the Conservators' Palace; ASL 16 (Conc. Acc. 1694).

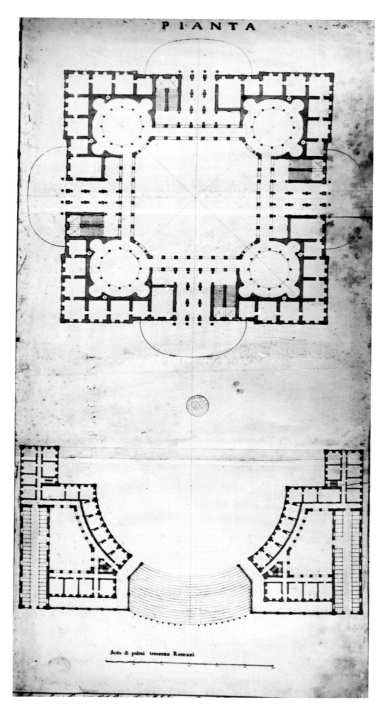

41 POMPEO FERRARI: plan for a villa for four dignitaries; ASL 45 (Conc.
Acc. 1696).

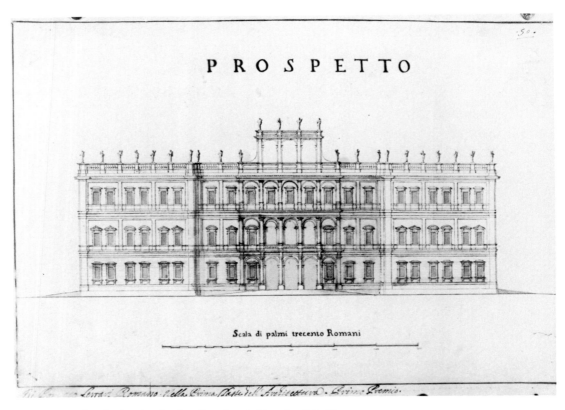

42 FERRARI: facade elevation for the villa palace in Plate 41; ASL 46.

43 FERRARI: longitudinal section for the villa palace in Plate 41; ASL 47.

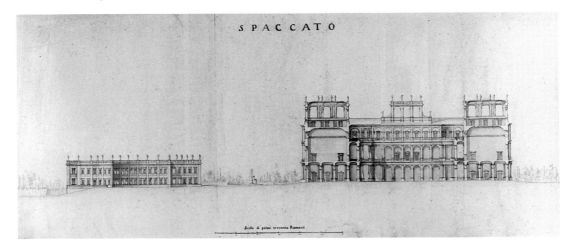

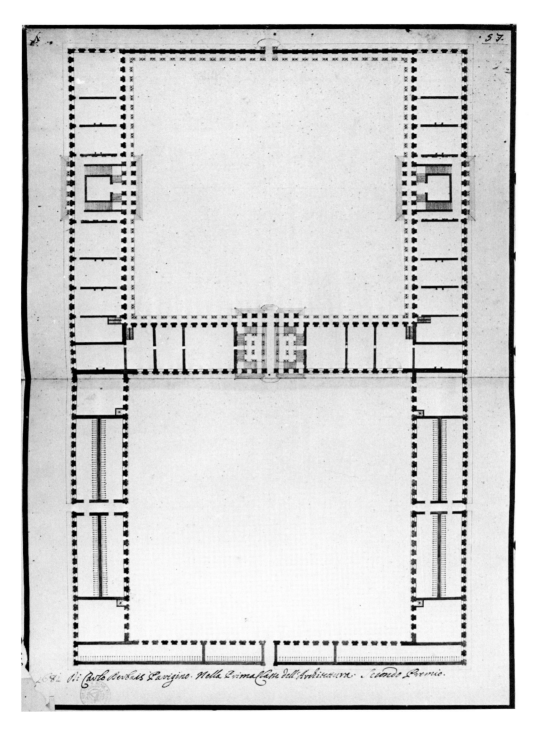

44 CHARLES DERBAIS: plan for a villa for four dignitaries; ASL 48 (Conc. Acc. 1696).

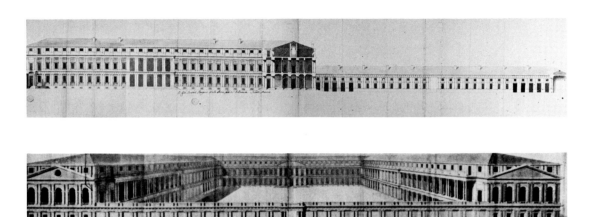

45 DERBAIS: longitudinal section for the villa in Plate 44; ASL 49.

46 DERBAIS: perspective for the villa in Plate 44; ASL 50.

47 CARLO PACENTI: plan for a villa for four dignitaries; ASL 51 (Conc. Acc. 1696).

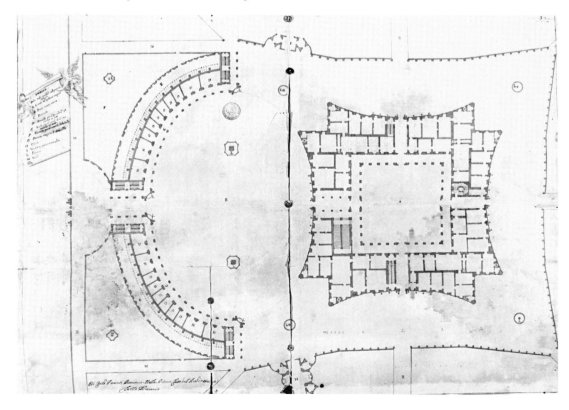

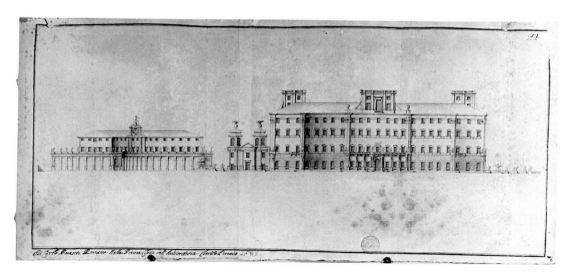

48 PACENTI: elevation for the villa in Plate 47; ASL 52.

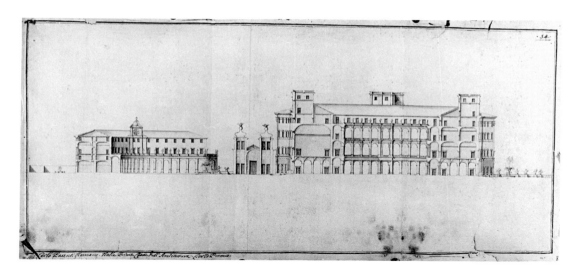

49 PACENTI: longitudinal section for the villa in Plate 47; ASL 53.

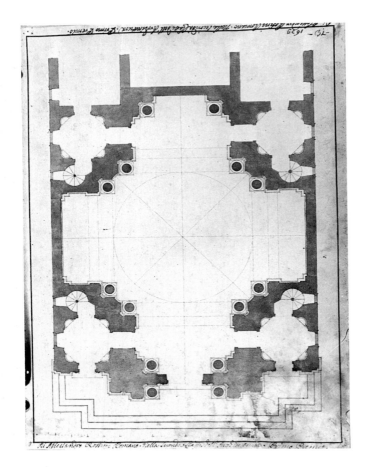

50 ALESSANDRO ROSSINI: plan for a chapel for the same villa; ASL 32 (Conc. Acc. 1696, second class).

51 ROSSINI: facade elevation for the chapel in Plate 50; ASL 33.

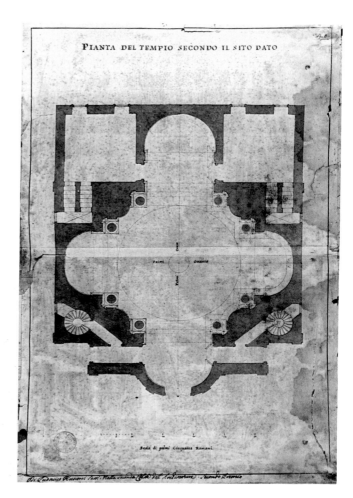

PIANTA DEL TEMPIO SECONDO IL SITO DATO

52 ROSSINI: lateral section for the chapel in Plate 50; ASL 34.

53 LUDOVICO RUSCONI-SASSI: plan for a chapel for the same villa; ASL 35 (Conc. Acc. 1696).

54 RUSCONI-SASSI: facade elevation for the chapel in Plate 53; ASL 36.

55 RUSCONI-SASSI: lateral section for the chapel in
Plate 53; ASL 37.

56 BASILIO SPINELLI: plan for a chapel for the same
villa; ASL 38 (Conc. Acc. 1696).

57 SPINELLI: facade elevation for the chapel in Plate 56; ASL 39.

58 SPINELLI: lateral section for the chapel in Plate 56; ASL 40.

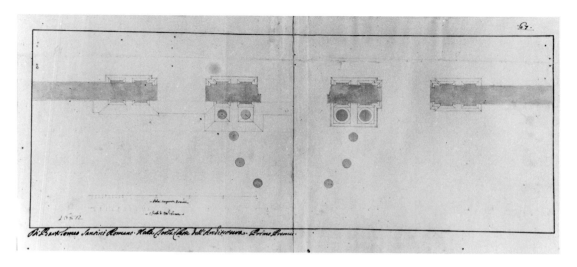

59 BARTOLOMEO SANTINI: plan for a gate for the same villa; ASL 59 (Conc. Acc. 1696, third class).

60 SANTINI: elevation for the gate in Plate 59; ASL 60.

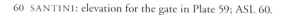

61 GIOVANNI ANTONIO SEVALLE: plan and elevation for a gate for the same villa; ASL 61 (Conc. Acc. 1696).

62 GIUSEPPE PARÀ: plan and elevation for a portal for the same villa; ASL 62 (Conc. Acc. 1696).

NOTES

NOTES TO CHAPTER I

1. Rudolf Wittkower, *Art and Architecture in Italy: 1600 to 1750,* revised ed., the Pelican History of Art (Baltimore, Md.: Penguin Books, 1973), 434. Wittkower admits that Roman *gravitas* continues in sculpture into the eighteenth century, but that after 1676 foreign influences are no longer simply absorbed, they are acknowledged and championed.

2. Wittkower (1973), 363.

3. Anthony Blunt, *Art and Architecture in France: 1500 to 1700,* 2nd revised ed., the Pelican History of Art (Baltimore, Md.: Penguin Books, 1973), 325–26. Sixteen seventy-five is the date Blunt uses for the election of LeBrun to the principate of the Accademia, but as this happens only in December, LeBrun himself was not informed of it, nor did his duties begin, until early in 1676 (see later text). Speaking on behalf of the French, Blunt is understandably more emphatic than Wittkower about the acute importance of this event for the future status of French taste.

4. Wittkower (1973), 369f.

5. This is admirably demonstrated by Nina Ayala Mallory in her published dissertation *Roman Rococo Architecture from Clement XI to Benedict XIV (1700–1758),* diss., Columbia University, 1965, Outstanding Dissertations in the Fine Arts (New York: Garland Publishing, 1977).

6. Nikolaus Pevsner, *Academies of Art: Past and Present* (Cambridge: Cambridge University Press, 1940), 64–65. The first statutes of the Accademia put forth in 1593, and revised in 1596, 1607, 1617, and 1620, maintain the separation between it as the forum for "disegno" with control over the valuation of artworks, and the traditional roles of the guilds in forming the skills of artists and determining licenses. But in 1621 a *breve* of Gregory XV reshaped the two into a general congregation of artists ruled by the Council of the Colletta chaired by the *principe,* in which the Compagnia had the upper hand and the achievements of the Accademia for the freedom of artists were reversed. Urban VIII's reforms in 1627 had the opposite effect, reestablishing the Accademia's ascendancy in the arbitration of all artistic production in Rome on behalf of the pope, with the support of taxes on every work of art.

7. Pevsner, 112.

8. Indeed, the premise behind every academy of art was that post-Renaissance artists must be versed in theories of beauty as well as the mechanics of their art, which requires that academic instruction take over where the workshops necessarily leave off. So it was that the predecessor of the Roman academy, the Accademia del Disegno in Florence, was conceived originally as an organism as much for the education of artists as for their protection (Pevsner, 46–47). But there, too, this mission had been eclipsed by mundane matters to the point that Zuccari, a member in Florence from 1575–78, petitioned for the revival of instruction (Pevsner, 51). He had hoped also at the outset to make this one of the principal functions of the Roman academy when he was given control of it in 1592. To this end the earliest statutes put particular emphasis on education, and give the Accademia a monopoly on life drawing in Rome (Pevsner, 61). The tenuous foothold this gave to such instruction, however, is evident in the fact that the first published statutes of the Accademia (*Ordini dell'Accademia de Pittori et Scultori di Roma* [Rome: 1609]) make no mention of its role as educator. See also: Melchior Missirini, *Memorie per Servire alla Storia della Romana Accademia di S. Luca* (Rome: De Romanis, 1823), 29f, and Carlo Pietrangeli, "Origini e Vicende dell'Accademia," in *L'Accademia Nazionale di San Luca* (Rome: De Luca, 1974), 12–14. The former is still the best source on the history of the Roman academy.

9. Pevsner, 47.

10. Pevsner, 60.

11. Pevsner, 80. On page 53, Pevsner laments the absence of mention in the minutes of the Florentine academy of any instructional activity during the first half of the 1600s: "The transactions of the academy meetings [after 1585] contain hardly anything beyond reports of the election of functionaries, decisions on litigations, and estimates given by appointed *stimatori* [in] disputes between artists and their 'customers' … " I would echo this complaint with regard to the Accademia's minutes (the *verbali*) for the same period.

12. Pevsner, 84–87. In 1643, LeBrun had returned from his sojourn in Rome, where he had for several years observed the activities of the Accademia during an early peak following the principate of Pietro da Cortona. But it was not his intention to see a French academy work in harmony with the guilds, as was the case in Rome, but rather to see it shut them out completely from any controlling interest. This was effectively achieved by 1660, after which the *Maîtrise* is relegated to the execution of Royal commissions by their various trades, to the designs and specifications of academy members.

13. Colbert had already put his stamp on the academies of Dance (1661) and *Belles Lettres* (1663), and he would do likewise for the academies of Sciences (1666) and Music (1669), as well as the Academy of Painters and Sculptors in their revised constitution of 1664. At the time he was its vice-protector and the nominal superior of LeBrun, under whom were the Rectors (4), Counselors (6), and Professors (12). Pevsner, 17, 89–90.

14. Pevsner, 112.

15. Pevsner (p. 96) states: "For the casual and semiprivate practice into which the Roman academy had relapsed so soon after its foundation, a reign of rule was now substituted [in Paris]."

16. Pevsner, 80. An indication of the hunger for instructional reforms at the Royal Academy is given by the students themselves, who in 1662 literally rebelled against the authority of their masters on the issue of course offerings and the posing of the nude. One of their complaints was that unlike the first years of the academy, lectures in geometry, perspective, architecture, and anatomy were no longer, or inadequately, being taught (the same condition prevailed at the Accademia by this time; see subsequent text). It was at this point that Colbert took over, and the reforms necessary to restore order and satisfy the obligations of academicians to teach were made. Reginald Blomfield, *A History of French Architecture* (1921; rpt., New York: Hacker Art Books, 1973), III, 8–9.

17. Gaetano Scano, "Insegnamento e Concorsi," in *L'Accademia Nazionale di San Luca,* 31; Pevsner, 62. The quote is from the rules of 1607, and may refer to such fundamental courses as geometry or mathematics.

18. ASL, vol. 44, fol. 57. The reference is to the lecturers responsible "per mettere l'atto," who are to supervise the conduct of the students during the posing of the nude and draped models.

19. Pevsner, 111. This had been attempted once before by Pietro da Cortona (*principe* from 1634 to 1638), which resulted in the famous debate between the advocates of "disegno" and "colore." But other than similar revivals in 1673 and 1681 (see subsequent text), routine lectures on theory do not begin until the centennial year.

20. ASL, vol. 44, fol. 16. The entry is for 21 September, near the end of Maratti's first year as *principe.*

21. ASL, vol. 43, fol. 169; vol. 44, fol. 22; Missirini, Titolo 81, 131.

22. While Pietro da Cortona had been made *principe* in 1634 in honor of his work on the Accademia's new church, his principal fame rested on his painting, as Bernini's rested on his sculpture. The only other architects *per se* on the roster of *principi* before Rainaldi were his father, Girolamo (1640–41), and Giovan Battista Soria (1648–51).

23. Pevsner, 60–61. The *brevi* were those of Gregory XIII (1577) and Sixtus V (1588).

24. Missirini, Titolo 81, 131; ASL, vol. 43, fol. 222 and vol. 44, fol. 92; misc. docs., Secolo XVII. Significantly, de Rossi was nominated for *Accademico di Merito* by then *principe* Charles Errard in August 1672 (see subsequent text). ASL, vol. 43, fol. 216; vol. 44, fol. 72. De Rossi's lectures on the orders are preserved in the archives of the Accademia in the form of fifteen loose folios (see subsequent text).

25. Missirini, Titolo 83, 133. The captain was Pietro Stroppa, whose membership had been accepted in August 1664 (ASL, vol. 44, fol. 14); a course in military architecture had recently been proposed but not effectuated. ASL, vol. 43, fol. 163; vol. 44, fol. 12.

26. ASL, vol. 45, fol. 1; vol. 46, fol. 2.

27. ASL, vol. 43, fol. 230. R. Wittkower, "Carlo Rainaldi and the Architecture of the Full Baroque," *Art Bulletin,* 19 (1937), 284. Tomassini had been admitted to membership in 1660 (ASL, vol. 43, fol. 129). Though he may have owed his promotion to lecturer to Rainaldi, the diagrams of the orders he later produced (see Figs. 56, 57) prove he was competent to hold that position as often as he eventually would. There is very little that survives to document his talents as an independent designer, however, and what there is recommends his draftsmanship more than his originality. See G. Matthiae, "Un progetto di chiesa di Gregorio Tomassini," *Roma,* 20 (1943), 418–21. That, and his command of architectural detail, may have been all that the Accademia was looking for at the time. Another possible clue to his background may lie in an entry of the *verbali* dated 22 July 1696 (ASL, vol. 45, fol. 165; vol. 46, fol. 87), two years before his death, which credits him with the donation to the Accademia of two reliquaries in gilt wood of his manufacture, and indicates that he had skills as a cabinet or perhaps model maker. He also seems to have been adept at designing metalwork (Matthiae, 419), another measure of his craft orientation. However, his one surviving building design, an unexecuted project for S. Salvatore in Onda (Ibid., tav. LXXIII–LXXIV), from the reign of Alexander VII, is a rather somber one.

28. ASL, vol. 45, fol. 17; vol. 46, fol. 4. Fontana was made *Accademico di Merito* on 15 May 1667, and not 1665 as is often misstated due to the difficulty of reading the manuscript (ASL, vol. 44, fol. 40). But he does not begin making an appearance in the general meetings until early in 1675 (already as Cavaliere Carlo Fontana; ASL, vol. 46, fol. 3). See also Braham/Hager, p. 8.

29. Hellmut Hager, "The Accademia di San Luca and the Precedents of the *Concorsi Clementini,*" in *Architectural Fantasy and Reality* (University Park, Pa.: The Pennsylvania State University Museum of Art, 1981), 5. The other member architects, aside from Rainaldi who is not mentioned on the roster, are Sbringa, Tomassini, Bufalini, and Felice della Greca, who was to be the lecturer in 1676 (see subsequent text).

30. Scano, 32.

31. Pevsner, 51.

32. Pevsner, 61.

33. Pietrangeli, 14–15. Exhibiting the *concorso* designs was not always possible during the celebration of the feast day, particularly if, as in 1663, insufficient notice was given of changes in the routine. In that year, the display of the designs was scheduled for "the last Sunday before Christmas." App. B, 1663, n. 2.

34. The Accademia must have been under considerable criticism at this time with regard to their need for the quite unpopular tax settled on all artists and artisans by the *breve* of Urban VIII. Maratti's speech as *principe* in 1664 (see previous text) expressed the value of the education at the Accademia which the taxes funded, and in that year he did succeed in holding the Accademia's end up. In 1666, the congregation hit upon the idea of sending one of the competition designs to the Cardinal Protector to "represent [to him] the expenses and requirements … of maintaining studies [at the Accademia]," so that he might better understand the need for the tax (App. B, 1666, n. 2). But by that time interest was flagging not only in the offering of courses or in the continuation of competition, but in any participation in the Accademia's activities. In December of 1666, three artists, among them Pietro da Cortona, declined the position of *principe* before it was accepted by Orfeo Bosselli, an ancient member who had only ten months to live (ASL, vol. 44, fol. 37). In view of this, and despite the outrage of the academicians, the tax was reduced by a bull of Clement X in 1670 (Missirini, Titolo 78, 118).

35. ASL, vol. 44, fol. 4. In April it was decided to give prizes not only to the participants in the *concorso* ("che fanno li disegni d'Inventione" as the *soggetti* were then called), but also to classwork in copying and drawing (App. B, 1664, n. 1).

36. Appendix B, 1664, n. 2. It must have been difficult to stretch this five *scudi* over the prizes in the three fields of painting, sculpture, and architecture (if indeed the latter two were included as per the new decrees). This may explain the trouble Domenico Guidi had in acquiring the prizes as mentioned in the above document.

37. ASL, vol. 43, fol. 159; vol. 44, fols. 5, 6.

38. Appendix B, 1664, nn. 5, 6. Piscuglia is later requested to resubmit the *soggetto* since his first proposal was inordinately difficult.

39. Only Orfeo Bosselli, on behalf of the sculptors, is specifically mentioned in the minutes as author of a *soggetto*. ASL, vol. 44, fol. 10.

40. The stipulation of a "soggetto … per copiare" refers to what was also a classroom practice: the assigning of students to the precise rendering of details of famous frescoes, carvings, or monuments. This will later become the usual third-class *soggetto,* at first in painting but in time also in architecture and sculpture; this is the earliest suggestion that there was to be competition at more than one level of difficulty.

41. ASL, vol. 43, fol. 168; vol. 44, fol. 19.

42. ASL, vol. 43, fol. 172; vol. 44, fol. 27.

43. ASL, vol. 43, fol. 222; vol. 44, fol. 92.

44. Little more of substance has been written on Errard since the entry in Guillet de St. Georges, *Mémoires inedits sur la Vie et les Ouvrages des Membres de l'Académie Royale de Peinture et de Sculpture,* ed. Dussieux et al. (Paris: 1854), I, 73–84. This biography was originally read by St. Georges to the Royal Academy in 1690, the year after Errard's death, as *Mémoire Historique des principaux ouvrages de M. Errard.* It is, therefore, virtually a contemporary account. Errard had been accepted to membership in the Accademia in the late 1630s, during a second trip to Rome to study architectural ornament, but after returning again in 1666 he does not appear at its meetings until 1670. At that time he is called upon (as "Carlo Herrard") to submit a design for part of the new vault for the Accademia's salon. The architect for this was Giovanni Grimaldi, and a program of fifteen allegorical paintings was suggested by G. B. Passeri, for which Errard was to deal with the subject of "Painting," one of three devoted to the major arts. This was indeed an honor for a relative newcomer and a foreigner, but also a wise expedient for the Accademia as it made use of his experience. The ceiling was never executed, however, and in any case the original buildings no longer exist. ASL, vol. 44, fol. 59.

45. The date usually given for Errard's birth is 1606, as reported in the biography above. But based on the epitaph carved on his tomb in S. Luigi dei Francesi, Rome, where his age at the time of his death in 1689 is given as eighty-eight, the date of his birth would be 1601. There is still more confusion, however, in that he gives his age as sixty on the documents related to his second marriage in 1675 (to a woman of eighteen), but this is probably the least reliable source.

46. Guillet de St. Georges, I, 75.

47. The main title reads *Parallèle de l'architecture antique et de la moderne, avec un recueil des dix principaux autheurs qui ont écrit des cinq ordres* (Paris: Chez Martin, 1650), and the "parallels" are drawn between antiquity and the treatises of Palladio, Scamozzi, Serlio, Vignola, Barbaro, Cataneo, Alberti, Viola, Bullant, and De l'Orme. Errard is credited with having prepared the drawings from which the plates were made, and which set the standard for precision in later tracts on architecture.

48. The two also worked together on a translation of Leonardo's treatise on painting, which was not as favorably received. Given Errard's principle function as illustrator for the *Parallèle,* and his clerical or administrative functions elsewhere, it is difficult to pinpoint where he stood with regard to theoretical questions. But his skills were definitely more those of an organizer and technician than a great thinker.

49. Blomfield, III, 101–2.

50. Blomfield, III, 103.

51. Jean-Paul Alaux, *L'Académie de France à Rome* (Paris: Editions Ducharte, 1933), I, 1–2.

52. Alaux, I, 9–11. Only one of the letters drafted by the secretary, Charles Perrault, may have been sent by Colbert, and given Poussin's expatriate status and his advanced age it is not certain how well even one would have been received by him. Neither question bears on the issues, however, since Poussin died at the end of the following year.

53. Alaux, I, 13. In the April competition, on the subject of Moses' destruction of the Tablets of the Law, Pierre Meunier took first place, Jean-Baptiste Corneille second, and Jean-Charles Friquet de Vaurose third. In July, Corneille took first, and Friquet de Vaurose second, with third going to Roger Lienard. The subject at that time was the ransoming of Dunkirk from the English conceived as an allegory of Jupiter and Danae, a rather ingenious reversal of the meaning of the event so that England becomes the exploited

party. Here begins the application of the resources of the academy to Colbert's larger propagandistic purpose. This topic was stipulated again in 1664, with Pierre Meunier taking first prize, and Corneille second.

54. Alaux, I, 14. The prize in sculpture in 1664 went to Roger Lienard, for his design on the subject of the flaying of Marsyas by order of Apollo. This could also be read as allegory, since Louis XIV was often identified as the Apollo of his age, if one reads Marsyas as any presumptuous contender.

55. Bernini's remarks to the French academy on 5 September 1665, near the end of his stay in Paris, are recorded in Paul Fréart de Chantelou, *Journal du voyage du cavalier Bernini en France,* ed. George Banner (Princeton: Princeton University Press, 1985). Bernini cites specifically the distribution of prizes during the celebration of the Accademia's *concorso,* perhaps the one to which he himself was invited some few weeks before his departure for France. But, as has been seen, competitions held with some kind of rigor had only been established by Maratti in that previous year. It is, then, a bit pretentious of Bernini to have set the Accademia up as an example, especially since he had shown no interest in its activities before this.

56. Alaux, I, 13–14. LeBrun is supposed to have recommended the idea of a competition and prize-giving to select the candidates for Rome, while the cost of the prizes was donated by the *Surintendant des Batiments.* The total value of the medals awarded in September of 1664 was four hundred *livres,* as compared to the five *scudi* spent on the Accademia's prizes that year.

57. Jules Guiffrey, "Les origines de l'Académie de France à Rome," *Journal des Savants,* NS 5, n. 6 (June 1907), 294. In this year, the prizes in painting went to François Bonnemer and Nicolas Rabon, and in sculpture to François Lespingola.

58. Guillet de St. Georges, I, 81–82.

59. Alaux, I, 13.

60. Guiffrey (1907), 295. The roster of students can presumably be reconstructed from the prizewinners for the past three years, but this does not explain the presence of the architect DuVivier among Errard's entourage. As yet there was no competition to select architects for the privilege of going to Rome, and would not be until the *Prix-de-Rome* was officially established for architects in

1720 (Alaux, I, 14). He may have been picked by Errard himself from the number of his own assistants as deserving of some experience abroad, but nothing certain is known of him.

61. Cecil Gould, *Bernini in France* (Princeton, N.J.: Princeton Univ. Press, 1982), 93, 122. After his return to Rome in 1666, Bernini continued to provide his council to the new academy in partial consideration of the pension then coming to him from Louis (which was also to pay for the equestrian statue of the king).

62. Alaux, I, xiv.

63. Alaux, I, 19. Time and again Colbert's letters to Errard refer to shipments of casts, etc., from the port at Civita Vecchia to the Seine. These references are more numerous than those to the educational functions of the academy. See *Correspondance des directeurs de l'Académie de France à Rome avec les Surintendants des Batiments,* ed. Anatole de Montaiglon (Paris: Charavay Freres, 1887), I, passim.

64. Robert W. Berger, "Charles LeBrun and the Louvre Colonnade," *Art Bulletin,* 52 (1970), 394–403.

65. Henri Lemonnier, *Procès-Verbaux de l'Académie Royale d'Architecture* (Paris: Jean Schemit, 1911–29), I, vii. The first faculty of the Academy of Architecture included François LeVau (Louis's brother), François D'Orbay (his brother-in-law), Libéral Bruant, Daniel Gittard, Antoine LePautre, and Pierre Mignard. The first director was François Blondel, and the first secretary was the historian André Felibien des Avaux. Claude Perrault was added to their number in 1673, and in 1675 Jules Hardouin-Mansart, who took over at Versailles upon LeVau's death.

66. Claude Perrault, ed., *Les dix livres d'architecture de Vitruve corrigez et traduite novellement en Français, avec des notes et des figures* (Paris: J. B. Coignard, 1673).

67. *P-V,* I, viii–ix. Blondel first prepared himself with a trip to Italy beginning in January of 1671, to add to his knowledge of its architecture and to learn something of its academics, before the first meeting of the Académie d' Architecture in December.

68. *P-V,* I, 2–3. The lectures in architecture were to be held on Tuesdays and Fridays, with the membership meeting in the Palais Royal (where the Academy of Painters and Sculptors also met) on Thursdays.

69. Nicolas-François Blondel, *Cours d'architecture enseigné dans l'Académie Royale d'Architecture,* Part 1 (Paris: Lambert Roulland, 1675); Parts 2–5 (Paris: chez l'Auteur, 1683). The preface to Part 1 contains remarks on the origins of the academy, and the text of Blondel's opening discourse. An expanded edition of all parts was published in 1698, but by then the utility of Blondel's *Cours* was being eroded by D'Aviler's (see Chapter II).

70. Claude Perrault, *Ordonnance des cinq espèces de colonnes selon la methode des anciens* (Paris: J. B. Coignard, 1683).

71. Wolfgang Herrmann, *The Theory of Claude Perrault* (London: Zwemmer, 1973).

72. *P-V,* I, 1, n. 1.

73. Alaux, I, 14. Very probably competitions were still held as part of the usual internal business of the academy, in deciding promotions for example. And these may in turn have been used to justify the recommendations of members in choosing candidates for the sessions in Rome. But in a letter of Colbert's from 1679 (App. B, 1679, n. 7), in which he solicits LeBrun and Perrault for their suggestions for adding to the complement of students in Rome, it is clear that nothing quite so objective was being used to make the choice. Colbert, in this as in everything, had the final word.

74. Blunt (1973), p. 344.

75. Louis Hautecoeur, *Histoire de l'architecture classique en France* (Paris: A. & J. Picard, 1943–50), II, 419.

76. Blomfield, III, 105.

77. *Corr.,* I, 12, n. 16.

78. Auguste Castan, "Les premieres installations de l'Académie de France à Rome," *Réunion des Sociétés des Beaux-Arts des Départments* (1889), 91. It was not until 1677 (App. B, 1680, n. 1) that a tenure of three years was firmly established for students of the academy in Rome. This was probably intended to address the overcrowding it had faced a few years before, and to provide a better opportunity to those students in Paris hoping to have a chance to go to Rome.

79. Alaux, I, 19.

80. The sources (Alaux and Castan) name both the Cafarelli and Capranica palaces as locations for the academy in the late Seicento, either together, or separately, as in times when rents were in dispute, which was often. More secure lodgings, at the Palazzo Mancini, were not available until the next century.

81. The 1673 inventory is given in full in Castan (100–115).

82. Castan, 91. At this time the *pensionnaires* were comprised of nine painters, five sculptors, an engraver, and the two architects which the statutes allowed (DuVivier and one named Vollant who had just arrived). This must be a rather fair assessment of the relative lack of emphasis put on architecture at this point. See also *Corr.,* I, passim.

83. Alaux, I, 30. Overcrowding may have brought tempers to the breaking point, especially since these young artists were forced to be in each other's company daily for many hours. Since they conceived of themselves as gentlemen, they always carried swords, and in the heat of argument these were often drawn, despite frequent demands from above that the practice cease. When such disputes came to arbitration, the fact that Errard was himself a master swordsman must have carried considerable weight.

84. ASL, vol. 44, fol. 59.

85. ASL, vol. 43, fols. 200, 203.

86. *Ordini* (1609), 10.

87. ASL, vol. 44, fol. 65. Both Poussin and Vouet had been voted to this post previously (Blunt [1973], 325), but they refused the honor. The Fleming Luigi Gentile was the only other non-Italian ever actually to hold the office of *principe* (1651) before Errard (Pevsner, 65).

88. "Francesco Bernetti Architetto" was made *Accademico di Merito* in June 1666 (ASL, vol. 44, fol. 33). It is tempting to suggest that his membership was based on his performance in a *concorso* of 1664 or 1665, as was allowed by Maratti's revised statutes. There is absolutely nothing known about him that would support this, however, unless it was his previous experience in competition that recommended him to propose the *soggetto* for architecture for the *concorso* that followed six years later.

89. ASL, vol. 44, fol. 77. The new date was initially set for the first Sunday after the Feast of All Souls. In the meantime, students were encouraged to use the delay to their advantage in finishing their designs.

90. ASL, vol. 44, fol. 83.

91. ASL, vol. 43, fol. 216; vol. 44, fol. 72.

92. Gould, 109–15 and passim.

93. Pietrangeli, 14.

94. Alaux, I, 20. It was at one time assumed that Errard was in trouble with the crown, presumably with regard to his management of the academy, but this is unsubstantiated. In fact, in the letter to Errard of 6 January 1673, posted at a time when Coypel had already been sent to replace him, Colbert praises Errard's efforts in his position and his obedience to the wishes of the crown (App. B, 1673, n. 1). That the letter was addressed to Errard at all, rather than to his successor, is taken to indicate that Errard was still in Colbert's good graces, as the bureaucrat in Colbert would not have allowed him to do so otherwise.

95. *Corr.*, I, 47–49, nn. 83, 85.

96. Alaux, I, 31. That Errard had the power to see the process through, and that the process had already been roughed out, is evident from the very little communication that was necessary between Errard and Paris during the aggregation proceedings in 1675–76.

97. ASL, vol. 43, fol. 222; vol. 44, fol. 92. Missirini (App. B, 1673, n. 2) names Passeri in this regard, but as secretary in 1673 he only passed the *soggetti* on to the membership on behalf of Brugueres. Brugueres (or Burgheres) was made *Accademico di Gratia* in 1670 (ASL, vol. 43, fol. 199), which carries with it the implication that he was no more than a gifted amateur.

98. This document also lists the topics in painting (1st class, Hannibal crossing the Alps; 2nd class, Hercules and the centaur Chiron) and sculpture (Hercules wrestling Achelous). It was apparently in this year that competition at lower levels was standardized for students in their first years, which included making copies after works by Raphael, Caracci, and Domenichino. In addition, those who worked for the guilds or *botteghe*, who practiced a "mechanical or manual art," were expressly forbidden to participate. This last in particular smacks of the rhetoric of the French academicians, who used the same argument in proposing their authority over the Parisian guilds.

99. ASL, vol. 44, fol. 97. There was mention of prizes of money or goods, but no final stipulation was made.

100. ASL, vol. 44, fol. 110. Ghezzi was a painter of some academic repute, several of whose works still survive in Roman collections.

101. Hager (1981), 4–6. With regard to the *concorsi,* the new statutes specifically stipulate prizes of drawing instruments, and require members to submit works of their own for display during the *concorso* for comparison with the competition designs. The latter was intended to give the public an appreciation of the Accademia's potentials at all levels. But it is also intriguing since it means that the winning designs were not to be read against the background of history, since works by deceased masters could not be displayed, but in the context of the work of their masters. As the subsequent text points out, the "authority" for these students was not the past but the present.

102. Missirini, Titolo 83, 133. Carlo Cesi was *principe* for most of 1675, but during his absence in the last quarter of the year his place was filled by the *vice-principe,* Domenico Guidi. No excuse is given for this transfer of power, so the possibility exists that Cesi in fact abnegated his authority in order to disassociate himself and the office of *principe* from the process of aggregation which followed. No complicity could therefore be charged on the part of the *principe,* and that high office could in Roman eyes remain above accusations of servility that might follow as a result.

103. *Corr.*, I, 39–40, n. 69.

104. Guillet de St. Georges, I, 83–84. Errard also brought with him more students for the program in Rome (*Corr.*, I, 55, n. 99).

105. Pietrangeli, 17.

106. Jean Arnaud, *L'Académie de St.-Luc à Rome: considérations historique depuis son origine jusqua nos jours* (Rome: Herrmann Loescher, 1886), p. 40.

107. Missirini, Titolo 84, 133–35. Carlo Emmanuele died a few months later, on 12 June. Pier Francesco Garolli, a Piedmontese specialist in perspective then living in Rome, was chosen to act as deputy on behalf of the Turin academy in the matter of its aggregation. Afterward, the doors of the Accademia were open to him, and in time he became an important part of their faculty (see Chapter IV).

108. Pevsner, 102.

109. LeBrun had been in Rome for only a short time during the early 1640s. Given the magnitude of

his responsibilities in Paris, it was inconceivable in 1675 that he would soon be free to take on others which would require him to travel elsewhere.

110. ASL, vol. 45, fol. 28; vol. 46, fol. 8.

111. Wittkower (1973), 434. Wittkower was mistaken in two regards as far as Guidi's involvement in the events of 1675 is concerned. Guidi was *vice-principe,* not *principe,* when LeBrun's nomination was put forward, and that proposal was made by Maratti, not by Guidi. Arnaud (p. 42) even proposes Bernini as the source for the nomination, since he and LeBrun were impressed with each other in Paris, but Bernini still had little interest in academic affairs beyond what he was obliged to devote to the advisement of French students of the academy in Rome. Also, though Guidi was *principe* earlier, in 1670, he held that post with no distinction, and so in that sense cannot be put "on an equal footing with Charles LeBrun."

112. Despite their supposed transcendence of the Italian Baroque, it is interesting to note how often French artists are referred to as "clones" of Italian artists. LeBrun is called the Giulio Romano of France (Missirini, p. 135), which was not just a way of equating their styles, but their classicist Roman training and subsequent success as decorators at a foreign court as well. Other curious parallels are drawn: Jean Goujon is called the Correggio of sculpture, and Pierre Puget is called the Michelangelo of France (Blunt, passim). Some of the associations are difficult to accept, but they all point up the fact that French art was still being conceived of in Italian terms.

113. It is also relevant that the posts of *consigliere* and *censore* were filled by appointment of the *principe,* in this case Errard. The *censori* had a great deal of power over the membership, since in this day the strict observation of the amenities was even more important than the observation of law.

114. Missirini, Titolo 85, 135–36.

115. Ibid.

116. The funds were set aside for repairs to the salon, and a plaque was erected in the Accademia "con iscrizzione concernente questo regalo." ASL, vol. 45, fol. 36.

117. Della Greca (1626–77) had for the previous two decades been employed by the papal camera, along with Bernini and Fontana, as a "misuratore," which could mean "architect," but in his case more likely refers to the function of appraiser.

Richard Krautheimer, *The Rome of Alexander VII* (Princeton: Princeton University Press, 1985), passim. His principal building effort for Alexander was at the Palazzo Chigi on Piazza Colonna, where he was responsible for the courtyard. Paolo Portoghesi, *Roma Barocca,* trans. Barbara La Penta (Cambridge, Mass.: The MIT Press, 1970), 543. While on the face of it della Greca's election to his position as instructor does not fit into the picture of a diplomatic or Francophilic agenda at the Accademia in 1676, neither does it detract from it. His effect on the curriculum would have been fundamentally neutral.

118. Missirini, Titolo 86, 140–41; Arnaud, 48–51.

119. Wittkower (1973), 434. For the details of Guidi's dealings with the French, see *Corr.,* I, passim.

120. Pietrangeli, p. 17.

121. Alaux, I, 31; Blomfield, III, 30.

122. Pevsner, 102.

123. Missirini, Titolo 86, 139–40; Arnaud, 45–47.

124. ASL, vol. 45, fol. 43.

125. Missirini, Titolo 86, 137–38.

126. ASL, vol. 45, fol. 45.

127. *Corr.,* I, 108–9, nn. 195, 196. Poerson's painting is now housed in the Trianon at Versailles. Coincidentally, Poerson himself would hold the office of *principe* of the Accademia from 1714 to 1718, and again from 1721 to 1722, while in Rome as director of the French academy there. This would be the only other time in the history of both academies that links were forged between them that were as strong as those first made by Errard (see Chapter V).

128. *Corr.,* I, 60–61, n. 109.

129. ASL, vol. 45, fols. 44, 46.

NOTES TO CHAPTER II

1. ASL, vol. 45, fol. 51. The drawings were submitted and the *prove* executed on the Thursday before the celebration of the concorso, which was set for Sunday, 14 November. See Appendix B, 1677, n. 5.

2. ASL, vol. 45, fol. 44. During the first year of Errard's stewardship for LeBrun, Mattia de Rossi was *primo rettore,* Tomassini was *stimatore d'architettura,* and according to the citation they

would have remained so for 1677. ASL, vol. 45, fol. 30; vol. 46, fol. 8.

3. The academic season had already begun in 1676 before della Greca was appointed instructor on 25 May (App. B, 1676, n. 3), but by 7 June he had yet to begin lecturing (Ibid., n. 6). There is no record of his ever having assumed these duties, and his last testament was filed on 2 August 1677. This suggests a long illness prior to his death at about age fifty. See: Ulrich Thieme and Felix Becker, *Allgemeines Lexicon der Bildenden Kunstler* (Leipzig: Verlag von E. A. Seemann, 1907), XIV, 562.

4. A. J. Braham and Hellmut Hager, *Carlo Fontana: Drawings at Windsor Castle* (London: A. Zwemmer, 1977), 9–11. No architect during the reign of Innocent XI was completely occupied with commissions, but Fontana faired better than the others in Rome. As well as the church of Santa Maria dei Miracoli, where his modifications to Rainaldi's design were being carried out, there were private commissions like the Cappella Ginetti and projects on paper for the pope (see later text). Most significant, however, is the fact that Fontana seems to have had a thriving studio with students of his own by this time.

5. Appendix B, 1678, n. 3. This announcement of the "Prix décernés par l'Académie de Saint-Luc de Rome aux pensionaires du Roi" is to be found in a *Mercure galant* of April 1678.

6. Wittkower (1973), 266.

7. The full texts of Bellori's *soggetti* can be found in the *verbali*, ASL, vol. 45, fol. 48. For the painters the subject was the story of the Gordian Knot; for the sculptors, each bas-relief was to depict the meeting between Alexander and the eccentric architect Denocrates, who claimed to be able to reshape a mountain into the form of a man, as described by Vitruvius in his second book. The competition winners in painting from the seventeenth century have now been published by the Accademia Nazionale di San Luca: Angela Cipriani and Enrico Valeriani, *I Disegni di Figura nell'Archivio Storico dell'Accademia di San Luca*, I, Concorsi e Accademie del Secolo XVII (Rome: Casa Editrice Quasar, 1988).

8. Not being an artist himself, Bellori would not have expected the same financial benefits of such recognition that others might have hoped to receive in the form of royal commissions or appointments. His motives may have indeed been higher, as expressed in his discourse given on the day of the concorso (App. B, 1677, n. 5), in which he linked the greatest advantage for the arts not only to the pursuits of the academies but also to the attitudes of rulers. He mentions specifically the benefits Louis's favor had brought to the joined institutions, and may have been looking ahead to a time when autocratic control might favor his theories. His very "eloquent and studied" oration does appear to have made an impression in Paris, judging by the document cited in note 5 and the commendation given him by Henri Testelin, secretary of the Académie Royale, in a report to Errard (App. B, 1678, n. 4).

9. Appendix B, 1678, n. 1. Another is again the document in note 5, which refers to " … les prix envoyés *tous les ans* par le Roy." This may also mean the prize money sent yearly to the Académie de France in Rome for its own competitions, as there is no record of any stipend for prizes sent to the Accademia in any year but 1677. In that year the prize money, used to purchase the gold medals mentioned later in the minutes (App. B, 1677, n. 6), must have totaled more than 100 *scudi* for all classes of competition in the three arts. This represents quite an incentive, not only for the competitors who could normally have expected a pen of modest cost at best, but also to the academicians themselves to guarantee at every opportunity the goodwill of the crown.

10. Appendix B, 1677, n. 1. In this entry the secretary only acknowledges the task Tomassini had proposed "some years before," the year being 1674, when he had suggested a "temple." Nothing came of it as the *concorso* for that year was cancelled (App. B, 1674, nn. 1, 2).

11. Appendix B, 1677, n. 2. The text was first published by Paolo Marconi, Angela Cipriani, and Enrico Valeriani, "Archival notes concerning the architectural drawings of the seventeenth century, preserved in the St. Luke Academy in Rome," *Architectural Fantasy and Reality* (1981), 167.

12. The dimensions were 90 by 100 *palmi*. Providing dimensions for the site was already a routine part of architectural competition at the Accademia, as is suggested by an entry in the *verbali* for 28 May 1673, which calls for the stipulation of the size ("grandezza") of the task in architecture (App. B, 1673, n. 7).

13. Tomassini required the execution of a "rincontro" by the candidate to be compared to the hand in his drawings to verify their authenticity. This is his wording for the *prova* drawing, which has much the same purpose, and is apparently routine by 1677 (see later text) though not documented by examples until the 1690s. The *prova* is formalized in the eighteenth century, particularly after its inclusion in the statutes of 1715. Hager (1981), 3.

14. Appendix B, 1677, n. 3. This *soggetto,* which like the other was apparently intended to be posted publicly as it is also carefully written and drawn, was discovered in the Accademia's archive by Dr. Cipriani. At the time, however, it could not be linked to any specific *concorso;* it bears Tomassini's name, but he authored several *soggetti* in different years. Much of the wording and the arrangement of this "secondo soggetto"—with task description, cautions on method, dimensioning, and a site plan—is identical to that in the first dated *soggetto.* The best indication that they are from the same competition is the reference in the second to the "preceding design for the octangular temple," which is, I think, conclusive enough.

15. It is possible, and indeed likely, that academic competition in all other classes went on as usual at the Accademia, separated from the *concorso* of 1677 which presented only the first classes to the public.

16. This tradition begins with Philibert De l'Orme's chapel at Anet (1549) and is so firmly established by the time of the elder Mansart (see below) that the octagon plan is readily distinguished as Italianate in derivation.

17. The author throughout this volume accepts the corrected attributions and design history for S. Agnese put forth on strong evidence by Gerhard Eimer in *La Fabbrica di S. Agnese in Piazza Navona,* 2 vols. (Stockholm: Almqvist and Wiksell, 1971).

18. Early projects (June 1652) for S. Agnese by Rainaldi and his father Girolamo did include vestibules (Eimer, I, 58–65; Wittkower [1973], 217). It is also of interest that the dimensions of the site Tomassini describes are approximately the same as those of the site of S. Agnese and its annexes, though the churches in the *concorso* designs are oriented to the short rather than the long sides.

19. Both the *verbali* for 15 August and Tomassini's *soggetti* refer to the *concorso* on the "giorno ... di S. Luca" (App. B, 1677, nn. 1, 2).

20. ASL, vol. 45, fol. 51–52.

21. Appendix B, 1678, n. 3; Ferdinand Boyer, "Les artistes français, étudiants, lauréats ou membres de l'Académie romaine de St.-Luc entre 1660-1700," *Bulletin de la Société de l'Histoire de l'Art Française* (1950), 127–29. First prize in painting went to Arnaud de Vuez of St.-Omer, second to Alessandro Alessandri of Paris (from a Polish expatriate family, Ubeleski), and third to Louis de Boulogne.

22. The French winners were Simon Hurtrelle (first) and Jean-Baptiste Théodon (third). Francesco Nouchieri of Ancona, who took the second prize, was a student of the Francophile Domenico Guidi, and may therefore still be considered part of the rule rather than the exception.

23. Chupin is referred to as "Sciupagn" in the Italian documents.

24. Appendix A, II, nn. 1, 4, 7. The usual procedure upon receipt of the designs was to inscribe on the back of each plan the number of the entry (as well as the number of sheets, or *pezzi,* pertaining to it) to assure anonymity. The reverse of Chupin's plan is numbered as six, which is the highest of the three surviving designs. But the *verbali* (ASL, vol. 45, 51v) record submissions from only the three French prizewinners. The only explanation is that submissions in painting and sculpture were numbered in sequence with those in architecture. See also note 109.

25. Appendix A, II, nn. 1–9.

26. Appendix B, 1678, nn. 3, 4.

27. Appendix B, 1677, n. 6. Compare these numbers to the value of the prizes in the first *concorso* of 1664, the only time before 1677 when such values were recorded. The total value of the prizes at that time was not to exceed *five scudi* (App. B, 1664, n. 2).

28. For example, in a letter to Colbert in 1676, Errard refers to him as "le Sr. Cheupein," but he was always rather cavalier about spelling, even by seventeenth-century standards (App. B, 1676, n. 9). Ghezzi entered his name as "Sciupagn" on his drawings, and in that form it was reported to Paris, to appear in a document of 1678 praising his success (App. B, 1678, n. 3). But neither

D'Aviler nor Desgots fared any better when their names appeared in writing while they were students.

29. *Corr.*, I, 39, n. 69.

30. Jules Guiffrey, *Comptes des Batiments du Roi sous le règne de Louis XIV* (Paris: Impr. Nationale, 1881–1901), II (1681–87), passim. The references are to payments made for services rendered as draftsman.

31. It was Montaiglon and Guiffrey who connected Chupin with the draftsman listed in the *Comptes*, having noticed that he had "escaped the researches of Lance" (*Corr.*, I, 40, note). Guiffrey later presumes that as Chupin had accompanied Coypel in an entourage of painters he was himself originally a painter. Guiffrey and Barthelemy, *Liste des pensionnaires de l'Académie de France à Rome* (Paris: 1908). There may be something to be said for this otherwise unfounded assumption after seeing his drawings, but for the rest of this century speculation about the unknown quantity Chupin has ceased. Louis Hautecoeur included him (as "Cheupin") among the early architectural *pensionnaires* of the academy in Rome only for the sake of completeness in his commodious *Histoire* (II, 472). Boyer's investigations into French artists at the Accademia in the seventeenth century do not go beyond the available written archival material, Chupin's name appearing only once in his essay, but I have chosen his spelling of the name as the most concise.

32. Appendix B, 1676, n. 9. The *pensionnaires* then numbered thirteen: four painters, five sculptors, and four architects. These last, two more than the usual complement of architects stipulated by the statutes, included the three prizewinners from 1677, and one Mesier who had apparently earned the wrath of Errard by some undisclosed indiscretion. He is called disrespectful, disobedient, a troublemaker, and extravagant, with no application to his studies. He is recommended for separation from the academy along with Louis Le Conte, a sculptor who had sown dissension among his fellows with regard to the statute which allowed students to work only on projects sanctioned by Errard or destined for the court. Le Conte survived this episode to earn some later distinction at Versailles, but Mesier did not, and he disappears, deprived of even the 200 *livres* he might otherwise have received to permit his return to France.

33. ASL, vol. 45, fol. 57; vol. 46, fol. 21. The three were proposed for membership, along with six Italians, in the meeting of 10 July 1678. They were the painter Alexander Ubeleski, and the sculptors Simon Hurtrelle and Jean-Baptiste Théodon. The latter two remained in Rome to work and to actively participate in the functions of the Accademia for some time before being repatriated (see Chapter IV for Théodon).

34. The interior of Chupin's design also shares an affinity with Michelangelo's St. Peter's in its pure geometric volumes.

35. *P-V,* III, 26–27. In the meeting of 23 December 1697, the members of the Académie d'Architecture discussed that part of the elder Blondel's *Cours* dealing with domes (Part 4, Book 5). The consensus reached was that the domes of St. Peter's and LeVau's chapel of the Collège des Quatre Nations in Paris were the best examples in their respective locations, remembering that at the time of Blondel's writing there was as yet no dome for Hardouin-Mansart's Chapel of the Invalides.

36. Of course there was the Pantheon, to which Maderno had added campanili: Howard Hibbard, *Carlo Maderno* (London: A. Zwemmer, 1971), 230–31. As a whole this ancient temple would not at this early date have made an appropriate model. But it certainly may have been an inspiration to Tomassini, and perhaps even the competitors, in searching out a modern version reflecting contemporary needs and tastes.

37. Yvan Christ, "Église de l'Assomption," *Dictionnaire des Églises de France,* ed. Jacques Brosse (Paris: 1968) IVc, 33. Outside of the usual mention in guidebooks and dictionaries Errard's church has received little attention and very little praise. Thieme and Becker's lexicon does not refer to the church at all in the entry on Errard. See Hautecoeur, II, 714–15; Blomfield, III, 105–6. Errard actually designed the building in 1666, the year of his departure for Rome, but construction did not begin until 1670, under the direction of the insensitive builder Cheret. As Errard's one attempt at architecture *per se,* and what with Cheret's mishandling of the project, it is safe to assume that the church was on Errard's mind and the minds of his students up to its completion.

38. W. H. Ward attributes part of this to the influence of Jean Marot's church of Notre Dame des Ardilliers, near Saumur (ca. 1650). See *The*

Architecture of the Renaissance in France, 2nd ed. (1926; rpt. New York: Hacker Art Books, 1976), II, 345.

39. Blondel's criticism is found in the part of the *Cours* dealing with domes (Part 4, Book 5): "tout (the dome) à fait extravagant aussi bien que le reste de l'édifice." For the reference to "sot dome" see Alaux, I, 12; Christ, loc. cit. More dispassionately, the younger Blondel later echoes these criticisms: " … ne pouvant dissimuler que la partie supérieure de cet édifice est tout à fait hors de proportion, étant lourde, pésante et d'une forme aussi materielle que peu ingenieuse. Cela provient sans doute du grand diamètre qu'on a donné à ce dome. Mais en ce cas sa hauteur auroit du être mieux proportionnée pour satisfaire aux règles de l'Art et aux principes du goût." *Architecture Française* (Paris: 1752–56; facs. Paris: Librarie Centrale des Beaux-Arts, 1904), III, 132–33.

40. Hautecoeur, II, 733. The association between the portico and the dome in either case was quite different, however, as the interior vaults of LeMercier's chapel carry the cupola quite high above the portico at the transept facade, with a pitched roof and thermal window intervening.

41. Christ, op. cit. For Hautecoeur (II, 714), the Assumption was at least better received by the French than Guarini's Theatine church in Paris, Ste.-Anne-la-Royale (1662). It is also true that in the following century neo-classical taste would praise Errard's portico with its flanking bays as an attractive facade for a basilican church, without the dome of course. See Hautecoeur, IV, 347; Joseph Rykwert, *The First Moderns* (Cambridge, Massachusetts: The MIT Press, 1980), 84.

42. The intrados of the dome of Errard's church is decorated with an Assumption, the first religious work of Charles de La Fosse, also completed in 1676. Together, Errard's Assumption and Mansart's Visitation might be said to constitute part of a series of French churches that conforms to a Marian type, of which Chupin's is an Italianate variant. And the theme can be linked to the Christian dedication of the Pantheon as well.

43. Several Parisian domes take their cue from the Vatican basilica, and may have been the starting point for Chupin. One such is the dome of LeMercier's Sorbonne chapel again, which is comparable to Chupin's in the treatment of the splayed windows of the drum. The greater impression was made by the Italian example however.

44. Biographies of D'Aviler exist in several sources, though with little variation from the earliest, which are found in the Mariette editions of his *Cours* after 1738: Pierre-Jean Mariette ed., *Cours d'Architecture,* by C.-A. D'Aviler (Paris: C. A. Jombert, 1756), xxxv–xxxviii. More accessible, if no more informative, is the version in the posthumous edition of Mariette's *Abecedario,* ed. Ph. de Chennevieres and A. de Montaiglon (1851–60; facs. Paris: Chez de Nobele, 1966), II, 65–67. See also: Adolphe Lance, *Dictionnaire des architectes français* (Paris: 1872), I, 182–84; Blomfield, IV, 15–20; Hautecoeur, II, 646–48.

45. On 19 September 1674, D'Aviler was awarded the usual sum of 200 *livres* for his trip to Rome (Blomfield, IV, 15–16; *Comptes,* I, 781). No mention of this is made in the *procès-verbaux,* but of course while there was as yet no *Prix-de-Rome* for students of architecture, such action was still in the hands of Colbert and the king. It may be, however, that at this point D'Aviler had the favor of one of the academicians, possibly François D'Orbay who would prove so important to his later career.

46. Mariette (1756), xxxvi.

47. H. Brauer and R. Wittkower, *Die Zeichnungen des G. Bernini* (Berlin, 1931), 41, and D. Frey, "Berninis Entwürfe für die Glockentürme von St. Peter in Rome," *Jahrbuch der kunsthistorischen Sammlungen, Wien,* 12 (1928), 224.

48. Wittkower (1973), 190–93.

49. H. Hager, "Zur Plannungs- und Baugeschichte der Zwillingskirchen auf der Piazza del Popolo," *RJK,* 11 (1967–68), 212.

50. There is such a portico attached to François Mansart's facade of the Val-de-Grace in Paris (1645–46), but the motif is also quite common in French palace architecture.

51. D'Aviler, *Cours d'Architecture,* 30.

52. There are the vault of the staircase of the Orleans Wing of the Château of Blois (1635–38), and Mansart's project for the crossing vault of the church of the Val-de-Grace (1645), to name two.

53. A. Braham and P. Smith, *François Mansart* (London: A. Zwemmer, 1973), I, 26–30.

54. André Gutton, "La restauration de la coupole de l'Institut," *Monuments historiques de la France* (1963), 1–7.

55. Even the most Italianate of central-plan churches in France, Jules Hardouin-Mansart's Chapel of the Invalides (1680–91), has a crossing of circular plan, and pendentives which are not sections of a sphere but sections of a cylinder. This could be looked upon as flouting the French dictum of *convenance,* or propriety, but it is a paradox which existed in French architecture since the chapel at Anet. D'Aviler quite effectively avoids the paradox.

56. Appendix A, II, nn. 4–6.

57. Mariette (1756), xxxvi.

58. Blomfield, III, 171–73.

59. Portions of D'Aviler's *Explication des Termes d'Architecture* (Paris: Chez Langlois, 1691), the companion volume to his *Cours,* are devoted to hydraulics, and enough of his material existed to expand the treatment of the subject in later editions. D'Aviler, *Dictionnaire d'Architecture Civile et Hydraulique, et des Arts qui en Dependant, comme ... la construction des Ponts & Chauffées, des Ecluses, et de tous les ouvrages hydrauliques,* Nouv. Ed. (Paris: Chez Jombert, 1755).

60. Lance, I, 215–16; Blomfield, IV, 21–25. Desgodetz, an excellent draftsman himself, was not a *pensionnaire* of the Royal Academy during his stay in Rome (1676–77), and so did not compete in the *concorso.* Nonetheless, his career presents an interesting comparison with those of the three prizewinners. By 1671 he was already in the service of the royal building works, and in 1672 he was allowed to attend the meetings of the new Académie d'Architecture, though he was the same age as D'Aviler and not yet a member. By his own telling, it was the Academy that sent him to Rome in 1674, and on his return he turned over to it some of the carefully measured and beautifully rendered drawings of Roman architecture he had created in little more than a year. Colbert then commissioned him to turn these into illustrations for a book, *Les Édifices antiques de Rome dessinés et mesurés très exactement* (1682), and it is to Colbert that the book is dedicated. This work gained him immediate esteem and financial profit, in addition to the income he had had as *Controleur des Batiments* at Chambord since 1680. Despite the magnitude of his accomplishment (*Les Édifices* remained an important sourcebook on Roman architecture and an example of drafting precision for more than a century), Desgodetz's relations with the Academy cooled for a time, as academic concerns became more pragmatic. Hardouin-Mansart's monopolization of the architectural scene in Paris kept him from commissions; and though he became *Controleur a Paris* in 1694, and *Architecte du Roi* in 1698, it was not until he became a member of the Academy in 1699 that he could pursue his scholarly career in earnest. He tried his hand at a treatise on the Orders, lectured in architecture at the Academy after 1714, and was a recognized authority on Roman architecture and decoration. But by then the greatest age of French building had passed him by. Though he had early revealed an innate genius, had powerful patronage, and advanced himself outside the usual channels, his progress, like that of each of the three prizewinners in 1677, was arrested during the tyranny of Hardouin-Mansart.

61. *P-V,* I, 125, n. 3. D'Aviler completed this translation in abridged form in 1685. The other chapters were finished by Du Ry in 1713 (see note 80).

62. *P-V,* I, 306.

63. *P-V,* II, 34–36. The members present were Blondel, Bruand, Gittard, D'Orbay, and Felibien. They not only praised D'Aviler's work, but added their own commentary.

64. Blomfield (IV, 17–18) points out that it was not Blainville speaking here, but his father, who was always impatient to see the Academy serve the practical needs of the royal building works.

65. *P-V,* I, 300.

66. *P-V,* I, 308–9. The academicians were otherwise pleased with these designs, and so Blomfield (IV, 7) believes they handled D'Aviler "very gently." Perhaps D'Aviler was guilty of errors, but there must have been disappointment on his part even so.

67. *P-V,* I, 320. The date was 4 August. The dome as executed to some other design appears near the canal between Paris and S. Denis on early eighteenth-century maps, and is referred to by Felibien in his history of the abbey (1706). It is quite possible that D'Aviler had hoped to propose himself as the architect, and his design for a domed Marian church in the line of the Visitation and Assumption churches would have made an interesting comparison with his *concorso* design. This is one of the more unfortunate lacunae in his career.

68. *P-V,* II, 55. This design bears upon no real project, since there were no plans to add such a chapel at the time. It was more likely only a proposal or demonstration on D'Aviler's part.

69. Blomfield, IV, 18.

70. It is unfortunate that the contributions of this architect as a scholar, draftsman, and teacher have for the most part been overlooked due to the dearth of buildings attributable to him. However, it is even more unfortunate that a true picture of him is overshadowed by exaggerated claims for his authorship of major monuments of the reign of Louis XIV, like the Louvre colonnade and the garden front of Versailles. See: Albert Laprade, *François d'Orbay, architecte de Louis XIV* (Paris: Vincent-Freal, 1960). Hautecoeur critiques Laprade's "adventurous" scholarship in: "François d'Orbay," *Journal des Savants* (April–June, 1960), 59–66. The association between D'Orbay and D'Aviler seems to have been the longest and most pleasant of the younger architect's life. D'Orbay had been in Rome in the early 1660s, and may have arranged for D'Aviler to be sent there, as well as been instrumental in his acceptance as a student at the new Académie d'Architecture. D'Orbay was also assistant to LeVau in the 1660s, and may have communicated the gist of projects like the Collège chapel to D'Aviler for later use in the *concorso* of 1677. In the 1680s and 1690s, D'Orbay was principal assistant to Hardouin-Mansart, with D'Aviler working closely beside him, almost as an equal. What D'Orbay's role was in mediating between the *Surintendant* and the ambitious subordinate is uncertain, but it seems to have been climaxed by his arranging for D'Aviler to go to Montpellier.

71. The full title reads: *Cours d'Architecture qui comprend les Ordres de Vignole avec des commentaires, les figures & descriptions de ses plus beaux batimens, & de ceux de Michelange* (Paris: Nicolas Langlois, 1691). The second volume was a dictionary: *Explication des Termes d'Architecture qui comprende l'Architecture, les mathematiques, la geometrie, la mecanique, l'hydraulique, le dessein, la peinture, la sculpture, les mesures, les instrumens, la coutume, &c.* (Paris: Langlois, 1691). Blomfield (IV, 25) calls the *Cours* "the direct result of Colbert's academies (and the Accademia, I would add), and the embodiment of all that was soundest in their teaching." But it was also a very daring move, given that the elder Blondel's *Cours* (see Chapter I) was already in use, with the backing of the Académie d'Architecture and the status derived from Blondel's name. Blondel's *Cours* was not complete, however, consisting only of introductory terms, principles, and comparisons of the

Orders, until four additional parts were published by Langlois in 1683. This was just about the time D'Aviler conceived his own *Cours,* intent, I would think, on a more practical demonstration of method beyond the mathematics and triumphal arches of Blondel.

72. Hautecoeur, *Architecture Classique,* II, 447; Blomfield, IV, 20.

73. Hautecoeur, II, 128.

74. Oddly enough, though he had no reason to love him, D'Aviler also professed to admire Hardouin-Mansart for his work at the Château de Clagny, near Versailles.

75. D'Aviler even included some valuable remarks on garden design in the *Cours,* ranging from the specific flowers to be grown, to recommendations on type: *niveau,* like the Tuileries; *en pente,* like Versailles; or *en gradins,* like Marly. There would seem to have been no art or science involved in building untouched by his interest.

76. Blomfield, IV, 20, plates CII–CVI.

77. Lance, I, 183. This impatience he had now felt for almost twenty years, since his initial acceptance to the Académie Royale d'Architecture.

78. Hautecoeur, II, 123; Blomfield, IV, 19; Mariette, *Cours,* xxxviii. Called the "Arc du Peyrou" and dedicated to Louis XIV's military victories, Ward (II, 326, Fig. 312), among others, refers to it as an architect's arch, compared to the Porte St.-Denis in Paris, by Blondel, which was only an armature for sculpture. It is then perhaps fitting that D'Aviler, an architect's architect, should have realized his first practical effort in France with this design provided by his friend and confidant, D'Orbay. The request for an overseer had come from Montpellier, and D'Aviler may very well have been recommended for this by D'Orbay, to get him out from under Hardouin-Mansart's shadow at last.

79. It is true that this mode, the one employed by D'Aviler in the *Cours* as well, is obsolete within a very short time in Paris, where tastes were in rapid flux. This does not mean D'Aviler was a provincial talent (Blunt, *Art and Architecture in France,* 438, n. 34), but rather that he was a cosmopolitan architect cut off from the mainstream by circumstance. D'Aviler's church architecture has received rare attention, the one notable instance being Ed.-J. Ciprut's "Un projet inédit de D'Aviler pour l'agrandissement de la Cathédrale

d'Ales," *Bulletin de l'Art Française* (1955), 110–19. This is informative of D'Aviler's patronage in the south, and the adaptability of his methods to a Gothic context, but is not otherwise pertinent to this study. There is, however, no question of the need for further work on D'Aviler beyond the mere preface contained here.

80. *P-V,* II, 151 and passim. Since 1687, the Academy had already been reading from D'Aviler's translation of Scamozzi (see note 61). The return to theoretical discussions in the late 1680s came about as the wave of building activity set in motion by Colbert subsided after his death.

81. The changing tastes of the early eighteenth century might have meant the end of the *Cours*'s usefulness beyond the publication of a second edition in 1710. But rather than discard this most practical textbook, the edition of 1720, revised by Jean-Baptiste LeBlond (Paris: Chez Mariette), was merely altered in stylistic content, with passages (on staircases, woodwork, planning, etc.) added to conform to existing modes. This also had the advantage of outmaneuvering the bootleggers producing editions out of the Netherlands, which indirectly speaks of the demand for D'Aviler's work. The reasons behind the adaptability of the *Cours* are cited by Ward (II, 275–78). In the age of Louis XIV, decorators like LeBrun were required to fit their work within the limits of a classical architecture which was the product of a long history of continuous refinement of the measuring of details, without concern for ornament. D'Aviler, who as his *concorso* design shows was not among the decorators, was nonetheless sympathetic to their needs, both there and in the *Cours*. He applied the rigor of his classicism only to the main articulation of his buildings, leaving considerable leeway for ornament, and coincidentally for those who later amended his text. Since the Rococo constituted changes in decorative taste for the most part, it was possible in the *Cours* to accommodate those variations in fashion for the next several decades.

82. Thieme/Becker, IX, 127.

83. *Dizionario Enciclopedico de Architettura e Urbanistica,* ed. Paolo Portoghesi (Rome: 1968), II, 161.

84. Desgots was awarded his stipend of 200 *livres* for the trip to Rome on 7 July 1675. *Comptes,* I, 854.

85. Hellmut Hager, "Carlo Fontana's Project for a Church in Honour of the 'Ecclesia Triumphans'

in the Colosseum, Rome," *JWCI,* 36 (1973), 319–37. Hager considers the Holy Year 1675 to be a turning point in the history of the Colosseum, when it was finally recognized for its Christian significance as a place of martyrdom. In that year, Innocent, then Cardinal Benedetto Odescalchi, must have envisaged a suitable monument to that fact, which he took up in earnest after his election in September 1676, and placed in the hands of Fontana. The *terminus ante quem* for the start of Fontana's project is the end of 1679, at the death of the church's second patron, Cardinal Francesco Barberini, who was also protector of the Accademia (ASL, vol. 45, fol. 73). A date closer to early 1677 is more likely, however, based on the wording of the source used by Hager. This is the introduction by Fontana to the album of his drawings in the Soane Museum, London (AL/7A), executed in preparation for the engravings of *L'Anfiteatro Flavio.* The introduction reads: "Giunse poi il predetto Emo. Odescalchi al Pontificato, e mi fece imporre dal prenominato Sig. Card. Barberini, che pensassi il modo per fare in quell'ambito un sontuoso edificio Sacro invece del Profano."

86. See again the album of drawings in the Soane Museum, and Carlo Fontana, *L'Anfiteatro Flavio* (The Hague: 1725). The project was proposed anew to Innocent XII (1690s), and Clement XI (ca. 1707): Hager, "Colosseum," 331–32. It was to attract the interest of the latter to his plans for the Roman edifice that Fontana published the history of the Colosseum and his projected alterations. But warfare once more precluded any attempt to realize his ideas, and the project (though not its influence, I would stress) came to an end with Fontana's death in 1714.

87. Hager believes Fontana's plan may also have been a criticism of Bernini at the Piazza of St. Peter's. Hager, "Colosseum," 330.

88. There is also some of the plan and portico of S. Maria dei Miracoli (Fig. 41) in Desgots's church, the former being solely Fontana's responsibility after 1676 (Hager, "Zwillingskirchen," 256). It may be that D'Aviler had access to Fontana's studio as well, and borrowed his tetrastyle portico from an example found there having to do either with the facades of the Twin Churches or Bernini's projected portico for the facade of St. Peter's (see note 53). It is doubtful that his choice of the Doric Order derived from any such source, given his antipathy for current Roman usage.

89. Hager, "Colosseum," 331.

90. Alaux, I, 34. There may have been several reasons behind LeNôtre's trip to Italy, an investigation into his errant nephew's activities being one. His principal duties, in his capacity as overseer of the Versailles gardens, were to inspect the progress of Bernini's equestrian portrait of Louis, and to study Italian landscape architecture in general. It may be for this reason that D'Aviler was released from his own researches into fountains and allowed to leave Italy that summer.

91. Appendix B, 1679, n. 1. Any number of offenses may have provoked the gentleman Errard, but Desgots's error most likely involved the rules of the Academy, where forgiveness encouraged by his superiors would have been acceptable to Errard. It may have been a transgression on the order of Mesier's, or his obvious dependence on D'Aviler's design in 1677 may have required disciplinary action as well (see note 32).

92. Appendix B, 1680, n. 1. The passport mentions that Desgots had fulfilled the rule of 28 October 1677, requiring him to stay three years in Rome in the service of the crown. But as he had arrived there in the summer of 1675, it may be that a two-year suspension was the cost of his unknown indiscretion.

93. Desgots was also granted extra funds for an extended stay in Lombardy during his return home (App. B, 1680, n. 1), where D'Aviler had been left to his own resources aside from the usual 200 *livres* stipend. At least at this stage, Desgots's relationship to LeNôtre seems to have made a friend of Colbert.

94. Thieme/Becker, IX, 127.

95. Lance, I, 216–17; Hautecoeur, II, 398.

96. In general, Desgots's greatest debt was still owed to his uncle, who had interceded for him in Rome, had chosen him for dispatch to England, and had procured for him his first independent stipend as a designer in 1692 (Blomfield, III, 165).

97. Desgots is first recorded in attendance on 4 January 1707 (*P-V,* III, 262), but he may have been admitted earlier, during the restructuring of the Academy that took place in 1699. Looking after the loose ends left by his uncle may well have occupied him for several years.

98. Hautecoeur, II, 114–16. There was also a minor commission from the Duc de Vendôme for a stair-case at Château Anet, and, according to Hautecoeur, the possibility of other works by him as yet unattributed.

99. Ward (II, 383–84) compares Sable, in elevation and planning, to the seventeenth-century hotels of the Faubourg St. Germain. Hautecoeur (II, n. 134) believed Perrigny to be more advanced ("less solemn") in its detailing, but the inclusion of a monumentally enclosed *cours d'honneur* is a dated practice, even though Desgots replaced the screening wall with a more open colonnade.

100. *P-V,* IV, 191–92. Desgots was nominated, along with Robert de Cotte, de Fontainebleau, and de L'Espine, to fill a vacancy left on the death of a member. From their illustrious number, Desgots was chosen by the regent on 11 March 1720.

101. At the Palais Royal, Desgots introduced a broad expanse of mown lawn, in the English fashion, sprinkled by jets fed from underground (Champion-Sandoz, *Le Palais Royal* [1910], I, 344).

102. Jacques-François Blondel, *Architecture Française* (1752; facs. Paris: Librairie Centrale des Beaux-Arts, 1904), III, 45. In his description of the Palais Royal, Blondel ranks Desgots among the greatest of French landscape architects, including LeNôtre, LeBlond, Cottart, and Bouteux. Later (p. 239) he laments the passing of their kind in his remarks on the gardens of the Hotel de Conty: "La distribution des jardins est plus singulière que belle, les formes en général sont bizarres … (garden design) a beaucoup dégénéré depuis la mort des célèbres le Nautre & Desgots."

103. *P-V,* V, 100. On 30 June 1732, a vacancy was announced to the assembly due to the death of Desgots. He was then very likely in his eighties, the last half of his life having been spent at the apex of his trade.

104. Paolo Marconi, Angela Cipriani, and Enrico Valeriani, *I disegni di architettura dell'Archivio storico dell'Accademia di San Luca* (Rome: De Luca, 1974), I, 3, nn. 10–12. Di Leti's drawings are in fact dated "1677" (see App. A, nn. 13–15).

105. Marconi et al. (1981), 167. The catalogers were unable to find a place for di Leti's design in the *Concorsi Accademici,* and so in this revision of their earlier work they simply delete it. The author addresses this problem in Chapter III.

106. Marconi et al. (1974), II, nn. 2178–82.

107. For instance, Chupin's octangular ambulatory could be read as loosely based on the Salute's; or the aediculae around the exterior of both D'Aviler's and Desgots's churches may be related to Longhena's building. So might the sceno-graphic axial vistas of the Salute explain the radi-ating plans of the second- and third-prize designs, but these associations are probably only coinci-dental, or at best cosanguineous.

108. Anthony Blunt, "Roman Baroque Architecture: The Other Side of the Medal," *Art History,* 3, n. 1 (March, 1980), 61–80. An interesting aside is pro-vided in this article in reference to a series of drawings for church facades by Domenichino, apparently a frustrated architect, which are housed at Windsor Castle (p. 64, n. 13). Illustrating his ideas for the facade of S. Ignazio, three of them employed classical porticoes, and one a "bold" ser-liana. It is curious, but as yet no more than this, that among the designs coming out of the *concorso* of 1677 those devices are distributed similarly. For now, it suggests that such facades have a lineage that extends throughout the seventeenth century, to include the academic ambiance that generated the *concorso* designs in 1677.

109. Unlike the competition entries (see note 24), the *dono* drawings are numbered on the front of the elevations. This set is numbered "no. 3, pezzi 3," and the other "no. 9, pezzo 1" (the plan was apparently missed). This allows the possibility that the design now under discussion was in fact submitted earlier than the other.

110. Della Greca would have had a grace period of up to six months to complete his *dono,* but by June he was missing his lectures in architecture, and it is doubtful that he met any other obligations.

111. Hager, "Colosseum," 328–29.

112. Aside from the churches already mentioned, S. Maria dei Miracoli and the Colosseum church, there was the church of the Jesuit college at Loyola in Spain, Fontana's most important com-mission of the 1680s (see Chapter IV). Among the chapels were the Cappella dell'Assunta of the Collegio Clementino in Rome (1685–87: Hager, "Un riesame di tre cappelle di Carlo Fontana," *Commentari,* 27 (1976), nn. 3–4, 252–89, and the Cappella Cybo (see subsequent text).

113. H. Hager, "La Cappella del Cardinale Alderano Cybo in S. Maria del Popolo," *Commentari,* 25 (1974), 48–50, Fig. 2.

114. H. Hager, "Balthasar Neumann's Schoenborn Chapel at Wurzburg Cathedral and Its Berninesque prototype," *Architectural History,* 26 (1983), 77–78, Pl. 37b, c. The reconstruction is based on the assumption that the first project would still have had to relate to Raphael's Chigi Chapel across the nave, and be adjusted to the architecture of the side aisle of the basilica. Pendentives are therefore presumed, which due to the geometry would have been cylindrical sections like those in the *dono.*

115. This annular corridor was a magnified version of those which circumscribe the interiors of Fontana's Colosseum and Loyola churches. It may reflect an Early Christian prototype, the mau-soleum of Sta. Costanza, and provide the sort of link with the past so favored by Bernini and his circle.

116. This would explain why this project is known from a copy in the Martinelli albums of the Bertarelli collection, Milan. Domenico Martinelli was a student, a competitor, and eventually an instructor in architecture at the Accademia in the 1680s (see Chapter III).

117. The practice of petitioning works from academy members for the decoration of the salon during the *concorsi* was stipulated by the new statutes of 1675 (see Chapter I, note 101). This purpose is implied in the minutes of 31 October 1677 (App. B, 1677, n. 5), when three members were assigned to see to those decorations.

118. ASL, vol. 45, fol. 57; vol. 46, fol. 21.

119. ASL, vol. 43, fol. 229.

120. Wittkower (1973), 539, n. 23; G. Borghini and G. Scarfone, "S. Carlo al Corso," *Alma Roma,* 15 (1974), nn. 1–2, 28–30; G. Drago and L. Salerno, *SS. Ambrogio e Carlo al Corso,* Chiese di Roma Illustrate, No. 96 (Rome: Marietti, 1967).

121. Thieme/Becker, XXIV, 393.

122. ASL, vol. 45, fol. 65; vol. 46, fol. 25 (16 April 1679); vol. 45, fol. 80 (8 April 1680).

123. This plan, with concave side walls anchored by engaged columns, may reflect an early idea of Fontana's for the Cappella Ginetti (1671–84) in S. Andrea della Valle, reconstructed in plan by Hager in "Un riesame di tre cappelle di Carlo Fontana" (see note 112), Fig. 3.

124. Menicucci first attempted to enter the Accademia in 1673, at which time he must have been at least

thirty years old. The year of his birth would therefore fall in the early 1640s.

125. Blunt (1980), 69–71.

126. In the last few pages of his article, Blunt several times misreads the nature of Fontana's style post-Bernini, losing track particularly of the frequency with which he turned to concentric schemes (n. 75).

127. Over the next seventy-five years the centralized church type would be of continual interest to the Accademia. During that period, in twenty-five competitions held with varying frequency, there would be seventeen occasions, either in the first or second classes, when the *soggetto* or the competing architects included a centrally planned church as all or part of the task. In all that time only four architects did not choose a centralized plan when the church type was not otherwise specified, and only one *soggetto,* that of 1679 (see Chapter III), asked specifically for a longitudinally planned church. Beyond the middle of the eighteenth century, the frequency with which churches are called for at all by the *soggetti* diminishes, while the scale of the projects expands to often impractical degrees. In 1754 and 1771 the first-class *soggetti* for the *Concorsi Clementini* call for cathedrals of the usual Latin-cross type, but immense in size and with numerous annexes. The simple concerns of centralized planning seem insignificant by comparison, and in any case the stylistic requisites after 1750 had sufficiently altered so as to negate the pertinence of a S. Agnese type altogether.

128. Marconi et al. (1974), I, 5, Figs. 63–67. The architect, Rossini, has earlier competition successes to his credit, which will be discussed in Chapter IV.

129. There were three occasions when an existing situation was called up by a *soggetto,* requiring an exceptional problem-solving effort on the part of the competitors. This happened in 1705 when one of the tasks was to design a facade for the Lateran basilica, in 1706 in designs for a public fountain (the Trevi), and in 1711 when a new sacristy was being considered for St. Peter's (Hager et al., *Architectural Fantasy and Reality,* passim). All three instances occurred during the pontificate of Clement XI (d. 1721), the most energetic period of architectural competition at the Accademia, and such serious intentions are rare in *concorsi* after the first quarter of the Settecento. Where the only test of an architect's ability to overcome

obstacles in design meant dealing with vast complexes, some ingenious solutions to adapting multiple functions to the plan were realized. But when faced with incorporating a centralized church in such a project, students took one of two routes to reduce the time devoted to its invention. They could model their designs on preexisting monuments (as was the case in the second-class *concorso* of 1728; Marconi et al. [1974], I, 14–15, nn. 345–370), or confine themselves to the simple Greek-cross plan, the course that was taken increasingly as the century progressed. This would have diluted the utility of the designs from 1677 in their researches.

130. Marconi et al. (1974), I, 11, nn. 262–77.

131. The latter design was modified by reference to a work by Filippo Juvarra, then Demangeot's instructor in architecture at the Accademia. Juvarra's *dono* of 1707, from which Demangeot in particular derived the location of his towers on the lateral axis of the cupola, will be considered subsequently as it bears on the question of the impact of the *concorso* of 1677.

132. Marconi et al. (1974), I, 12–13.

133. Marconi et al. (1974), I, nn. 123–34. Only two of the four prizewinners included campanili (P. P. Scaramella, first; Ferdinando Reif, third), placing them at the facade. All four architects chose to give their otherwise centralized plans a longitudinal emphasis, and as a result the view of the dome is subordinated in each design to the facade and/or towers. It should also be noted that though the designs range from the traditional to the adventurous in conception, each falls back on the feature of the pendentive.

134. The drawings are inscribed: "Del Seg. Antonio Valerij Architetto ammesso alli 3 Maggio 1696" (Marconi et al. [1974], II, nn. 2106–7). See also: ASL, vol. 45, fol. 164.

135. ASL, vol. 45, fol. 93; vol. 46, fol. 42. The date was 5 October.

136. Valerii was already forty-eight when he earned his membership in the Accademia, and it would be nearly another twenty years before any substantial activity on his part was recorded. He did serve as *principe* at the Accademia in 1726, but in view of his advanced age this was probably only an honorarium (Thieme/Becker, XXXIV, 68). On the basis of his skill at rendering, it is reasonable to assume that he was primarily occupied as a draftsman prior to 1696.

137. In their bi-apsidal plan, and their functions as sac-risties and links between altar spaces, these "corri-dors" may be compared to the sacristies of Desgots's design as well (cf. Pl. 7). The section drawing suggests that Valerii may also have aban-doned pendentives on the example of the French, avoiding their use through the continuity of the interior octagon. The conventions are otherwise Italianate, however, and he may instead have been in line with Carlo Fontana in this regard.

138. Hellmut Hager, *Filippo Juvarra e il concorso di modelli del 1715 bandito da Clemente XI per la nuova sacrestia di S. Pietro* (Rome: Quaderni di Commentari, 1970).

139. Gil R. Smith, "Accademico di Merito of 1707: Design for a Church of Central Plan by Filippo Juvarra," *Architectural Fantasy and Reality,* 141–56.

140. Susan Scott Munshower, "Concorso Clementino of 1705: Design for a Royal Palace in a Villa for Three Important Persons," *Architectural Fantasy and Reality,* 30–42. The tripartite scheme was contrived to relate to the Accademia's most recently adopted symbol, the equilateral triangle, which referred to the equality of the three Arts. As Munshower points out, this generated a number of similarly planned projects, even churches; again the academic inclinations of the Settecento seem more pretentious than practical.

141. Henry A. Millon, "Filippo Juvarra and the Accademia di San Luca in Rome in the Early Eighteenth Century," *Projects and Monuments in the Period of the Roman Baroque,* ed. Hellmut Hager and Susan S. Munshower, Papers in Art History from The Pennsylvania State University, Vol. I (University Park, Pa.: 1984).

142. The intensity of Juvarra's interest in this theme is evident in the number of finished drawings he produced that are nearly identical to his *dono* design. There are two versions in Turin, two in Berlin, and one in Stockholm, all of the same approximate date, though A. E. Brinckmann con-siders the Berlin drawings, made for Card. Alessandro Albani, to be the originals. Brinckmann, *Die Baukunst des 17. und 18. Jahrhunderts in den romanischen Landern* (Berlin: 1915), 6; Sabine Jacob, *Italienische Zeichnungen der Kunstbibliothek Berlin* (Berlin: 1975), 146, nn. 751–52.

143. N. Carboneri, *La Reale Chiesa di Superga di Filippo Juvarra,* Corpus Juvarrianum (Turin:

Accademia delle Scienze, 1979), 5–6.

144. It is also possible to compare productively Juvarra's *dono* to Longhena's Salute, one of the possible models for the competitors in 1677. As usual, there is no one Italian prototype sufficient to explain more than one element of Juvarra's design; it is inarguably unique.

145. In actuality, the foremost section of the drum colonnade and the portico are so integrated—by the spacing of the articulation, the superimposi-tion of the pediments, and the dynamic contrast of the convexly projecting apses and obliquely receding drum—as to present another unique variation on the "typical" two-storied Baroque facade.

146. Richard Pommer, *Eighteenth-Century Architecture in Piedmont: The Open Structures of Juvarra, Alfieri, and Vittone* (New York University Press, 1967).

147. Carboneri, 6–7. Juvarra replaced the architect Antonio Bertola of Palermo on the project.

148. The Superga was intended by Vittorio Amadeo as a victory church, dedicated in gratitude for divine intervention in his defeat of the French near Turin in 1706. Coincidentally or not, Juvarra's *dono* of 1707 was conceived as a votive church, suitable to such a function.

149. Pommer, 38.

150. Though completed as a temple-front portico *in antis* between two bays framed by pilasters, the facade elevation of S. Filippo Neri can still recall Chupin's, and through it Errard's Assumption. The facade of the latter has already been pointed out (see note 45) as being considered well suited to a longitudinal church by eighteenth-century critics. Since the facade of the Turin church was once intended to have towers, Chupin's design may have sorted itself out of Juvarra's memory when he returned to his designs for S. Filippo Neri, after a lapse in building during the 1720s. The unusually stark classicism of this facade has heretofore been loosely attributed to Juvarra's experience of Palladian architecture in London, ca. 1720 (Pommer, 87–88).

151. Millon (1984), 15; ASL, vol. 46A, passim.

152. See the entries for the *concorsi* in the first class of architecture for the years 1725, 1732, and 1739 in Marconi et al. (1974), I, 12–18. In 1732, Bernardo Vittone, one of the most ardent follow-

ers of Juvarra, favored the Superga and other Juvarresque motifs in the design of one church as part of a vast project for an island city (see Chapter IV).

153. Evidence of Eigtwedt's familiarity with Juvarra's *dono* exists in a copy of the plan in his hand that is also in the collection of the Royal Danish Academy. It is illustrated in Frederick Weilbach, "Filippo Juvarra und die Marmorkirche in Kopenhagen," in *Architectura: Jahrbuch für Geschichte der Baukunst,* I (1933), 17–21. Later projects for the completion of Eigtwedt's church would even involve the French architect Anges-Jacques Gabriel: Christian Elling, *Documents inédits concernants les projets de Gabriel & Jardin pour l'église Frederic à Copenhague* (Copenhagen: 1931); *Monumenta Architecturae Danicae: Danish Architectural Drawings, 1660–1920,* ed. C. Elling and K. Fisker (Copenhagen: Den Gyldendalske Boghandel, 1961), Pls. 47–62.

154. E.g., Hans Sedlmayr, "Zwei Beispiele zur Interpretation," *Kunst und Wahrheit: Zur Theorie und Methode der Kunstgeschichte* (Munich: Maander Kunstverlag, 1978); Frances Fergusson, "St. Charles' Church, Vienna: The Iconography of Its Architecture," *JSAH,* 29 (1970), 318–26.

155. Fergusson, 320.

156. H. Sedlmayr, *J. B. Fischer von Erlach* (Vienna: 1956), 57. If Juvarra did submit a competition design, it does not survive as such.

157. Carboneri (p. 6) does take the *dono* into account, but rather than find in favor of Juvarra on the question of precedence, he explains the coincidence as a result of the architects' shared experiences under Carlo Fontana. This comes close to a complete explanation, but he is unaware of events in 1677.

158. H. Aurenhammer, *J. B. Fischer von Erlach* (London: Allen Lane, 1973), 18.

159. Aside from being secretary of the Accademia, and author of the *soggetti* in painting and sculpture for 1677, Bellori was also custodian of the collections of Queen Christina of Sweden. While in exile in Rome, she was patroness of a group of intellectuals and antiquarians which had an important influence on Fischer's own scholarship.

160. The connection between Fischer and the *concorso* of 1677 has also been verified independently by Hellmut Lorenz in another context: "Das 'Lustgartengebäude' Fischers von Erlach—

Variationen eines architektonischen Themas," in *Wiener Jahrbuch für Kunstgeschichte,* Bd. XXXII (1979), 59–76. See Chapter III.

161. A. Braham, "L'Église du Dome," *JWCI,* 23 (1960), 216–24. It was because the Dome was originally intended as a Bourbon sepulcher that François Mansart's earlier projects were revived. It is interesting to note that the Superga was also initially intended by Vittorio Amadeo to be a tomb for his dynasty (Pommer, 41), perhaps in emulation of Louis XIV's chapel at the Invalides. Aside from the fact that both churches are attached at the rear to another building, there are few formal links between them, except that they, like the Karlskirche, draw from the same pool of motifs derived for centralized churches in France and Italy as had the competitors in 1677. It is tempting to propose that the theme for the *concorso* of 1677 was actually motivated by the Invalides project, but the timing makes it unlikely. If this *were* the case, then bringing the students in on such an important project at this initial stage would have been more honor than they deserved, and more insult than Hardouin-Mansart could have borne.

162. A. Braham (1960), 216. The building was actually begun in March 1679, to new designs which take into account the abandonment of the sepulcher concept. Further adjustments were made to the cupola when the ring of lights around the crowning vault was added, destroying the proportions of the original (p. 217). It was at this point that D'Aviler was present in Hardouin-Mansart's office, and may have felt he had something to impart. But there were no other major changes to Mansart's original scheme, and the fabric of the church was completed in 1691. The previous projects for the chapel at S. Denis, which date to the early 1660s, may have been within the ken of Errard or his students, and the changes which came with the change in venue may have been communicated to D'Aviler, and through him to the others, by D'Orbay, who was Hardouin-Mansart's assistant in the late 1670s. See also: P. Reutersward, *The Two Churches of the Hotel des Invalides* (Stockholm: Almqvist and Wiksell, 1965); and Blunt, *Art and Architecture in France,* 364.

163. B. Kerber, "Ein Kirchen Project des Andrea Pozzo als Vorstufe vor Weltenburg," *Architettura,* 2 (1972), 34–47.

164. Pozzo used the truncated dome again in the side chapels of the Jesuit church in Vienna (after 1702, see note 175). By then J. B. Fischer von Erlach had incorporated the device in the diagonal chapels of the Kollegienkirche in Salzburg (1694–1707). Whether he had discovered it independently in Rome about 1680, or had it communicated to him by Pozzo, the truncated dome thereafter becomes part of Austrian practice.

165. M. Elizabeth Garza, "Antonio Gherardi," *MEA*, II, 189–90; Thomas Pickrel, *Antonio Gherardi*, Diss., University of Kansas, 1981.

166. Hellmut Hager has unravelled the complex design history of the baptismal chapel: Braham/Hager, *Fontana*, 39–44, Fig. 9 (see Chapter IV).

167. Anthony Blunt, *Baroque and Rococo Architecture and Decoration* (New York: Harper & Row, 1978), 227. The implication is that if the Asams were interested in architecture while at the Accademia, they would not have neglected to make use of the archives, or the advice of Carlo Fontana.

168. Blunt, *Baroque and Rococo*, 228–33. The architecture of Weltenburg is usually attributed to Cosmas Damian. The Asams' other masterpiece, St. John Nepomuk in Munich (after 1733), is the product of Egid Quirin's equivalent architectural talent, but is thoroughly Bavarian in pedigree.

169. Carl Albert, the Elector of Bavaria, was responsible for the funding of the Weltenburg church on behalf of the Order of St. George. This church, the Superga, and the Karlskirche, therefore, all have aristocratic patronage in common.

170. L. Rovere, V. Viale, A. E. Brinckmann, *Filippo Juvarra*, Comitato per la Onoranze a Filippo Juvarra, vol. I (Milan: Casa Editrice Oberdan Zucchi, 1937); Vittorio Viale, *Mostra del Barocco Piemontese: Palazzo Madama, Palazzo Reale, e Palazzina di Stupinigi* (Turin: Architettura e Scenografia, 1963); Pommer, op. cit.; Luigi Malle, *Stupinigi: Un capolavoro del Settecento europeo tra barochetto e classicismo* (Turin: 1968); Salvatore Boscarino, *Juvarra Architetto* (Rome: 1973).

171. Hans Sedlmayr, *Epochen und Werke, gesammelte Schriften zur Kunstgeschichte*, Bd. II (Vienna/Munich: Verlag Herold, 1960); H. Sedlmayr, *J. B. Fischer von Erlach* (1956; rpt. Vienna: Verlag Herold, 1978); H. Sedlmayr (1978), op. cit.; H. Sedlmayr, "Die Kollegienkirche und die Kirche der Sorbonne: Metamorphosen der Kreuzkuppelkirche im Übergang zum Frühbarock," in *Mitteilungen der Gesellschaft für Salzburger Landeskunde*, 120/121 (1980–81).

172. P. Bourget and G. Cattaui, *Jules Hardouin Mansart* (Paris: Editions Vincent, Freal, & Cie., 1956).

173. E. Hanfstaengl, *Die Bruder Cosmas Damian und Egid Quirin Asam* (Munich: 1955).

174. Bernhard Kerber, *Andrea Pozzo* (Berlin/New York: De Gruyter, 1971); Andrea Pozzo, *Perspectiva Pictorum et Architectorum*, 2 vols. (Rome: Komareck Bohemi, 1693–1700).

175. Pozzo reused the truncated dome, by means quite similar to those employed by Carlo Fontana in the baptistry of St. Peter's, in the remodeling of the side chapels of the Jesuit University church in Vienna (1703–9, see note 164).

176. Ragnar Josephson, *Nicodemus Tessin d. y.: Tiden, Mannen, Verket*, 2 vols. (Stockholm: 1930–31); R. Josephson, *L'Architecte de Charles XII, Nicodeme Tessin, a la Cour de Louis XIV* (Paris/Brussels: Van Oest, 1930); Bjorn R. Kommer, *Nicodemus Tessin der jüngere und das Stockholmer Schloss: Untersuchungen zum Hauptwerk der Schwedischen Architektur*, Heidelberger Kunstgeschichtliche Abhandlungen, N.S. 11 (Heidelberg: Carl Winter Universitats Verlag, 1974). The royal palace at Stockholm, Tessin's most important commission, is rich with references to French and Italian church and palace design. The references call up several of the themes pursued in the *Concorsi Accademici*, which is an indication of how universal that pursuit was. In fact the parallels are so close as to suggest a more direct contact between the Accademia and Tessin than has heretofore been presumed; the author must reserve that investigation for a later date.

NOTES TO CHAPTER III

1. The date was 28 November 1677 (App. B, 1678, n. 1; ASL, vol. 45, fol. 53). Errard was nominated by Carlo Maratti, who had been party to the aggregation on behalf of the Romans, and he in turn was elected *vice-principe* for 1678. Ostensibly, this would have maintained a balance of authority in the Accademia, shared at its highest office between the Italians and the French, in keeping with the articles of 1676. Curiously, however, Maratti refused the position, as the meeting of 17

July (see note 5) records his censure at the hands of the congregation for giving insufficient grounds for his refusal. Usually those grounds involved the heavy workload of a prospective officer, and since Maratti was himself increasingly in demand, it is not necessary to assume that he had somehow become disenchanted with Errard or the French. One legitimate conclusion, though, is that Maratti was willing to leave the work of restructuring the Accademia to the French without at least his supervision. Giovanni Maria Morandi was named *vice-principe* in Maratti's stead, and in fact served as *principe* in the later part of 1678 during an extended illness of Errard's.

2. The date was 16 January (App. B, 1678, n. 2). The letter was signed by Errard, and by Domenico Guidi and Giovanni Battista Gaulli acting as *primo* and *secondo consiglieri* respectively.

3. ASL, vol. 45, fol. 56; vol. 46, fol. 20.

4. ASL, vol. 45, fol. 57; vol. 46, fol. 21. The French were Simon Hurtrelle, who had won the first prize in sculpture in 1677, Jean-Baptiste Théodon, winner of the third prize in sculpture, and the painter Alessandro Alessandri (see Chapter II, notes 21, 22). The two prizewinners in sculpture (the third was Italian) may also have been chosen for a possible association with Bernini during the work on Louis XIV's equestrian portrait. The Polish expatriate Alessandri can be considered a "qualified Frenchman." Three Roman sculptors were also nominated, as well as one from Burgundy, and a Venetian painter.

5. ASL, vol, 45, fol. 58; vol. 46, fol. 21. Letters of patent were forwarded via Paris to all three of the French, but Hurtrelle and Théodon had actually stayed in Rome and continued to be active at the Accademia for some time. All of the new members were put in charge of the festivities on the Feast of St. Luke (meeting of 2 October; ASL, vol. 45, fol. 59) to partially fulfill their obligations as initiates.

6. Missirini, Titolo LXXXVIII, 143.

7. The first of the latter, which were more consistently published during the papacy of Clement XI, was produced in honor of the centenary of 1696 and its *concorso*. See Chapter IV. In Ghezzi, the Accademia must have felt itself provided with the equivalent of a Testelin or Felibien, the capable secretaries and historians of the French academies of art and architecture respectively.

8. Examples of lecture outlines for courses in perspective and geometry are preserved in the Accademia's archive from earlier in the century, but no demonstrations of the Orders of architecture before the efforts of Mattia de Rossi in 1673. Before there was an official curriculum in architecture at the Accademia, architects would often be invited in to supplement the meager instruction that the painters and sculptors could give by discoursing on their own ideals and methods for the Orders. Vincenzo della Greca's lectures in 1636 (Blunt [1980], 69–71) were preserved only by chance in the manuscript notes of one of the students, which were graciously illustrated and annotated by the architect himself. Blunt states:

> There is no theory, strictly speaking, in the lectures, but a fairly clear attitude towards architecture is implied in them. What Della Greca offers his students is a selection of models which are mainly drawn from respectable sources of the mid- and late-sixteenth century (p. 71)....

Vincenzo della Greca's manuscript thesis, unpublished but dated 1641, is preserved in the Vaduz Castle collections in Liechtenstein; the author's thanks to Hellmut Lorenz for this reference. What Portoghesi (537, n. 57) identifies as the fragment of a thesis by Felice della Greca in the National Museum in Stockholm, may only be lecture notes from his brief tenure as instructor in 1676. See G. Curcio, "La 'Breve Relazione' inedita di Felice della Greca e la trattatistica funzionale fra il cinquecento e il seicento," *Ricerche de storia dell'arte*, 8 (1978–79), 99–118. For the lessons produced by later instructors as permanent source material, see the subsequent text, and Henry Millon, "Filippo Juvarra and the Accademia di San Luca in Rome in the Early 18th Century," in *Projects and Monuments*, 15.

9. The Accademia acknowledged its gratitude to the embroiderers for this service in the meeting of 12 November 1678 (ASL, vol. 45, fol. 10).

10. Missirini, Titolo LXXXIX, 144.

11. The date was 28 May (ASL, vol. 45, fol. 67). Errard returned to the relative ease of his post as director of the Académie de France in Rome, but he continued to make known his presence within the Accademia in 1679. Early that year he presented to the congregation a large engraving after LeBrun's very successful painting of Alexander's victory over Porus. This gift was received with "sommo applauso" and displayed in the Accademia's main salon.

12. For the painters, the subject in the first class was the finding of Moses. The first-class *soggetto* in sculpture, "quando esso Moise amor bambino calpesto la Regia corona postare in testa dal Rè Faraone," is intriguing. It is tempting to propose that this was an allegorical response to the blatantly monarchical propaganda of the *soggetti* in 1677, and an assertion of Italian independence. See the subsequent text.

13. Colbert wrote to LeBrun on 15 September to request his recommendations for new *pensionnaires* to send to Rome in order to bring student numbers up to the mandated levels. See Appendix B, 1679, n. 7.

14. Appendix B, 1679, n. 4. It was usually the practice for new members in architecture to assume the task of lecturing, since as less established artists they would have had the time and needed the experience and compensation. This was not always in the best interest of the curriculum, however. Menicucci was made one of the two chaplains on 3 May (ASL, vol. 45, fol. 66). He was, therefore, an example of a priest/architect that establishes a precedent for Filippo Juvarra, who would later fill much the same role at the Accademia, albeit with considerably more distinction. Juvarra was at least not as unique in his having taken Holy Orders as a first reading of his brother's biography might indicate. V. Viale, ed., *Filippo Juvarra, Architetto e Scenografo* (Messina: 1966), 16–30.

15. Ward, II, 283; Hautecouer, *Architecture Classique,* III, 358. At one time, however briefly, facade towers *were* a part of the project for Rainaldi's S. Maria in Campitelli: Carlo Antonio Erra, *Storia dell'Immagine e Chiesa di Santa Maria in Portico in Campitelli* (Rome: Komarek, 1750), 55. Their tentative inclusion was by no means definitive, and they do not appear in either the completed facade, or the earlier foundation-medal project: R. Wittkower, "Carlo Rainaldi and the Roman Architecture of the Full Baroque," in *Art Bulletin* 19 (1937); Furio Fasolo, *L'Opera di Heronimo e Carlo Rainaldi* (1961). The greater weight of this early project's relevance to the *concorso* in 1679 lies with its colonnaded portico, convex but in two stories, and in that regard Pietro da Cortona's facade of S. Maria in Via Lata has precedence (see subsequent text). Maderno's and Bernini's projects for towers on the facade of St. Peter's (Figs. 10, 11) address exceptional circumstances, which relate more to the theme of 1677 than that of 1679.

16. The assumption is by no means certain with regard to St.-Sulpice. Lack of funds halted construction there in 1675 before the facade was begun, and no design by LeVau has survived (Hautecouer, II, pt. 1, 95). But given the similarities in general type and patronage between St.-Sulpice and St.-Eustache, it is likely that they shared similarities with regard to LeVau's facade projects as well.

17. Hautecouer, II, pt. 1, 96, Fig. 85. LeVau's design was never executed.

18. ASL, vol. 45, fol. 71. It is worthwhile to question why six prizes were awarded in this category rather than the customary three. It is almost as though it was intended to give the Italians an inevitable majority.

19. Ghezzi notes on 18 June (ASL, vol. 45, fol. 67) that in regard to his role in publishing the *concorso,* "in oltre si notifichi me a d'o *concorso* non saranno ammessi qui giovani che lavarano per le botteghe."

20. ASL, vol. 45, fol. 73; Missirini, Titolo LXXXIX, 144. Carlo Barberini's letter accepting the responsibilities of protector was read to the congregation on 21 January 1680 (ASL, vol. 45, fol. 77).

21. ASL, vol. 45, fol. 75; Missirini, Titolo LXXIX, 130.

22. Appendix B, 1680, n. 2. Errard was also chosen at this time to conduct the life-drawing classes for June.

23. It was as symbol (Star of Wisdom) that Borromini had employed the hexagon at S. Ivo (1642–50). Formally, it had had no serious consideration for church design since Sebastiano Serlio's treatise (1574, Book V, fol. 6).

24. The use of triangular geometries to form architectural symbols of the Accademia's composition does, in fact, associate several projects executed under its aegis. See Susan Scott Munshower, "Concorso Clementino of 1705," *Architectural Fantasy and Reality,* 30–42, and "Project by Giuseppe Ercolani," Ibid., 74–75; Gil R. Smith, "Concorso Clementino of 1750," Ibid., 131–40.

25. ASL, vol. 45, fol. 87. Prizes were awarded in the first classes as follows:

Painting-	Luigi Sceron (Fr.). 1°
	Guiseppe Nicola Natini (It.) 2°
	Michele Probenor (Gr.) 3°
	Raimondo LaFaye (Fr.) 4°
Sculpture-	Stefano Massone
Architecture-	Domenico Martinelli

26. The Accademia had earlier taken exception to a remark in a recently printed book, Abbate Carlo Bartolomeo Piazza's *Opere Pie di Roma,* to the effect that all financial gifts to the Accademia were used every year to buy the prizes for the *concorsi* (ASL, vol. 45, fol. 83). The congregation vehemently denied this calumny, and apparently went on to prove it by in fact spending very little (it could afford no more) on the prizes in 1680.

27. ASL, vol. 45, fol. 81. The biblical reference is to 2 Kings 12:17f.

28. There was more to the story than this. Jehoash's military power had also diminished since the death of his capable advisor Jehoiada, and much of his ill fame derived from his buying off foreign invaders with the treasures of the temple just recently restored. This may also be a factor in the metaphor to be developed from this iconography, having to do with the fact that Louis was content to treat with the infidel Turks rather than join a European alliance against them that might have diminished his status. This severely affected Louis's popularity in Europe, in much the same way Jehoash's popularity had been affected.

29. The issue of diplomacy between France and Rome as it relates to the competitions in painting and sculpture, and to activity at large in the figural arts, is a subject all its own and too large to deal with adequately here. The work of cataloging the Accademia's archive of competition designs in painting, and of wading through the records and sources pertaining to them, has only just been begun by scholars in the field. See ASL, *I premiati dell'Accademia, 1682–1754,* ed. Angela Cipriani (Rome: Quasar, 1989); ASL, *I disegni di figura nell'Archivio Storico dell'Accademia di San Luca,* 2 vols., ed. A Cipriani and E. Valeriani (Rome: Quasar, 1988–89). A third volume of the latter catalog, on the competitions in painting from the late-eighteenth and nineteenth centuries, awaits publication. The much thornier problem of cataloging the terra-cotta submissions in sculpture has yet to begin.

30. An inkling of Roman attitudes toward the feud between Innocent and Louis on the issue of church vs. state may also have been given in Ghezzi's *soggetto* for sculpture in 1679: Moses trampling the crown of Pharoah. At the least there can be no mistaking where Ghezzi's sympathies lay.

31. ASL, vol. 45, fol. 86; vol. 46, fol. 38. This election of his most illustrious successor may very well have been prompted in part as a tribute to Bernini, who died just three days earlier on 28 November. If so, it is the *only* tribute or even mention that the Accademia records in its minutes with regard to the passing of the most singular genius of the age. Regrettably, he was not *their* genius.

32. Missirini, LXXXVI, 141.

33. Missirini (Titolo LXXXIX, 144) does mention that a debate of this kind was scheduled by Lazzaro Baldi during the previous year, on the Feast of the Assumption during a general reunion of the Accademia, " … ma nulla fu scritto di quel congresso."

34. Appendix B, 1681, n. 1. Missirini assumes here that the document had only recently come into the Accademia's possession, but the inference should be that it was brought into debate for the first time in 1681. It had actually been submitted in 1672, when Errard was first *principe* and de Rossi first became a member.

35. Missirini, Titolo XCI, 145–46. While invoking Raphael and Poussin, the debates established the ultimate authority in antiquity. And despite the participation of Bellori, Maratti, and Morandi, the tone, at least as communicated secondhand by Missirini, was considerably less Francophilic than in 1677.

36. Competition was also scheduled again in this year in the third classes of painting and sculpture, both of which required a copy after an antique relief or a work of Raphael's.

37. Carapecchia's master, Carlo Fontana (Braham/Hager, 16, 21), would have likely held the same opinions, and was quite probably covetous of Mattia's status with the French, which had boosted his public esteem after Bernini's death far beyond his achievements as an architect. The consequences of this are to be seen in the *concorsi* during Fontana's reign as *principe* in the 1690s (see Chapter IV).

38. Appendix B, 1681, n. 5. Tomassini and Menicucci were again the judges in architecture (ASL, vol. 45, fol. 94).

39. Appendix B, 1682, n. 1; ASL, vol. 45, fol. 97.

40. ASL, vol. 45, fol. 95.

41. Eighteen voting members were present; Errard and Menicucci received 11 votes each, Fontana 10, and Contini 14.

42. Missirini, Titolo XCII, 146–47.

43. The *verbali* of 24 May 1682 (ASL, vol. 45, fol. 101), read: "Non solo fu risoluto si faccino legare li (detti) disegni ma si consegnino al Se. Tomassini le sue lettioni d'Architettura, acciò possi terminarli, e circa la legatura degli altri disegni si debbano sceglierli migliori col farli legare al che s'offerse far fare il Sige. Luigi Garzi … e quanto à gli altri esser bene esitargli, e che ciò debba farsi con l'assistenza di Si. G. M. Morandi e Mattia de Rossi." This establishes the *terminus ad quem* for the dating of Tomassini's drawings on the Orders.

44. ASL, vol. 45, fol. 102.

45. J. Starzynski, "Augustyn Locci, inzynier i artystyczny doradça Jana III," *Bjuletin historii sztuki,* 1 (1932–33), 119–27; Starzynski, *Wilanów: Dzieje Budowy Palacuza Jana III* (Warszawa: 1933); V. Z. Rewski, "Architekci G. B. Colombo i D. Martinelli a Jan III Sobieski," *Bjuletin historii sztuki,* 9 (1947), 322–40; Starzynski, "Dwor artystyczny Jana III," *Zycie Sztuki,* 2 (1965), 138–40; Wojciech Fijalkowski, "Rezydencja Jana III w Wilanówie w swietle materialow z czasów saskich," *Bjuletin historii sztuki,* 29 (1967), 365; Mariusz Karpowicz, "Il filone italiano dell'arte polacca del Seicento ed i suoi rappresentanti maggiori," in *Barocco fra Italia e Polonia,* ed. Jan Slaski, Comitato degli Studi sull'Arte, Accademia Polacca delle Scienze (Warszawa: 1977); Fijalkowski, "L'arte e gli artisti italiani alla corte di Jan III Sobieski," in *Polonia—Italia, relazioni artistiche dal medioevo al XVIII secolo,* Biblioteca e Centro di Studi a Rome, Accademia Polacca delle Scienze (Wrocław/Warszawa: 1979), 83–116.

46. This date had been established on 22 September, at which time the judges in architecture were also chosen: Tomassini, de Rossi, and Menicucci (ASL, vol. 45, fol. 104; vol. 46, fol. 46).

47. ASL, vol. 45, fol. 106.

48. In an uncharacteristic lapse, or perhaps in a fit of pique at not being the orator himself, Ghezzi neglects to note the doctor's first name (he leaves a blank space as though there were no reason he *should* know the name) and his topic.

49. ASL, vol. 45, fols. 99, 108; vol. 47, fol. 47. Mattia de Rossi was the other *stimatore* for 1682.

50. Missirini, Titolo XCIII, 147; Hager, "The Accademia di San Luca and the Precedents of the Concorsi Clementini," *Architectural Fantasy and Reality,* 3; Alessandro del Bufalo, *Giovanni Battista Contini e la tradizione del tardomanierismo nell'architettura tra '600 e '700* (Rome: Edizioni Kappa, 1982). Contini's principal preoccupation at the time was the Loggia del Paradiso at the Benedictine monastery of Montecassino, his first major commission independent of Bernini (Braham/Hager, 11). Unlike his fellows, Fontana and de Rossi, Contini would not accept the role of *principe* again until 1719, when it was offered him in token of a long and by then distinguished life. He would never demonstrate the academic ambitions that Bernini's other two successors made quite obvious.

51. ASL, vol. 45, fol. 114.

52. Appendix B, 1683, n. 3. In fact, Martinelli was expected to produce his own renderings of the lessons in architecture, as Tomassini had previously, to serve as his *dono accademico*. Tomassini had earlier been called to Naples in the temporary service of the Spanish viceroy (App. B, 1683, n. 2) to be replaced as treasurer by Agostino Scilla. He would return a few years later, but to a considerably diminished academy (see the subsequent text).

53. ASL, vol. 45, fol. 116; Missirini, Titolo XCIII, 147.

54. ASL, vol. 45, fol. 116; vol. 46, fol. 51.

55. The notes for the minutes as they were taken down in ASL, vol. 46, are in a hand different from Ghezzi's, and are almost indecipherable as a result. The minutes as transcribed into the permanent record (vol. 45) are more clearly written (now by Ghezzi), and are corrected for accuracy (Martinelli was called "Agostino" in vol. 46), but are still quite sparse. The conclusion is that Ghezzi himself was not in attendance throughout much of 1684, and may have fulfilled only the minimal duties of his post, the rest being delegated to an assistant.

56. ASL, vol. 45, fol. 119.

57. ASL, vol. 45, fols. 120–21; vol. 46, fol. 54.

58. ASL, vol. 45, fol. 122. Hamerani, perhaps an expatriate German, was also made master of ceremonies for the Feast of St. Luke. He became *Accademico di Merito* on 2 December (ASL, vol. 45, fol. 124).

59. Alaux, 33; *Corr.*, I, 67, n. 111.

60. Alaux, 35–36.

61. *Corr.*, I, passim; Wittkower (1973), 434. Bernini, Maratti, and Guidi are also mentioned specifically as guiding the efforts of French *pensionnaires* in painting and sculpture in 1680 (*Corr.*, I, 93, n. 163).

62. *Corr.*, I, 105–6, nn. 189–90.

63. Castan, 87–89; Alaux, 36; *Corr.*, I, 103, 128, nn. 188, 235.

64. *Corr.*, I, 71, n. 119.

65. *Corr.*, I, 88, n. 152; Lance, I, 139.

66. *Corr.*, I, 93–94, n. 164; Lance, I, 203–4; Blomfield, IV, 57, n. 1.

67. *Corr.*, I, 112, n. 203.

68. *Corr.*, I, 120–22, n. 227.

69. Blomfield, IV, 49, n. 3.

70. Lance, I, 108; Blomfield, III, 147.

71. Mignard would eventually have LeBrun's position as director of the academy when the latter died in 1690. To qualify for the office, however, he had to be promoted into the academy and up through the ranks, by royal authority (Blunt [1973], 352–53; Pevsner, 103).

72. Alaux, p. 36; Lance, I, 254–55; Thieme/Becker, IV, 12; *Corr.*, I, 144, n. 241.

73. *Corr.*, I, 129–41, n. 239.

74. He is buried in St. Luigi dei Francesi, though his will (Bertolotti, 83–86) requested that he be interred in SS. Trinità dei Monti, the church of the French Trinitarians. A traditional and pious man, Errard dispensed his wealth to relatives and religious houses in France and Rome rather than to the academies, to which he had otherwise dedicated his life but where his efforts over two decades had apparently come to nothing by the time of his death. *Corr.*, I, 183–84, n. 285.

75. *Corr.*, I, 144–45, n. 242.

76. *Corr.*, I, 126, 128, nn. 228, 237.

77. *Corr.*, I, passim. The academy was reimbursed for its expenses in 1685 to a total of 45,483 *livres* (Ibid., 153, n. 254). The following year the total was down to 37,000 *livres* (Ibid., 159, n. 265).

78. Pevsner, 104.

79. *Corr.*, I, 176, n. 276.

80. *Corr.*, I, 151–52, n. 250. The source is a letter from the cleric Dom Michel Germain in Rome to Dom Placide Percheron, 2 October 1685.

81. *Corr.*, I, 153–54, nn. 255, 259.

82. La Teulière cleverly circumvented the ordinance for a time by using English ships, which were not, apparently, as direly affected.

83. Domenico Guidi seems also to have suffered from the shift in the affections of the French. Twice in 1688 he was forced to recall to them the contract they had made for his Versailles group, which had been dispatched to Paris, but for which he had not yet received full payment. The matter was eventually settled in November (*Corr.*, I, 177–83, nn. 278, 281, 283), after which French commissions no longer came to Italian artists by way of the Académie.

84. *Corr.*, I, 169, n. 271.

85. *Corr.*, I, 177, n. 279.

86. Anatole de Montaiglon, *Procès-Verbaux de l'Académie Royale de Peinture et Sculpture* (1875), II, 310. Patronage appointments continued as well, of course.

87. *Corr.*, I, 203–5, nn. 301, 303.

88. *Corr.*, I, 204, n. 302.

89. *Corr.*, I, 189, n. 289.

90. *Corr.*, I, 182, n. 282.

91. *Corr.*, I, 209–10, n. 307. Later in this same letter from La Teulière to Villacerf (212–13), the former qualifies the value of this sort of copying, stating that it would be too intimidating for any but the most advanced students. As such, he feels that they would learn just as well from more recent work executed under the patronage of French kings. It was common practice for La Teulière to denigrate the achievements and abilities of the Italians, while working so hard at the same time to maintain a French presence among them. His servility in this is only another indication of his costly lack of confidence in his position, brought on by inexperience.

92. ASL, vol. 45, fol. 71; vol. 46, fol. 28.

93. The reverse of Martinelli's plan bears the numeration "15" put there by the secretary to identify what was meant to be an anonymous submission (App. A, no.10), though one submission could hardly have been anonymous. Since this number does not appear to indicate a field of at least fifteen competitors in architecture, it may include entries in other media or in the previous *concorso* (1677).

94. The date of "1679" inscribed on all three of Martinelli's drawings has been called into question by the fact that so many of the seventeenth-century *concorso* designs were incorrectly dated at the time they were labeled and entered into the *Rubrica,* or inventory of the archive, in 1756. This problem was tentatively corrected on the basis of better evidence, like the *verbali* and *soggetti,* by Professors Marconi, Cipriani, and Valeriani of the Accademia Nazionale di San Luca, in the appendix of the catalog *Architectural Fantasy and Reality* (1981, 166–69). Based on their reading of the *soggetto* in 1680 (App. B, 1680, n. 4), when Martinelli again took first prize, they argued that his drawings should be dated to that year since his design included the stipulated five altars and two towers at the facade. But this *soggetto* calls specifically for an hexagonal design, which Martinelli's is not, and so it seems more likely that it should be dated to the previous year, even though no text of that *soggetto* survives to corroborate this.

95. The eighteenth-century biography of Martinelli is still the most complete: Giambattista Franceschini, *Memorie della vita di Domenico Martinelli, sacerdote Lucchese e insigne Architetto* (Lucca: 1772). See also: Thieme/Becker, XXIV, 164; *DEAU,* III, 497–99. A definitive monograph on Martinelli has appeared in print just as the present study goes to press: Hellmut Lorenz, *Domenico Martinelli und die österreichische Barockarchitektur* (Vienna: Österreichische Akademie der Wissenschaften, 1991). Born in Lucca late in 1650, Martinelli, like Filippo Juvarra, was first ordained a priest (1673) and probably sometime shortly thereafter entered the Accademia's program in architecture at the usual age of 23 (1674). At that time Gregorio Tomassini was lecturer for the first time in architecture (see Chapter I). The following year Carlo Fontana, who would later take Martinelli into his studio (1678), was lecturer, but then Tomassini resumed the position between 1676 and 1678. Menicucci's

brief instructorship (1679) would have meant little to Martinelli, and thus the greater impression on his early training would have been made by Tomassini.

96. Of course, Martinelli had Tomassini's lessons readily available as a resource, but rather than simply copying he did produce an entirely different set of drawings, using a different format, and included his own tract on geometry and terminology.

97. Wilhelm G. Rizzi, "Erganzungen zur Baugeschichte des Stadtpalais Lichtenstein in Wien—Bankgasse," *Österreichische Zeitschrift für Kunst und Denkmal,* 31 (1975), 57–63; Zdenek Kudelka, "Zur Frage der Beziehung des D. Martinelli zu J. B. Fischer von Erlach," *Sbornik Praçi Filozoficke Faculty Brnenske University,* Ser. F, 23–24 (1979–80), 47–60; Hellmut Lorenz, *Liechtenstein Palaces in Vienna* (New York: The Metropolitan Musuem of Art, 1985), 11–15. The dome of Martinelli's *concorso* design (Pl. 12) may already show the influence of the Bernini circle, as it is of a kind with the dome of G. B. Contini's Cappella d'Elci in S. Sabina (1671, Fig. 135).

98. Hautecouer, II, 94–97; Blomfield, III, 125–26.

99. Hautecouer, II, 171–72.

100. That the topic of towered and porticoed facades was very much in the air in Paris during the last decade of LeVau's life can be illustrated by a development in English architecture. Wren's facade of St. Paul's conforms to that type, and as it happens his only direct experience of European ideas came in 1665 when he was in Paris and became intimate with the French architectural establishment, especially LeVau. The tendency in the past has been to explain the colonnaded loggias of the London facade as derivatives of the East front of the Louvre, but it would be more appropriate to expect issues of ecclesiastic architecture to inform him in this instance. He could still have been introduced to those issues, and indeed to possible solutions, on his trip to Paris, which taught him so much of the rest of his eclectic vocabulary.

101. Blomfield, IV, 108–12; Hautecoeur, III, 362–66. The absence of the pediment in Servandoni's facade may be fortuitous. It could have been deleted by the architects who completed his work above the second cornice after 1745, but it is also true that this assumption is based on earlier designs of his own that Servandoni himself may have preempted. In any case, Blomfield's criticism

that St.-Sulpice is devalued by the loss of the pediment is true only from his quite puristic classicist standpoint.

102. Braham/Hager, 14. See also Chapter IV.

103. Even so, Martinelli's elevated status within the Accademia was not guaranteed, for upon his return he immediately ran afoul of Carlo Fontana's son Francesco, who was not only his father's favorite but the real power behind the principate of the aged Maratti (see Chapter V). Perhaps jealous of what his rival had achieved in his absence, Martinelli put himself at odds with Francesco in 1706 with regard to one of the Accademia's more heated controversies. Martinelli was instructor in architecture in June when the congregation resolved to bar competitions in the third class "a cagione dell'insolenze ogni anno fatte nelli Palazzi, e Chiese con scandali e resentimenti grandi" (ASL, vol. 46A, fol. 57). It seems that the freshman competitors were chafing at the idea of copying rather than creating for their part in the *concorsi,* and were expressing their aggravation in an unseemly fashion. This debate will be more fully developed in Chapter IV. Francesco, who had been absent when the resolution was passed, tried to overturn it by his authority as *vice-principe,* as he felt it to be prejudicial to the advancement of young architects, for whom competition in the third class was now essential. The rest of the membership, including Martinelli, argued vehemently against his intervention in the matter, until Ghezzi proposed petitioning the pope, Clement XI, for his ruling as the ultimate authority. On 9 July (fol. 59), Ghezzi reported that the pope favored Francesco, and he, Ghezzi, and Maratti proceeded to define new topics for the third class for 1707 (in architecture it was to be a rendering of the facade of the Palazzo Barberini: Marconi et al. [1974], I, 8). When these were posted, and students were taking note of them, Martinelli happened in and was immediately engaged in a violent (drunken?) argument first with them, and then with academicians who tried to subdue him after he had removed and destroyed the *soggetti.* Martinelli was of the faction, presumably a majority, who were appalled at student conduct in the matter and the idea of their dictating policy, and who had opposed Francesco's decision to appease them. But regardless of how much support Martinelli or his motives might have had (and it included that of the *principe,* Maratti) his passionate methods condemned him. He was censured by the congregation, and given the maximum punishment for his behavior: a three-year suspension. By the time he was reinstated in September of 1709 (fol. 108), Francesco Fontana had been dead for a year, and Martinelli could peacefully resume his post as lecturer in architecture and perspective.

104. The drawing in question is in volume IX (fol. 8) of the Martinelli collection in the Civico Gabinetto dei Disegni in Milan. As his lecture notes in architecture would become his *dono,* and since the Accademia was already in possession of his earlier prizewinning entry, there would have been less reason to retain the competition design for 1680 and it could easily have been returned to the hands of the artist. Also among the same drawings in Milan is a plan for a hexagonal church (vol. I, fol. 11), but it is not worked out to a degree suitable for competition and does not otherwise correspond to Figure 67.

105. In the interest of being thorough, there was one architect, Bernardo Vittone of Piedmont, who passed through the Accademia as a student (1732) and later made use of a hexagonal plan for his first church, the Sanctuary at Vallinotto (1738–39). Exercises using hexagonal geometries may have been a routine part of his and other students' experiences at the Accademia, and may have been a point of departure for him. But there is in his mature work more of Guarini, whose treatise he edited and published (1737), than of the Accademia, and the hexagon more probably was influenced by his predecessor's mathematical approach.

106. See note 94. Faced with the inconsistencies of date and theme, and the fact that di Leti was not listed as a prizewinner in any year, Drs. Marconi, Valeriani, and Cipriani chose simply to delete di Leti's project from their revised "catalog." Dr. Cipriani was herself aware of the close association between his project and the *soggetto* of 1680, and so it is hoped they will accept the redefinition of di Leti's submission as a *dono,* which is respectfully proposed herein.

107. ASL, vol. 45, fol. 85; vol. 46, fol. 36.

108. The *verbali* make no mention of di Leti submitting a *dono* during the following year, though the *dono* of a painter nominated with him was recorded in July (ASL, vol. 45, fol. 92). See note 112.

109. ASL, vol. 45, fol. 165; vol. 46, fol. 87. Whatever

this *dono* was, di Leti felt compelled in July of 1696 to present another in its place: a reliquary in gilt wood which he had decorated as assistant to Tomassini, who presented it to the congregation along with one of his own. This one entry in the *verbali* is enlightening on several points about di Leti, who is a very poorly documented architect. He appears to have had a craft orientation to his art, and even in cabinet work he was still second to Tomassini as late as 1696. It would also appear that he was not himself entirely pleased with the work he had done on his first *dono*, and wanted to replace it with something that might better withstand the scrutiny of his peers. The date of 1680 for di Leti's induction into the Accademia was perpetuated by Thieme/Becker (XXIII, 139) on the basis of earlier incomplete readings of the *verbali*, but it applies in fact only to his induction into the Congregazione dei Virtuosi.

110. Alfonso Gambardella, *Architettura e Commitenze nello Stato Pontificio tra Barocco e Rococo: un amministratore illuminato Giuseppe Renato Imperiali*, Studi e Testi di Storia e Critica dell'Arte, vol. XII (Napoli: Società Editrice Napoletana, 1979), 106, 185–87. Gambardella is not a completely reliable source (he impossibly dates di Leti's *birth* to 1680), but the evidence of the inscription *in situ* on which the attribution is based is irrefutable. He also makes use of the Imperiali archive for his documentation; that family was di Leti's only significant source of patronage. Di Leti died on 8 December 1711.

111. *Ordini dell'Accademia* … (1609), 32.

112. The painter nominated with di Leti was accepted into membership within the year. The targets of the crackdown were apparently the architects, di Leti and Pioselli, and the actions of the Accademia were enough of a discouragement to the latter that nothing more is mentioned of him in the *verbali* after 12 October 1681 (ASL, vol. 45, fol. 94; vol. 46, fol. 42) when the two of them were rebuked by the membership for failing to submit their *doni*.

113. ASL, vol. 45, fol. 177; vol. 46, fol. 97; vol. 46A, fol. 12.

114. Much the same could be said of Francesco Fontana and his church of the SS. Apostoli in Rome, which was his only independent accomplishment prior to his death in 1708.

115. Even though the *verbali* required that at least four students compete in each class for there to be a prize (App. B, 1681, n. 3), this stipulation may not after all have carried much weight, and such numbers cannot be verified for the *concorso* in architecture. On the reverse of Plate 17 (see App. A), Carapecchia's entries are labeled "no. 19." Since nineteen students could not have been available to compete in architecture in 1681, this probably refers to a consecutive numbering system inclusive of entries in painting and sculpture, as had been the case in the earlier competitions. In the final analysis, it is impossible to say whether any architect other than Carapecchia competed in 1681.

116. L. Pascoli, *Vite dei pittori, scultori, ed architetti moderni* (Rome: 1730–36), II, 549. Pascoli was particularly enthusiastic about Carapecchia's drafting ability. Autographed examples of his work in pen and ink still survive in collections of his master's folios (like those at Windsor Castle: Braham/Hager, 21–22, nn. 468–470). His hand is otherwise largely indistinguishable from the uniformly high quality of work produced by all draftsmen under Fontana's tutelage. His *concorso* design, for example, displays the sepia line and gray wash technique common to his school, and is indeed rendered admirably.

117. The nearest parallel is the Palazzo Pamphili on the Piazza Navona (1645–50, Fig. 2), which just happens to be another of Carlo Rainaldi's buildings, as was S. Agnese, the church that inspired the *soggetto* in 1677. Carapecchia's belvedere was brought into line with the general Berninian sense by including a perspectively splayed arch motif in the arcading of its three bays. In spirit this is similar to Bernini's treatment of the uppermost story of the facade of the Palazzo Barberini (Fig. 114), and to the outside bays of Fontana's facade of S. Rita (1665, Fig. 86). The belvedere was apparently mandated by the *soggetto* in 1681, but it has a rather detached appearance in Carapecchia's drawing, due to its coarser rendering, as though it were an afterthought.

118. R. W. Berger, "Antoine LePautre and the motif of the drum-without-dome," *JSAH*, 25 (1966), 165–80.

119. Berger, 173. The alternative design by Rainaldi for the Louvre, which to Colbert expressed the image of a "closed" crown in its central mansarded pavilion, was preferred by him to Bernini's because that form related more directly to the crown of France. This was a typically supercilious com-

ment, and may have had nothing to do with any serious emblematic purpose he might already have formed for the Louvre. Still, Berger traces the rhetoric of the "crown" motif to this point.

120. Another was for Prince Eugene: the Schloss Rackeve (1702) near Budapest. Hildebrandt's patron in this instance chose a mansarded central pavilion for the executed design, since this form was analogous to the Imperial crown which he had so heroically served in the wars with the Turks and the French. See also: Bruno Grimschitz, *Johann Lucas von Hildebrandt* (Wien: 1932), 21–30, Figs. 8, 18.

121. Aurenhammer, 98; Hellmut Lorenz (1979), op. cit. In his article, Lorenz is the first to make the connection between Fischer and the *concorsi* Accademici, which he also does with respect to the competition in 1677 (see Chapter II, n. 160).

122. Aurenhammer, 22. Fischer accompanied Philipp Schorr (and perhaps Gregorio Tomassini; see previous text) to the court of the new Spanish viceroy in Naples no earlier than 1683. From there he left for Vienna in 1685.

123. Cf. Germain Boffrand's *château* La Malgrange, and works by Boullée and Ledoux (Berger, 178). Ledoux's *L'architecture considerée* (1804) revitalized interest in the "drum-without-dome" for Neo-classical purposes, but even so it is awkward to use this to explain the appearance of the motif in exactly contemporary projects, like Giuseppe Bonomi's Rosneath House (1802–6) in England. See John Harris, *The Architect and the British Country House: 1620–1920* (AIA: 1986). Bonomi was born in Rome, attended the Collegio Romano, and was a student of Marchese Teodoli, a lecturer in architecture at the Accademia in the late 1700s. That the circular rooftop belvedere he envisioned for Rosneath is nearly identical to Carapecchia's version suggests that he, too, may have had a direct experience of the Accademia's archive to draw upon.

124. It is well that the record can now be set straight as far as the relationship between Carapecchia's two drawings and these later projects are concerned. His entry, though accurately dated 1681, has been erroneously labeled a second-class project (App. A, no. 16) by the same archivist who misdated many of the seventeenth-century drawings in 1756 (see n. 94). This step was taken because the archivist had also mistakenly dated the palace designs from the *concorsi* of 1691 and 1696 to

1681 (Marconi et al. [1974], nn. 41–55). Because his project was indeed smaller in scale than the others, and consisted of only two facade drawings, it would have appeared to be a second-class entry by comparison. But in fact, as the subsequent text will show, his project was ancestral to the others, and not their inferior.

125. Munshower (1981), 33.

126. Carlo Stefano's employment of the domeless drum was repeated substantially without change by the winner of the first prize in the first class of architecture in 1707, Filippo Vasconi (Marconi et al. [1974], nn. 174–77), for a garden villa on an island in a lake. Here the motif reaches a dead end, and would not continue in use in Italian architecture beyond the death of Carlo Fontana.

127. Braham/Hager, 176–77; John Varriano, "Martino Longhi the Younger and the Facade of San Giovanni Calibità in Rome," *Art Bulletin,* 52, No. 1 (March 1970), 71–74. The date for Carapecchia's facade and a restoration of the church is 1711. See also: L. Heutter and R. Montini, *San Giovanni Calibità,* Chiese di Roma Illustrate, vol. 37 (Rome: 1956).

128. It is also unfortunate that Marconi et al. (1981, p. 167), missed the *verbali's* reference to Reissner's having won the first prize in this year (ASL, vol. 45, fol. 105; App. B, 1682, n. 5), and called into question the *Rubrica* of 1756, and the labels on the drawings, which conferred this honor on him. They may have been misled by the different spellings of Reissner's name that appear in these documents ("Raisner" and "Reizner" respectively), having themselves settled on the form of "Reitzner." For the purposes of this paper, the spelling used by contemporary Polish scholarship based on documents from that country (see n. 130) will be used, without, it is hoped, adding to the confusion.

129. An inventory of the Accademia's archive from 1682–83 (the same referenced in App. B, 1683, n. 1), lists two paintings then in their possession by recently admitted Polish artists: an allegory of Painting by Giorgio Simonnovich (Jerzy Eleuter Szymonowicz-Siemiginowski, first-class/first-prize winner in painting in 1681, and *Accademico di Merito* as of 6 September 1682; ASL, vol. 45, fol. 103), and a John the Baptist by Reissner.

130. See all references in previous note 45, and Adam Milobedzki, *Architektura Polska XVII Wieku* (Warsaw: 1980), II, 387, 404–5. If Reissner had

reached the prescribed age of thirty upon receiving membership in 1682, he may have been born in 1652: his death came in 1713. At Wilanów, he and the other decorators were under the direction of Stefan Szwaner, a student of Andreas Schluter. An unattributed quadratura ceiling in the "Stanza Silente" at Wilanów (Fijalkowski [1979], p. 100) depicting an illusionistic cupola could be Reissner's. He may also have filled in time as a surveyor and geographer (Thieme/Becker, XVIII, 144–45), but no architecture has been attributed to him.

131. The dome fresco indicated in the section, depicting the Fall of the Rebel Angels, is in fact one of the most original aspects of his design. It was an iconography only recently popularized by Milton's *Paradise Lost* (1667), and had as yet no precedence in the visual arts. It must have been an early ambition of Reissner's to create such a ceiling when the opportunity arose, so much so that he included it here in disregard of the general iconography of the Community of Saints to which the church is manifestly dedicated.

132. This was no doubt a wise strategy. At Wilanów, for example, the majority of the painters and stuccodors with whom Reissner worked were Italian and French (Milobedzki, II, 405). It was only his cosmopolitan training that separated him from the native craftsmen whom the foreigners had otherwise supplanted. While such practical motivations may have operated in determining Reissner's two-sided training, it is also true that Andrea Pozzo's style, consisting of a unity of thinking applied to real and painted architecture, would later have considerable influence in Poland. See: Jerzy Kowalczyk, "Andrea Pozzo e il tardo Barocco in Polonia," *Barocco Fra Italia e Polonia,* ed. Jan Slaski (Warsaw: Polish Academy of Science, 1977), 111–29. Perhaps Reissner in some way anticipates the advent of this taste.

133. Brian Knox, *The Architecture of Poland* (New York: Praeger Publishers, 1971), 138–39.

134. Pompeo Ferrari, first-prize/first-class winner in 1694 and 1696 (see Chapter IV), would be able to turn his equivalent experience and Italian patrimony into quite a successful career in Poland after the turn of the century.

135. The vault over the main altar mimics the form of the truncated dome introduced in the *concorso* of 1677 (see Chapter II), though of oblong plan, to support a lantern of rather curious shape.

136. Fontana's facade for the church of the Jesuit sanctuary at Loyola in Spain (see Chapter IV and Fig. 96) is similarly planned, but as it is of only one story it is less pertinent to Reissner's design. Still, it had been conceived only a year prior to Reissner's participation in the *concorso* of 1682, and was one of Fontana's most important commissions at the time.

137. The shrine which Reissner indicated at the center of the nave of his church (though only in plan) may be a link to Fontana's concentrically planned project for the Colosseum church (cf. Fig. 17).

138. Where militantly Catholic Poland would not have favored such a translation from Eastern Orthodox models a century before, in its decline as a European power it was increasingly subject to Russian (and Prussian) political and cultural influence.

139. V. Z. Rewski, "Rysunki architektoniczne z Polski w Mediolanie," *Bjuletin historii sztuki y kultury,* 9 (1947), 138; Fijalkowski (1979), 110. Fijalkowski raises the interesting possibility that Martinelli actually visited Jan III's court at Wilanów, and perhaps himself advised on the addition of the belvedere (n. 133).

140. ASL, vol. 45, fols. 102, 104. It had been two years since the *concorso* was celebrated on time. The judges were Tomassini, Mattia de Rossi, and G. B. Menicucci.

141. ASL, vol. 45, fol. 107; vol. 46, fol. 47.

142. This della Greca's association with the Accademia suggests he was somehow related to Felice, who was lecturer in Architecture in 1676 but died a year later, and through him to Vincenzo della Greca, who was also a papal architect and a pupil of G. B. Montano. R. Lefèvre, "Due architetti Siciliani a Roma nel 1600: I della Greca," *Studi Meridionali,* 4 (1971), 387. See also note 8.

143. ASL, vol. 45, fol. 125; vol. 46, fol. 55.

144. Braham/Hager, 11–12.

145. Missirini, Titolo XCIV, 148.

146. ASL, vol. 45, fol. 132; vol. 46, fol. 59.

147. ASL, vol. 45, fols. 137–39.

148. Domenico Ruberti, possibly a relation of Mattia de Rossi's, was accepted into membership as a perspective artist on 3 October 1688. Both Missirini (p. 148) and the *verbali* (ASL, vol. 45, fol. 142; vol. 46, fol. 64) put an inordinately large

emphasis on this accomplishment for its own sake.

149. ASL, vol. 45, fol. 144.

150. It is even possible that de Rossi took over the duties of instructor, though Tomassini was available and would be back in that position by the following year.

151. Tomassini and Domenico Ruberti (n. 148) were the judges in architecture. ASL, vol. 45, fol. 151.

152. This despite the fact that he was singled out by Pascoli (*Vite*, I, 330) as a distinguished contemporary. Nina Mallory's otherwise comprehensive dissertation on Roman architects of the early eighteenth century (op. cit. [1965]) does not mention him at all though it is illustrated by some of his works. An appreciation of Barigioni's worth does not expand beyond the scope of the biographical dictionaries (see n. 153) until Tod Marder's "Piazza della Rotonda e la fontana del Pantheon: un rinnovamento urbanistico di Clemente XI," *Arte Illustrata*, 7 (1974), 310–20. Barigioni is given lengthy mention and illustration in Alfonso Gambardella's book on Imperiali patronage (op. cit. [1979], 76–86). Not until 1983 was what amounts to a monograph on Barigioni published by Bianca Maria Santese as *Palazzo Testa Piccolomini alla Dataria: Filippo Barigioni architetto romano* (Rome: De Luca, 1983).

153. Thieme/Becker, II, 497.

154. H. Hager (1970), 54, n. 88. Hager was the first to call attention to the discrepancy between the dates on the drawings from the *concorsi* Accademici and their apparent chronology.

155. He was a saddler, in fact (Santese, 118).

156. ASL, vol. 45, passim. An Antonio Barigioni won second prize in the first class of painting in 1692 (ASL, misc. docs., Secolo XVII). Two of the goldsmiths in attendance in February of 1694 (ASL, vol. 45, fol. 156) were Domenico and Francesco Barigioni, who may have been Filippo's brothers (Santese, 118, n. 19).

157. Braham/Hager, 23. The Fontana studio commonly used color for coding plans, but rarely used it for pictorial purposes.

158. Hager (1970), 54.

159. Werner Oechslin, "Il soggiorno romano di Bernardo Antonio Vittone," *Atti del Convegno:*

Bernardo Vittone e la disputa fra classicismo e barocco nel Settecento (Turin: 1972), I, 413–39.

160. Wittkower (1973), 395. The palace designs were engraved, annotated, and presented to Charles III by Luigi Vanvitelli as *Dichiarazione dei disegni del Reale Palazzo di Caserta alle Sacre Reale Maestà di Carlo Re della due Sicilie e di Gerusalemma* (Napoli: 1756).

161. Wittkower (1973), 397–98. Cesare de Seta connects the interior wings of Caserta to Rome in the 1690s via Carlo Fontana's projects for the Liechtenstein garden palace: "I disegni di Luigi Vanvitelli per la Reggia di Caserta ed i progetti di Carlo Fontana per il Palazzo del Principe di Lichtenstein," in *Architettura, Ambiente, e Società a Napoli nel '700* (Torino: Einaudi Editore, 1981). The reference to Fontana, eventually head of the Accademia and Barigioni's master, comes close to the mark. Also, the Liechtenstein project will prove to have significant effect on the *concorso* of 1696, the year it was on the drawing board (see Chapter IV), and on much else that follows. But in all other respects, as well as the radiating wings, the greater precedent for Caserta belongs to Barigioni's project of 1692.

162. Barigioni's facade project for S. Giovanni is illustrated in: Elizabeth Kieven, *Ferdinando Fuga e l'architettura romana del settecento* (Rome: Multigrafica Editrice, 1988), 83–84, Fig. 96; Kieven's monograph on Alessandro Galilei and the competition for the Lateran facade is due for publication as this book goes to print.

163. Santese, 190.

164. ASL, vol. 45, fol. 153.

165. ASL, vol. 45, fol. 154. Tomassini was again appointed to lecture in architecture. To hold down the expense, instead of draped and nude models being provided simultaneously, for example, they would each be available for half of the time allotted for posing (ASL, vol. 45 fol. 156; vol. 46, fol. 76).

166. ASL, vol. 45, fol. 154; vol. 46, fols. 72–73.

NOTES TO CHAPTER IV

1. It should be recalled at this point that Mattia came to the office of *principe* both times by acclamation, while Fontana came to his first tenure by default (see Chapter III).

2. See the subsequent text, and in particular his references to Mattia in his volume on the history of St. Peter's: *Il Tempio Vaticano e sua origine* (Rome: 1694).

3. Fontana had, since Alexander VII's reign, been an assistant to Bernini on the Piazza di S. Pietro, and both *misuratore* and *stimatore* for the *Fabbrica* of the Vatican (Braham/Hager, 8), and as such was also a legitimate heir to Bernini's position there. Whether he could see it or not, the lion's share of Bernini's studio which he inherited was by far the more important legacy, however.

4. Braham/Hager, 34.

5. Projects for the font itself had already been commissioned from Fontana by Alexander VIII in 1690, but nothing came of this (Braham/Hager, 39).

6. Braham/Hager, 39–40; *Corr.*, I, 269, 434–35, nn. 337, 445.

7. Braham/Hager, 44. Fontana's first projects did not go without criticism from the pope, who did not appreciate their expense. The decision on his part late in 1693 to incorporate an antique porphyry basin as the font for the chapel superseded all of its earlier history, however, by requiring the complete reworking of the design, but by then Fontana was fully in charge.

8. *Corr.*, I, 451, n. 641. For Théodon's connection with the Accademia, see Chapters II and III.

9. It was not quite this way with the Romans, who still complained that there were "northern artists" (meaning perhaps either their origin or stylistic affiliation) at work on the baptistry (Braham/Hager, 42).

10. Carlo Fontana, *Descrizione della nobile Cappella della Fonte Battesimale in S. Pietro* (Rome: 1697). A more comprehensive report made by Fontana in 1704 is published in Braham/Hager (46–51).

11. Braham/Hager, 1–4. There is an even larger body of images compiled by Fontana in anticipation of publication (the thirteen volumes of drawings housed at Windsor Castle for a start) than were ever in fact published. As for Palladio, three of his *Four Books of Architecture* (1570) illustrated his own designs or studies after the antique, while only one, the first, was devoted to the Orders.

12. *Corr.*, I, 259, n. 337. Already here La Teulière puts Fontana on an equal footing with Mattia de Rossi as one of "les deux plus habiles Architectes de Rome."

13. *Corr.*, I. 434–35, n. 445. La Teulière begins his reference to the baptistry by mentioning Fontana's kinsman and antecedent at St. Peter's, Domenico Fontana, and his transportation of the Vatican obelisk for Sixtus V. It is this kind of information, along with the details of the baptistry competition (including payments made to Domenico Guidi), which La Teulière could most readily have had from Carlo Fontana's history. It is also illuminating to note that La Teulière words his remarks as though this were the first time Villacerf should have heard of Fontana.

14. *Corr.*, I, 434, 445–56, nn. 448, 466; Braham/Hager, 35.

15. *Corr.*, II, 10, 22, nn. 487, 494. La Teulière returned Fontana's slight by remarking that while Fontana's book may have been "bien imprimé pour ce pays" (the patronizing tone was typical and deliberate), it was not worth the asking price of twelve *écus*, which gave it a monetary value greater than Perrault's edition of Vitruvius, "qui est incomparablement plus charge d'ouvrage." *Corr.*, II, 34–37, n. 504. The relationship between Fontana and La Teulière was obviously not entirely amicable, but La Teulière placed some of the blame for high prices on the hostility of Roman merchants toward foreign customers, particularly the French. In any case, he refrained from buying the copy of *Il Tempio Vaticano* that he once thought to forward to Villacerf.

16. *Corr.*, II, 111, n. 568. His source at this point seems again to have been Lorenzo Ottoni, whose design for a medallion relief destined for the palace was included on the drawing.

17. *Corr.*, II, 113, n. 570.

18. Braham/Hager, 113. A later and more expanded report is given by Fontana in *Discorso sopra l'antico Monte Citatorio* (Rome: 1708).

19. Fontana's archeology turns out to have been faulty. Rather than the site having been occupied by ancient Roman law courts, it was (as revealed by excavations made as early as 1703) in fact dedicated to a funerary purpose: the *ustrina* of the Antonine dynasty. See Ernest Nash, *A Pictorial Dictionary of Ancient Rome,* 2nd ed. (London: Thames and Hudson, 1968), II, 487.

20. *Corr.*, II, 113, n. 570.

21. Braham/Hager, 114.

22. *Corr.*, II, 161, n. 634. A commemorative medal

for the *Dogana di Terra* was also dispatched to Paris the following year (Ibid., 243, n. 718), and then on 14 August 1696, two engravings of the *dogane* (Ibid., 256, n. 730).

23. *Corr.*, II, 204–5, n. 672.

24. Fontana's excuse for this lapse was that he had returned to his efforts at the promotion and publication of his Colosseum researches and designs (perhaps in anticipation of the upcoming Holy Year: see Chapter II and *Corr.*, II, 237, n. 712). Despairing of ever seeing the proofs for the theater, La Teulière forwarded engravings after the two customs houses instead (see n. 22), though "ne doutant point que le Cavalier Fontana n'en fasse graver d'autres qui seront mieux; je n'ay pas creu devoir les attendre, m'imaginant que vous (Villacerf) auries du plaisir de voir ces bastimens tels qu'ils sont."

25. One of La Teulière's rare, and inadvertently quite insightful, pronouncements on architecture came in a letter to Villacerf of 9 August 1696 (*Corr.*, II, 253–4, n. 728), in which he points to Greece as the ultimate source of what was good in architecture. He lifted this opinion from Jacob Spon's *Voyage d'Italie, de Dalmatie, de Grece, et du Levant fait aux années 1675 et 1676* (Lyon: 1678) as a rationale for his having effectively turned his back on architecture in Rome, ancient or modern.

26. Braham/Hager, 105.

27. Braham/Hager, 35–36. Augustus was said to have been moved to convert to Catholicism by the entries in Fontana's book which proved that the funds raised by selling indulgences, a spur to Luther's rebellion, truly did go to the enormous expense of rebuilding St. Peter's rather than to the lining of papal pockets. But a much greater inducement was the throne of Poland, for which he was a candidate in 1696 and to which only a Catholic nobleman could aspire.

28. Braham/Hager, 125–27; Hellmut Lorenz, "Carlo Fontanas Plane für ein Landschloss des Fürsten Johann Adam Andreas von Liechtenstein," *Jahrbuch der Liechtensteinischen Kunstgesellschaft,* Bd. 3 (1978–79), 43–88. The prince's request was quite specific with regard to the elements required for the palace, and they and the projects which Fontana generates will have some bearing on the *concorso* designs for 1696. See the subsequent text.

29. Braham/Hager, 129–31.

30. Fontana lost the first to his own student, Domenico Martinelli, who was the architect of the Liechtenstein palace in Vienna (see Chapter III). The second fell through on the death of its patron in 1700.

31. Braham/Hager, 133–34. The building may very well have been executed to these designs, though they were much altered by local workmen.

32. Braham/Hager, 114. Even in Rome, however, Fontana was often frustrated by the mercurial nature of his principal patron, Innocent XII, who could praise him for his ideas while condemning them for their expense, or raise his hopes for ambitious projects and then reduce their scope or find fault with trivial details. Fontana would even be passed over as architect to St. Peter's after Mattia de Rossi's death, in favor of the latter's brother, Domenico. Fontana was not awarded this distinction until 1697.

33. Riario may have first come in contact with Fontana in the entourage of Queen Christina, who while in Rome kept her residence and held her intellectual salons in his family palace. Braham/Hager, 183.

34. Documents both in and apart from the *verbali* (App. B, 1694, nn. 4, 5; Marconi et al. [1981], 168) establish that the ceremonies were, in fact, held on the Campidoglio in 1694. This belies the notion that the *concorso* of 1696 was the first to be celebrated there (G. Scano, "Insegnamento e concorsi," in *L'Accademia Naz. di S. Luca,* 33), or that the centenary celebrations in 1695 were the first time the Accademia was allowed the use of the great hall.

35. Appendix B, 1694, n. 5. All of those named, it will be noted, incidentally, are specified as Romans, and for three of them very little else is known. There is the possibility that one or more of them came to Fontana from Mattia de Rossi's studio, as the latter withdrew from the scene in 1694, but they conceivably would have had the same start there (cf. Barigioni, Chapter III). Fontana's workshop, large as it was and operated in many respects like a "school" or a traditional *bottega,* would have provided the more meaningful experience and quickly shaped their methods to conform to its own. By contrast, the crude methods of the other two prizewinners in the first class, the provincials Andrea della Valle and Carlo Ravassi, will more deeply underscore the advantages of a "Fontanesque" education. Ferrari's advanced

standing in 1694 suggests that he entered the architecture curriculum as early as Fontana's first principate in 1686–87, with the others joining him in succeeding years. See note 104.

36. H. Hager, "Carlo Fontana and the Jesuit Sanctuary at Loyola," *JWCI,* 37 (1974), 280–81. Hager, in collaboration with other authors, has, as the present volume goes to press, produced a full monographic study on the Loyola sanctuary: José Ramón Eguillor, S. J., Hellmut Hager, and Raffael Maria Hornedo, S. J., *Loyola, Historia y Arquitectura* (San Sebastián: Donostia, 1991).

37. Before judging Fontana too harshly, it should be remembered that the Accademia also had to accept Francesco's *soggetto,* and doing so was not entirely gratuitous. By such means the members acknowledged the stature of their *principe,* and his gift of the prizes, but they also recovered some of the value of the competition topic. The *soggetti* in 1681, 1682, and 1691 were too closely linked to the work of Bernini in palace and church design to advance those fields to any extraordinary degree. On the other hand, the motive behind the *soggetti* in 1677 and 1679, and again in 1694 and 1696, seems to have been exactly that.

38. Millon (1984), 15–16; V. Viale, ed., *Filippo Juvarra. Architetto e Scenografo* (Messina: 1966), 16–30. The shorter "life" is by Scipione Maffei (publ. 1738), and the longer possibly by Juvarra's brother, Francesco (publ. as anonymous by A. Rossi, 1874).

39. It should be noted that Fontana's drawings otherwise have a very "finished" quality to them: they are penned, signed, and accompanied by explanatory texts. In other words, they, too, are not the demonstrations produced for temporary audiences that lessons before Tomassini had been.

40. ASL, vol. 45, fol. 158; vol. 46, fol. 79. Filippo di Leti was called upon to act for Mattia in the event his failing health prevented him from participating. Indeed, di Leti had already appeared in Mattia's stead to present a set of vestments to the Accademia's church. It is not certain, therefore, that de Rossi was in fact among the judges on 10 October.

41. ASL, vol. 45, fol. 159; vol. 46, fol. 80. Fontana had thus finally been honored in the same way that Charles LeBrun and Mattia de Rossi had in earlier instances (see above). For an impression of the higher *personal* regard in which de Rossi was held by the Accademia, compare the eulogies

recorded in the *verbali* for him (ASL, vol. 45, fol. 162–63) and for Fontana (ASL, vol. 46A, fol. 165).

42. The year of the centennial was figured from 1595, the year in which Federico Zuccari's first statutes for the Accademia were approved, though its first meeting had been held nearly two years earlier (Pietrangeli et al., 12).

43. ASL, vol. 45, fols. 163–4.

44. Missirini, Titolo XCVII, 149–50.

45. Missirini, Titolo XCVIII, 150–53.

46. ASL, vol. 45, fol. 164.

47. G. Ghezzi, *Il Centesimo dell'anno MDCXCV celebrato in Roma dell'Accademia del Disegno* (Rome: 1696). The *relazioni* were published yearly only from 1702 to 1711, during the heyday of the *Concorsi Clementini* (see Chapter V). They were resumed again sporadically, as were the *concorsi,* a few years after the deaths of both Clement XI and Ghezzi in 1721.

48. If there was not a practical intent, there may have been a symbolic one, but in that sense the number "three," standing for the three visual arts, had more meaning for the Accademia. In 1705, when Francesco Fontana was still authoring *soggetti* (and Juvarra was winner of the first prize), the task in the first class was the design of a villa palace for *three* dignitaries, and Susan Munshower makes clear elsewhere the symbolic connection with the Accademia. The dignitaries in that case may have been the Accademia's *consiglieri,* its counselors in the affairs of the three arts it served and next in line to the *principe,* whose number in 1705 just happened to include Carlo Fontana. See Chapter III, note 24. The present author has also drawn attention (same note) to the point at the Accademia where a fourth discipline, mathematics, was added to the concept of the ideal academy to make the symbolism more convenient to a quadrilateral architecture, but this happens too late (1750) to have relevance for 1696.

49. Outside of the academic context, the project would more reasonably provide residence for individuals of higher rank, perhaps ambassadors.

50. Since the *soggetti* may this time have been established as much as a year in advance (Scano, 33), this expectation is all the less unreasonable.

51. ASL, vol. 45, fol. 166. Carlo Fontana and Antonio Valerii are also mentioned in Ghezzi's *relazione* (n.

47) as judges in architecture. The former may be taken for granted because of his station, but Valerii, who had been admitted to membership only four months earlier (ASL, vol. 45, fol. 164), may not have been more than an interested bystander.

52. The second-prize winner in the third class was inserted among the winners in the first class, a competitor not appearing on the judges' list (Giuseppe Rossi) was added to the winners in the second class but crossed out later, and Giuseppe Parà was mistakenly identified as competitor "M" in the third class. It is also of interest to note that the French prizewinner, Charles Derbais, had his name added to a blank space on this list later, in a different ink and hand. It may have taken some time to find out just exactly who he was.

53. ASL, vol. 45, fol. 166.

54. Missirini, Titolo XCVIII, 152–53. The medals are illustrated in: J. Varriano & N. Whitman, *Roma Resurgens: Papal Medals from the Age of the Baroque* (Ann Arbor: Ann Arbor Press, 1983).

55. ASL, vol. 45, fol. 167.

56. ASL, vol. 45, fol. 170. The date was 4 October 1697. The three were sworn in on 24 November, and their *doni* were submitted within the year (Bizzacheri's, a proposal for the facade of S. Carlo al Corso which was his own attempt at a fusion of styles, is the only one preserved: Marconi et al. [1974], II, n. 2098). At this same time, Fontana asked permission to construct a chapel in SS. Martina e Luca, but nothing came of this.

57. ASL, vol. 45, fol. 171; vol. 46, fol. 91. Unfortunately, there were no *concorsi* scheduled for the immediate future, and Tomassini's parting gesture would eventually be eclipsed when Clement XI diverted papal funds for the prizes for the *Concorsi Clementini* (see Chapter V).

58. ASL, vol. 45, fol. 173. The date was 14 September 1698. Baldi was acting as *vice-principe* in the absence of both Fontanas. There seems to have been an element at the Accademia awaiting just such an opportunity to break Carlo's stride.

59. ASL, vol. 45, fol. 175.

60. ASL, vol. 45, fol. 178. Giuseppe Ghezzi nearly participated in this "changing of the guard" at the Accademia, having asked permission to retire in January of 1699. Fortunately he was convinced to stay on as secretary, to the benefit of the coverage in the *verbali* and *relazioni* of the impressive

events at the Accademia during the reign of Clement XI (see n. 47).

61. Pevsner has enumerated the reasons for the decline of the French academies at this time in *Academies of Art,* 103–5.

62. The grant was doubled after the war, but it would be some time before it would return to or exceed the level of 6,000 *livres* it had reached under Colbert.

63. This is why D'Aviler's more pragmatic *Cours d'Architecture* could so immediately replace Blondel's in the affections of the Académie Royale (see Chapter II).

64. This is what was meant earlier in the text by the equation in this sense of Fontana and Hardouin-Mansart: Both had achieved a similar station for their workshops, but by different means and for different ends because of their different situations. By 1699, Hardouin-Mansart would be the supreme authority in Paris *de jure,* as *Surintendant des Bâtiments du Roi.*

65. *P-V,* II, 280–81.

66. *Corr.,* II, 10–11, 20–21, nn. 488, 491.

67. *Corr.,* II, 226, n. 313.

68. Guiffrey/Barthelemy, *Liste des pensionnaires,* 52.

69. In truth, La Teulière *had* to allow this just so they could survive. Pierre LeGros was the only one of the four who, in his subsequent and distinguished career as a sculptor in Rome, proved himself truly deserving of this recognition, however.

70. *Corr.,* II, 222–25, n. 312.

71. For example: *Corr.,* II, nn. 355, 360.

72. Glorified accountant that he was, La Teulière's principal evidence for the hostility of the Roman populace were the usurious rates of exchange often charged to the French by merchants when accepting their notes. La Teulière remarks on this in a large proportion of his letters, and indeed the rates seem to have fluctuated quite contemptibly (for example: *Corr.,* II, n. 469).

73. *Corr.,* II, n. 344. La Teulière bore the disgrace of his superiors in this incident, as the one who had to face papal chastisement for the slight to Maratti. La Teulière had not been responsible, but he was the one to make amends, and this obviously rankled. For his part, Maratti cannot entirely be blamed for playing the French against the pope to get what was due him.

74. *Corr.*, II, passim.

75. *Corr.*, I, 143–44. Montaiglon and Guiffrey rightly point out in this reference that though the articles of aggregation permitted such an expedient, it was not likely to happen. The principate was an annually elected post, while the directorship was an extended court appointment that would not have readily descended upon a foreigner.

76. *Corr.*, II, 21, n. 492. In this and later exchanges between Louis XIV and his ambassador in Rome, Cardinal Forbin-Janson (Ibid., nn. 501, 503), the king expressed his wish not to interfere with the pope's intentions. Here is a measure both of his willingness to bend for this pope (see Chapter III) and of his disdain for the fate of his academy in Rome.

77. *Corr.*, II, 23–24, nn. 495, 496. Elsewhere throughout his correspondence La Teulière complains of the sorry conditions prevailing at the academy. It seems the diligence of its students and administrators had made it quite rich in models and casts but the neglect of Paris had made it quite poor in its furnishings.

78. It is no proof against this that La Teulière makes no mention whatsoever of the Accademia in his letters to Paris; quite to the contrary it strengthens the premise. To have hinted at any collaboration with the Romans would only have further undermined his status with his superiors and led to the withdrawal of more support on the grounds that he could have it from others. Besides, with Colbert and LeBrun gone, it was unlikely that anyone in Paris, even the king, had a full recollection of what the aggregation had made possible. As long as La Teulière remained mute about contacts between the Accademia and his academy, even when a young French architect won a prize in the *concorso* of 1697 (see the text), he could take advantage of the aggregation accords, which were still on the books, after all, with no one at home the wiser about how he was able to cope. A great many of his own inadequacies could be covered up in this fashion. And at the same time the appearance of a functioning, if struggling, academy could be created to keep the attention of Paris.

79. *Corr.*, II, 10–11, n. 488.

80. *Corr.*, II, 25–31, n. 497.

81. *Corr.*, II, passim.

82. Wend Graf Kalnein and Michael Levy, *Art and Architecture of the Eighteenth Century in France,* The Pelican History of Art (Baltimore: Penguin Books, 1972), 239; Hautecoeur, III, 251; Blomfield, IV, 83–87. Typical for himself and for his day, Blomfield considered Oppenord to have misused his stay in Rome to perfect a style which would contribute to the advent of the Rococo, and therefore to the overthrow of his beloved French classicism. Historians since have been considerably more objective.

83. *Corr.*, I, 300, 335, nn. 354, 371. Oppenord shared an apartment nearby with other French students who were unattached to the academy. He was allowed to take meals at the academy, though, and to participate in the drawing classes, without a fee.

84. *Corr.*, I, 327, n. 365.

85. *Corr.*, I, 344, n. 370. La Teulière repeats this generalized assessment continuously, varying the wording only slightly, right up to his last report on Oppenord in 1699, to the new *Surintendant des Bâtiments,* Hardouin-Mansart (*Corr.*, II, 453, n. 967).

86. *Corr.*, II, 66, n. 532. He was then one of the four *pensionnaires,* soon to be three (he and the sculptors, LePautre and LeGros) with the departure of the painter Sarabat. The painters Favannes and St.-Yves, and the sculptor Fremin would be admitted in 1696, after the departure of LeGros. These five would then constitute the enrollment through 1698.

87. *Corr.*, II, 62, 153, nn. 528, 624. Villacerf was so out of touch with what Oppenord was up to in Rome, that he even required Oppenord to work at his handwriting and spelling, as if these skills were extremely important to his art (Ibid., 170, n. 647). His sketchbooks show him to have had a perfectly acceptable penmanship at this time.

88. *Corr.*, II, 84, n. 550.

89. *Corr.*, II, passim.

90. La Teulière was always sure that these would impress Villacerf and the king, but in the end they found them only "curious."

91. *Corr.*, II, 234–35, 247, nn. 709, 721. These sound suspiciously like the make-work occupations Colbert had devised to try to discipline D'Aviler in the 1670s (see Chapter II).

92. *Corr.*, II, 239–41, n. 716.

93. *Corr.*, II, 258, n. 732. Oppenord was even allowed to travel to Venice and Vicenza for three months in his last year in Italy, in order to check Palladio's monuments against the *Four Books*. This would have been unthinkable twenty years earlier, and indeed he would have found the favorite of the French academy to have been far less doctrinaire than his text. Oppenord also visited Florence, Bologna, Mantua, Verona, and other cities, to experience more of modern Italian architecture outside of the literature. Bramante, Sansovino, Giulio Romano, and Pirro Ligorio are architects specifically mentioned as having his attention in this regard (Ibid., 400–430).

94. This opportunity may have implications for other young French architects in Rome at this time. Jean Silvain Cartaud, a minor luminary of the Rococo, arrived in 1695 as just another cipher to Villacerf ("je ne sais pas sa profession": *Corr.*, II, 128, n. 589) and was never granted a pension. He stayed on in Rome, however, supported by his friend, the *pensionnaire* Fremin, and may have made his way to Fontana's studio in the hope of continuing his education on his own. Such action was more of a necessity for Thomas Laine and Jacques-Denis Antoine, who arrived in Rome in their teens (1696 and 1697 respectively; Ibid., nn. 703, 800) with little grasp of even the rudiments of their art. The Accademia or Fontana's studio were the only places they might have had access to remedial training, though Antoine seems to have attached himself to Oppenord as well (Ibid., n. 823, passim). The question of Charles Derbais's experiences in Rome, in the three years he was there before winning a prize in the *concorso* of 1697 (App. B, 1697, n. 1), will be considered in the subsequent text. A specific occasion for communication between Oppenord and Fontana came in 1698. Innocent XII had asked Cardinal de Bouillon, then ambassador for France, to look in on the restorations to the harbor of Anzio while on his way to his diocese in Albano (*Corr.*, II, 385–86, n. 894). The cardinal took Oppenord along to make a record of the progress on the repairs, which were Carlo Fontana's responsibility. Oppenord very likely, therefore, had been briefed for his trip by Fontana, and reported to Fontana on his return, as not even the pope could consider it politic to solicit an independent *foreign* assessment of a project by his own chief architect. That both the pope and the cardinal commented favorably on Oppenord's conduct shows how smoothly things went, presumably without ruffling Fontana's feathers.

95. *Corr.*, II, 440–42, nn. 958–59.

96. Kalnein/Levy, 239–40.

97. Braham/Hager, 43. The fact that Oppenord also used color to enhance his drawing—an unusual practice in France—with blue wash for the mirror, red for the mantel and chimney, and brown for the carpentry of the vaults, further suggests his familiarity with the methods of Fontana's studio, where tinted washes were employed for similar purposes (Ibid., 20).

98. Much the same action on Oppenord's part has been proposed earlier to connect the design history of the facade of St.-Sulpice in Paris to Domenico Martinelli's prizewinning project for 1679 (see Chapter III).

99. *Corr.*, II, 32, n. 499.

100. *Corr.*, II, 382, n. 890.

101. *Corr.*, II, 442–48, nn. 960–63.

102. Blomfield, III, 32. La Teulière died in Rome, unrequited and destitute, in 1702.

103. The only (but well-deserved) monograph on Ferrari, published in Poland just before World War II, has never been reprinted, and is extremely rare: Witold Dalbor, *Pompeo Ferrari, działalnosc architektoniczna w polsce* (Warsaw: 1938). Few sources since have made use of it, even though it was illustrated by a number of Ferrari's own drawings and provided a summary in Italian. Indeed, with the first flurry of interest in Polish architecture after the war, it was difficult for any scholarship to rise above the level of a survey: Stanislaw Szymanski, *Die Sakrale Kunst in Polen: Architektur,* Ars Christiana (1956); Zbigniew Dmochowski, *The Architecture of Poland* (London: Polish Research Centre, 1956); Jan Zachwatowicz, *Polnische Architektur bis zur Mitte des XIX.Jhs.* (Warsaw: Budownictwo i Architektura, 1956). The same was true even for more specialized investigations: Ladislao Tatarkiewicz, "Dodici generazione di architetti italiani in Pologna," *Palladio,* 7 (1957), 119–25. Eberhard Hempel took the first earnest scholarly look at the material for the seventeenth and eighteenth centuries in *Baroque Art and Architecture in Central Europe,* Pelican History of Art (Baltimore: Penguin Books, 1965), followed by Wladyslaw Tatarkiewicz, *Osztuce Polskiej XVII i XVIII Wieku: Architektura, Rzezba* (Warsaw: 1966), and Brian Knox, *The Architecture of Poland* (New York: Praeger Publishers, 1971). Not until 1980 was a com-

mendable specialized approach taken to the Polish Baroque, but it is in need of translation if it is to have the audience abroad that it deserves: Adam Milobedzki, *Architektura polska XVII wieku,* 2 vols. (Warsaw: 1980). An appropriate first step in this direction for eighteenth-century Polish architecture has recently been made: A. Milobedzki, "The Main Trends and Phenomena in Polish Architecture, 1697–1733," trans. Jerzy Dlutek, in *Polish Art Studies,* VII, Polskiej Akademii Nauk (Wroclaw: 1986) 27–33. The author's thanks are due Dr. Christine Challingsworth for her help with some of these references. An article on Pompeo Ferrari by the author is in volume 8 of Papers in Art History from The Pennsylvania State University, currently in press.

104. The author prefers a date circa 1670. This would put Ferrari in his twenties when competing in the first class in 1694 and 1696, which was more usual. It would also have been usual for him to join a workshop in his teens, i.e., in the late 1680s. If that workshop was Fontana's, as the subsequent text concludes, he may have joined both it and the classes at the Accademia during Fontana's first principate (1686–87). He would also, therefore, have had the benefit of Martinelli's and Tomassini's lectures.

105. Dmochowski, 262–63; Hempel, 141; Knox, 124.

106. Vittone's sketchbooks, which include copies of and variations on other projects (some by Fontana and Juvarra, for example), are housed in the Musée des Arts Décoratifs, Paris. They are the subject of an essay by R. Wittkower in *Studies in the Italian Baroque* (London: Thames & Hudson, 1974), 223–34.

107. Hellmut Hager points to one Borrominesque episode in Fontana's career, but he was younger then (ca. 1670): "Die Kuppel des Domes in Montefiascone zu einem borrominesken Experiment von Carlo Fontana," *RJK,* 15 (1975), 145–61. If Fontana later equated his more mature age with a classical dignity of style, this does not preclude his encouraging his own young students to strike out in other directions. In this he was distinct from Contini, who once severely derided a student for taking too much license from Borromini: Pascoli, *Vite,* II, 551–60.

108. He may still have been following a lead from Borromini in this. S. Agnese was to be increasingly identified with Borromini's name, to the exclusion of Rainaldi's, though his part was comparatively small.

109. A. Braham, "L'Église du Dome," *JWCI,* 23, nn. 3–4 (1960), 216–24.

110. Ferrari may have had recourse to Lejeune de Bellencourts's *Description Générale de l'Hostel Royal des Invalides* (1683), which reproduced Hardouin-Mansart's first project (it differed from the executed one primarily in the dome). But Ferrari's church has no indication of even that degree of familiarity. The gist of the plan of the dome may have been passed on to him through Nicodemus Tessin, the Swedish architect who had frequented Fontana's studio, the last time in 1687–88 just after a visit to France. His may in fact be the drawings done after Mansart's first project that are now in the Nationalmuseum, Stockholm. Tessin's activities in Paris, Rome, and northern Europe continually relate to subject matter raised in the *Concorsi Accademici* (see Chapter II, n. 173), since he, too, is a substantial thread tying the Late Baroque traditions of France and Italy together. In his own way, distinct from the academic relations highlighted in this volume, he personifies the same dialogue.

111. It is not even a structurally feasible whole. There is insufficient buttressing at the drum, or mass of masonry in the piers, to hope to carry the dome. This also shows up Ferrari's ignorance, this time of the static integrity of Mansart's design, and by contrast his greater success with the rest of the college, where the practicalities of construction are well considered.

112. Again, it is not surprising that in his correspondences La Teulière is mute on the subject of the *concorso* of 1694, and what it had to say about his academy's status relative to the Romans. The bearer could very well have been blamed for the tidings.

113. George Kubler, *Building the Escorial* (Princeton: Princeton University Press, 1982), Fig. 7. The fact that both della Valle and Ravassi submitted perspective views suggests they may have been training in this at the Accademia under Pier Francesco Garolli, lecturer in the subject since 1682 (ASL, vol. 45, fol. 104). Since he would be succeeded in this capacity after 1710 by worthies like Martinelli and Juvarra, it would not be surprising to find that it was he who professed to be able to instruct della Valle and Ravassi in architecture, but neither would it surprise to find him failing in it.

114. As there is no drum in Ravassi's church, it is also possible to link his design for it to the Sanctuary

of the Madonna in Mondovì, which had been begun by Ascanio Vitozzi in 1596 but was still incomplete. It may have formed part of Ravassi's experiences before leaving the north of Italy: Gil R. Smith, "Concorso Accademico of 1694," in *Architectural Fantasy and Reality,* 8–11. For that matter, della Valle's reference to Pietro da Cortona's church may have been his way of remembering his origins, as they were from neighboring towns in Tuscany.

115. Achievement in two successive first-class *concorsi* was still a requirement for admission to membership (see Chapter I). This would not change officially until the framing of the statutes of 1715.

116. Wittkower (1973), 112–14; see also Howard Hibbard, *Carlo Maderno and Roman Architecture, 1580–1630* (University Park, PA: 1971). In fact, Ferrari's reference to the Palazzo Barberini for his villa concept in a way verifies Hibbard's and Wittkower's assumptions about the nature of Maderno's design.

117. Sebastiano Serlio, *L'Architettura* (1537–51), Book III, fol. 18.

118. Braham/Hager, 125–27. Prince Liechtenstein's specific requirements for the project did not arrive in Rome until after Fontana had begun to rough out an idealized solution. Hiding under a flap on Fontana's proposed plan (Fig. 104) is another variation on his ideal, which he no doubt preferred, and which he perhaps hoped might influence the prince's decision. His dogged pursuit of such ideals may be what eventually cost him the commission to build.

119. In altering his design, Pacenti may have been responding to Fontana's commission from Liechtenstein, rather than to the *soggetto.* The prince had asked Fontana to provide for two sets of apartments on two separate floors, with only one two-story salon bridging them, and one grand vestibule and staircase, which describes Pacenti's revisions exactly. Pacenti seems also to have had the prince's stipulations in mind when he secured the site (with a precinct wall rather than a moat); when he positioned a clock tower over the stable wing in section and elevation; and when he added to his project the chapel (H) and gateway (C) that had been required only of the competitors in the lower classes. There are Germanic mannerisms in his design—the bulbous domes of the church towers crowned by imperial eagles and the herms supporting the colossal pilasters of the palace—

that again seem intended for Liechtenstein's eye. But since the prince's commission called for restraint in ornamentation, one has to wonder why Pacenti included so much figural sculpture above the first cornice when he had noticeably less talent for it.

120. Among the studies after Roman buildings in the Oppenord sketchbook at the Cooper-Hewitt Museum in New York, there is an original *pensiero* for a villa/*château* in a French style (fol. 19 verso). It is difficult to imagine any other reason why this design should appear among his Roman sketches, if it is *not* indeed his prelude to a competition entry in 1696. If that is what it is, it is unfortunate that he took it no further.

121. Milobedzki (1986); Knox, 124; Hempel, 141; Dmochowski, 306.

122. The addition of two stable wings of semicircular plan to the north of the palace at this later date does, coincidentally, bring the complex even closer in line with Ferrari's project in 1696. Knox, 126.

123. Catenacci was the son of a Comesque father (Giorgio) who came to Poland around 1660 (Knox, 122–24). He may not, then, have been Ferrari's senior by many years, but he did have more practical experience behind him. He had been cut off from the mainstream of Baroque architecture for all of his professional life, however, and so even Ferrari's youthful worldliness would have been a boon to his practice. Ferrari, on the other hand, needed to join a workshop in order to establish his credentials with the Polish guilds, lest noble patronage fail him, and in the end it was fortunate he had.

124. E. Bassi and J. Kowalczyk, "Longhena in Polonia: la chiesa dei Filippini," *Arte Veneta,* 26 (1972), 1–13. Construction was interrupted at Gostyn during the Northern War, and when work resumed in 1726 under Ferrari alone it was he who completed the cupola. Milobedzki, II, 414–16; Hempel, 71; Zachwatowicz, nn. 304, 305. Toward the end of his career, Ferrari inherited another project from Catenacci which must have been an occasion for *déjà vu.* For the Jesuit college in Poznan he was again involved on a complex identical in function to that of his *concorso* design for 1694. It was no preparation, however, since most of the work was complete before his arrival (1727), and only the entrance portal and high altar are attributed to him. Milobedzki, II, 416; Syzmanski, 363; Zachwatowicz, n. 300.

125. Knox, 125; Dmochowski, 261.

126. Zachwatowicz, n. 352. Zachwatowicz considered the Leszno church to be Ferrari's masterpiece. See the English edition of his researches: *Polish Architecture* (Warsaw: Arkady, 1967), 231–35.

127. Knox, 124–25; Dmochowski, 267.

128. Milobedzki, II, 411; Hempel, 141; Zachwatowicz (1956), n. 350.

129. Cathie C. Kelly, "Ludovico Rusconi Sassi and Early Eighteenth-Century Architecture in Rome," Diss., The Pennsylvania State University, 1980. Kelly's analysis leads up to the *Concorso Clementino* of 1702, in which Rusconi-Sassi again competed with Alessandro Rossini in the first class. Taken as a whole, then, their activities as students at the Accademia should all the more be associated with the Settecento, and less with the *Concorsi Accademici* (see Chapter V).

130. In this the author does not agree with Kelly that it is necessary to look deeply for precedents for Sperone's action (Kelly, 35–37). In fairness, she was working without benefit of the more accurate dating of the *Concorsi Accademici* that was available after 1981 (see Chapter III, note 92). Before that, Sperone's drawings were grouped together with the second-class winners from 1696 (Marconi et al. [1974], I, 3–4) since they all bore the erroneous date of 1679. Kelly was therefore being compassionate when she assumed that there must have been as much behind Sperone's first-prize design as there was behind the others (see subsequent text). This need no longer be the case, and in fact the church designs from 1696 will have to be considered as removed from Sperone's by more than just their date.

131. It may also be that he delved into the Accademia's archive of drawings to find a similar usage in Martinelli's project for 1679 (Pl. 12; see Chapter III, n. 95) to reinforce his choice. Carlo Rainaldi's architecture, specifically the cupola of S. Maria in Campitelli (1663–67), may be the ultimate source for all the examples mentioned (Kelly, 30), but this would also not be unexpected of the Accademia's students (see Chapters II and III).

132. Sperone had an undistinguished career, the only highlight of which was the Cappella S. Michele in S. Eustachio (1716–19; Portoghesi, 552). If anything, though, this is much more unremarkable than his *concorso* design. His work on some ephemeral architecture in 1727 is recorded in the Vatican archives (Kelly, 69, n. 68).

133. Ensuring their right to advance to a higher class may have been part of the reason Rossini and Rusconi-Sassi were both given a first prize in 1694. Filippo Ottoni will not advance to the second class until the *Concorso Clementino* of 1702, or to the first class until 1704, and so his history at the Accademia belongs even more to the next century.

134. According to his drawing, Sevalle was from Turin, and may therefore have been one of the students given access to the Accademia by its aggregation with the ducal academy in Turin in 1675 (see Chapter I). If so, he does not seem to have been well prepared for this venture, nor to have learned a great deal from it. In this he was not unlike Charles Derbais, and so his design became another convenient demonstration to the spectators in 1696 of what it meant to be Roman.

135. Blomfield, III, 210–11; Hautecouer, II, 636–41, Fig. 431.

136. Marconi et al. (1974), I, 5, nn. 72–81.

137. Thieme/Becker, XXIX, 75; *DEAU,* III, 345. Rossini may have done some work for the Odescalchi family before leaving Rome.

138. Kelly (1981), 15–16.

139. H. Hager, "Il modello di Ludovico Rusconi Sassi del concorso per la facciata di San Giovanni in Laterano (1732) ed i progetti a convessità centrale durante la prima metà del Settecento a Roma," *Commentari,* XXII (1971), 36–67; Kelly (1981), 103–10.

140. Kelly (1981), 129–52.

141. C. Kelly, "Rusconi Sassi, Ludovico," *MEA,* III, 620–21.

142. C. Kelly, "Accademico di Merito of 1724," in *Architectural Fantasy and Reality,* 157–61.

143. Kelly (1981), 166–95. Lengthy consideration of the design history of the facade of the Lateran basilica does not fit the purpose of this book. The reader is referred instead to Vincenzo Golzio, "La Facciata di S. Giovanni in Laterano e l'architettura del Settecento," *Miscellanea Bibliothecae Hertzianae,* XVI (1961), 450–63. Elizabeth Kieven's book on Gallilei, which will inevitably shed further light on the subject, is currently in press.

144. Susan Munshower, "Concorso Clementino of 1705," in *Architectural Fantasy and Reality,* 43–47.

145. Hager (1971), passim.

146. H. Hager, "On a Project Ascribed to Carlo Fontana for the Facade of San Giovanni in Laterano," *The Burlington Magazine*, 117 (1974), 105–9. James Gibbs, a student of Fontana's during the first decade of the eighteenth century, may have produced a copy of Fontana's competition design, which is now in the Ashmolean at Oxford. The competition had no result due to the untimely death of the pope in 1700.

147. Wittkower (1973), 240–42.

148. Kelly (1981), 15.

149. Bernadette Balco, "Concorso Clementino of 1704," in *Architectural Fantasy and Reality*, 17–29. Winner of the first prize in this year, the Pole Kaspar Barzanka brings a multifarious stylistic repertoire equivalent to Ferrari's back to Poland upon his return, learned at Carlo Fontana's feet: Jerzy Kowalczyk, "Andrea Pozzo e il tardo Barocco in Polonia," in *Barocco fra Italia e Polonia* (op. cit.) 111–29; Hempel, 141.

150. It could even be said that Jan Reissner's project introduced new motifs—a vault fresco based on Milton, or the domed expression around the cupola—under similar conditions. Cf. Pls. 18–20.

151. See Chapter III, n. 104.

152. The crucial significance of Filippo Juvarra's sojourn in Rome, and his learning experience under Carlo Fontana and the aegis of the Accademia, are fully considered in: Henry Millon, *Filippo Juvarra: Drawings from the Roman Period 1704–1714,* Accademia delle Scienze di Torino, Corpus Juvarrianum, Part I (Rome: Edizioni dell'Elefante, 1984); H. Hager, "Juvarra nella scuola di Carlo Fontana," in *Studi Juvarriani* (Rome: 1985).

153. Carboneri, *Superga,* 6–7.

154. Richard Pommer, *Eighteenth-Century Architecture in Piedmont* (New York: NYU Press, 1967), 23–35.

155. Pommer, 1–2.

156. Windsor F. Cousins, Jr., "Accademico di Merito of 1733," in *Architectural Fantasy and Reality*, 162–65; Werner Oechslin, *Bildungsgut und Antikenrezeption des frühen Settecento in Rom. Studien zum Römischen Aufenthalt Bernardo Antonio Vittones* (Zurich: 1972), 160–64.

1. Braham/Hager, 17–18.

2. Alaux, 31.

3. Pevsner, *Academies of Art,* 102.

4. Ibid., 104.

5. Scano, "Insegnamento e concorsi," in *L'Accademia Nazionale di S. Luca,* 33.

6. ASA, vol. 45, fol. 178. The date was 9 June 1700.

7. Braham/Hager, 15. Maratti himself was not entirely pleased with the honor. On occasion he even begged the pope to permit his retirement, for reasons of advanced age and overwork, but he was admonished by Clement that only God could release him from his responsibilities. ASL, vol. 45A, fol. 51.

8. Later on, Fontana could act through his son Francesco, who was Maratti's *vice-principe* after 1700, and in 1706 was given all of the failing Maratti's authority. When Francesco died in 1708, Carlo became *vice-principe,* with full administrative powers, but he was spiritually disinclined to exercise them. His son's sudden demise was a devastating blow.

9. Marconi et al. (1974), I, 5, nn. 63–81. See also the references to this *concorso* in Chapters II and IV.

10. Marconi et al. (1974), I, 5–6, nn. 82–105. Filippo Juvarra also had occasion to turn to this theme later in his career, with designs in 1725 for a palace for the papal conclave: Vittorio Viale, "I disegni di Filippo Juvarra per il Palazzo del Conclave," in *Atti della Accademia delle Scienze,* vol. 103 (Torino: 1969).

11. For discussions and illustrations of selected *Concorsi Clementini* from 1704 on, the reader is referred to: Hellmut Hager, ed., *Architectural Fantasy and Reality* (University Park: The Pennsylvania State University, 1981); Marconi et al. (1974), I, 6f, n. 106f.

12. ASL, vol. 46A, fols, 57–59. For Domenico Martinelli's part in this episode, see Chapter III, note 101.

13. Braham/Hager, 17; ASL, vol. 46A, fol. 165.

14. Hellmut Hager, "The Accademia di San Luca in Rome, and the Academie Royale d'Architecture in Paris: A Preliminary Investigation," in *Projects and Monuments,* 129–61.

Selected Bibliography

Accademia di San Luca. *Congregationi dell'Accademia dei Pittori, Scultori, et Architetti di Roma, Registrate dal Notaro della Mede'ma Accademia (G. Ghezzi): 19 Nov. 1674 – 21 Giun. 1711.* MS. vol. 46. Rome: Archive of the Acc. di S. Luca, 1711.

Accademia di San Luca. *Congregationi dell'Accademia di S. Luca dall'Anno 1664 a tutto 1674.* MS. vol. 44. Rome: Archive of the Acc. di S. Luca, 1674.

Accademia di San Luca. *Liber Accademie/Sa. Luce/Congreg. 1634 al 1674.* MS. vol. 43. Rome: Archive of the Acc. di S. Luca, 1674.

Accademia di San Luca. *Ordini dell'Accademia de Pittori et Scultori di Roma.* Rome: Acc. di S. Luca, 1609.

Accademia di San Luca. *Propositioni, resolutioni e decreti fatti nelle Congregat'ni dell'Accademia del Pittori, Scultori, e Architetti di Roma, Registrate dal Segretario della med'ma Accademia (G. Ghezzi): 1674 al 1699.* MS. vol. 45. Rome: Archive of the Acc. di S. Luca, 1699.

Alaux, Jean-Paul. *L'Académie de France à Rome, ses Directeurs, ses Pensionnaires.* 2 vols. Paris: Editions Duchartre, 1933.

Algarotti, Conte Francesco. *Essai sur la Peinture et sur l'Académie de France établie à Rome.* 1769; rpt. Geneva: Minkoff Reprints, 1972.

Anon. *L'Accademia di Francia a Roma: 1666–1903.* Rome: Tipografia Cooperativa Sociale, 1903.

Anon. *La Reale Insigne Accademia di San Luca nella inaugurazione della sua nuova sede.* Rome: Societa Tipografia Castaldi, 1934.

Arnaud, Jean. *L'Académie de St. Luc à Rome: considérations historiques depuis son origine jusqu'à nos jours.* Rome: Herrmann Loescher, 1886.

Barthelemy, Marie-Joseph, and Jules Guiffrey. *Liste des pensionnaires de l'Académie de France à Rome.* Paris: Académie des Beaux-Arts de l'Institut de France, 1908.

Beaurne, Georges. *L'Académie de France à Rome: La Villa Medici.* Paris: Librairie Garnier Frères, 1923.

Bertolotti, Antonino. *Artisti Francesi in Roma nei Secoli XV, XVI, e XVII.* 1886; rpt. Bologna: A. Forni, 1975.

Blondel, Nicolas-François. *Cours d'Architecture enseigné dans l'Académie Royale d'Architecture.* 5 pts. Paris: 1675–83.

Boyer, Ferdinand. "Les Artistes Français, étudients, lauréats ou membres de l'Académie romaine de St-Luc entre 1660–1700, d'après des documents inédits." *Bulletin de la Société de l'Histoire de l'Art Français* (1950), 117–32.

Braham, A. J., and Hellmut Hager. *Carlo Fontana: The Drawings at Windsor Castle.* London: A. Zwemmer, 1977.

Castan, Auguste. "Les Premières installations de l'Académie de France à Rome." *Réunion des Sociétés des Beaux-Arts des Departments,* 1889, 83–115.

Cipriani, Angela and Valeriani, Enrico, eds. *I Disegni di Figura nell'Archivio Storico dell'Accademia di San Luca: I, Concorsi e Accademie all Secolo XVII.* Roma: Casa Editrice Quasar, 1988.

Dalbor, Witold. *Pompeo Ferrari.* Warsaw: 1938.

D'Aviler, Charles-Augustin. *Cours d'Architecture qui comprend les Ordres de Vignole avec des commentaires, les figures & descriptions de ses plus beaux Batimens, & de ceux de Michelange.* Paris: Nicolas Langlois, 1691.

D'Aviler, Charles-Augustin. *Cours d'Architecture, revu & augmenté de plusiers desseins & preceptes conformes a l'usage present, & d'un grand nombre de termes & de remarques.* Revised ed. Paris: Jean Mariette, 1720.

Fontana, Carlo. *Discorso sopra l'antico Monte Citatorio situato nel Campo Marzio.* Roma: 1708.

Fontana, Carlo. *L'Anfiteatro Flavio.* The Hague: Isaac Vaillant, 1725.

Fontana, Carlo. *Templum Vaticanum.* Roma: 1694.

Ghezzi, Giuseppe. *Il Centesimo dell'anno MDCXCV celebrato in Roma dall'Accademia del Disegno.* Rome: Acc. di S. Luca, 1696.

Gould, Cecil. *Bernini in France: An Episode in Seventeenth-Century History.* Princeton, NJ: Princeton University Press, 1982.

Guiffrey, Jules. *Comptes des Batiments du Roi sous le règne de Louis XIV.* Paris: Imprimerie Nationale, 1881–1901.

Guiffrey, Jules. "Les Origines de l'Académie de France à Rome." *Journal des Savants,* NS 6, 5 (1907), 289–97.

Guiffrey, Jules, and Anatole de Montaiglon. *Correspondance des Directeurs de l'Académie de France à Rome avec les Surintendants de Batiments.* 18 vols. Paris: Librarie de la Société de l'Histoire de l'Art Français, 1887–1907.

Hager, Hellmut. "Il modello di Ludovico Rusconi Sassi del concorso per la facciata di San Giovanni in Laterano (1732) ed i prospetti a convessità centrale durante la prima metà del Settecento a Roma." *Commentari,* NS 22, 1 (1971), 36–37.

Hager, Hellmut and Munshower, Susan, eds. *Architectural Fantasy and Reality: Drawings from the Accademia Nazionale di San Luca in Rome, Concorsi Clementini 1700–1750.* University Park: The Pennsylvania State University Museum of Art, 1981.

Herrmann, Wolfgang. "Antoine Desgodetz and the Académie Royale d'Architecture." *Art Bulletin,* 40 (1985), 23–53.

Kelly, Cathie Cook. "Ludovico Rusconi Sassi and Early Eighteenth-Century Architecture in Rome." Diss., The Pennsylvania State University, 1980.

Lapauze, Henri. *Histoire de l'Académie de France à Rome.* 2 vols. Paris: Librairie Plon, 1924.

Lemonnier, Henri. *Procès-Verbaux de l'Académie Royale de Architecture: 1671–1793.* 9 vols. Paris: Librairie de la Société de l'Histoire de l'Art Français et l'Académie des Beaux-Arts, 1911–29.

Lorentz, Stanislaw. *Relazioni Artistiche fra l'Italia e la Polonia.* Conferenze del'Accademia Polacca di Scienze e Lettere, Fasc. 15. Rome: Signorelli, 1961.

Marconi, Paolo, Angela Cipriani, and Enrico Valeriani. *I disegni di architettura dell'Archivio Storico dell'Accademia di San Luca.* 2 vols. Rome: De Luca, 1974.

Millon, Henry A. "Filippo Juvarra and the Accademia di San Luca in Rome in the Early Eighteenth Century." *Projects and Monuments in the Period of the Roman Baroque.* Ed. Hellmut Hager and Susan S. Munshower. Papers in Art History from The Pennsylvania State University, vol. 1. University Park: The Pennsylvania State University, 1984, 12–24.

Missirini, Melchior. *Memorie per servire alla Storia della Romana Accademia di S. Luca, fino alla Morte de Antonio Canova.* Rome: De Romanis, 1823.

Montaiglon, Anatole de. *Mémoires pour servir a l'Histoire de l'Académie Royale.* Paris: 1853.

Montaiglon, Anatole de. *Procès-Verbaux de l'Académie Royale de Peinture et Sculpture.* 11 vols. 1875.

Pascoli, Lione. *Vite de'Pittori, Scultori, ed. Architetti Moderni.* 2 vols., 1730–36; rpt. Rome: E. Calzone, 1933.

Pevsner, Nikolaus. *Academies of Art, Past and Present.* Cambridge: The Cambridge University Press, 1940.

Pietrangeli, Carlo, ed. *L'Accademia Nazionale di San Luca.* Rome: De Luca Editore, 1974.

Pirotta, Luigi. "Contributo alla Storia della Accademia Nazionale de S. Luca: Alunni Stranieri delle scuole accademiche premiati nei vari concorsi." *L'Urbe,* 25, n. 1 (1962), 5–9.

Pirotta, Luigi. "Francesco Fontana assistente di Carlo Maratti nel principato della Accademia di San Luca." *L'Urbe,* 31, n. 2 (1968), 16–21.

Rocchi, Giuseppe. *Memorie della vita di Domenico Martinelli sacerdote Lucchese e insigne architetto.* Lucca: 1772.

Santese, Bianca Maria. *Palazzo Testa Piccolomini alla Dataria: Filippo Barigioni Architetto Romano.* Rome: De Luca, 1983.

Slaski, Jan, ed. *Barocco fra Italia e Polonia.* Accademia Polacca delle Scienze, Comitato degli Studi sull'Arte. Warsaw: 1977.

Smith, Gil R. "The *Concorso Accademico* of 1677 at the Accademia di San Luca." *Projects and Monuments in the Period of the Roman Baroque.* Ed. Hellmut Hager and Susan S. Munshower. Papers in Art History from The Pennsylvania State University, vol. 1. University Park: The Pennsylvania State University, 1984, 26–45.

Vagnetti, Fausto. *La Regia Accademia di Belle Arti di Roma.* Florence: Felice le Monnier, 1943.

Valeri, Ugo. *L'ultimo allievo del Bernini: Antonio Valeri.* Rome: Societa Tipologia Italia (1958).

Valetta, Giuseppe Ippolito, Count Franchi-Verney della. *L'Accademia di Francia a Roma.* Rome: 1903.

Zachwatowicz, Jan. *Polish Architecture.* Warsaw: Arkady, 1967.

Selected Glossary

aggregati: It., the guilds officially affiliated with the Accademia di San Luca, e.g., the *Aggregati degli Indoratori* (gilders); these groups attended meetings but had no voting rights.

breve: It., a papal brief or letter, such as that from Clement VIII establishing the Accademia di San Luca in 1593.

bussola: It., literally a compass; at the Accademia di San Luca the term referred to the ballot from which the name of the next year's *principe* would be drawn by lot; names were entered into the *bussola* upon nomination and receipt of a two-thirds majority vote from the membership.

compagnia: It., a company or association of craft guilds; when capitalized it signifies the Roman guild association.

concorso: It., a design competition; at the Accademia di San Luca the competitions were called the *Concorsi Accademici* until 1702, when they became the *Concorsi Clementini* in honor of Pope Clement XI.

disegno: It., a drawing, or an entire project design; the term also has abstract meaning with regard to the formal elements of the visual arts.

dono: It., literally a donation; at the Accademia di San Luca it was the term for a new member's original work presented at or following his or her induction, as a condition of his or her membership (though this condition was often neglected).

fabbrica: It., a building or construction; when capitalized it signifies a building committee or office of works, e.g., *Fabbrica di S. Pietro*.

maitrise: Fr., literally mastership; when capitalized it signifies the Parisian association of guildmasters (see *compagnia*).

paciere: It., literally a peacemaker; at the Accademia di San Luca the term applied to the officers responsible for arbitrating disputes between members and/or students.

pensionnaire: Fr., literally a boarder; at the Académie de France in Rome, the term referred to a student whose stay in Rome had the sanction and financial support of the French crown.

principe: It., literally a prince; at the Accademia di San Luca it was the title reserved for their annually elected head.

prova: It., an examination; at the Accademia di San Luca the term referred to the extemporaneous design examination administered to competitors in the *concorsi* after their entries were submitted, as proof of their qualifications.

recteur: Fr., rector; at the Académie Royale de Peinture et Sculpture there were four, two from each medium, who were responsible for instruction and were second in authority only to the chancellor; *directeur* was the next lowest rank at the Académie Royale.

relazione: It., a report; at the Accademia di San Luca the term was used to refer to its competition accounts, published for the first time in 1696, which contained the discourse and poetry recited at the prize ceremony.

soggetto: It., the subject (task, topic, theme) of a class of academic competition (*concorso*) at the Accademia di San Luca.

stimatore: It., an appraiser; at the Accademia di San Luca the term applied to the officers responsible for valuating works of art or building contracts, e.g., *Stimatore d'Architettura*.

Surintendant des Batiments: Fr., the chief royal minister for building construction and public works in the French dominions.

verbali: It., the minutes of the Accademia's meetings (*congregazioni*); the meetings were of two kinds: for the general membership and, less frequently, for the officers.

visitatore: It., a visitor; at the Accademia di San Luca the term applied to the officers responsible for attending to the needs of sick members or the families of deceased members.

INDEX

Figure numbers and plate numbers appear in italics following page numbers.